Register Your Book
at www.ibmpressbooks.com/ibmregister

Upon registration, we will send you electronic sample chapters from two of our popular IBM Press books. In addition, you will be automatically entered into a monthly drawing for a free IBM Press book.

Registration also entitles you to:

- Notices and reminders about author appearances, conferences, and online chats with special guests

- Access to supplemental material that may be available

- Advance notice of forthcoming editions

- Related book recommendations

- Information about special contests and promotions throughout the year

- Chapter excerpts and supplements of forthcoming books

Contact us

If you are interested in writing a book or reviewing manuscripts prior to publication, please write to us at:

Editorial Director, IBM Press
c/o Pearson Education
One Lake Street
Upper Saddle River, New Jersey 07458

e-mail: IBMPress@pearsoned.com

Visit us on the Web: www.ibmpressbooks.com

Apache Derby— Off to the Races

DB2® Books

DB2® Universal Database V8 for Linux, UNIX, and Windows Database Administration Certification Guide, Fifth Edition
Baklarz and Wong

Understanding DB2®
Chong, Liu, Qi, and Snow

Integrated Solutions with DB2®
Cutlip and Medicke

High Availability Guide for DB2®
Eaton and Cialini

DB2® Universal Database V8 Handbook for Windows, UNIX, and Linux
Gunning

DB2® SQL PL, Second Edition
Janmohamed, Liu, Bradstock, Chong, Gao, McArthur, and Yip

DB2® Universal Database for OS/390 V7.1 Application Certification Guide
Lawson

DB2® for z/OS® Version 8 DBA Certification Guide
Lawson

DB2® Universal Database V8 Application Development Certification Guide, Second Edition
Martineau, Sanyal, Gashyna, and Kyprianou

DB2® Universal Database V8.1 Certification Exam 700 Study Guide
Sanders

DB2® Universal Database V8.1 Certification Exam 703 Study Guide
Sanders

DB2® Universal Database V8.1 Certification Exams 701 and 706 Study Guide
Sanders

DB2® Universal Database for OS/390
Sloan and Hernandez

The Official Introduction to DB2® for z/OS®, Second Edition
Sloan

Advanced DBA Certification Guide and Reference for DB2® Universal Database v8 for Linux, UNIX, and Windows
Snow and Phan

DB2® Express
Yip, Cheung, Gartner, Liu, and O'Connell

Apache Derby — Off to the Races
Zikopoulos, Baklarz, and Scott

DB2® Version 8
Zikopoulos, Baklarz, deRoos, and Melnyk

On Demand Computing Books

Business Intelligence for the Enterprise
Biere

On Demand Computing
Fellenstein

Grid Computing
Joseph and Fellenstein

Autonomic Computing
Murch

Rational® Software Books

Software Configuration Management Strategies and IBM Rational ClearCase®, Second Edition
Bellagio and Milligan

WebSphere® Books

IBM® WebSphere®
Barcia, Hines, Alcott, and Botzum

IBM® WebSphere® Application Server for Distributed Platforms and z/OS®
Black, Everett, Draeger, Miller, Iyer, McGuinnes, Patel, Herescu, Gissel, Betancourt, Casile, Tang, and Beaubien

Enterprise Java™ Programming with IBM® WebSphere®, Second Edition
Brown, Craig, Hester, Pitt, Stinehour, Weitzel, Amsden, Jakab, and Berg

IBM® WebSphere® and Lotus
Lamb, Laskey, and Indurkhya

IBM® WebSphere® System Administration
Williamson, Chan, Cundiff, Lauzon, and Mitchell

Enterprise Messaging Using JMS and IBM® WebSphere®
Yusuf

More Books from IBM Press

Irresistible! Markets, Models, and Meta-Value in Consumer Electronics
Bailey and Wenzek

Service-Oriented Architecture Compass
Bieberstein, Bose, Fiammante, Jones, and Shah

Developing Quality Technical Information, Second Edition
Hargis, Carey, Hernandez, Hughes, Longo, Rouiller, and Wilde

Performance Tuning for Linux® Servers
Johnson, Huizenga, and Pulavarty

RFID Sourcebook
Lahiri

Building Applications with the Linux Standard Base
Linux Standard Base Team

An Introduction to IMS™
Meltz, Long, Harrington, Hain, and Nicholls

Search Engine Marketing, Inc.
Moran and Hunt

Inescapable Data
Stakutis and Webster

IBM PRESS

Apache Derby— Off to the Races

Includes Details of IBM® Cloudscape™

Paul C. Zikopoulos, George Baklarz, Dan Scott

IBM Press
Pearson plc

Upper Saddle River, NJ • Boston • Indianapolis • San Francisco
New York • Toronto • Montreal • London • Munich • Paris • Madrid
Capetown • Sydney • Tokyo • Singapore • Mexico City

ibmpressbooks.com

IBM Press Program Managers: Tara Woodman and Ellice Uffer
IBM Press Consulting Editors: Susan Visser and Roman B. Melnyk
Cover design: IBM Corporation

Published by Pearson plc
Publishing as IBM Press

Library of Congress Cataloging-in-Publication Data

Zikopoulos, Paul.
  Apache Derby : off to the races : includes details of IBM Cloudscape DB2 information management
software / Paul C. Zikopoulos, Dan Scott, George Baklarz.
     p. cm.
  ISBN 0-13-185525-5
  1. Open source software. 2. Apache Group. I. Scott, Dan, 1972- II. Baklarz, George. III. Title.
  QA76.76.S46Z55 2005
  005.3—dc22

                                                          2005020022

ISBN 0-13-185525-5
Text printed in the United States on recycled paper at R. R. Donnelley in Crawfordsville, Indiana.
First printing, November 2005

When going through the late nights and extra hours that seem to accompany any book we write, the thought of whom the book is written for sometimes keeps us going. Of course, this book is written for you, but personally, we'd like to make the following dedications:

From Paul Zikopoulos

From a professional perspective, a certain group of IBMers that have become mentors to me over the years (even though they didn't necessarily sign up for it): Bob Picianno, Alyse Passarelli, Leon Katsnelson, Chris Eaton, Jim Stittle, Pat Selinger, and George Baklarz. The thing that's so great about this group is that they lead even when they don't know they're doing it. I wonder if others are as privileged as I am to work with folks who have this kind of talent. As well, to Mary Anne MacKenzie (VP Franklin Templeton) for her continual advice from a career development perspective, but more importantly, being such a precious friend to my family.

At a personal level, my wife Kelly Donata for just being my wife, and delivering Chloë Alyse in a safe and what seems to be an ever-growing (and cost-increasing) fashion. I'm not so convinced Kelly ever gave me words of encouragement on this book, but I *really* want to thank her for giving me the distraction! Finally, I don't have the fragmented pet family that George Baklarz has, but I'll follow George's lead and thank Chachi (my dog) for hanging out with me at 2:00 a.m. while writing this book.

From George Baklarz

I'd like to thank Katrina, Andrew, Geoff, Tristan (cat), Ellie (dog), and Basil (dog-in-law) for their continued patience and support while writing this book. Their words of encouragement ("Are you still working on that?") were much appreciated!

From Dan Scott

To my mother, who scrimped and saved to buy me my first and second computers: I know the sacrifices you made, and I will never be able to thank you enough.

To Spook the cat: Thank you for curling up on my lap through those late night debugging and writing sessions.

To my incredible wife, who encouraged me to tackle this project and patiently dealt with my chronic procrastination and soaring stress levels: Thank you, Lynn, for inspiring me, supporting me, making me laugh, and enhancing my life beyond measure. I am an extremely lucky man to have you by my side.

Table of Contents

Part 3

Chapter 9   Developing Apache Derby Applications with JDBC   233

Preface

Executive Letter from Bob Picciano (Vice President of Database Servers, IBM)

Whether you are just starting with Apache Derby or you've been using the IBM Cloudscape offering for some time, what most people convey to me about this specific database product is admiration for the rich function and gratitude for the simplicity of deployment, management, and maintenance. As you'll read in this book, Apache Derby and IBM Cloudscape have been on an interesting evolutionary journey and the benefactors of the journey are those individuals who want to develop robust applications that require a true, full function, open source database, but want the simplicity and management characteristics of an embedded offering. Apache Derby is unique in its capability to deliver these attributes, and it does so on a true open source code base that is vibrant, and it continues to evolve to meet the requirements of a growing community.

Paul, George, and Dan have crafted an excellent overview and vista-filled tour of Apache Derby that will allow the reader to get a solid grasp of the product's broad capabilities. Whether you are developing in PHP, C, Java, .NET, or anything in between, Apache Derby has a great deal to offer you and we hope you will join the ranks of those developing their applications with this elegant and capable offering. This book makes learning the many facets of this mature, but rapidly evolving product, easy and fun.

Aside from completing this book with a confident sense of understanding of Apache Derby, we also hope that you are inspired to give something back to the Apache Derby project or open source at large. We are very excited about the course, prospects, and progress of true open source offerings because of their power to foster stable, open interfaces and tackle the many challenges of today's heterogeneous computing environments. Please enjoy your Apache Derby journey and we sincerely look forward to hearing from you about your experiences or ideas at iloveapachederby@yahoo.com.

About This Book

This book is written for everyone! Well, that may be a broad statement, but it's partially true. For the most part, we've tried to put a little bit of everything in this book. From a discussion on the open source movement, to the benefits of relational database technology for those of you who leverage a file system to persist data, to a primer on SQL, to step-by-step tutorials on building sample applications, you'll find it all in this book.

In Part I, we introduce you to the open source world, and we talk about such fundamental concepts as the Apache process, why IBM contributes to the open source movement, IBM's significant role with respect to open source software, why someone would want to use a relational database, the differences between the IBM Cloudscape and the Apache Derby databases, and more. You don't have to be technical to benefit from Part I. However, even if you're a developer and you don't think that you'll find this information useful, read it: you're going to learn some key information that will prove invaluable as you work your way through the rest of this book.

Part II introduces you to the different ways that you can use the IBM Cloudscape database (also known as Apache Derby) in the "real world." You don't know the difference between IBM Cloudscape and Apache Derby? That's what Part I is for! In Part II we talk about deployment and functional considerations for development environments, client/server environments, multi-threaded applications, Web servers, and more. After giving you a foundation in the ways that you can use Apache Derby, we present you with a general overview of this database and database technology in general. (After all, not everyone who reads this book is a database expert—we'll give you enough to get going.) The "meat" of this part of the book takes you through step-by-step examples of how to install the Apache Derby code on a Windows or Linux workstation for developmental purposes. (We cover how to install it on any operating system and production deployment as well.) Finally, this part ends with important concepts such as managing the Apache Derby database (for all you DBAs out there), securing the database, and a really good primer on SQL. After reading Part II, you'll not only have a great foundation that's applicable to most databases in general, you'll also have the Apache Derby code installed on your workstation, at which point you'll be ready to really get the Apache Derby database working for you. For the most part, we aren't expecting most of you to be DBAs, so we'll take the time to give you a good enough DBA foundation. The best part of the Apache Derby and IBM Cloudscape databases are that they don't require DBAs—just basic database knowledge.

Part III prepares you for the tutorials in Part IV. You'll learn about each of the programming languages that are supported by Apache Derby and how their elements interact with the Apache Derby database engine.

Part IV shows you how to build a sample application called "Your Momma Loves Drama" (YMLD). It's shown in Figure Preface-1.

The YMLD application is designed to give you a general feel for how to build a real-world application (and its supporting database) using the Apache Derby database. YMLD is a basic ticket booking system for a theater. If you follow the tutorials, you'll learn how to leverage many of the different features in the Apache Derby database using its supported programming languages. Part IV first shows you, in great detail, how to build the YMLD application using the JDBC API; it then gives you a detailed example of building this application using the Windows programming interfaces (specifically .NET and ODBC). The final three chapters in this part give you examples (although they aren't presented in the same detailed end-to-end manner like the JDBC and Windows chapters) of how to use the most popular open source languages (Python, PHP, and Perl) to build the YMLD application.

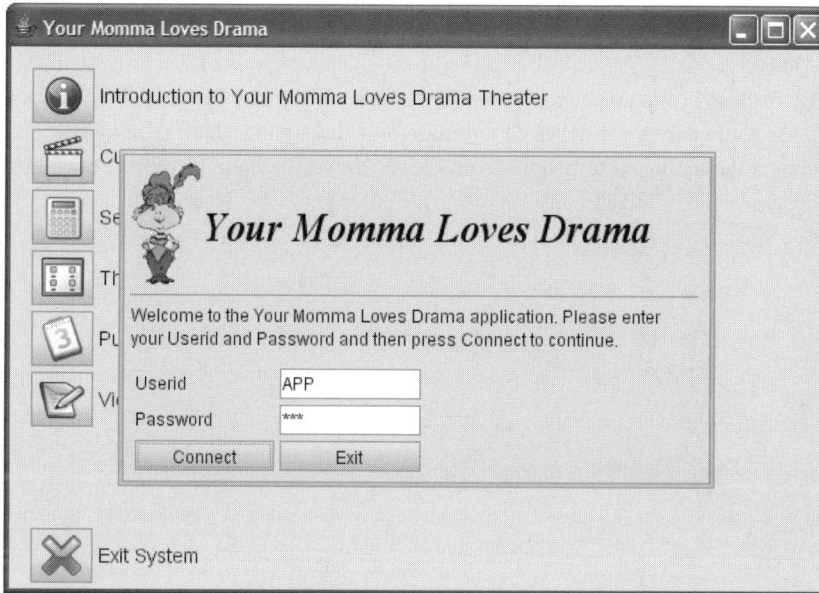

Figure Preface-1   The "Your Momma Loves Drama" Application

The appendices provide information about the book's Web site (www.ibmpressbooks.com/title/0131855255) where we've got links to lots of great stuff for you, such as downloadable code, tutorials, lots of articles, a whole whack of resources where you can learn more about Apache Derby (and find an ever-increasing domain of knowledge and tutorials—brought to you by your fellow community members, of course!), and some troubleshooting hints and tips to help you through the most common "sticking points."

We hope that you enjoy this book and learn just how powerful this free, open source database can be. And don't forget, when you learn how to build applications to the Apache Derby database, you're also learning how to build DB2 Universal Database (DB2 UDB) applications because the SQL API is fully compatible with DB2 UDB for Linux, UNIX, and Windows (which is about 95 percent compatible with the DB2 family)—now that's resume padding!

So, are you ready? On your marks... Get set... Go!... It's "off to the races with Apache Derby!" By the way, if you're using Apache Derby to power up your applications (even if you didn't use our book to get started—but especially if you did), let us know—we'd love to hear from you at: iloveapacherderby@yahoo.com.

Acknowledgments

Books don't get written overnight, and they don't get written without the support of a community— be it for moral support, technical advice, reviews, edits, and so on.

Overall, we have to thank the Apache Derby developers and community who have helped make this database a serious contender in a very small amount of time—thank you.

As a group, we'd really like to thank the following people for contributing and helping deliver what's in your hands now—we could not have done it without you: Susan Visser (for her words of encouragement and support of this book since its inception), Roman Melnyk (for agreeing to edit the book at a moment's notice—we liked him better as an author), Grant Hutchison (for his continual reviews of the book), Tim Bunce (for bringing clarity to the Perl world of databases with the Perl DBI driver), Man-Yong Lee (for bringing the first version of the PyDB2 module to the world over the course of a weekend), Wez Furlong (for running the gauntlet of standardizing database access in PHP with PDO, creating PDO_ODBC, and introducing Dan to the PHP community: he says he'll gladly buy you the beverage of your choice any time you want), and finally, Jean Anderson, Kathy Saunders, and Andrew McIntyre (for always taking the the time to answer questions, reviewing some of the chapters, and most of all loving what they do—it really shows).

In addition to this group, we'd like to thank the following people who helped us as well: Patricia Selinger, Daniel Debrunner, Bernard Goodwin, Michael Thurston, Mary Kate Murray, Robin O'Brien, Frank Koconis, Kevin Foster, Tammy Cannizza, David Fallside, Rajesh Kartha, Tom Christopher, Ron Reuben, Bernard Cadogan, Stanley Bradbury, Sumit Varshney, and anyone else we may have missed.

About the Authors

Paul C. Zikopoulos, BA, MBA, is an award-winning writer and speaker with the IBM Database Competitive Technology team. He has more than 10 years of experience with DB2 UDB and has written over 60 magazine articles and several books about it. Paul has co-authored the books *DB2 Version 8: The Official Guide, DB2: The Complete Reference, DB2 Fundamentals Certification for Dummies, DB2 for Dummies*, and *A DBA's Guide to Databases on Linux*. Paul is a DB2 Certified Advanced Technical Expert (DRDA and Cluster/EEE) and a DB2 Certified Solutions Expert (Business Intelligence and Database Administration). In his spare time, he enjoys all sorts of sporting activities, running with his dog Chachi, and trying to figure out the world according to Chloë—his new daughter. You can reach him at paulz_ibm@msn.com.

George Baklarz, B Math, M Sc (Comp Science) is a senior manager in the DB2 Worldwide Pre-sales Support Group. He works closely with customers to help them understand new information management technology and to gain their feedback for improving DB2 products. He has more than 20 years of experience with DB2 and has co-authored a number of books, including *DB2 UDB Version 8.1 Database Administration Certification Guide* (Prentice Hall, 2003) and *DB2 UDB Version 8: The Official Guide* (Prentice Hall, 2003). In addition, he is a member of the International DB2 Users Group Speaker and Volunteer Hall of Fame. In his spare time, he lectures at the University of Guelph (database theory) and presents at a variety of user conferences, including the International DB2 Users Group. You can reach George when he's not traveling at baklarz@gmail.com.

Dan Scott has been working for IBM on DB2 Universal Database since 1998, and currently holds the position of product manager. He has been involved in the intersection of DB2, Linux, and open source scripting languages as a user, author, public speaker, and occasionally a developer since 1999. In addition to authoring technical manuals for IBM and contributing articles to IBM developerWorks, Dan wrote the original "DB2 for Linux HOWTO" and tested and documented the PHP Data Objects (PDO) extension for www.php.net. Dan has presented internationally on the subject of developing applications with scripting languages that connect to Apache Derby, IBM Cloudscape, and IBM DB2 Universal Database. He lives in Toronto with his wife, cat, a coffee roaster, and a wide range of outdoor sporting equipment. You can reach him at dan.scott@acm.org.

## CHAPTER 1

On Your Marks …
Get Set … Go!!!
An Introduction to the Apache Derby and IBM Cloudscape Community

Introduction

Welcome to the Apache Derby and IBM Cloudscape family! We are glad to have you join our community of thousands, all dedicated to open standards and open source computing.

On August 3, 2004, IBM released a technical preview of IBM Cloudscape Version 10. While this in itself is exciting news, more importantly, IBM also made one of the most significant contributions in the history of the open source database community by contributing the source code for IBM Cloudscape to the Apache Software Foundation as the Apache Derby database. The Apache Software Foundation subsequently accepted Apache Derby as an incubator project. At the time this book was published, Apache Derby and IBM Cloudscape Version 10.1 was released and the Apache Derby project graduated from an incubator project (more on that in a bit) to an Apache sub-project.

The history of the Cloudscape technology is an interesting one indeed. In 1997, Cloudscape Inc. released what was perhaps the world's first real Java-based database, well before Java became the darling of the information technology (IT) community. The Cloudscape database began to carve its reputation as a pure Java-based relational database with just a 2 MB "fingerprint" that simplified application development. It made applications easier to deploy on any platform and represented the first truly relational database for which a DBA was not a requirement! Its significance went well beyond a "lights out" no management database. Cloudscape opened the doors for application developers (who are not generally database savvy) to leverage the benefits of a persistent data store for their applications.

In 1999, Informix bought Cloudscape Inc. and continued to enhance this database server, seeding it with even richer self-managing, ease of deployment, and open standards features—many of which were ahead of their time. IBM acquired the Cloudscape technology in July 2001 by purchasing the assets of Informix Software. As you can see, the IBM Cloudscape (formerly just Cloudscape) database has been around for a long time, which accounts for its maturity, robustness, and functionally rich feature set.

After the Informix acquisition, the IBM Cloudscape development teams have reported into IBM's Database Technology Institute, under the direction of Don Haderle and Dr. Patricia Selinger, two of the founders of relational database technology. In fact, since IBM acquired this technology, it has funded a continually expanding development team through several new versions and added compatibility with the IBM DB2 Universal Database (DB2 UDB) family through a fully compliant SQL application programming interface (API). This means that applications written for IBM Cloudscape (and subsequently Apache Derby—more on that in a bit) can easily be migrated to the DB2 UDB platform if necessary.

You might be surprised to know just how many partners, customers, and software packages use IBM Cloudscape in their technology—the very technology you're about to learn how to program to. In fact, over 80 different IBM products use IBM Cloudscape for many different reasons, including ease of deployment, portability, "hands-free" operation, an open standards-based Java engine, the small footprint, and more. For example, IBM Cloudscape powers products such as WebSphere Application Server, DB2 Content Manager, WebSphere Portal Server, IBM Director, Lotus Workplace, and many others. The IBM Cloudscape engine is a transparent component of all these products, and that is the whole point! Despite its application-transparency, you should be able to sense the power of this database engine because it is trusted to support these enterprise products.

As you probably have figured out by now, IBM has open sourced the IBM Cloudscape technology as Apache Derby and remains solidly committed to its future success. Throughout this book, we will use the term Apache Derby to represent both the IBM Cloudscape and Apache Derby databases because they are identical. There are some add-ons for IBM Cloudscape that you can freely download; where appropriate, we will identify them as such.

Specifically, IBM supports the Apache Derby open source database by:

- Contributing the IBM Cloudscape code to serve as the code base for the Apache database

- Donating resources to host a central Web-based location for add-on code, educational materials, support, the IBM DB2 Universal JDBC Driver, interfaces for ODBC, PHP, Perl, .NET, and more. The IBM Cloudscape Web site is available on IBM's developerWorks at: www.ibm.com/developerworks/cloudscape.

- Funding a dedicated open source project team that includes a complete development group with database development experience. Some members of this team are Apache Derby committers

- Providing hardware resources for nightly builds and testing of the open source code lines

- Running a full set of software and function verification test cases, and creating a fully functional open source test suite for Apache Derby

- Monitoring multiple Apache- and IBM-based forums and mail lists to offer free advice and best practice information to support the Apache Derby community

Why should you be interested in developing on the Apache Derby platform? The Apache Derby platform:

- *Is easy to deploy.* This database requires no installation: just copy a 2 MB .JAR file and set the CLASSPATH environment variable. Because it is Java-based, the database runs anywhere a standard JVM (J2SE 1.3 or higher) can be installed: from Macintosh to mainframe, and all points in between. In addition to this Apache Derby databases (and their data) are platform-independent and can be moved to any machine by simply zipping up your files and emailing them.

- *Requires no DBA skills or administration effort.* When using Apache Derby as an embedded solution, the application automatically starts the relational engine. Upgrades to future versions are done in-place, at connection time. Apache Derby automatically reclaims space, updates statistics, and much more. Quite simply, you do not need to staff your project with a DBA.

To be a player in the open source movement, you must be a proponent of open standards. Arguably, no other large IT company in the world has done more for the open source movement and open standards than IBM. In fact, today IBM backs over 150 different open source projects.

Specifically, Apache Derby uses open standards technology such as the American National Standards Institute's Structured Query Language (ANSI SQL), JDBC, SQLJ, and more. In fact, because Apache Derby is open source, future plans could include distributing Apache Derby with various mainstream Linux distributions as an accompanying database.

The IBM user community provides valuable feedback to this open source project, including bug reports and feature requests. Although IBM Cloudscape is the same database as the Apache Derby database available to the open source community, the IBM Cloudscape product has a separately purchasable service and support contract, and comes with a graphical-based installation and setup wizard to make full platform deployments (which include binary add-on features from IBM, such as an ODBC interface) easier and more consolidated.

Apache Derby addresses a unique market need and is a great fit for many workloads. Although Apache Derby enriches an environment steeped with a heavy Java investment and an open source middleware stack, it isn't just for Java developers. APIs are provided (either directly or through a download) for PHP, Perl, CLI, ODBC, and .NET.

In this chapter, we'll discuss the Apache Derby and IBM Cloudscape platforms, differences between them (again, there is nothing from a code perspective), why IBM is involved, why now, more than ever, you should consider a relational storage engine for your applications if you're not already using one, and more.

If You're Not the Kind of Person Who Reads Introduction Chapters ...

We recommend that you read this chapter anyway to get a good level of detail about Apache Derby, the motivation behind what IBM is doing in the open source space (it's a continuation of previous works actually), why open source in the first place, and more.

If you're not going to read this chapter, but you want a one-minute overview of Apache Derby and IBM Cloudscape, the following paragraphs, courtesy of Kathy Saunders (Release and QA Manager for IBM Cloudscape) and Jean Anderson (Architect for IBM Cloudscape) summarize this product quite well:

"Apache Derby is a lightweight, embeddable relational engine in the form of a Java class library. Its native interface is Java Database Connectivity (JDBC), with Java-relational extensions. It implements the SQL92E standard as well as many SQL 99 extensions. The engine provides transactions and crash recovery, and allows multiple connections and multiple threads to use a connection. Apache Derby can be easily embedded into any Java application program or server framework without compromising the Java-ness of the application because it is a Java class library. Derby's support for complex SQL transactions and JDBC allows your applications to migrate to other SQL databases, such as IBM DB2Universal Database (UDB), when they need to grow.

Apache Derby Network Server provides multi-user connectivity to Apache Derby databases within a single system or over a network. The Apache Derby Network Server receives and replies to queries from clients using the standard Distributed Database Architecture (DRDA) protocol. Databases are accessed through the Apache Derby Network Server using the IBM JDBC driver and the DB2 UDB JDBC universal driver.

There are several technical aspects that differentiate Apache Derby from other database systems:

- *It's easy to administer. When embedded in a client application, a Derby system requires no administrative intervention.*

- *It's embeddable. Applications can embed the Database Management System (DBMS) engine in the application process, eliminating the need to manage a separate database process or service.*

- *It can run as a separate process, using the Network Server framework or a server framework of your choice.*

- *It is a pure Java class library: This is important to Java developers who are trying to maintain the advantages of Java technology, such as platform independence, ease of configuration, and ease of installation.*

- *It needs no proprietary Java Virtual Machine (JVM). Written entirely in the Java language, it runs with any certified JVM.*

- *The engine is lightweight. It is about 2 MB of class files, and it uses as little as 4 MB of Java heap.*

- *It provides the ability to write stored procedures and functions in Java that can run in any tier of an application. Derby does not have a proprietary stored procedure language; it uses JDBC.*

Apache Derby is also like other relational database systems. It has transactions (commit and rollback), supports multiple connections with transactional isolation, and provides crash recovery.

The unique combination of technical capabilities allows application developers to build data-driven applications that are pervasive (run anywhere), deployable (downloadable), manageable, extensible, and connectable."

Let Me Get This Straight, Apache Derby Is IBM Cloudscape?

IBM contributed the IBM Cloudscape database technology to the Apache Software Foundation as *Apache Derby* while at the same time announcing the *IBM Cloudscape Version 10* database (the commercial offering based on the same open source technology).

What does all this mean? As far as the code goes—how you use it, class names, files names, and practically anything else you can think of—you can use the terms Apache Derby and IBM Cloudscape interchangeably (the exception to this is Apache-specific licensing rules that are governed by the Apache Software Foundation). Both Apache Derby and IBM Cloudscape are built from the same open source Apache Derby codebase. For the most part, all packages (class names, command names, stored procedure names, and so on) use the same naming convention under the Apache Derby name.

There are some minor differences between Apache Derby and IBM Cloudscape with respect to surrounding (or add-on) technologies that you should be aware of, and we will cover them later in this chapter.

The Apache Derby database, at the time this book was written, is available from the Incubator page on the Apache Web site (http://incubator.apache.org/projects/index.html) as both source code and compiled binaries. If you download Apache Derby, your usage of Apache Derby is bound by the Apache License Version 2.0. The Apache License is friendly to commercial businesses (which makes this a great product that provides a zero-cost, rich, and robust data runtime). In fact, anyone who binds to it can create his or her own commercial product. You can learn more about the Apache Software Foundation's licensing terms at: www.apache.org/licenses.

As previously mentioned, the Apache Derby database is distributed both in open source code and in compiled binary format on the Apache Web site. To become a full-fledged Apache project, a project (like Apache Derby) must start in the Apache incubator, where it is given the opportunity to demonstrate that it can become part of a viable Apache community composed of individual contributors (you can see a list of the current contributors for Apache Derby at: http://incubator.apache.org/ projects/derby.html#Detailed+References%3A) from both within and outside of the contributing company (in this case IBM). To learn more about how Apache incubator projects work, see http:// incubator.apache.org/. Apache Derby will not be fully accepted by the Apache Software Foundation until it graduates from the incubator project. Incidentally, during the production phase of this book, Apache Derby graduated from the incubator phase to an official Apache sub-project.

At the time this book was written, the Apache Derby contribution was in a "Podling" stage and therefore requires the accompanying disclaimer (from http://incubator.apache.org/derby):

"Apache Derby is an effort undergoing incubation at the Apache Software Foundation (ASF), sponsored by IBM. Incubation is required of all newly accepted projects until a further review indicates that the infrastructure, communications, and decision making process have stabilized in a manner consistent with other successful ASF projects. While incubation status is

not necessarily a reflection of the completeness or stability of the code, it does indicate that the project has yet to be fully endorsed by the ASF."

In contrast, the IBM Cloudscape database is only available in binary format; however, you do not need to pay for this license either. You can freely download and use the IBM Cloudscape database from the IBM developerWorks Web site at: http://www.ibm.com/developerworks/cloudscape.

Whether you're developing an Apache Derby, IBM Cloudscape, .NET, open source (Python, PHP, or Perl), or Java application, bookmark this site. It is the most comprehensive developer resource for the IBM databases.

This Web site provides resources for developers contributed by Apache Derby community members from inside and outside IBM, such as technical articles, sample code, user forums, documentation, and links to the IBM Cloudscape add-ons.

One difference between Apache Derby and IBM Cloudscape is that you can purchase a support contract for IBM Cloudscape. A support contract delivers a service level agreement (SLA) from IBM that comes from its award winning, 24 × 7 'best-of-breed' service support team. Most of the personnel on this support team also contribute time and effort to the Apache Derby project by monitoring forums and newsgroups. However, a support contract enables businesses to rely on a paid support structure for critical application deployments in the same way they would receive support for proprietary products—this means defect repudiation, committed response times, severity classifications, and so on.

Other differences between IBM Cloudscape and Apache Derby are that IBM Cloudscape has:

- A graphical installation wizard that lets you optionally select add-on IBM Cloudscape functional components like the ones detailed in this list. It is very well suited for developer workstation deployments.

- The DB2 Universal JDBC driver, commonly referred to as the Java Common Client (JCC). This JCC driver is available for download from the IBM Cloudscape Web site. The JCC driver can perform Type 2 and Type 4 JDBC connections, and it shares a common codebase that can be used for JDBC connections across the entire DB2 and IBM Cloudscape family (there are licensing considerations for some of these connections). The benefit is portability if the need ever arises for a more enterprise-class database like DB2 UDB. Because the same code manages the connection and application flow between the hosting application and the database, you can be assured that migration efforts are trivial.

- The IBM DB2 Plug-In for Eclipse (available as a free download from the IBM developerWorks Web site). This download includes:

  - The base Eclipse software developer's kit (SDK).

  - An Eclipse-based plug-in for Apache Derby, IBM Cloudscape, DB2, or Informix schema and SQL statement development. This tool enriches functions previously delivered by the old Cloudscape `Cview` utility.

- • An Eclipse-based plug-in for schema and data migration (with validity checking) from Apache Derby to DB2 for Linux, UNIX, and Windows.

- • Additional data access APIs like ODBC, PHP, Perl, and .NET interfaces. These interfaces can all be downloaded from developerWorks (although we've included links to them on the book's Web site [www.ibmpressbooks.com/title/0131855255] to make it easier to get going). White papers and other supporting collateral will accompany them as they become available. For example, the ODBC collateral will explain how to interface with Perl, PHP, and .NET applications using the ODBC driver.

- • Preloaded sample databases, including the traditional Cloudscape TOURSDB database and the DB2 SAMPLE database (these are included in the installation package).

- • Scripts to help you get up and running more quickly by setting your CLASSPATH environment variable, or by running some of the data utilities, and so on (these are included in the installation package).

- • Sample programs that test your database server.

- • An installation program that includes an IBM Java Runtime Environment (JRE) which is automatically installed with IBM Cloudscape for Windows and Linux (IBM Cloudscape also ships a Java-based installer for other platforms, but you have to ensure that a JRE is installed and configured on your server.)

- • Documentation in PDF format, and online access to an information center built on the Eclipse help system framework. For Apache Derby, because you will have access to the documentation source files, you could use Apache Forrest to build and publish the documentation in HTML format to your own Web site or help system.

Keep in mind that because Apache Derby and IBM Cloudscape are the same product, any of the IBM Cloudscape add-ons mentioned in the previous list can be downloaded from IBM for use with Apache Derby.

Development of the Apache Derby Database—Who Can Contribute and How?

In this section, we will briefly discuss who can contribute to Apache Derby and how contributions are made. The goal of this section is not to make you an expert in how the Apache Software Foundation process works; rather, it will briefly describe how your work could end up in Apache Derby. For complete details on the concepts outlined in this section, see http://www.apache.org/foundation/how-it-works.

While you read this section, keep in mind that because Apache Derby and IBM Cloudscape share the same codebase, any changes to the host Apache Derby code are automatically reflected in the IBM Cloudscape binaries. The add-ons provided by IBM with IBM Cloudscape are proprietary, and their source code is not being made available; however, they can be freely used with Apache Derby. For example, IBM's Java Common Client is not open source code.

Because Apache Derby is an open source database project, its success relies on an ecosystem to enrich and mature the quality of its code base. The development of Apache Derby is peer-based, and these development peers come from an ecosystem that includes personnel from IBM, current Cloudscape customers, and a host of other developers who have previous Cloudscape experience or who choose to become experts in this field because of its obvious advantages. The introduction of new features into the base source code must strictly follow Apache guidelines.

Anyone can be included in the Apache mailing lists and submit code. These developers are known as Apache Derby *contributors*. The actual code for Apache Derby is maintained in a Subversion (SVN) repository that is restricted to a smaller set of *committers*. (You can learn more about SVN at http://subversion.tigris.org/.)

The Apache meritocracy determines which members of the Apache Derby community can become committers. This ascension path is the nucleus of the Apache organization and its projects. The Apache Software Foundation has five different levels, as shown in Figure 1-1.

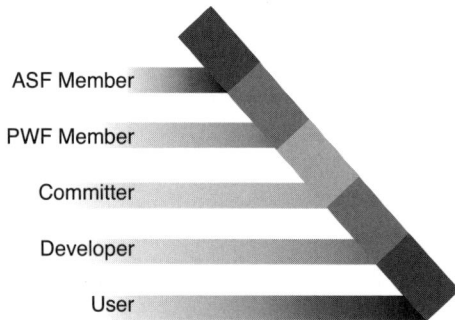

Figure 1-1   The Apache Software Foundation hierarchy

After contributors "earn their stripes" through meritable contributions and overall technical leadership for the direction of the source code, they can be promoted to committers. When a developer is considered a committer, he or she is granted access to the SVN repository. On their Web site, the Apache group calls this process *meritocracy;* literally, "govern of merit." You earn rights in accordance to your worth and efforts.

Committers get to vote on what contributed features make it into the build tree (again, the source code for the product is stored in the SVN repository). In this way, an experienced committee directs future innovations for the Apache Derby project (this is all part of the Apache process). Of course, because Apache Derby is open source, you are free to develop your own derivative works and use them for yourself, but we encourage all developers to become active in the development of Apache Derby—we are a community after all!

Each committee member can vote for a new feature, abstain from voting, or vote against a new feature for Apache Derby. Any negative votes must include an alternative proposal or a detailed explanation for the negative vote. (Bug fixes do not go through this process, but they do require review at check-in.) In essence, the community tries to come to agreement before moving forward with any changes. The Apache Software Foundation refers to this process as "consensus gathering," and it is a key construct in any Apache community.

IBM assigned six committers to the Apache Derby project when it released this product to the open source community. These committers are all steeped in IBM Cloudscape skills. In fact, they also have a deep understanding of other databases, such as DB2, Informix, Sybase, and SQL Server. Some of these committers are the original architects of the Cloudscape database. For Apache Derby to graduate from an Apache incubator project to a full-fledged Apache project (the project currently sits as an official Apache sub-project only one year before it is accepted as an incubator project), the committer ratio of IBMers to non-IBMers needs to "strike balance." Who will be among the committers that will join the Apache Derby project and help it become a full-fledged Apache project? It could be you!

How Can IBM Sell a Product for Profit and Contribute the Same Product to the Open Source Community?

Some members of the community might be skeptical about how IBM could possibly open source the code base for a product that is a source of revenue. Remember, if you choose to use IBM Cloudscape instead of Apache Derby, you are not paying for the right to use the database; you are only paying for a support contract (if you want one).

IBM has long been a strong contributor of open source software and open standards, especially in the areas of XML, Linux, Web Services, HTML, IP, HTTP, J2EE, true grid computing, and more. For example, IBM invented and donated the Distributed Relational Database Architecture (DRDA) standard for client/server communications.

The XML4J processor is another example of software that was developed in an IBM proprietary manner and later successfully open sourced. If you go to the Apache Web site, you will find the Xerces XML projects in the project list—those came from IBM. IBM actually helped start the Apache Software Foundation, so Apache Derby and Apache Xerces are great examples of the synergy that can be leveraged between open source and the for-profit business sector. This can work as long as the for-profit side of the equation is committed to open standards.

One of the best known contributions from IBM to the open source community is the Eclipse project (www.eclipse.org), a very successful open source integrated development environment (IDE) that was donated by IBM after they invested over 40 million dollars into it, and it not only lives on today, but has developed into a thriving community into the millions.

Other examples include IBM's extensive contributions to the Globus Alliance Grid specification (http://www.globus.org/ogsa/), the millions of dollars contributed toward the Linux movement, and the fact that IBM has led or co-led the creation of Web Service foundation technologies. IBM has also made significant contributions to Java; in fact, by contributing the IBM Cloudscape technology to the open source community as Apache Derby, IBM is enabling Java to expand into new market segments. This is not market posturing; this is real code that has changed (and is changing) the IT landscape forever.

The Apache Derby contribution represents over 500,000 lines of code, estimated to be worth over 85 million dollars!

So, in a nutshell, IBM is a significant force supporting open source innovation and collaboration. The company participated in more than 120 collaborative projects that have been contributed to the open source community. IBM contributed 500 patents into a "patent commons" for development and innovation. IBM has invested more than $1 billion in Linux development. IBM drives the adoption of and migrations to Linux among the development community, and expands enterprise-class tools for open source developers. So indeed, one can say that IBM is involved in open source!

How an Open Source Database Like Apache Derby Can Help

Several vendors are open sourcing their databases these days. Some have yet to publish their source code. The Apache Derby initiative is unique in that the entire source code is published. IBM believes that delivering this code to the Apache Derby community enables a richer and more robust feedback mechanism by which more functions, features, and benefits can be driven into the Apache Derby database.

Another unique and differentiating feature of Apache Derby is that this database was born out of a very successful proprietary initiative and consumer adoption lifecycle. Many features in this product resulted from specific business needs, and customers paid for the right to have these features. Since the Informix acquisition, IBM has continued to invest in this database, and it now powers much of the IBM software middleware stack. An open source Apache Derby database is interesting from both business and technical perspectives.

Open Source Software from a Business Perspective

From a business perspective, the Apache Derby database provides a way for individuals and companies to collaborate on projects that result in a greater sum than each could accomplish on their own: in short, it is synergistic.

It also flattens the "time to value" curve for projects by allocating fixed and variable costs across a greater sum of resources (most of which are not yours, which is a good thing from a cost allocation perspective). This effect drives down the marginal (per unit) cost of new features that are continuously driven into a product and would otherwise cost the recipient more money to obtain and leverage.

For example, consider maintenance programs such as Microsoft's Software Assurance (SA), which are used to deliver technology updates with new features to Microsoft software. Agreements like this come with their own usage terms but no promise with respect to the delivery of new features. However, new features are prepaid in advance, without credit. For example, SQL Server has a built-in five-year gap between SQL Server 2000 and SQL Server 2005. During this time, Microsoft did not release a significant amount of new functionality because of the business unit's release schedule, in spite of a user base that required a technology update. (They did deliver some new features. For example, their 64-bit engine was delivered outside of a scheduled release to remain competitive in the database space.) The point here isn't to besmirch Microsoft, but rather to point out that the delivery of new technology had nothing to do with technological innovation. In fact, some would argue that there has been limited technological innovation with this product (because there wasn't a release) in the last four years (until the release of SQL Server 2005)—yet not only was the right for these new features prepaid for, but there was also an opportunity cost of not having access to them.

On the other hand, the Apache Derby formula gives access to innovations from their earliest inception, as soon as they become part of the stable build stream. The point is that users of Apache Derby can take advantage of a new feature independently of its location in the product lifecycle, individual business unit goals, corporate funding, and so on. Rather, the decision to take advantage of a feature is based on need—early adopters will gravitate to new features earlier, whereas others might choose to wait until new features are more mature and tested—with a database like Apache Derby, you can do this.

Because this book is written with the Apache Derby application developer in mind, it is beyond our scope to discuss in detail the business benefits of the open source movement. There is a host of information on the Web about the business value of open source software. A good place to start is at www.ibm.com/developerworks/rational/library/1303.html.

Open Source Software from a Technical Perspective

From a technical perspective, because the source code for Apache Derby is readily and fully available to an "interested" and participatory community, the open source model has the advantage of transforming application developers into Apache Derby co-developers. Code bugs have a better chance of being detected, and the community serves as a quality assurance tier beyond the test buckets engineered by function verification testing (FVT) and system verification testing (SVT) units in the proprietary model. Beyond the mere detection of problem code, the fix for any issue can be delivered when the code is ready, outside of the complexities of a release cycle, costly hot fix schedules, or emergency rating systems.

The open source model also helps drive key technical features into the product more quickly because more developers are working on solutions to today's problems, and they get these improvements into the code at the same time (and not in correlation to profit center results). Quite simply, when software like the Apache Derby database is open source, it is free from business conditions and acts as a propellant for new features. In addition, the open source model enables end users to leverage features in a granulized and "as-needed" fashion (some applications will need urgent access to a performance feature, whereas others can wait), with full and open access to the build tree.

When discussing the benefits of open source software, we found the following quote quite interesting: "Source-level debugging saves valuable time throughout the embedded development process by eliminating the guesswork about how the code is interacting with the kernel or other low level operating system code." This quote (from Microsoft: http://msdn.microsoft.com/embedded/prevver/ce3/download/source/default.aspx) captures one of the key technical advantages of open source software. It's our point exactly.

The Apache Derby project delivers where other companies' marketing collateral tailors off.

Why the Need for a Local Data Store?

There are many reasons why more and more application developers and architects are turning to embeddable or lightweight databases. Before answering "why use a relational engine underneath an application?" which draws you to the Apache Derby platform, let's first discuss some of the benefits of just having a localized engine to store and manage your data.

Applications sometimes need to persist data, yet operate as an occasionally connected client (OCC). Such applications require intermittent access to the corporate network to refresh, upload, or pull data changes. For example, a traveling insurance agent might fill out reports throughout the day and want to manage the data locally until a time when the data can be uploaded to the corporate server. During the day, however, that user will need fast and efficient local access to data that pertains to his or her region.

Local data stores have become more popular recently for security reasons as well. Having a database available to an application, but not over a network, minimizes many security concerns. Today's economy is governed by more and more regulatory compliance rules concerning data persistence, such as the Health Insurance Portability and Accountability Act (HIPAA), Sarbanes-Oxley (SOX), the Basel II accord, and others. Another example of this is the challenge that many lines of business are facing with the new corporate reporting requirements in the United States. A lot of reporting is handled and stored in Microsoft Excel files, which might trigger compliance issues. Apache Derby can be used to provide a secure and robust repository for this data (alleviating the issues surrounding file repositories), while providing transparent access for end users who won't really know that the data isn't in a file.

In the past, data storage engines were under the complete control of IT departments, which had a number of implications. These engines had to be resourced from IT (which meant jumping through hoops to get a DBA's attention or resource); you consumed corporate CPU cycles, storage, and more. A self-managing and self-contained database such as Apache Derby has a "rounding error" of significance with respect to IT budgets and skill allocations, so you can avoid that lengthy process altogether.

Geographic isolation might also drive the requirement for a local data store. For example, many of today's cars have built-in computers that gather information that will subsequently be dumped to a certified mechanic's computer. These databases are being enhanced in many ways. Computers that collect driving characteristics data will run algorithms and queries that will adjust the performance characteristics of the car (suspension, torque, air/fuel ratios, and so on) to match the owner's driving patterns in real time.

Another example is Rolls-Royce. Although Rolls-Royce may be well known for its spectacular cars and artisanship (though the reality is that Rolls-Royce hasn't been making Rolls-Royces since the early 1980s), its real business is producing aero-engines, along with marine engines, power generators, nuclear submarine power plants, and so on. Rolls-Royce attaches drives to some of these engines that literally record gigabytes of information during operation. This data has to be stored somewhere. Sounds like a great opportunity for a database! Take for example an airplane whose engines record data through an entire flight pattern, which then is dumped for analysis to the safety engineer at the destination airport—it makes us feel safe when someone sending our plane on to the next destination knows how that engine performed that whole way!

Having data managed locally can increase performance, deliver better and more convenient access to vital data, and provide many other benefits that we will not cover here.

Estimates point to data collection rates of around 450 megabytes for every man, woman, and child per year, and in the three years prior to 2004, the world collected more data than it did in the last ten thousand years. There are a multitude of factors driving unprecedented data storage requirements, and these data requirements can only be handled by a relational database management system (RDBMS).

Why Use a Relational Database?

Now that it is apparent how applications and business processes can benefit from a functional place to persist and manage data, it is interesting to briefly comment on why a relational database is the best choice (as opposed to other approaches, like a file system, etc.).

There are many applications out there today that use some sort of local storage format to keep data collocated with the application, or to address any of the issues mentioned in the previous section. However, without a database, most of the proposed solutions cannot handle the atomicity of multiple changes (all or nothing, and the management of transactions that may impact each other), and there is no built-in recovery mechanisms in case of a failure during the transaction, no parallelism, no set-oriented data access API, no ability to share the same data at the same time between applications or users based on the business rules, and so on.

The most common format—perhaps due to legacy decisions and the lack of an embeddable, small-footprint database like Apache Derby in the past—is the flat file. Some databases even build on a flat file system, like FileMaker Pro. In the past, developers might have used a flat file system for their data storage requirements because it was perceived to be simple (for operational and management reasons, not from a coding standpoint) and fast. However, this architecture comes with its disadvantages: namely, it requires a lot of hand coding and is prone to errors.

Another common approach is XML; most programming languages implement standard programming interfaces for reading and writing XML (the XML specification itself is an open standard maintained by the World Wide Web Consortium). Like flat files, XML files can be easy to understand when you open them in an XML editor; however, as your data and the relationships between your data elements become more complex, designing a single XML file to store your data becomes a non-trivial exercise.

Storing data in XML files forces you to implement locking mechanisms to ensure that the files are always in a consistent state. In addition, as the amount of data you have to store in the file grows, your application will either require more system resources to store the entire XML file in memory, or have to reread and parse the XML file every time it has to retrieve data.

XML files are a great means of communicating between applications who don't know each other. In fact, XML is great for a lot of reasons. But as a data store, it requires a lot of effort for anything more than trivial data persistence scenarios. Of course advanced databases like DB2

UDB have the capability to provide XML repositories in combination with all the benefits that accrue from years of experience in the relational world.

One of the most significant benefits of using a database such as Apache Derby is that it delivers *atomicity, consistency, isolation, and durability (ACID)* compliance. Not all open source or proprietary databases do that. Databases exist for the purpose of providing a reliable and permanent storage mechanism that encompasses very strict properties embodied by these ACID characteristics. Although it is outside the scope of this chapter to discuss relational theory, you can learn more about ACID transactional processing and why it is so important from the "bible" of database theory: *An Introduction to Database Systems*, by C. J. Date (Addison-Wesley, 2004).

Another benefit of a relational data store is the concept of *relationships*. In fact, that is what relational databases (as the name would imply) are all about: set relationships. Whereas mathematicians can use algebra and set theory to no end for theoretical proofs, what a relational database delivers is a mechanism by which entities can be easily traversed and assembled, in any direction, with minimal coding effort. Need to know all the accounts with a last name that contains a specific group of characters? What about folks in the Eastern region? What happens to your application logic and pointer files when you move this data to another storage device in a flat file system? All this is transparently retrievable and navigable using a relational database, without code changes.

How is this possible? What is this 'magic' language by which you can interact with your data in an abstracted way without caring about its location? *Structured Query Language (SQL):* it can be used (in one form or another) to access all sorts of relational databases. SQL is a declarative language in that it does not contain any variables, loops, or other programming constructs (though there are procedural cousins that incorporate these entities). It is easy to learn, even for the non-programming kind.

Using a data store that can process SQL makes the data model more dynamic and flexible than it could ever hope to be when using a flat file system or some other approach. For example, if new information is deemed to be important, a query can be quickly written and implemented into the application. The methods by which the data needs to be accessed, or where it resides, are not issues. Typically, with a flat file system, this information was only well known to the original application developer; it's just not an issue with a relational database system. With a relational database system, access to the data and how to get to that data is abstracted from the developer.

With a flat file system, adding a new structure to the data model requires a new file (or the editing of an existing one), the registration of (or pointer updates to) the file, and so on. With an XML file system, you would have to modify your existing XML file structure and all of the methods that make assumptions based on the existing structure, or add another XML file to contain the new structure, and then implement a complex (and customized) join operation between the two XML files. Today, with Apache Derby relational database technology, it is as simple as a `CREATE TABLE` statement to add a new structure and a `SELECT` statement to return the new data.

The use of SQL also opens up a database to a wide variety of interfaces and access methods that would all have to be hand-coded when working with a flat file system. These interfaces mean a shortened and less expensive development cycle for applications, along with a readily available talent pool of developers and administrators.

Today's computers are orders of magnitude more *powerful* than those of the previous two generations. Many decisions were made to use flat files as opposed to a relational database some years ago due to the cost/power ratio for computers. When an Intel x486 processor with 64 MB of RAM was the most powerful (and expensive) computer around, you can see why economics would dictate the use of a flat file system. Today, computers and personal devices have moved far from the early adopters' phase of their respective product lifecycle curves such that they are capable of hosting a lot of data at relatively inexpensive costs.

Relational databases are very *scalable* as well. You can start with a database that resides on a tablet for a single user and move it to a large symmetric multiprocessor (SMP) machine that is used to support thousands of users and literally millions of transactions per minute.

Finally, the *manageability* of a relational database was thought to require an expert skill set, and thus it was deemed inappropriate for many applications. Databases like Apache Derby do not require users to perform table reorganizations or know anything about heap-related tuning parameters (if you do not know what these are, don't worry—that is the point).

How the Apache Derby Platform Can Help Your Business

There are many reasons why an Apache Derby platform decision can benefit your company, project, or infrastructure. In this section, we will give you some examples of how Apache Derby can be used in today's marketplace.

From a market perspective, not all client/server or Web applications require the muscle of an enterprise-class infrastructure database. In fact, 20–30% of applications might only need basic relational database capabilities, and their hosting environments might not have the system requirements to grab IT allocations (or attention for that matter) for these full-fledged data engines. However, they still require the scalability and robustness for data integrity that are associated with such databases, and Apache Derby gives them a way to do that.

In addition, as the amount of data being collected literally grows logarithmically and developers learn to leverage the benefits of a relational storage model, there are more and more demands for relational engines to be easy to use, easy to deploy, and embeddable. Developers will use databases, but they have overwhelmingly communicated that they are not interested in becoming DBAs.

Java has become a mainstay of the IT community; it is the write once, run anywhere imperative that helps to encourage platform independence and drives down the cost of computing. In fact, over 40% of all developers have Java-based skills. Coupled with other open source movements like Linux, the market screams for a true Java-oriented database from implementation through to the API. (Apache Derby can also support other programming languages and interfaces like .NET and ODBC, too, so it isn't just for Java developers.)

Finally, more than ever, the open source community is literally changing the landscape of information technology. Open source communities drive timely innovation into operating systems; Web servers can deliver this innovation in a rapidly adoptable model at minimal costs. As other proprietary software companies deliver an infrastructure under predatory pricing schemes, the market is turning to the open source community to "break the chains that bind."

The Apache Derby database delivers the true database technology that the market has been asking for on many fronts. Apache Derby is a Java-based embeddable database. Because it is written in Java, it can be embedded within your Java applications and deployed anywhere. This means that moving your application from a mainframe to a Linux- or Windows-based server is as simple as deploying a JAR file: "just drop-and-go." Further adding to its portability, Apache Derby uses an SQL92 and SQL99 entry level compliant SQL API (in fact, its SQL API is 100% compliant with the DB2 family).

There are no DBA requirements for managing Apache Derby. It could truly be hosted on those irritating late-night infomercials that claim to take the hassle out of various day-to-day chores. What little management there is (or that you can take advantage of for more granular tuning) can be controlled programmatically from the application itself. For example, a database backup can be executed through a native API call.

Finally, heavy investments in tooling create a feature-rich open source Eclipse environment for Apache Derby application development. This allows Java developers to remain productive in a comfortable open source environment, yet still leverage the benefits of a database.

Specifically, Apache Derby can be used for workloads such as:

- **Small business client database applications:** Many small businesses do not require a database that can support thousands of simultaneous users. For these businesses, Apache Derby may be a perfect fit, especially because it does not require a DBA—a luxury many small businesses cannot afford.

- **Embedded applications:** Because the database is only about 2 MB in size and is implemented as a Java .JAR file, it simply becomes a part of the application that is running it.

- **Client database applications:** Many client applications need the power and reliability of a fully transactional (ACID compliant) SQL database, without the unwanted overhead of a DBA. Java applications built on the Apache Derby platform will pretty much run on any platform that supports a JVM.

- **Local registries and repositories:** Application Servers use Apache Derby to store dynamic registries such as UDDI or meta-data stores. Because these databases are fully transactional engines, developers do not have to worry about data corruption and system crashes destroying their critical configuration data.

- **Small business client/server and Web-based applications:** Small businesses need Web sites that are low on maintenance and high on reliability, with plenty of head room for seasonal business spikes. Apache Derby delivers a robust performance engine suitable for many small business needs; for example, Web shopping carts, recommendation engines, and so on.

- **Java development databases:** Apache Derby makes it easy to put a relational database on every developer's desktop. Apache Derby is just 2 MB, requires no DBA, and the support for JDBC allows for an easy switch to an open standards enterprise database during the later stages of development and testing. This means that you can leverage this database for development at no cost and write applications to be deployed on more industrial-strength databases such as DB2, Informix, and so on. In the past, many shops addressed the development database requirement with a client/server database. However, this introduced the need for a DBA and opened up the possibility of one developer's "bad code" compromising the entire development team's productivity by accidentally erasing test databases or corrupting the database. It also forced system administrators to develop software deployment strategies and to obtain the bandwidth to support them. With Apache Derby, developers can simply copy the Apache Derby .JAR file to a local directory, set their `CLASSPATH` environment variable so that it points to the .JAR file, and they are ready for development. Even moving data around is a snap.

- ***Demonstration or proof-of-concept applications:*** Apache Derby is an ideal database to use for demonstrations of your software (when a database is required) and proofs of concept. Because of its small size, Apache Derby adds very little to the download size of your demo, and it can be invisibly embedded into your application. Your potential customers and evaluators can run your application just as they would against an enterprise database without having to download, configure, and run one. Think of all those applications that run on a multitude of databases but require a significant investment for a simple proof-of-concept or demonstration. Apache Derby can solve these problems.

A High-Level View of the Apache Derby Database

Apache Derby is a relational database management system that is written in Java. Java and the open source movement go hand-in-hand. Java is an attractive language in which to write such software because its "write once, run anywhere" mantra allows for seamless portability. People that like Java will love Apache Derby because the engine is very portable: again, from Mac to mainframe, and all parts in between. For example, Apache Derby is heavily leveraged on mainframes for applications that require a lightweight meta-data storage engine.

The moment many application developers or project managers hear the word "database," they start looking for a database administrator (DBA), and questions along the line of "how do I implement an incremental backup" and só forth arise. The Apache Derby database is not for DBAs (and they're likely not to like it very much because they'll be looking for the wrong things). In fact, Apache Derby is unique in that it does not require professional DBAs, or DBA skills for that matter, to run. It is truly a "lights-out" database management system. Think of Apache Derby as that "black box" in the corner. But don't let the "behind the scenes" characteristics of the Apache Derby platform fool you: there are customers today with Cloudscape databases that hold tens of gigabytes of data.

Apache Derby delivers an efficient "next to no compromise" database engine in a "fingerprint-sized" engine of only 2 MB. Along with its tiny size, it has generally minimized resource requirements too. For example, in some environments, it can run with as little as 4 MB of RAM on a J2SE/J2EE 1.3 or later platform. In addition, the number and size of tables are pretty much limited only by the disk space available to them. (The maximum number of indexes per table is 32,767, and the maximum number of columns in a table is 1,012.) This makes Apache Derby not only easy to deploy but also easy to embed within applications as well. In fact, it literally disappears into its hosting application.

Apache Derby packs a lot of punch in its tiny 2 MB allocation. It provides a fully relational database engine, including complete support for SQL92E and JDBC (2.0 and 3.0), and partial support for SQL99. It has many advanced features that experienced database developers may be accustomed to with larger databases, such as:

- Identity columns (sometimes referred to as auto-incremented columns) for key generation
- Fast query compilation through a cost-based optimizer that supports hash joins, sort avoidance, and row- or table-level locking based on a percentage of data selected
- Automated statistics collection, automatic table reorganization and space reclamation, programmatic backups (no DBA required), and more
- Binary large objects (BLOBs) for complex non-traditional data handling
- Referential constraints (primary and foreign key), general constraints (unique and check), and default values for business rules enforcement
- Transactional processing (it's ACID-compliant; see the "Why Use a Relational Database?" section for more details) with isolation levels such as repeatable-read and uncommitted-read
- Objects to encapsulate business logic and promote code reuse and best practices, such as stored procedures, user-defined functions (UDFs), and triggers
- Views
- Bulk load utility
- Scrollable cursors for more efficient result set processing
- Concurrent access by any number of program threads or processes
- Multi-user access
- JDBC (both an embedded driver and an external driver that's the same one used with DB2 UDB for z/OS and DB2 UDB for Linux, Unix, and Windows—called the Java Common Client), ODBC, CLI, .NET, PHP, and Perl connectivity (add-on interfaces are available from the IBM Cloudscape Web site). In fact, IBM contributed the Apache Derby Network Client during the writing of this book—learn more at: http://incubator.apache.org/derby/faq.html#netclient.
- Rich security features, such as signed Java Archive (.JAR) files, encryption of stored data (through the Java Cryptography Extension, or JCE, and other providers), ability to run with a Java 2 security manager enabled, optional LDAP authentication, and more

- Unlimited table size (though many operating system's 2 GB file limits could theoretically come into play because Cloudscape stores each table as a separate file)

- The IBM Integration Plug-in for Apache Derby; a free Eclipse-based plug-in to implement Apache Derby functionality as user interface component (http://www-106.ibm .com/developerworks/db2/library/techarticle/dm-0501cline/)

- National language support for program integrated information (for example, error messages, program output, and so on), and documentation for the following languages: Spanish (es), German (de_DE), French (fr), Italian (it), Brazilian Portuguese (pt_BR), Korean (ko_KR), Japanese (ja_JP), Traditional Chinese (zh_TW), and Simplified Chinese (zh_CN)

Officially, Apache Derby supports any standard JVM (J2SE 1.3 or higher). Whereas most applications detail operating system support prerequisites, the JVM is really the run-time platform for this database.

All Apache Derby components and future enhancements will adhere to the *Apache Derby Charter*. This charter is a statement of direction or purpose. It dictates a course of action that everyone involved in this community will adhere to in order to create the best possible underlying data store for their applications. Specifically, it decrees that any contributions to the Apache Derby code base must be completely written in Java, easy to use, have a small footprint, and be secure.

Details on SQL Support in Apache Derby and IBM Cloudscape

Apache Derby and IBM Cloudscape implement the SQL92E language standard and many features that are found in the SQL99 specification (with extensions for Java). Although not complete, the following list details most of the features that you're likely to leverage when building your own application:

- Basic database types, such as: CHAR, DECIMAL, DOUBLE PRECISION, FLOAT, INTEGER, NUMERIC, REAL, SMALLINT

- Datetime data types (from SQL92T): DATE, TIME, TIMESTAMP (with JDBC date/ time escape syntax)

- Other types: BIGINT, VARCHAR, CHAR FOR BIT DATA, VARCHAR FOR BIT DATA, LONG VARCHAR, LONG VARCHAR FOR BIT DATA, BLOB, CLOB

- Basic operations: +,*,-,/,unary +,unary -

- Basic comparisons: <,>,<=,>=,<>,=

- Datetime literals

- Built-in functions: ABS or ABSVAL, CAST, LENGTH, CONCATENATION (‖), NULLIF and CASE expressions, CURRENT_DATE, CURRENT_ISOLATION, CURRENT_ TIME, CURRENT_TIMESTAMP, CURRENT_USER, DATE, DAY, HOUR, IDENTITY_VAL_LOCAL, LOCATE, LCASE or LOWER, LTRIM, MINUTE,

MOD, MONTH, RTRIM, SECOND, SESSION_USER, SQRT, SUBSTR, TIME, TIMESTAMP, UCASE or UPPER, USER, YEAR

- Basic predicates: BETWEEN, LIKE, NULL
- Quantified predicates: IN, ALL, ANY or SOME, EXISTS
- CREATE and DROP SCHEMA
- CREATE and DROP TABLE
- Check constraints
- ALTER TABLE: ADD COLUMN and ADD or DROP CONSTRAINT
- CREATE and DROP VIEW
- Constraints: NOT NULL, UNIQUE, PRIMARY KEY, CHECK, FOREIGN KEY
- Cascade delete
- Column defaults
- Delimited identifiers
- Updatable cursors (through JDBC)
- Dynamic SQL (through JDBC)
- INSERT, UPDATE, and DELETE statements
- Positioned updates and deletes
- WHERE qualifications
- GROUP BY
- HAVING
- ORDER BY
- UNION and UNION ALL
- Subqueries as expressions (from SQL92F)
- Joins in the WHERE clause
- Joins (SQL92T): INNER, RIGHT OUTER, LEFT OUTER, named column join, conditional join
- Aggregate functions (with DISTINCT): AVG, COUNT, MAX, MIN, SUM
- SELECT *, SELECT table.* (SQL92T), SELECT DISTINCT, select expressions
- Named select columns
- SQLSTATE
- UNION in views (SQL92T)
- CAST (SQL92T)
- INSERT expressions (SQL92T): insert into T2 (COL) select col from T1

- VALUES expressions: select * from (values (1, 2)) as foo(x, y), and so on
- Triggers

The Apache Derby Components

Developers, line of business (LOB) managers, and IT professionals have chosen and will continue to choose the Apache Derby database in countless scenarios and for numerous vertical applications. Apache Derby can be entirely embedded within an application, used in a client/server architecture, or even embedded in an application server.

Three major components are shipped with Apache Derby: the Apache Derby database engine, the Apache Derby network server, and the Apache Derby ij JDBC scripting tool (there are some other tools, but this is the main one). As previously mentioned, the Apache Derby Network Client is a recent IBM contribution that will become the mainstay for many of your applications that leverage a traditional client/server environment. You can get it at: http://incubator.apache.org/derby/faq.html#netclient.

The Apache Derby Database Engine

The core of an Apache Derby solution lies within the *Apache Derby database engine*. As you have seen, the Apache Derby database engine is a full-featured, fully functional, embeddable relational database engine. Having been part of IBM for three years, the Apache Derby SQL dialect is a subset of that used for DB2. This means that Apache Derby applications are, for the most part, fully portable to DB2. In addition, an Apache Derby database can interact with the DB2 Everyplace SyncServer (both as a client and as a backend data store), which allows it to be part of a mobile solution that includes synchronization logic.

Apache Derby can be easily embedded within a Java application because it is implemented as a Java class library. For example, Apache Derby is usually delivered as part of an application's .JAR file in which the Apache Derby .JAR file has been included.

The database is started when the Java virtual machine (JVM) that hosts the application is started, and it is subsequently shut down when the JVM hosting the application is terminated. Because a JVM can be multi-threaded, any threads that are spawned within the JVM hosting the Apache Derby database engine can access the database. Concurrent access to this database, without the use of the Apache Derby network server, *must* be made from within the same JVM.

It is possible to have multiple JVMs running on a machine and even to have separate Apache Derby databases in each JVM. In this case, the environments are considered to be completely separate.

Apache Derby Network Server

The Apache Derby network server increases the reach of the Apache Derby database engine by providing traditional client/server functionality across JVMs, expanded data access interface options, as well as concurrent access between JVMs on the same machine. The Apache Derby network server allows clients to connect over TCP/IP.

When developers refer to Apache Derby as an embeddable database, they are referring to the fact that the Apache Derby database runs within a JVM process. Without the Apache Derby network server, there would be no networking services, data access outside of the embedded JDBC driver in the database engine, or other infrastructure requirements; this accounts for its small footprint.

Understanding what the embedded concept entails is critical when developing applications. For example, one common misconception that developers have when they work with Apache Derby as a standalone database is that it's only a single-user database and does not have communication capabilities. They believe that it is a single-user, single-connection, single-threaded system and develop their applications accordingly. This is not true. Apache Derby as a standalone database can support as many connections as desired, so long as they are established from the same JVM hosting the Apache Derby engine.

For an Apache Derby database to be accessed from a process that resides outside the hosting JVM that loaded the Apache Derby database initially (even if the JVM process resides on the same server), you need to load the Apache Derby network server. Read that last sentence twice to ensure you understand it because it is often a source of confusion for Apache Derby developers when multiple JVMs reside on the same machine. The Apache Derby network server allows for communications between JVM processes. This means that this communication infrastructure isn't solely required to communicate between machines; it is needed even if two different JVM processes reside *on the same machine* and want to talk to the same database.

Using the Apache Derby network server, you could have a number of Java programs or JVMs interacting with a number of Apache Derby databases (or a single database for that matter). The Apache Derby network server is also required to support interfaces other than JDBC, like ODBC or .NET. The Apache Derby database engine comes with an embedded JDBC driver (this is not the JCC driver that we talked about earlier)—so you will not need the network server for intra-JVM JDBC connections. The Apache Derby Network Client works with the Apache Derby Network Server.

ij—The Apache Derby JDBC Scripting Tool

The `ij` tool is a JDBC-based scripting tool that allows SQL scripts to be executed against an Apache Derby database. This is one of the few tools used with Apache Derby. We will use this tool throughout the book to create a database and some tables, populate those tables, and retrieve data from the Apache Derby database.

It is important to remember the role of the Apache Derby network server when using this tool because many application developers end up with a connection error when using it for the first time. For example, let's assume a developer has created an application and is invoking that application to test it. Starting the application starts a JVM where the application resides and where the Apache Derby database engine runs. When testing the application, the developer might want to add some data or work with the database schema, so what better tool with which to connect to the database than the `ij` tool? If you do not have the Apache Derby network server loaded, you are going to get an error because the i j tool is a Java tool that runs in its own JVM. For the most part, if you are a developer, we recommend that you include the Apache Derby network server in your environment. Otherwise, you will have to concern yourself with these sorts of issues, which can sneak up on you if your integrated development environment (IDE) makes multiple connections to the target database.

Developing Apache Derby Applications

Because Apache Derby is a Java-based database engine, most application developers will choose to program their applications using the JDBC API. Cloudscape supports Java applications written in JDBC 2.0 and 3.0.

An Apache Derby application follows the same general methodology as other Java-based applications in that a proper JDBC driver is loaded, a connection is made to the required database, a statement object is created, and finally the statement object is used to execute some business logic (generally an SQL statement or a stored procedure). Prepared statements are also supported in Apache Derby, as well as parameter markers, which deliver an excellent performance boost for your applications. In addition, the Apache Derby database leverages the Java just-in-time (JIT) compiler for better performance through native operational profiling.

The only Apache Derby-specific code outlined in the previous paragraph is the loading of the JDBC driver and the uniform resource locator (URL) you would specify in the connection string. This means your Apache Derby applications can be easily altered to use other JDBC-compliant databases, such as DB2, Informix, and so on, by loading the appropriate driver class.

One very strong feature of Apache Derby is that the SQL API is 100% compatible with DB2, so if you ever decide to trade up for a full-fledged database, the migration to DB2 would be effortless. (There is also a free Eclipse-based migration toolkit for Apache Derby-to-DB2 migrations!) We bet you did not know that being an Apache Derby developer meant you were a DB2 developer too. Investing your skills in Apache Derby is definitely a resume-builder!

You can use almost any Java-based IDE to develop your Apache Derby-based applications. For example, you can use WebSphere Studio Application Developer (WSAD), Borland JBuilder, netBeans, and so on.

In keeping with the open source tradition, a plug-in is available for the Eclipse framework to equip application developers with a rich toolset for developing Apache Derby applications. Of course, you can also choose to write your applications the old-fashioned way, using your favorite editor such as emacs or vi—whatever suits your needs. When using a separate tool to help with application development, remember that you should probably have the Apache Derby Network Server installed as well.

The IBM DB2 plug-in for Eclipse lets you explore and create schemas for your DB2, Apache Derby, IBM Cloudscape, and Informix databases. An example of the Eclipse IDE with this plug-in is shown in Figure 1-2.

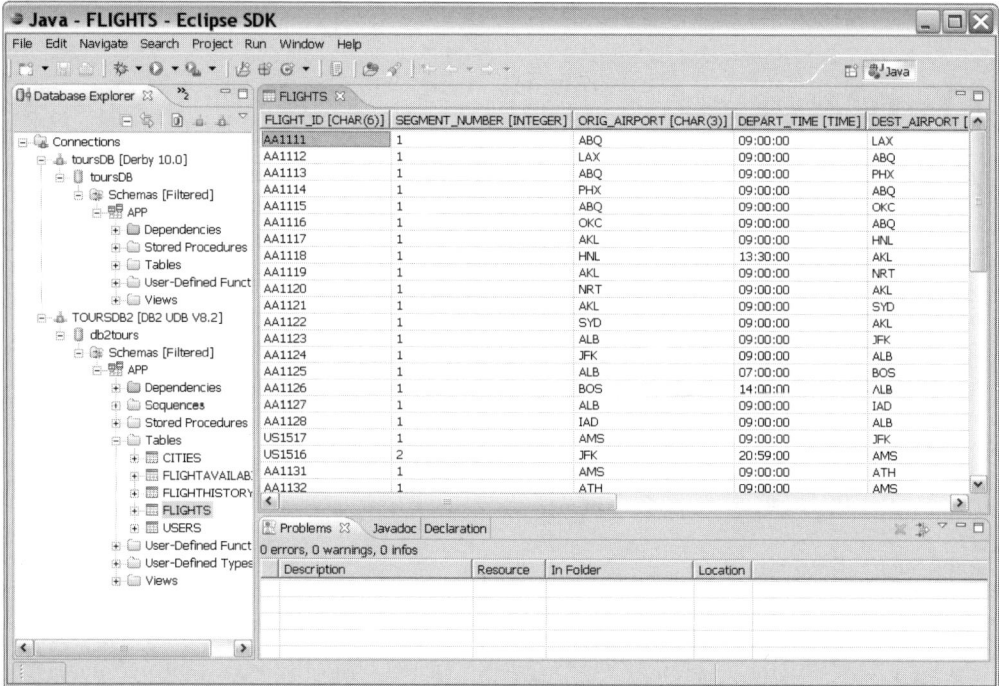

Figure 1-2 Using free open source Eclipse-based IDEs to work with Apache Derby databases

This plug-in also comes with a migration toolkit that allows you to migrate your Apache Derby schema to a DB2 database. Over time, expect to see more and more features driven into the plug-in and the Eclipse framework. (It is open source after all, so we are counting on some of you to contribute!)

Of course, there are other programming interfaces that you can use to develop applications and the tooling that goes along with it: for example, ODBC, CLI, .NET, Perl, and PHP will all be supported. You're going to learn a whole lot about application development with Apache Derby from this book.

## CHAPTER 2

Deployment Options for Apache Derby Databases

Before you install an Apache Derby database, it's important to understand the deployment options, prerequisites, and restrictions that are associated with the deployment model you pick. In this chapter, we'll introduce you to the different ways that you can deploy an Apache Derby database. Unless stated otherwise, references to the Apache Derby database also refer to IBM Cloudscape because they are the same database, as discussed in Chapter 1, "On Your Marks... Get Set... Go!!! An Introduction to the Apache Derby and IBM Cloudscape Community."

Apache Derby has a rich deployment model that makes it suitable for embedded, client/server, or multi-tiered applications. You can use the Apache Derby database engine to build:

- Applications that need to persist data and that want to leverage the services of a database engine, but also want to have those services run within the Java application itself. Because Apache Derby is almost transparent to end users, requires no administration, and can run in the same Java Virtual Machine (JVM) as your application, it's a great choice for embedded frameworks.

- Applications that need to leverage a server framework with the Apache Derby database to provide client/server connectivity, enable communications with an application server, or permit access to application programming interfaces (APIs) that are outside of the application's JVM.

Using the Embedded Framework for Apache Derby Applications

Some applications require a persistent data store but want to completely hide the fact that a relational-based data storage engine is "under the hood." The Apache Derby database engine is ideally suited to this scenario, and it shines when these are the primary requirements.

Because Apache Derby is simply a Java class library (called `derby.jar`), it can be embedded transparently into any Java application or server framework without affecting its "Javaness." This is in stark contrast to many other data management options that are currently available. There is nothing to additionally install besides your application, and there are no connections to configure or networking components to set up.

The fact that Apache Derby is embedded means that your application and the database engine can run in the same process and therefore run within the same JVM. Your Java application and the database are literally the same entity. In this framework, your application talks to Apache Derby through an embedded JDBC driver and makes corresponding API calls to the database engine. Because the JDBC driver is embedded within Apache Derby, there is no need for network communications, instantiation of transmission packets, memory context switches, or the traversal of additional code paths. This makes your embedded Apache Derby database very fast and efficient. In fact, from the operating system's perspective, your application and Apache Derby are seen as one process—you can't get more invisible than that!

When your application starts, it loads the local JDBC driver, which in turn starts the Apache Derby engine. When your application shuts down, it also shuts down the Apache Derby engine. This further illustrates the simplicity of leveraging this powerful relational database in your embedded application—who would have thought that using a database could be so easy?

In an embedded framework, *only a single application (or JVM) can access a database at one time.* That is why this framework is sometimes referred to as a single-user implementation. When references are made to the term *user* in this context, it means the application itself, which can be confusing at times. When you embed Apache Derby in your applications, the database engine will support multiple simultaneous connections and data access from multiple application threads from *the same application running within the same process (JVM).*

The points made in the previous paragraphs are very important points to remember in an embedded framework and we're going to repeat them a number of times in this section because people always get it wrong. Call it a simple rule that confuses everyone, but only one JVM at a time can access a database without the Apache Derby Network Server. You will know that you've forgotten this fact if you encounter `ERROR XJ040: Failed to start database` ... while working with Apache Derby. In the following example, we started an application that uses the TESTDB database and then tried to connect to this same database using the `ij` tool:

```
ij> connect 'jdbc:derby:testdb';
ERROR XJ040: Failed to start database 'testdb', see the next
  exception for details.
ERROR XSDB6: Another instance of Cloudscape may have already
  booted the database C:\cloudscape\cloud1001a\lib\testdb.
```

You receive this message because Apache Derby locks the db.lck file when it starts in order to protect the integrity of the database.

Examples of the Embedded Framework for Apache Derby Applications

This section provides some examples of the Apache Derby database in an embedded framework. Many more deployment options are available to you, but these examples will give you a good idea of what you will need to consider when designing your application.

The simplest way to use Apache Derby is to embed it within your application—we call this the *embedded framework.* Figure 2-1 shows the Apache Derby database engine deployed in an embedded framework. This figure serves as a building block for other options.

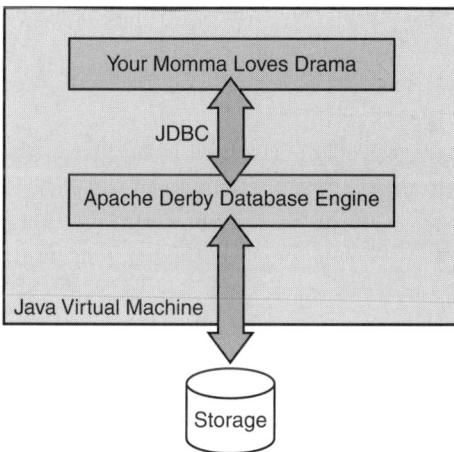

Figure 2-1   An application with an embedded Apache Derby database engine

In Figure 2-1 we start with a Java-based application (called "Your Momma Loves Drama"— you're going to learn how to build this application using various approaches and programming languages later in this book). This application in Figure 2-1 is written in Java, and when it starts, it runs within a JVM (the run-time service provider for any Java application).

In this scenario, users interact with the database through the Your Momma Loves Drama application—the fact that a database is busy at work behind the scenes is really unknown to them. The embedded JDBC driver communicates with the Apache Derby database engine. The Apache Derby database manages the data that is contained in the attached storage device.

When your application starts, it makes a call to the embedded Apache Derby JDBC driver and starts the database engine. Unlike typical database deployments, you don't need to set up any special network connections, install a proprietary client, or spend time configuring connections so that the application can talk to the database (because the database engine is an integral part of the application).

There are some interesting characteristics of the storage cylinder in Figure 2-1 that apply to Apache Derby databases in any deployment model. The data is "hardened" to your storage containers in such a way that the files are very portable. This allows you to agnostically move your database among workstations, servers, or hybrid devices without concern for complexities like bit encoding (big- and little-endian) or CPU architecture. For example, moving an Apache Derby database from a Macintosh computer to a mainframe or from an AIX box to a Windows machine can be done with no special considerations at all (just make sure that if you move databases, you move the entire database hierarchy).

In fact, if you are building a read-only application, Apache Derby can use read-only media as the storage unit for your data. This makes the Apache Derby database even more deployable for a wide array of applications.

For example, a ticket kiosk may have its own Java application and a need to support transactions (see Figure 2-2). Each quarter, a movie company publishes information about its upcoming releases for their application. The kiosk running the Apache Derby database can be configured with a media reader to read each quarter's shows, including trailers and promotions. When it's time to load a quarter's data into the application, you simply insert the CD-ROM containing the new movie listings, and the Apache Derby database can read data from it.

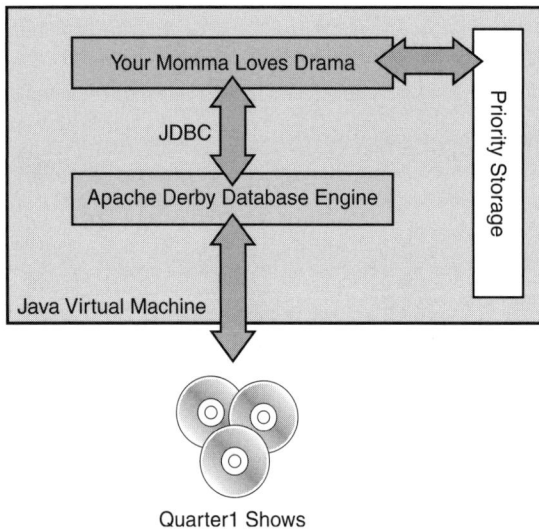

Quarter1 Shows

Figure 2-2   Connecting to read-only media and other non-Apache Derby resources

Figure 2-3 shows multiple Your Momma Loves Drama client threads running in the same process as the Apache Derby database. In this case, the Apache Derby database is acting like a client/ server database for a single application within the same JVM. This is a source of confusion for many new Apache Derby developers because they often hear references to a single-user topology.

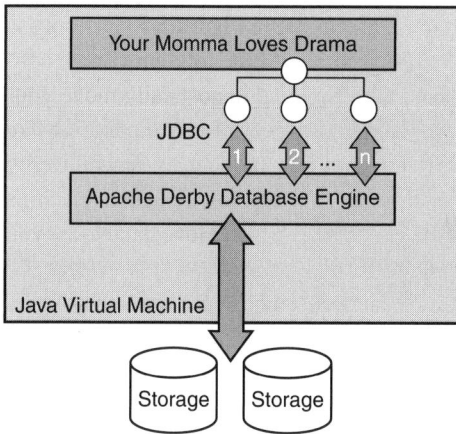

Figure 2-3 An application spawning multiple threads to the Apache Derby engine using a single connection

For example, in the environment shown in Figure 2-3, your application is multithreaded. However, you have to manage these threads programmatically yourself (what thread to run, when to run it, and so on). The standard way of doing this is to start multiple threads and assign each thread its own connection.

The Apache Derby database provides persistence of data by storing the data in disk files. The database engine can manage one or more database files, but each file can only be accessed by a single instance of the engine. In a client/server configuration, the engine provides multi-user access to the databases under its control. All threads that access the database do so through the database engine.

Another sample scenario is shown in Figure 2-4. Note that separate `DriverManager` `.getConnection()` calls for each database are required.

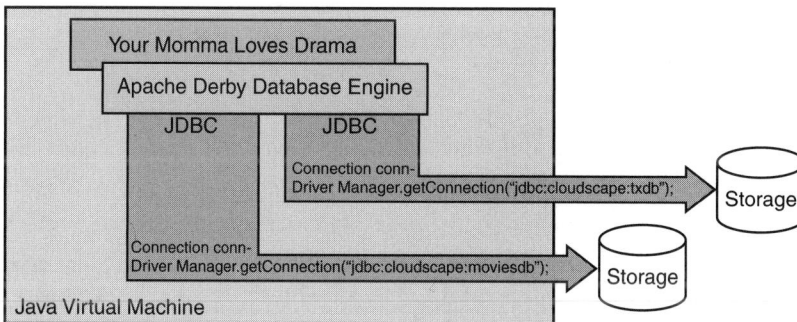

Figure 2-4 Connecting to multiple Apache Derby databases

It's just as easy to embed the Apache Derby database inside a Java-based application server (for example, IBM WebSphere Application Server or Apache Tomcat) as it is within your own applications. This allows you to take advantage of the services provided by these programs, such as connection pooling, connection concentration, etc. Browser-based clients can then access a database through Hypertext Transfer Protocol (HTTP) requests to servlets, Enterprise Java Beans (EJBs), Java Server Pages (JSPs), and so on.

In fact, IBM WebSphere Application Server and lots of other IBM software products use an embedded copy of the Apache Derby database in the form of IBM Cloudscape (refer to Chapter 1 if you don't know the difference) to manage state-based data. An example of Apache Derby embedded within an application server is shown in Figure 2-5.

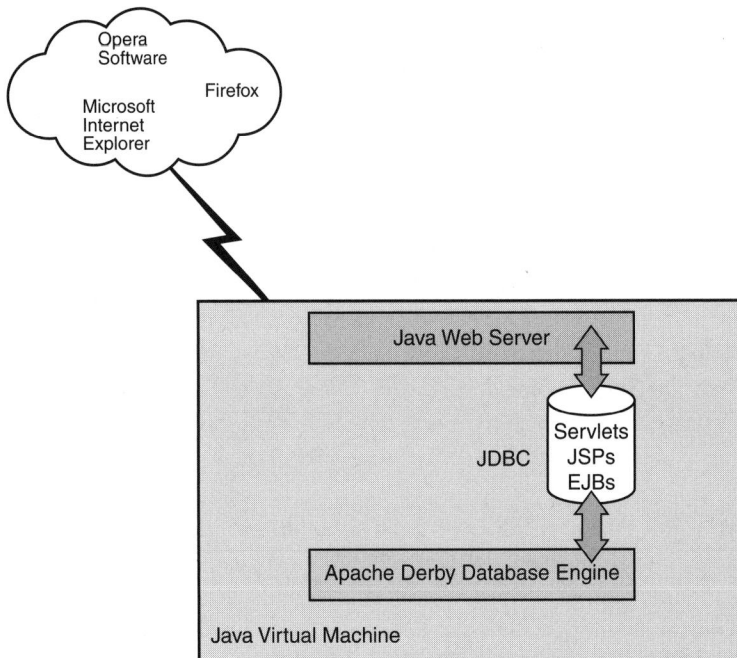

Figure 2-5   Connecting to an Apache Derby database that is embedded in a Web server

When your application requests data from the Apache Derby database, the embedded JDBC driver makes a copy of this data for the application. This programming model is often referred to as a *disconnected model with optimistic locking*. Changes to the data in the application layer do not affect the data in the database until your application specifically makes a JDBC call to send the changes back to the database. Because Apache Derby is transactionally safe, complex data manipulations can be grouped together as transactions. Apache Derby guarantees the atomicity of data transactions by ensuring that either all or none of the transaction will harden to disk—even after a failure.

Some Final Comments About the Embedded Framework for Apache Derby Applications

You can see the benefits of simply including the Apache Derby database Java archive file in your application. It is only about 2 MB in size, it is invisible, it performs very well because there is no network I/O to deal with, and so on. In fact, this is how the Apache Derby database was designed to run.

The term "single-user" often causes confusion for first-time Apache Derby users. To ensure we're clear, regardless of the deployment option used, Apache Derby supports multi-user access (as in connections), or independent database connections by the same application. A server framework implementation of Apache Derby differentiates itself from an embedded framework in that the database engine can support multiple isolated transactions as needed. With the embedded framework, each connection to an Apache Derby database represents a transaction. Therefore, independent connections by the same application, within the same JVM, allow you to execute multiple independent transactions for which you can specify isolation levels to control the concurrency of your application. These isolation levels include read committed, read uncommitted, repeatable read, and serializable.

GOLDEN RULE

You can't have more than one JVM access the database at the same time without using an embedded server framework unless you also have the Apache Derby Network Server installed.

The Apache Derby .JAR file contains no networking code. This doesn't mean that Apache Derby is a single-user database (which is how some people interpret it). For communications outside of the JVM, Apache Derby requires the Apache Derby Network Server (`derbynet.jar`), which is shipped in a separate .JAR file and is just as easily embedded as the Apache Derby database itself.

With the embedded framework, the only API that you can use to talk to your Apache Derby database is JDBC whose driver that is built into the database engine. If you want to use other APIs, you need to include the Apache Derby Network Server in your application.

DEVELOPERS AND THEIR TOOLS

Developers often run into problems when they use tools like `ij` or the Eclipse-based plug-in for development. They start their application and then want to use another tool to work with the database—but you can't do that in the embedded framework. This won't work even if you're using an Explorer window in your favorite IDE because that IDE is spawning a separate connection to the Apache Derby database from a separate JVM. To support this environment, you would need an Apache Derby Network Server. In fact, we recommend that all application development workstations include this component, even if the application will be deployed in an embedded framework.

Using the Server Framework for Apache Derby Applications

The Apache Derby Network Server (`derbynet.jar`) provides a server framework for Apache Derby databases (`derby.jar`). It uses the DB2 UDB Java Common Client JDBC driver (`db2cc.jar`). You can read about the differences between this driver and the embedded JDBC driver discussed in the previous section in the product documentation. Of course, the JCC is just one of the many options available, including the new Apache Derby Network Client (see http://incubator.apache.org/derby/faq.html#netclient) and C-JDBC by ObjectWeb (see http://c-jdbc.objectweb.org/).

There are many reasons why you might want to include the Apache Derby Network Server in your application. Here are some of the more important ones:

- You want to use other APIs to access the Apache Derby database. For example, CLI, ODBC, .NET, PHP, Python, or Perl all require the use of the Apache Derby Network Server.

- You are setting up an Apache Derby development environment and would like to be able to concurrently test your application and work with the database's schema using an assortment of tools in your integrated development environment (IDE).

- You want to be able to communicate with the Apache Derby database engine across different JVMs running on your device or workstation. This scenario resembles the traditional client/server model.

There are a number of different scenarios for which this framework is appropriate, and we'll discuss them in this section. What's important to keep in mind is that without the Apache Derby Network Server, multiple JVMs cannot access the same database. When used with your application, this component starts a server process that controls access to your database and connections to it.

In community feedback and newsgroups, we've noticed that a number of developers get really hung up on the restriction of only one JVM accessing a database. They wonder how the Apache Derby Network Server could magically bypass this requirement. Well, there's no magic that allows multiple processes to open the same operating system file—not for Apache Derby, Oracle, DB2, or anything else. The Apache Derby Network Server starts up the one JVM that connects to the physical database and then functions as a coordinator for the applications in other JVMs that want to connect to it. In short: multiple JVMs can connect to the Apache Derby Network Server, which routes JDBC requests to the database.

You are probably wondering why the Apache Derby database itself doesn't provide client/server functionality—after all, it's a database, and that's what databases do—they serve up data. Remember, however, that in the embedded version of the Apache Derby database, you can indeed have client/server functionality—it just has to use JDBC and come from within the same Java process as the application.

> **TIP**
>
> During the writing of this book, the Apache Derby Network Client was released, which gives you additional options for connectivity. This client allows for simplified database application development by combining the ease of use with tools like Eclipse and Apache Derby into one environment. After installing the Apache Derby Network client, the Apache Derby database and .JAR files can be added to any Eclipse Java project. The Apache Derby Network client also provides access to the IBM Cloudscape `ij` SQL scripting tool from within Eclipse. SQL commands can be executed or whole SQL scripts can be run from `ij` using the Eclipse console. The Apache Derby Network Server can be configured to listen on different ports of the local host machine using the Eclipse project properties and started from a menu item in Eclipse. This enables both clients from within the Eclipse environment and standalone client applications to connect to the Apache Derby Network Server. Learn more at http://www-106.ibm.com/developerworks/db2/library/techarticle/dm-0501cline/.

The Apache Derby database was developed with different frameworks because many applications are designed to run on a single system within a single process and don't require client/server capabilities (beyond the multiple threads that we talked about earlier). Because Apache Derby is invisible, it provides opportunities to robustly persist data in ways that many application developers might not have considered previously.

For example, standalone kiosks that provide directions through a single-user interaction might not need the capabilities provided by the Apache Derby Network Server, nor would an address book application for a PDA. Adding the extra footprint for unnecessary function would not be a good idea either. So if you need this function (which is what we are going to talk about in this section), you have to add it in.

If your application doesn't need the Apache Derby Network Server, don't use it. An application using an embedded framework will always perform better than one using a server framework.

> **DEVELOPERS! MAKE DEBUGGING EASIER**
>
> If you are a developer, we want to set up your Apache Derby environment with the server framework to make application development and debugging easier—even if the application will be deployed in an embedded framework. If you use the IBM Cloudscape GUI-based installation tool (which we link to from this book's Web site [www.ibmpressbooks.com/title/0131855255]), it will provide everything you need for Apache Derby database development.

You can use the Apache Derby Network Server in a traditional client/server framework, or you can embed it in the same manner as you would embed the database engine, as described in the previous section. Once the Apache Derby Network Server is running, your connection code is the same—the difference is in the way you get this framework running.

Examples of the Server Framework for Apache Derby Applications

The Apache Derby Network Server provides multi-user connectivity to Apache Derby databases within a single system or over a network. To support a traditional client/server configuration, you will need the .JAR files for both the database and the network server. In addition, your CLASSPATH environment variable setting will need to be updated to point to both of these files. (You can learn more about this environment variable in the installation chapters.) A traditional client/server model using the Apache Derby Network Server is shown in Figure 2-6.

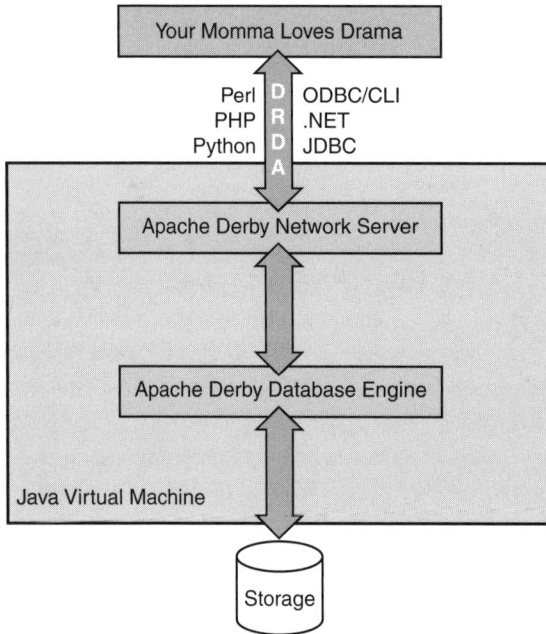

Figure 2-6   The Apache Derby database and the Apache Derby Network Server are required in a traditional client/server environment

Note that there is still only a single JVM accessing the database where the network server is running.

In this scenario, the Apache Derby Network Server receives and replies to API requests from clients. Applications that make JDBC calls are handled by the DB2 UDB Java Common Client, and internal connections are handled by the embedded Apache Derby JDBC driver. There are some differences between these drivers; refer to the Apache Derby Administration Guide for details. In Figure 2-6, you can see that the application is not embedded with the Apache Derby components.

Figure 2-7 builds on Figure 2-3 by adding multiple threads from an external process (JVM), which is supported by the addition of the Apache Derby Network Server.

If you are building an embedded application, as depicted in Figure 2-1, but want to connect to your database using a third-party tool, or the ij tool to produce some quick reports and browse, you need the Apache Derby Network Server.

Figure 2-8 is really a combination of Figure 2-6 and Figure 2-1. The model in Figure 2-8 is especially useful when developing and debugging an embedded database solution. It gives you the flexibility to connect to your running application and use schema browsing tools like the Eclipse plug-in or ij for data-centric work.

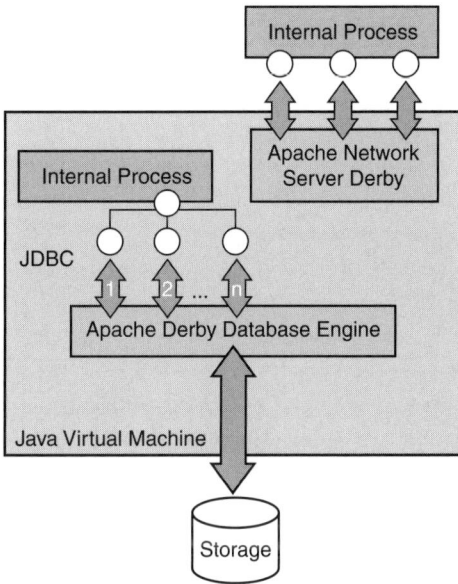

Figure 2-7   Using multiple threads from a separate process with the Apache Derby Network
Server

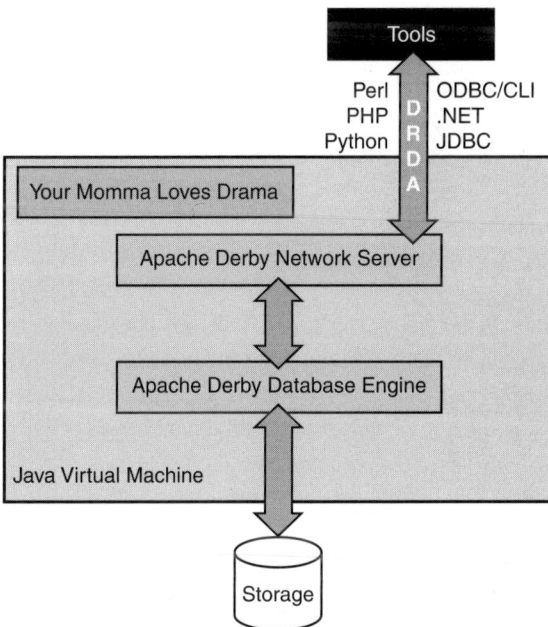

Figure 2-8   The Apache Derby database and the Apache Derby Network Server in a single
embedded solution

In Figure 2-8, the application is hosted in the JVM. When the application starts, it starts the Apache Derby database. You can start up the Apache Derby Network Server programmatically by opening a port for the network server to listen for client requests. In this example, your application, the database engine, and the network server all reside within the same JVM. Clients or tools can talk to the database through the network server. This is a very popular deployment model for developing Apache Derby applications, and it's a nice way to circumvent the development conundrum of the embedded solution discussed in the previous section.

Figure 2-9 shows a deployment model that uses a Java-based application server like WebSphere Application Server (WAS), which has no idea how to communicate with Apache Derby tools such as ij. In Figure 2-9, you can see that WAS uses the embedded driver, and that external tools leverage the Apache Derby Network Server. As previously mentioned, WAS actually uses the IBM Cloudscape version of Apache Derby when processing session-based data. In this example, the applications are actually WebSphere Application Server and other various external tooling applications.

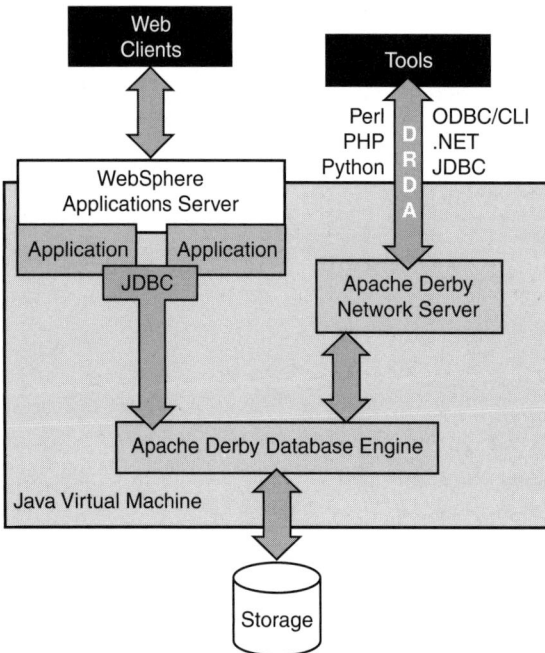

Figure 2-9   Apache Derby in a typical application server deployment.

## CHAPTER 3

Apache Derby Databases

Introduction

This chapter discusses the structure and content of an Apache Derby database. An Apache Derby database is an organized collection of objects. Each database has its own system catalog, log files, security, and tuning parameters. There are a number of basic components or objects that are defined for each Apache Derby database. These objects include:

- Tables
- Schemas
- Views
- Indexes
- Triggers
- Stored procedures
- Log files

We first examine what an Apache Derby database is, and how it is created. A database object, for the purpose of this book, is any component of an Apache Derby database, such as tables, views, indexes, schemas, triggers, and procedures. How the database objects are created and manipulated is discussed in Chapter 8, "SQL."

Database Structure

An Apache Derby database contains dictionary objects such as tables, columns, indexes, and .JAR files. An Apache Derby database can also store its own configuration information.

An Apache Derby database is stored in files that live in a directory with the same name as the database (that is, the SAMPLE database is found in the SAMPLE directory). Database directories typically live in system directories. A database directory contains the following objects:

- log directory—This directory contains files that make up the database transaction log, used internally for data recovery.

- seg0 directory—This directory contains one file for each user table, system table, and index.

- service.properties file—This is a text file with internal configuration information.

- tmp directory (optional)—A temporary directory used by Apache Derby for large sorts, deferred updates, and deletes. Sorts are used by a variety of SQL statements. For databases on read-only media, you might need to set a property to change the location of this directory.

- jar directory (optional)—This directory contains .JAR files that are stored when you use database class loading.

There are some limitations on the number and size of Apache Derby databases and database objects. Table 3-1 lists these limitations.

Table 3-1   Size Limits for Apache Derby Database Objects

Object	Limit
Tables per database	java.lang.Long.MAX_VALUE Some operating systems impose a limit on the number of files allowed in a single directory.
Indexes per table	32,767 or storage
Columns per table	1,012
Number of columns in an index key	16
Rows per table	No limit
Size of table	No limit Some operating systems impose a limit on the size of a single file.
Size of row	No limit, because rows can span pages. Some operating systems impose a limit on the size of a single file, and therefore limit the size of a table and the size of a row in that table.

The next section describes how databases can be created, dropped, and managed within the Apache Derby environment.

Creating an Apache Derby Database

There is no `CREATE DATABASE` command within the Apache Derby environment. Instead, databases are created and accessed via the Apache Derby connection URL.

SETTING UP THE PROPER APACHE DERBY ENVIRONMENT

Before attempting any of the examples in this section, make sure that you have issued the `SETEMBBEDEDCP` command in Windows or `setEmbeddedCP.sh` in Linux. These commands are case sensitive in Linux, so make sure that you type the shell command correctly. This command sets up the appropriate environment variables for running Apache Derby on your operating system.

The connection URL contains various options that get passed to the JDBC driver. The most important option is the name of the database, which follows the driver name:

```
jdbc:derby:SAMPLE
jdbc:derby:databaseName=SAMPLE
```

Either of these forms of the connection URL is acceptable. The database name can also contain an explicit reference to the location of the database. In the prior example, the `SAMPLE` database is assumed to be in the system directory, or the location where the application is running. If this is not the case, the location of the database needs to be explicitly defined, as shown in the following example:

```
jdbc:derby:d:/databases/SAMPLE
```

Note that this example uses a Windows file name, but this can also be a file system in Linux. If the database does not exist, an additional parameter needs to be added to the connection string to force the creation of the database:

```
jdbc:derby:d:/databases/SAMPLE;create=true
```

If the database already exists, and the `create=true` parameter is used, Apache Derby issues an error message but will not re-create the database. This prevents someone from inadvertently destroying an existing database.

Additional parameters are available to the user, and they are discussed later in this chapter. The name of the database itself can be any combination of letters in the range A–Z, digits in the range 0–9, and underscore (_) characters. The only restriction on the name is that it must start with a character (A–Z).

Database names within Apache Derby can cause you grief depending on your environment. Database names in a Windows environment are not case sensitive, so `SAMPLE` and `sample` are exactly the same database from an Apache Derby perspective. However, if you are running on Linux, names are case sensitive, so make sure that you spell the name exactly the way you created it. To minimize confusion on local and remote applications, you should use uppercase names for databases. The SQL standard forces the database name to uppercase when a DB2 client tries to connect to the Apache Derby database running in network server mode, so a best practice is to always specify an uppercase database name in your connection string and when you are actually creating the database.

> **DATABASE NAMES**
> A good practice in Apache Derby is to always use uppercase letters when naming a database. This will eliminate any difficulties when connecting from a network client or when moving the database between different operating systems.

One of the tools supplied with Apache Derby is `ij`. This tool is Apache Derby's interactive JDBC scripting tool. It is a simple utility for running scripts against an Apache Derby database. The `ij` tool is a Java application that you start from an MS-DOS command window or the UNIX shell. The tool provides several commands to help you access a variety of JDBC features through scripts.

To create a new database through `ij`, issue the following command from a command window or shell:

```
java -Dij.protocol=jdbc:derby: -Dij.database=SAMPLE;create=true
    org.apache.derby.tools.ij
```

In this example, two parameters are specified on the `ij` command. Note that the database name is not included in the protocol section, as would be the case if you were using a normal connection. When the utility is used from a command line, output similar to the following is produced:

```
ij version 10.0 (C) Copyright IBM Corp. 1997, 2004.
CONNECTION0* -  jdbc:derby:SAMPLE
* = current connection
ij>
```

Up to this point, the `ij` tool has created and connected you to the SAMPLE database. Note that no message is produced during the creation of the database. Apache Derby will connect to the new database, unless an error occurs during the creation step. If the database already exists, the `ij` tool returns the following warning:

```
WARNING 01J01: Database 'SAMPLE' not created, connection made to
existing database instead.
```

The `ij` utility will not re-create the database, so you will not lose any data if you issued this command by mistake. An alternative approach to creating a database is to use the connection command from within the `ij` utility. If you invoke the `ij` command without a database name, it will start in a "disconnected" state.

```
java -Dij.protocol=jdbc:derby: org.apache.derby.tools.ij
ij version 10.0 (C) Copyright IBM Corp. 1997, 2004.
ij>
```

The `CONNECT` command is part of the `ij` tool syntax, and it supports the same parameters as the `ij` startup command.

```
java -Dij.protocol=jdbc:derby: org.apache.derby.tools.ij
ij version 10.0 (C) Copyright IBM Corp. 1997, 2004.
ij> connect 'jdbc:derby:SAMPLE;create=true';
ij>
```

The database is available for access as soon as the `ij` prompt returns.

Deleting an Apache Derby Database

Apache Derby does not have a `DROP DATABASE` command. Instead, you must use operating system commands to delete the directory in which the database resides. The Apache Derby catalog tables for the deleted database are independent of any other database that you might have created. Other databases have their own unique directory structure and do not share catalog tables.

Database Contents

When a database has been created by Apache Derby, it generates a number of files underneath the database directory. By default, the directory containing the database will have the same name as the database. Within this directory, Apache Derby will create:

- `log` directory—Transaction log
- `seg0` directory—Contains files for each user table, system table, and index
- `service.properties` file—Internal configuration information
- `tmp` directory—Temporary sort space
- `jar` directory—Contains .JAR files that are stored when you use database class loading

In addition to these files, Apache Derby creates a number of system tables that are required to manage the contents of the database. These system tables are:

- `SYSALIASES`—Describes procedures and functions within the current database
- `SYSCHECKS`—Describes check constraints within the current database
- `SYSCOLUMNS`—Describes columns within all tables in the current database

- SYSCONGLOMERATES—Describe conglomerates within the current database, where a conglomerate is a unit of storage (a table or an index)
- SYSCONSTRAINTS—Contains information common to all types of constraints within the current database, including primary key, unique, foreign key, and check constraints
- SYSDEPENDS—Describes the dependency relationships between persistent objects in the database
- SYSFILES—Describes .JAR files that are stored in the database
- SYSFOREIGNKEYS—Describes information that is specific to foreign key constraints in the current database; Apache Derby generates a backing index for each foreign key constraint
- SYSKEYS—Describes specific information for primary key and unique constraints within the current database; Apache Derby generates an index on the table to back up each constraint
- SYSSCHEMAS—Describes schemas within the current database
- SYSSTATISTICS—Contains statistics on various objects within the database
- SYSSTATEMENTS—Contains one row of information for each prepared statement
- SYSTABLES—Describes tables and views within the current database
- SYSTRIGGERS—Describes database triggers within the current database
- SYSVIEWS—Describes view definitions within the current database

Additional information on these tables can be found in the Apache Derby manuals found at http://incubator.apache.org/derby/manuals/index.html. Chapter 8 also contains definitions and examples of some of these important tables.

Although all of these tables are necessary for Apache Derby to run, SYSTABLES and SYSCOLUMNS are of particular interest to a developer or user of the system. Because every system table can be manipulated with regular SQL expressions, you can find the name of every table within the database by issuing a simple SQL SELECT statement:

```
SELECT * FROM SYS.SYSTABLES;
```

All of the system tables are created with a schema name of SYS. Unless otherwise specified, tables created by an application have a schema name of APP.

Additional Database Connection Options

For most applications, connecting to a database without any additional options will give you all of the capabilities that you require. However, there are some additional connect line options that will be of interest to those users who need a higher level of security and encryption in the database or who need to maintain the database. The options can be divided into three categories: security, maintenance, and environment.

Security

Apache Derby includes a number of options for encrypting the database and for securing access to it. By default, the database can be accessed by any application, with no restriction on who can view the contents. This may be an appropriate level of access for an embedded database, where all data requests are handled through an application that already authenticates users. However, if the database is open to multiple users or requires strong encryption of its contents, you might want to consider using these options.

- `dataEncryption`—Specifies data encryption on disk for a new database. This parameter must be specified, along with the `create=true` parameter, the `boot-Password` parameter, and optionally, the encryption provider and algorithm.

- `bootPassword`—Specifies the key to use for encrypting a new database or booting an existing encrypted database. The password must be an alphanumeric string that is at least eight characters long. When creating a database, the `bootPassword` parameter must be specified, along with the `dataEncryption` parameter. On subsequent access to the database, only the `bootPassword` parameter must be specified.

- `encryptionProvider`—Any alternate encryption routine can be specified at database creation time by specifying an encryption provider and the algorithm that is to be used. If this parameter is not specified, the default encryption provider is `com.sun.crypto.provider.SunJCE`.

- `encryptionAlgorithm`—Specifies the algorithm for data encryption. The format of this parameter is `algorithmName/feedbackMode/padding`. In Apache Derby, the only padding type allowed is `NoPadding`. If no encryption algorithm is specified, the default value is `DES/CBC/NoPadding`.

- `user, password`—A user ID and password can also be specified on the connection string. These parameters are optional, but they must be specified if you have turned on authentication checking within the database. User IDs and passwords can be checked in a variety of ways, including the Lightweight Directory Access Protocol (LDAP), a user-defined class, or Apache Derby's built-in user IDs. For more information on security, see Chapter 7, "Security," or refer to the Apache Derby Developer's Guide.

Maintenance

Although an Apache Derby database is mostly maintenance-free, there are a number of connect options that are used to recover a database and to set logging information for the transactions that take place.

- `logDevice`—The `logDevice` specifies the path to the directory in which the database logs are to be stored during database creation or restoration.

- `rollForwardRecoveryFrom`—You can specify the `rollForwardRecoveryFrom=Path` option in the boot time URL to restore the database using a backup copy, and perform roll-forward recovery using archived and active logs.

- createFrom—You can specify the createFrom=Path option in the boot time connection URL to create a database using a full backup image from the specified location.

- restoreFrom—You can specify the restoreFrom=Path option in the boot time connection URL to restore a database using a full backup image from the specified location.

- shutdown—Shuts down a database if you specify a databaseName. (Reconnecting to the database reboots it.) This option shuts down the entire Apache Derby system if, and only if, you do not specify a databaseName. When you are shutting down a single database, Apache Derby performs a final checkpoint on the database. When you are shutting down a system, Apache Derby performs a final checkpoint on all system databases, deregisters the JDBC driver, and shuts down within the JVM before the JVM exits.

The location of the log files will have the largest impact on database performance. By default, the log files are placed in the same directory as the database tables. This means that there will be disk contention on the same device, as the system attempts to log insert, update, and delete operations at the same time as it is retrieving data from the database. To improve performance in high-maintenance applications, you should consider placing the log files on an alternate device. At database creation time, the log directory location can be specified with the logDevice parameter, as in the following example:

```
java -Dij.protocol=jdbc:derby:
 -Dij.database=d:\databases\SAMPLE;create=true;logDevice=e:\logs
  org.apache.derby.tools.ij
```

The database will reside in the d:\databases\SAMPLE directory, and the logs will be placed in the e:\logs\log directory. The log files are always placed in a separate log directory, rather than within the database directory itself. A log file can be moved manually later if log and database contention becomes an issue. To accomplish this, move the logs physically from their current location and place them in the new log location. This step must be done when the database has been stopped; otherwise your logs will become corrupted and the database might be left in an inconsistent state!

```
move d:\databases\SAMPLE\log\*.* e:\logs\log
```

After the logs have been moved, the services.properties file found within the database directory needs to be modified to have the log file point to the new location. The required line in this file is:

```
logDevice=e:\\logs or logDevice=e:/logs
```

SPECIAL CHARACTERS IN THE APACHE DERBY PROPERTIES FILE
When editing the Apache Derby `services.properties` file, remember that forward and backward slashes can be interchanged in file definitions. However, two backward slashes are required instead of one because the backward slash is considered an escape character: two characters are required to represent one backward slash.

You must use double backward slashes or single forward slashes when specifying a directory name. This keyword may not exist in the `services.properties` file if you did not specify an alternative log file location during the creation of the database. This line only exists if you created a database with the `logDevice` parameter.

Note that backup and recovery of a database might require additional steps if the logs are not in the default location. In addition, you must ensure that you have placed the logs for a database in its own unique location. For example, the `logDevice` parameter specified in the earlier example should only be used by the `SAMPLE` database. Because the log files for different databases have the same names, having two databases point to the same directory will cause problems.

For more information on how to maintain an Apache Derby database, see Chapter 6, "Managing an Apache Derby Database."

Environment

The territory of a database is usually dependent on the territory defined for the operating system or the Java locale being used. If the database needs to be defined for a different territory, the territory parameter can be set to a different country code.

The default system territory is found using `java.util.Locale.getDefault()`. Specify a territory in the form ll_CC, where ll is the two-letter language code, and CC is the two-letter country code. Language codes consist of a pair of lowercase letters that conform to ISO-639. For a list of ISO-639 codes, visit http://www.ics.uci.edu/pub/ietf/http/related/iso639.txt.

Database Objects

An Apache Derby database is an organized collection of objects. Each database has its own system catalog, log files, security, and tuning parameters. SQL is used throughout the database industry as a common method of issuing database queries. Before we examine the SQL language, we need to understand some Apache Derby terminology. We will be referring to the basic components or objects that are defined for each Apache Derby database. These objects include:

Tables

Data Types

Schemas

Views

Indexes

Triggers

Procedures

The following sections give a brief overview of each object and describe how it is used.

Tables

A table is an unordered set of rows. Rows consist of columns. Each column is based on a data type. Tables, once created and populated with data, are referenced in the FROM and INTO clauses of data manipulation language (DML) statements. Tables are created using the CREATE TABLE statement, and each table is a logical representation of the way the data is physically stored on disk.

Data Types

Each column in an Apache Derby table must be associated with a data type. The data type indicates the kind of data that is valid for the column. Apache Derby supports a number of built-in data types, including:

- Integer Types—These include the SMALLINT, INTEGER, and BIGINT data types. These types are exact representations of integer values.

- Decimal Types—The DECIMAL and NUMERIC data types are identical and are used for storing currency values that typically have a decimal point associated with them.

- Floating Point—FLOAT, REAL, and DOUBLE PRECISION data types allow you to store floating point values that include a significant value and a mantissa. These types are generally used for scientific computing, which requires extremely large or small values with unknown precision.

- Character Types—CHAR, VARCHAR, LONG VARCHAR, BLOB, and CLOB are variations of character-based values. These data types contain character strings of various lengths. A number of these data types can also be modified to ignore codepage conversion between a client and a server (FOR BIT DATA).

- Date and Time Types—There are three data types that are used to track date and time: DATE, TIME, and TIMESTAMP.

Apache Derby supports all of these built-in data types, and their structure and usage are described later in Chapter 8.

Schemas

Schemas are database objects used in Apache Derby to logically group other database objects. Most database objects are named using a two-part naming convention (schema_name. object_name). The first part of the name is referred to as the schema or the qualifier for the database object. The second part is the object name. When you create an object and do not specify a schema, the object is associated with the implicit schema APP.

When an object is referenced in an SQL statement, it is also implicitly qualified with the APP schema if no schema name is specified in the SQL statement. The CURRENT SCHEMA (or CURRENT SQLID) special register contains the default qualifier to be used for unqualified objects referenced in dynamic SQL statements. You can modify this value with the `SET CURRENT SCHEMA` statement.

Views

Views are virtual tables that are derived from one or more tables or views and can be used interchangeably with tables when retrieving data. Views do not contain real data. Only the definition exists in the database. Views can be created to limit access to sensitive data while allowing more general access to other data.

Views are not updateable in Apache Derby. This means that you cannot `INSERT`, `UPDATE`, or `DELETE` rows through a view.

Indexes

Indexes are physical objects that are associated with individual tables. Any table can have one or more indexes defined on it. A view cannot have an index defined on it, but Apache Derby can use the indexes that are defined on the underlying table on which the view is based.

Indexes are used to:

- Ensure the uniqueness of data values
- Improve SQL query performance

Indexes can be used to access data more quickly and avoid the time-consuming task of sorting the data using temporary storage. Indexes are maintained automatically by Apache Derby as data is inserted, updated, and deleted.

Indexes can be defined in ascending or descending order. They can be defined as unique or not unique, and they can be defined on a single column or multiple columns. Note that the maintenance overhead of indexes can negatively impact the performance of `INSERT`, `UPDATE`, and `DELETE` statements, so care should be taken to weigh improved `SELECT` performance against data maintenance functions.

In some situations, Apache Derby will automatically generate an index on your behalf. When unique, primary, and foreign key constraints are specified in a table, Apache Derby generates indexes that enforce or "back" these constraints. If a column or set of columns has a unique or primary key constraint defined on it, you cannot create an index on those columns. Apache Derby has already created it for you with a system-generated name.

Triggers

A trigger is a set of actions that will be executed when a defined event occurs. The triggering events can be the following SQL statements:

- `INSERT`
- `UPDATE`
- `DELETE`

Along with constraints, triggers can help to enforce data integrity rules with actions such as cascading deletes or updates. Triggers can also perform a variety of functions such as updating other tables, issuing alerts, and sending email.

Triggers are defined for a specific table, and once defined, a trigger is automatically active. A table can have multiple triggers defined on it, and if multiple triggers are defined on a given table, the order of trigger activation is based on the trigger creation timestamp (the order in which the triggers were created).

Procedures

Methods invoked within Apache Derby are commonly called database-side procedures, or stored procedures. The CREATE PROCEDURE statement allows you to create Java stored procedures, which you can then call using the CALL PROCEDURE statement.

Stored procedures are useful for encapsulating logic that you might want to reuse between applications. In addition, stored procedures might be able to manipulate the data more efficiently, especially in a client-server environment. A stored procedure can manipulate data locally at the server, rather than passing individual rows back to an application to process remotely. The use of stored procedures can result in considerable performance benefits.

Summary

An Apache Derby database contains a variety of objects, including tables, indexes, schemas, views, log files, and triggers. There are a variety of options available to you for modifying the behavior of the database, including security, performance, recovery, and language support. Finally, Apache Derby databases are self-contained and can easily be moved or deleted using standard operating system commands.

Installing Apache Derby and IBM Cloudscape on Windows

In this chapter, we walk you through the steps involved in setting up your environment to run the Apache Derby or IBM Cloudscape database on a Windows-based workstation. If you want to install either of these products on a Linux-based workstation, we cover that process in Chapter 5, "Installing Apache Derby and IBM Cloudscape on Linux." For all other operating systems, you can use the manual method or the universal Java installation program (both of which are also covered in this chapter).

Because we've included a copy of IBM Cloudscape in the back of this book, we'll assume that the source you are using to install your environment comes from the IBM Cloudscape image that is linked to from this book's Web site (www.ibmpressbooks.com/title/0131855255). In addition, as described in Chapter 2, "Deployment Options for Apache Derby Databases," an IBM Cloudscape installation will automate the tasks for setting up your environment, and because that product is especially well suited for developers, it makes sense to detail that process in this chapter.

In this chapter, unless otherwise noted, we'll only refer to the IBM Cloudscape version of the Apache Derby database. Where other paragraphs warrant differences, we'll point them out to you and then continue with our assumption.

We're assuming in this chapter that you are aware of the differences between the IBM Cloudscape and Apache Derby packages. If the details are a little sketchy, see Chapter 1, "On Your Marks . . . Get Set . . . Go!!! An Introduction to the Apache Derby and IBM Cloudscape Community."

You can install IBM Cloudscape on Windows by using the generic graphical Windows packaged installer, or manually by updating a couple of environment variables so that they point to the location of the Java archive (.JAR) file that contains the IBM Cloudscape database engine and network server. The Windows installation program requires approximately 65 MB of free space on your system, and it is invoked by double-clicking on an .EXE file. We recommend that you use the native program for your operating system whenever you can.

If you are installing the Apache Derby database engine from the Apache Web site, you can only use the manual method. Installing Apache Derby manually is as simple as copying over the required .JAR files to your disk and updating the `CLASSPATH` for your JRE.

Migration from Previous Versions of Cloudscape

Apache Derby and IBM Cloudscape Version 10.0 do not support the automatic upgrade of databases from previous versions of Cloudscape. The IBM Cloudscape database engine and SQL API have been rewritten so that applications built on these platforms are fully compatible with IBM DB2 Universal Database for Linux, UNIX, and Windows Version 8.1. For information on migrating databases created with previous versions of Cloudscape, see http://publib.boulder.ibm .com/epubs/html/c1894710.html.

If you have an existing pre-Version 10.0 installation of Cloudscape installed on your machine, *do not* install IBM Cloudscape Version 10.0 on top of it. You must uninstall the previous version of the product by running the uninstall program, or you must manually remove the files. The Cloudscape uninstaller will not remove your databases.

If you are installing IBM Cloudscape on an existing IBM Cloudscape Version 10.0 instal-lation or adding one of the components shipped in this package to your existing installation, you might see a size of 0 MB if you elect to customize the installation using the graphical installation program.

IBM CLOUDSCAPE AND CLOUDSCAPE—IS THERE A DIFFERENCE?
Note the difference between IBM Cloudscape and Cloudscape databases. IBM Cloudscape and Apache Derby databases are the same. References to Cloudscape on its own refer to a version of the code before the release where IBM Cloudscape and Apache Derby converged and became an open source product.

Before You Begin

Whether you plan to use the IBM Cloudscape installer to create a development environment or directly deploy an IBM Cloudscape database engine (or an application with the engine built into it), you need to set up your system for the installation of the database engine code (and any add-on components). In this section, we'll introduce you to some key terms that you need to under-stand and the steps you can take to ensure that your environment is ready for installation.

Not all of these steps are necessary, and some may have been done already for you in the course of your day-to-day interactions with other software packages. In short, the installation of IBM Cloudscape isn't as cumbersome as the length of this chapter might imply, but we want to ensure that you have a good understanding of the IBM Cloudscape environment and its interac-tion with your system.

When you install IBM Cloudscape, the main components that you need to understand are the product .JAR files, the database files, and the database log file. These three components exist in all IBM Cloudscape installations and need to be known to your system before you can use the database.

The Java Runtime Environment

The environment in which you want to deploy your application must have a Java Runtime Environment (JRE) at the Version 1.3 level or later to support an IBM Cloudscape database or network server (we recommend running at Version 1.4.2 or higher).

If you don't have a JRE on your system (although chances are most of you will), the IBM Cloudscape installation program for Windows gives you the option to install IBM's JRE for Windows, which is provided as part of the installation image. Of course, you can always install your own JRE or Java Developer's Kit (JDK).

IBM provides JREs and JDKs for the AIX, Linux, Windows, and z/OS operating systems. You can download them at http://www-106.ibm.com/developerworks/java/jdk/. If you need a JRE or JDK for another platform, or if you want to use a specific vendor's JRE or JDK, you should refer to that vendor's Web site or documentation for more information.

If your system does not have a JRE already installed, the IBM Cloudscape installation program will automatically load one because it relies on a JRE to support the graphical installation process. If the IBM Cloudscape installation program has to load a JRE from its own image (in other words, a JRE doesn't exist on your system), it will install it on your workstation—unless you specifically ask it not to.

Again, you may already have a running JRE in your environment, because you have a Java-based integrated development environment (IDE), or because you just have software that uses Java and one was subsequently installed, but if you don't, the IBM Cloudscape installation program has you covered.

WHEN YOU MIGHT WANT TO USE THE GENERIC INSTALLATION PROGRAM
If you know that you have a JRE running on your system, you can use the generic installation program to graphically set up an IBM Cloudscape environment. This is a useful option if your workstation or target device has a shortage of available disk space because this installation program has a significantly smaller footprint than its Windows-native counterpart.

J Who? How Do I Set It Up? How Do I Know I've Got One?

If you're not familiar with some of the terms that we mentioned in the previous section, let's spend some time distinguishing between a JDK, a JRE, a JVM, and so on. If you feel right at home in a Java environment, you can skip this section.

As its name implies, the JRE provides the runtime environment for Java-based applications. Specifically, it provides a Java Virtual Machine (JVM), which is a protected execution environment where Java applications actually run. At a higher level, it can be thought of as a piece of software that interprets Java programs, class files, and .JAR files and allows them to run in a safe and protected environment. The counterpart to Java's JVM in the Microsoft programming model is the Common Language Runtime (CLR). So, even if you are not a Java expert, think CLR and you know all you need to know for now.

The JRE, which always includes a JVM, is actually the minimal file set you need to run any Java application, and that is why it is often installed as part of different applications that use Java. For example, our test workstation could have a JRE because we also have the IBM DB2 Universal Database for Linux, UNIX, and Windows product running on it, and that product would install a JDK.

In contrast, a JDK is a superset of a JRE. A JDK contains all of the components of a JRE, with additional utilities and tools for Java application development. People who want to develop Java-based applications almost always require a JDK. If you have a Java-based IDE such as IBM WebSphere Studio Application Developer (WSAD), IBM Rational Application Developer, or any Eclipse-based tooling, you likely already have a JDK installed and running on your system.

Checking the Version of the JRE on Your System

You can check to see if you have a JRE installed, what version or edition it is, and more by simply entering the `java -version` command from any Windows command prompt, as shown in Figure 4-1.

```
D:\Program Files\IBM\SQLLIB\BIN>java -version
java version "1.4.1"
Java(TM) 2 Runtime Environment, Standard Edition (build 1.4.1)
Classic VM (build 1.4.1, J2RE 1.4.1 IBM Windows 32 build cn1411-20040301a (JIT enabled: jitc))

D:\Program Files\IBM\SQLLIB\BIN>_
```

Figure 4-1   Using the `java -version` command to find information about your Java environment (if it exists)

You can see that this particular workstation has a Java environment already installed. The JRE conforms to the Java 2 Standard Edition (J2SE) specification and is provided by IBM. It runs at the 1.4.1 level. Again, if you don't have a Java environment on your machine (in which case you'll receive an error when running the command), don't worry: the IBM Cloudscape installation program for Windows will take care of this for you.

Setting the *PATH* Environment Variable

Your IBM Cloudscape solution—and all of your Java applications for that matter—need to be able to find a JRE to run correctly. In Windows, the PATH system variable is used to denote a set of directories where Windows will search for any executable (.EXE) files. Because the JRE is an .EXE file on your system (for example, `java.exe`), you can use the PATH system variable to tell Windows where to find the appropriate runtime to support your IBM Cloudscape database and Java-based applications.

You may have more than one JRE installed on your workstation as a result of different products installing a JRE or JDK with them. If you have more than one JRE, the one that you want to use for IBM Cloudscape must appear *before* any others defined by your PATH system variable. In addition, you need to point to the \bin directory that resides in the path of the JRE that you want to use. (If you are going to use the JRE that comes with IBM Cloudscape, you can still update this variable now: just enter the directory where you plan to install the IBM Cloudscape files. The JRE installs into a subdirectory inside $CLOUDSCAPE_INSTALL$: ibm-jre-n142p directory.)

To set the PATH system variable in Windows, perform the following steps:

1. Click **Start** and select **Control Panel**. Then double-click on the **System** icon. (Alternatively, you can right-click on the **My Computer** icon and select **Properties**.)

2. Select **Advanced**.

3. Click **Environment Variables**. The Environment Variables window opens, as shown in Figure 4-2.

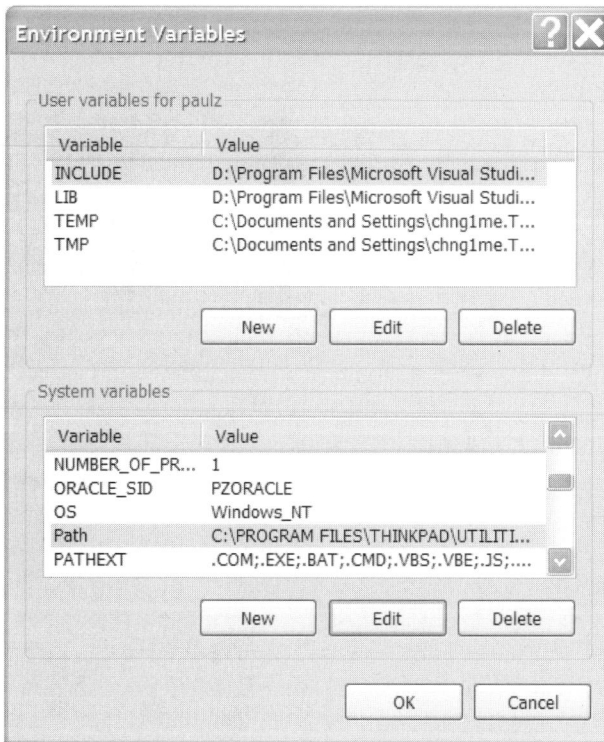

Figure 4-2 The Windows Environment Variables window, where you can set your PATH (and other) variables for your IBM Cloudscape environment

4. Select the **Path** variable from the **System variables** box (as shown in Figure 4-2) and click the corresponding **Edit** button. The Edit System Variable window opens. Add the path to your JRE's \bin directory to the front of the variable declaration, as shown in Figure 4-3. In a Windows environment, you separate entries for variables using a semicolon (;).

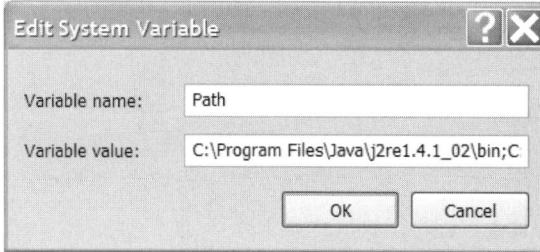

Figure 4-3   Editing the PATH system variable in Windows

TIP
Don't forget to include the semi-colon (;) separation character between directory paths and ensure that you enter the path to the JRE that you want to use at the start of the PATH system variable declaration. Also, note that the path to your JRE must include the \bin directory.

---

5. Click **OK**.

To ensure that you have correctly set your PATH system variable, enter the java -version command in different directories on your system.

If you look back at Figure 4-1, you'll recall that the JRE running on our system was at the 1.4.1 level. If you run this command in a new command window, it should indicate that you are using the JRE that you specified for the PATH system variable. (Your system might require a reboot in order for your changes to take effect.)

In Figure 4-4, you can see that the version of the JRE being used is different from the one in Figure 4-1—we specifically set our machine up to point to this JRE. In Figure 4-1, the JRE defaults to the one that was installed with DB2 Universal Database, which we also happen to have on our test machine. That is why you should always put the JRE that you want to use for IBM Cloudscape, if it matters, at the start of the PATH system variable declaration.

We could choose to use the JRE that comes with DB2 Universal Database (or any other software package for that matter) because it meets the requirements for an IBM Cloudscape installation.

However, we chose a different JRE to illustrate the use of this variable. You can see that the setting of the PATH system variable (Figure 4-3) has taken effect from the output of the java -version command shown in Figure 4-4.

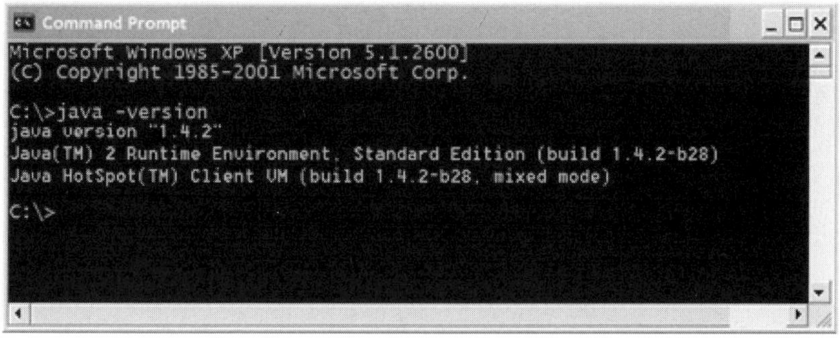

Figure 4-4 An updated PATH system variable in Windows that points to the JRE that you want to use for your IBM Cloudscape installation

The best way to see your environment's PATH system variable settings is to run the echo %PATH% command in a Windows command prompt. An example is shown in Figure 4-5.

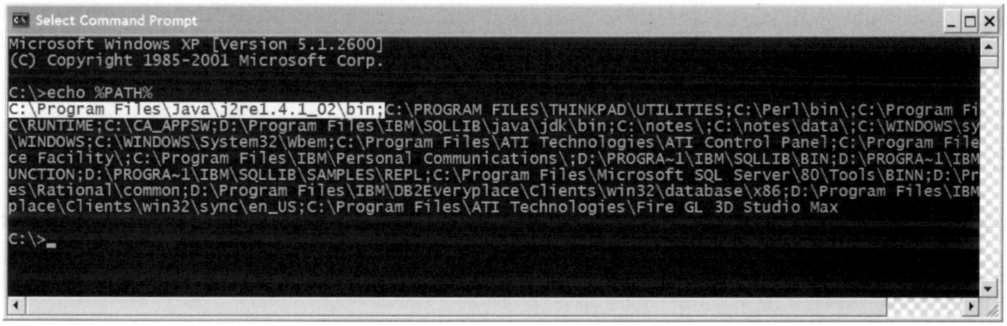

Figure 4-5 Viewing the PATH setting on your Windows system

Using the Windows Installer to Install IBM Cloudscape on Windows—Attention Developers!

One of IBM Cloudscape's extra features is a Java-based graphical installation program. If you were to install Apache Derby, you would not have access to this program (though remember, the code that is ultimately placed on your system or device is the same).

The installation program for IBM Cloudscape really installs a development environment, not a single program or just the database. Consequently, the IBM Cloudscape installation program is targeted at developers and comes with very little configuration for the programmer or power user.

When deploying Apache Derby or IBM Cloudscape for production purposes, chances are that you will not use the graphical installation program because you are not likely to need the specific add-on features that this method provides.

The IBM Cloudscape installation program for Windows is built using InstallShield MultiPlatform Version 5.0 and has a similar look and feel to most other installers on each platform. IBM chose to use this infrastructure because it provides a consistent interface and acts the same on all platforms (though some platforms have some amount of native support built into them). If you plan to use this installation program to set up an IBM Cloudscape environment, you will need to ensure that you have about 60 MB of free disk space on your workstation.

There is also a generic graphical installation program—but it requires that a JRE be installed on your machine before you can run it (unlike the Windows version, which provides one if it is not found on your system). You can, of course, use this version on Windows too—but for the most part, we recommend using the installer that is built for your platform (if one exists).

If you plan to use the generic installation program to set up an IBM Cloudscape environment, you will need to ensure that you have about 15 MB of free disk space on your workstation (because it doesn't include a JRE, this installation program doesn't have as large a footprint as the native Windows installer). In addition to this, because it doesn't come with a JRE, you will need to ensure that the JVM on your system is at version 1.3 or later. To start the generic IBM Cloudscape installation program, enter the `java -jar 10.0-IBM-Cloudscape.jar` command in the directory where the installation image resides.

The generic installation program for IBM Cloudscape works on any platform that has a standard JRE, although support and testing efforts have specifically been done for Windows, Linux, AIX, Solaris, and Mac OS X.

Installing IBM Cloudscape is a pretty simple and transparent process. The installation program just places some files on your machine, edits the scripts in the `framework/` directory (these are optionally used to set up your environment) for your chosen installation directory, and creates an uninstaller program. That's it. There are no modifications to the Windows registry, and this provides the flexibility to have multiple IBM Cloudscape applications on a system and helps to retain portability. Because no information is stored in the registry, and all necessary runtime information can be stored inside a database, a developer does not need to worry about potential conflicts with other IBM Cloudscape applications from third parties.

In the future, you will likely see the IBM Cloudscape installation program built on InstallShieldX, which should allow for better integration into the Windows environment and some nicer cross-platform features. In addition, any binary add-ons that will be delivered (for example, ODBC) will be added to this installation method too.

IBM Cloudscape for Windows Installer Prerequisites

If you are planning to use the graphical IBM Cloudscape installer program on Windows, you need to ensure that you have enough disk space on your system to accommodate not only the image, but also any temporary space the installer might need to set up your environment.

Although it will always depend on the components that you select for installation, a "Typical" (or full) installation using the IBM Cloudscape installer requires approximately 65 MB of disk space and about 130 MB of temporary disk space.

NOT ENOUGH FOOTPRINT FOR THE NATIVE-WINDOWS INSTALLER?
If you have a running JRE on your system and you are concerned about the footprint of the graphical Windows installation program, you can use the generic graphical installation program as an alternative.

The IBM Cloudscape installer will install files that are not listed as features in the Feature Selection window (see Figure 4-11). In addition, auxiliary files are dynamically created at runtime. Even though these files do affect the size of the features listed in Figure 4-11, their sizes are incorporated into the total disk space calculation that appears in the Installation Summary window (see Figure 4-12). That is why the sum of the features might add up to less than the total disk space required. This feature guarantees that the disk space required is checked before the installation proceeds.

Finally, for the graphical installation program to function correctly, you need to ensure that your screen's resolution is set no lower than 640 × 480 and that it supports at least 256 colors (often referred to as color quality) or higher.

Performing the Windows Installation

To install IBM Cloudscape on Windows using the IBM Cloudscape graphical installation program, perform the following steps:

1. Ensure that you are logged on as a user with the authority to install a program on your Windows workstation.

2. Access the media where the IBM Cloudscape code is located (we're assuming this to be the unpacked image linked to from this book's Web site) and double-click on the **10.0-IBM-Cloudscape-Win32.exe** file to start the IBM Cloudscape for Windows installer. The Welcome window opens, as shown in Figure 4-6. Click **Next**.

3. You are given the option to read the release notes. If you select **Yes, I would like to read the release notes now** and then click **Next**, you will be able to browse the release notes, as shown in Figure 4-7. Otherwise, you'll be asked to accept the licensing agreement, as shown in Figure 4-8.

4. Before you can install the software, you have to accept the license agreement. Select the **I accept the terms in the license agreement** (as shown in Figure 4-8) radio button, and click **Next**.

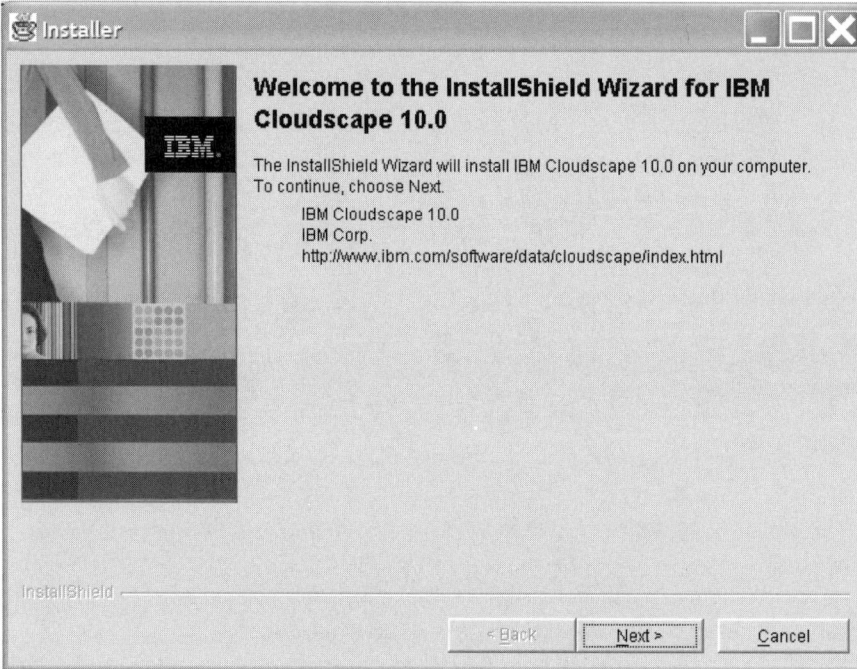

Figure 4-6   The IBM Cloudscape Windows Welcome window

Figure 4-7   The Release Notes—read them!

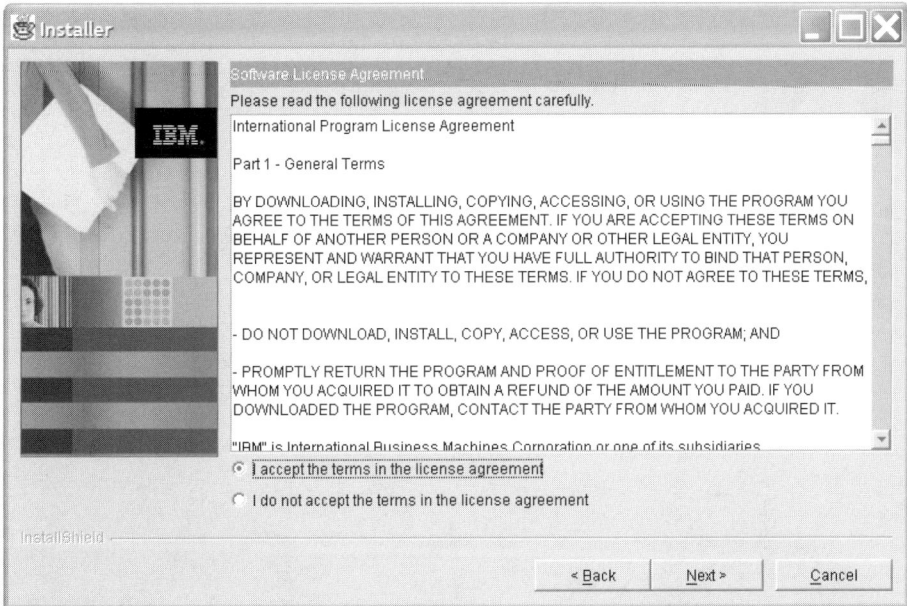

Figure 4-8   You must accept the licensing agreement to install IBM Cloudscape

5. Select the target directory where you want to install the IBM Cloudscape development environment using the **Browse** button, and then click **Next**. This is shown in Figure 4-9.

   The installation program will use the **Directory Name** field to set an environment variable called CLOUDSCAPE_INSTALL (which you'll learn more about later in this chapter).

ENVIRONMENT AND SYSTEM VARIABLES—THE VARIABLES

It's helpful to understand the difference between environment variables and system variables. The value of the CLASSPATH environment variable is whatever the setting of CLASSPATH happens to be in the particular command prompt, Integrated Development Environment (IDE), and so on in which you are running.

A system variable is a global default that can be overridden in the current execution environment. Knowing this distinction helps developers better understand the transient nature of an environment variable, as opposed to the more permanent nature of a system variable.

SPACES IN YOUR PATH NAME

You should not select a path name that includes spaces because this could cause problems when executing some of the scripts that are provided for your Apache Derby environment.

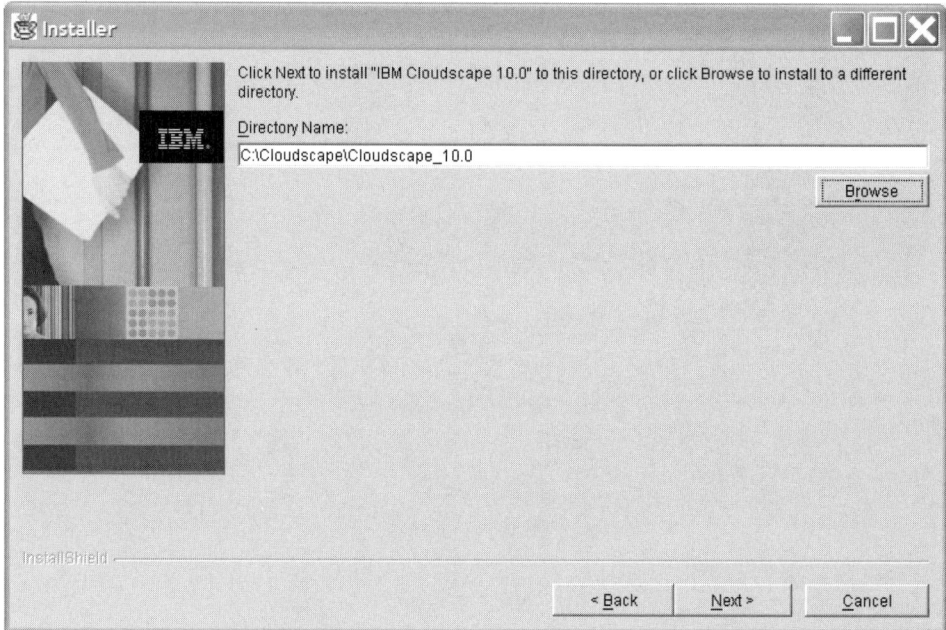

Figure 4-9   Choosing the target installation directory

6. The installation program now gives you the choice of performing a **Typical** or a **Custom** installation, as shown in Figure 4-10.

   A Typical installation will, by default, install all of the add-on components available in the IBM Cloudscape package. A Custom installation will allow you to pick and choose the components that you want to install on your system. For example, you might not want the documentation (approximately 5 MB) to be installed on your machine. Although this example installs all of the IBM Cloudscape components, select the **Custom** radio button and click **Next** to see your options.

7. Select the components that you want to install. Figure 4-11 shows you a list of all the components that you can install as part of an IBM Cloudscape installation. When you are finished, click **Next**.

   To follow along with the examples in this book, select all of the components—we only selected this option to show the granularity that you have when using this installation method.

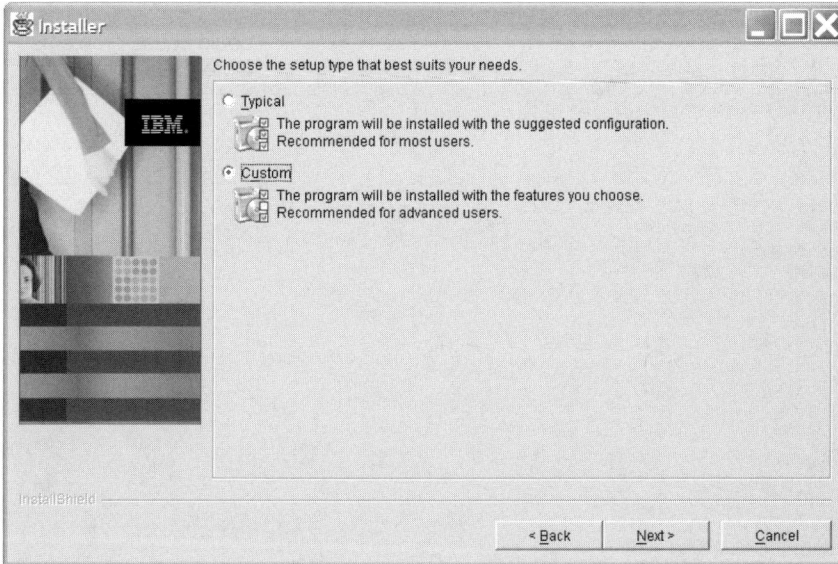

Figure 4-10   A Custom installation allows you to select the components that you want as part of your IBM Cloudscape environment

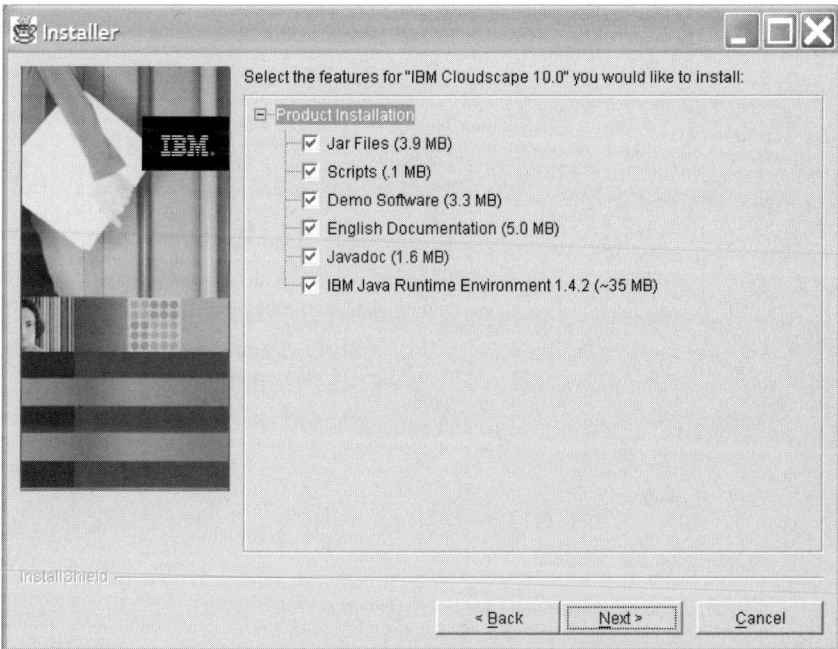

Figure 4-11   A Custom installation allows you to select the components that you want as part of your IBM Cloudscape environment

---

THE JRE THAT WE GIVE YOU

One of the components included in an IBM Cloudscape for Windows installation is the IBM Java Runtime Environment (JRE) Version 1.4.2. This JRE is installed by default. If you already have a JRE installed and you want to use it, you can remove the JRE from the installation.

---

8. Next, you are presented with a summary of the options that you selected, as shown in Figure 4-12. Click **Next**, and you're "off to the races with Apache Derby and IBM Cloudscape!"

9. When the installation completes, click **Next**, then **Finish**. You can see that the components that you selected have been installed in the target directory, as shown in Figure 4-13.

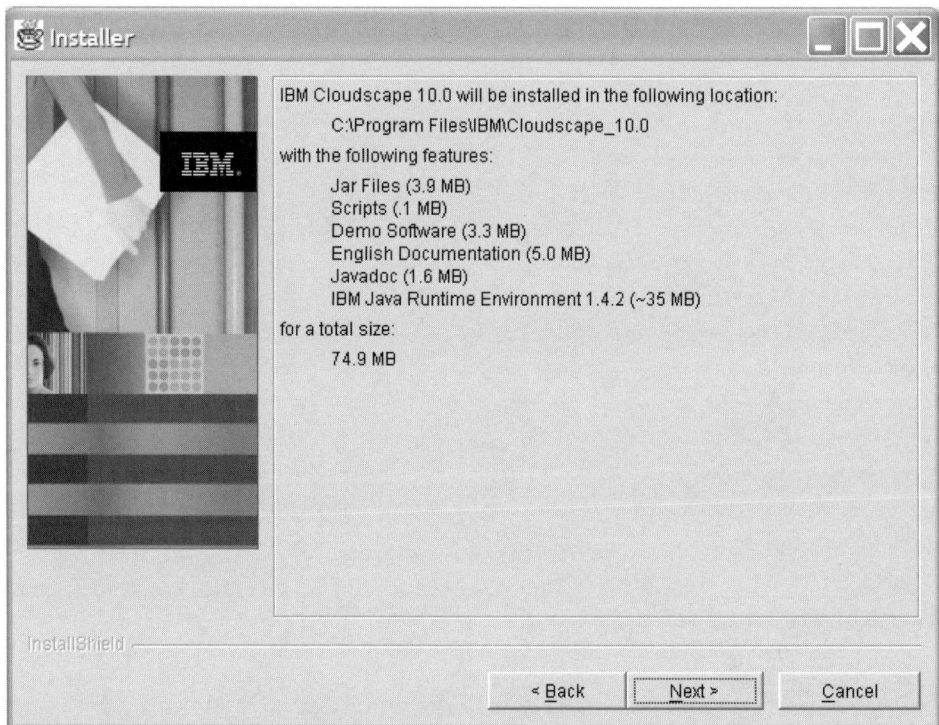

Figure 4-12   The summary panel—the last step before installing IBM Cloudscape on your workstation

Post-Installation Tasks for Graphical Installation Programs

When you have finished setting up an IBM Cloudscape environment using one of the graphical installation programs, you need to define the CLASSPATH system variable so that the list of class libraries

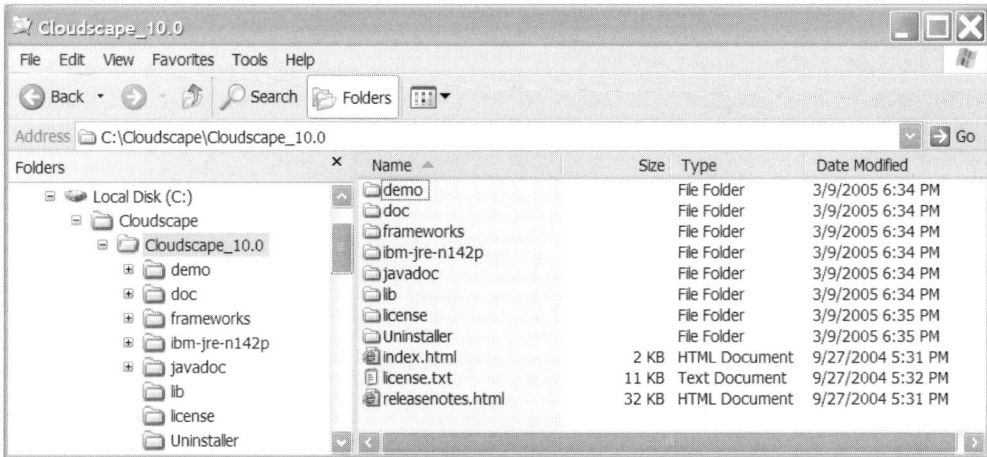

Figure 4-13   Your IBM Cloudscape installation

needed by your application is known to your JVM. On Windows, you can use the `setEmbeddedCP`
`.Bat` script file (located in the `x:\<IBM Cloudscape Installation Directory>\`
`frameworks\embedded\bin` directory) to set this environment variable. If you are using the
IBM Cloudscape Network Server, you'll find the scripts you need in the `x:\<IBM Cloudscape`
`Installation Directory>\frameworks\NetworkServer\bin` directory.

These script files rely on the correct setting of the `CLOUDSCAPE_INSTALL` environment
variable that was automatically set for you when you specified the directory for your IBM Cloudscape installation (refer to Figure 4-9).

For more information on the `CLASSPATH` and `CLOUDSCAPE_INSTALL` environment
variables, see the "Installing Apache Derby or IBM Cloudscape on Windows Manually" section.

The point is that when you use the graphical installation program, you don't have to worry
about this kind of stuff.

IF YOU NEED A LITTLE HELP
If you can't seem to get your IBM Cloudscape database to start correctly, try running the
appropriate scripts to solve the problem.

Installing Apache Derby or IBM Cloudscape on Windows Manually

Although we recommend using the graphical IBM Cloudscape installation program to set up
your application development environment, you should familiarize yourself with the steps to
set up an IBM Cloudscape environment manually. Having a good understanding of the manual
installation method will be especially helpful when you deploy your applications.

Remember, the IBM Cloudscape graphical installation program is ideal for setting up an application development environment. However, its footprint may not make it the ideal choice for application deployment. For example, you might only want to have multiple applications accessing your database to support application development. Without the use of the IBM Cloudscape Network Server, you could not start your application (which also starts the database) and connect to it with your IDE or the `ij` tool at the same time.

Installing IBM Cloudscape using the manual method is easy, which in turn makes it easy to deploy your application. Just copy the required .JAR files, set the `CLOUDSCAPE_INSTALL` and `CLASSPATH` variables, and you're ready to go.

Creating and Setting the *CLOUDSCAPE_INSTALL* Environment Variable

When you install Apache Derby manually, we recommend that you create the `CLOUDSCAPE_INSTALL` environment variable. The `CLOUDSCAPE_INSTALL` environment variable is used to define the base directory where the IBM Cloudscape product will be installed. (In this chapter, we use the `c:\cloudscape\cloudscape_10.0` directory that we used in the "Using the Windows Installer to Install IBM Cloudscape on Windows—Attention Developers!" section; refer to Figure 4-9.) This directory is often referred to as the **IBM Cloudscape system home directory**. The IBM Cloudscape system home directory is the default directory for all files (log files, database files, and so on).

CLOUDSCAPE_INSTALL IN THE FUTURE

In the future, the name of this environment variable will likely change to `DERBY_INSTALL`.

You can set `CLOUDSCAPE_INSTALL` at the system or at the user level as a system variable. System variables are preset environment variables for the Windows command line environment. System variables can be overridden later by setting a new value for the environment variable in the command line environment whenever necessary. If you do not set this variable, the default home directory for your database will be the working directory of the Java process running the database engine.

We recommend that you set up a home directory for your environment (for any deployments) because it provides consistency, simplicity, and, best of all, allows you to leverage the setup scripts detailed in the "Post-Installation Tasks for Graphical Installation Programs" section, which can save you time and help you to avoid errors.

On Windows, you can use the **Environment Variables** dialog box (as you did in Figure 4-2 to define the `PATH` system variable) to create a `CLOUDSCAPE_INSTALL` system variable, as shown in Figure 4-14. (This time you need to click the **New** button, instead of the **Edit** button, unless this system variable already exists.)

A BACKWARD SLASH IN YOUR SYSTEM VARIABLES

We recommend that you do not put a backward slash (\) at the end of this variable, as some information resources do. If you were to set `CLOUDSCAPE_INSTALL=C:\CLOUDSCAPE\CLOUDSCAPE_10.0\`, you would likely end up with two backward slashes when the variable resolves, which isn't correct and would more than likely lead to a Java exception being thrown when you start your application.

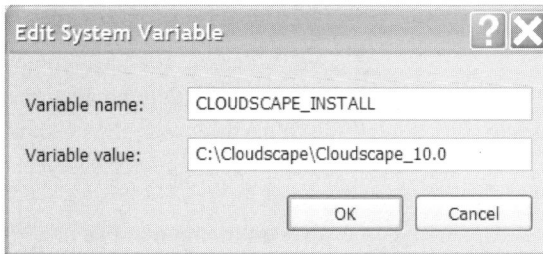

Figure 4-14   Creating the CLOUDSCAPE_INSTALL system variable

In Figure 4-14, we set the CLOUDSCAPE_INSTALL system variable at the system level; however, it could be set at the user level (refer to the upper portion of Figure 4-2). If set at the user level, this environment variable only applies to the user for whom it is set.

You can also set the CLOUDSCAPE_INSTALL system variable for a single session using your operating system's set command. We cover this method later in this chapter.

When you are finished creating and setting the CLOUDSCAPE_INSTALL system variable, verify that it was set correctly by starting a *new* command window and issuing the echo %CLOUDSCAPE_INSTALL% command as you did for the PATH system variable in Figure 4-5. It is important that you start a new command window when verifying a new setting for a system variable because any existing sessions or open applications will not pick up the new settings.

Setting the *CLASSPATH* Environment Variable

The CLASSPATH environment variable is the most important environment variable that you need to understand when manually deploying an IBM Cloudscape solution. IBM Cloudscape provides scripts that you can use to set up this variable, which we covered in the "Post-Installation Tasks for Graphical Installation Programs" section under "Using the Windows Installer to Install IBM Cloudscape on Windows—Attention Developers!".

If you've used any Java programs before, you should be somewhat familiar with the CLASSPATH environment variable. The CLASSPATH is a list of the class libraries needed by the JVM and other Java applications to run your program. Quite simply, CLASSPATH tells the Java interpreter and compiler (provided by the JRE) where to find the classes they need to run your Java program (be it IBM Cloudscape, Apache Derby, or something completely unrelated to a database). So, although you can deploy your database as standalone files in a directory, within a JAR, or a combination of the two, without defining this environment variable, nothing is going to work.

For example, the derby.jar file contains the IBM Cloudscape engine code. If this file isn't in your CLASSPATH, your application won't be able to load and start the database. Any tools or features (for example, the IBM Cloudscape Network Server or some of the database tools that come with IBM Cloudscape) have to be in your CLASSPATH in order to work.

As with any environment variable, you can set it permanently or for a single session. If you plan to set this (or any other environment variable for that matter) for a single session, you must explicitly set it each and every time you start your application.

You can permanently set the CLASSPATH environment variable by creating or updating the corresponding system variable in the Windows System control panel, the same way you set the PATH system variable in Figure 4-2.

> **TIP**
> We recommend permanently setting the CLASSPATH system variable for the exercises in this book.

Because they tend to work with multiple databases, developers often like to set this environment variable for a single session only. Typically, you set operating system-specific variables by using the set command.

For example, the following command:

```
SET CLASSPATH=C:\Cloudscape\Cloudscape_10.0\lib\derby.jar;
 %CLOUDSCAPE_INSTALL%\lib\derbytools.jar;
 %CLOUDSCAPE_INSTALL%\lib\derbynet.jar;
```

would set the CLASSPATH for the database tools, the network server, and the database engine for the current session only. This means that you would need to reset this variable each time you opened a new command prompt.

> **DIFFERENT WAYS TO SPECIFY A *PATH***
> Notice that we used two different methods to specify the path to the IBM Cloudscape components. For the database engine, we used the full path name. For the tools and the network server, we used the CLOUDSCAPE_INSTALL system variable detailed in the previous section. As you can see, using the CLOUDSCAPE_INSTALL system variable makes the up and running process easier and minimizes input errors.

To make things easier for session-level settings of the CLASSPATH environment variable, IBM Cloudscape provides scripts to do this for you (we actually asked you to run them if you set up your IBM Cloudscape environment using the graphical installation program). You can find these scripts in the x:\<IBM Cloudscape Installation Directory>\frameworks\ embedded\bin and x:\<IBM Cloudscape Installation Directory>\frameworks\NetworkServer\bin directories, respectively. Ensure that you run these .BAT scripts each time you open a new command window (there is one for the network server and one for the database; run the ones that correspond to the components you plan to use) if you're not going to permanently set the CLASSPATH system variable.

Verifying the Installation

In this section, we'll cover some different tests that you can perform to ensure that you set up your IBM Cloudscape environment correctly. The test scenarios in this section can be used to validate both manual and graphical installations.

Verifying a Database Installation

An easy way to test whether you've correctly set up your environment for an IBM Cloudscape database is to use the `SimpleApp` application that's found in the `x:\<IBM Cloudscape Installation Directory>\Cloudscape_10.0\demo\programs\simple` directory. This program will not run if the `CLASSPATH` or `PATH` system variables are not set correctly.

When you run the `SimpleApp` application, it will:

1. Launch a JVM to host the application (it is a Java program, after all)
2. Start the Apache Derby database engine
3. Create a database called `CLOUDSCAPEDB`
4. Populate a table within the `CLOUDSCAPEDB` database
5. Shut down the database
6. Terminate the application

An example of running this program when the `CLASSPATH` variable is set only for a session is shown in Figure 4-15. If you set the `CLASSPATH` variable permanently, you can still run this program: just omit the statements that explicitly set the variable.

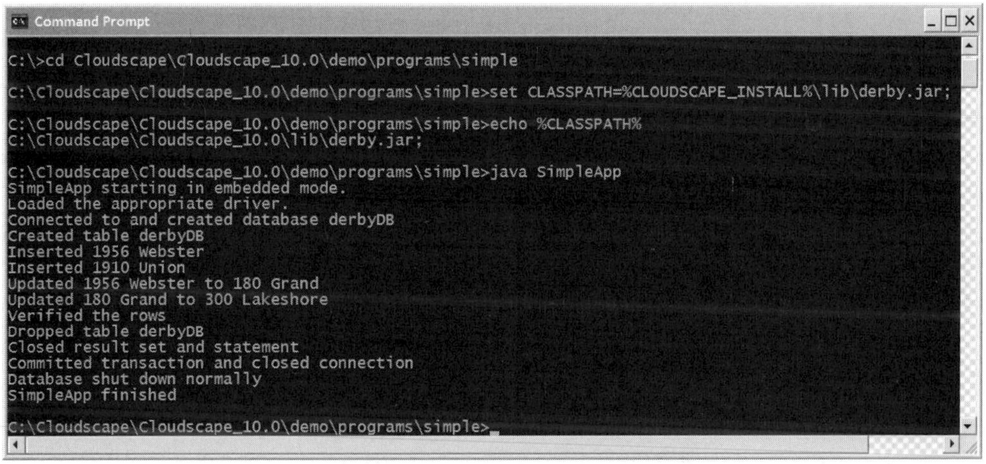

Figure 4-15 Verifying the installation of an Apache Derby database

Verifying a Network Server Installation

To verify that you've correctly installed an environment that accepts multiple connections to your database, you can run a sample program that obtains an embedded connection and allows client connections at the same time.

Remember that to ensure consistency, only one JVM is allowed to access the database at any one time. When you start the IBM Cloudscape Network Server, the IBM Cloudscape embedded database driver is also loaded. This means that your application can get an embedded connection to the same database that the network server is accessing to serve up client requests for data.

The `SimpleNetworkServerSample` application starts the IBM Cloudscape Network Server, as well as the embedded driver, and waits for clients to connect to the database. The `SimpleNetworkClientSample` application interacts with the IBM Cloudscape Network Server from another JVM. Both of these sample applications are located in the `x:\<IBM Cloudscape Installation Directory>\demo\programs\nserverdemo` directory.

When you start the `SimpleNetworkServerSample` application, it will:

1. Start the IBM Cloudscape Network Server and set a property that also loads the embedded JDBC driver
2. Check to see whether the IBM Cloudscape Network Server is running
3. Create the NSSIMPLEDB database (if it does not already exist)
4. Obtain a database connection using the embedded JDBC driver, and execute a sample query to test it
5. Allow client connections to connect to the IBM Cloudscape database until you decide to stop the server and exit the program
6. Shut down the IBM Cloudscape Network Server before exiting the program

To run the `SimpleNetworkServerSample` application, ensure that both the `derbynet.jar` and `derby.jar` files are properly noted in your `CLASSPATH` system variable (we'll assume at this point that you know how to do this) and then issue the `java SimpleNetwork-ServerSample` command, as shown in Figure 4-16.

Once the IBM Cloudscape Network Server is started, you're ready to start the `Simple-NetworkClientSample` application, which will connect to the NSSIMPLEDB database from an external JVM.

Specifically, the `SimpleNetworkClientSample` application will:

1. Load the DB2 JDBC Universal Driver
2. Obtain a client connection to the database using the driver manager
3. Obtain a client connection to the database using a data source
4. Test both database connections by executing a simple query
5. Close the connection and exit the program

To run the `SimpleNetworkClientSample` application, you're going to have to do something a little different because it relies on a different set of .JAR files to run. All of the previous verification

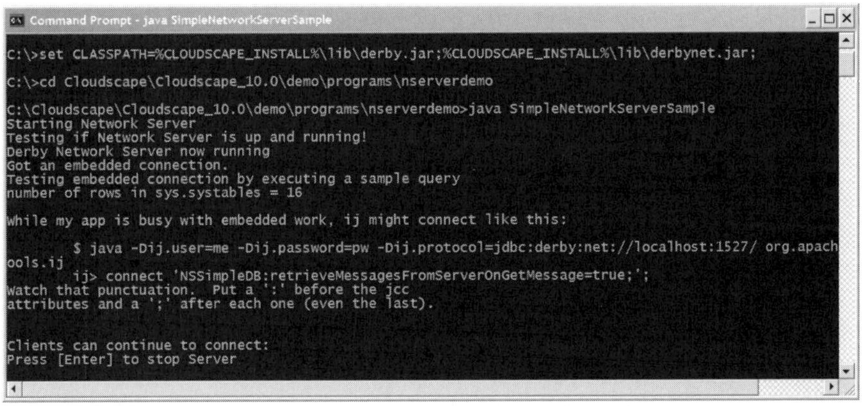

Figure 4-16 Verifying the installation of an IBM Cloudscape Network Server

scenarios have connected you to an embedded IBM Cloudscape database. Because this application runs in an external JVM, you must point to the driver files that it will use to make the connection. In this case, you need to add both the db2jcc.jar and db2jcc_license_c.jar files to your CLASSPATH system variable in the same way that you added files in the previous examples. (These files are located in the same directory as the database and network server files.)

TIP

The frameworks\NetworkServer\bin\setNetworkClientCP.bat script will set the CLASSPATH to include the db2jcc.jar and db2jcc_license_c.jar files.

An example of running the SimpleNetworkClientSample application is shown in Figure 4-17.

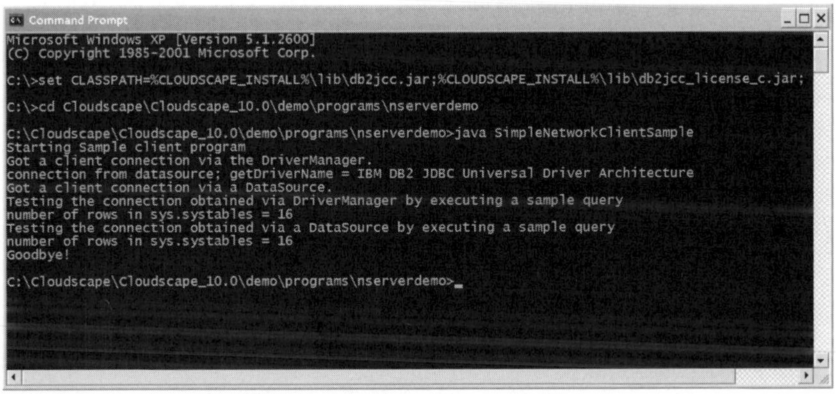

Figure 4-17 Verifying that a client application can connect to the IBM Cloudscape Network Server

Troubleshooting an Installation

If you've read through the steps in this chapter, Apache Derby and IBM Cloudscape installations will be a snap. For an easily installable product, we may have overdone the details in this chapter, but we wanted to ensure that you know the "ins" and "outs" of installing this software.

Nine times out of ten, an installation problem has to do with that pesky CLASSPATH environment variable. That's why we recommend that you use the script files provided by IBM Cloudscape to set this variable for either a graphical or manual installation (and, of course, it uses the CLOUDSCAPE_INSTALL system variable too . . . so set it).

The most common CLASSPATH issue occurs when the Java class that your application is trying to use cannot be found in the current setting of the CLASSPATH environment variable. When this happens, the JVM throws a java.lang.ClassNotFoundException error, as shown in Figure 4-18. Figure 4-18 shows the error that would have occurred if the test case in Figure 4-15 had not found the required derby.jar file.

```
Microsoft Windows XP [Version 5.1.2600]
(C) Copyright 1985-2001 Microsoft Corp.

C:\>cd Cloudscape\Cloudscape_10.0\demo\programs\simple

C:\Cloudscape\Cloudscape_10.0\demo\programs\simple>set CLASSPATH=%CLOUDSCAPE_INSTALL%\lib\cs.jar;.;

C:\Cloudscape\Cloudscape_10.0\demo\programs\simple>echo %CLASSPATH%
C:\Cloudscape\Cloudscape_10.0\lib\cs.jar;.;

C:\Cloudscape\Cloudscape_10.0\demo\programs\simple>java SimpleApp
SimpleApp starting in embedded mode.
exception thrown:
java.lang.ClassNotFoundException: org.apache.derby.jdbc.EmbeddedDriver
        at java.net.URLClassLoader$1.run(Unknown Source)
        at java.security.AccessController.doPrivileged(Native Method)
        at java.net.URLClassLoader.findClass(Unknown Source)
        at java.lang.ClassLoader.loadClass(Unknown Source)
        at sun.misc.Launcher$AppClassLoader.loadClass(Unknown Source)
        at java.lang.ClassLoader.loadClass(Unknown Source)
        at java.lang.ClassLoader.loadClassInternal(Unknown Source)
        at java.lang.Class.forName0(Native Method)
        at java.lang.Class.forName(Unknown Source)
        at SimpleApp.go(SimpleApp.java:64)
        at SimpleApp.main(SimpleApp.java:48)
SimpleApp finished

C:\Cloudscape\Cloudscape_10.0\demo\programs\simple>
```

Figure 4-18   The JVM throws a Java exception because it cannot find the required .JAR file in the CLASSPATH

Another common error occurs when the class that you are trying to access is found, but one of the .JAR files it imports cannot be found. This typically has to do with a CLASSPATH issue and will throw a java.lang.NoClassDefFoundError error. The error often occurs when you create and compile your application on a development workstation where the CLASSPATH was set globally as a system variable, and then you attempt to deploy your application on another workstation.

Whenever you experience a problem trying to start your database, always check the value of CLASSPATH in the current environment. In Figure 4-18, you can see that the CLASSPATH was set to point to a file called cs.jar, instead of the derby.jar file that is required (cs.jar was the original name of the database file before it was donated to the Apache user community).

To see a list of files contained within a .JAR file, use the jar -tvf <jar_file> command. For example, Figure 4-19 shows the results of running the jar -tvf derby.jar | more command.

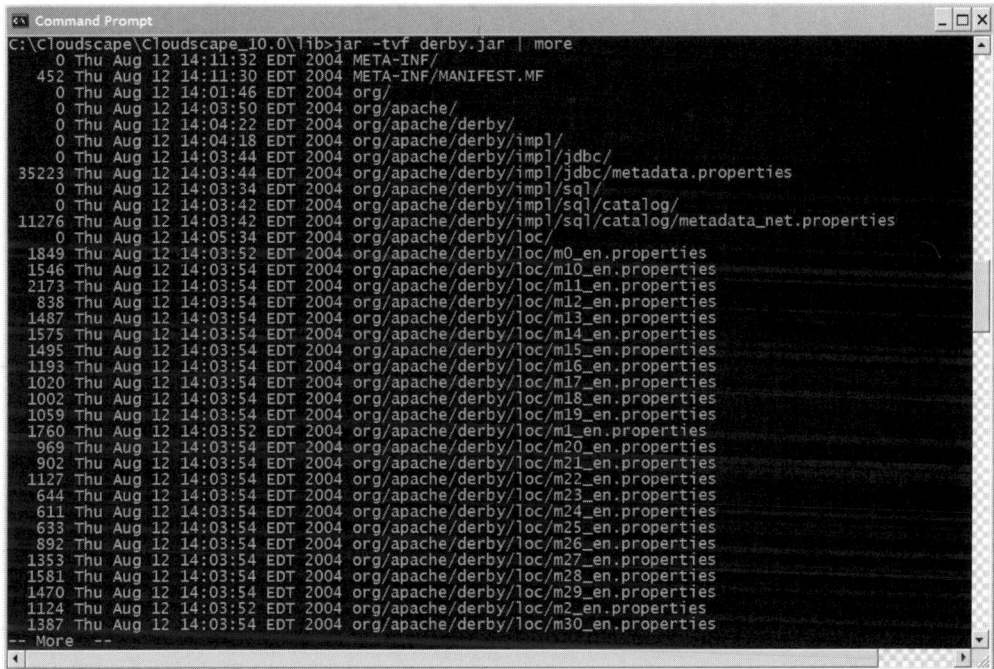

Figure 4-19   The contents of the derby.jar file

Another useful tool that you can use to troubleshoot an IBM Cloudscape installation is sysinfo, located in the x:\<IBM Cloudscape Installation Directory>\frameworks\embedded\bin directory. You can use this tool to test for all the libraries that can be found and those that can't. An example of using sysinfo is shown in Figure 4-20.

You can append -cp <filename.class> to the end of sysinfo to look for a specific class in the CLASSPATH environment variable.

Another common problem occurs when people try to access an IBM Cloudscape database (that was started in an application) from an external IDE or tools such as ij (we covered this in Chapter 2) without first starting the IBM Cloudscape Network Server.

Figure 4-20   Using the sysinfo tool to test for the libraries that you need

Odds and Ends About Your Installation

In this section, we'll give you some additional installation details that should prove helpful as you make your way through the rest of this book.

Files on Disk

The installation program laid down a number of files, including the IBM Cloudscape database engine, the IBM Cloudscape Network Server, some samples, and a host of other files in your target directory. A list of these directories is shown in Figure 4-21.

The lib directory contains the actual database server (derby.jar) and network server (derbynet.jar) files. The DB2 Java Common Client (JCC) JDBC driver (db2cc.jar) is installed in this directory too (including the license file as well). The IBM Cloudscape tools (derbytools.jar) are also located here. Tools such as dblook (a utility to view or dump the data definition language, or DDL, for objects in your databases) or ij (an interactive JDBC scripting tool and SQL command line interface) are part of the derbytools.jar file.

In Figure 4-21, you can see that the installation has two databases. One is the sample database for DB2 Universal Database called SAMPLE, and the other is the Cloudscape sample database called TOURSDB.

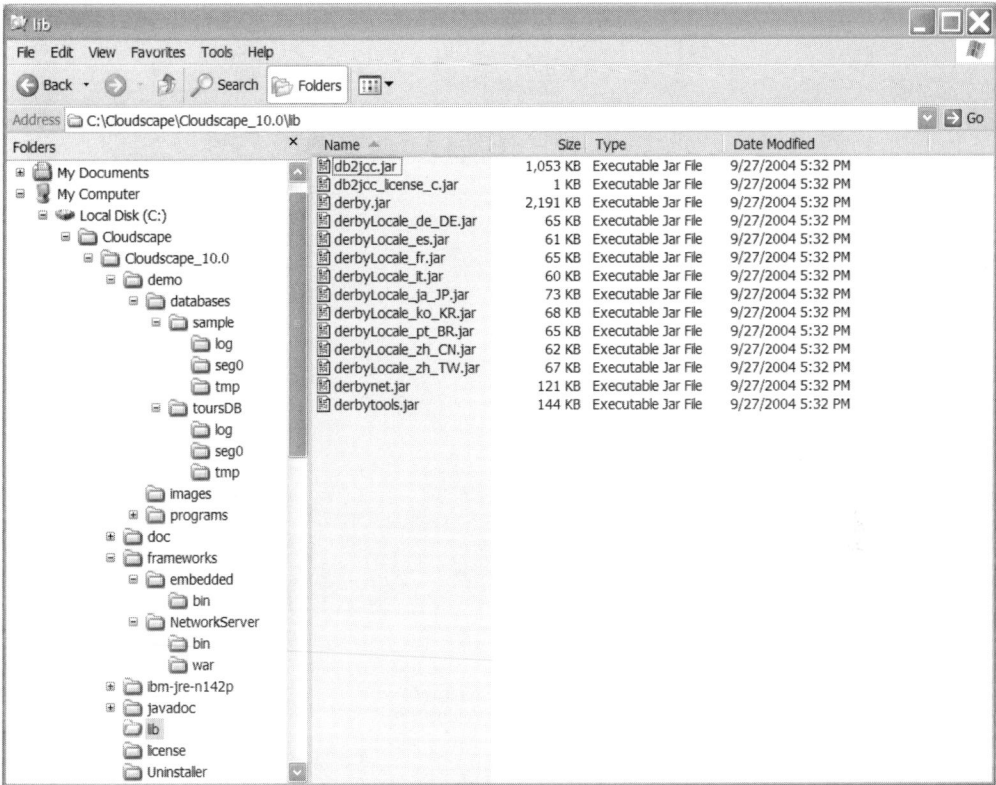

Figure 4-21 The on-disk file structure after completing an IBM Cloudscape installation

Within each database directory (which always has the same name as the database itself) are three sub-directories. You will need to know the path to a database when you want to start it with your application. The `seg0` directory contains the data files for a database (and represents the actual location of the data on disk), and the log directory contains the transaction log files. You should never directly access these files.

Installing Apache Derby and IBM Cloudscape on Linux

In this chapter, we walk you through the steps involved in setting up your environment to run the Apache Derby or IBM Cloudscape database on a Linux-based workstation. If you want to install either of these products on a Windows-based workstation, see Chapter 4, "Installing Apache Derby and IBM Cloudscape on Windows." For all other operating systems, you can use the manual method or the universal Java installation program (both of which are also covered in this chapter).

Because we've included a copy of IBM Cloudscape in the back of this book, we'll assume that the source you are using to install your environment comes from the IBM Cloudscape image that's linked to from this book's Web site (www.ibmpressbooks.com/title/0131855255). In addition to this, as described in Chapter 2, "Deployment Options for Apache Derby Databases," an IBM Cloudscape installation will automate the tasks for setting up your environment, and because that product is especially well suited for developers, it makes sense to detail that process in this chapter.

In this chapter, unless otherwise noted, we'll only refer to the IBM Cloudscape version of the Apache Derby database. Where other paragraphs warrant differences, we'll point them out to you and then continue with our assumption.

We're assuming that you are aware of the differences between the IBM Cloudscape and Apache Derby packages. If the details are a little sketchy, see Chapter 1, "On Your Marks ... Get Set ... Go!!! An Introduction to the Apache Derby and IBM Cloudscape Community."

You can install IBM Cloudscape on Linux by using the graphical Linux packaged installer, a generic graphical installation program, or manually by updating a couple of environment variables so that they point to the location of the Java archive (.JAR) file that contains the IBM Cloudscape database engine and network server. The Linux installation program requires approximately 85 MB of free space on your system and is invoked by double-clicking on the `10.0-IBM-Cloudscape-Linux.bin` file. We recommend that you use the native installation program for your operating system whenever you can.

If you are installing the Apache Derby database engine from the Apache Web site, you can only use the manual method. Installing Apache Derby manually is as simple as copying over the required .JAR files to your disk and updating the `CLASSPATH` for your JRE.

Migration from Previous Versions of Cloudscape

Apache Derby and IBM Cloudscape Version 10.0 do not support the automatic upgrade of databases from previous versions of Cloudscape. The IBM Cloudscape database engine and SQL API have been rewritten so that applications built on these platforms are fully compatible with IBM DB2 Universal Database for Linux, UNIX, and Windows. For information on migrating databases created with previous versions of Cloudscape, see http://publib.boulder.ibm.com/ epubs/html/c1894710.html.

If you have an existing pre-Version 10.0 installation of Cloudscape installed on your machine, *do not* install IBM Cloudscape Version 10.0 on top of it. You must uninstall the previous version of the product by running the uninstall program, or you must manually remove the files. The Cloudscape uninstaller will not remove your databases.

If you are installing IBM Cloudscape on an existing IBM Cloudscape Version 10.0 installation or adding one of the components shipped in this package to your existing installation, you might see a size of 0 MB if you select to customize the installation using the graphical installation program.

IBM CLOUDSCAPE AND CLOUDSCAPE— IS THERE A DIFFERENCE?
Note the difference between IBM Cloudscape and Cloudscape databases. IBM Cloudscape and Apache Derby databases are the same thing and are based on the Version 10.0 release of IBM Cloudscape. References to Cloudscape on its own refer to a version of the code before the release where IBM Cloudscape and Apache Derby converge.

Before You Begin

Whether you plan to use the IBM Cloudscape installer to create a development environment, or directly deploy an IBM Cloudscape database engine (or an application with the engine built into it), you need to set up your system for the installation of the database engine code (and any add-on components). In this section, we'll introduce you to some key terms that you need to understand and the steps you can take to ensure that your environment is ready for installation.

Not all of these steps are necessary, and some may have been done already for you in the course of your day-to-day interactions with other software packages. In short, the installation of IBM Cloudscape isn't as cumbersome as the length of this chapter might imply, but we want to ensure that you have a good understanding of the IBM Cloudscape environment and its interaction with your system.

When you install IBM Cloudscape, the main components that you need to understand are the product .JAR files, the database files, and the database log file. These three components exist in all IBM Cloudscape installations and need to be known to your system before you can use the database.

The Java Runtime Environment

The environment in which you want to deploy your application must have a Java Runtime Environment (JRE) at the version 1.3 level or later to support an IBM Cloudscape database or network server (we recommend running at version 1.4.2 or higher).

If you don't have a JRE on your system, the IBM Cloudscape installation program for Linux gives you the option to install IBM's JRE for Linux, which is provided as part of the installation image. Of course, you can always install your own JRE or Java Developer's Kit (JDK).

IBM provides JREs and JDKs for the AIX, Linux, Windows, and z/OS operating systems. You can download them at http://www-106.ibm.com/developerworks/java/jdk/. If you need a JRE or JDK for another platform, or if you want to use a specific vendor's JRE or JDK, you should refer to that vendor's Web site or documentation for more information.

If your system does not have a JRE already installed, the IBM Cloudscape installation program will automatically load one because it relies on a JRE to support the graphical installation process. If the IBM Cloudscape installation program has to load a JRE from its own image, it will install it on your workstation—unless you specifically ask it not to.

Again, you may already have a running JRE in your environment, because you have a Java-based integrated development environment (IDE), or because you have software that uses Java and one was subsequently installed; but if you don't—the IBM Cloudscape installation program has you covered.

WHEN YOU MIGHT WANT TO USE THE GENERIC INSTALLATION PROGRAM

If you know that you have a JRE running on your system, you can use the generic installation program to graphically set up an IBM Cloudscape environment. This is a useful option if your workstation or target device has a shortage of available disk space because the generic installation program has a significantly smaller footprint than its Linux-native counterpart.

J Who? How Do I Set It Up? How Do I Know I've Got One?

If you're not familiar with some of the terms that we mentioned in the previous section, let's spend some time distinguishing between a JDK, a JRE, a JVM, and so on. If you feel right at home in a Java environment, you can skip this section.

As its name implies, the JRE provides the runtime environment for Java-based applications. Specifically, it provides a Java Virtual Machine (JVM), which is a protected execution environment where Java applications actually run. At a higher level, it can be thought of as a piece of software that interprets Java programs, class files, and .JAR files and allows them to run in a safe and protected environment.

The JRE, which always includes a JVM, is actually the minimal file set you need to run any Java application, and that is why it is often installed as part of different applications that use Java. For example, our test workstation could have a JRE because we also have the IBM DB2 Universal Database for Linux, UNIX, and Windows product running on it, and that product installs a JDK.

In contrast, a JDK is a superset of a JRE. A JDK contains all of the components of a JRE, with additional utilities and tools for Java application development. People who want to develop Java-based applications almost always require a JDK. If you have a Java-based IDE such as IBM WebSphere Studio Application Developer (WSAD), IBM Rational Application Developer, or any Eclipse-based tooling, you likely already have a JDK installed and running on your system.

Checking the Version of the JRE on Your System

You can check to see if you have a JRE installed, what version or edition it is, and more by simply entering the `java -version` command from any Linux terminal session, as shown in Figure 5-1.

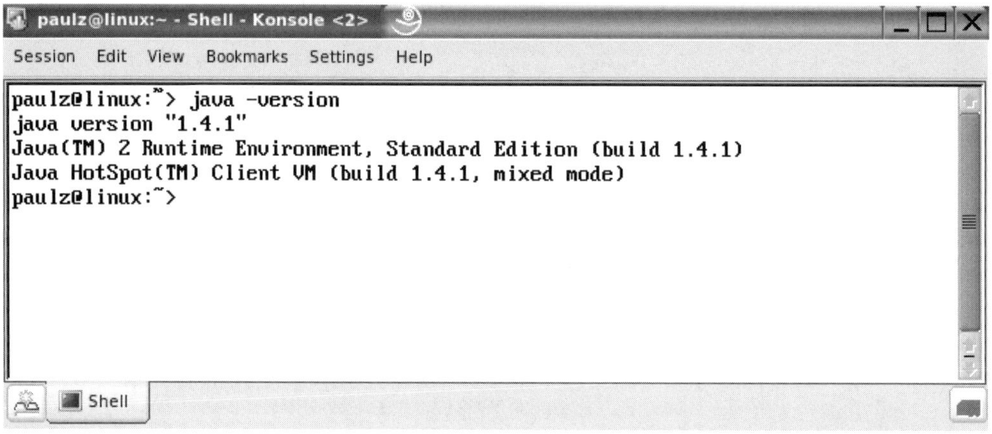

Figure 5-1   Using the `java -version` command to find information about your Java environment (if it exists)

You can see that this particular workstation has a Java environment already installed. The JRE conforms to the Java 2 Standard Edition (J2SE) specification. It runs at the 1.4.1 level. Again, if you don't have a Java environment on your machine, don't worry: the IBM Cloudscape installation program for Linux will take care of this for you.

Setting the *PATH* Environment Variable

Your IBM Cloudscape solution—and all of your Java applications for that matter—need to be able to find a JRE to run correctly. In Linux, the PATH environment variable is used to denote a set of directories where Linux will search for any executable files. Because the JRE is a file on your system (there is no extension for this file in Linux), you can use the PATH environment variable to tell Linux where to find the appropriate runtime to support your IBM Cloudscape database and Java-based applications.

You may have more than one JRE installed on your workstation as a result of different products installing a JRE or JDK with them. If you have more than one JRE, the one that you want to use for IBM Cloudscape must appear *before* any others defined by your PATH environment variable. In addition, you need to point to the /bin directory that resides in the path of the JRE that you want to use. (If you are going to use the JRE that comes with IBM Cloudscape, you can still update this variable now: just enter the directory where you plan to install the IBM Cloudscape files.)

To set the PATH environment variable on Linux, perform the following steps:

1. Open the profile for the user that you want to use to start the IBM Cloudscape installation program. Depending on the implementation of Linux you are using, there are a number of ways to do this. For example, if you are using the bash shell, you might set this in the .bash_profile file or the .bashrc file in your home directory. If the file doesn't exist, you can create it.

2. Add the path to your JRE's /bin directory to the front of the variable declaration, as shown in Figure 5-2. In a Linux environment, you separate entries for variables using a colon (:).

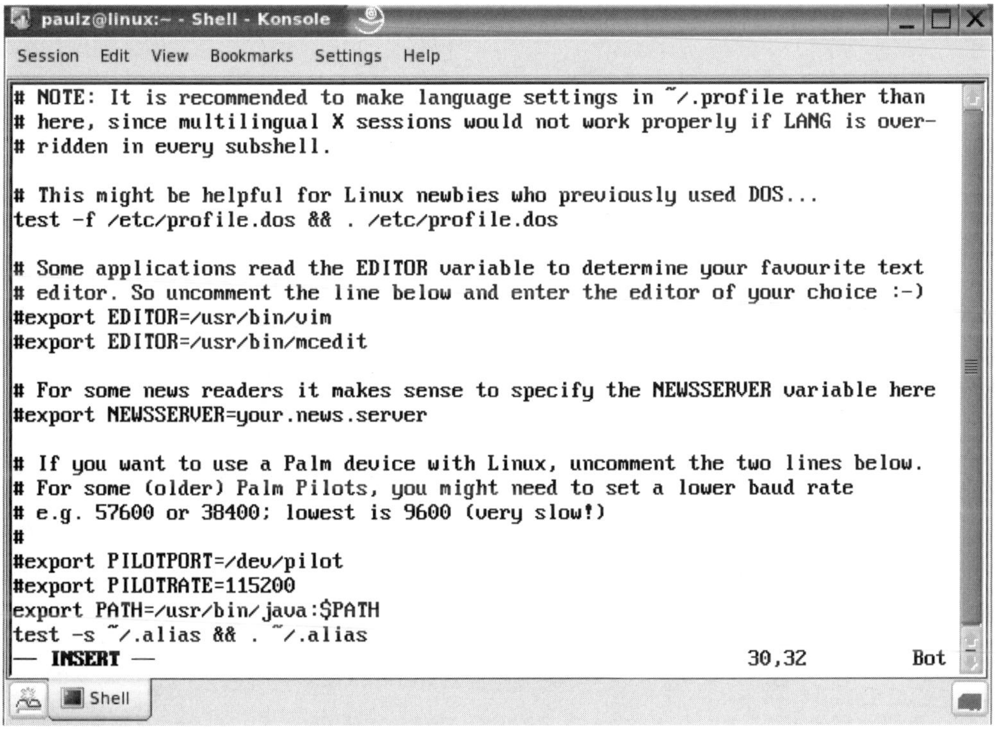

Figure 5-2 Setting the PATH environment variable in Linux

Don't forget to include the colon (:) separation character between directory paths and ensure that you enter the path to the JRE that you want to use at the start of the PATH environment variable declaration. Also, note the path to your JRE must include the /bin directory.

TIP

Ensure that you append the $PATH parameter after the colon (:) that separates entries in this variable on Linux. Otherwise, all paths will resolve to this location. And remember, Linux is case sensitive.

---

3. Close and save the changes to your profile.

To ensure that you have correctly set your PATH environment variable, enter the java -version command in different directories on your system.

If you look back at Figure 5-1, you'll recall that the JRE running on our system was at the 1.4.1 level. If you run this command in a new command window, it should indicate that you are using the JRE that you specified for the PATH environment variable.

In Figure 5-3, you can see that the version of the JRE being used is different from the one in Figure 5-1—we specifically set our machine up to point to this JRE. In Figure 5-1, the JRE defaults to the one that was installed with our SuSE Linux system. That is why you should always put the JRE that you want to use for IBM Cloudscape, if it matters, at the start of the PATH environment variable declaration.

We could choose to use the JRE that comes with SuSE Linux (or any other software package for the matter) because it meets the requirements for an IBM Cloudscape installation. However, we chose a different JRE to illustrate the use of this variable. You can see that the setting of the PATH environment variable (Figure 5-2) has taken effect from the output of the java -version command shown in Figure 5-3.

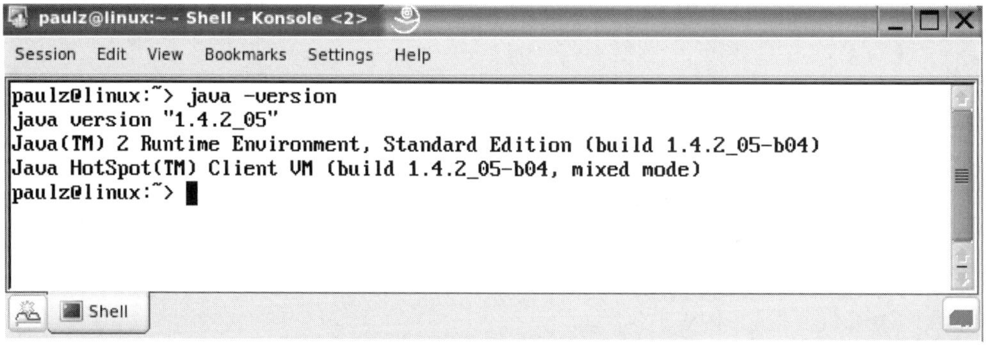

Figure 5-3   An updated PATH environment variable in Linux that points to the JRE that you want to use for your IBM Cloudscape installation

The best way to see your PATH environment variable setting is to run the echo $PATH command in a Linux session. An example is shown in Figure 5-4.

TIP

Ensure that you've sourced your profile so that the kernel will pick up the changes that you made. For example, use the source .bashrc command.

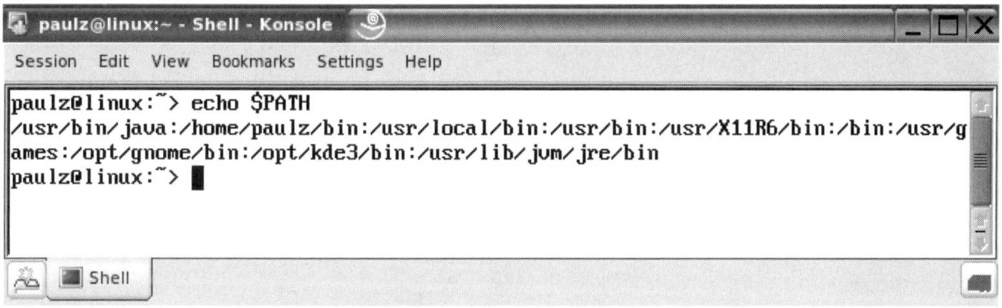

Figure 5-4 Viewing the PATH setting on your Linux system

Using the Linux Installer to Install IBM Cloudscape on Linux—Attention Developers!

One of IBM Cloudscape's extra features is a Java-based graphical installation program. If you were to install Apache Derby, you would not have access to this program (though remember, the code that is ultimately placed on your system or device is the same).

The installation program for IBM Cloudscape really installs a development environment, not a single program or just the database. Consequently, the IBM Cloudscape installation program is targeted at developers and comes with very little configuration requirements for the programmer or power user.

When deploying Apache Derby or IBM Cloudscape for production purposes, chances are that you will not use the graphical installation program because you are not likely to need the specific add-on features that this method provides.

The IBM Cloudscape installation program for Linux is built using InstallShield MultiPlatform Version 5.0 and has a similar look and feel to most other installers on each platform.

IBM chose to use this infrastructure because it provides a consistent interface and acts the same on all platforms (though some platforms have some amount of native support built into them). If you plan to use this installation program to set up an IBM Cloudscape environment, you will need to ensure that you have about 85 MB of free disk space on your workstation.

There is also a generic graphical installation program—but it requires that a JRE be installed on your machine before you can run it (unlike the native Linux installer, which provides one if it is not found on your system). You can, of course, use this version on Linux too—but for the most part, we recommend using the installer that is built for your platform (if one exists).

If you plan to use the generic installation program to set up an IBM Cloudscape environment, you will need to ensure that you have about 15 MB of free disk space on your workstation (because it doesn't include a JRE, this installation program doesn't have as large a footprint as the native Linux installer). In addition, because it doesn't come with a JRE, you will need to ensure that the JVM on your system is at version 1.3 or later. To start the generic IBM Cloudscape installation program, enter the `java -jar 10.0-IBM-Cloudscape.jar` command in the directory where the installation image resides.

The generic installation program for IBM Cloudscape works on any platform that has a standard JRE, although support and testing efforts have specifically been done for Windows, Linux, AIX, Solaris, and Mac OS X.

Installing IBM Cloudscape is a pretty simple and transparent process. The installation program just places some files on your machine, edits the scripts in the framework directory (these are optionally used to set up your environment) for your chosen installation directory, and creates an uninstaller program. That's it. There are no modifications to your system, and this provides the flexibility to have multiple IBM Cloudscape applications on a system and helps to retain portability. Because no information is stored in your system, and all necessary runtime information can be stored inside a database, a developer does not need to worry about potential conflicts with other IBM Cloudscape applications from third parties.

In the future, you will likely see the IBM Cloudscape installation program built on InstallShieldX, which should allow for better integration into the Linux environment and some nicer cross-platform features. In addition, any binary add-ons that will be delivered (for example, ODBC) will be added to this installation method too.

IBM Cloudscape for Linux Installer Prerequisites

If you are planning to use the graphical IBM Cloudscape installer program on Linux, you need to ensure that you have enough disk space on your system to accommodate not only the image but also any temporary space the installer might need to set up your environment.

Although it will always depend on the components that you select for installation, a Typical (or full) installation using the IBM Cloudscape installer requires approximately 95 MB of disk space and about 160 MB of temporary disk space.

NOT ENOUGH FOOTPRINT FOR THE LINUX INSTALLER?
If you have JRE on your system and you are concerned about the footprint of the graphical Linux installation program, you can use the generic graphical installation program as an alternative.

The IBM Cloudscape installer will install files that are not listed as features in the Feature Selection window (see Figure 5-11). In addition, auxiliary files are dynamically created at runtime. Even though these files do affect the size of the features listed in Figure 5-11, their sizes are incorporated into the total disk space calculation that appears in the Installation Summary window (see Figure 5-12). That is why the sum of the features might add up to less than the total disk space required. This feature guarantees that the disk space required is checked before the installation proceeds.

Finally, for the graphical installation program to function correctly, you need to ensure that your screen's resolution is set no lower than 640 × 480 and that it supports at least 256 colors (often referred to as color quality) or higher.

Performing the Linux Installation

To install IBM Cloudscape on Linux using the IBM Cloudscape graphical installation program, perform the following steps:

> **ATTENTION 2.6 KERNEL USERS**
>
> As of the writing of this book, the IBM Cloudscape installation program does not work with the 2.6 kernel and certain JVMs. The 2.6 kernel changes the threading model and creates the incompatibility. Certain distributions (for example, RHEL3, SuSE Linux Pro 9.2) either backport the 2.6 kernel or ship with it—the IBM Cloudscape installation program may not work with these distributions. If you start the IBM Cloudscape installation program for Linux and it doesn't start, use the `export LD_ASSUME_KERNEL=2.4.19` command to set the kernel level for the session that will perform the installation, as shown in Figure 5-5. By the time this book hits publication, especially with the IBM Cloudscape Version 10.1 release and the proliferation of the 2.6 kernel, this might not be an issue for your installation.

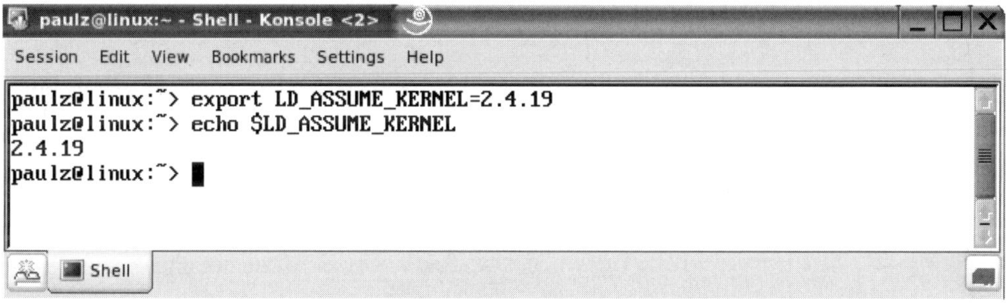

Figure 5-5   Enabling a session to use the IBM Cloudscape installation program for Linux on a distribution using the 2.6 kernel

1. Ensure that you are logged on to your system with `root` authority (this isn't required, but it removes the need to worry about permissions when installing on your workstation).

2. Access the media where the IBM Cloudscape code is located (we're assuming this to be the unpacked image linked to from this book's Web site) and enter the `./10.0-IBM-Cloudscape-Linux.bin` command in a command prompt to start the Cloudscape for Linux installer.

> **TIP**
>
> In most cases, if you aren't using the 2.6 kernel, you can simply double-click on the icon when viewing the media in an explorer window to start the installation program.

3. After the JVM is prepared to run the IBM Cloudscape installation program, the Welcome window opens, as shown in Figure 5-6. Click **Next**.

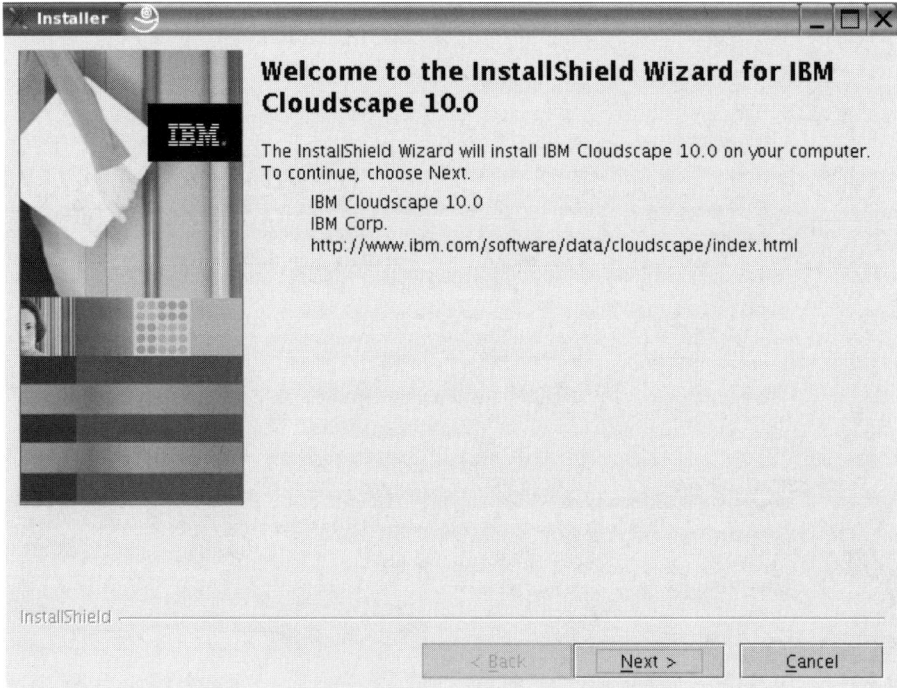

Figure 5-6   The IBM Cloudscape on Linux Welcome window

4. You are given the option to read the release notes. If you select **Yes, I would like to read the release notes now**, and then click **Next**, you will be able to browse the release notes, as shown in Figure 5-7. Otherwise, you'll be asked to accept the licensing agreement, as shown in Figure 5-8.

5. Before you can install the software, you have to accept the license agreement. Select the **I accept the terms in the license agreement** radio button as shown in Figure 5-8, and click **Next**.

6. Select the target directory where you want to install the IBM Cloudscape development environment using the **Browse** button and click **Next**. This is shown in Figure 5-9. The default directory is /opt/ibm/Cloudscape_10.0.

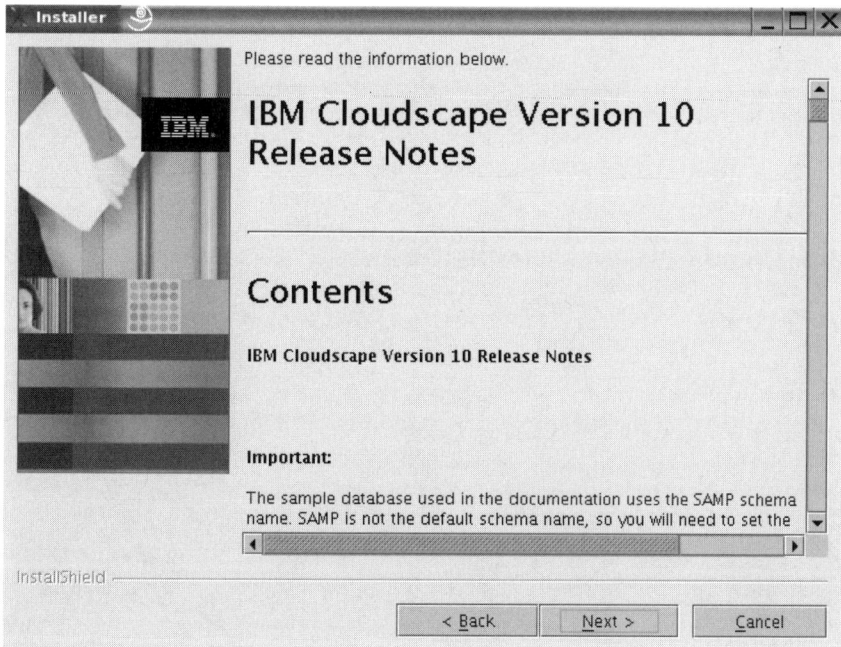

Figure 5-7 The Release Notes—read them!

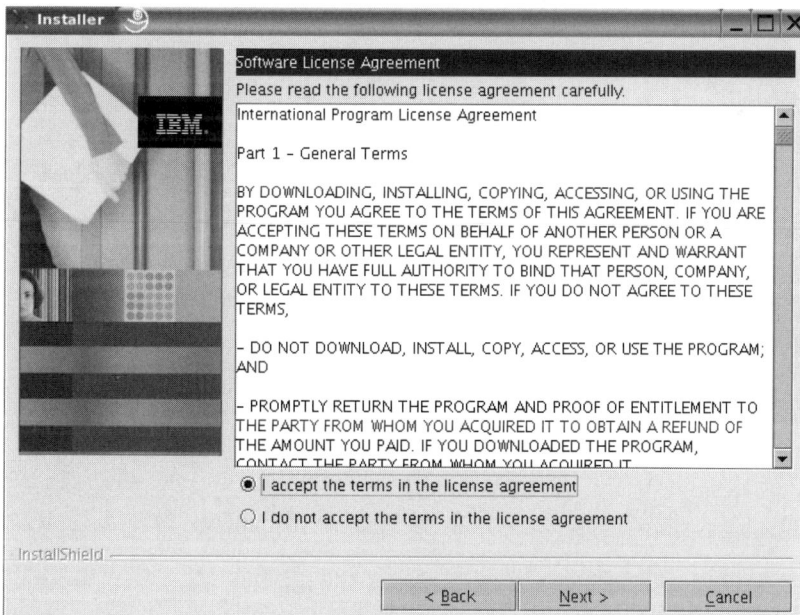

Figure 5-8 You must accept the licensing agreement to install IBM Cloudscape

---

CHOOSING A DIRECTORY TO INSTALL THE PRODUCT

The `/opt/ibm/Cloudscape_10.0` directory is the mandated IBM default installation directory on Linux for this product (in other words, IBM has a company-wide default installation directory for any products on Linux). However, this directory may not exist on every UNIX or Linux-based installation (it's fairly standard for this directory to be created at installation time when Linux is installed on a machine).

You can install this product in any directory you want; however, if you don't choose the default directory (or it doesn't exist), then `root` permissions may be required to perform the installation because you need to create a directory (of course you can install the code in a directory that you already have required permissions for as well; for example, a user's `/home` directory).

The installation program will use the **Directory Name** field to set an environment variable called CLOUDSCAPE_INSTALL (which you'll learn more about later in this chapter).

TIP

You *cannot* select a path name that includes spaces.

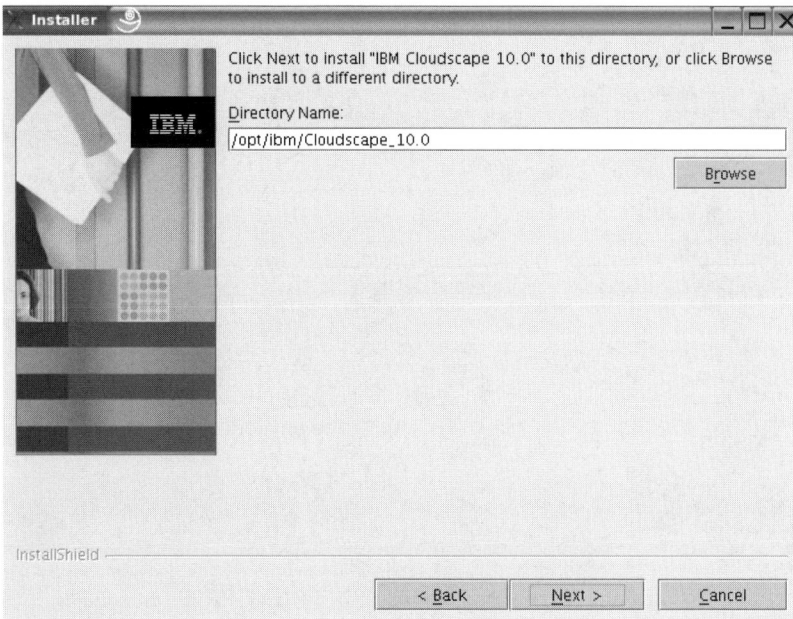

Figure 5-9   Choosing the target installation directory

7. The installation program now gives you the choice of performing a **Typical** or a **Custom** installation, as shown in Figure 5-10.

A Typical installation will, by default, install all of the add-on components available in the IBM Cloudscape package. A Custom installation will allow you to pick and choose the components that you want to install on your system. For example, you may not want the documentation (approximately 5 MB) to be installed on your machine. Although this example installs all of the IBM Cloudscape components, select the **Custom** radio button and click **Next** to see your options.

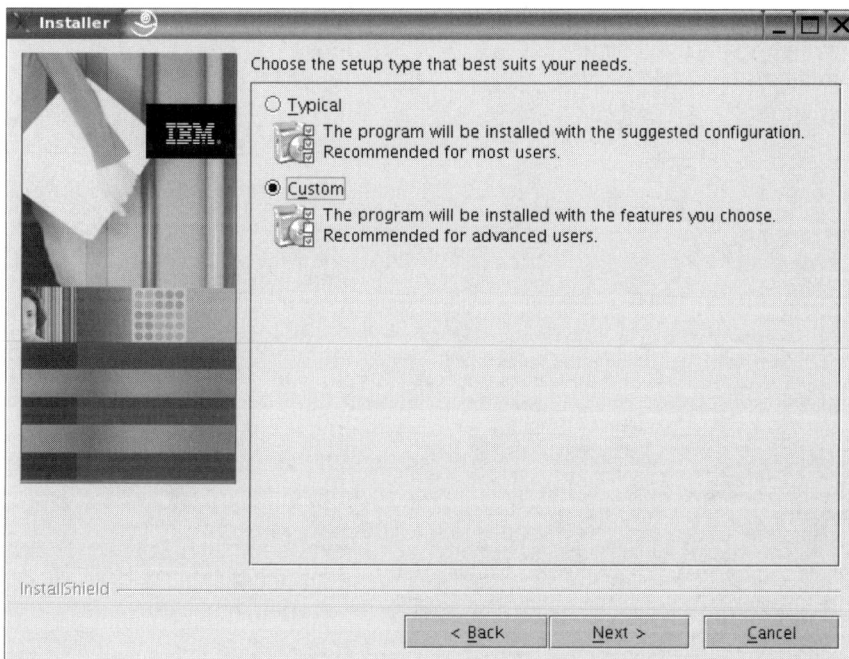

Figure 5-10   A Custom installation allows you to select the components that you want as part of your IBM Cloudscape environment

8. Select the components that you want to install. Figure 5-11 shows you a list of all the components that you can install as part of an IBM Cloudscape installation. When you are finished, click **Next**.

To follow along with the examples in this book, select all of the components—we only selected this option to show the granularity that you have when using this installation method.

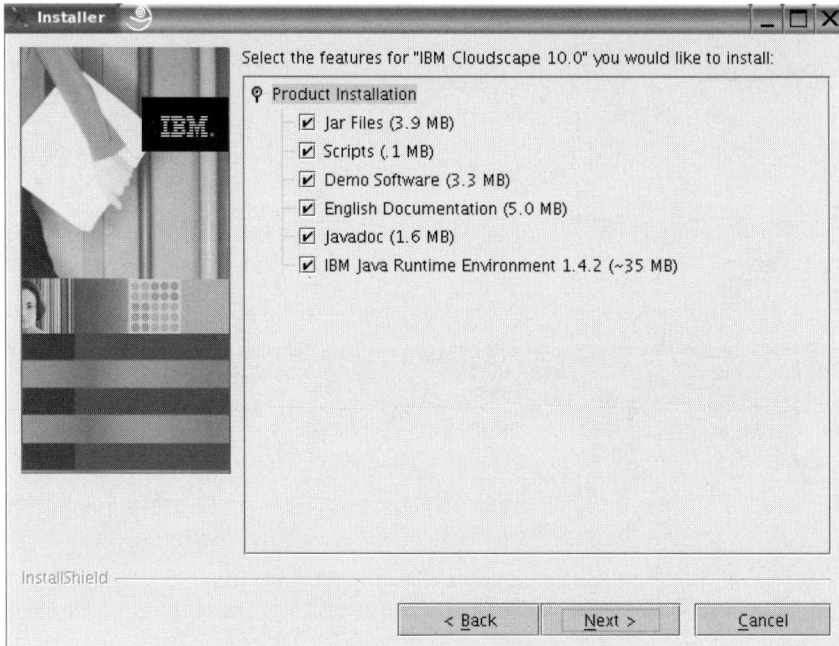

Figure 5-11 A Custom installation allows you to select the components that you want as part of your IBM Cloudscape environment

---

THE JRE THAT WE GIVE YOU

One of the components included in an IBM Cloudscape for Linux installation is the IBM Java Runtime Environment (JRE) Version 1.4.2. This JRE is installed by default. If you already have a JRE installed and you want to use it, you can remove the JRE from the installation.

---

9. Next, you are presented with a summary of the options that you selected, as shown in Figure 5-12. Click **Next,** and you're "off to the races with Apache Derby and IBM Cloudscape!"

10. When the installation completes, click **Next**, then **Finish**. You can see that the components that you selected have been installed in the target directory as shown in Figure 5-13.

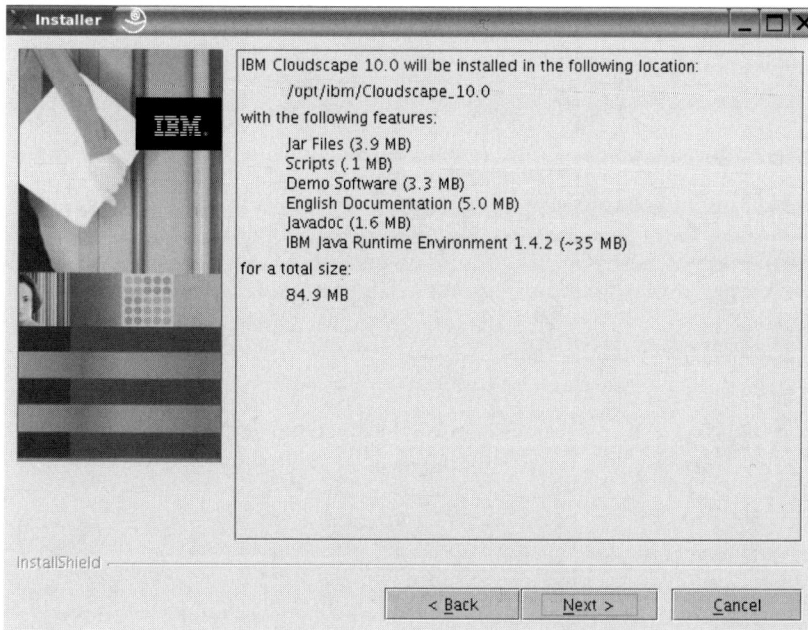

Figure 5-12 The summary panel—the last step before installing IBM Cloudscape on your workstation

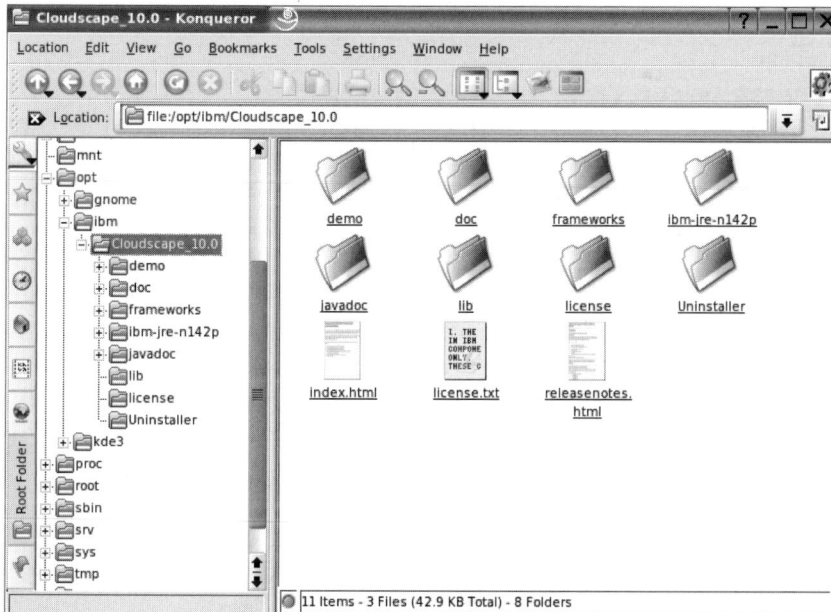

Figure 5-13 Your IBM Cloudscape installation

Post-Installation Tasks for Graphical Installation Programs

When you have finished setting up an IBM Cloudscape environment using one of the graphical installation programs, you need to define the `CLASSPATH` environment variable so that the list of class libraries needed by your application is known to your JVM. On Linux, you can use the `setEmbeddedCP.ksh` script file (located in the `<IBM Cloudscape Installation Directory>/frameworks/embedded/bin` directory) to set this environment variable. If you are using the IBM Cloudscape Network Server, you'll find the scripts you need in the `<IBM Cloudscape Installation Directory>/frameworks/NetworkServer/bin` directory.

These script files rely on the correct setting of the `CLOUDSCAPE_INSTALL` environment variable that was automatically set for you when you specified the directory for your IBM Cloudscape installation (refer to Figure 5-9).

For more information on the `CLASSPATH` and `CLOUDSCAPE_INSTALL` environment variables, see the "Installing Apache Derby or IBM Cloudscape on Linux Manually" section. The point is that when you use the graphical installation program, you don't have to worry about this kind of stuff.

IF YOU NEED A LITTLE HELP
If you can't seem to get your IBM Cloudscape database to start correctly, try running the appropriate scripts to solve the problem.

Installing Apache Derby or IBM Cloudscape on Linux Manually

Although we recommend using the graphical IBM Cloudscape installation program to set up your application development environment, you should familiarize yourself with the steps to set up an IBM Cloudscape environment manually. Having a good understanding of the manual installation method will be especially helpful when you deploy your applications.

Remember, the IBM Cloudscape graphical installation program is ideal for setting up an application development environment. However, its footprint may not make it the ideal choice for application deployment. For example, you might only want to have multiple applications accessing your database to support application development. Without the use of the IBM Cloudscape Network Server, you could not start your application (which also starts the database) and connect to it with your IDE or the `ij` tool at the same time.

Installing IBM Cloudscape using the manual method is easy, which in turn makes it easy to deploy your application. Just copy the required .JAR files, set the `CLOUDSCAPE_INSTALL` and `CLASSPATH` environment variables, and you're ready to go.

Creating and Setting the *CLOUDSCAPE_INSTALL* Environment Variable

When you install Apache Derby manually, we recommend that you create the `CLOUDSCAPE_INSTALL` environment variable. The `CLOUDSCAPE_INSTALL` environment variable is used to define the base directory where the IBM Cloudscape product will be installed. (In this chapter, we use the `opt/ibm/cloudscape_10.0` directory that we used in the "Using the Linux Installer to Install IBM Cloudscape on Linux—Attention Developers!" section; refer to Figure 5-9.) This directory is often referred to as the IBM Cloudscape system home directory. The IBM Cloudscape system home directory is the default directory for all files (log files, database files, and so on).

CLOUDSCAPE_INSTALL IN THE FUTURE
In the future, the name of this environment variable will likely change to `DERBY_INSTALL`.

We recommend that you set up a home directory for your environment (for any deployments) because it provides consistency, simplicity, and best of all, it allows you to leverage the setup scripts detailed in the "Post-Installation Tasks for Graphical Installation Programs" section, which can save you time and help you to avoid errors.

On Linux, set the `PATH` environment variable for your profile (as you did in Figure 5-2) to create the `CLOUDSCAPE_INSTALL` environment variable.

A FORWARD SLASH IN YOUR SYSTEM VARIABLES
We recommend that you do not put a forward slash (/) at the end of this variable, as some information resources do. If you were to set `CLOUDSCAPE_INSTALL=/opt/ibm/cloudscape_10.0/`, you would likely end up with two forward slashes when the variable resolves, which isn't correct and would more than likely lead to a Java exception being thrown when you start your application.

You can also set the `CLOUDSCAPE_INSTALL` environment variable for a single session using the appropriate command to set environment variables for your shell: usually `set`, `setenv`, or `export`. We cover this method later in this chapter.

When you are finished creating and setting the `CLOUDSCAPE_INSTALL` environment variable, verify that it was set correctly by starting a *new* command window and issuing the `echo $CLOUDSCAPE_INSTALL` command as you did for the `PATH` environment variable in Figure 5-5. It is important that you start a new command window when verifying a new setting for an environment variable, because any existing sessions or open applications will not pick up the new settings.

Setting the *CLASSPATH* Environment Variable

The `CLASSPATH` environment variable is the most important environment variable that you need to understand when manually deploying an IBM Cloudscape solution. IBM Cloudscape provides scripts that you can use to set up this variable, which we covered in the "Post-Installation Tasks for Graphical Installation Programs" section under "Using the Linux Installer to Install IBM Cloudscape—Attention Developers!".

If you've used any Java programs before, you should be somewhat familiar with the CLASSPATH environment variable. The CLASSPATH environment variable represents a list of the class libraries needed by the JVM and other Java applications to run your program. Quite simply, CLASSPATH tells the Java interpreter and compiler (provided by the JRE) where to find the classes they need to run your Java program (be it IBM Cloudscape, Apache Derby, or something completely unrelated to a database). So, although you can deploy your database as standalone files in a directory, within a .JAR file, or a combination of the two, without defining this environment variable, nothing is going to work.

For example, the derby.jar file contains the IBM Cloudscape engine code. If this file isn't in your CLASSPATH, your application won't be able to load and start the database. Any tools or features (for example, the IBM Cloudscape Network Server or some of the database tools that come with IBM Cloudscape) have to be in your CLASSPATH in order to work.

As with any environment variable, you can set CLASSPATH permanently or for a single session. If you plan to set this (or any other environment variable for that matter) for a single session, you must explicitly set it each and every time you start your application.

You can permanently set the CLASSPATH environment variable the same way you set the PATH environment variable in Figure 5-2.

TIP

We recommend permanently setting the CLASSPATH system variable for the exercises in this book.

Because they tend to work with multiple databases, developers often like to set this environment variable for a single session only. Typically, you set operating system-specific variables by using the set command.

For example, the following command:

```
SET CLASSPATH=opt/IBM/Cloudscape/Cloudscape_10.0/lib/derby.jar;
   $CLOUDSCAPE_INSTALL/lib/derbytools.jar;
   $CLOUDSCAPE_INSTALL/lib/derbynet.jar;
```

would set the CLASSPATH for the database tools, the network server, and the database engine for the current session only. This means that you need to reset this variable each time you open a new command prompt.

KNOW YOUR SHELL

This example was for the bash shell. The command you may need to enter on your distribution may be different in other shells.

Notice that we used two different methods to specify the path to the IBM Cloudscape components. For the database engine, we used the full path name. For the tools and the network server, we used the CLOUDSCAPE_INSTALL environment variable detailed in the previous section. As you can see, using the CLOUDSCAPE_INSTALL environment variable makes the up and running process easier and minimizes input errors.

   To make things easier for session-level settings of the CLASSPATH environment variable, IBM Cloudscape provides scripts to do this for you (we actually asked you to run them if you set up your IBM Cloudscape environment using the graphical installation program). You can find these scripts in the <IBM Cloudscape Installation Directory>/frameworks/ embedded/bin and <IBM Cloudscape Installation Directory>/frame- works/NetworkServer/bin directories, respectively. Ensure that you run these .ksh scripts each time you open a new command window (there is one for the network server and one for the database; run the ones that correspond to the components you plan to use) if you're not going to permanently set the CLASSPATH environment variable.

Verifying the Installation

In this section, we'll cover some different tests that you can perform to ensure that you set up your IBM Cloudscape environment correctly. The test scenarios in this section can be used to validate both manual and graphical installations.

Verifying a Database Installation

An easy way to test whether you've correctly set up your environment for an IBM Cloudscape data-base is to use the SimpleApp application that's found in the <IBM Cloudscape Instal- lation Directory>/Cloudscape_10.0/demo/programs/simple directory. This program will not run if the CLASSPATH or PATH environment variables are not set correctly.

   When you run the SimpleApp application, it will:

1. Launch a JVM to host the application (it is a Java program, after all)
2. Start the Apache Derby database engine
3. Create a database called CLOUDSCAPEDB
4. Populate a table within the CLOUDSCAPEDB database
5. Shut down the database
6. Terminate the application

An example of running this program when the CLASSPATH variable is set only for a session is shown in Figure 5-14. If you set the CLASSPATH variable permanently, you can still run this program: just omit the statements that explicitly set the variable.

Verifying a Network Server Installation

To verify that you've correctly installed an environment that accepts multiple connections to your database, you can run a sample program that obtains an embedded connection and allows client connections at the same time.

```
Shell - Konsole <2>
Session  Edit  View  Bookmarks  Settings  Help
linux:~ # cd /opt/ibm/Cloudscape_10.0/demo/programs/simple/
linux:/opt/ibm/Cloudscape_10.0/demo/programs/simple # export CLASSPATH=/opt/ibm/Cloudscape_10.0/lib/derby.jar:
linux:/opt/ibm/Cloudscape_10.0/demo/programs/simple # echo $CLASSPATH
/opt/ibm/Cloudscape_10.0/lib/derby.jar:
linux:/opt/ibm/Cloudscape_10.0/demo/programs/simple # java SimpleApp
SimpleApp starting in embedded mode.
Loaded the appropriate driver.
Connected to and created database derbyDB
Created table derbyDB
Inserted 1956 Webster
Inserted 1910 Union
Updated 1956 Webster to 180 Grand
Updated 180 Grand to 300 Lakeshore
Verified the rows
Dropped table derbyDB
Closed result set and statement
Committed transaction and closed connection
Database shut down normally
SimpleApp finished
linux:/opt/ibm/Cloudscape_10.0/demo/programs/simple # ▮

  Shell
```

Figure 5-14   Verifying the installation of an Apache Derby database

Remember that to ensure consistency, only one JVM is allowed to access the database at any one time. When you start the IBM Cloudscape Network Server, the IBM Cloudscape embedded database driver is also loaded. This means that your application can get an embedded connection to the same database that the network server is accessing to serve up client requests for data.

The SimpleNetworkServerSample application starts the IBM Cloudscape Network Server, as well as the embedded driver, and waits for clients to connect to the database. The SimpleNetworkClientSample application interacts with the IBM Cloudscape Network Server from another JVM. Both of these sample applications are located in the <IBM Cloudscape Installation Directory>/demo/program/nserverdemo directory.

When you start the SimpleNetworkServerSample application, it will:

1. Start the IBM Cloudscape Network Server and set a property that also loads the embedded JDBC driver

2. Check to see whether the IBM Cloudscape Network Server is running

3. Create the NSSIMPLEDB database (if it does not already exist)

4. Obtain a database connection using the embedded JDBC driver, and execute a sample query to test it

5. Allow client connections to connect to the IBM Cloudscape database until you decide to stop the server and exit the program

6. Shut down the IBM Cloudscape Network Server before exiting the program

To run the SimpleNetworkServerSample application, ensure that both the derbynet.jar and derby.jar files are properly noted in your CLASSPATH environment variable (we'll assume at this point that you know how to do this) and then issue the java SimpleNetworkServerSample command, as shown in Figure 5-15.

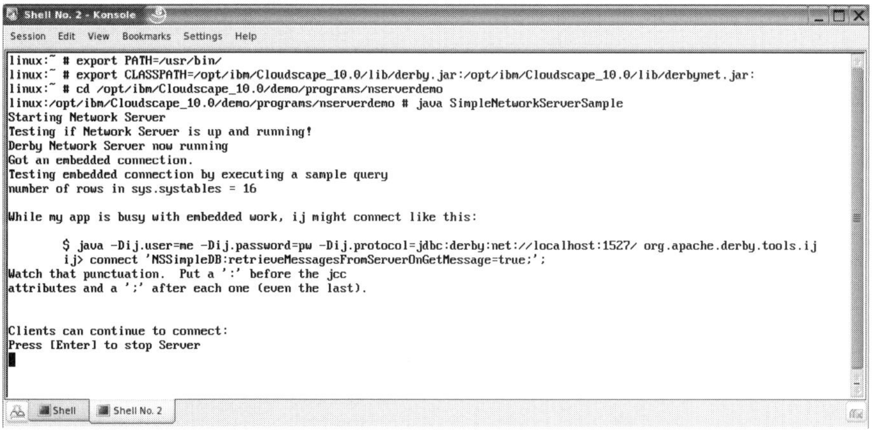

Figure 5-15 Verifying the installation of an IBM Cloudscape Network Server

Once the IBM Cloudscape Network Server is started, you're ready to start the `Simple-NetworkClientSample` application, which will connect to the NSSIMPLEDB database from an external JVM.

Specifically, the `SimpleNetworkClientSample` application will:

1. Load the DB2 JDBC Universal Driver

2. Obtain a client connection to the database using the driver manager

3. Obtain a client connection to the database using a data source

4. Test both database connections by executing a simple query

5. Close the connection and exit the program

To run the `SimpleNetworkClientSample` application, you're going to have to do something a little different because it relies on a different set of .JAR files to run. All of the previous verification scenarios have connected you to an embedded IBM Cloudscape database. Because this application runs in an external JVM, you must point to the driver files that it will use to make the connection. In this case, you need to add both the `db2jcc.jar` and `db2jcc_license_c.jar` files to your `CLASSPATH` environment variable in the same way that you added files in the previous examples. (These files are located in the same directory as the database and network server files.)

TIP

The `frameworks/NetworkServer/bin/setNetworkClientCP.bat` script will set the `CLASSPATH` to include the `db2jcc.jar` and `db2jcc_license_c.jar` files.

An example of running the `SimpleNetworkClientSample` application is shown in Figure 5-16.

```
Shell No. 2 - Konsole <2>

Session   Edit   View   Bookmarks   Settings   Help

linux:~ # export PATH=/usr/bin/
linux:~ # export CLASSPATH=/opt/ibm/Cloudscape_10.0/lib/db2jcc.jar:/opt/ibm/Cloudscape_10.0/lib/db2jcc_license_c.jar:
linux:~ # cd /opt/ibm/Cloudscape_10.0/demo/programs/nserverdemo/
linux:/opt/ibm/Cloudscape_10.0/demo/programs/nserverdemo # java SimpleNetworkClientSample
Starting Sample client program
Got a client connection via the DriverManager.
connection from datasource; getDriverName = IBM DB2 JDBC Universal Driver Architecture
Got a client connection via a DataSource.
Testing the connection obtained via DriverManager by executing a sample query
number of rows in sys.systables = 16
Testing the connection obtained via a DataSource by executing a sample query
number of rows in sys.systables = 16
Goodbye!
linux:/opt/ibm/Cloudscape_10.0/demo/programs/nserverdemo # █



   Shell      Shell No. 2
```

Figure 5-16   Verifying that a client application can connect to the IBM Cloudscape Network Server

Troubleshooting an Installation

If you've read through the steps in this chapter, Apache Derby and IBM Cloudscape installations will be a snap. For an easily installable product, we may have overdone the details in this chapter, but we wanted to ensure that you know the "ins" and "outs" of installing this software.

Nine times out of ten, an installation problem has to do with that pesky CLASSPATH environment variable. That's why we recommend that you use the script files provided by IBM Cloudscape to set this variable for either a graphical or manual installation (and, of course, it uses the CLOUDSCAPE_INSTALL environment variable too ... so set it).

The most common CLASSPATH issue occurs when the Java class that your application is trying to use cannot be found in the current setting of the CLASSPATH environment variable. When this happens, the JVM throws a java.lang.ClassNotFoundException error, as shown in Figure 5-17. Figure 5-17 shows the error that would have occurred if the example in Figure 5-14 had not found the required derby.jar file.

Another common error occurs when the class that you are trying to access is found, but one of the .JAR files it imports cannot be found. This typically has to do with a CLASSPATH issue and will throw a java.lang.NoClassDefFoundError error. This error often occurs when you create and compile your application on a development workstation where the CLASSPATH environment variable was set globally, and then you attempt to deploy your application on another workstation.

Whenever you experience a problem trying to start your database, always check the CLASSPATH environment variable. In Figure 5-17 we experienced an error because there wasn't a setting for the CLASSPATH environment variable that pointed to the required .JAR files.

To see a list of files contained within a .JAR file, use the jar -tvf <jar_file> command. For example, Figure 5-18 shows the results of running the jar -tvf derby.jar | more command.

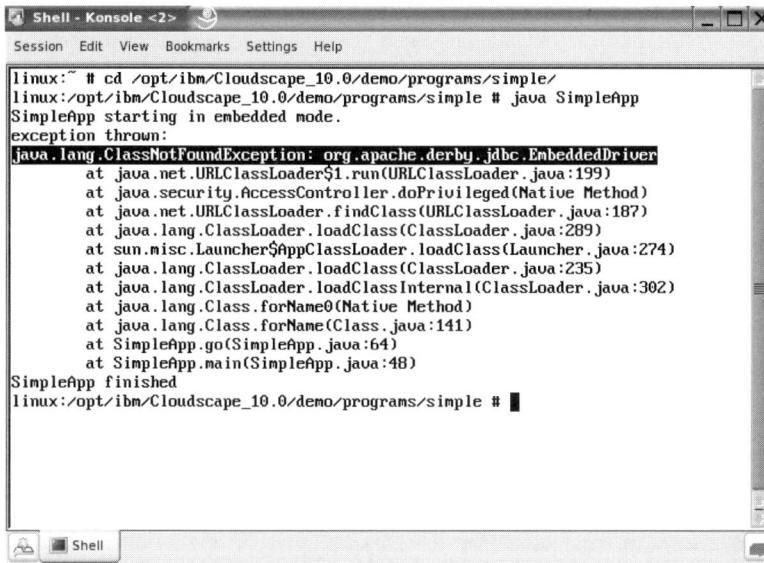

Figure 5-17 The JVM throws a Java exception because it cannot find the required .JAR file in the CLASSPATH

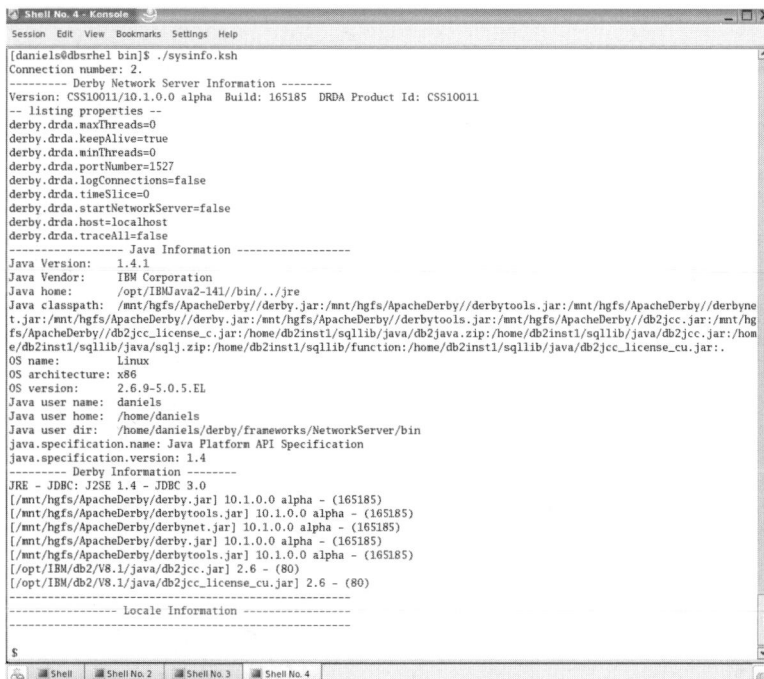

Figure 5-18 The contents of the derby.jar file

Another useful tool that you can use to troubleshoot an IBM Cloudscape installation is the sysinfo program, located in the x:/<IBM Cloudscape Installation Directory>/ frameworks/embedded/bin directory. You can use this tool to test for all the libraries that can be found and those that can't. An example of using sysinfo is shown in Figure 5-19.

```
Shell No. 4 - Konsole

Session  Edit  View  Bookmarks  Settings  Help

linux:~ # cd /opt/ibm/Cloudscape_10.0/frameworks/embedded/bin
linux:/opt/ibm/Cloudscape_10.0/frameworks/embedded/bin # ./sysinfo.ksh
------------------ Java Information ------------------
Java Version:    1.4.2_05
Java Vendor:     Sun Microsystems Inc.
Java home:       /usr/lib/jvm/java-1.4.2-sun-1.4.2.05/jre
Java classpath:  /opt/ibm/Cloudscape_10.0/lib/derby.jar:/opt/ibm/Cloudscape_10.0/lib/derbytools.ja
r:
OS name:         Linux
OS architecture: i386
OS version:      2.6.8-24-default
Java user name:  root
Java user home:  /root
Java user dir:   /opt/ibm/Cloudscape_10.0/frameworks/embedded/bin
--------- Derby Information --------
[/opt/ibm/Cloudscape_10.0/lib/derby.jar] 10.0.2.0 - (30301)
[/opt/ibm/Cloudscape_10.0/lib/derbytools.jar] 10.0.2.0 - (30301)
---------------------------------------------------------
---------------- Locale Information ------------------
---------------------------------------------------------
linux:/opt/ibm/Cloudscape_10.0/frameworks/embedded/bin # █



  Shell      Shell No. 2    Shell No. 3    Shell No. 4
```

Figure 5-19   Using the sysinfo tool to test for the libraries that you need

You can append -cp <filename.class> to the end of the sysinfo command to look for a specific class in the CLASSPATH environment variable.

Another common problem occurs when people try to access an IBM Cloudscape database (that was started in an application) from an external IDE or tools such as ij (we covered this in Chapter 2) without first starting the IBM Cloudscape Network Server.

Odds and Ends About Your Installation

In this section, we'll give you some additional installation details that should prove to be helpful as you make your way through the rest of this book.

Files on Disk

The installation program laid down a number of files, including the IBM Cloudscape database engine, the IBM Cloudscape Network Server, some samples, and a host of other files in your target directory. A list of these directories is shown in Figure 5-20.

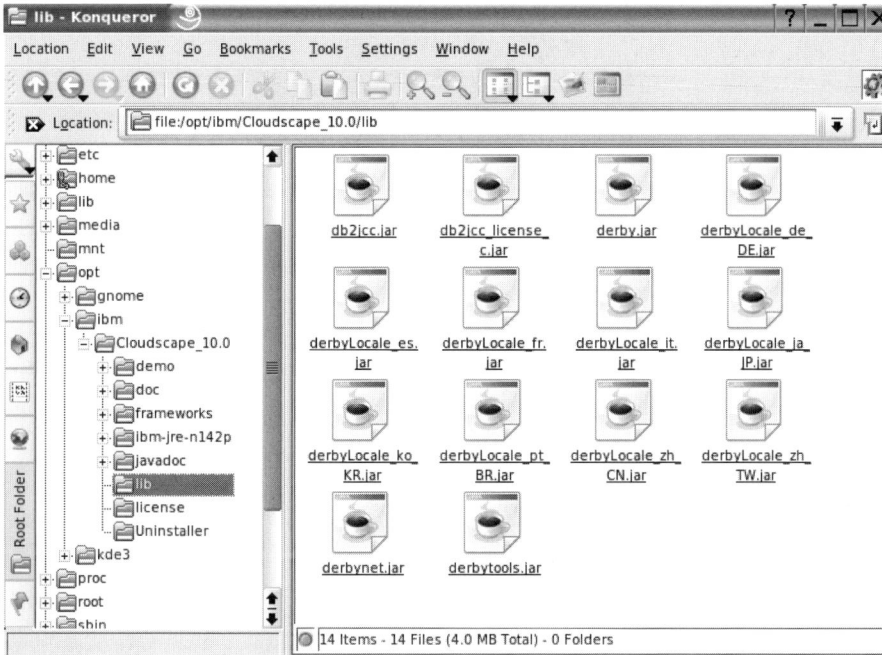

Figure 5-20   The on-disk file structure after completing an IBM Cloudscape installation

The /lib directory contains the actual database server (derby.jar) and network server (derbynet.jar) files. The DB2 Java Common Client (JCC) JDBC driver (db2cc.jar) is installed in this directory too (as well as any required license files). The IBM Cloudscape tools (derbytools.jar) are also located here. Tools such as dblook (a utility to view or dump the data definition language, or DDL, for objects in your databases) or ij (an interactive JDBC scripting tool and SQL command line interface) are part of the derbytools.jar file.

The Linux graphical installation program creates two databases for you. One is the sample database for DB2 Universal Database called SAMPLE, and the other is the Cloudscape sample database called TOURSDB.

Within each database directory (which always has the same name as the database itself) are three sub-directories. You will need to know the path to a database when you want to start it with your application. The /seg0 directory contains the data files for a database (and represents the actual location of the data on disk), and the log directory contains the transaction log files. You should never directly access these files.

Managing an Apache Derby Database

Apache Derby has been designed and developed as a database that requires little or no administration or maintenance. In the simplest case, where Apache Derby is running as a small database embedded directly within a Java application, this goal has been achieved: you can run the application for years without ever having to perform a backup or compress the data in the database. In more complex cases, where the size of the database is larger or Apache Derby is running in network server mode, there are some administration tasks that you must consider when you design your application and deployment strategy.

Disaster Prevention and Recovery

After designing your database schema, your most important database administration task is defining a database backup and recovery strategy. If your application crashes or your database server hangs and requires a reboot, there is a chance that the file system will suffer such severe damage that Apache Derby's built-in crash recovery support will not be able to restore your database to a consistent state. To prepare for such an unfortunate event, you want to be able to restore your data from a known point in time. A good database backup and recovery strategy gives you and your database users the confidence that, in the event of a disaster, their hard work or content will not be lost.

Backing Up a Database

Apache Derby gives you several different options for creating a backup copy of your database, ranging from an entirely offline backup, during which users can neither read data from nor write data to the database, to an entirely online backup, during which users can read data from the database, but writes to the database are blocked.

Online Backup with Read Access (Built-in Copy)

This approach provides the greatest level of database availability to your users: they can read data from the database while the backup operation is running in the background. "So," you may ask, "why would Apache Derby provide any other database backup methods?" There are two reasons why you might not want to use the online backup with built-in copy:

- The copy operations at the core of the online backup method are implemented in Java and might be somewhat slower than the native file copying utilities that are available at the operating system level. For a very large database, the time Apache Derby takes to perform a full-access online backup might be much greater than if you simply issued the copy commands from a batch file or shell script.

- An online backup operation requires its own system resources (including memory and disk input/output operations) that might interfere with Apache Derby's ability to serve requests to database users. For a large database with a number of active users, the performance degradation of the overall system during an online backup with built-in copy operation might be less tolerable than one of the other backup options that provide less access to users but that take less time to perform.

Even with those potential disadvantages, you should strongly consider using online backup with built-in copy as your default backup strategy. The online backup with built-in copy maintains a log that indicates when a backup occurred and whether or not the backup was successful. The potential performance disadvantages do not significantly impact real-life database management scenarios. Over the course of testing this option with a ~100 MB database on a 1700 Mhz processor, an online backup operation (while a database client was continuously inserting rows into the database) took approximately 20 seconds to complete in the worst case. That is an impressive display of online availability, and it suggests that online backup with built-in copy might be all that you ever need.

To perform a full-access online backup operation, call the SYSCS_UTIL.SYSCS_BACKUP_DATABASE() stored procedure using the following syntax:

```
CALL SYSCS_UTIL.SYSCS_BACKUP_DATABASE(backup-directory)
```

where `backup-directory` represents the full path to the directory in which the database backup will be placed. For example, to create a backup of the YMLD database in the /home/lynn/data/backups directory, issue the following command:

```
CALL SYSCS_UTIL.SYSCS_BACKUP_DATABASE('/home/lynn/data/backups/')
```

This backup operation:

- Creates a new directory called /home/lynn/data/backups/YMLD/
- Copies the existing YMLD database into the backup database directory

- Creates or appends to the BACKUP.HISTORY file a set of entries describing the backup operation in both the original YMLD database directory and in the backup database directory

If a backup for the same database has already been performed in the target backup directory, the Apache Derby backup operation temporarily renames the existing directory to *backup-directory*.OLD, performs the backup into the new directory, and then deletes the *backup-directory*.OLD directory. This process ensures that the old backup directory is still available if your new backup operation is interrupted.

BACKING UP DATABASES MAY PROVE HARMFUL TO YOUR HEALTH

Although backing up critical data in databases is encouraged, be aware that Apache Derby does not distinguish between a directory containing a backup of an Apache Derby database and any other directory with the same name as the Apache Derby database you are backing up. Therefore, if your database is named WINDOWS and you decide to place the backup in the C:\ directory, Apache Derby will quite willingly try to rename the C:\ WINDOWS directory to C:\WINDOWS.OLD, create the backup in C:\WINDOWS, and delete the C:\WINDOWS.OLD directory.

File permissions or operating system self-preservation might prevent you from entirely destroying your operating system, but be aware that the same situation can occur for any directory with the same name as your Apache Derby database. To prevent accidental or deliberate damage to your system, ensure that your Apache Derby database runs with the minimal permissions possible on your operating system.

Online Backup with Read Access (Native Copy)

If you decide that the performance advantages of the native operating system file access and copy operations outweigh the advantages of the Apache Derby built-in backup procedure, you can perform an online backup operation while your users are restricted to read-only operations on the database data. To complete an online backup operation with read-only access, perform the following steps:

1. Set the database to a read-only state by calling the SYSCS_UTIL.SYSCS_FREEZE_ DATABASE() stored procedure.

2. Issue the native operating system copy command to copy the complete database directory to your new location.

3. Return the database to a writable state by calling the SYSCS_UTIL.SYSCS_ UNFREEZE_DATABASE() stored procedure.

For example, on Linux you could write a simple Perl script to perform an online backup operation with read access and add the script to your cron jobs as a daily scheduled event to automate your backups:

```perl
#!/usr/bin/perl
use strict;
```

```perl
use DBI;
use File::Spec;

my ($sec,$min,$hour,$mday,$mon,$year,$wday,$yday,$isdst) =
    localtime();
my $date = sprintf("%d.%02d.%02d", $year + 1900, $mon + 1,
    $mday);
my $source = '/home/dan/derbydb';
my $destination = File::Spec->catdir('/home/dan/backup/',
    $date);

my $dbh = DBI->connect('dbi:DB2:YMLD', 'dan', 'm8mb0', {
    AutoCommit => 1,
    RaiseError => 1
});
$dbh->do('CALL SYSCS_UTIL.SYSCS_FREEZE_DATABASE()');
system("cp -r $source $destination");
$dbh->do('CALL SYSCS_UTIL.SYSCS_UNFREEZE_DATABASE()');
$dbh->disconnect();
```

In this script, we use the Perl DBI to connect to the YMLD database and call the SYSCS_UTIL
.SYSCS_FREEZE_DATABASE() stored procedure. We then invoke the system() function to
call the operating system cp -r recursive file copy command to create a backup of the YMLD
database in a directory identified by today's date. Finally, we use the Perl DBI to call the SYSCS_
UTIL.SYSCS_UNFREEZE_DATABASE() stored procedure and disconnect from the database.
For more information on writing Perl scripts that interact with Apache Derby databases, see
Chapter 14, "'Your Momma Loves Drama' in Perl."

Offline Backup

Performing an offline backup is relatively simple. The process consists of two basic steps:

1. Ensure that the database is offline.

   If you are running Apache Derby in network server mode, stop the network
   server to ensure that no clients are connected, or can connect, during the backup
   operation.

   If you are running Apache Derby embedded in an application, shut down the
   Derby system by issuing the following JDBC call:

   ```java
   String shutdown = "jdbc:derby:YMLD;shutdown=true";
   DriverManager.getConnection(shutdown);
   ```

2. Make a copy of the database directory.

   After stopping the network server or shutting down the Derby system, you can use any file copying commands or utilities to make a copy of the database directory. On a Windows operating system, for example, you can issue the `xcopy /s /i source destination` command to create a backup of your database.

Restoring a Database from a Backup Image

To restore a database from a backup image, shut down the Apache Derby system, remove or rename the directory containing the current "live" database, and copy or move the backup directory into its place. For example, to restore one of the daily backups from the "Online Backup With Read Access" scenario, you could perform the following steps:

1. Shut down the Apache Derby network server.

2. Rename the current live database:

   `mv /home/dan/YMLD /home/dan/YMLD.corrupt`

3. Move the backup into the place of the live database:

   `mv /home/dan/backup/2004.03.10 /home/dan/YMLD`

4. Start the Apache Derby network server.

Apache Derby will automatically use the restored database upon the next connection to the database. If the backup database image was corrupted, Apache Derby has no way of correcting the problems in the image. To ensure that the database structure and data are consistent, consider checking the consistency of the database after restoring the database image, as described in the "Checking Database Consistency" section later in this chapter.

Data Movement

Data movement refers to database operations that move large amounts of data from a file into a database or copy large amounts of data out of a database into a file. A data movement operation that moves large amounts of data into a database from a file is called an *import* operation. A data movement operation that copies large amounts of data from the database into a file is called an *export* operation.

A database without data is like a library without books: there may be structure, layout, and agents ready to retrieve information and add to the collection, but without data, there is nothing useful that you can do. When setting up an Apache Derby database, you can add data to the database in one of two ways. On a day-to-day basis, database applications can insert rows into the database using `INSERT` statements as part of their regular operations. Sometimes, however, you want to add a massive number of records to the database at one time—for example, you might want to migrate your database to Apache Derby from a different database system or convert an application built on top of spreadsheets into a more efficient Apache Derby application. In those cases, you want to avoid the overhead of issuing hundreds of thousands of INSERT statements, so you should instead consider using the bulk import stored procedures to add data.

For similar reasons, there are times when you want to export the data from one or more tables in your Apache Derby database to a file format that can be consumed by other databases or applications. For example, when you create a report for management, it might be to your advantage to load the data into a spreadsheet so that you can create ad-hoc charts and graphs that simplify the data for your management audience, or you might want to provide a subset of your data to associates so that they can concentrate on an intensive analysis of that data without affecting your Apache Derby network server. In those cases, you can use the bulk export stored procedures to efficiently generate the output files.

Apache Derby's data movement operations offer some significant advantages over applications built on simple INSERT or SELECT statements: they offer great performance, work with a standard file format, and automatically convert all of the data into your required code set. However, there are a number of restrictions to consider:

- You can only import and export data of the non-binary data types. BLOB, CLOB, and FOR BIT DATA types cannot be imported through the import routine.

- Import operations lock the table into which data is being inserted, which can affect the concurrency of the database in any Apache Derby application that supports multiple connections.

- The import and export commands are treated as a single unit of work, and they will issue a COMMIT or ROLLBACK when they finish processing. To avoid inadvertently committing or rolling back any previous transactions, you should commit or roll back any current transactions before issuing an import or export command.

Importing Data

Apache Derby offers bulk import stored procedures that enable you to import data into one table, or a subset of columns in a table, at a time. The entire table is exclusively locked during import. The table must exist before you import data. If the table is not empty, and you have chosen to append rows to the existing data rather than use the REPLACE option to completely replace the contents of the table, the import procedure will insert a single row at a time. For large amounts of data, the append operation will be noticeably slower than using the REPLACE option.

Importing Data into a Table

The syntax for the import table procedure is as follows:

```
CALL SYSCS_UTIL.SYSCS_IMPORT_TABLE (IN schemaName VARCHAR(128),
IN tableName VARCHAR(128), IN fileName VARCHAR(32672),
IN columnDelimiter CHAR(1), IN characterDelimiter  CHAR(1),
IN codeset VARCHAR(128), IN replace SMALLINT)
```

Table 6-1   *SYSCS_UTIL.SYSCS_IMPORT_TABLE* arguments

Argument	Description
schemaName	Name of the schema. A value of null defaults to the default schema for the current connection.
tableName	Name of the table. The table name is case-sensitive.
fileName	Full path name for the file containing the data to import. Use forward slashes (/) as path delimiters on both Windows and UNIX-based operating systems.
columnDelimiter	Character used to separate columns in the data file. A value of null defaults to the comma (,) character.
characterDelimiter	Character used to enclose character data. A value of null defaults to the double quotation mark (") character.
codeset	Character encoding set of the data file. The import procedure converts the data from the specified character encoding set to the database code set (UTF-8). A value of null defaults to the code set of the JVM in which the import procedure has been invoked.
replace	A value of 0 indicates that the contents of the data file should be appended to any existing rows in the table. A value of 1 indicates that any existing rows of the table should be deleted and replaced by the contents of the data file.

For example, to insert the contents of the file `/home/lynn/productions.dat` into the `PRODUCTIONS` table in the `APP` schema of the `YMLD` database using the `REPLACE` option, issue the following SQL statement in an application or from the `ij` tool:

```
CALL SYSCS_UTIL.SYSCS_IMPORT_TABLE
  ('APP','PRODUCTIONS','/home/lynn/productions.dat',
    null,null,null,1);
```

Because the column and character delimiters were left as defaults, a subset of the `produc-tions.dat` file might look like the following:

```
1,"Lilly of the Valley","2005-01-01","2005-02-25"
2,"My New Title",       "2005-01-25","2005-04-05"
3,"Desperate Houses",   "2005-03-06","2005-06-25"
```

Importing Data into a Subset of Columns in a Table

Apache Derby also gives you the option of inserting data into a subset of the columns in a table using the `SYSCS_UTIL.SYSCS_IMPORT_DATA` stored procedure. The syntax for the `SYSCS_UTIL.SYSCS_IMPORT_DATA` stored procedure is as follows:

```
SYSCS_UTIL.SYSCS_IMPORT_DATA (IN schemaName VARCHAR(128),
IN tableName VARCHAR(128), IN insertColumns VARCHAR(32672),
IN columnIndexes VARCHAR(32672), IN fileName VARCHAR(32672),
IN columnDelimiter CHAR(1), IN characterDelimiter  CHAR(1),
IN codeset VARCHAR(128), IN replace SMALLINT)
```

Table 6-2   *SYSCS_UTIL.SYSCS_IMPORT_DATA* arguments

Argument	Description
schemaName	Name of the schema. A value of null defaults to the default schema for the current connection.
tableName	Name of the table. The table name is case-sensitive.
insertColumns	Comma-delimited list of columns, in the order in which the data is to be imported. A value of null specifies all of the columns in the table.
columnIndexes	Comma-delimited list of 1-indexed columns found in the data file, in the order in which the data is to be imported. A value of null specifies all of the columns in the data file.
fileName	Full path name for the file containing the data to import. Use forward slashes (/) as path delimiters on both Windows and UNIX-based operating systems.
columnDelimiter	Character used to separate columns in the data file. A value of null defaults to the comma (,) character.
characterDelimiter	Character used to enclose character data. A value of null defaults to the double quotation mark (") character.

Table 6-2 *SYSCS_UTIL.SYSCS_IMPORT_DATA arguments (continued)*

Argument	Description
`codeset`	Character encoding set of the data file. The import procedure converts the data from the specified character encoding set to the database code set (UTF-8). A value of null defaults to the code set of the JVM in which the import procedure has been invoked.
`replace`	A value of 0 indicates that the contents of the data file should be appended to any existing rows in the table. A value of 1 indicates that any existing rows of the table should be deleted and replaced by the contents of the data file.

The most challenging part of the SYSCS_UTIL.SYSCS_IMPORT_DATA syntax to understand is the `columnIndexes` field. To create the "1-indexed list of columns," imagine that all of the columns in the data file are numbered from left to right, starting at 1, and increasing by 1 for every subsequent column. Then, select the columns into which the data will be imported and create a list that is delimited by commas. For example, to insert only the production ID and production name into the PRODUCTIONS table from a data file containing all four columns for the table, where the production ID is the first column and the production name is the second column, issue the following command:

```
CALL SYSCS_UTIL.SYSCS_IMPORT_DATA  ('APP','PRODUCTIONS',
  'PRODUCTION_NO, PRODUCTION_TITLE', '1, 2',
  '/home/lynn/productions.dat', null, null, null, 1);
```

Exporting Data

Apache Derby offers export stored procedures that enable you to export one table, or the results of a SELECT statement, into a file. Just like the import stored procedures, the export stored procedures are locale-sensitive and default to reasonable values for column and character delimiters for the output file that will be recognized by other applications as a comma-separated value (.csv) file format.

Exporting Data from a Single Table

The syntax for the SYSCS_UTIL.SYSCS_EXPORT_TABLE stored procedure is as follows:

```
SYSCS_UTIL.SYSCS_EXPORT_TABLE (IN schemaName VARCHAR(128),
IN tableName VARCHAR(128), IN fileName VARCHAR(32672),
IN columnDelimiter CHAR(1), IN characterDelimiter CHAR(1),
IN codeset VARCHAR(128))
```

Table 6-3   *SYSCS_UTIL.SYSCS_EXPORT_TABLE* arguments

Argument	Description
schemaName	Name of the schema. A value of null defaults to the default schema for the current connection.
tableName	Name of the table. The table name is case-sensitive.
fileName	Full path name for the file to which the data is to be exported. Use forward slashes (/) as path delimiters on both Windows and UNIX-based operating systems.
columnDelimiter	Character used to separate columns in the data file. A value of null defaults to the comma (,) character.
characterDelimiter	Character used to enclose character data. A value of null defaults to the double quotation mark (") character.
codeset	Character encoding set of the data file. The export procedure converts the data from the database code set (UTF-8) to the specified character encoding set. A value of null defaults to the code set of the JVM in which the export procedure has been invoked.

For example, to export the contents of the PRODUCTIONS table in the APP schema of the YMLD database into the file C:\TEMP\productions.dat, issue the following SQL statement in an application or from the ij tool:

```
CALL SYSCS_UTIL.SYSCS_EXPORT_TABLE
    ('APP','PRODUCTION','C:\TEMP\productions.dat',
      null,null,null);
```

Because the column and character delimiters were left as defaults, part of the productions .dat file might look like the following:

```
1,"Lilly of the Valley","2005-01-01","2005-02-25"
2,"My New Title",       "2005-01-25","2005-04-05"
3,"Desperate Houses",   "2005-03-06","2005-06-25"
```

Exporting Data from the Results of a *SELECT* Statement

Although exporting the complete set of data from a single table to an output file is extremely useful, there are many situations in which you might want to export either a subset of data from a table, or a set of data generated from values that have been selected from more than one table in the database. The syntax for the SYSCS_UTIL.SYSCS_EXPORT_QUERY stored procedure is as follows:

```
SYSCS_UTIL.SYSCS_EXPORT_QUERY(IN selectStatement
    VARCHAR(32672), IN fileName VARCHAR(32672),
    IN columnDelimiter CHAR(1),IN characterDelimiter CHAR(1),
    IN codeset VARCHAR(128))
```

Table 6-4 *SYSCS_UTIL.SYSCS_EXPORT_QUERY* arguments

Argument	Description
selectStatement	SELECT statement that generates the rows to be exported.
fileName	Full path name for the file to which the data is to be exported. Use forward slashes (/) as path delimiters on both Windows and UNIX-based operating systems.
columnDelimiter	Character used to separate columns in the data file. A value of null defaults to the comma (,) character.
characterDelimiter	Character used to enclose character data. A value of null defaults to the double quotation mark (") character.
codeset	Character encoding set of the data file. The export procedure converts the data from the database code set (UTF-8) to the specified character encoding set. A value of null defaults to the code set of the JVM in which the export procedure has been invoked.

For example, to export the list of performances for a single production in the YMLD database into the file D:\cloudscape\stuff.dat using the default column delimiter, character delimiter, and code set, issue the following command:

```
call SYSCS_UTIL.SYSCS_EXPORT_QUERY(
  'SELECT a.Performance_No, a.Performance_Date, b.Production_
    Title
  FROM PERFORMANCES a INNER JOIN PRODUCTIONS b
  ON a.Production_No = b.Production_No
  WHERE a.Production_No = 1',
'D:/cloudscape/stuff.dat', null, null, null);
```

Some of the data in the resulting file might look like the following:

```
1,"2005-01-01","Lilly of the Valley"
2,"2005-01-02","Lilly of the Valley"
3,"2005-01-03","Lilly of the Valley"
```

Database Maintenance and Tuning

Checking Database Consistency

In perfectly normal environments and situations, you can be confident that the tables within an Apache Derby database are consistent. However, we live in a world in which events such as power surges or power loss can occur, or ruthless system administrators can prematurely terminate an Apache Derby process. Events that cause an unexpected interruption of the Apache Derby processes can, unfortunately, cause one or more tables in a database to be placed in an inconsistent state. After such an event, you should check the state of the tables in your database with the SYSCS_UTIL.SYSCS_CHECK_TABLE function. If you discover that one or more of your tables is in an inconsistent state, you will have to recover your data from one of your database backups (as described in the first section in this chapter, "Disaster Prevention and Recovery").

The syntax for the SYSCS_UTIL.SYSCS_CHECK_TABLE function is as follows:

```
SYSCS_UTIL.SYSCS_CHECK_TABLE(IN schemaName VARCHAR(128),
    IN tableName VARCHAR(128))
```

Both parameters must be supplied. Passing a value of null for either *schemaName* or *table-Name* results in a usage error being returned by the Apache Derby database server. The function always returns a SMALLINT value of 1, but if the table is in an inconsistent state, Apache Derby will raise an error describing the reason that the table is not consistent.

For example, to check the consistency of the PRODUCTIONS table in the YMLD database, issue the following command:

```
ij> VALUES SYSCS_UTIL.SYSCS_CHECK_TABLE('APP', 'PRODUCTIONS');
```

If the table is in an inconsistent state because, for example, a Perl script went awry and appended data to the data files in the Apache Derby database, the output from this command might look something like the following:

```
ij> values syscs_util.syscs_check_table('APP', 'PRODUCTIONS');
1
-----------
ERROR XSDB0: Unexpected exception on in-memory page null
```

To check the consistency of every table in the database, you can issue a SELECT statement that joins the system catalogs for the database schemas and tables and runs the SYSCS_UTIL .SYSCS_CHECK_TABLE function against each returned table, as follows:

```
ij> SELECT schemaname, tablename,
SYSCS_UTIL.SYSCS_CHECK_TABLE(schemaname, tablename)
FROM sys.sysschemas INNER JOIN sys.systables
ON sys.sysschemas.schemaid = sys.systables.schemaid;
```

To check the consistency of every table in a specific schema, simply add a `WHERE` clause specifying the name of the schema. For example, to check the consistency of the tables within the APP schema, issue the following `SELECT` statement:

```
ij> SELECT schemaname, tablename,
SYSCS_UTIL.SYSCS_CHECK_TABLE(schemaname, tablename)
FROM sys.sysschemas INNER JOIN sys.systables
ON sys.sysschemas.schemaid = sys.systables.schemaid
WHERE sys.sysschemas.schemaname = 'APP';
```

Investigating Performance Issues with Database Statistics

Attempting to tune your database performance for the typical applications you plan to deploy against it without actual performance data can be a frustrating exercise. You could use the simplistic approach of extracting the SQL statements from your applications to simulate a typical workload, then running and timing the workload after every change you make to your database schema or SQL statements. This would give you a black box understanding of how your changes have affected the performance of the workload, but it cannot give you the data you need to address specific performance issues. Fortunately, Apache Derby includes the capabilities you need (database statistics) to peer inside that block box and understand why specific issues occur and how to address those issues with precision.

Statistics can help you to understand the execution plan of the SQL statements being issued against your database. An execution plan describes how Apache Derby will retrieve or update the data requested or used by the SQL statement, identifying which database elements it uses to speed up data access. For example, the execution plan shows when Apache Derby uses an index scan to quickly access just the rows in a table that correspond to specific index values. The execution plan also shows when Apache Derby has to perform a table scan, which requires the database server to retrieve every row in a table to determine which values meet the requirements of the SQL statement. If many of your SQL statements result in table scans for specific predicates, you might be able to improve the performance of your queries by creating a new index, or you could consider rewriting the SQL statement to avoid the table scan.

Gathering Runtime Statistics

Collecting SQL statement statistics negatively affects the performance of the database, so by default, Apache Derby does not collect database statistics. To collect statistics, call the `SYSCS_UTIL.SYSCS_SET_RUNTIMESTATISTICS` stored procedure with an input value of 1. Apache Derby collects the statistics for a single SQL statement at a time and enables you to display the statistics and execution plan for that statement by retrieving the value of the `SYSCS_UTIL.SYSCS_GET_RUNTIMESTATISTICS` function.

PREVENTING DATA TRUNCATION IN *IJ*

By default, the `ij` tool truncates text that is wider than 128 characters. When you retrieve statistics using the `SYSCS_UTIL.SYSCS_GET_RUNTIMESTATISTICS()` table function, the returned text will almost always be wider than 128 characters, resulting in truncation of much of the important statistics information.

To avoid truncating your statistics, set the `MaximumDisplayWidth` variable in `ij` to 32762 characters to match the `VARCHAR(32762)` return value of the `SYSCS_UTIL.SYSCS_GET_RUNTIMESTATISTICS()` table function:

```
ij> MaximumDisplayWidth 32762;
```

You should also ensure that your terminal or DOS prompt has enough history buffer to be able to scroll back and display the complete set of runtime statistics.

The following set of statements demonstrates how to collect and display the statistics and execution plan for a relatively complex SQL query against the YMLD database. To preserve space, only the section of the results showing the table scan has been included in the output.

```
ij> CALL SYSCS_UTIL.SYSCS_SET_RUNTIMESTATISTICS(1);

ij> SELECT COUNT(*) FROM app.seats INNER JOIN app.performances
ON seats.performance_no = performances.performance_no
WHERE performances.performance_no IN
(SELECT production_no FROM app.productions
WHERE production_title = 'Lilly of the Valley');

ij> VALUES SYSCS_UTIL.SYSCS_GET_RUNTIMESTATISTICS();

Left result set:
        Table Scan ResultSet for PRODUCTIONS at read committed
          isolation level using instantaneous share row locking chosen
          by the optimizer
        Number of opens = 1
        Rows seen = 1
        Rows filtered = 0
        Fetch Size = 16
                constructor time (milliseconds) = 0
                open time (milliseconds) = 0
                next time (milliseconds) = 0
                close time (milliseconds) = 0
                next time in milliseconds/row = 0
```

```
      scan information:
            Bit set of columns fetched={0, 1}
            Number of columns fetched=2
            Number of pages visited=2
            Number of rows qualified=1
            Number of rows visited=9
            Scan type=heap
            start position:
null                                          stop position:
null                                          qualifiers:
Column[0][0] Id: 1
Operator: =
Ordered nulls: false
Unknown return value: false
Negate comparison result: false


            optimizer estimated row count:      1.40
            optimizer estimated cost:          55.40
```

Within the left result set in the execution plan, you can see the table scan that Apache Derby uses to retrieve the appropriate value for the PRODUCTION_TITLE column in the PRODUCTIONS table. Creating an index on the PRODUCTION_TITLE column of the PRODUCTIONS table should enable future queries of a similar nature to use an index scan instead of a table scan:

```
ij> CREATE INDEX title_index ON productions (production_title);
```

After creating an index on the PRODUCTION_TITLE column, we can reissue the SELECT statement and check the execution plan to ensure that the new index resolves the potential performance bottleneck of the table scan.

Adding Timing to Runtime Statistics

As you might have noticed in the previous extract of statistics gathered for a complex query against the YMLD database, all of the times reported for every operation were exactly 0 milliseconds. Although the amount of data in the YMLD database is small, we know that table scans are expensive operations, and we would expect to see some measurable impact even on the smallest sets of data. Apache Derby does not collect timing statistics by default when statistics collection has been turned on. Just as with regular statistics, the reason timing statistics are not collected is that the overhead of collecting timing statistics interferes even more significantly with the actual performance of your production database. The designers and developers of Apache Derby appear to be quite concerned about the quantum effect when it comes to relational databases!

To add timing information to your runtime statistics, call the SYSCS_UTIL.SYSCS_
SET_STATISTICS_TIMING() stored procedure with an input value of 1. You can then issue
an SQL statement and retrieve the runtime statistics. In the following example, we turn on timing statistics, delete the index that we created previously, and repeat the previous SQL query. In
the small section of retrieved statistics that is displayed, you can see that the close time for the
table scan on the PRODUCTIONS table has been timed at 10 milliseconds—a significant amount
of time indeed, when the rest of the operations for the table scan and the other (output omitted)
index scans are still timed at 0 milliseconds.

```
ij> CALL SYSCS_UTIL.SYSCS_SET_STATISTICS_TIMING(1);
0 rows inserted/updated/deleted

ij> DROP INDEX title_index;
0 rows inserted/updated/deleted

ij> SELECT COUNT(*) FROM app.seats INNER JOIN app.performances
ON seats.performance_no = performances.performance_no
WHERE performances.performance_no IN
(SELECT production_no FROM app.productions
WHERE production_title = 'Lilly of the Valley');

ij> VALUES SYSCS_UTIL.SYSCS_GET_RUNTIMESTATISTICS();

Left result set:
        Table Scan ResultSet for PRODUCTIONS at read committed
          isolation level using instantaneous share row
          locking chosen by the optimizer
        Number of opens = 1
        Rows seen = 1
        Rows filtered = 0
        Fetch Size = 16
                constructor time (milliseconds) = 0
                open time (milliseconds) = 0
                next time (milliseconds) = 0
                close time (milliseconds) = 10
                next time in milliseconds/row = 0

        scan information:
                Bit set of columns fetched={0, 1}
                Number of columns fetched=2
                Number of pages visited=2
                Number of rows qualified=1
```

```
              Number of rows visited=9
              Scan type=heap
              start position:
null                                              stop position:
null                                              qualifiers:
Column[0][0] Id: 1
Operator: =
Ordered nulls: false
Unknown return value: false
Negate comparison result: false

              optimizer estimated row count:         1.40
              optimizer estimated cost:             55.40
```

By re-creating the index and reissuing the SQL statement, we can see that the table scan has been replaced by an index scan, with estimates of 0 milliseconds for all operations and a significantly lowered estimated optimizer cost. After seeing such a dramatic decrease for an extremely small table, the negative impact of table scans on database performance should be quite clear. And with Apache Derby's tools for collecting and displaying statistics, as well as your knowledge of the value of creating indexes or rewriting SQL statements to avoid table scans, you are well equipped to keep your Apache Derby database a lean, mean, SQL statement crunching machine.

```
Ij> CREATE INDEX table_index ON PRODUCTIONS(Production_Title);
0 rows inserted/updated/deleted

ij> SELECT COUNT(*) FROM app.seats INNER JOIN app.performances
ON seats.performance_no = performances.performance_no
WHERE performances.performance_no IN
(SELECT production_no FROM app.productions
WHERE production_title = 'Lilly of the Valley');

ij> VALUES SYSCS_UTIL.SYSCS_GET_RUNTIMESTATISTICS();

Left result set:
      Index Row to Base Row ResultSet for PRODUCTIONS:
      Number of opens = 1
      Rows seen = 1
      Columns accessed from heap = {0, 1}
            constructor time (milliseconds) = 0
            open time (milliseconds) = 0
            next time (milliseconds) = 0
            close time (milliseconds) = 0
```

```
optimizer estimated row count:           1.00
optimizer estimated cost:                8.70


Index Scan ResultSet for PRODUCTIONS using index
   TITLE_INDEX at read committed isolation
      level using
    instantaneous share row locking chosen by the
      optimizer
Number of opens = 1
Rows seen = 1
Rows filtered = 0
Fetch Size = 16
           constructor time (milliseconds) = 0
           open time (milliseconds) = 0
           next time (milliseconds) = 0
           close time (milliseconds) = 0
           next time in milliseconds/row = 0


     scan information:
           Bit set of columns fetched=All
           Number of columns fetched=2
           Number of deleted rows visited=0
           Number of pages visited=1
           Number of rows qualified=1
           Number of rows visited=2
           Scan type=btree
           Tree height=-1
           start position:
>= on first 1 column(s).
Ordered null semantics on the following columns:


           stop position:
> on first 1 column(s).
Ordered null semantics on the following columns:


           qualifiers:                      None
           optimizer estimated row count:   1.00
           optimizer estimated cost:        8.70
```

Reorganizing Data

Although achieving maximum performance (or more realistically, avoiding major performance bottlenecks) is one aspect of database tuning, another aspect that concerns some database administrators is maintaining a small footprint on disk. For example, on a server that runs a multitude of Apache Derby network server databases, you might be more interested in minimizing the disk footprint for each of your databases than in optimizing the performance of those databases. If you are interested in minimizing disk footprint, it is critical to know that Apache Derby does not automatically return disk space to the operating system after delete operations. For example, if you deleted 1,000,000 rows with an average of 128 bytes per row, 128 megabytes of disk space would be waiting in reserve for the next data to be inserted into the database.

You can force Apache Derby to return space for a single table by calling the `SYSCS_UTIL` `.SYSCS_COMPRESS_TABLE` stored procedure. The syntax for the stored procedure is as follows:

```
CALL SYSCS_UTIL.SYSCS_COMPRESS_TABLE (
  IN schemaName VARCHAR(128), IN tableName VARCHAR(128),
  IN sequentialCompression INTEGER)
```

Table 6-5 *SYSCS_UTIL.SYSCS_COMPRESS_TABLE* arguments

Argument	Description
schemaName	Name of the schema. A value of null defaults to the default schema for the current connection.
tableName	Name of the table. The table name is case-sensitive.
sequentialCompression	Specifies whether to use concurrent compression (value = 0) or sequential compression (value = 1). Concurrent compression uses multiple threads, more temporary disk space, and finishes faster, but sequential compression uses less memory.

For example, to compress the `PERFORMANCES` table in the YMLD database using concurrent compression, you can issue the following command:

```
CALL SYSCS_UTIL.SYSCS_COMPRESS_TABLE ('APP', 'PERFORMANCES', 0);
```

Summary

Although Apache Derby is a zero- or low-maintenance database, there are scenarios where it makes sense to invest some effort in learning the administration capabilities that Apache Derby has to offer. In this chapter you have learned:

- The importance of developing a backup and recovery strategy

- How to back up and recover Apache Derby databases, with online and offline options for performing your backup operations

- How to import data to and export data from tables in an Apache Derby database

- How to investigate long, slow-running SQL statements through Apache Derby's run-time statistics utilities

- How to reorganize your database tables to save disk space

With this knowledge, you can ensure that users of your Apache Derby databases—whether embedded within an application or accessed through a network server—have safe and efficient access to their data.

Security

Introduction

Security is an important consideration whenever data is stored in a relational database management system. In this chapter, we discuss controlling data access using many different methods.

Security for a database can be configured at a physical or a logical level:

- Physical—Physical security refers to the underlying disk and file structures on which the database depends. Access to these objects is typically restricted by the operating system. Access to the system might also be limited by the connectivity that is allowed from outside clients. The system could be configured to restrict use to local users or applications only.

- Logical—Logical security refers to security that is implemented within the database or an outside security manager that manages access to objects within the database. This can be as simple as authenticating the user through a user ID and password or placing controls on tables and objects themselves.

Apache Derby databases are deployed in many types of environments, so they have different security needs from what a traditional database might require. These databases are not always locked away in machine rooms where it is difficult for someone to tamper with the physical media. Apache Derby databases are typically found on desktops, laptops, and kiosks, as well as servers. In practice, many of these databases are encrypted to prevent the media from being examined. Once an Apache Derby application is deployed, most of the access is through the application itself, so extensive security features (like GRANT and REVOKE) are typically not required.

The various options available for securing a database are discussed next.

Database File Security

Physical security for an Apache Derby database is controlled through the operating system and the database startup parameters. Most operating systems will allow a form of control over the underlying files in the Apache Derby database. An Apache Derby database places all of the data and control information within a directory structure in the underlying file system. Control to the file system is then established through operating system commands, so that only specific applications or users can access the data. For instance, in a Windows XP environment, the following steps will allow you to set specific file privileges on a directory.

1. In any Explorer window, click `Tools` and then `File Options`.
2. Click the `View` tab.
3. Scroll to the bottom, and uncheck `Use simple file sharing (Recommended)`.

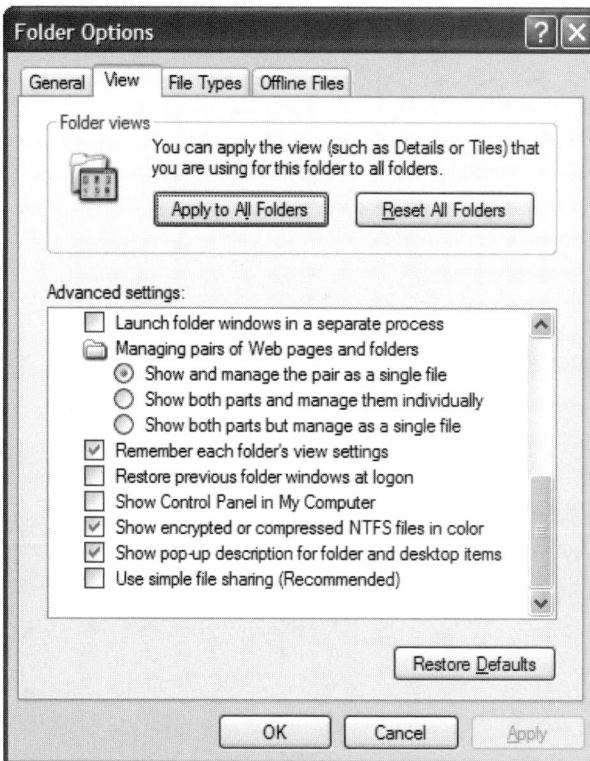

Figure 7-1   Folder Options

4. Click `OK`.
5. Permissions can now be set on files and directories by clicking the `Security` tab of the properties window (right-click on the file/directory and click `Properties`).

The primary reason for placing controls on file access is maintenance, not necessarily user access. Users will access the data through the Apache Derby engine, not directly through the file system. However, these same users should not access the files directly so that they cannot delete, move, or corrupt data that might be important for the operation of the database.

Database File Encryption

Apache Derby includes a number of options for encrypting the database. Encrypting the database might be a requirement for many sensitive applications, especially if unauthorized users could access the actual database files. Encryption must be turned on at database creation time. There is no option to encrypt a database after it has been created.

Four options are associated with encryption, and they are specified as part of the connection string:

- `dataEncryption`—Specifies data encryption on disk for a new database. This parameter must be specified, along with the `create=true` parameter, the `boot-Password` parameter, and optionally, the encryption provider and algorithm.

- `bootPassword`—Specifies the key to use for encrypting a new database or booting an existing encrypted database. The password must be an alphanumeric string that is at least eight characters long. When creating a database, the `bootPassword` parameter must be specified, along with the `dataEncryption` parameter. On subsequent access to the database, only the `bootPassword` parameter needs to be supplied.

- `encryptionProvider`—Any alternate encryption routine can be specified at database creation time by specifying an encryption provider and the algorithm to be used. If this parameter is not specified, the default encryption provider is `com.sun.crypto` `.provider.SunJCE`.

- `encryptionAlgorithm`—This parameter specifies the algorithm for data encryption. The format of the parameter is `algorithmName/feedbackMode/padding`. In Apache Derby, the only padding type allowed is `NoPadding`. If no encryption algorithm is specified, the default value is `DES/CBC/NoPadding`.

For example, to create a database with encryption, the following string would be passed to the `ij` utility:

```
java -Dij.protocol=jdbc:derby: org.apache.derby.tools.ij
ij version 10.0 (C) Copyright IBM Corp. 1997, 2004.
ij> connect 'tst;create=true;dataEncryption=true;bootPassword=test1234';
```

The database `tst` is created with encryption and a boot password of 'test1234'. Once this database is created, the only way to access it is to supply the boot password on the connect statement. If the password is not supplied, the program or the `ij` utility fails with a corresponding error message.

```
java -Dij.protocol=jdbc:derby: org.apache.derby.tools.ij
ij version 10.0 (C) Copyright IBM Corp. 1997, 2004.
```

```
ij> connect 'tst';
ERROR XJ040: Failed to start database 'tst', see the next exception for
details.
ERROR XBM06: Startup failed, an encrypted database cannot be accessed
without the correct boot password.
```

The initial access to an encrypted database will always require a password. Note that if the password is supplied without encryption, it will have no effect on the database. The password will be ignored on subsequent connections to the database. Care should also be taken when selecting the password. The password needs a minimum of eight characters and should contain a combination of letters and numbers.

Encrypted databases cannot be booted automatically, along with all other system databases, on system startup. Instead, encrypted databases are booted when you first connect to them. Once a database is booted, all connections can access the database without the boot password. The boot password is not meant to prevent unauthorized connections to the database once it has been booted. The encryption of the database is meant to prevent fraudulent access to data outside of the database engine.

The two other parameters that are available for encryption are `encryptionProvider` and `encryptionAlgorithm`. The default encryption routine provided in Apache Derby is `com.sun.crypto.provider.SunJCE`. At the time of publication, the Sun site lists eight additional providers of security plug-ins (http://java.sun.com/products/jce/jce14_providers.html).

- Assembla Trust Technology AB has released a JCE provider that supports PKI-related operations for Microsoft's key stores through JNI. It implements the KeyStore, Cipher, and Signature SPI classes. For more information, see https://download.assembla.se/jceprovider/.

- IAIK of Austria has developed a JCE 1.4-compliant provider that includes key generation, cipher, message digest, and signature services. It implements many algorithms and standards. For more information, see http://jce.iaik.tugraz.at.

- INTESIGROUP has released a JCE provider that supports pkcs#11 tokens. For more information about the Intesi JCE provider, see: http://www.intesigroup.com/en/secur_PkJce.html.

- Pheox has released a JCE provider that supports access to Microsoft's certificate stores through Microsoft's CAPI. For more information, see http://www.jcapi.com.

- The Legion of the Bouncy Castle has released a JCE 1.4-compliant provider that implements a collection of cryptography algorithms and provides tools for generating and processing X.509 certificates, PKCS12 files, CMS (PKCS7), S/MIME, OpenPGP, and OCSP (RFC 2560). For more information, see http://www.bouncycastle.org.

- nCipher Ltd. has released a JCE 1.4-compliant provider to support its FIPS 140-2-compliant hardware security modules with the nForce and nShield products. The nCipher provider contains all of the standard cryptographic algorithms that the security industry uses. Also, this provider—in conjunction with nCipher hardware—provides key security and cryptographic acceleration for asymmetric operations. For more information, see http://www.ncipher.com/toolkits/ciphertools.html.

- Uwe Guenther has released a JCE provider that implements all the relevant crypto algorithms, such as DES, Triple-DES, RSA, and RIPEMD160. For more information, see http://www.jhbci.de.

- Wedgetail Communications has released a JCE 1.4-compliant provider for implementing industry-standard algorithms for public and symmetric key cryptography. For more information, see http://www.vintela.com/company/wt_wedgetail.php.

For most applications, the supplied encryption routines included with the JCE will be sufficient. However, the default encryption level uses 56-bit DES encryption, so you might want to specify a more secure encryption level.

There are three specifications that make up the `encryptionAlgorithm` parameter: algorithm, feedback mode, and padding. These specifications are combined to create a string `algorithmName/feedbackMode/padding`. The `padding` parameter can only be `NoPadding`, but `algorithmName` and `feedbackMode` can have other values.

Algorithm

The following values can be specified for `algorithmName`:

- `DES`—The Digital Encryption Standard, as described in FIPS PUB 46-2
- `DESede`—Triple DES encryption (DES-EDE)

Apache Derby supports any encryption algorithm that:

- Is symmetric
- Is a block cipher, with a block size of 8 bytes
- Uses the `NoPadding` padding scheme
- Has a secret key that can be represented as an arbitrary byte array
- Requires exactly one initialization parameter, an initialization vector of type `javax.crypto.spec.IvParameterSpec`
- Can use `javax.crypto.spec.SecretKeySpec` to represent its key

More details on these algorithms can be found in the Sun documentation at http://java.sun.com/j2se/1.4.2/docs/guide/security/jce/JCERefGuide.html.

To use triple DES encryption, the `encryptionAlgorithm` string should be set to:

```
DESede/CBC/NoPadding
```

The encryptionAlgorithm value is not enclosed by quotation marks.

```
java -Dij.protocol=jdbc:derby: org.apache.derby.tools.ij
ij version 10.0 (C) Copyright IBM Corp. 1997, 2004.
ij> connect 'test3333;create=true;dataEncryption=true;
bootPassword=test3333;encryptionAlgorithm=DESede/CBC/NoPadding;'
```

Feedback Mode

The following values can be specified for feedbackMode:

- CBC—Cipher Block Chaining Mode, as defined in FIPS PUB 81
- CFB—Cipher Feedback Mode, as defined in FIPS PUB 81
- ECB—Electronic Codebook Mode, as defined in: The National Institute of Standards and Technology (NIST) Federal Information Processing Standard (FIPS) PUB 81, "DES Modes of Operation," U.S. Department of Commerce, Dec 1980
- OFB—Output Feedback Mode, as defined in FIPS PUB 81

More details on these modes and the JCE implementation can be found in the Sun documentation at http://java.sun.com/j2se/1.4.2/docs/guide/security/jce/JCERefGuide.html.

User Authentication

By default, there is no user authentication within Apache Derby. In some cases, this can cause a problem, especially when accessing Apache Derby from a remote client. The client that is used to communicate with the database requires the specification of a user ID and password as part of the connection. In this case, any user ID and password is acceptable to the database.

Apache Derby provides support for user authentication so that the user's name and password are authenticated before the user is allowed to access the system. When user authentication is enabled, the user requesting a connection must provide a valid name and password, which Apache Derby verifies against the repository of users defined on the system. Once the user is authenticated, Apache Derby grants the user access to the system, but not necessarily access to the database that is specified in the connection request.

In Apache Derby, access to a database is determined by user authorization. More details on how to authorize a user for database access are provided in the later section "User-defined Authorization." Authentication can be handled through an external directory service (like LDAP), through user-defined code, or using Apache Derby's mechanism for creating a built-in repository of users.

Before going into the details of how to set up security mechanisms, some knowledge of user names within Apache Derby is required. User names within the Apache Derby system are known as authorization identifiers. The authorization identifier is a string that represents the name of the user (if one was provided). The special register CURRENT_USER returns the authorization identifier for the current user. If a user connects without the specification of a user ID, the default name of APP is used instead.

When an authorization identifier is passed to the Apache Derby system, it becomes an SQL92 identifier. SQL92 identifiers are converted to uppercase characters (unless they were delimited with double quotation marks) and have a maximum length of 128 characters. User names must be valid authorization identifiers, even if user authentication is turned off, and even if all users are allowed access to all databases.

When working with both user authentication and user authorization, you need to understand how user names are treated by the system. If an external authentication system is used, the conversion of a user name to an authorization identifier does not happen until after authentication has occurred.

The authentication system is probably case-sensitive, so a user ID such as "Andrew", for example, is valid. The user ID "Andrew" would be passed on to the authentication system, and when it is properly validated, Apache Derby would allow this user to connect to the system. However, within the database itself, the user ID is converted to uppercase ("ANDREW"), and this is what Apache Derby will use for authorization within the database. In other words, "Andrew", "ANDREW", and "andrew" are unique from an authentication perspective but identical from an authorization perspective.

Enabling Authentication

If you want to use an external authentication mechanism, the Apache Derby system or database properties must be set. Which property to set depends on how the database will be used.

- System-wide—Most properties can be set on a system-wide basis; that is, you set a property for the entire system and all of its databases. Some properties, such as error handling and automatic booting, can be configured only in this way because they apply to the entire system.

- Database-wide—Some properties can also be set on a database-wide basis; that is, a property is applicable to the selected database only, and not to other databases in the system, unless it is set individually for each of them. When you change these properties, the changes affect only the objects within the specified database.

System-wide properties can be set either from the command line or in the derby.properties file. If a system property is changed from a command line, it is effective only while the system is running. The change is not recorded in the derby.properties file.

You can set persistent system-wide properties in a text file called derby.properties, which must be placed in the directory specified by the derby.system.home property. There should be one derby.properties file per system, not per database. The file must be created in the system directory. If derby.system.home is not specified, the current directory from which the system was started is assumed to contain the properties file.

To set up authentication for all users in the system, add the following string to the `derby`
`.properties` file, or include it as part of the start command for the database:

```
derby.connection.requireAuthentication=true
```

The `SET_DATABASE_PROPERTY` function should be used to set up authentication at the database level. There must already be a connection to the database before you issue this command:

```
connect 'YMLD';
CALL SYSCS_UTIL.SYSCS_SET_DATABASE_PROPERTY(
  'derby.connection.requireAuthentication', 'true');
```

After the change has been made, any connection attempt will fail unless a valid user ID and password are specified.

```
connect 'ymld';
ERROR 08004: Connection refused : Invalid authentication.
```

Before setting up authentication at the database level, ensure that at least one user is defined in
the database. Otherwise, there will be no way to connect to the database because Apache Derby
does not have the concept of a system administrator or a super-user to access the database.

LDAP Directory Service Authentication

A typical use for a directory service is to store user names and passwords for a computer system.
Apache Derby uses the Java Naming and Directory Interface (JNDI) to interact with external
directory services that can provide authentication of user names and passwords.

You can allow Apache Derby to authenticate users against an existing LDAP (lightweight
directory access protocol) directory service within your enterprise. LDAP provides an open directory access protocol running over TCP/IP. An LDAP directory service can quickly authenticate
a user name and password. To use an LDAP directory service, set `derby.authentication`
`.provider` to LDAP. Examples of LDAP service providers are:

- Netscape Directory Server
- UMich slapd (freeware for the UNIX platform from the University of Michigan)
- AE SLAPD for Windows NT, from AEInc

To use an LDAP directory service with Apache Derby, you need the following libraries in your
class path:

- `jndi.jar`—JNDI classes
- `ldap.jar`—LDAP provider from Sun
- `providerutil.jar`—JNDI classes for a provider

Apache Derby does not provide these libraries; they are available from Sun on the JNDI page at http://java.sun.com/products/jndi/. You must use the 1.1x versions of these libraries.

When specifying LDAP as your authentication service, you must specify the location of the server and its port number. Set the `derby.authentication.server` property to the location and port number of the LDAP server.

```
derby.authentication.server=geoffrey:389
```

Additional LDAP settings are listed in Table 7-1.

Table 7-1 LDAP Settings

Property Name	Use
`derby.authentication.provider`	Specifies the kind of user authentication to use (LDAP)
`derby.authentication.server`	For LDAP and NIS+ user authentication; specifies the location of the server
`derby.authentication.ldap` `.searchAuthDN, derby.authentication` `.ldap.searchAuthPW, derby` `.authentication.ldap.searchFilter,` and `derby.authentication.ldap` `.searchBase`	Configure the way that DN searches are to be performed
`javax.naming`	JNDI properties

Some external directory services might have specific JNDI properties that can be set. These are set at either the database or the system level, depending on how the external service was configured. Each JNDI provider has its own set of properties that you can set within the Apache Derby system. For example, you can set the `java.naming.security.authentication` property to allow user credentials to be encrypted on the network if the provider supports this encryption. You can also specify that SSL should be used with LDAP (LDAPS).

Additional considerations regarding LDAP user IDs, performance, and filtering of user IDs can be found in the Apache Derby Developer's Guide at http://incubator.apache.org/derby/manuals/index.html.

User-Defined Authentication

You can define your own class to implement authentication within Apache Derby. Set `derby` `.authentication.provider` to the full name of a class that implements the public interface `org.apache.derby.authentication.UserAuthenticator`. By writing your own class, you can hook Apache Derby up to an external authentication service other than LDAP. An example of this can be found in the Apache Derby Developer's Guide.

Built-In Authentication

The simplest authentication scheme is provided within Apache Derby itself. Apache Derby provides a simple, built-in repository of user names and passwords. To use the built-in repository, set `derby.authentication.provider` to BUILTIN. Using this built-in repository is an alternative to using an external directory service such as LDAP.

System-Level Users

When you create users with system-level properties, those users are available to all databases in the system. You set the value of this system-wide property once for each user, so you don't have to set it for each database.

To delete a user, remove that user from the file. This property can be set in the `derby` `.properties` file. Create one line for each user, according to the following format:

```
derby.user.UserName=password
```

For example, the following file creates a group of user IDs and passwords. The pound (#) character is used to comment out a line.

```
# Accounting Group
derby.user.andrew=my1psp
derby.user.Katrina=ell1ed0g
# Administration
derby.GEOFFREY=gh0strcnrulZ
```

The user IDs are case-sensitive from an authentication perspective, but not from an SQL identifier perspective. For example, the following connection through the `ij` utility illustrates the difference:

```
01   connect 'ymld' user 'katrina' password 'ellied0g';
     ERROR 08004: Connection refused : Invalid authentication.
02   connect 'ymld' user 'GEOFFREY' password 'gh0strcnrulz';
     ERROR 08004: Connection refused : Invalid authentication.
03   connect 'ymld' user 'fred' password 'notincluded';
     ERROR 08004: Connection refused : Invalid authentication.
04   connect 'ymld' user 'Katrina' password 'ell1ed0g';
05   values current_user;

1
---------
KATRINA

1 row selected
```

- [01] connect 'ymld' user 'katrina' password 'elliedOg'
  This connection fails because the user ID is incorrect. The user ID is case-sensitive.
- [02] connect 'ymld' user 'GEOFFREY' password 'gh0strcnrulz'
  This connection fails because the password is incorrect. The password is also case-sensitive.
- [03] connect 'ymld' user 'fred' password 'notincluded'
  This connection fails because the user ID is not known to the system.
- [04] connect 'ymld' user 'Katrina' password 'ell1edOg'
  This is a valid connection.
- [05] values current_user
  This command returns a value of 'KATRINA', an SQL92 identifier. Note that the user ID has been folded to uppercase characters.

Database-Level Users

Authentication can also be set at the database level. When you create users with database-level properties, those users are available to the specified database only. A user is added to the database by using the SYSCS_UTIL.SYSCS_SET_DATABASE_PROPERTY() command.

This command has two parameters: a property name and its corresponding value. The first parameter is derby.user.UserName, and the second parameter corresponds to a password. For example:

```
call syscs_util.syscs_set_database_property
    ('derby.user.andrew','my1psp');
call syscs_util.syscs_set_database_property
    ('derby.user.Katrina','ell1edOg');
call syscs_util.syscs_set_database_property
    ('derby.user.GEOFFREY','gh0strcnrulZ');
```

To delete a user, set the password to null.

```
call syscs_util.syscs_set_database_property
    ('derby.user.GEOFFREY',null);
```

If the system has not been enabled for authentication, you must set authentication at the database level using the following commands:

```
call syscs_util.syscs_set_database_property
    ('derby.connection.requireAuthentication','true');
call syscs_util.syscs_set_database_property
    ('derby.authentication.provider','BUILTIN');
```

Security Hierarchy

Because Apache Derby supports two levels of authentication, you need to know which level takes precedence and how they interact.

- Authentication set at the system level only

  When the derby.properties file contains requireAuthentication=true, all users defined at the system level will have access to all databases. Attempting to connect to any database will fail unless a user ID and password are specified.

- Authentication set at the database level only

  When requireAuthentication is set to true for an individual database (and not set in the derby.properties file), access to the database is restricted to users who are defined in the database. Therefore, it is a good idea to create a user in the database before restricting access to the database! If you've made a mistake and this hasn't been done, you can turn on system-level authentication, add the user ID, and then connect to the database.

- Authentication set at both the system and the database level

  System-level users can connect to the database, along with users identified at the database level. If there is a conflict involving passwords, the database-level password takes precedence. For example, you might have created user T1 with password t1 at the system level, and user T1 with password t2 at the database level. Connecting as T1 with the t1 password fails because the database-level password takes precedence over the system-level password.

Database Authorization

Apache Derby provides the ability to configure user authorization for the system. This can be used to secure default access to all databases in the system. To control access to a particular database, you can set database-level properties that specify which users have full (read-write) access to the database and which users have read-only access to the database. Users that are not specified by either property will inherit the default access to the database, which is full (read-write) access.

To specify the access mode for a database, use the derby.database.default-ConnectionMode property. This property can be set to one of three values:

- noAccess
- readOnlyAccess
- fullAccess (the default)

The following example sets the connection mode to readOnlyAccess:

```
call syscs_util.syscs_set_database_property
     ('derby.database.defaultConnectionMode','readOnlyAccess');
```

To specify which users have full (read-write) access to a database, use the `derby.database` `.fullAccessUsers` property. For example:

```
call syscs_util.syscs_set_database_property
    ('derby.database.fullAccessUsers','Katrina,andrew');
```

To specify which users have read-only access to a database, use the `derby.database` `.readOnlyAccessUsers` property. For example:

```
call syscs_util.syscs_set_database_property
    ('derby.database.readOnlyAccessUsers','GEOFFREY');
```

Users are specified in a comma-separated list (with no spaces on either side of each comma). For users that are not specified by either property, access is determined by the `derby.database` `.defaultConnectionMode` property.

It is possible to configure a database so that it cannot be changed (or even accessed) using the `derby.database.defaultConnectionMode` property. If you set this property to `noAccess` or `readOnlyAccess`, be sure to define at least one full-access user.

Permissions

The following table summarizes what read-only and full-access users can do.

Table 7-2   Allowable Actions by Access Type

Action	Read-Only User	Full-Access User
Execute SELECT statements	x	x
Read database properties	x	x
Load database classes from .JAR files	x	x
Execute INSERT, UPDATE, or DELETE statements		x
Execute DDL statements		x
Add or replace .JAR files		x
Set database properties		x

Errors

If a user is not authorized to connect to the database that is specified in the connection request, SQLException 04501 is raised. If a user with read-only access attempts to write to a database, SQLException 08004 - connection refused is raised.

Summary

Apache Derby offers a number of ways of securing your database, including encryption, user authentication, and authorization. Authentication can be performed with LDAP, a user-defined class library, or Apache Derby's built-in facilities. Users can be authenticated at the system or database level. In addition, access to databases can also be controlled at the read-only or the read-write level.

More details on how to implement LDAP and user-defined authentication can be found in the Apache Derby Developer's Guide at http://incubator.apache.org/derby/manuals/index.html.

## CHAPTER 8

SQL

Introduction

The standard language of relational database access is SQL (Structured Query Language). SQL is not a conventional programming language. It was designed for the purpose of accessing tabular data. Every Relational Database Management System (RDBMS) implements a slightly different version of SQL. In this chapter, we examine the Apache Derby implementation of the SQL language. If you are familiar with other RDBMS products, you will already understand many aspects of the Apache Derby implementation of SQL, thanks to the industry acceptance of the ISO/ANSI SQL standard.

SQL is divided into three major categories:

- DDL (Data Definition Language)—Used to create, modify, or drop database objects
- DML (Data Manipulation Language)—Used to select, insert, update, or delete database data (records)
- DCL (Data Control Language)—Used to provide data object access control

We first examine the Apache Derby database objects and how they are created. A database object is any component of an Apache Derby database, such as tables, views, indexes, schemas, triggers, and procedures.

Next, we will explore the ways in which these objects can be referenced in SQL statements, including SELECT, INSERT, UPDATE, and DELETE.

Finally, we will examine the SQL language elements and some of the more sophisticated features within the Apache Derby database. As SQL has evolved, many new statements have been added to provide a more complete set of data management methods. We explore some of these advanced features, including constraints, triggers, views, and outer joins.

Your Momma Loves Drama Database

Many of the examples in this book contain references to the "Your Momma Loves Drama" database. This fictitious database contains information about productions that are held in a small theater. Figure 8-1 is a graphical representation of the tables in this database.

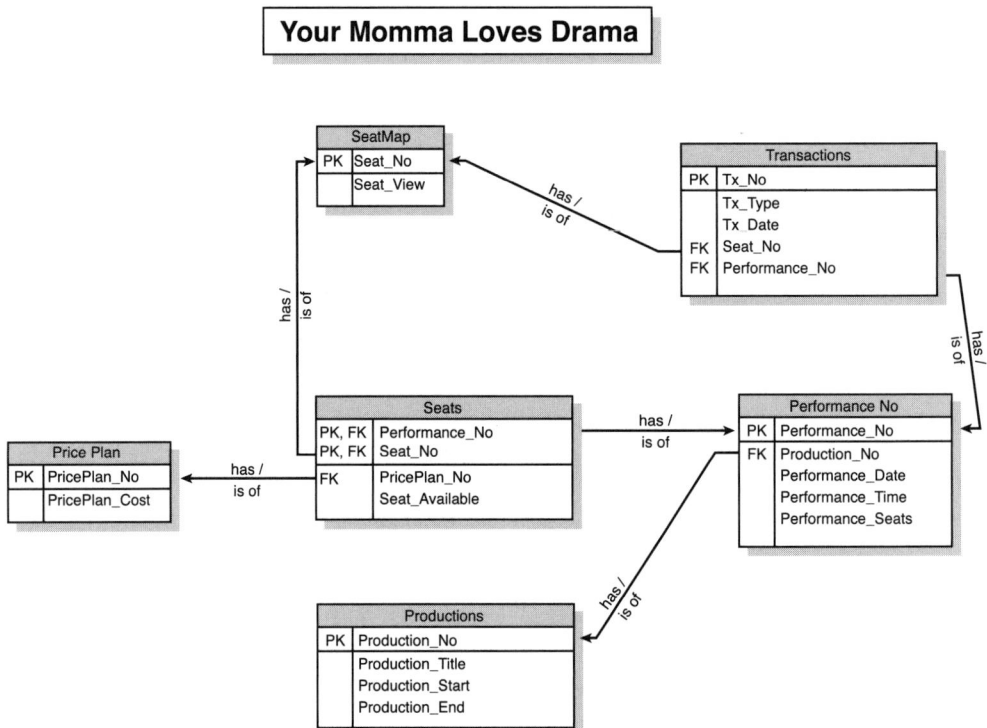

Figure 8-1   Your Momma Loves Drama Tables

The tables and their usage are described below. The Web site for this book (www.ibmpressbooks .com/title/0131855255) contains scripts that will create the YMLD database for you, as well as many of the examples found within this chapter. In order to create this database on your system, you first need to create a directory on your local system and then copy the contents of the Chapter 8 link into this directory. Once that step is complete, you can run the database creation step as shown (this assumes a Windows environment).

```
md \databases
cd \databases
... copy the files from the Chapter 8 link to this directory ...
ij <create-YMLD.sql
```

Make sure that you run the `ij` command from the directory in which the database is going to reside. Otherwise, the database will be created in the directory from which the `ij` command was issued. The `create-YMLD.sql` script contains a number of SQL statements that will create the YMLD database and supporting tables, as well as load the tables with sample data.

SETTING UP THE PROPER APACHE DERBY ENVIRONMENT

Before attempting any of the examples in this section, make sure that you have issued the `SETEMBBEDEDCP` command in Windows, or `setEmbeddedCP.sh` in Linux. This Linux command is case-sensitive, so make sure that you type the shell command correctly. These commands set up the appropriate environment variables for running Apache Derby on your operating system.

The script generates these tables:

- `PRODUCTIONS`—This table contains the title and date of all the productions that are being performed at the theater.

- `PERFORMANCES`—Each production will have a number of performances associated with it. Each performance has date and time information, along with a current count of the number of seats available. Although the number of seats available for a performance can easily be calculated, this column can be used for quick searches of available performances.

- `SEATS`—Each performance has a number of seats assigned to it. Performances can have a different number of seats available to them, depending on whether they are matinee performances or evening performances. In this particular theater, we have limited the number of available seats to twenty.

- `PRICEPLAN`—Each seat has a particular price associated with it, depending on the location of the seat and the date and time of the performance.

- `SEATMAP`—The `SEATMAP` table is used during the booking process to allow patrons to see what the view of the stage will be from the seats that they are purchasing.

- `TRANSACTIONS`—All purchases made through the system are logged in the `TRANS-ACTIONS` table—This allows for the auditing of purchases, as well as queries about transaction volumes.

Data Definition Language (DDL)

SQL Data Definition Language (DDL) is used to create, modify, or delete objects in an Apache Derby database. DDL includes four basic SQL statements:

- `CREATE`
- `ALTER`

- DECLARE

- DROP

The DECLARE statement is unusual in that it is only used for temporary tables. Normally a table is "created" and a permanent copy of it is placed in the database. Applications use the DECLARE statement when there is a need to hold temporary data.

All SQL statements are case-insensitive. For example, the following statements are equivalent:

```
CREATE TABLE EMPLOYEE;
create table employee;
```

The objects that you create, whether they are tables, views, or column names, must adhere to Apache Derby naming standards. Ordinary identifiers are identifiers that are not surrounded by double quotation marks. Delimited identifiers are surrounded by double quotation marks. An ordinary identifier must begin with a letter and contain only letters, underscore characters (_), or digits. The permitted letters and digits include all Unicode letters and digits. Ordinary identifiers can be up to 128 characters long and are case-insensitive because they are automatically converted to uppercase. For example:

```
SALARY_42, Salary_42, salary_42
```

Each of these identifiers is identical from an SQL perspective. Enclosing the identifier in double quotation marks allows you to include special characters as part of the name. However, spaces at the end of a delimited identifier are ignored. Apache Derby interprets two consecutive double quotation marks within a delimited identifier as one double quotation mark. For example:

```
"Base Salary", "Holiday.Pay.Rate", "Quotes "" Inside"
```

Periods within delimited identifiers are not separators but are part of the identifier. So, "EMPLOYEE.SALARY" is a valid identifier but completely different from EMPLOYEE.SALARY. The first example is an identifier name, but the second is a reference to the SALARY column in the EMPLOYEE table. Although the use of delimited identifiers can give you more flexibility in the naming of columns, they require more consideration when building SQL statements. Each delimited identifier must be spelled correctly, or the SQL statement will fail. To simplify the SQL statements in this chapter, we do not use delimited identifiers.

The next section looks in detail at some of the objects that can be created in a database, including tables, views, and indexes. One useful technique to remember when creating objects within Apache Derby is to store all of the DDL statements in a script file to allow for easier creation of the database objects in the future. This script can then be executed by using the Apache Derby ij utility.

The *CREATE* Statement

The CREATE statement is used to create database objects. The database objects that can be created are:

- Table
- Index
- Schema
- View
- Trigger

The creation of any database object updates the catalog tables. Specific authorities and privileges are required to create database objects.

The *ALTER* Statement

The ALTER statement allows you to change some characteristics of an existing table. The ALTER TABLE statement allows you to:

- Add a column to a table
- Add a constraint to a table
- Drop an existing constraint from a table
- Increase the size of a VARCHAR column
- Add a default value for an existing column in a table
- Override row-level locking for the table

The ALTER statement is usually used during the testing of applications, but it is very rarely used in production systems because of the possible impact on existing applications. For example, adding a column to a table will make a SELECT * statement return a different number of columns and can cause an existing application to return incorrect results.

The *DECLARE* Statement

The DECLARE statement is very similar to the CREATE statement, except that it is used to create temporary tables that are used only during a session. The only object that can be declared is a table, and it exists only for the current user who created it.

The creation of a temporary table does not update the catalog, so locking, logging, and other forms of contention are avoided when using this object.

Declared tables have a number of restrictions against them. The following features are not available with declared tables:

- Indexes
- Triggers on the declared table, or triggers that refer to a declared table
- Views

- `LOCK TABLE` command (which is unnecessary anyway)
- Column constraints or primary keys
- Generated columns

Declared tables can be dropped just like a regular table. Once a table is declared, it can be referenced like any other table. More details on the usage of the `DECLARE` statement can be found in the section on table creation.

The *DROP* Statement

The `DROP` statement is used to delete objects from the database. Because database objects can be dependent on other database objects, the act of dropping an object can result in a related object being rendered invalid. You can drop any object that was created with the `CREATE` or `DECLARE` statement.

Apache Derby Data Types

Every column in a table must be assigned a data type from among the various data types supplied by Apache Derby. Knowledge of the possible data values and their usage is required to be able to select the correct data type. Specifying an inappropriate data type when defining a table can result in:

- Wasted disk space
- Improper expression evaluation
- Degraded performance

When using character data types, the choice between `CHAR` and `VARCHAR` is determined by the range of column length. For example, if the range of column length is relatively small, use a fixed `CHAR` with the maximum length. This will reduce storage requirements and could improve performance. Using a `CHAR` column for an address field wastes space if the contents are usually empty or don't use the full size of the field.

The built-in data types can be divided into three major categories:

- Numeric
- String (Unicode and binary)
- Datetime

Details about these data types are provided in the following sections.

Numeric Data Types

The six Apache Derby data types that can be used to store numeric data are:

- `SMALLINT` (2 bytes)
- `INTEGER` (4 bytes)
- `BIGINT` (8 bytes)

- DECIMAL/NUMERIC
- REAL (4 bytes)
- DOUBLE PRECISION (8 bytes)
- FLOAT (alias for DOUBLE PRECISION or REAL)

These data types are used to store different numeric types and precisions. The precision of a number is the number of digits that are used to represent its value. The data is stored in the Apache Derby database using a fixed amount of storage for all numeric data types. The amount of storage required increases as the precision of the number goes up.

You must also be aware of the range limits of the data types and the corresponding application programming language when you are manipulating these numeric fields.

Some data values are of the INTEGER type by nature, such as an age. It would be unusual to have a value representing a number of people that contains fractional data (numbers to the right of the decimal). On the other hand, some values require decimal places to accurately reflect their value, such as salary. These two examples should use different Apache Derby data types to store their values (SMALLINT and DECIMAL, respectively).

Numeric values should not be enclosed by quotation marks. If they are, the values are treated as character strings. Even if a field contains numbers in its representation, an Apache Derby numeric data type should be used to represent the data only if arithmetic operations are allowed.

Small Integer (*SMALLINT*)

A small integer uses the least amount of storage in the database for each value. An integer does not allow any digits to the right of the decimal point.

The data value range for a SMALLINT is -32,768 to 32,767. The precision for a SMALLINT is 5 digits (to the left of the decimal point). Two bytes of database storage are used for each SMALLINT column value.

Example: AGE SMALLINT

Integer (*INTEGER*)

An INTEGER requires twice as much storage as a SMALLINT but has a greater range of possible values.

The data value range for an INTEGER is -2,147,483,648 to 2,147,483,647. The precision for an INTEGER is 10 digits (to the left of the decimal point). Four bytes of database storage are used for each INTEGER column value.

Example: STREET_NO INT

Big Integer (*BIGINT*)

The BIGINT data type is available to support 64-bit integers. The data value range for a BIGINT is -9,223,372,036,854,775,808 to +9,223,372,036,854,775,807. As platforms include native support for 64-bit integers, the processing of large numbers with BIGINT is more efficient than processing with DECIMAL, and more precise than DOUBLE or REAL. Eight bytes of database storage are used for each BIGINT column value.

Example: TRANSACTION_NO BIGINT

Decimal (*DECIMAL/NUMERIC*)

The DECIMAL or NUMERIC data type is used for numbers with fractional and whole parts. DECIMAL data is stored in a packed format.

The precision and scale must be provided when a decimal data type is used. The precision is the total number of digits (range from 1 to 31), and the scale is the number of digits in the fractional part of the number. For example, a decimal data type to store currency values of up to $1 million would require a definition of DECIMAL(9,2). The terms NUMERIC, DECIMAL, and DEC can all be used to declare a decimal/numeric column. If a decimal data type is to be used in a C program, the host variable must be declared as a double. A DECIMAL number takes up p/2 + 1 bytes of storage, where p is the precision used. For example, DEC(8,2) would take up 5 bytes of storage (8/2 + 1), whereas DEC(7,2) would take up only 4 bytes (truncate the division of p/2).

Example: SALARY DEC(13,2)

Single-Precision Floating-Point (*REAL/FLOAT*)

The REAL data type is an approximation of a number. The approximation requires 32 bits or 4 bytes of storage. To specify a single-precision number using the REAL data type, its length must be defined between 1 and 24 (especially if the FLOAT data type is used, because it can represent both single- and double-precision and is determined by the integer value specified).

Example: LATITUDE REAL or LATITUDE FLOAT(20)

Double-Precision Floating-Point (*DOUBLE/FLOAT*)

The DOUBLE or FLOAT data type is an approximation of a number. The approximation requires 64 bits or 8 bytes of storage. To specify a double-precision number using the FLOAT data type, its length must be defined between 25 and 53.

Example: DISTANCE DOUBLE or DISTANCE FLOAT(50)

String Data Types

This section discusses the string data types, which include CHAR, VARCHAR, and LONG VARCHAR. All strings within Apache Derby are stored in Unicode (2 bytes), so although your application might refer to the third character in a string, it will actually be stored in the fifth and sixth position of the physical string. Normally this will not impact the way your application will see the data, but you will need to take into consideration the additional size of the field if you are copying it to a binary-based field.

The Unicode character encoding standard is a fixed-length character encoding scheme that includes characters from almost all the living languages of the world. Unicode characters are usually shown as U+xxxx, where xxxx is the hexadecimal code of the character. Each character is 16 bits (2 bytes) wide, regardless of the language, and the resulting 65,536 code elements are sufficient for encoding most of the characters of the major languages of the world.

Fixed-Length Character String (*CHAR*)

Fixed-length character strings are stored in the database using the entire defined amount of storage. If the data being stored always has the same length, the CHAR data type should be used.

Using fixed-length character fields can potentially waste disk space if the data is not using the defined amount of storage. However, overhead is involved in storing varying-length character strings. The term CHARACTER can be used as a synonym for CHAR.

The length of a fixed-length string must be between 1 and 254 characters. If you do not specify a value for the length, a value of 1 is assumed.

Example: LAST_NAME CHAR(10)

Varying-Length Character String (*VARCHAR*)

Varying-length character strings are stored in the database using only the amount of space required to store the data. For instance, individual names should be defined as varying-length strings (VARCHAR) because each person's name has a different length (up to a maximum length). The term CHAR VARYING or CHARACTER VARYING can be used as a synonym for VARCHAR.

If a varying-length character string is updated, and the resulting value is larger than the original, the record might need to be restructured to another page in the table. This might result in more processing time for changes to VARCHAR columns. Records in Apache Derby can span multiple pages, so there is no need to worry about the record size. The maximum length of a VARCHAR column is 32,672 bytes.

Example: ADDRESS VARCHAR(128)

Varying-Length Long Character String (*LONG VARCHAR*)

LONG VARCHAR is a historical data type that was used for large character strings before the VARCHAR limit was extended. This data type is used to store character data with a varying length of up to 32,700 characters. This is extremely close to the VARCHAR limit of 32,672 characters, so this data type is rarely used. The LONG VARCHAR data type does not require a length field, so it is specified without any additional parameters. If you need to store data greater than 32,700 characters in length, use the CLOB data type.

Example: RESUME LONG VARCHAR

Character String Considerations

Character strings in Apache Derby are delimited by a single quotation mark character ('). Double quotation marks delimit special identifiers in SQL. A double quotation mark does not require an escape character when it is used in an SQL string, but it requires an escape character within a Java or C program.

Example: `'This is a valid "quote" in a string'`

In a Java application, this string would require special escape characters.

Example: `SQL_String = "'This is a valid \"quote\" in a string'";`

Binary String Data Types

The three string types (`CHAR`, `VARCHAR`, and `LONG VARCHAR`) can be modified with the `FOR BIT DATA` attribute. Without this attribute, the length specification determines the number of Unicode characters that can be placed into a field. For example, `CHAR(5)` indicates that only five characters can be stored in this string. However, the underlying storage for this field actually requires 10 bytes because of the Unicode representation. In addition, when the string is retrieved by an application, the client code might need to "translate" the string into an appropriate representation for that client workstation. A Unicode "£" (pound sign) would be displayed as "œ" on a Windows system if the byte representation remains the same. The client translates this character automatically so that the intended character is found in the string that is retrieved. If you do not want character translations to occur, or if you need to store a precise number of bytes, then the `FOR BIT DATA` specification must be used.

The `FOR BIT DATA` specification is appended to the string field that you are defining.

Example: `EMPLOYEE_IMAGE VARCHAR(2000) FOR BIT DATA`

When the space is allocated in the table, the field will take up exactly 2000 bytes. If the `FOR BIT DATA` specification were not present, the field would take up 4000 bytes because of the Unicode character encoding. In addition, this string would not be translated when it is retrieved by an application. This is particularly important if the string does not contain character data.

Large Objects

Traditionally, large unstructured data was stored somewhere outside of the database. Therefore, the data could not be accessed using SQL. Apache Derby implements data types that will store large amounts of unstructured data. These data types are known as large objects (LOBs). Multiple LOB columns can be defined for a single table.

You might choose to use `BLOB`s for the storage of pictures, images, audio, or video objects, along with large documents, in a database. `BLOB` columns will accept any binary string without regard to its content.

If you want to manipulate textual data that is greater than 32 KB in length, you would use the `CLOB` (character large object) data type. For example, if you need to store an employee's resume, the resume could be stored in a `CLOB` column, along with the rest of the employee's information. There are many SQL functions that can be used to manipulate large character data columns, but there are a few restrictions that you should know.

- `LOB` types cannot be compared for equality (=) or non-equality (!=, <>)
- `LOB` values cannot be ordered, so <, <=, >, >= tests are not supported

- LOB types cannot be used in indices or as primary key columns
- DISTINCT, GROUP BY, and ORDER BY clauses are prohibited on LOB types
- LOB types cannot be involved in implicit casting to other base types
- CLOBs and LONG VARCHARs are not allowed as parameters to many of the conversion functions
- CREATE FUNCTION and CREATE PROCEDURE statements do not permit LONG VARCHARs, CLOBs, or BLOBs

Character Large Object (*CLOB*)

Character large objects are varying-length Unicode character strings that are stored in the database. CLOB columns are typically used to store more than 32 KB of text. The maximum size of each CLOB column is 2,147,483,647 characters (not bytes!). Because this data type is of varying length, the amount of disk space allocated is determined by the amount of data in each record. Therefore, you should create the column specifying the length of the longest string. The size of the string can be specified in bytes, or as an integer value followed by K (thousands), M (millions), or G (billions).

Example: COURSE_ABSTRACT CLOB (50 K)

Binary Large Object (*BLOB*)

Binary large objects are varying-length binary strings. The data is stored in a binary format. There are restrictions when using this data type, including the inability to sort this type of column. The BLOB data type is useful for storing nontraditional relational data, such as images or video.

The maximum size of each BLOB column is 2 GB (gigabytes). Because this data type is of varying length, the amount of disk space allocated is determined by the amount of data in each record, not by the defined maximum size of the column in the table definition. The size of the string can be specified in bytes, or as an integer value followed by K (thousands), M (millions), or G (billions).

Example: LOCATION_MAP BLOB (2 M)

Date and Time Data Types

There are three Apache Derby data types specifically used to represent dates and times:

- DATE—This data type is stored internally as a (packed) string of 4 bytes. Externally, the string has a length of 10 bytes (YYYY-MM-DD).
- TIME—This data type is stored internally as a (packed) string of 3 bytes. Externally, the string has a length of 8 bytes (HH:MM:SS).
- TIMESTAMP—This data type is stored internally as a (packed) string of 10 bytes. Externally, the string has a length of 23 characters (YYYY-MM-DD-HH:MM:SS.NNN), although a timestamp can have up to 6 microseconds specified as part of the number.

From the user perspective, these data types can be treated as character or string data types. Every time you want to use a datetime attribute, you will need to enclose it with quotation marks. However, datetime data types are not stored in the database as fixed-length character strings.

Creating a column with a datetime format is relatively straightforward because no optional length arguments are associated with the type:

```
HIRE_DATE         DATE
TRANSACTION_TIME  TIMESTAMP
START_TIME        TIME
```

Apache Derby provides special functions that allow you to manipulate these data types. These functions allow you to extract the year, month, day, hour, minute, and second from a datetime value, and they should always be used instead of substring functions. This ensures that the application will continue to work even if the underlying representation of the date or time value changes.

```
YEAR('2005-03-01') = 2005
HOUR('15:12:45') = 15
DAY('2005-02-28 13:00:05.223') = 28
```

The values that are returned from these functions are treated as large integers, so you can perform arithmetic operations on them.

Although date and time values are always stored in the same way, they can be specified in a variety of ways, which are discussed in the following.

Date String (*DATE*)

There are a number of valid ways to represent a DATE value as a string. A date is always stored in YYYY-MM-DD format, but the value can be input as follows:

- ISO: 'yyyy-mm-dd'
- North American: 'mm/dd/yyyy'
- European: 'dd.mm.yyyy'

The year must always be supplied as a 4-digit value, whereas month or day does not require the full two digits.

Example: '2005-03-01', '01.03.2005', '03/01/2005'

When the data is retrieved (using a SELECT statement), the output string will be always be in YYYY-MM-DD format.

Time String (*TIME*)

There are a number of valid ways to represent a TIME value as a string. A time value can be input as follows:

- ISO: 'hh.mm.ss'

- North American: 'hh:mm AM or PM'

- European: 'hh.mm.ss'

Note that the North American format does not allow seconds. If you intend to include seconds as part of a time value, you must use the ISO format. The North American time format includes the letters AM or PM to signify morning or evening. For the other two formats, a 24-hour clock is used, so times after 12 noon have the value 12 added to them. Therefore, 1 PM becomes 13:00:00 in the 24-hour clock.

Example: `'13:20:15'`, `'5:20 PM'`

Timestamp String (*TIMESTAMP*)

The timestamp data type has a single external format and takes up 10 bytes of storage. Timestamps have an external representation as YYYY-MM-DD-HH.MM.SS.NNNNNN (Year-Month-Day-Hour-Minute-Seconds-Microseconds). The least significant digits (microseconds) will not display if they are zero. In other words, a value of '2005-03-10-11.15.20.300000' will not display the last 5 zeros when retrieved using the `ij` utility.

Example: `'2005-01-05-21.15.23.123456'`

Creating User Tables

The `CREATE TABLE` statement allows you to define tables. The definition must include the table name and the column attributes. The definition can include other attributes of the table, such as its primary key or check constraints. Primary keys and check constraints are described in the section on constraints.

After the table is defined, column names and data types cannot be modified. Exceptions to this include increasing the length of a `VARCHAR` column. New columns can be added to the table, but you need to be careful because default data values will be used for all of the existing records. In addition, after a table is created, you can change table options such as constraints, identity column values, and lock granularity.

The maximum number of columns that a table can have is 1012.

Sample Table Create Statements

The following example shows two `CREATE TABLE` statements: one creates a `DEPARTMENT` table and the other an `EMPLOYEE` table.

```
CREATE TABLE DEPARTMENT
  (
  Deptnumb    SMALLINT,
  Deptname    VARCHAR(20),
  Mgrno       SMALLINT
  );
```

```
CREATE TABLE EMPLOYEE
  (
  ID           SMALLINT,
  Name         VARCHAR(9),
  Dept         SMALLINT,
  Hiredate     DATE,
  Salary       DECIMAL(7,2)
  );
```

The simplest form of the CREATE TABLE statement is quite straightforward:

```
CREATE TABLE schema.table_name ( column 1 [, column 2 ...] )
```

The table name must be a valid SQL identifier and can contain a schema name. If an application starts up the database, or if you use the ij command, the default schema name is APP. This means that all objects belong to the schema called APP. You can override this by prefixing the name of the table with the schema name that you want. The following two SELECT statements are identical if you use the default connection to Apache Derby:

```
CREATE TABLE EMPLOYEE (NAME VARCHAR(20));
SELECT * FROM EMPLOYEE;
SELECT * FROM APP.EMPLOYEE;
```

Schemas can be useful when logically grouping objects in a single collection because they provide a unique namespace for the objects. To create a schema, use the CREATE SCHEMA statement:

Example: CREATE SCHEMA Productions

After the schema has been created, you can use the schema name in CREATE TABLE statements, as well as all subsequent SQL statements.

The portion between the parentheses () in the CREATE TABLE statement contains the individual column definitions. Each column definition is separated from the others with a comma. The column definition contains the name of the column, the data type, and then any additional constraints associated with that column. Constraints are modifiers to the data type that further restrict what can be placed into the field. Once the table has been created, it can be accessed using SQL statements such as INSERT, UPDATE, DELETE, and SELECT.

Additional Data Type Modifiers

Additional modifiers are available within Apache Derby that can change the type of data that goes into a column. One modifier lets Apache Derby know whether or not null values are allowed, and the other modifier determines whether the system should automatically increment column values.

Null Considerations

A null represents an unknown state. Therefore, when columns containing null values are used in calculations, the result is unknown. All of the data types discussed in the previous section support the presence of nulls. During table definition, you can specify that a value must be provided. This is accomplished by adding a phrase to the column definition. The CREATE TABLE statement can contain the NOT NULL clause as part of the definition of a column. This will ensure that the column contains a value (is not null). By default, all columns are considered to be able to contain nulls, so there is no need to use the NULL clause as part of the column definition.

Special considerations are required to properly handle nulls when coding an Apache Derby application. Apache Derby treats nulls differently than it treats other values. To define a column not to accept nulls, add the NOT NULL clause to the end of the column definition:

Example: CREATE TABLE T1 (C1 INT NOT NULL)

In this example, Apache Derby will not allow any nulls to be stored in the C1 column. In general, avoid using nullable columns unless they are required to implement the database design. You must also consider overhead storage. An extra byte per nullable column is necessary if nulls are allowed.

Not Null with Default

When you insert a row into a table and omit the value of one or more columns, these columns can either be null (if the column is defined as nullable) or given a default value. If the column is defined as not nullable, the insert operation will fail unless a value has been provided for the column. Apache Derby has a defined default value for each of the Apache Derby data types, but you can explicitly provide a default value for any column. The default value is specified in the CREATE TABLE statement.

Example: BONUS DECIMAL(7,2) NOT NULL WITH DEFAULT 1000.00

By defining your own default value, you can ensure that the column has been populated with appropriate values. The original EMPLOYEE table definition can be modified to include default values, as shown here.

```
CREATE TABLE EMPLOYEE
  (
  ID         SMALLINT NOT NULL,
  NAME       VARCHAR(9) NOT NULL,
  DEPT       SMALLINT,
  HIREDATE   DATE NOT NULL WITH DEFAULT CURRENT_DATE,
  SALARY     DECIMAL(7,2) NOT NULL DEFAULT 10000.00
  );
```

In this example, all of the columns except the DEPT column require a value (NOT NULL). If no value is specified, the hire date is set to the current date in the system, and the salary is set to 10,000.00. The default value can be either a constant or one of the special built-in functions.

These functions can be very useful in setting column values based on the current environment in which the application is running.

- CURRENT_TIMESTAMP (CURRENT TIMESTAMP) returns a valid timestamp value with the current date and time.
- CURRENT_DATE (CURRENT DATE) returns a date value with the current system date.
- CURRENT_TIME (CURRENT TIME) returns a time value with the current system clock time.
- CURRENT_USER (USER, SESSION_USER) returns the authorization identifier of the current user (the name that was passed in when the user connected to the database). If there is no current user, it returns APP.
- CURRENT_SCHEMA (CURRENT_SQLID, CURRENT SCHEMA) returns the schema name that is used to qualify database object references.

To ensure that the default value is being used during an insert operation, the DEFAULT keyword should be specified in the VALUES portion of the INSERT statement. A nullable column also requires a value if you have specified it in the column list of an INSERT statement. In this situation, the NULL keyword can be used to indicate that no value should be placed into this field. For example:

```
INSERT INTO EMPLOYEE VALUES
    (12,'Paul',NULL,DEFAULT,20000.0),
    (13,'Dan',125,DEFAULT, 15500.00),
    (14,'George',412,'2005-03-01',DEFAULT);

SELECT * FROM Employee;

ID      |NAME     |DEPT  |HIREDATE   |SALARY
--------------------------------------------------
12      |Paul     |NULL  |2005-03-06|20000.00
13      |Dan      |125   |2005-03-06|15500.00
14      |George   |412   |2005-03-01|10000.00

3 rows selected
```

If the INSERT statement did not specify the DEPT, HIREDATE, or SALARY column, Apache Derby automatically fills in these fields with the default values:

```
INSERT INTO EMPLOYEE(ID, NAME) VALUES
    (15,'Alyse'),
    (16,'Susan');
```

```
SELECT * FROM EMPLOYEE;

ID     |NAME      |DEPT   |HIREDATE   |SALARY
-----------------------------------------------
12     |Paul      |NULL   |2005-03-06|20000.00
13     |Dan       |125    |2005-03-06|15500.00
14     |George    |412    |2005-03-01|10000.00
15     |Alyse     |NULL   |2005-03-06|10000.00
16     |Susan     |NULL   |2005-03-06|10000.00

5 rows selected
```

The second example works, even though we did not supply a DEPT, HIREDATE, or SALARY value. The DEPT column does not require a value (NULL), and the values for HIREDATE and SALARY were supplied by the DEFAULT clause in the column definition. INSERT statements do not need to have every column accounted for in the syntax, but it is generally good practice to supply values for every column, even if a column contains DEFAULT or NULL values. Anyone who has to read the SQL statement will easily recognize what values are being supplied to the database.

Identity Column

The previous section discussed how columns can be populated with values even if no value is supplied by the user. It is also possible to have Apache Derby generate sequence numbers or other values during record insertion.

Often, a single column within a table represents a unique identifier for that row. This identifier is a number that is sequentially updated as new records are added.

Apache Derby can automatically generate sequential values. The following example shows the EMPLOYEE table definition with the ID column being generated automatically.

```
CREATE TABLE EMPLOYEE
  (
  ID        SMALLINT GENERATED ALWAYS AS IDENTITY,
  Name      VARCHAR(9) NOT NULL,
  Dept      SMALLINT,
  Hiredate  DATE NOT NULL WITH DEFAULT CURRENT_DATE,
  Salary    DECIMAL(7,2) NOT NULL DEFAULT 10000.00
  );

INSERT INTO EMPLOYEE(NAME) VALUES 'George','Paul','Dan';

SELECT * FROM EMPLOYEE;
```

```
ID     |NAME      |DEPT  |HIREDATE  |SALARY
-------------------------------------------------
1      |George    |NULL  |2005-03-06|10000.00
2      |Paul      |NULL  |2005-03-06|10000.00
3      |Dan       |NULL  |2005-03-06|10000.00
```

3 rows selected

An identity column is always defined with the GENERATED ALWAYS clause. The INSERT statement cannot specify a value for the identity column. By default, the numbering will start at 1 and increment by 1. The range and increment can be specified as part of the column definition.

```
CREATE TABLE EMPLOYEE
  (
  ID           SMALLINT GENERATED ALWAYS AS IDENTITY
                  (START WITH 100, INCREMENT BY 10),
  Name         VARCHAR(9) NOT NULL,
  Dept         SMALLINT,
  Hiredate     DATE NOT NULL WITH DEFAULT CURRENT_DATE,
  Salary       DECIMAL(7,2) NOT NULL DEFAULT 10000.00
  );

INSERT INTO EMPLOYEE(NAME) VALUES 'George','Paul','Dan';

SELECT * FROM EMPLOYEE;
```

```
ID     |NAME      |DEPT  |HIREDATE  |SALARY
-------------------------------------------------
100    |George    |NULL  |2005-03-06|10000.00
110    |Paul      |NULL  |2005-03-06|10000.00
120    |Dan       |NULL  |2005-03-06|10000.00
```

3 rows selected

Identity columns are restricted to numeric values (SMALLINT, INT, and BIGINT) and can only be defined once per table. Identity columns can be modified after they are created to change the increment value (INCREMENT BY). For instance, the following ALTER statement will change the increment value for the EMPLOYEE table to 50:

```
ALTER TABLE EMPLOYEE ALTER ID SET INCREMENT BY 50;
```

The sequence numbers can start with a negative number and can be decremented instead of incremented (a negative INCREMENT). The sequence number will continue to be generated by the system until the range of values is exhausted. If an attempt is made to insert past the largest number, an error occurs. For this reason, you should consider using a data type that will support the largest sequence number that the system could possibly require.

IDENTITY_VAL _LOCAL Function

In many instances, an application will need to know the last generated value in a table. This information might be required if the application needs to update other tables based on a newly generated value. You can use the IDENTITY_VAL_LOCAL function to retrieve this information.

The IDENTITY_VAL_LOCAL function is a non-deterministic function that returns the most recently assigned value for an identity column, where the assignment occurred as a result of a single row INSERT statement using a VALUES clause. The IDENTITY_VAL_LOCAL function has no input parameters. The result is a DECIMAL (31,0), regardless of the actual data type of the corresponding identity column. The value returned by the IDENTITY_VAL_LOCAL function is the value assigned to the identity column of the table identified in the most recent single row INSERT statement. The INSERT statement must contain a VALUES clause on a table containing an identity column. The function returns a null value when a single row INSERT statement with a VALUES clause has not been issued for a table containing an identity column.

The VALUES clause can be used to retrieve the last generated value in a table. For example:

```
VALUES IDENTITY_VAL_LOCAL;
```

Declared Tables

The DECLARE statement is very similar to the CREATE statement, except that it is used to create temporary tables that are used only during a session. The only object that can be DECLARED is a table, and it is only for the use of the program or individual who created it. The statement used to create a temporary table is as follows:

```
DECLARE GLOBAL TEMPORARY TABLE table-name
( column-definitions  [ , column-definition ] * )
[ ON COMMIT {DELETE | PRESERVE} ROWS ]
NOT LOGGED [ON ROLLBACK DELETE ROWS]
```

The table name has the same restrictions as a normal table name. However, the schema that is always associated with a declared table is SESSION. To refer to a temporary table, the SESSION schema must be used as part of the table name.

All data types except LONG VARCHAR, BLOB, and CLOB are supported.

ON COMMIT specifies the action taken on the table when a commit operation is performed. This action can be either DELETE ROWS or PRESERVE ROWS. DELETE ROWS means that all rows of the table will be deleted if a cursor that cannot be held is open on the table. This is the default value for ON COMMIT. PRESERVE ROWS means that the rows of the table will be preserved during a commit operation.

NOT LOGGED specifies the action taken when a rollback operation is performed. If the table was created during the unit of work that is being rolled back, the table will be dropped. If the table was dropped during the unit of work, the table will be restored with no rows.

ON ROLLBACK DELETE ROWS is the default value for NOT LOGGED. NOT LOGGED ON ROLLBACK DELETE ROWS specifies the action that is to be taken on the table when a ROLLBACK operation is performed. If the table data has been changed, all the rows will be deleted.

The creation of a temporary table does not update the catalog, so locking, logging, and other forms of contention are avoided with this object. Declared tables can be dropped but not altered. No other database objects (such as views or triggers) can be created to act against temporary tables. Temporary tables do not allow for the creation of indexes to improve performance.

After a table is declared, it can be referenced like any other table. The following example shows a temporary table being declared and then used in a subsequent SQL statement.

```
DECLARE GLOBAL TEMPORARY TABLE T1
  (
  EMPL VARCHAR(10),
  DEPTNO INT,
  SALARY INT,
  BONUS INT
  )
ON COMMIT PRESERVE ROWS NOT LOGGED;

INSERT INTO SESSION.T1(EMPL, DEPTNO, SALARY)
  SELECT * FROM EMPL;

SELECT * FROM SESSION.T1;
```

EMPL	DEPTNO	SALARY	BONUS
George	1	10000	NULL
Paul	2	15000	NULL
Dan	3	30000	NULL
Bernard	NULL	22000	NULL
John	2	21000	NULL
Susan	3	11000	NULL
Alyse	3	31000	NULL

```
7 rows selected
```

Modifying a Table

The `ALTER TABLE` statement lets you modify an existing table to:

- Add a column
- Add a constraint
- Drop an existing constraint
- Increase the width of a `VARCHAR` column
- Override row-level locking for the table (or drop the override)

Some of the attributes of a table can be changed only after the table has been created. For example, you need to use the `ALTER TABLE` statement if you want to change the default lock level. The basic syntax is as follows:

```
ALTER TABLE <table> <function>
```

Adding a Column to a Table

To add a new column to a table, use the `ADD COLUMN` clause. For example, the following statement adds a new `BONUS` column to the `EMPL` table:

```
ALTER TABLE EMPL ADD COLUMN BONUS INT;
```

The information after the `ADD COLUMN` clause includes the column name and the attributes associated with that column. All columns are added at the end of the row. Subsequent `SELECT *` statements will show this column appearing at the end of the original columns in the table.

Adding a Constraint to a Table

`ALTER TABLE ADD CONSTRAINT` adds a table-level constraint to an existing table. Any supported table-level constraint type can be added using `ALTER TABLE`. The following are limitations when adding a constraint to an existing table.

When adding a foreign key or check constraint to an existing table, Apache Derby checks the table to make sure existing rows satisfy the constraint. If any row is invalid, Apache Derby throws a statement exception, and the constraint is not added.

All columns included in a primary key must contain non-null data and must be unique. `ALTER TABLE ADD UNIQUE` or `PRIMARY KEY` provides a shorthand method of defining a primary key composed of a single column. If `PRIMARY KEY` is specified in the definition of column C, the effect is the same as if the `PRIMARY KEY(C)` clause were specified as a separate clause. The column cannot contain null values, so the `NOT NULL` attribute must also be specified.

Dropping an Existing Constraint on a Table

ALTER TABLE DROP CONSTRAINT drops a constraint on an existing table. To drop an unnamed constraint, you must specify the generated constraint name stored in SYS.SYSCON-STRAINTS as a delimited identifier. Dropping a primary key, unique, or foreign key constraint drops the physical index that enforces the constraint.

Altering the Size of a *VARCHAR* Column

The size of an existing VARCHAR column can be increased by specifying the SET keyword. To increase the size of a column, specify the data type and new size after the column name.

```
ALTER TABLE EMPL ALTER NAME SET DATA TYPE VARCHAR(20)
```

You cannot decrease the size or change the data type. You are not allowed to increase the size of a column that is part of a primary key or unique key referenced by a foreign key constraint, or that is part of a foreign key constraint.

Overriding Row-Level Locking

The LOCKSIZE option specifies the granularity of locks used when the table is accessed. By default, row-level locks are used when tables are accessed. This option of the ALTER TABLE statement allows locking to be pushed up to the table level. Using table-level locks can improve the performance of queries by reducing the number of locks that need to be obtained and released. However, concurrency might be reduced because all locks are held over the entire table.

Removing a Table

When you want to remove a table, issue the DROP TABLE statement, which will delete the contents of the table and remove its description from the catalog tables. Any objects that are directly or indirectly dependent on this table (for example, indexes, triggers, or views) are deleted or made inoperative. The following example drops the EMPL table:

```
DROP TABLE EMPL
```

Constraints

Tables are composed of rows; rows are composed of columns. Tables can have constraints to guarantee the uniqueness of rows that maintain relationships between tables. A constraint is a rule that the Apache Derby database manager enforces. There are three types of constraints:

- Unique constraint—Ensures unique values for a key in a table. Any changes to the columns that comprise the unique key are checked for uniqueness.

- Referential integrity constraint—Enforces referential constraints on insert, update, and delete operations. It is the state of a database in which all values of all foreign keys are valid.

- Table check constraint—Verifies that changed data does not violate conditions that were specified when a table was created or altered.

Unique Constraint

A unique constraint is the rule that the values of a key are valid only if they are unique within the table. Each column making up the key in a unique constraint must be defined as NOT NULL. Unique constraints are defined in the CREATE TABLE statement or the ALTER TABLE statement using the PRIMARY KEY clause or the UNIQUE clause.

A table can have any number of unique constraints; however, a table cannot have more than one unique constraint on the same set of columns.

When a unique constraint is defined, the database manager creates (if needed) a unique index and designates it as either a primary or unique system-required index. The enforcement of the constraint is through the unique index. Once a unique constraint has been established on a column, the check for uniqueness during multiple row updates is deferred until the end of the update (deferred unique constraint).

A unique constraint can also be used as the parent key in a referential constraint.

Referential Integrity

Referential integrity (RI) allows you to define required relationships between and within tables. The database manager maintains these relationships, which are expressed as referential constraints, and requires that all values of a given attribute or table column also exist in some other table column. Figure 8-2 illustrates the referential integrity relationship between the EMPLOYEE and DEPT tables.

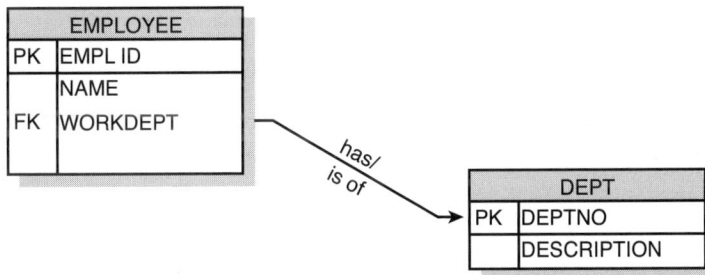

Figure 8-2 Employee and Department relationship

This constraint requires that every employee in the EMPLOYEE table must be in a department that exists in the DEPT table. No employee can be in a department that does not exist.

A unique key is a column or a set of columns for which no values are duplicated in any other row. Only one unique key can be defined as the primary key for each table. The unique key can also be known as the parent key when referenced by a foreign key.

A primary key is a special case of a unique key. Each table can only have one primary key. In this example, DEPTNO and EMPL_ID are the primary keys of the DEPT and EMPLOYEE tables, respectively.

A foreign key is a column or a set of columns in a table that refer to a unique key or primary key of the same or another table. A foreign key is used to establish a relationship with a unique key or primary key and enforces referential integrity among tables. The WORKDEPT column in the EMPLOYEE table is a foreign key because it refers to the primary key (DEPTNO) in the DEPT table. The names of the columns do not have to be the same for these relationships to be defined. It is good practice to use the same names for identical columns in different tables to minimize the possibility of error.

A parent key is a primary key or unique key of a referential constraint.

A parent table is a table containing a parent key that is related to at least one foreign key in the same or another table. A table can be a parent in an arbitrary number of relationships. In this example, the DEPT table, which has a primary key DEPTNO, is a parent of the EMPLOYEE table, which contains the foreign key WORKDEPT.

A dependent table is a table containing one or more foreign keys. A dependent table can also be a parent table. A table can be a dependent in an arbitrary number of relationships. For example, the EMPLOYEE table, which contains the foreign key WORKDEPT, is dependent on the DEPT table (which contains the associated primary key DEPTNO).

A referential constraint is an assertion that non-null values of a designated foreign key are valid only if they also appear as values of a unique key in a designated parent table. The purpose of referential constraints is to guarantee that database relationships are maintained and that data entry rules are followed.

Enforcement of referential constraints has special implications for some SQL operations that depend on whether the table is a parent or a dependent. The database manager enforces referential constraints across systems based on the following referential integrity rules:

- INSERT rule
- DELETE rule
- UPDATE rule

INSERT Rule

The INSERT rule is implicit when a foreign key is specified. You can insert a row at any time into a parent table without any action being taken in the dependent table.

You cannot insert a row into a dependent table unless there is a row in the parent table with a parent key value equal to the foreign key value of the row that is being inserted, unless the foreign key value is null.

If an INSERT operation fails for one row during an attempt to insert more than one row, all rows inserted by the statement are removed from the database.

The following SQL defines the `RI_EMPLOYEE` and `RI_DEPT` tables to demonstrate how referential integrity rules work on `INSERT`.

```
CREATE TABLE RI_DEPT
  (
  DEPTNO INT NOT NULL PRIMARY KEY,
  DESCRIPTION VARCHAR(10)
  );

CREATE TABLE RI_EMPLOYEE
  (
  EMPL_ID INT,
  NAME VARCHAR(10),
  WORKDEPT INT,
  FOREIGN KEY(WORKDEPT) REFERENCES RI_DEPT(DEPTNO)
  );
```

Before any records can be added to the `RI_EMPLOYEE` table, the `RI_DEPT` table needs to be populated.

```
INSERT INTO RI_DEPT
  VALUES
    (1,'Plumbing'), (2,'Accounting'), (3,'Sales');
```

The following three insert operations will work properly because the department number being inserted has a matching department number in the `RI_DEPT` table.

```
INSERT INTO RI_EMPLOYEE
  VALUES
    (1,'George',1), (2,'Katrina',3), (3,'Ellie',2);
```

The next `INSERT` statement tries to insert an employee into department 4. Because this department does not exist in the `RI_DEPT` table, an error occurs.

```
INSERT INTO RI_EMPLOYEE
  VALUES
    (4,'Andrew',4);
```

```
ERROR 23503: INSERT on table 'RI_EMPLOYEE' caused a violation
   of foreign key constraint 'SQL050310092749470' for key (4).
   The statement has been rolled back.
```

To fix this problem, department 4 must be added to the `RI_DEPT` table before the insert operation is attempted again.

```
INSERT INTO RI_DEPT VALUES (4,'Systems');
INSERT INTO RI_EMPLOYEE VALUES(4,'Andrew',4);
```

DELETE Rules

When you delete a row from a parent table, the database manager checks if there are any dependent rows in the dependent table with matching foreign key values. If any dependent rows are found, several actions can be taken. You determine which action will be taken by specifying a `DELETE` rule when you create the dependent table.

- `RESTRICT`—This rule prevents any row in the parent table from being deleted if any dependent rows are found. If you need to remove both parent and dependent rows, delete dependent rows first.

- `NO ACTION`—This rule enforces the presence of a parent row for every child after all the referential constraints are applied. This is the default. The difference between `NO ACTION` and `RESTRICT` is based on when the constraint is enforced.

- `CASCADE`—This rule ensures that deleting a row in the parent table automatically deletes any related rows in the dependent table.

- `SET NULL`—This rule ensures that deletion of a row in the parent table sets the values of the foreign key in any dependent row to null (if nullable). Other parts of the row are unchanged.

The two RI tables defined earlier did not specify any delete rules. The default rule is `NO ACTION`, which is similar to `RESTRICT`. If we try to delete department number 3 from the system, we encounter an error.

```
DELETE FROM RI_DEPT WHERE DEPTNO = 3;
```

```
ERROR 23503: DELETE on table 'RI_DEPT' caused a violation of
   foreign key constraint 'SQL050310092749470' for key (3).
   The statement has been rolled back.
```

Before this department can be deleted, each employee in the department must become associated with a different department. Once there are no values in the `RI_EMPLOYEE` table that are associated with department number 3, the department can be deleted.

```
UPDATE RI_EMPLOYEE
   SET WORKDEPT = 4 WHERE WORKDEPT = 3;
```

```
DELETE FROM RI_DEPT WHERE DEPTNO = 3;
```

If the DELETE rule had been specified as SET NULL, deletion of department number 3 would have changed the department number of all employees in that department to the null value.

If the DELETE rule had been specified as CASCADE, all of the employees working in department number 3 would have been deleted. Care must be taken when specifying CASCADE because it can cause many rows to be deleted, especially when many tables are related through referential integrity rules.

UPDATE Rules

The database manager prevents the update of a unique key in a parent row. When you update a foreign key value in a dependent table, and the foreign key is defined with the NOT NULL option, the value must match some parent key value in the parent table. Two options exist:

- RESTRICT—The update of the parent key will be rejected if a row in the dependent table matches the original values of the key.
- NO ACTION—The update of the parent key will be rejected if any row in the dependent table does not have a corresponding parent key when the update operation (excluding after triggers) completes. This is the default.

Check Constraints

A check constraint is used to enforce data integrity at either the column or the table level. Once a table check constraint has been defined for a table, every update or insert operation will involve checking that constraint. If the constraint is violated, the row will not be inserted or updated, and an SQL error will be returned.

A table check constraint can be defined at table creation time or later, using the ALTER TABLE statement.

Table check constraints can help implement business rules for data by specifying the values that are allowed in one or more columns of every row in a table. This can save time for the application developer because the validation of each data value can be performed by the database and not by each of the applications accessing the database.

A check constraint is added after a column definition in a CREATE TABLE statement. The following example places a constraint on the SALARY column that restricts the range of values that can be inserted into it.

```
CREATE TABLE T1
 (
 DEPTNO INT,
 SALARY INT CHECK (SALARY BETWEEN 10000 and 20000)
 );

INSERT INTO T1 VALUES (1,15000);
```

```
INSERT INTO T1 VALUES (2,25000);
```

```
ERROR 23513: The check constraint 'SQL050309000758470' was
    violated while performing an INSERT or UPDATE on table 'APP.T1'.
```

Adding Check Constraints

When you add a check constraint to a table that contains data, one of two things can happen:

- All of the rows satisfy the check constraint
- Some or all of the rows do not satisfy the check constraint

In the first case, in which all of the rows satisfy the check constraint, the constraint will be created successfully. Future attempts to insert or to update data that does not satisfy the constraint will be rejected.

When there are some rows that do not satisfy the check constraint, the constraint will not be created (that is, the ALTER TABLE statement will fail). An ALTER TABLE statement that adds a new constraint to the T1 table is shown next. The check constraint, named CHECK_DEPT, ensures that the department number is greater than 5. Apache Derby will use this name to inform us which constraint was violated if an INSERT or UPDATE statement fails. The CHECK clause is used to define a table check constraint.

```
ALTER TABLE T1 ADD CONSTRAINT check_dept CHECK (DEPTNO > 0);
```

```
ERROR X0Y59: Attempt to add or enable constraint(s) on table
    'APP.T1' failed because the table contains 1 row(s) that
    violate the following check constraint(s): CHECK_DEPT.
```

The ALTER TABLE statement (used because the table already exists) has failed because there already is a record in the T1 table that violates the constraint.

Modifying Check Constraints

You might need to change the check constraints that are used to implement business rules in your organization from time to time, especially when those rules change.

However, there is no way to change an existing check constraint. Whenever a check constraint needs to change, you must drop it and then create a new one. Check constraints can be dropped at any time, and this action will not affect your table or the data within it.

When you drop a check constraint, you must be aware that data validation performed by the constraint will no longer be in effect. The statement used to drop a constraint is the ALTER TABLE statement.

The following example shows how to drop an existing constraint. After dropping the constraint, you can re-create it with a new definition.

```
ALTER TABLE T1 DROP CONSTRAINT CHECK_DEPT;
```

System Catalog Tables

There are special tables used by Apache Derby that contain information about all objects within the database, and that are created for you when the database is created (for instance, using the `CREATE TABLE` command). These tables are called system catalog tables, and they are examined by Apache Derby during query processing. Some of the information contained in the system catalog tables includes:

- Table/index definitions
- Column data types
- Defined constraints
- Object dependencies
- Object privileges

When DDL statements are issued, the system catalog tables might, in fact, be updated for you. There are a number of base system tables and views in an Apache Derby database, and they always have a special schema called SYS.

The system catalog data cannot be modified using an `INSERT` or a `DELETE` statement. The system tables also contain statistical information about the tables in the database. For example, the number of physical pages allocated for each table is stored in the system catalog tables.

Database object privileges, such as `INSERT` and `SELECT`, are also maintained within the system catalog tables. The privileges are established using special SQL statements known as Data Control Language (DCL) statements. The primary DCL statements are `GRANT` and `REVOKE`.

The system catalog tables are primarily for read-only purposes because they are maintained by Apache Derby.

In general, there is at least one system catalog table for each of the database object types. Following is a quick description of these tables:

- `SYSALIASES`—Describes procedures and functions in the database
- `SYSCHECKS`—Describes check constraints for the database
- `SYSCOLUMNS`—Describes columns within all tables in the database
- `SYSCONGLOMERATES`—Describes conglomerates in the current database, where a conglomerate is a unit of storage that is either a table or an index
- `SYSCONSTRAINTS`—Contains information common to all types of constraints in the current database, including primary, unique, foreign key, and check constraints

- SYSDEPENDS—Describes the dependency relationships between persistent objects in the database
- SYSFILES—Describes .JAR files stored in the database
- SYSFOREIGNKEYS—Describes the information specific to foreign key constraints in the current database; Apache Derby generates a backing index for each foreign key constraint
- SYSKEYS—Describes the information specific to primary key and unique constraints in the current database; Apache Derby generates an index on the table to enforce each constraint
- SYSSCHEMAS—Describes schemas in the current database
- SYSSTATISTICS—Contains statistical information about various objects in the database
- SYSSTATEMENTS—Contains one row of information for each prepared statement
- SYSTABLES—Describes tables and views in the current database
- SYSTRIGGERS—Describes triggers in the current database
- SYSVIEWS—Describes view definitions in the current database

SYSTABLES is especially useful for determining the tables that are in the current database. Use the following SELECT statement to retrieve a list of table names.

```
SELECT TABLENAME FROM SYS.SYSTABLES;
```

If you want information about the columns that belong to a particular table, you can use a query that is similar to the following:

```
SELECT SC.COLUMNNUMBER AS COL_NO,
       SC.COLUMNNAME AS NAME,
       SC.COLUMNDATATYPE AS TYPE
FROM
  SYS.SYSCOLUMNS SC, SYS.SYSTABLES ST
WHERE
  SC.REFERENCEID = ST.TABLEID AND
  ST.TABLENAME = 'EMPL'
ORDER BY 1;
```

```
COL_NO      |NAME            |TYPE
-------------------------------------------------
1           |NAME            |VARCHAR(20)
2           |DEPTNO          |INTEGER
3           |SALARY          |INTEGER
4           |BONUS           |INTEGER

4 rows selected
```

Views

Views are virtual tables that are created using the CREATE VIEW statement. Once a view is defined, it can be accessed (as though it were a table) using SELECT statements. A view is a temporary result and is available only during query processing. With a view, you can make a subset of table data available to an application program. A view can have column names that are different from the names of corresponding columns in the original tables.

Views provide flexibility in the way that application programs and end-user queries look at table data. Note that views in Apache Derby are only for SELECT statements. No INSERT, UPDATE, or DELETE statements can be issued against a view.

A sample CREATE VIEW statement is shown here. There are two tables, EMPL and DEPT, that contain information about a department in which an employee might work. The EMPL table only contains the department number, but the DEPT table contains a description of the department. The view will combine these two tables to show employee names and the names of the departments in which they work. The sensitive SALARY column will not be included as part of the view, and the records will be restricted to only those employees working in department number 3.

```
CREATE VIEW EMPLDEPT AS
  (
  SELECT EMPL.NAME, DEPT.DESCR
    FROM EMPL, DEPT
  WHERE
    EMPL.DEPTNO = DEPT.DEPTNO AND
    EMPL.DEPTNO = 3
  );

SELECT * FROM EMPLDEPT;

NAME                          |DESCR
------------------------------------
Dan                           |Sales
Susan                         |Sales
Alyse                         |Sales

3 rows selected
```

After the view has been defined, access privileges can be specified. This provides data security because only a restricted view of the base table is accessible. As this example shows, a view can contain a WHERE clause to restrict access to certain rows, or it can contain only a subset of the available columns.

The column names in the view do not have to match the column names in the base table. The table name has an associated schema, as does the view name. The previous

CREATE VIEW statement could be modified to change the column names to EMPL_NAME and EMPL_DEPT.

```
CREATE VIEW EMPLDEPT(EMPL_NAME,EMPL_DEPT) AS
  (
  SELECT EMPL.NAME, DEPT.DESCR
    FROM EMPL, DEPT
  WHERE
    EMPL.DEPTNO = DEPT.DEPTNO AND
    EMPL.DEPTNO = 3
  );
```

```
select * from empldept;
```

```
EMPL_NAME                     |EMPL_DEPT
------------------------------
Dan                           |Sales
Susan                         |Sales
Alyse                         |Sales
```

```
3 rows selected
```

After a view has been defined, it can be used in any SELECT statement.

Nested View Definitions

A view can be based on another view. In many cases, a user might not know that he or she is creating a view that is already based on an existing view. The complexity of view materialization is handled automatically by Apache Derby.

The EMPLDEPT view could be used to create another view that returns a count of the employees in the original view.

```
CREATE VIEW GETEMPCNT(EMPL_COUNT) AS
  (
  SELECT COUNT(*) FROM EMPLDEPT
  );
```

```
SELECT * FROM GETEMPCNT;
```

```
EMPL_COUNT
-----------
3
```

```
1 row selected
```

Modifying a View

Views are virtual table definitions. The view definitions are stored in the system catalog; therefore, if you back up your database, the view definitions are contained in the backup image. The data contained in the view is only available when the view is being referenced in a SELECT statement.

Unlike some other Apache Derby objects, a view cannot be altered using the ALTER statement. If a view definition needs to be changed in any way, the original view must be dropped and re-created with the desired configuration. A view can become inoperative if any of the referenced database objects have been dropped from the database.

Removing a View

When you want to remove a view, issue the statement:

```
DROP VIEW view_name
```

If another view depends on the view that is being dropped, Apache Derby will issue an error message and cancel the drop operation.

```
ERROR X0Y23: Operation 'DROP VIEW' cannot be performed on object
 'EMPLDEPT' because VIEW 'GETEMPCNT' is dependent on that object.
```

To fix the problem in this example, first drop the view that is dependent on the EMPLDEPT view.

Indexes

An index is a list of the locations of rows sorted by the contents of one or more specified columns. Indexes are typically used to improve query performance. However, they can also support logical database design. For example, a primary key does not allow duplicate values in columns, thereby guaranteeing that no two rows in a table are the same. Indexes can be created in ascending or descending order of the values in a column. Indexes contain a pointer to the physical location of the rows in a table.

These are two main purposes for creating indexes:

- To ensure uniqueness of values
- To improve query performance

More than one index can be defined on a particular table, which can have a beneficial effect on the performance of queries. However, the more indexes there are, the more the database manager must work to keep the indexes current during update, delete, and insert operations. Creating a large number of indexes for a table that receives many updates can slow down processing.

Unique Index and Non-Unique Index

A unique index guarantees the uniqueness of the data values in one or more columns. The unique index can be used during query processing to perform faster retrieval of data. The uniqueness is enforced at the end of the SQL operation that updates rows or inserts new rows. Uniqueness is also checked during the execution of the CREATE INDEX statement. If the table already contains rows with duplicate key values, an index is not created.

A non-unique index can also improve query performance by maintaining a sorted order for the data.

The following are types of keys used to implement constraints:

- A unique key is used to implement unique constraints. A unique constraint does not allow two different rows to have the same values on the key columns.

- A primary key is used to implement referential integrity constraints. A primary key is a special type of unique key. There can be only one primary key per table. The primary key column must be defined with the NOT NULL attribute.

- A foreign key is used to implement referential integrity constraints. Referential constraints can only reference a primary key or unique constraint. A foreign key can only have values that exist in the primary key or unique constraint they are referencing, or null values. (A foreign key is not an index.)

Referential Integrity and Indexes

We have discussed how defining a primary key will ensure the uniqueness of rows and that the primary key is maintained using an index. The index supporting a primary key is known as the primary index of the table. If a constraint name is not provided, Apache Derby-generated indexes are given the name SQL<timestamp>.

Indexes supporting primary or unique key constraints cannot be dropped explicitly. To remove primary or unique key constraint indexes, you need to use the ALTER TABLE statement. Primary key indexes are dropped using the DROP PRIMARY KEY clause. Unique key indexes are dropped using the DROP UNIQUE constraint-name clause.

Null Values and Indexes

It is important to understand the difference between a primary key or unique constraint and a unique index. Apache Derby uses two elements to implement the relational database concept of primary and unique keys: unique indexes and the NOT NULL constraint. Therefore, unique indexes by themselves do not enforce the primary key constraint because they can allow null values. A null value, when it comes to indexing, is treated as equal to all other null values. You cannot insert a null value twice if the column is a key of a unique index because that would violate the uniqueness rule for the index.

General Indexing Guidelines

Indexes consume disk space. The amount of disk space will vary depending on the size of the key columns and the number of rows being indexed. The size of an index will increase as more data is inserted into the table. Therefore, consider the disk space required for indexes when planning the size of the database. Some of the indexing considerations include:

- Primary key and unique constraints will always create a system-generated unique index.
- It is usually beneficial to create indexes on foreign key constraint columns.

Creating an Index

Creating an index is relatively simple. The basic statement syntax is:

```
CREATE [UNIQUE] INDEX index-Name
  ON table-Name
 (Simple-column-Name [ASC|DESC] [ , Simple-column-Name
   [ASC|DESC]] *
```

The column list can contain up to 16 columns in the table. Each one of these columns can be in either ascending or descending order. By default, Apache Derby uses the ascending order of each column to create an index. Specifying ASC after the column name does not alter the default behavior. Specifying DESC after the column name causes Apache Derby to use descending column order when creating the index. This can help improve the performance of queries that require the results to be in mixed sort order or in descending order, and queries that select the minimum or maximum value of an indexed column.

The following statement creates a descending index on department number for the EMPL table.

```
CREATE INDEX EMPL_INDEX ON EMPL(DEPTNO)
```

Modifying an Index

Index attributes cannot be changed without re-creating the index definition. For example, you cannot add a column to the list of index key columns without dropping the previous definition and creating a new index. If you want to modify your index, you have to drop the index first and then create the index again. There is no ALTER INDEX statement.

Removing an Index

When you want to remove an index, issue the following statement:

```
DROP INDEX <index-name>
```

If you did not assign a name to the index at creation time, you will need to determine the system generated name from the catalog tables. For easier maintenance, it is good practice to explicitly name all constraints and indexes.

Data Retrieval

The previous section discussed the creation of various database objects using DDL. This section describes how to manipulate database objects using the part of SQL known as Data Manipulation Language (DML). The majority of the SQL statements within an Apache Derby application involve DML statements. Therefore, application developers must understand the various methods of inserting, updating, and retrieving data from the database. We will examine the four main DML statements: `SELECT`, `INSERT`, `UPDATE`, and `DELETE`.

The "Your Momma Loves Drama" (YMLD) database described at the beginning of this chapter will be used to demonstrate many of the features of SQL. Six tables are associated with this database:

- `PRODUCTIONS`—Titles and dates of all the productions
- `PERFORMANCES`—Date and time information, as well as the number of seats available, for each performance
- `SEATS`— Seats available for a performance
- `PRICEPLAN`—Seat price plan
- `SEATMAP`—Seat view
- `TRANSACTIONS`—All purchase transactions

The `PRODUCTIONS`, `PERFORMANCES`, and `SEATS` tables are the main tables of YMLD, whereas the `PRICEPLAN`, `SEATMAP`, and `TRANSACTION` tables are used as support tables for the database.

Retrieving an Entire Table

The most basic of all retrieval operations involves the `SELECT` statement with no clauses other than `FROM`. The `FROM` clause specifies the name of the table from which to retrieve data. The following `SELECT` statement retrieves all of the productions scheduled at the theater. The requested information is contained in the `PRODUCTIONS` table.

```
SELECT * FROM PRODUCTIONS
```

SQL is a data access language that consists of statements. There are many optional clauses that can be used to modify a statement. The `SELECT` statement is referred to as a query, and the results are known as a result set or result table.

```
PRODUCTION&|PRODUCTION_TITLE           |PRODUCTIO&|PRODUCTIO&
-------------------------------------------------------------
1          |Lilly of the Valley        |2005-01-01|2005-02-25
2          |My New Title               |2005-01-25|2005-04-05
3          |Desperate Houses           |2005-03-06|2005-06-25
4          |Icing the Puck             |2005-01-10|2005-08-03
```

```
5              |Heroes not Zeros          |2005-06-17|2005-10-27
6              |Rubber Sacks              |2005-07-23|2005-09-22
7              |Couched in Leather        |2005-09-10|2005-12-31
8              |Backsplash                |2005-08-08|2005-11-21
9              |Naughty or Nice?          |2005-11-06|2005-12-31

9 rows selected
```

This SELECT statement was issued from within the ij utility. The column headings are truncated because they are longer than the data fields being displayed.

In SQL, the asterisk (*) is used to indicate that all columns of a table are being referenced. In this example, the SELECT statement refers to all of the columns in the PRODUCTIONS table. The order of the columns in the result table is the same as the order that was specified in the CREATE TABLE or CREATE VIEW statement. If multiple tables are involved in a SELECT statement, all columns from one table can be specified with table-name.* in the select list.

```
SELECT EMPL.* FROM EMPL
```

If the table is altered, and a new column is added, the result set would contain the new column.

Because the result of a SELECT * statement varies according to the table definition, it is recommended that you explicitly specify the names of the columns that you want to see.

```
SELECT
   PRODUCTION_NO,
   PRODUCTION_TITLE,
   PRODUCTION_START,
   PRODUCTION_END
FROM
   PRODUCTIONS
```

This query will return a similar result set even if new columns are added to the table. The formatting of the SQL statement is not important. Although the columns and the table name have been placed on separate lines, this is not required to run the statement properly. The entire SELECT statement could have been placed on one line, but it would have been much more difficult to read.

Projecting Columns from a Table

Projection is a relational operation that allows you to retrieve a subset of the columns from a table. The next example limits the output from a SELECT statement so that only the production title and start date are shown.

```
SELECT PRODUCTION_TITLE, PRODUCTION_START FROM PRODUCTIONS
```

The result of this query is shown in the following example. The order of the columns in the result table will always match their order in the select list. The order of the columns as they were defined in the CREATE TABLE or CREATE VIEW statement is ignored when a select list is provided.

```
PRODUCTION_TITLE                        | PRODUCTIO&
-------------------------------------------------------

Lilly of the Valley                     |2005-01-01
My New Title                            |2005-01-25
Desperate Houses                        |2005-03-06
Icing the Puck                          |2005-01-10
Heroes not Zeros                        |2005-06-17
Rubber Sacks                            |2005-07-23
Couched in Leather                      |2005-09-10
Backsplash                              |2005-08-08
Naughty or Nice?                        |2005-11-06

9 rows selected
```

Changing the Order of the Columns

Permutation is the relational operation that allows you to change the order of the columns in your result table. Permutation is used every time you select columns in an order that is different than their order in the CREATE TABLE statement. For example, to display the start date prior to the production title, you could execute the following SELECT statement.

```
SELECT PRODUCTION_START, PRODUCTION_TITLE FROM PRODUCTIONS
```

This query retrieves the columns in a different order than the previous result.

```
PRODUCTIO&|PRODUCTION_TITLE
-------------------------------------------------------

2005-01-01|Lilly of the Valley
2005-01-25|My New Title
2005-03-06|Desperate Houses
2005-01-10|Icing the Puck
2005-06-17|Heroes not Zeros
2005-07-23|Rubber Sacks
2005-09-10|Couched in Leather
2005-08-08|Backsplash
2005-11-06|Naughty or Nice?

9 rows selected
```

Restricting the Rows That Are Returned from a Table

Restriction is a relational operation that filters the result set. Restriction is accomplished through the use of conditions (predicates) that are specified in a WHERE clause. The predicates must be evaluated by Apache Derby before the result table is returned. There are many types of predicates. In the following example, the equality (=) predicate is used to restrict the result to display only the title of production number 2.

```
SELECT
  PRODUCTION_TITLE
FROM
  PRODUCTIONS
WHERE
  PRODUCTION_NO = 2
```

The columns in the select list do not have to include the columns that are used in the predicate. Other comparison operators, such as greater than (>), less than (<), greater than or equal to (>=), less than or equal to (<=), and not equal to (<>) can be used in a WHERE clause. This statement is an example of a basic predicate. A basic predicate compares two values.

Restricting Rows Using Multiple Conditions

It is possible to combine multiple predicates in a single WHERE clause. The predicates can be combined using Boolean operators, such as the AND operator. The order in which the predicates are specified does not affect the result table. The Apache Derby optimizer decides the order in which the conditions are applied to maximize query performance. This decision is based on statistical information and other factors.

The next example retrieves the productions that have a production number that is greater than 5 and an end date that is earlier than December 1, 2005. The rows that satisfy the predicates are known as the qualifying rows.

```
SELECT
  PRODUCTION_NO, PRODUCTION_TITLE, PRODUCTION_END
FROM
  PRODUCTIONS
WHERE
  PRODUCTION_NO > 5 AND
  PRODUCTION_END < '2005-12-01';

PRODUCTION&| PRODUCTION_TITLE                           | PRODUCTIO&
-------------------------------------------------------------------
6          |Rubber Sacks                                |2005-09-22
8          |Backsplash                                  |2005-11-21

2 rows selected
```

Searching for String Patterns

SQL has a powerful predicate that allows you to search for patterns in character string columns. This is the LIKE predicate.

For instance, a theater patron might only want to attend productions that have the word "the" in the title. Not a particularly good reason to attend a production, but you can determine which productions qualify by using the LIKE keyword.

```
SELECT PRODUCTION_TITLE FROM PRODUCTIONS
WHERE
   PRODUCTION_TITLE LIKE '%the%';


PRODUCTION_TITLE
-------------------
Lilly of the Valley
Icing the Puck
Couched in Leather


3 rows selected
```

In this query, the string '%the%' uses a wildcard character with the LIKE predicate. In SQL, the percent character (%) represents zero or more characters. The search string ('%the%') can be matched with strings like 'there', 'leather', and so on. (Because the percent character can match zero or more characters, the search string can also match the single word 'the'.)

The percent character can be used anywhere in the search string. It can also be used as many times as required. The percent character is not case-sensitive, so it can take the place of uppercase or lowercase letters. However, the constant characters included in the search string are case-sensitive.

Another wildcard character used with the LIKE predicate is the underline character (_). This character represents one, and only one, character. The underline character can take the place of any character. However, the underline character does not represent (and cannot match) an empty character.

The previous query can be modified to include all productions that have the lowercase letter 'a' as the second letter in the production name.

```
SELECT PRODUCTION_TITLE FROM PRODUCTIONS
WHERE
   PRODUCTION_TITLE LIKE '_a%';


PRODUCTION_TITLE
-------------------
Backsplash
Naughty or Nice?


2 rows selected
```

This example uses two wildcard characters that work with the LIKE predicate. The search string in this example can include any character in the first position (_), followed by the lowercase letter 'a', and then any number of characters following the 'a' (%). If your query needs to find one of the special characters (_,%), you can use the ESCAPE clause. In that case, the LIKE string would include the ESCAPE keyword followed by the character that Apache Derby is supposed to treat as a normal character rather than a special search directive. The following example searches for production titles that contain a percent sign character (%).

```
SELECT Production_Title FROM Productions
  WHERE PRODUCTION_TITLE LIKE '%\%%' ESCAPE '\'
```

In our example, there are no titles with a '%' in them.

Searching for Data in Ranges

SQL also offers a range operator that you can use to restrict rows to a particular range of values.

Consider the requirement to list all productions that are being run during the months of July through October. This logic could be coded explicitly by listing all of the months in the query.

```
SELECT PRODUCTION_TITLE, PRODUCTION_START FROM PRODUCTIONS
WHERE
  MONTH(PRODUCTION_START) = 7 OR
  MONTH(PRODUCTION_START) = 8 OR
  MONTH(PRODUCTION_START) = 9 OR
  MONTH(PRODUCTION_START) = 10
```

This process could become very tedious, especially if there is a wide range of values. The BETWEEN predicate could be used instead to create a lower and upper limit for comparison. An important fact about the BETWEEN predicate is that it can work with character ranges as well. The previous query can be modified to use boundary values, as follows:

```
SELECT PRODUCTION_TITLE, PRODUCTION_START FROM PRODUCTIONS
WHERE
  MONTH(PRODUCTION_START) BETWEEN 7 AND 10;
```

```
PRODUCTION_TITLE                    | PRODUCTIO&
------------------------------------
Rubber Sacks                        |2005-07-23
Couched in Leather                  |2005-09-10
Backsplash                          |2005-08-08

3 rows selected
```

Searching for a Set of Values

In SQL, it is possible to select rows based on a set of values. The previous example used the BETWEEN predicate to select the set of records. However, instead of using the BETWEEN predicate, the possible values could have been identified using the IN predicate. The IN predicate contains a list of values that the column in the result set can include.

```
SELECT PRODUCTION_TITLE, PRODUCTION_START FROM PRODUCTIONS
WHERE
  MONTH(PRODUCTION_START) IN (7,8,9,10);
```

PRODUCTION_TITLE	PRODUCTIO&
Rubber Sacks	2005-07-23
Couched in Leather	2005-09-10
Backsplash	2005-08-08

```
3 rows selected
```

You can also use the NOT clause with the IN predicate. In this case, the condition is true when a value is not present in the set of values identified by the IN predicate.

You can use as many values as you want with the IN predicate. However, there will be cases when the list of values is very long, and it would be better to retrieve them using another query.

The IN predicate can also be used to define a set of values based on conditions. In this case, the IN predicate accepts a query that defines the set of values. When you define the set of values using a query, the SQL statement that defines that set is called a subquery.

Searching for Null Values

A null value represents an unknown value for a particular occurrence of an entity. You can use a null value when you don't know a particular value in a column. For example, the EMPL table includes an employee who does not have a department number.

```
SELECT NAME, DEPTNO FROM EMPL;
```

NAME	DEPTNO
George	1
Paul	2
Dan	3
Bernard	NULL
John	2
Susan	3

```
Alyse    |3
```

```
7 rows selected
```

To select records that have null values in a column, you must use the `IS NULL` predicate rather than the equality operator. Similarly, use the `IS NOT NULL` predicate to select records that have non-null values in a column. The following query selects those records that have a null value for the department number.

```
SELECT NAME, DEPTNO FROM EMPL
WHERE
  DEPTNO IS NULL;
```

```
NAME      |DEPTNO
--------------------
Bernard  |NULL
```

```
1 row selected
```

The `IS NULL` predicate is used to search for the null value in this example. Remember that the null value means "unknown." Because it has no particular value, it can't be compared with other values. You can't use relational operators, such as equals (=), with null values.

Searching for Negative Conditions

The `LIKE`, `BETWEEN`, and `IS NULL` predicates always look for values that satisfy a particular condition. These predicates can also be used to look for values that don't satisfy a particular condition.

The `NOT` clause, combined with the `LIKE`, `BETWEEN`, or `IS NULL` predicate, can be used to look for the opposite condition or to perform negative searches. The following example has a `LIKE` predicate combined with the `NOT` clause. This query will find all productions that have a title without the word "the" in them.

```
SELECT PRODUCTION_TITLE FROM PRODUCTIONS
WHERE
  PRODUCTION_TITLE NOT LIKE '%the%';
```

```
PRODUCTION_TITLE
--------------------
My New Title
Desperate Houses
Heroes not Zeros
Rubber Sacks
Backsplash
```

```
Naughty or Nice?
```

```
6 rows selected
```

The next example has a BETWEEN predicate combined with the NOT clause. This query will list
all employees whose salary is not within the range of 20000 to 30000.

```
SELECT NAME, SALARY FROM EMPL
WHERE
   SALARY NOT BETWEEN 20000 and 30000;
```

```
NAME      | SALARY
-------------------
George    | 10000
Paul      | 15000
Susan     | 11000
Alyse     | 31000
```

```
4 rows selected
```

Negation can also be applied to the null value. The following query returns a list of employees
who have a valid department number.

```
SELECT NAME, DEPTNO FROM EMPL
WHERE
   DEPTNO IS NOT NULL;
```

```
NAME      | DEPTNO
-------------------
George    | 1
Paul      | 2
Dan       | 3
John      | 2
Susan     | 3
Alyse     | 3
```

```
6 rows selected
```

Selecting Columns from Multiple Tables

There are basically two operations that retrieve columns from multiple tables in a single SELECT
statement. These operations are:

- Cartesian product
- Join

Cartesian Product

A Cartesian product is a relational operation that merges all the rows from one table with all the rows from another table. This operation is primarily of theoretical interest. In theory, any multi-table access can be performed by constructing the Cartesian product and then removing extraneous rows and columns. In practice, this is almost always the most expensive way to do things.

The number of rows in the result table is always equal to the product of the number of rows in each of the tables being accessed.

The following example uses two small tables, EMPL and DEPT. EMPL contains the names of three employees, and DEPT contains the names of three departments. The following DDL creates these two tables:

```
CREATE TABLE EMPL (NAME VARCHAR(8), DEPTNO INT, SALARY INT);
INSERT INTO EMPL VALUES
   ('George',1,10000),('Paul',2,15000),('Dan',3,30000);
CREATE TABLE DEPT (DEPTNO INT, DESCR VARCHAR(10));
INSERT INTO DEPT VALUES (1,'Plumbing'),(2,'Accounting'),(3,'Sales');
```

The following query returns all of the records from the EMPL table:

```
SELECT * FROM EMPL;
```

```
NAME      |DEPTNO      |SALARY
--------------------------------
George    |1           |10000
Paul      |2           |15000
Dan       |3           |30000
```

3 rows selected

The following query returns all of the records from the DEPT table:

```
SELECT * FROM DEPT;
```

```
DEPTNO       |DESCR
----------------------
1            |Plumbing
2            |Accounting
3            |Sales
```

3 rows selected

The Cartesian product of these two tables is shown in the next example:

```
SELECT
  EMPL.NAME, EMPL.DEPTNO, DEPT.DESCR
```

```
FROM
  EMPL, DEPT;
```

```
NAME      |DEPTNO        |DESCR
------------------------------
George   |1            |Plumbing
George   |1            |Accounting
George   |1            |Sales
Paul     |2            |Plumbing
Paul     |2            |Accounting
Paul     |2            |Sales
Dan      |3            |Plumbing
Dan      |3            |Accounting
Dan      |3            |Sales
```

```
9 rows selected
```

Two tables are referenced in the FROM clause of this SELECT statement. The table names are separated by a comma. There is no predicate limiting the rows to be retrieved.

The result table is a representation of all possible combinations of the input tables. The EMPL table has three rows, and the DEPT table has three rows; therefore, the query returns nine rows. Note the second column in the select list. It is necessary to fully qualify the column name with the schema and table name because the DEPTNO column exists in both the EMPL and DEPT tables. In this case, the SQL statement needs to specify that the DEPTNO column is to be retrieved from the EMPL table and not from the DEPT table.

By adding a predicate to the original statement, the result table becomes a more useful representation of the data. The following example requests all employees who work in department number 1.

```
SELECT
  EMPL.NAME, EMPL.DEPTNO, DEPT.DESCR
FROM
  EMPL, DEPT
WHERE
  EMPL.DEPTNO = 1;
```

```
NAME      |DEPTNO        |DESCR
------------------------------
George   |1            |Plumbing
George   |1            |Accounting
George   |1            |Sales
```

```
3 rows selected
```

Adding a WHERE clause to your query does not always provide the desired result. In this example, it appears that the employee works in three departments. The query attempted to filter out rows that only apply to employees in department 1, but there was no filter on the DEPT table. Therefore, the result of the query is a multiple of the number of departments. Usually, when multiple tables are referenced, a cross-table relationship using a table join is required. Table joins are described in the next section.

```
SELECT
  EMPL.NAME, EMPL.DEPTNO, DEPT.DESCR
FROM
  EMPL, DEPT
WHERE
  EMPL.DEPTNO = 1 AND
  EMPL.DEPTNO = DEPT.DEPTNO;


NAME     |DEPTNO      |DESCR
------------------------------
George   |1           |Plumbing


1 row selected
```

Joins

The EMPL table in the previous example provided department numbers but not the complete names of the departments. The department names are stored in the DEPT table. To obtain the name of a department, the data must be retrieved from the DEPT table using a relationship or join strategy.

Consider a query that lists everyone who works in the "Sales" or "Plumbing" department. To accomplish this, data from two tables, EMPL and DEPT, needs to be selected.

The DEPT table contains a description field that can be used to search for the department name. The first query retrieves only those rows that contain "Sales" or "Plumbing" as a description.

```
SELECT * FROM DEPT
WHERE
  DESCR='Plumbing' or DESCR='Sales';


DEPTNO      |DESCR
----------------------
1           |Plumbing
3           |Sales


2 rows selected
```

The DEPTNO column is critical for the second query. This column will be used as the join column to tie the two tables together. The rows from the EMPL table must match the rows in the DEPT table. This is accomplished by specifying that the DEPTNO value in the EMPL table must be the same as the DEPTNO value in the DEPT table.

```
SELECT
  DEPT.DESCR, EMPL.NAME
FROM
  DEPT, EMPL
WHERE
  DESCR='Plumbing' OR DESCR='Sales' AND
  DEPT.DEPTNO = EMPL.DEPTNO;
```

```
DESCR      |NAME
-------------------
Plumbing   |George
Plumbing   |Paul
Plumbing   |Dan
Sales      |Dan

4 rows selected
```

The results appear to indicate that three people work in the plumbing department. This result is incorrect because of the order of precedence of relational operators. The AND operator takes precedence over the OR operator. The query was executed with the following logic:

```
DESCR='Plumbing' OR (DESCR='Sales' AND DEPT.DEPTNO = EMPL.DEPTNO)
```

The query should have been written as follows:

```
SELECT
  DEPT.DESCR, EMPL.NAME
FROM
  DEPT, EMPL
WHERE
  (DESCR='Plumbing' OR DESCR='Sales') AND
  DEPT.DEPTNO = EMPL.DEPTNO;
```

```
DESCR      |NAME
-------------------
Plumbing   |George
Sales      |Dan

2 rows selected
```

It is always good practice to use parentheses to specify the order of operations for any mathematical or logical expressions in your SQL. In addition, query performance can significantly improve if the join columns are appropriately indexed.

A table join requires a predicate that includes an expression based on columns from the tables referenced in the FROM clause. This is known as a join predicate. The FROM clause has not changed from the Cartesian product examples. The only difference is in the join predicate DEPT.DEPTNO = EMPL.DEPTNO. This kind of join operation is also known as an inner join. An inner join returns only the rows that are present in both of the joined tables.

The table names need to be qualified because there is a column named DEPTNO in both of the referenced tables. When multiple tables are being accessed in a single query, you have to qualify the column names with the appropriate table name. An error will occur if the columns being referenced are ambiguous (not properly qualified).

There is no defined limit, except in storage, to the number of tables that can be referenced in a single SQL statement. However, there is a 1012-column limit on the select list of a query.

Outer Join

The most common join operation is the inner join, as discussed in the previous section. Although this type of join works in the majority of cases, it does not produce the correct results if any of the values in the join columns are missing.

The result set for an inner join consists only of those matched rows that are present in both joined tables. What happens when we need to include those values that are present in one or another joined table, but not in both of them? In this case, we need to use an outer join operation. Outer joins are designed to generate a result set that includes those values that are present in joined tables and those that are not.

Before examining the outer join in detail, let's consider the explicit syntax of a join operation. Recall the implicit join of the EMPL and DEPT tables that we discussed earlier:

```
SELECT DEPT.DESCR, EMPL.NAME FROM DEPT, EMPL
   WHERE (DESCR='Plumbing' OR DESCR='Sales') AND
         DEPT.DEPTNO = EMPL.DEPTNO;

DESCR      |NAME
------------------
Plumbing   |George
Sales      |Dan

2 rows selected
```

The statement DEPT.DEPTNO = EMPL.DEPTNO tells Apache Derby that these two columns from the DEPT and EMPL tables are common, and that records should be combined using these columns. An alternative way of coding this is to use the INNER JOIN clause:

```
SELECT DEPT.DESCR, EMPL.NAME
   FROM DEPT
```

```
   INNER JOIN EMPL
    ON    (EMPL.DEPTNO = DEPT.DEPTNO)
   WHERE
    (DESCR='Plumbing' OR DESCR='Sales');
```

```
DESCR       |NAME
------------------
Plumbing    |George
Sales       |Dan
```

```
2 rows selected
```

In this example, you specify the tables that will be joined, along with the join operation, and the join columns that are required.

Observe the INNER JOIN operator in this example. It belongs to the FROM clause of the statement. The ON keyword is used to specify the join conditions for the tables being joined. In our example, the join condition is based on the join columns, DEPTNO in the DEPT table, and DEPTNO in the EMPL table.

The explicit join syntax also allows you to specify an outer join, as you will see in the next section.

Left Outer Join

A left outer join operation, also known as a left join, produces a result set that includes the matching values of both joined tables and those values that are only present in the left joined table. The left joined table is the table that is used in the left part of the LEFT OUTER JOIN operator when coding the join operation.

The reason for using a left outer join will become evident in the following example. To fully demonstrate join behavior, one record will be added to both the DEPT and the EMPL table. A new department that doesn't have a number yet but that does have a valid description will be added to the DEPT table. A new employee who has not yet been assigned to a department will be added to the EMPL table.

```
INSERT INTO DEPT VALUES (NULL, 'Electrical');
INSERT INTO EMPL VALUES ('Bernard',NULL,22000);
SELECT * FROM DEPT;
```

```
DEPTNO      |DESCR
---------------------
1           |Plumbing
2           |Accounting
3           |Sales
```

```
NULL       |Electrical

4 rows selected

SELECT * FROM EMPL;

NAME      |DEPTNO      |SALARY
---------------------------------
George  |1          |10000
Paul    |2          |15000
Dan     |3          |30000
Bernard |NULL       |22000

4 rows selected
```

Suppose you are asked to produce a report that includes employee names, salaries, and the names of the departments in which they work. An inner join operation returns the following result set:

```
SELECT EMPL.NAME, EMPL.SALARY, DEPT.DESCR
   FROM EMPL
     INNER JOIN DEPT
     ON    (EMPL.DEPTNO = DEPT.DEPTNO);

NAME      |SALARY      |DESCR
---------------------------------
George  |10000       |Plumbing
Paul    |15000       |Accounting
Dan     |30000       |Sales

3 rows selected
```

Unfortunately, the report is incorrect because Bernard is missing. The INNER JOIN clause requires that the joining column value be present in both tables. In this case, Bernard has not yet been assigned a department number, so there is no DEPTNO to join with the DEPT table.

The problem can be solved by specifying the LEFT OUTER JOIN clause instead:

```
SELECT EMPL.NAME, EMPL.SALARY, DEPT.DESCR
   FROM EMPL
     LEFT OUTER JOIN DEPT
     ON    (EMPL.DEPTNO - DEPT.DEPTNO);
```

```
NAME      | SALARY     | DESCR
------------------------------
George    | 10000      | Plumbing
Paul      | 15000      | Accounting
Dan       | 30000      | Sales
Bernard   | 22000      | NULL
```

```
4 rows selected
```

Observe the syntax that is used to indicate a left outer join. In this example, the result set includes employees who are not represented in the DEPT table. In other words, the result set includes all of the rows in the left table (EMPL), even if there is no match with records in the joined table (DEPT).

Right Outer Join

A right outer join operation, also known as a right join, produces a result set that includes the matching values of both joined tables and those values that are only present in the right joined table. The right joined table is the table that is used in the right part of the RIGHT OUTER JOIN operator when coding the join operation.

In the previous example, the LEFT OUTER JOIN clause can be changed to a RIGHT OUTER JOIN clause to produce a list of all departments and their employees:

```
SELECT EMPL.NAME, EMPL.SALARY, DEPT.DESCR
   FROM EMPL
     RIGHT OUTER JOIN DEPT
     ON    (EMPL.DEPTNO = DEPT.DEPTNO);
```

```
NAME      | SALARY     | DESCR
------------------------------
George    | 10000      | Plumbing
Paul      | 15000      | Accounting
Dan       | 30000      | Sales
NULL      | NULL       | Electrical
```

```
4 rows selected
```

This result set tells us which employees are reporting to the different departments. In this example, the Electrical department does not have any employees. Bernard is missing from this list because he does not yet belong to a department.

Using Correlation Names

If each column needed to be fully qualified with the table name, such as table-schema.table-name. column-name, queries would become very large and cumbersome. Fortunately, there is an easier way to disambiguate columns in multi-table SELECT statements.

Columns can be qualified using correlation names. A correlation name is an alias for a table in an SQL statement. The previous SQL example can be rewritten using correlation names:

```
SELECT D.DESCR, E.NAME FROM DEPT D, EMPL E
   WHERE (DESCR='Plumbing' OR DESCR='Sales') AND
         D.DEPTNO = E.DEPTNO;
```

The correlation name immediately follows the name of the table in the FROM clause. In this example, the correlation name for the DEPT table is D, and the correlation name for the EMPL table is E.

Correlation names are accessible within the SQL statement only. Following the execution of the SQL statement, the correlation name is no longer defined. Once a correlation name has been defined, it can be referenced in place of the table name throughout the rest of the query.

Sorting Output

Data in an Apache Derby database is stored in tables without regard to order. To retrieve data in a particular order, the ORDER BY clause must be added to a SELECT statement. Similarly, if the data is to be grouped, the GROUP BY clause must be added to the statement.

The order of the rows in the result table has not been specified in any of the examples so far. The following example produces a list of productions in alphabetical order:

```
SELECT PRODUCTION_TITLE FROM PRODUCTIONS
ORDER BY PRODUCTION_TITLE;


PRODUCTION_TITLE
-----------------------
Backsplash
Couched in Leather
Desperate Houses
Heroes not Zeros
Icing the Puck
Lilly of the Valley
My New Title
Naughty or Nice?
Rubber Sacks

9 rows selected
```

The following example contains an ORDER BY clause, followed by a list of the columns that specify the sort order, and the direction of the sort (descending):

```
SELECT PRODUCTION_TITLE FROM PRODUCTIONS
ORDER BY PRODUCTION_TITLE DESC;
```

```
PRODUCTION_TITLE
----------------------
Rubber Sacks
Naughty or Nice?
My New Title
Lilly of the Valley
Icing the Puck
Heroes not Zeros
Desperate Houses
Couched in Leather
Backsplash


9 rows selected
```

In this example, the DESC keyword that follows the PRODUCTION_TITLE column indicates that the result table should be in descending order based on the title. Ascending order is the default.

The ORDER BY clause can refer to more than one column in the result set. Each column in the ORDER BY clause can also have an ASC or DESC specification associated with it. The next example adds three additional records to the EMPL table and then selects all the department numbers in descending order, with employees by department sorted in ascending order:

```
INSERT INTO EMPL VALUES
   ('John',2,21000),('Susan',3,11000),('Alyse',3,31000);
SELECT DEPT.DEPTNO, EMPL.NAME FROM DEPT, EMPL
   WHERE DEPT.DEPTNO = EMPL.DEPTNO
   ORDER BY 1 DESC, 2 ASC;


DEPTNO        |NAME
--------------------
3             |Alyse
3             |Dan
2             |John
2             |Paul
2             |Susan
1             |George


6 rows selected
```

You can reference the column that should be used to sort the data by using the column name or by specifying its position in the select list. Using the column position is very useful when the column in the select list is made up of derived (calculated) columns that have no explicit name.

The following example sorts the employees on the basis of the bonus that they will get at the end of the year. The bonus is defined as 10% of their salary.

```
SELECT NAME, SALARY/10 FROM EMPL
   ORDER BY 2;


NAME      |2
--------------------

George   |1000
Susan    |1100
Paul     |1500
John     |2100
Bernard  |2200
Dan      |3000
Alyse    |3100


7 rows selected
```

It would be impossible to sort this result set without the ability to specify the column position. You can also rename a column using an alias. The alias can then be referenced in the ORDER BY clause. The following example sorts the result set using an alias for the salary calculation.

```
SELECT NAME, SALARY/10 AS BONUS FROM EMPL
   ORDER BY BONUS;
;
NAME      |BONUS
--------------------

George   |1000
Susan    |1100
Paul     |1500
John     |2100
Bernard  |2200
Dan      |3000
Alyse    |3100


7 rows selected
```

Derived Columns

There are cases in which you will need to perform calculations on the data. SQL has some basic built-in mathematical and string functions. Mathematical operations include addition, subtraction, multiplication, and division.

A calculation can be defined in the WHERE clause of the SQL statement or in the select list. The next example returns the names of all employees who would be eligible for a raise this year and the raise amount. Eligible employees are those whose current salary is less than 20,000, and their raise would be based on a sliding scale calculated as 10% of the difference between their existing salary and 20,000.

```
SELECT NAME, (20000-SALARY)*0.10 FROM EMPL
WHERE
   SALARY < 20000
ORDER BY 2;


NAME      |2
--------------------------
Paul      |500.00
Susan     |900.00
George    |1000.00


3 rows selected
```

In this example, the second column of the result set is a calculated column. Remember that you must use the column position if you want to use this calculated column in an ORDER BY clause (unless you name it). Occasionally, the values of a derived column might not display as expected. The example uses (20000-SALARY)*0.10 as the calculation. Even though 20,000 and SALARY are integer values, the result displays as a decimal value because of the last term in the calculation (0.10). If the statement had been changed to (20000-SALARY)/10, the result would have been displayed as an integer. Apache Derby will "promote" a result to the most accurate data type in the expression. If this is not what you want, you should use the CAST function to change the representation of the result.

In addition to the problem of referring to a calculation in an ORDER BY clause, the results do not describe what the calculation in the answer set represents. The second column heading only displays the number "2". Any calculation done in an SQL statement will have a column heading of "n" where n represents the position of the column in the output. Although this might be acceptable for applications retrieving data, it isn't very descriptive for users. To fix this, SQL allows any column to be renamed. If you name the derived (calculated) column, the ORDER BY clause can reference that name to allow for more readable SQL.

In the following example, the previous query has been rewritten to rename the output column of the calculation as RAISE and to use that name as part of the ORDER BY clause:

```
SELECT NAME, (20000-SALARY)*0.10 AS RAISE FROM EMPL
WHERE
   SALARY < 20000
ORDER BY RAISE;
```

```
NAME     |RAISE
-----------------------
Paul     |500.00
Susan    |900.00
George   |1000.00


3 rows selected
```

The AS clause is used to override the default name of a column in the select list. In this example, we are giving the name RAISE to the calculation (20000-SALARY)*0.10. This column name is used in the query to specify the column that should be used for sorting the output.

Apache Derby Functions

Apache Derby provides different types of functions, including scalar and column functions. Scalar functions (also known as row functions) provide a result for each row of the result table. A scalar function can be used anywhere an expression is allowed.

Column functions (also known as vector functions) work on a group of rows to provide a result. The rows are specified using a fullselect and can optionally be grouped using the GROUP BY clause.

This section introduces some of the SQL functions provided by Apache Derby. SQL functions are categorized by their implementation type. They are either built-in functions, or extensions of Apache Derby known as user-defined functions.

Built-in functions are provided by Apache Derby. These can be either scalar or column functions. User-defined functions (UDFs) are extensions of the current SQL language. These functions can be developed by an Apache Derby administrator or application developer. After a UDF has been created, it can be invoked by any user with the proper privileges.

Scalar Functions

Scalar functions are applied to each row of data, and they return one result per row. For example, you could use the substring (SUBSTR) function to retrieve the first letter of each person's name in the EMPL table. The arguments for this function include a string data type column, beginning offset, and length. The output data type is dependent on the definition of the function.

```
SELECT NAME, SUBSTR(NAME,1,1) FROM EMPL;
NAME     |2
-------------
George   |G
Paul     |P
Dan      |D
Bernard  |B
John     |J
```

```
Susan    |S
Alyse    |A
```

7 rows selected

In this example, SUBSTR returns a string of one character. This function is known as a string function because it works with any string data type. If the output column requires a meaningful name, you can use the AS clause.

In this example, the substring starts from the beginning of the string because 1 was used as the second argument of the function. The length of the output string is indicated by the third argument. In this example, the length is 1.

The following query uses the MONTH scalar function to return the month in which each production is scheduled to start at the YMLD theater:

```
SELECT PRODUCTION_TITLE, MONTH(PRODUCTION_START)
   FROM PRODUCTIONS;
```

```
PRODUCTION_TITLE                      |2
---------------------------------------
Lilly of the Valley                   |1
My New Title                          |1
Desperate Houses                      |3
Icing the Puck                        |1
Heroes not Zeros                      |6
Rubber Sacks                          |7
Couched in Leather                    |9
Backsplash                            |8
Naughty or Nice?                      |11
```

9 rows selected

Numerous functions are available in Apache Derby. The following is a current list of scalar functions that are supplied with the database.

- Math Functions—These are standard mathematical functions, such as ABS (ABSVAL), MOD, and SQRT.

- Casting Functions—These functions change one data type into another. They include BIGINT, CAST, CHAR, DATE, DOUBLE, INTEGER, SMALLINT, TIME, TIMESTAMP, and VARCHAR.

- String Functions—String functions manipulate character strings and return information about the strings. These functions include LENGTH, LOCATE, LCASE (or LOWER), LTRIM, RTRIM, SUBSTR, and UCASE (or UPPER).

- Date Functions—Individual elements of a date or time field can be retrieved using these functions. DAY, MONTH, and YEAR retrieve information from DATE or TIMESTAMP values, and HOUR, MINUTE, and SECOND retrieve information from TIME or TIMESTAMP values.
- Miscellaneous Functions—These functions return values based on system information. This list of functions includes CURRENT_TIMESTAMP, CURRENT_DATE, CURRENT_TIME, CURRENT_USER, and SESSION_USER.

Column Functions

Column functions provide a single result for a group of qualifying rows in a specified table or view. Many common queries can be satisfied using column functions, such as finding the smallest value, the largest value, or the average of a group of values.

For example, you can use the MAX function to obtain the maximum salary in the EMPL table.

```
SELECT MAX(SALARY) FROM EMPL;

1
-----------
31000

1 row selected
```

A WHERE clause can also be added to the query to make the MAX function more selective. For example, the following query determines the highest salary in department number 2.

```
SELECT MAX(SALARY) FROM EMPL
  WHERE DEPTNO = 2;

1
-----------
21000

1 row selected
```

The next example calculates the average salary of all employees. Notice that the AVG column function is used in this example:

```
SELECT AVG(SALARY) FROM EMPL;

1
-----------
20000

1 row selected
```

Apache Derby provides many more built-in functions, including:

- COUNT—The number of qualifying records
- SUM—Sum of all the values in a set of rows
- AVG—Average of all the values in a set of rows
- MAX—Maximum value in a set of rows
- MIN—Minimum value in a set of rows

Grouping Values

Many queries require some level of data aggregation. This is accomplished in SQL through the use of the GROUP BY clause.

The following query returns the average number of seats that are available for each performance.

```
SELECT PRODUCTION_NO, AVG(PERFORMANCE_SEATS) FROM PERFORMANCES
GROUP BY PRODUCTION_NO;


PRODUCTION& | 2
-----------------------
1            | 9
2            | 10
3            | 10
4            | 9
5            | 9
6            | 10
7            | 10
8            | 9
9            | 10


9 rows selected
```

The GROUP BY clause tells Apache Derby to group those rows that have the same values in the columns that are specified in the group by list. In this example, the grouping is done by PRODUCTION_NO. Apache Derby calculates the average of each of those groups (in this case, each production).

When you combine column functions and other elements, such as column names, scalar functions, or calculated columns, you must use the GROUP BY clause. In this case, you must include every element that is not a column function in the group by list. Constant values are the only elements that can be omitted from a group by list.

The following query retrieves the minimum, maximum, and average number of seats available by production.

```
SELECT PRODUCTION_NO, MIN(PERFORMANCE_SEATS) AS SEATS_MIN,
       MAX(PERFORMANCE_SEATS) AS SEATS_MAX,
       AVG(PERFORMANCE_SEATS) AS SEATS_AVG
FROM PERFORMANCES
GROUP BY PRODUCTION_NO;
```

```
PRODUCTION&|SEATS_MIN  |SEATS_MAX  |SEATS_AVG
-------------------------------------------------
1          |5          |15         |9
2          |7          |14         |10
3          |6          |15         |10
4          |4          |15         |9
5          |5          |16         |9
6          |5          |14         |10
7          |5          |15         |10
8          |6          |14         |9
9          |6          |15         |10

9 rows selected
```

It is possible to sort the output of this query by using an ORDER BY clause. Note that the ORDER BY clause should always be the last clause in an SQL statement.

Restricting Results with Column Functions

Up to now, our examples have restricted rows based on row conditions. It is also possible to restrict rows using column functions and the GROUP BY clause.

For example, the EMPL table has a total of seven rows, and there are two departments that have more than one employee:

```
SELECT * FROM EMPL;
```

```
NAME     |DEPTNO      |SALARY
---------------------------------
George   |1           |10000
Paul     |2           |15000
Dan      |3           |30000
Bernard  |NULL        |22000
John     |2           |21000
Susan    |3           |11000
```

```
Alyse    |3                    |31000
```

```
7 rows selected
```

Suppose that you need to create a report that lists departments with more than one employee. To do this, you can use the COUNT function and a GROUP BY clause, as follows:

```
SELECT DEPTNO, COUNT(*) FROM EMPL
GROUP BY DEPTNO;
```

```
DEPTNO       |2
----------------------
1            |1
2            |2
3            |3
NULL         |1
```

```
4 rows selected
```

The COUNT column function is used to get the total number of employees in every department. When the asterisk (*) is used with the COUNT function, the result will include the number of rows in the table that meet the selection or aggregation criteria in the WHERE or GROUP BY clause. In this example, the grouping is done by department number.

To select only those departments that have more than one employee, add the HAVING clause after the GROUP BY clause to restrict the records that are returned.

```
SELECT DEPTNO, COUNT(*) FROM EMPL
GROUP BY DEPTNO
   HAVING COUNT(*) > 1;
```

```
DEPTNO       |2
----------------------
2            |2
3            |3
```

```
2 rows selected
```

The HAVING clause for groups is analogous to the WHERE clause for tables. The HAVING clause restricts the result to include only those groups of rows that meet the specified conditions.

Eliminating Duplicates

When you execute a query, you might get duplicate rows in the result. SQL provides a special keyword to remove the duplicate rows from your output.

For example, the PRODUCTIONS table contains information about the productions that will be running at the YMLD Theater. One of the columns contains the production start date (PRODUCTION_START). The theater manager might want to run a query that tells her what months will have the opening of a new show. The following query uses the MONTH function to return the month of each production at the theater:

```
SELECT MONTH(PRODUCTION_START) AS OPENING
FROM PRODUCTIONS;

OPENING
--------------
1
1
3
1
6
7
9
8
11

9 rows selected
```

The resulting output contains duplicate information, and the rows are not sorted according to the month. You can eliminate duplicate rows by using the DISTINCT keyword, as shown in the following example:

```
SELECT
   DISTINCT MONTH(PRODUCTION_START) AS OPENING
FROM
   PRODUCTIONS
ORDER BY OPENING;

OPENING
--------------
1
3
6
7
8
9
11

7 rows selected
```

When you use the DISTINCT keyword inside a COUNT function, the function will not count duplicate column entries. The following queries return results from a COUNT(*) and a COUNT(DISTINCT) function:

```
SELECT
  COUNT(MONTH(PRODUCTION_START))
FROM
  PRODUCTIONS;


1
--------------
9

1 row selected


SELECT
  COUNT(DISTINCT MONTH(PRODUCTION_START))
FROM
  PRODUCTIONS;

1
--------------
7

1 row selected
```

Make sure that you understand the difference between COUNT(*) and COUNT(DISTINCT). They are similar in syntax but differ in function.

Subqueries

Subqueries can be used within an IN clause to specify the search arguments for an SQL statement.

Consider the difficulty in producing a report that lists the productions that have less than 50% of their total seats sold. Multiple calculations need to be done to determine the current seat count. Each performance has a PERFORMANCE_SEATS column that lists the current seats available. The total number of performances for a production has to be calculated from the PERFORMANCES table by counting up the number of rows for a performance and multiplying that by 20 (the number of seats in the theater). Then the total number of seats available for these performances must be calculated by adding up all of the values in the PERFORMANCE_SEATS column. This value divided by the total seat count will give us a percentage. Then the Productions that are related to these performances must be retrieved.

SQL of this complexity can best be handled by breaking up the request into a number of discrete chunks. The first query calculates the number of performances by production number:

```
SELECT
  PRODUCTION_NO, COUNT(*)
FROM
  PERFORMANCES
GROUP BY PRODUCTION_NO;


PRODUCTION&|2
---------------
1          |22
2          |23
3          |54
4          |93
5          |44
6          |21
7          |37
8          |41
9          |30


9 rows selected
```

This query can include a SUM function that adds up the number of seats available by PRODUCTION_NO. The following query shows some of the intermediate results, which helps confirm that the calculation is correct:

```
SELECT
  PRODUCTION_NO, COUNT(*),
  SUM(PERFORMANCE_SEATS) AS SEAT_COUNT,
  COUNT(*)*20 AS MAX_SEATS,
  (SUM(PERFORMANCE_SEATS)* 100) / (COUNT(*) * 20) AS PCNT_FULL
FROM
  PERFORMANCES
GROUP BY PRODUCTION_NO;


PRODUCTION&|2         |SEAT_COUNT |MAX_SEATS  |PCNT_FULL
-----------------------------------------------------------
1          |22        |214        |440        |48
2          |23        |234        |460        |50
3          |54        |560        |1080       |51
4          |93        |896        |1860       |48
5          |44        |431        |880        |48
```

6		21		215		420		51
7		37		374		740		50
8		41		399		820		48
9		30		320		600		53

```
9 rows selected
```

From this intermediate list, we need to extract those productions that are less than 50% full. This can be done with one of two methods. One method is to select values into a temporary table and then to select values from that table. Another method is to use the HAVING clause to restrict the result set:

```
SELECT
  PRODUCTION_NO, COUNT(*),
  SUM(PERFORMANCE_SEATS) AS SEAT_COUNT,
  COUNT(*)*20 AS MAX_SEATS,
  (SUM(PERFORMANCE_SEATS)* 100) / (COUNT(*) * 20) AS PCNT_FULL
FROM
  PERFORMANCES
GROUP BY PRODUCTION_NO
HAVING
  ((SUM(PERFORMANCE_SEATS)* 100) / (COUNT(*) * 20)) < 50;
```

PRODUCTION&	2	|SEAT_COUNT	|MAX_SEATS	|PCNT_FULL
1		22		214		440		48
4		93		896		1860		48
5		44		431		880		48
8		41		399		820		48

```
4 rows selected
```

It would be a lot easier to read this query if the HAVING clause allowed an alias (PCNT_FULL) to be used, but Apache Derby does not support this functionality. Now that the list of productions is available, a subselect can be used to retrieve the names of the productions that are less than 50% booked. The final SQL statement is as follows:

```
SELECT
  PRODUCTION_NO, PRODUCTION_TITLE
FROM
  PRODUCTIONS
WHERE
  PRODUCTION_NO IN
```

```
(
SELECT
  PRODUCTION_NO,
  (SUM(PERFORMANCE_SEATS)* 100) / (COUNT(*) * 20) AS PCNT_FULL
FROM
  PERFORMANCES
GROUP BY PRODUCTION_NO
HAVING
  ((SUM(PERFORMANCE_SEATS)* 100) / (COUNT(*) * 20)) < 50
);
```

```
PRODUCTION&|PRODUCTION_TITLE
------- -----------------------
1         |Lilly of the Valley
4         |Icing the Puck
5         |Heroes not Zeros
8         |Backsplash
```

```
4 rows selected
```

In this example, the subquery appears as part of the IN clause. The subquery is retrieving the productions that have less than 50% of their seats sold.

The subquery looks like a standard SQL statement. The only difference here is that the subquery is used to define selection criteria. You will never see its results. We are only using the subquery to create a list of values that will be used later by the outer SELECT statement.

The subquery used in this example is known as an uncorrelated subquery. In an uncorrelated subquery, the retrieved values are not directly related to the rows that are processed by the outer SELECT statement, whereas a correlated subquery references values that are returned by the outer SELECT statement.

The theater manager might decide that productions later in the year are not a concern from a ticket sales perspective. Instead, she wants to concentrate on productions that run from January to August. Our query can be rewritten so that the WHERE clause only returns productions that meet these date criteria:

```
SELECT
  PRODUCTION_NO, PRODUCTION_TITLE
FROM
  PRODUCTIONS PROD
WHERE
  PRODUCTION_END < '2005-08-31' AND
```

```
    (
    SELECT
      (SUM(PERFORMANCE_SEATS) * 100) / (COUNT(*) * 20) AS PCNT_FULL
    FROM
      PERFORMANCES PERF
    WHERE
      PERF.PRODUCTION_NO = PROD.PRODUCTION_NO
    ) < 50;
```

```
PRODUCTION& | PRODUCTION_TITLE
------------------------------
1            |Lilly of the Valley
4            |Icing the Puck
```

```
2 rows selected
```

Note the WHERE clause in this subquery. It references a table in the outer FROM clause. The outside table (PRODUCTIONS) and the inside table (PERFORMANCES) need to have correlation names assigned to them so that the SELECT statement will work properly. The PERF .PRODUCTION_NO = PROD.PRODUCTION_NO statement gets the production number from the outer loop. Think of the first SELECT statement as the outer loop and the second SELECT statement as the inner loop that gets its values from the outer loop.

You should understand the difference between subselects and subqueries. Subselects are queries that do not include an ORDER BY clause, an UPDATE clause, or UNION operators. Subqueries are used with the IN clause to specify the search arguments for an SQL statement.

Quantified Predicates

A quantified predicate is used to compare a value or values with a collection of values. There are three types of quantified predicates:

- ALL—The comparison must be true for all values returned by the table subquery.
- SOME—The comparison must be true for at least one value of the table subquery.
- ANY—ANY is equivalent to SOME.

These comparison operators are always used with a subselect that returns one or more records. For instance, a manager might want to find the names of those employees who make more money than anyone in a certain department. The following DDL creates a table with a list of employees and salaries.

```
DROP TABLE WORKERS;
CREATE TABLE WORKERS
  (
  NAME VARCHAR(8),
```

```
DEPTNO INT,
SALARY INT DEFAULT 10000
);
INSERT INTO WORKERS VALUES
('Jean',1,15000),('Pete',2,20000),('Brunis',5,18000),
('Lottie',5,19000),('Geoffrey',2,25000),('Andrew',3,11000),
('Ellie',5,9000);
```

One way to find all employees who make more than the maximum salary of employees in department 5 is to use a subselect with the MAX function:

```
SELECT * FROM WORKERS
WHERE
  SALARY >
    (SELECT MAX(SALARY) FROM WORKERS
     WHERE
       DEPTNO = 5
    );
```

```
NAME      |DEPTNO      |SALARY
--------------------------------
Pete      |2           |20000
Geoffrey|2             |25000
```

2 rows selected

Another way to accomplish this is to use the ALL predicate. The ALL predicate means that the comparison must be true for all records in the subselect. In this case, each salary in the base table must be greater than all salaries in the select list.

```
SELECT * FROM WORKERS
WHERE
  SALARY > ALL
    (SELECT SALARY FROM WORKERS
     WHERE
       DEPTNO = 5
    );
```

```
NAME      |DEPTNO      |SALARY
--------------------------------
Pete      |2           |20000
Geoffrey|2             |25000
```

2 rows selected

As is typical with most queries, the results can be obtained using a variety of techniques! Changing the predicate to SOME results in a list of employees who have a higher salary than at least one employee in department 5.

```
SELECT * FROM WORKERS
WHERE
  SALARY > SOME
    (SELECT SALARY FROM WORKERS
     WHERE
       DEPTNO = 5
    );
```

```
NAME      |DEPTNO       |SALARY
----------------------------------
Jean      |1            |15000
Pete      |2            |20000
Brunis    |5            |18000
Lottie    |5            |19000
Geoffrey  |2            |25000
Andrew    |3            |11000

6 rows selected
```

When SOME or ANY is specified for the fullselect, the predicate is true if the relationship is true for at least one value returned by the fullselect. The ALL predicate would only be true if the comparison were true for all values returned by the fullselect.

Note that if you use an equality predicate (=) with the ALL clause, the subselect must only return one row; otherwise, an error occurs. This is due to the SQL restriction that only one value can be compared using the equality predicate.

Case Expressions

You can add some logic to your SQL using CASE expressions. Consider the generation of a list of employees categorized by salary. Those employees who make less than $15,000 would be considered 'Junior', between $15,000 and $20,000 would be considered 'Intermediate', and more than $20,000 would be considered 'Senior'. The SQL that accomplishes this uses the CASE expression to produce columns with these headings.

```
SELECT
  NAME,
  CASE
    WHEN SALARY < 15000 THEN 'Junior'
    WHEN SALARY < 20000 THEN 'Intermediate'
    ELSE 'Senior'
```

```
  END AS Level
FROM
  WORKERS;

NAME     |LEVEL
---------------------
Jean     |Intermediate
Pete     |Senior
Brunis   |Intermediate
Lottie   |Intermediate
Geoffrey|Senior
Andrew   |Junior
Ellie    |Junior

7 rows selected
```

The order of the conditions for the CASE expression is very important. Apache Derby will process the first condition first, then the second, and so on. If you do not pay attention to the order in which the conditions are processed, you might retrieve the same result for every row in your table. For example, if you coded the "< 20000" option before the "< 15000", all of the data that is less than 20,000 will display the message 'Intermediate'.

Every condition in the CASE expression starts with the WHEN clause, and the set of conditions finishes with the END clause. The ELSE clause is optional but recommended in the event that none of the conditions is met.

Nested Table Expressions

A nested table expression is a special kind of subquery. This subquery is used in the FROM clause to create local temporary tables that are only known in the SQL that defines them.

Consider the problem of obtaining the average salary of all of the departments in a company. The first approach would be to use the AVG function in a select list:

```
SELECT AVG(SALARY) FROM WORKERS;

1
-----------
16714

1 row selected
```

The problem with this approach is that this gives us an average across all employees, rather than individual departments. What is really required is the average of the following department averages.

```
SELECT DEPTNO, AVG(SALARY) FROM WORKERS
GROUP BY DEPTNO;
```

```
DEPTNO      |2
------------------
1           |15000
2           |22500
3           |11000
5           |15333
```

4 rows selected

This "average of averages" can be accomplished with a nested table expression (sometimes referred to as an inline view):

```
SELECT AVG(DEPT_AVERAGE) FROM
  (
  SELECT DEPTNO, AVG(SALARY) AS DEPT_AVERAGE FROM WORKERS
  GROUP BY DEPTNO
  ) AS AVGCALC;
```

```
1
-------------
15958
```

1 row selected

In this example, the nested subselect creates a temporary table that will be used by the outer SELECT to obtain the overall average score. This temporary table is called AVGCALC. The inside SELECT must be named with the AS clause; otherwise, an error occurs.

The DEPTNO column is included in the subquery so that you can calculate the average for each department. After the subquery executes, the outer SELECT will be able to obtain the average value of the averages calculated in the nested table expression. The calculated average column (DEPT_AVERAGE) must be named so that the outer SELECT knows what value it is averaging.

An advantage of using nested table expressions over views is that nested table expressions exist only during the execution of the query, so you don't have to worry about their maintenance. They reduce contention over the system catalog tables, and because they are created at execution time, they can be defined using variables in an application.

Scalar Fullselect

A scalar fullselect is a SELECT statement that returns only one value. This type of SELECT can be used in different parts of an SQL statement. It can be used in the select list or in the WHERE clause.

Scalar fullselects can be used to combine grouped information, such as averages or sums, with detailed information in a single query.

Occasionally, you might need to use row data in a report that includes information based on the entire table. For instance, a company might keep a separate table of bonus payments that are given to employees. The base employee table contains their current salary and bonus amounts, while the bonus table contains all of the bonus payments. In other words, the total in the employee bonus column should equal the sum of bonus payments in the BONUSES table. The following DDL creates these two tables.

```
DROP TABLE EMPL_BONUSES;
CREATE TABLE EMPL_BONUSES
  ( NAME VARCHAR(10), SALARY INT, BONUS INT );
INSERT INTO EMPL_BONUSES(NAME, SALARY)
  VALUES
    ('Jean',15000),('Ellie',18000),('Pete',20000),
    ('Geoffrey',25000),
    ('Andrew',3000);


DROP TABLE BONUSES;
CREATE TABLE BONUSES
  ( NAME VARCHAR(10),BONUS INT );
INSERT INTO BONUSES
  VALUES
    ('Jean',1000),('Ellie',500),('Pete',2000),('Pete',3000),
    ('Ellie',2000),('Jean',300),('Andrew',3000);

UPDATE EMPL_BONUSES
  SET BONUS =
  (SELECT SUM(BONUSES.BONUS) FROM BONUSES
    WHERE
      BONUSES.NAME = EMPL_BONUSES.NAME
  );

SELECT * FROM EMPL_BONUSES;
```

NAME	SALARY	BONUS
Jean	15000	1300
Ellie	18000	2500
Pete	20000	5000

```
Geoffrey  |25000          |NULL
Andrew    |3000           |3000
```

5 rows selected

The next example uses scalar fullselects to retrieve employee bonuses, along with the average, minimum, and maximum bonuses across all employees in the company:

```
SELECT
  NAME, BONUS,
  (SELECT AVG(BONUS) FROM BONUSES) AS AVG_BONUS,
  (SELECT MIN(BONUS) FROM BONUSES) AS MIN_BONUS,
  (SELECT MAX(BONUS) FROM BONUSES) AS MAX_BONUS
FROM
  EMPL_BONUSES;
```

NAME	BONUS	AVG_BONUS	MIN_BONUS	MAX_BONUS
Jean	1300	1685	300	3000
Ellie	2500	1685	300	3000
Pete	5000	1685	300	3000
Geoffrey	NULL	1685	300	3000
Andrew	3000	1685	300	3000

5 rows selected

In this example, three scalar fullselects are used to retrieve the aggregated data. The first scalar fullselect calculates the average bonus, the second one calculates the minimum bonus, and the third one calculates the maximum bonus, all from the BONUSES table.

Note how the SQL statements that produce the average, minimum, and maximum values are scalar fullselects. The results returned by these fullselects are not correlated to the original SELECT statement. Suppose that the manager who produced the original report now wants to see an employee's minimum and maximum bonuses, rather than a company-wide value. To produce this report, the average, minimum, and maximum values have to be tied back to the employee record that is being displayed. To accomplish this request, a correlated subselect is required. The subselect must ensure that it returns only one value at a time.

The following query uses a correlated subselect to determine the average, minimum, and maximum bonuses for each employee:

```
SELECT
  NAME, BONUS,
  (SELECT AVG(BONUS) FROM BONUSES
     WHERE BONUSES.NAME = EMPL_BONUSES.NAME) AS AVG_BONUS,
```

```
(SELECT MIN(BONUS) FROM BONUSES
    WHERE BONUSES.NAME = EMPL_BONUSES.NAME) AS MIN_BONUS,
(SELECT MAX(BONUS) FROM BONUSES
    WHERE BONUSES.NAME = EMPL_BONUSES.NAME) AS MAX_BONUS
FROM
  EMPL_BONUSES;
```

NAME	BONUS	AVG_BONUS	MIN_BONUS	MAX_BONUS
Jean	1300	650	300	1000
Ellie	2500	1250	500	2000
Pete	5000	2500	2000	3000
Geoffrey	NULL	NULL	NULL	NULL
Andrew	3000	3000	3000	3000

```
5 rows selected
```

Examine the columns in the select list. These columns are made up of SELECT statements against the BONUSES table, and each statement makes reference to the table of the outer SELECT so that it can obtain separate average, minimum, and maximum values for each employee. It is important to fully qualify the columns that are being joined (BONUSES.NAME) so that Apache Derby knows from which table to take each column value.

Union

The UNION operator lets you combine the results of two or more different SELECT statements into one result table. You can combine as many tables as you want using the UNION operator. The only restriction is that every table produced by the SQL statement must be UNION-compatible; that is, it must have the same type, number, and order of columns.

Suppose you want to create a report that lists an employee's salary and bonus in the same column. A regular select list won't work because the columns appear beside one another:

```
SELECT * FROM EMPL_BONUSES;
```

NAME	SALARY	BONUS
Jean	15000	1300
Ellie	18000	2500
Pete	20000	5000
Geoffrey	25000	NULL
Andrew	3000	3000

```
5 rows selected
```

The UNION operator would allow the query to return both values in the same column. The SQL is split into two separate SELECT statements, one returning the SALARY value and the other returning the BONUS value.

```
SELECT NAME, SALARY FROM EMPL_BONUSES
UNION
SELECT NAME, BONUS  FROM EMPL_BONUSES;


NAME        |2
--------------------
Andrew      |3000
Ellie       |2500
Ellie       |18000
Geoffrey    |25000
Geoffrey    |NULL
Jean        |1300
Jean        |15000
Pete        |5000
Pete        |20000


9 rows selected
```

There are two interesting problems associated with this result. First of all, the record associated with Andrew appears to only have one result, although he does have a salary and a bonus. This is actually a result of how the UNION operator works. The UNION operator removes duplicate rows from the result table. Because Andrew has a bonus of $3000 and a salary of $3000, the UNION operator considered the second value to be a duplicate and eliminated it from the result set. There will be times when you want to list all of the rows that were processed by your queries. SQL provides a UNION ALL operator for this purpose:

```
SELECT NAME, SALARY FROM EMPL_BONUSES
UNION ALL
SELECT NAME, BONUS  FROM EMPL_BONUSES;
NAME        |2
--------------------
Jean        |15000
Ellie       |18000
Pete        |20000
Geoffrey    |25000
Andrew      |3000
Jean        |1300
Ellie       |2500
```

```
Pete        |5000
Geoffrey    |NULL
Andrew      |3000
```

```
10 rows selected
```

This result highlights the second problem that was encountered in the first result set. The original UNION result was sorted by NAME. This was probably the intended result, but not guaranteed by SQL. It just so happens that the UNION operator sorts results to eliminate duplicates in the answer set. If you need to sort the entire answer set, the ORDER BY clause must be placed after the final SQL statement. The following query also uses a CASE expression to convert null values into zeros. If an employee does not have a bonus, this can safely be assumed to mean zero.

```
SELECT NAME, SALARY
FROM
   EMPL_BONUSES
UNION ALL
SELECT NAME,
   CASE
     WHEN BONUS IS NULL THEN 0
     ELSE BONUS
   END
FROM
   EMPL_BONUSES
ORDER BY NAME;
```

```
NAME        |2
---------------------
Andrew      |3000
Andrew      |3000
Ellie       |2500
Ellie       |18000
Geoffrey    |0
Geoffrey    |25000
Jean        |1300
Jean        |15000
Pete        |5000
Pete        |20000
```

```
10 rows selected
```

Be sure to use a UNION operator only when you don't want duplicates in the result set. UNION
ALL offers better performance because it doesn't sort the results to eliminate duplicates. However, you can't always substitute a UNION for a UNION ALL.

The *EXISTS* Predicate

The EXISTS predicate is used in conjunction with a subquery. The predicate is considered to
be true if at least one record is returned by the subquery. NOT EXISTS is true if no records are
returned by the subquery. For example, the following query returns a list of all of the employees
who have been given a bonus:

```
SELECT * FROM EMPL_BONUSES E
WHERE
  EXISTS
   (SELECT * FROM BONUSES B
    WHERE
      B.NAME = E.NAME AND
      B.BONUS IS NOT NULL
   );
```

NAME	SALARY	BONUS
Jean	15000	1300
Ellie	18000	2500
Pete	20000	5000
Andrew	3000	3000

```
4 rows selected
```

This result could also have been obtained by using the COUNT function, as shown in the following example:

```
SELECT * FROM EMPL_BONUSES E
WHERE
  (SELECT COUNT(*) FROM BONUSES B
    WHERE
      B.NAME = E.NAME AND
      B.BONUS IS NOT NULL
  ) > 0;
```

Although both of these queries return identical results, they are handled in different ways by the
database. In the second example, every record found by the SELECT statement must be added up
to determine the final count. If this result is anything other than zero, it will be returned as a valid

record to the higher-level SELECT statement. In the first example, the EXISTS predicate is satisfied as soon as one record is found, and the scanning of additional records is unnecessary.

The opposite of EXISTS is NOT EXISTS. If the NOT EXISTS predicate is used in the first query, the result set represents all employees who have not been given a bonus.

```
SELECT * FROM EMPL_BONUSES E
WHERE
  NOT EXISTS
    (SELECT * FROM BONUSES B
     WHERE
       B.NAME = E.NAME AND
       B.BONUS IS NOT NULL
    );
```

```
NAME       | SALARY      | BONUS
---------------------------------
Geoffrey   | 25000       | NULL
```

```
1 row selected
```

Data Modification

Up to now, all of our SQL has focused on queries. The SELECT statement allows you to retrieve data from your database and assumes that the tables contain data. There are three SQL statements that you can use to add, change, or remove data stored in an Apache Derby database table: INSERT, UPDATE, and DELETE.

To perform these operations, you must have the required privileges on the tables being accessed. These privileges must be granted with caution because they allow end users to modify rows.

Inserting Rows

To initially populate an Apache Derby table with data, use the INSERT statement to store one or more rows at a time. Every row that is populated using the INSERT statement must adhere to table check constraints, data type validation, dynamic (trigger) constraints, and referential integrity constraints. An SQL error will occur if any of these conditions are violated during the processing of the INSERT statement.

The following example shows a simple INSERT statement. This statement inserts data into the WORKERS table.

```
DROP TABLE WORKERS;
CREATE TABLE WORKERS
```

```
(
NAME VARCHAR(8),
DEPTNO INT,
SALARY INT DEFAULT 10000
);
INSERT INTO WORKERS(NAME, DEPTNO, SALARY)
  VALUES ('Geoffrey',1,15000);
```

In this example, all of the column names are specified in the INSERT statement, and the contents of the row are enclosed in parentheses, with one value for each column.

In the VALUES clause, the number and order of the inserted elements must match the number and order of the column names specified in the INSERT column list. However, the order of the columns doesn't have to match the order in which they are defined in the table. For those columns that don't require a value, you can indicate a null or a default value. The following example inserts a record that contains a null value for the department number and the default value for the salary. This example also switches the order of the columns to demonstrate the ability to insert data in a different order than that specified in the original table definition.

```
INSERT INTO WORKERS(DEPTNO, NAME, SALARY)
  VALUES
  (NULL,'Andrew',DEFAULT);
```

Depending on your column definition, the default value can insert a system-defined default, a user-defined default, or a null value. Be aware that if the column doesn't accept null values (NOT NULL) and wasn't defined as WITH DEFAULT, you will receive an error message when using the DEFAULT keyword. This error is caused by NOT NULL columns receiving a default value of NULL.

When you want to insert values into all of the columns in a table, you do not have to provide a column list in the INSERT statement:

```
INSERT INTO WORKERS
  VALUES
  ('Katrina',3,20000);

SELECT * FROM WORKERS;

NAME     |DEPTNO     |SALARY
-------------------------------
Geoffrey|1          |15000
Andrew  |NULL       |10000
Katrina |3          |20000

3 rows selected
```

This method will only work if you specify a value for all of the columns in a table. If you miss a column, Apache Derby will not allow you to insert the row into the table.

Inserting Data into Specific Columns

There are times when you need to insert data only for specific columns. Every column that is not included in the INSERT statement will receive its default value.

　　　This operation can be accomplished only if the omitted columns accept null values or have a default value definition. This means that you must specify a value for the columns that are defined as NOT NULL. This restriction excludes columns that are defined as NOT NULL WITH DEFAULT.

　　　The following example inserts a new employee into the WORKER table, but with no department or salary information.

```
INSERT INTO WORKERS(NAME)
  VALUES
  ('Ellie');

SELECT * FROM WORKERS WHERE NAME='Ellie';

NAME     |DEPTNO      |SALARY
-------------------------------
Ellie    |NULL        |10000

1 row selected
```

Remember that columns defined using WITH DEFAULT that are not listed in the INSERT statement will receive the null value or a default value.

Inserting Multiple Rows

You can insert multiple rows into a table using a single INSERT statement. For example, you might want to add a number of new employees at the same time:

```
INSERT INTO WORKERS
  VALUES
  ('Tristan',NULL,20000),
  ('Basil',3,DEFAULT);

SELECT * FROM WORKERS;

NAME     |DEPTNO      |SALARY
-------------------------------
Geoffrey|1           |15000
Andrew  |NULL        |10000
```

```
Katrina  |3          |20000
Ellie    |NULL       |10000
Tristan  |NULL       |20000
Basil    |3          |10000
```

```
6 rows selected
```

All of the values for each row are enclosed in parentheses and are separated from each other with a comma. When inserting multiple rows with a single statement, you have to remember that all of the rows must have the same number, type, and order of columns. This means, for example, that you cannot insert values into one column in the first row and into five columns in the last row.

Inserting a Set of Values

You can insert the result of a subselect into the same or a different table. The subselect must follow these rules:

- The number of columns must equal the number of columns in the insert column list.
- The data type of each of the columns must match the data type of the corresponding columns in the insert column list.
- The insert column list can be omitted only if values are inserted into all of the columns in the table.
- Only columns defined to allow null values or defined as NOT NULL WITH DEFAULT can be omitted from the insert column list.

In some situations, it might be useful to create tables that are duplicates of others so that you can do multiple calculations against them. The following example creates a table that mimics the structure of the WORKERS table. This new table will be populated with those employees who currently do not have a valid department number.

```
DROP TABLE TEMP_WORKERS;
CREATE TABLE TEMP_WORKERS
  (
  NAME VARCHAR(8),
  DEPTNO INT,
  SALARY INT DEFAULT 10000
  );

INSERT INTO TEMP_WORKERS
  SELECT * FROM WORKERS
  WHERE
    DEPTNO IS NULL;
```

```
SELECT * FROM TEMP_WORKERS;

NAME     |DEPTNO       |SALARY
-------------------------------
Andrew   |NULL         |10000
Ellie    |NULL         |10000
Tristan  |NULL         |20000

3 rows selected
```

The select list used in the subselect in this example uses the asterisk (*) instead of the names of all of the columns. This is possible because the TEMP_WORKERS table has the same column structure as the WORKERS table. However, to keep this query independent of future table modifications, you should use an explicit select list instead of an asterisk.

Updating Rows

So far, we have looked at the INSERT statement as a method of loading data into your Apache Derby table. You might want to update only one column with values for a group of rows. There is an SQL UPDATE statement that you can use to specify the column and its new values. A table or a view can be referenced as the target for the UPDATE statement.

The UPDATE statement can be used in two forms:

- Searched update—This type of UPDATE statement is used to update one or more rows in a table. It requires a WHERE clause to select which rows are to be updated.
- Positioned update—This type of UPDATE statement is always embedded in a program. It uses cursors to update rows. As the cursor is repositioned (using the FETCH statement), the target row for the UPDATE statement changes.

This section focuses on the searched update feature. As is the case with an insert operation, all relevant constraints are enforced during an update operation. Update constraints can be different from insert constraints.

For example, the following is a transaction that updates all of the employees in the WORKERS table to have a valid department number (5):

```
UPDATE WORKERS
  SET DEPTNO = 5
  WHERE
    DEPTNO IS NULL;

SELECT * FROM WORKERS
  WHERE DEPTNO = 5;
```

```
NAME       |DEPTNO       |SALARY
-------------------------------
Andrew   |5           |10000
Ellie    |5           |10000
Tristan  |5           |20000
```

3 rows selected

It is very important that you provide the proper WHERE clause to avoid updating unintended rows. In this example, we needed to specify the predicate DEPTNO IS NULL to avoid changing the department number for any of the other employees.

The UPDATE statement can also be used with scalar fullselects. In this case, the fullselect must return a row with exactly the same number of columns and column data types of the row that will be updated. This scalar fullselect must return only one row.

Our next example will increase the salary of everyone in department 5 by 10% of the average salary of the employees in the other departments. The following query shows the current salaries of the employees in department 5 and the average salary of everyone working in the other departments:

```
SELECT * FROM WORKERS
   WHERE DEPTNO = 5;
```

```
NAME       |DEPTNO       |SALARY
-------------------------------
Andrew   |5           |10000
Ellie    |5           |10000
Tristan  |5           |20000
```

3 rows selected

```
SELECT AVG(SALARY) FROM WORKERS
   WHERE DEPTNO <> 5;
```

```
1
-----------
15000
```

1 row selected

We want to take 10% of the average salary of the other departments ($15,000/10) and add that to the salaries of everyone in department 5. A scalar fullselect can be used to calculate the average, and then that value can be added to each value in the SALARY column:

```
UPDATE WORKERS
   SET SALARY =
```

```
       SALARY +
         (
         SELECT AVG(SALARY) FROM WORKERS
         WHERE DEPTNO <> 5
         ) / 10
  WHERE DEPTNO = 5;

SELECT * FROM WORKERS
  WHERE DEPTNO = 5;

NAME     |DEPTNO       |SALARY
-----------------------------
Andrew   |5           |11500
Ellie    |5           |11500
Tristan  |5           |21500

3 rows selected
```

Notice that the last WHERE clause in the statement restricts the rows that will be updated. If you forget the WHERE clause in an UPDATE statement, all of the rows in your table will be updated.

The SQL statement that updates the salary column is known as a scalar fullselect because it returns only one row. The scalar fullselect can be considered a special case of a row fullselect.

Removing Data

Many methods are available for removing data from an Apache Derby database. To remove all of the data within a database, you can delete the directory in which the database was created. However, this might remove more data than you intended because the entire database, including its configuration, will be physically removed.

It is also possible to remove data using the DROP TABLE statement. If you want to remove all of the rows from a table, it is easier and quicker to execute the DROP TABLE statement. If the table is dropped, it must be re-created before any data can be added to it again.

The DELETE statement removes rows from tables. The syntax of the DELETE statement is different from the SELECT or INSERT statements because columns cannot be selected; only rows can be deleted.

In general, there are two kinds of DELETE statements:

- Searched delete—This type of DELETE statement is used to delete one or more rows from a table. It uses a WHERE clause to select the rows to be deleted.

- Positioned delete—This type of DELETE statement is always embedded in a program. It uses cursors to delete the row over which the cursor is positioned.

This section focuses on the searched delete feature.

The following example deletes employees whose department number is 1:

```
SELECT * FROM WORKERS WHERE DEPTNO = 1;

NAME     |DEPTNO      |SALARY
--------------------------------
Geoffrey|1            |15000

1 row selected

DELETE FROM WORKERS
   WHERE DEPTNO = 1;

SELECT * FROM WORKERS WHERE DEPTNO = 1;

ij> NAME     |DEPTNO      |SALARY
--------------------------------

0 rows selected
```

You can issue a SELECT statement with the same WHERE clause to verify the result of a delete operation. If the operation was successful, the query will return an empty result table.

A delete operation can become more sophisticated through the use of subselects. The following example deletes all employees whose salary is greater than the company average:

```
SELECT
   (SELECT AVG(SALARY) FROM WORKERS) AS AVG_SALARY,
    WORKERS.*
FROM WORKERS;

AVG_SALARY |NAME     |DEPTNO      |SALARY
-----------------------------------------------
14900      |Andrew  |5            |11500
14900      |Katrina |3            |20000
14900      |Ellie   |5            |11500
14900      |Tristan |5            |21500
14900      |Basil   |3            |10000

5 rows selected

DELETE FROM WORKERS
   WHERE SALARY > (SELECT AVG(SALARY) FROM WORKERS);
```

```
SELECT * FROM WORKERS;

NAME    |DEPTNO      |SALARY
--------------------------------
Andrew  |5           |11500
Ellie   |5           |11500
Basil   |3           |10000

3 rows selected
```

In this example, we are using a subselect to get the average salary of all employees. This value will be used to search for the employees that we want to delete. Note that the first SELECT statement uses a scalar fullselect as well. You can place values in the select list that are results from another SELECT statement.

Development SQL

There are a number of SQL features that are normally associated with application development or database administration. Although these features can be used with interactive programs such as ij, end users who only want to query the contents of a database don't normally use them. This section describes five of these features:

- Schemas
- User-defined functions (UDFs)
- Triggers
- Stored procedures
- Commit or rollback operations

Schemas

A schema is a database entity that represents a collection of named objects within an Apache Derby database. The schema name is actually part of the fully qualified name of the object being accessed. When database objects are being defined using the SQL CREATE <db-object> statement, a qualifier or schema name should be specified in the name of the database object. However, if no schema name is specified, the default is APP. All of the examples in this chapter omit the schema name. The following two statements are equivalent:

```
SELECT * FROM BONUSES;
NAME       |BONUS
--------------------
Jean       |1000
Ellie      |500
```

```
Pete       |2000
Pete       |3000
Ellie      |2000
Jean       |300
Andrew     |3000


7 rows selected

SELECT * FROM APP.BONUSES;

NAME       |BONUS
--------------------
Jean       |1000
Ellie      |500
Pete       |2000
Pete       |3000
Ellie      |2000
Jean       |300
Andrew     |3000


7 rows selected
```

Schemas can explicitly be created using the CREATE SCHEMA statement, with one user specified as the owner. If you wanted to create tables with a schema called MASTER, you could issue the following statement:

```
CREATE SCHEMA MASTER;
CREATE TABLE MASTER.EMPL (NAME VARCHAR(10));
```

In this example, the EMPL table is considered part of the MASTER schema, not the default APP schema.

Schema names are associated with many database objects, including tables, views, and indexes. For application development purposes, the table and view objects are of primary interest because indexes cannot directly be referenced in DML statements (INSERT, UPDATE, or DELETE). If the creator of a database object does not include the schema name in the database object definition, the object is created using the creator's authorization ID.

For example, assume that a table called T1 was created using the statement:

```
CREATE TABLE T1 (C1 CHAR(3))
```

The complete name of the database object would be APP.T1, and an application would have to specify the entire name.

The fully qualified name of a database object must be unique within the database. Thus, from the previous example, another table can exist with the name T1, as long as the schema name is something other than MASTER.

User-Defined Functions

User-defined functions (UDFs) form the basis of Object-Relational extensions to the SQL language. Fundamentally, a database function is a relationship between a set of input data values and a result value. Apache Derby comes with many built-in functions; however, it is possible to create your own scalar functions. Scalar functions take in one or more values and return another value. A UDF must be written in Java and then defined to the database. For example, the following SQL will register a SIN function using existing Java libraries.

```
CREATE FUNCTION SIN (DATA DOUBLE)
  RETURNS DOUBLE
  EXTERNAL NAME 'java.lang.Math.sin'
  LANGUAGE JAVA
  PARAMETER STYLE JAVA;

VALUES SIN(0), SIN(3.14159);

1
---------------------
0.0
2.65358979335273E-6

2 rows selected
```

If a specific function is not available in Apache Derby, there might be a function defined within the standard Java class libraries that could be used instead.

The syntax of the CREATE FUNCTION statement can be broken down into a number of sections. The first section contains the name of the function (in this example, SIN) followed by the parameters being sent to the function itself. Each parameter has a name and data type associated with it. The parameter names are optional, but naming the parameters makes it easier to associate a parameter with its purpose. The parameters can be of any data type except LONG VARCHAR, CLOB, and BLOB.

The RETURNS clause defines the type of value that will be returned by the function. In this example, the SIN function will return a DOUBLE value. The return value has the same restrictions as the input parameters.

The EXTERNAL NAME clause specifies the Java method that is to be called when the function is executed, and it takes the form class_name.method_name. The external name cannot have any extraneous spaces.

LANGUAGE JAVA tells the Apache Derby database manager to call the function as a public static method in a Java class.

PARAMETER STYLE tells Apache Derby that the function will use a parameter-passing convention that conforms to the Java language and SQL routines specification.

The SQL clause tells Apache Derby what SQL operatons the function can perform. There are three options for this parameter:

- CONTAINS SQL indicates that SQL statements that neither read nor modify SQL data can be executed by the function.

- NO SQL indicates that the function cannot execute any SQL statements.

- READS SQL DATA indicates that SQL statements that do not modify SQL data can be included in the function. This is the default setting.

The ON NULL INPUT clause specifies whether the function is called if any of the input arguments is null. There are two options for this parameter:

- RETURNS NULL ON NULL INPUT specifies that the function should not be invoked if any of the input arguments is null. The result is the null value.

- CALLED ON NULL INPUT specifies that the function should be invoked if any or all input arguments are null. This specification means that the function must be coded to test for null argument values. The function can return a null or a non-null value. This is the default setting.

A function definition must contain the EXTERNAL NAME, LANGUAGE, and PARAMETER STYLE clauses.

Triggers

A trigger is a set of actions that will be executed when a defined event occurs. The triggering events can be defined on INSERT, UPDATE, or DELETE statements.

Triggers are defined for a specific table, and once defined, a trigger is automatically active. A table can have multiple triggers defined for it, and if multiple triggers are defined for a given table, the order of trigger activation is based on the trigger creation timestamp (the order in which the triggers were created).

When a database event that fires a trigger occurs, Apache Derby performs actions in this order:

- It performs constraints checking (primary key, unique key, foreign key, table check).

- It performs the insert, update, or delete operation.

- It fires "after triggers."

Trigger definitions are stored in the system catalog tables. You can see them through the following catalog views:

- SYSTRIGGERS contains the trigger definition information; one row for each defined trigger

- SYSSTATEMENTS contains one row for the SQL statement that is part of a trigger

Triggers can be used for a variety of purposes, but one of the primary ones is to ensure that cross-table dependencies are maintained. The triggered action could involve updating rows in related tables. This is similar to referential integrity, but it is a more flexible alternative.

Trigger Activation

A trigger can only be defined to fire after an event occurs. This is called an after trigger, and it will fire for each row in the set of affected rows, or after the statement has successfully completed (depending on the defined granularity). Therefore, the trigger body sees the table as being in a consistent state. (All transactions have completed.)

Another important feature about triggers is that they can fire other triggers (or the same trigger) or other constraints. These are known as cascading triggers.

Depending on the nature of the trigger, new and old data values can be accessible to the trigger during its execution.

By using triggers, you can:

- Reduce the amount of application development and make development faster. Because triggers are stored in Apache Derby itself and are processed by Apache Derby, you do not need to code the triggers or their actions into your applications.

- Provide a global environment for your business rules. Because triggers only have to be defined once and are then stored in the database, they are available to all applications executing against the database.

- Reduce the maintenance of your applications. Again, because a trigger is handled by Apache Derby and is stored in the database itself, any changes to the trigger due to changes in your environment only need to occur in one (not multiple) application.

Trigger Body

The trigger body contains a single SQL statement that performs some type of action. The trigger statement has the following limitations:

- It must not contain any dynamic parameters (?).
- It must not create, alter, or drop the table upon which the trigger is defined.
- It must not add an index to or remove an index from the table on which the trigger is defined.
- It must not add a trigger to or drop a trigger from the table upon which the trigger is defined.
- It must not commit or roll back the current transaction or change the isolation level.
- It must not execute a CALL statement.

The trigger statement can reference database objects other than the table upon which the trigger is declared. If any object that the trigger depends upon is dropped, the trigger is invalidated. If the trigger cannot be successfully recompiled upon the next execution, the invocation throws an exception, and the statement that caused it to fire will be rolled back.

The best way to understand triggers is to see some in action. The next few sections demonstrate how triggers can be used.

Trigger Example—Updating Other Tables

Two tables were defined in a previous section: one contained employee salary information, and the other contained bonus payment information. These tables are re-created for this section, with the addition of a sequence column in the BONUSES table, as follows:

```
DROP TABLE EMPL_BONUSES;
CREATE TABLE EMPL_BONUSES
  ( NAME VARCHAR(10), SALARY INT, BONUS INT );
INSERT INTO EMPL_BONUSES(NAME, SALARY)
  VALUES
    ('Jean',15000),('Ellie',18000),('Pete',20000),('Geoffrey',
      25000),
    ('Andrew',3000);


DROP TABLE BONUSES;
CREATE TABLE BONUSES
  (TX INT GENERATED ALWAYS AS IDENTITY, NAME VARCHAR(10), BONUS INT );
INSERT INTO BONUSES(NAME, BONUS)
  VALUES
    ('Jean',1000),('Ellie',500),('Pete',2000),('Pete',3000),
    ('Ellie',2000),('Jean',300),('Andrew',3000);

UPDATE EMPL_BONUSES
  SET BONUS =
   (SELECT SUM(BONUSES.BONUS) FROM BONUSES
    WHERE
      BONUSES.NAME = EMPL_BONUSES.NAME
  );
```

There is a key relationship between these tables. The BONUS column in the EMPL_BONUSES table is the sum of all of the bonuses for that employee found in the BONUSES table. If a new bonus payment is added to the BONUSES table, the assumption is that the application or user will also update the EMPL_BONUSES table to reflect this change. Rather than leave the update to fate, we can define an appropriate trigger to take care of it.

```
CREATE TRIGGER UPDATE_EMP_BONUS
  AFTER INSERT ON BONUSES
```

```
  REFERENCING NEW AS n
  FOR EACH ROW MODE DB2SQL
UPDATE EMPL_BONUSES
  SET EMPL_BONUSES.BONUS =
    CASE
      WHEN EMPL_BONUSES.BONUS IS NULL THEN n.BONUS
      ELSE EMPL_BONUSES.BONUS + n.BONUS
    END
  WHERE
    EMPL_BONUSES.NAME = n.NAME;
```

The CREATE TRIGGER statement can be divided into two sections. The first section describes the role of the trigger, and the second section includes the logic that will be executed in the trigger. The first parameter is the name of the trigger (UPDATE_EMP_BONUS). This is followed by the action clause.

The UPDATE_EMP_BONUS trigger is an AFTER, INSERT, and FOR EACH ROW trigger. This trigger will fire every time a row is inserted into the BONUSES table. The trigger body section will perform an update operation to set the value of the BONUS column for the corresponding row in the EMPL_BONUSES table.

After a new bonus value is inserted into the BONUSES table, the corresponding employee record should be updated. The following example adds a new bonus value for Andrew:

```
SELECT * FROM EMPL_BONUSES
  WHERE NAME='Andrew';


NAME        |SALARY      |BONUS
----------------------------------
Andrew      |3000        |3000


1 row selected

INSERT INTO BONUSES(NAME,BONUS) VALUES ('Andrew',1000);

SELECT * FROM EMPL_BONUSES
  WHERE NAME='Andrew';

NAME        |SALARY      |BONUS
----------------------------------
Andrew      |3000        |4000


1 row selected
```

Trigger Example—Changing Inserted Values

In the previous example, a bonus was added to the BONUSES table, but no checking was done to see whether this was a valid bonus. A trigger could be defined to check whether the bonus value is within a range of acceptable values. In this example, we add a new trigger that checks the bonus value and changed it to an appropriate value.

```
CREATE TRIGGER CHECK_BONUS_VALUE
   AFTER INSERT ON BONUSES
   REFERENCING NEW AS n
   FOR EACH ROW MODE DB2SQL
   UPDATE BONUSES SET
     BONUS =
       CASE
         WHEN (n.BONUS < 500) THEN 500
         WHEN (n.BONUS > 5000) THEN 5000
         ELSE n.BONUS
       END
     WHERE
       TX = n.TX;
```

The UPDATE statement checks the inserted value, and if that value is outside of an acceptable range, it resets the value.

The next example creates a new employee (Paul) and then inserts some bonuses that are outside of the acceptable range. Note that the two triggers (CHECK_BONUS_VALUE and UPDATE_EMP_BONUS) must both fire when an insert operation occurs.

```
INSERT INTO EMPL_BONUSES(Name, Salary) VALUES ('Paul',28000);
INSERT INTO BONUSES(NAME,BONUS) VALUES ('Paul',-300),
   ('Paul',6000);
SELECT * FROM EMPL_BONUSES WHERE NAME='Paul';

NAME        |SALARY      |BONUS
----------------------------------
Paul        |28000       |5700

1 row selected
```

Something didn't work correctly here! The first insert operation into the BONUSES table had a value of -300. The trigger should have changed that value to 500. The second insert value was 6000, and that should have been changed to 5000. The following query reveals that these values were correctly placed into the BONUSES table:

```
SELECT * FROM BONUSES WHERE NAME='Paul';
```

```
TX          |NAME        |BONUS
--------------------------------
11          |Paul        |500
12          |Paul        |5000
```

2 rows selected

So what went wrong? Even though one trigger might fire after another, they both see the same image of the row. The CHECK_BONUS_VALUE trigger changed the value of the bonus, but this was not visible to the other trigger. So, when the bonus values of -300 and 6000 are added together, they result in a total bonus of 5700. The changes made by the second trigger were never seen by the first trigger. The best way to correct this type of problem is to delete the second trigger and use column constraints to check the data before the triggers are fired. In this case, a simple BONUS BETWEEN 500 AND 5000 would have caught this problem.

Trigger Example—Sets

Triggers can also be used on sets of values. The previous examples were based on individual records being inserted or changed. With sets, the trigger will fire after all of the records are updated or deleted. For instance, a trigger could be written to populate an additional table (TOTAL_SALARY) that is updated whenever the total salary paid out to employees is updated. This trigger would only need to fire when a transaction is complete because it could just query all of the employee records to determine the total salary.

```
CREATE TABLE TOTAL_SALARY (ALLSALARY INT);
INSERT INTO TOTAL_SALARY
  SELECT SUM(SALARY) FROM EMPL_BONUSES;

SELECT * FROM TOTAL_SALARY;

ALLSALARY
-----------
109000
```

1 row selected

The next trigger will run whenever there is an update against the EMPL_BONUSES table. A trigger on INSERT and DELETE statements would also be necessary to make sure that this value is properly updated.

```
CREATE TRIGGER CHECK_SALARY
   AFTER UPDATE OF SALARY ON EMPL_BONUSES
   REFERENCING NEW_TABLE AS NEW_SALARY
   FOR EACH STATEMENT MODE DB2SQL
```

```
UPDATE TOTAL_SALARY
  SET ALLSALARY =
     (SELECT SUM(SALARY) FROM NEW_SALARY);
```

The next SQL statement gives everyone in the company a 10% raise. The `CHECK_SALARY` trigger will fire and update the `ALLSALARY` column to contain the new value.

```
UPDATE EMPL_BONUSES
  SET SALARY = SALARY * 1.10;

SELECT * FROM TOTAL_SALARY;

ALLSALARY
-----------
119900

1 row selected
```

Triggers are a very powerful feature within the Apache Derby database, but you must ensure that you use constraints and triggers together appropriately.

Stored Procedures

A procedure, also called a stored procedure, is a database object that is created by executing the `CREATE PROCEDURE` statement. A procedure encapsulates logic and SQL statements. Procedures are used as subroutine extensions to applications, and other database objects that can contain logic.

Stored procedures enable the encapsulation of SQL statements, function invocations, and logic elements that can be reused by multiple programs. Procedures can be called from client applications using the `CALL` statement. Procedures can contain SQL statements that read or modify table data, and return result sets to the calling application.

When a procedure is called, the SQL and logic within the procedure is executed on the server. Data is only transferred between the client and the database server in the procedure call and in the procedure return. If you have a series of SQL statements to execute within a client application, and the application does not need to do any processing in between those statements, then this series of statements would benefit from being included in a procedure.

Creating stored procedures is a similar process to creating user-defined functions. The `CREATE PROCEDURE` statement allows you to create Java stored procedures, which you can then call using the `CALL` statement.

For example, the following DDL will register a stored procedure called `TOTAL_REVENUE` in an existing Java library:

```
CREATE PROCEDURE TOTAL_REVENUE
  (IN CURRENT_YEAR INTEGER, OUT TOTAL DECIMAL(10,2))
```

```
PARAMETER STYLE JAVA
READS SQL DATA
LANGUAGE JAVA
EXTERNAL NAME 'com.test.sales.TotalRevenue'
```

The syntax of the `CREATE PROCEDURE` statement can be broken down into a number of sections. The first section contains the name of the procedure (in this example, `TOTAL_REVENUE`), followed by some parameters. Each parameter has a name and data type associated with it. The `IN`, `OUT`, and `INOUT` keywords tell the system whether the parameters are for input, output, or both input and output. The parameters can be of any data type except `LONG VARCHAR`, `CLOB`, and `BLOB`.

`PARAMETER STYLE` tells Apache Derby that the procedure will use a parameter-passing convention that conforms to the Java language and SQL routines specification.

`DYNAMIC RESULT SETS` specifies the estimated upper bound of returned result sets for the procedure. The default is zero dynamic result sets.

The `SQL` clause tells Apache Derby what SQL operations the procedure can perform. There are three options for this parameter:

- `CONTAINS SQL` indicates that SQL statements that neither read nor modify SQL data can be executed by the procedure.

- `MODIFIES SQL DATA` indicates that the procedure can execute any SQL statement except statements that are not supported in stored procedures.

- `NO SQL` indicates that the procedure cannot execute any SQL statements.

`READS SQL DATA` indicates that SQL statements that do not modify SQL data can be included in the procedure. This is the default setting.

`LANGUAGE JAVA` tells Apache Derby to call the procedure as a public static method in a Java class.

The `EXTERNAL NAME` clause specifies the Java method that is to be called when the procedure is executed, and it takes the form `class_name.method_name`. The external name cannot have any extraneous spaces.

A procedure definition must contain the `EXTERNAL NAME`, `LANGUAGE`, and `PARAMETER STYLE` clauses.

Commit and *Rollback*

An application must establish a connection to the target database server before it can run any executable SQL statements. This connection identifies both the authorization ID of the user who is running the application and the name of the database server against which the application is to run. After the connection has been established, the application can issue SQL statements that manipulate data (`SELECT`, `INSERT`, `UPDATE`, or `DELETE`), define and maintain database objects (`CREATE`, `ALTER`, or `DROP`), and initiate control operations (`COMMIT` or `ROLLBACK`). These statements are considered parts of a transaction.

A transaction is a sequence of SQL statements (possibly with intervening program logic) that the database manager treats as a whole. An often-used alternative term is unit of work. To ensure the consistency of data at the transaction level, the system ensures that either all operations within a transaction are completed, or that none are completed.

A transaction begins implicitly with the first executable SQL statement and ends with either a commit operation or a rollback operation, or when the application ends. In Apache Derby, you cannot issue the SQL COMMIT or ROLLBACK statement explicitly; instead, you must use APIs or object methods to end transactions in a way that results in a commit or a rollback operation. A commit operation makes the changes that have taken place during the current transaction permanent, and a rollback operation restores the data to the state it was in prior to the beginning of the transaction.

To end properly, an application must:

- Complete the current transaction (if one is in progress) by explicitly issuing either a COMMIT statement or a ROLLBACK statement through the programming API
- Release the connection to the database server by using the appropriate function or method for your programming interface
- Clean up resources that it has used; for example, free any temporary storage

An important difference between Apache Derby and other databases is that the commit or rollback operation must be handled through the application APIs, rather than through the explicit issuing of these statements.

Summary

This chapter has covered a large amount of information about SQL. The first section described the various SQL statements that are used to create database objects, including tables, views, and indexes. The second section described data manipulation, including the SELECT, INSERT, DELETE, and UPDATE statements. Finally, features that are more suited to application development were covered at the end of the chapter.

All of the examples in this chapter can be found on the book's Web site. The best way to learn how to use SQL with Apache Derby is to try running the examples yourself and experimenting with different SQL statements.

Developing Apache Derby Applications with JDBC

Introduction

Apache Derby provides support for many different types of Java programs, including applications, applets, stored procedures, and user-defined functions. In addition, Apache Derby also supports the concept of an embedded JDBC application where the JDBC driver, application, and database library are in a single .JAR file.

Java programs that access and manipulate Apache Derby databases can use the Java Database Connectivity (JDBC) application programming interface (API). JDBC is a vendor-neutral SQL interface that provides data access to your application through standardized Java methods. The greatest benefit of using Java—regardless of the database interface—is its write once, run anywhere capability, allowing the same Java program to be distributed and executed on various operating platforms in a heterogeneous environment without recompiling. In addition, because the Java database interface supported by Apache Derby is an industry open standard, you have the added benefit of being able to use your Java program with a variety of database vendors.

For JDBC programs, your Java code passes dynamic SQL either directly to the database using the embedded JDBC driver that comes with the engine, or through a client JDBC driver that comes with the optional DB2 client. Apache Derby executes the SQL statements through JDBC APIs, and the results are passed back to your Java code. JDBC is similar to the DB2 call-level interface (CLI) or Open Database Connectivity (ODBC) because JDBC uses dynamic SQL, and you do not have to precompile or bind to a JDBC program.

Java programs written for Apache Derby offer:

- Increased portability to other database systems and operating platforms
- Easy access to databases across the Internet from multiple client platforms

- Representation of the NULL state built into Java types
- Object-oriented application development and data access model

Apache Derby supports many types of Java programs. Applications and applets are two main types of Java programs.

Java applications can run directly against the Apache Derby database in embedded mode, or they can rely on a client JDBC dirver, such as the Derby Network Client or the DB2 client code, to connect to the database. You can start an application from the desktop or a command line, like any other application. For remote requests, the Derby Network Client or DB2 JDBC driver can be used to handle the JDBC API calls from your application. The JDBC driver on the client communicates the requests to the Apache Derby Network server, receives the results, and passes them back to the Java application.

Java applets do not require any client JDBC driver code to be installed on the system where they execute. You need only a Java-enabled Web browser on the client machine to run your applet. Typically, you would embed the applet in a Hypertext Markup Language (HTML) page. When you load your HTML page, the browser downloads the Java applet to your machine, which then downloads the Java class files and appropriate JDBC driver. When your applet calls the JDBC API to connect to Apache Derby, the JDBC driver establishes a separate network connection to the database server.

Apache Derby also supports user-defined functions and stored procedures written in Java.

This chapter presents an overview of the JDBC specification and demonstrates how to call JDBC APIs to access a database and manipulate data in that database. In addition, this chapter introduces some commonly used terms and constructs to help you better understand JDBC programs for Apache Derby.

Many of the examples in this chapter contain references to the "Your Momma Loves Drama" database. This fictitious database contains information about theatrical productions held in a small theater. For more information about this database and how it is created, see Chapter 8, "SQL."

JBDC Program Structure

The following diagram shows the components of a JDBC application. Although not all of these components are required, there are three core actions in every application: loading the driver manager, connecting to the database, and issuing SQL statements.

The arrows represent the order in which the various JDBC calls are performed in an application. Solid lines represent steps that must be taken within an application. Broken lines represent optional steps available to the application developer. Connections, statements, and result sets should also be closed once they are no longer needed. This is highlighted by the close box symbols (☒) in the diagram.

When an application starts, it must load the JDBC driver associated with Apache Derby. After the driver has been loaded, a connection can be made to one or more databases. In the case of stored procedures and user-defined functions, this step is not required because it is assumed that the program is running under the control of an application that has already connected to the database engine. It would be a mistake to try to execute a user-defined function without already being connected to an Apache Derby database.

JBDC Calling Sequence

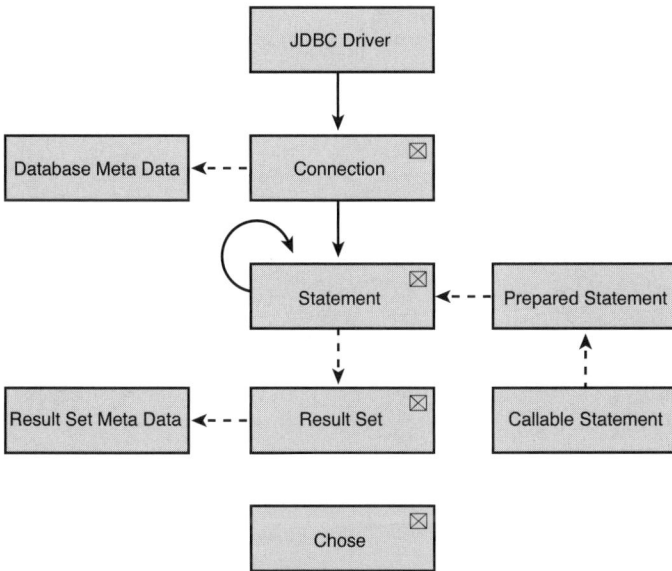

Figure 9-1   JDBC Calling Sequence

After the connection to a database has been made, the application can optionally request meta-data from the database. This meta-data contains information about the tables and other objects within the database. For most applications, programmers are aware of the database objects they expect to manipulate. The information returned from the database meta-data might be useful for generic applications that are used for querying or manipulating the database without any prior knowledge of the database structure.

The application can also issue various SQL statements, such as `SELECT`, `INSERT`, `UPDATE`, or `DELETE`. Statements can be prepared and re-used multiple times to reduce the overhead of statement optimization. This includes calling stored procedures and SQL functions, which encapsulate SQL logic in an external Java programs.

If the SQL statements return any data, the application can manipulate the result sets. A result set contains the rows and columns that are requested by an SQL statement. If the column and row structures are not known beforehand, the application can request meta-data about those structures.

When processing for a statement or connection is complete, the statement or connection should be explicitly closed in the application; this frees up resources in both the application and the database.

JDBC Imports

Every application that uses the JDBC API needs to include a number of import statements at the beginning of the program. These imports are required for the `javac` program to resolve JDBC references. The import libraries are listed in the following table. Note that at a minimum, the `java.sql.*` import is required.

Table 9-1   JDBC Import Statements

Import	Description
`java.sql.*`	This import is required for the core JDBC API and should be included in every program that uses JDBC.
`javax.sql.*`	This library is required for enterprise server-side support.
`java.io.*`	This library is required for any streaming of `BLOB` or `CLOB` objects.
`java.math.*`	This library is required for any BigDecimal support (`NUMERIC` and `DECIMAL` columns).
`java.text.*`	This library provides support for formatting dates and numbers.
`java.util.*`	This library is required for retrieving the property values of a database.

For a simple application, the `java.sql.*` import is usually sufficient.

```
import java.sql.*;
public class ShowProductions {
  public static void main(String argv[]) throws SQLException {
    ...
```

Using Embedded JDBC Drivers

Every Apache Derby embedded application must load the JDBC driver before issuing any connects or SQL statements. Stored procedures and user-defined functions do not need to load the JDBC driver because it is assumed that they are running under the context of another program that is executing an SQL statement.

By definition, an embedded Apache Derby application has a direct connection to the database. When the application starts, it is the only connection to the database, and when the application completes, the database is stopped. The other option is to run Apache Derby as a network database. In this case, the program can be one of many applications that are accessing the database.

The class that loads the Apache Derby local JDBC driver is the `org.apache.derby.jdbc` `.EmbeddedDriver` class. There are a variety of ways to create an instance of the Apache Derby driver class, but do not use the class directly through the `java.sql.Driver` interface. The preferred method is to use the `DriverManager` class to create connections using the `Class.forName()` method: `Class.forName("org.apache.derby.jdbc.EmbeddedDriver")`.

```
String DerbyDriver = "org.apache.derby.jdbc.EmbeddedDriver";

try {
  Class.forName(DerbyDriver).newInstance();
}
```

```
catch (Exception NoDriver) {
  System.out.println("Derby driver not found: " + DerbyDriver);
  NoDriver.printStackTrace();
  System.exit(1);
}
```

By creating an instance at the same time, this approach ensures that the class is loaded in all JVMs. The driver can also be loaded using either of the following two techniques:

```
new org.apache.derby.jdbc.EmbeddedDriver()
Class c = org.apache.derby.jdbc.EmbeddedDriver.class
```

Either of these techniques will work, but they both require that the class be found when the code is compiled. In addition, the driver can be loaded by setting the `jdbc.drivers` system property.

To set a system property, you alter the invocation command line or the system properties within the application. It is not possible to alter system properties within an applet. The following is an example of setting the driver through the JVM:

```
java -Djdbc.drivers=org.apache.derby.jdbc.EmbeddedDriver ShowProductions

Production Title
Lilly of the Valley
My New Title
Desperate Houses
Icing the Puck
Heroes not Zeros
Rubber Sacks
Couched in Leather
Backsplash
Naughty or Nice?
```

In this example, the `try` block (`Class.forName`) is not required in the application. However, the application must be started with this additional system property, or it fails.

```
java ShowProductions

Error = 08001
No suitable driver
```

IBM DB2 JDBC Universal Driver for Derby

The Apache Derby Network Server supports a traditional client-server framework in which many clients executing in different JVMs can connect to the same Apache Derby database. The

Network Server routes requests to the database and returns results to the clients. This requires a client JDBC driver that can talk to the Apache Derby Network Server, and many are available now, including the Derby Network Client and the IBM DB2 JDBC Universal driver mentioned in this section.

The IBM DB2 JDBC Universal Driver for Apache Derby is the same JDBC driver that is included with the Cloudscape 10.0 product. If Apache Derby is being used as a network server, you can use this driver to connect to the database with JDBC.

The DB2JCC network driver is available from the IBM download site. This book's Web site (www.ibmpressbooks.com/title/0131855255) also contains a link to this file. The `db2jcc_for_derby.zip` file includes the `db2jcc.jar` and `db2jcc_license_c.jar` files. Unzip the `db2jcc_for_derby.zip` file into either the `%DERBY_INSTALL%/lib` directory (where `%DERBY_INSTALL%` represents the directory where you installed Apache Derby) or another directory.

Both of these .JAR files are required to use the DB2 JDBC Universal Driver. Put both of them in your client class path to run your application. The following statement should be included in your program to load the network driver code: `Class.forName("com.ibm.db2.jcc` `.DB2Driver")`.

```
String DerbyDriver = "com.ibm.db2.jcc.DB2Driver";

try {
  Class.forName(DerbyDriver).newInstance();
}
catch (Exception NoDriver) {
  System.out.println("Derby driver not found: " + DerbyDriver);
  NoDriver.printStackTrace();
  System.exit(1);
}
```

Note the similarities between the embedded driver and the network driver. The same logic can be used for either type of connection. The only difference is the driver name that is passed to the `Class.forName` function.

Establishing a Database Connection

After an application has loaded the appropriate driver, it can establish a connection to the database. To connect to an embedded Apache Derby database, use the following `getConnection()` method:

```
Connection conn = null;
conn = DriverManager.getConnection("jdbc:derby:YMLD");
```

The getConnection URL takes the form jdbc:derby:[subprotocol:][database-name][;attributes].

- subprotocol is rarely used in the connection URL. This option specifies where Apache Derby should look for a database. This can be in a directory, a class path, or in a .JAR file. The majority of the time, this option is used for read-only databases.

- databasename specifies a database name, with or without a relative or absolute path.

- attributes specifies any additional options that are available when connecting to an Apache Derby database. Many of these options are described in Chapter 6, "Managing an Apache Derby Database."

The application code should include suitable try blocks around the connection statement to trap any errors that might occur.

```
try {
  conn = DriverManager.getConnection("jdbc:derby:YMLD");
  ...
}
catch (SQLException se) {
  String SQLState = se.getSQLState();
  String SQLMessage = se.getMessage();
  System.out.println("Error = "+SQLState);
  System.out.println(SQLMessage);
}
```

The alternative method for specifying properties in the connection string is to create a Properties() variable before issuing the connect command. To use the properties variable, you must include the java.util.Properties library. The following code illustrates how properties can be used.

```
import java.sql.*;
import java.lang.*;
import java.util.Properties;

String url = "jdbc:derby:YMLD";
Properties properties = new Properties();
properties.put("user", "APP");
properties.put("password", "APP");
properties.put("retrieveMessagesFromServerOnGetMessage", "true");
Connection conn = DriverManager.getConnection(url, properties);
```

Connecting with DB2 JDBC Drivers

When connecting to an Apache Derby Network server, an application needs to load a connection URL that is specific to the network server. In addition, a remote connection requires a user name and a password. If authentication has not been set up in Apache Derby, any user name and password can be used, and they are ignored. Refer to Chapter 7, "Security," for more information on security in Apache Derby.

The URL needed to access the network server is:

```
jdbc:derby:net://<server>[:<port>]/<databaseName>
    :user=<value>;password=<value>;
    [<Apache Derby URL attribute>=<value> [;...]]
    [:<Universal Driver attribute>=<value>; [...;]]
```

The syntax for connection to the network server differs slightly from the syntax used to connect to Apache Derby running in embedded mode. After the database name and attributes, you can include Apache Derby attributes, followed by attributes for the DB2 JDBC driver. The database name, Apache Derby, and JDBC driver attributes are separated by colons. The final JDBC attribute must include a semicolon at the end. The values for these different attributes are listed in the following section.

Server Name

The server name is the name of the machine on which the server is running. This value can be the name of the machine (for example, `DERBY`) or its address (for example, `127.0.0.1`). Unless the network server was started with the `-h` option, or the `derby.drda.host` property is set, this value should be `localhost`.

By default, the Apache Derby Network servers will only listen on the local host. Clients must use the `localhost` host name to connect. By default, clients cannot access the network server from another host. To enable connections from other hosts, you can set the `derby.drda.host` property, or you can start the network server with the `-h` option in the `java org.apache.derby.drda.NetworkServerControl start` command.

In the following example, the server will only listen on the local host, and clients cannot access the server from another host:

```
java org.apache.derby.drda.NetworkServerControl start
```

In the next example, the server runs on host machine `pook.apache.org`, and also listens for clients from other hosts. Clients should specify the server in the URL or DataSource as `pook.apache.org`:

```
java org.apache.derby.drda.NetworkServerControl start -h pook.apache.org
```

To start the network server so that it will listen on all interfaces, start with an IP address of `0.0.0.0`, as follows:

```
java org.apache.derby.drda.NetworkServerControl start -h 0.0.0.0
```

A server started with this IP address will listen to client requests that originate from both `localhost` and other machines.

Port Number

The port number represents the port to which the network server is listening. The default value is 1527. If the network server is started with a different port number, the corresponding catalog entry for the database must use that same port number. Otherwise, the connection will fail.

Database Name

The database name represents the name of the database to which you are connecting. The maximum length of a database name is 18 characters. If path information is associated with a database, double quotation marks must be used to enclose the path information in the database name. Alternately, you can specify path information by setting the `derby.system.home` property in either the `derby.properties` file or in the Java environment when starting the network server.

Apache Derby Attributes

The Apache Derby database options follow the server and database names. Each option must be terminated with a semicolon, and the database name must be separated from the options by a colon.

Two attributes, user and password, are required in this string. Without a suitable user or password, the Apache Derby connection will not work. If no authentication has been set up for the database, any user and password combination is allowed. For instance, the following string would be valid, even if user `APP` did not exist:

```
jdbc:derby:net://localhost/YMLD
    :user=APP;password=APP;
```

Universal Driver Attributes

The DB2 Universal JDBC Driver supports a number of optional database connection URL attributes. The DB2 Universal JDBC Driver requires that you set the Universal Driver user and password attributes to non-null values. Here's a list of the DB2 Universal JDBC Driver attributes available to you when running the network server:

- `user`—User name (required by the Universal JDBC Driver)
- `password`—User password (required by the Universal JDBC Driver)
- `portNumber`—The TCP/IP port number where the network server listens for connection requests to this data source. The default is 1527.
- `retrieveMessagesFromServerOnGetMessage`—Specifies that error messages from the server are to be displayed. The default is false.

- readOnly—Creates a read-only connection. The default is false.
- logWriter—The character output stream to which all logging and trace messages for the database are written. The data type of this property is java.io.PrinterWriter. The default value is null, which means that no logs or trace messages for the database are written.
- traceLevel—Specifies the granularity of logging messages to the logWriter property.

  This traceLevel value can be any of the following:

  TRACE_NONE
  TRACE_CONNECTION_CALLS
  TRACE_STATEMENT_CALLS
  TRACE_RESULT_SET_CALLS
  TRACE_DRIVER_CONFIGURATION
  TRACE_CONNECTS
  TRACE_DRDA_FLOWS
  TRACE_RESULT_SET_META_DATA
  TRACE_PARAMETER_META_DATA
  TRACE_DIAGNOSTICS
  TRACE_SQLJ
  TRACE_ALL

  To specify more than one value at a time, use the "or" operator (|) to combine them.
- traceFile—Specifies the name of a file to which the DB2 Universal JDBC Driver writes trace information. The data type of this property is String. The traceFile property is an alternative to the logWriter property for directing the output trace stream to a file.
- securityMechanism—Specifies what type of security mechanism is to be used.
- deferPrepares—Specifies whether to defer prepare operations until runtime. The data type of this property is boolean. The default is true for Universal Type 4 Connectivity. Deferring prepare operations can reduce network delays. However, if you defer prepare operations, you need to ensure that input data types match Apache Derby table column types.

There are two options that might be of interest to an application developer. The readOnly option will prevent the application from updating any tables in the database, and the retrieve-MessagesFromServerOnGetMessage option will retrieve the full SQL error messages from the server, rather than just the error code. This option is extremely useful when the reason for the error code is unknown, and the text of the message might be more meaningful.

The retrieveMessagesFromServerOnGetMessage is off by default because the IBM DB2 Universal JDBC Driver must invoke a separate stored procedure to get the message text. This will add overhead to the application when message text needs to be retrieved. This will be useful during the debugging of an application, but you may want to turn it off when the application has been placed into production.

The following code shows how to set these two options:

```
jdbc:derby:net://localhost/YMLD
   :user=APP;password=APP;
   :readOnly=true;retrieveMessagesFromServerOnGetMessage=true;
```

For example, the following error would be returned if a query could not find a particular table:

```
Error = 42X05
DB2 SQL error: SQLCODE: -1, SQLSTATE: 42X05, SQLERRMC:
PRODUCTIONSX  42X05
```

However, if the retrieveMessagesFromServerOnGetMessage option were set to true, the following message would be returned instead:

```
Error = 42X05
Table 'PRODUCTIONSX' does not exist.
```

The following sample application connects to the YMLD database using a network connection to the database. This example assumes that the database is on the local host rather than on an external machine.

```
Connection conn = null;
String DerbyDriver = "com.ibm.db2.jcc.DB2Driver";
String DatabaseConnection =
   "jdbc:derby:net://localhost/YMLD" +
   ":user=app;password=app" +
   ":retrieveMessagesFromServerOnGetMessage=true;" ;

try {
  Class.forName(DerbyDriver).newInstance();
}
catch (Exception NoDriver) {
  System.out.println("Derby driver not found: " + DerbyDriver);
  NoDriver.printStackTrace();
  System.exit(1);
}

try {
  conn = DriverManager.getConnection(DatabaseConnection);
  ...
}
```

```
catch (SQLException se) {
  String SQLState = se.getSQLState();
  String SQLMessage = se.getMessage();
  System.out.println("Error = "+SQLState);
  System.out.println(SQLMessage);
}
```

Allocating Statements

After successfully loading a driver and connecting to the database, the application can begin issuing some dynamic SQL statements.

Dynamic SQL statements are those statements that your application builds and executes at runtime. These statements are built and typically only used once. The application builds the SQL statement as a series of strings and then submits the statement for processing.

The first step in executing dynamic SQL is to allocate a statement. In other programming environments, this is sometimes referred to as getting a statement handle. This statement will be used for executing the SQL statements.

```
Connection conn = null;
Statement stmt = null;

conn = DriverManager.getConnection("jdbc:derby:YMLD");
stmt = conn.createStatement();
```

The variable stmt is assigned a statement handle that will be used for subsequent execution of SQL statements.

resultSetType and *resultSetCurrency*

The createStatement() method includes two additional parameters: resultSetType and resultSetCurrency. These parameters influence how a result set is handled by Apache Derby. A result set is the set of rows that is returned by a SELECT statement. By default, result sets have a forward scrollable cursor (TYPE_FORWARD_ONLY). A forward cursor is used for sequentially retrieving rows from a database.

Applications that need to retrieve rows from the result set in a random fashion would use a scrollable cursor (TYPE_SCROLL_INSENSITIVE). This method has much more flexibility than the default forward scrollable cursor, but it requires more logic in the application.

Whenever the createStatement() is specified with a resultSetType, the resultSetCurrency must also be specified. CONCUR_READ_ONLY is the only value for this parameter that is acceptable. The CONCUR_UPDATABLE option is also allowed as a value, but Apache Derby will issue a warning and set the value to CONCUR_READ_ONLY. A future release of Apache Derby will lift this restriction.

The following example sets the statement to have a scrollable cursor with the read-only attribute:

```
conn = DriverManager.getConnection("jdbc:derby:YMLD");
s = conn.createStatement(ResultSet.TYPE_SCROLL_INSENSITIVE,
                         ResultSet.CONCUR_READ_ONLY);
rs = s.executeQuery( "SELECT Production_Title FROM Productions");
```

Note that both of these parameter constants require the use of `ResultSet` as the interface name.

Closing Statements

When an application is finished using a statement, it is good practice to close the statement to free resources in the application and in the database. A statement is closed using the `close` method:

```
Statement s = conn.createStatement();
...
s.close();
```

Additional Statement Options

A statement can have additional options associated with it. There are four methods that are supported from a call perspective but that have no effect in Apache Derby. These methods are `getFetchDirection()`, `getFetchSize()`, `setFetchDirection()`, and `setFetchSize()`.
The remaining methods are:

- `void addBatch(String sql)`
  This method allows a programmer to batch a number of statements together in one call to the database. More details on this can be found in the section on Batch Processing.

- `void clearBatch()`
  After a set of statements executes in batch mode, the statements must be cleared before new statements can be added.

- `int[] executeBatch()`
  This method will send the entire set of SQL statements to the database engine for processing.

- `int getMaxFieldSize()`
  This method returns the size of the largest column in the result set. This information can be used to allocate any arrays or buffers that will be used to transfer information from the database to the application.

- `void getMaxRows()`

  This method returns the maximum number of rows that a result set can return. This is not equivalent to the number of rows that an SQL statement has produced.

- `void setEscapeProcessing(boolean enable)`

  This method turns on JDBC escape syntax processing. Escape processing is meant to allow an application developer to create SQL that will port across other database implementations. Some of these escape sequences are useful (like the date and time formats) but not strictly necessary to use Apache Derby. When using escape processing, the following strings are interpreted as described:

  - `{ d 'YYYY-MM-DD' }` Date field.
  - `{ t 'hh:mm:ss' }` Time field. Note that hh is in 24-hour clock format.
  - `{ ts 'YYYY-MM-DD hh:mm:ss.fff }` Timestamp field. The fff represents millseconds, and is not required as part of the timestamp field.
  - `{ ? = call storedprocedurename() }` Call a stored procedure or function. This syntax is used when preparing SQL `CALL` statements that require parameters be passed to them. This escape sequence can also be used to return results from a user-defined function.
  - `{ escape 'char' }` Escape character for `LIKE` clause. The standard `LIKE` clause in Apache Derby already supports the `ESCAPE` clause natively.
  - `{ oj }` Outer Join. This syntax is not required because outer joins are natively supported by the SQL.
  - `{ fn }` The `fn` keyword allows the use of several scalar functions. The function name follows the keyword. Any Apache Derby built-in function is allowed in this syntax.

- `void setMaxFieldSize(int max)`

  This method sets the maximum size for a column in a result set. This option has no effect on `BLOB`s and `CLOB`s.

- `void setMaxRows()`

  This method is an extremely useful option; it limits the total size of a result set, which can prevent a query from returning thousands of rows.

Executing Dynamic SQL

SQL statements can be submitted to the database for execution. The simplest form of SQL statement to handle within an application is a Data Manipulation Language (DML) statement, such as `INSERT`, `UPDATE`, or `DELETE`. Such statements return no rows from the database. With DML, the program is either creating or operating on an object. An `SQLException` will be raised if there is an error in executing the statement.

The following code fragment will issue a SET SCHEMA statement to the database for execution:

```
Connection conn = null;
Statement stmt = null;

try {
  conn = DriverManager.getConnection("jdbc:derby:YMLD");
  stmt = conn.createStatement();
  stmt.execute("set schema 'APP'");
}
```

The stmt.execute method will immediately execute the SQL statement that is specified in the argument. In this example, the database is being asked to set the schema to 'APP'.

A try block should always be placed around any SQL statements that can cause an error. Although it is unlikely that your SQL syntax would be incorrect, there is always the possibility that the underlying objects have been dropped or are missing. In addition, SQL that is submitted directly by a user can be error-prone.

The types of SQL that can be executed using the execute method include SET, INSERT, DELETE, UPDATE, CREATE, DROP, ALTER, CALL, VALUES, LOCK, and DECLARE statements. It is also possible to issue SELECT statements, although you will probably want to retrieve the results of the query. The execute method does not return results other than throwing SQL-Exceptions or SQLWarnings.

There are two additional forms of the execute method: executeUpdate() and execute-Query(); executeQuery() is best suited for retrieving result sets from a SELECT statement. This form of the execute method is discussed in detail in the section on retrieving query results.

The executeUpdate() method is used primarily for INSERT, UPDATE, and DELETE statements. The execute method can also be used to issue these statements, but the application must query the SQLWarnings method to determine whether a statement has changed any rows. The following section describes different methods of trapping errors from SQL statements. The difficulty with UPDATE statements is that updating zero rows returns a warning, not an error.

The executeUpdate() method returns the number of rows inserted, updated, or deleted as a result of the SQL statement. This allows the application to determine the next step to take without having to query the SQLWarnings method and check the SQLSTATE returned by the database. This technique helps to simplify the logic required in an application. The following example illustrates the use of the executeUpdate() method:

```
try {
  Statement s = conn.createStatement();
  rowsReturned = s.executeUpdate(
```

```
    "UPDATE PRODUCTIONS SET PRODUCTION_NO = 10 WHERE PRODUCTION_NO = 0");
    System.out.println("Rows updated=" + rowsReturned);
    s.close();
}
```

```
Rows updated=0
```

Trapping *SQLExceptions*

All SQL statements should have some form of `try` block around them. This will help the application trap any errors that can arise from improper SQL, missing database objects, or general database errors. The errors generated by SQL statements are referred to as SQLCODEs or SQLSTATEs. SQLCODEs arc used by other database managers, but the standard errors in Apache Derby are handled as SQLSTATEs.

All SQL that completes successfully will have a `'00000'` SQLSTATE. However, there might be situations in which a statement causes a warning that is acceptable to the application. For this reason, the SQLSTATE and error codes need to be examined to determine whether the application can continue running. An example of an error that can be safely ignored is SQL exception XJ015. A clean shutdown of Apache Derby will raise this exception.

There are three methods available from within an exception call to generate diagnostic information. The getMessage(), getSQLState(), and getErrorCode() methods can return valuable information to the user about what caused the statement to fail.

getMessage()

This method returns the full text of the error message. To get the full error description when using a network server connection, the `retrieveMessagesFromServerOnGetMessage` setting must be true. The default is false, which means that only SQLSTATE information is returned with some additional error parameter markers.

For example, the following error would be returned if a table was not found during the execution of a query:

```
Error = 42X05
DB2 SQL error: SQLCODE: -1, SQLSTATE: 42X05, SQLERRMC:
PRODUCTIONSX  42X05
```

If the message option were set to true, the following message would be returned instead:

```
Error = 42X05
Table 'PRODUCTIONSX' does not exist.
```

getSQLState()

This method returns the SQLSTATE value reported by Apache Derby. The SQLSTATE is a 5-character code, so you cannot assume that this will be a numeric value. Some of the more common SQLSTATEs are listed in Table 9-2. The values within braces { } represent the names of objects associated with the statement.

Table 9-2   SQLSTATE Values

SQLSTATE	Description
00000	Statement completed successfully.
02000	No row was found for FETCH, UPDATE, or DELETE, or the result of a query is an empty table.
04501	Database connection refused.
08004	User authorization error.
22001	A truncation error was encountered trying to shrink {0} "{1}" to length {2}.
23502	Column "{0}" cannot accept a null value.
23503	{2} on table "{1}" caused a violation of foreign key constraint "{0}" for key {3}. The statement has been rolled back.
23505	The statement was aborted because it would have caused a duplicate key value in a unique or primary key constraint or unique index identified by "{0}" defined on "{1}".
23513	The check constraint "{1}" was violated while performing an INSERT or UPDATE on table "{0}".
38xxx	External routine exception. The SQL standard reserves 38001–38004 and 38sxx, where s is '0–4' or 'A–H'. Derby throws 38000 if the method does not throw a specific SQLSTATE.
40001	A lock could not be obtained due to a deadlock, cycle of locks & waiters is: {0}. The selected victim is XID: {1}.

getErrorCode()

Apache Derby database exceptions are classified by severity. The severity of an SQLException is available through the getErrorCode() method call. Note that the error code defines the severity of the error and is not unique to each exception. The severities are summarized in Table 9-3.

Table 9-3   ErrorCode Values

ERROR CODE	Description
0	No error occurred, or the system was unable to determine the severity.
10000	STATEMENT_SEVERITY—The effects of the current statement, if any, on persistent data are undone.
20000	TRANSACTION_SEVERITY—The effects of the current transaction on persistent data are undone; a rollback is performed.
30000	SESSION_SEVERITY—A rollback is performed, and the current session is terminated; this closes the current connection.
40000	DATABASE_SEVERITY—A rollback is performed, the current session is terminated, and the database is closed.
50000	SYSTEM_SEVERITY—The system is shut down; all uncommitted transactions are rolled back; this error code is associated with internal errors that cause the system to shut down.

Using the ErrorCode can be an alternative to SQLSTATE, but it will not be as specific. However, this error code is useful when determining whether additional steps need to be taken to re-execute the query. For instance, an ErrorCode of 40000 indicates a severe database error that would be difficult to correct from within an application.

Multiple *SQLExceptions*

Apache Derby sometimes returns multiple SQLExceptions. Use the getNextException() chain to process all of the exceptions. The first exception is always the most severe exception, with SQL92 Standard exceptions preceding those that are specific to Apache Derby. Usually the most severe error is the one that the application should be dealing with, but for diagnostic purposes, it might be good practice to list all of the errors that occurred during the execution of an SQL statement.

```
catch (SQLException se) {
  while (se != null) {
    String SQLState = se.getSQLState();
    String SQLMessage = se.getMessage();
    System.out.println("Error = "+SQLState);
    System.out.println(SQLMessage);
    se = se.getNextException();
  }
}
```

SQLWarnings Versus *SQLExceptions*

Apache Derby can generate warnings in certain circumstances. A warning is generated if, for example, you try to connect to a database with the create attribute set to truc, but the database already exists. Aggregates such as SUM() also raise a warning if null values are encountered during the evaluation. A warning will also being raised if an UPDATE or a DELETE statement affects no rows.

The following code uses a catch statement to capture any errors that occur during the execution of an UPDATE statement.

```
try {
  conn = DriverManager.getConnection("jdbc:derby:YMLD");
  s = conn.createStatement();
  s.execute("UPDATE PRODUCTIONS SET PRODUCTION_NO = 10 WHERE
      PRODUCTION_NO = 0");
  s.close();
}

catch (SQLException se) {
  ...
}
```

There are no rows with a PRODUCTION_NO value of zero in the table. The UPDATE statement runs successfully, although it doesn't actually change any rows. From an SQL perspective, no SQLException is occurring. But to trap the fact that no rows were updated, a check against SQLWarning should have been used, in addition to the SQLException.

SQLWarnings are not trapped within a try block. Instead, the warning information must be examined after the SQL statement executes. This is handled through the use of the SQLWarning method.

```
SQLWarning sw = s.getWarnings();
```

SQLWarnings are similar to SQLExceptions because they inherit the same three methods: getSQLState(), getMessage(), and getErrorCode(). In addition, there can be multiple SQLWarnings in a statement, so there is a corresponding getNextWarning() method to cycle through all of the warnings that were raised.

The next example checks for warnings after execution of the UPDATE statement.

```
SQLWarning sw = null;

try {
  conn = DriverManager.getConnection("jdbc:derby:YMLD");
  s = conn.createStatement();
  s.execute("UPDATE PRODUCTIONS SET PRODUCTION_NO = 10 " +
            "WHERE PRODUCTION_NO = 0");
```

```
  sw = s.getWarnings();
  while (sw != null) {
    String SQLState = sw.getSQLState();
    String SQLMessage = sw.getMessage();
    System.out.println("Warning = "+SQLState);
    System.out.println(SQLMessage);
    System.out.println("ErrorCode="+sw.getErrorCode());
    sw = sw.getNextWarning();
  }
  s.close();
}
```

```
Warning = 02000
No row was found for FETCH, UPDATE or DELETE; or the result of a query
is an empty table.
ErrorCode=10000
```

Note that the example does not include the `catch` block. It is still good coding practice to include a `catch` block in the event that the statement fails for a completely unanticipated reason.

A simpler method for catching SQL warnings on `INSERT`, `UPDATE`, or `DELETE` statements is to use the `executeUpdate` method. This method returns the number of rows that were affected by the SQL, and the program can then determine what action to take if no rows were updated.

An `SQLWarning` will remain in affect until another SQL statement is issued. If you want to clear any warnings that might exist, use the `clearWarnings()` method.

Retrieving Query Results

At some point an application will want to retrieve some data from the database. The method that returns an answer set is `executeQuery()`. This method takes an SQL string as its argument and attempts to create a result set from the database.

```
ResultSet rs = null;
rs = s.executeQuery("SELECT Production_Title FROM Productions");
```

A result set will contain a number of rows, with each row containing the columns that are specified in the select list. A result set is very similar to an array of records. For instance, the previous example returns 10 rows, but with only one column (Production_Title) being returned from the Productions table.

To retrieve the values from the result set, a simple `while` loop can be created to process all of the rows.

```
rs = s.executeQuery( "SELECT Production_Title FROM Productions");
System.out.println( "Production Title");
```

```
while (rs.next()) {
  String production_title = rs.getString("PRODUCTION_TITLE");
  System.out.println( production_title);
}
rs.close();
```

The next () method moves a virtual pointer through a result set. This method returns true when it successfully moves to the next row. By default, the cursor points to a position before the first row. The initial call to the next () method moves it to the first row in the result set. An application could make repeated calls to next () until all of the rows in the result set were processed.

Apache Derby supports a number of other positioning calls in JDBC. The list of methods available is summarized in Figure 9-2.

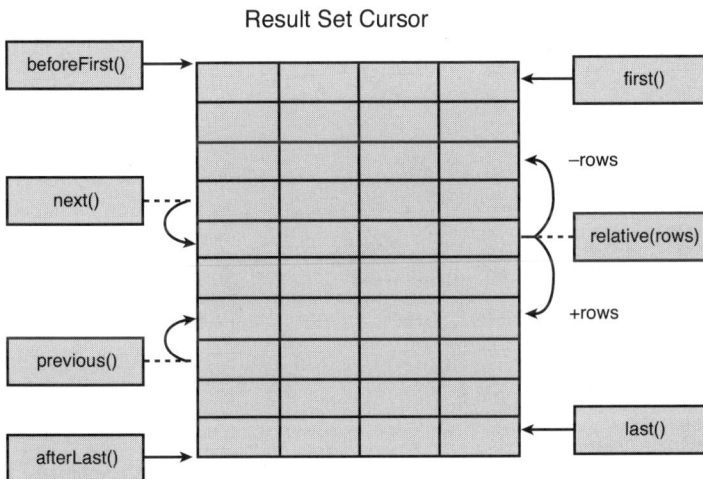

Figure 9-2 Result Set Cursor

An application can use any of these methods to position the cursor in the result set. Although next () is probably the most common method to use, the other methods allow the application to move to other records in the result set without access to any of the prior records. A summary of all of these methods follows.

- beforeFirst ()—The beforeFirst () method positions the result set cursor before the first row. At this position, none of the data is available. This method is useful when an application needs to reset the cursor to the beginning of the result set so that a next () loop functions properly.
- first ()—The first () method places the cursor at the first row in the result set. The application can subsequently access the data in the first row.
- last ()—The last () method places the cursor at the last row in the result set.

- `afterLast()`—When the `next()` method is called and the result set is exhausted, the cursor ends up in the `afterLast()` position.

- `next()`—The `next()` method is used to navigate through the result set one row at a time. If a row is available, `next()` returns true; otherwise, it returns false. If the database has been configured with autocommit on, the `next()` call closes the cursor to the result set after it scrolls past the last row. This is the only method that will implicitly close the result set. Even though this is the default behavior for Apache Derby, applications should issue an explicit `close()` against the result set.

- `previous()`—The `previous()` method goes back to the previous row in the result set. If the cursor is already on the first row, the `previous()` method puts the cursor into the `beforeFirst()` state.

- `relative()`—The `relative()` method gives the application a quick way of moving forward or backward in a result set. The `relative()` method takes one integer argument, which indicates the positive (forward) or negative (backward) movement that the cursor should take.

- `isAfterLast()`, `isBeforeFirst()`, `isFirst()`, `isLast()`—Each one of these methods returns true if its condition is met. These methods are useful for an interactive application. You might be examining one row at a time, randomly viewing rows in a result set. The behavior of the application might need to change when it reaches the last row in the result set. The `next()` call would not be appropriate in an application like this, so these methods can help determine when the cursor has reached the end of the result set.

None of the positioning functions will cause an `SQLException` to occur when they attempt to move the cursor beyond the end or before the beginning of a result set. An exception will only occur when one of the get routines (`getString()`, for example) tries to access the row in the result set.

The following application illustrates the use of these various methods to move around a result set, and it demonstrates some of the errors that will occur if attempts are made to access records that are outside the limits. Key statements are numbered and are discussed next.

```
01  public static void whereAmI(ResultSet rs) throws
    SQLException {
        System.out.println("isBeforeFirst=" + rs.isBeforeFirst() + " " +
                        "isFirst=" + rs.isFirst() + " " +
                        "isLast=" + rs.isLast() + " " +
                        "isAfterLast=" + rs.isAfterLast());
    }


02  conn = DriverManager.getConnection("jdbc:derby:YMLD");
03  s = conn.createStatement(ResultSet.TYPE_SCROLL_INSENSITIVE,
                        ResultSet.CONCUR_READ_ONLY);
```

```
04  rs = s.executeQuery( "SELECT Production_Title FROM Productions");
05  whereAmI(rs);

    try { // View record without positioning with next()
      System.out.println("Trying to access a record before a next()");
06    title = rs.getString("PRODUCTION_TITLE");
    }
    catch (SQLException se) {
07    System.out.println("No next:  "+ se.getMessage());
    }


08  rs.next(); // Next record successful
09  whereAmI(rs);
10  title = rs.getString("PRODUCTION_TITLE");
    System.out.println("next():    " + title);
11  rs.last(); // Last record successful
12  whereAmI(rs);
    title = rs.getString("PRODUCTION_TITLE");
    System.out.println("last():    " + title);
13  rs.next(); // Skip past end
14  whereAmI(rs);
15  rs.first();
16  title = rs.getString("PRODUCTION_TITLE");
    System.out.println("first():  " + title);
17  rs.relative(3);
    title = rs.getString("PRODUCTION_TITLE");
    System.out.println("+3 recs:  " + title);
18  rs.relative(-3);
    title = rs.getString("PRODUCTION_TITLE");
    System.out.println("-3 recs:  " + title);
19  System.out.println("Going past end of record set");
    try {
20    rs.relative(10);
21    whereAmI(rs);
22    title = rs.getString("PRODUCTION_TITLE");
    }
    catch (SQLException se) {
      System.out.println("Too far  :  "+ se.getMessage());
    }
```

The following shows sample output from this application.

```
isBeforeFirst=true isFirst=false isLast=false isAfterLast=false
Trying to access a record before a next()
No next:  Invalid cursor state - no current row.
isBeforeFirst=false isFirst=true isLast=false isAfterLast=false
next() :    Lilly of the Valley
isBeforeFirst=false isFirst=false isLast=true isAfterLast=false
last() :    Naughty or Nice?
isBeforeFirst=false isFirst=false isLast=false isAfterLast=true
first():  Lilly of the Valley
+3 recs:  Icing the Puck
-3 recs:  Lilly of the Valley
Going past end of record set
isBeforeFirst=false isFirst=false isLast=false isAfterLast=true
Too far  :  Invalid cursor state - no current row.
```

Following are some notes that are associated with the numbered lines of code in this application.

- [01] `public static void whereAmI(ResultSet rs) throws SQLException`
  The `whereAmI()` method is used to track the four Boolean functions: `isFirst()`, `isLast()`, `isBeforeFirst()`, and `isAfterLast()`. This method simplifies the development of the application code and illustrates a way that result sets or statements can be passed to other methods to handle certain conditions.

- [02] `conn = DriverManager.getConnection("jdbc:derby:YMLD");`
  A connection is made to the YMLD (Your Momma Loves Drama) database.

- [03] `s = conn.createStatement(ResultSet.TYPE_SCROLL_INSENSITIVE, ...)`
  To use the `first()`, `last()`, and other positioning methods, the statement must be defined with `TYPE_SCROLL_INSENSITIVE`. If the statement is not defined this way, the application ends with an XJ061 error: The `isBeforeFirst()` method is only allowed on scrollable cursors.

- [04] `rs = s.executeQuery("SELECT Production_Title FROM Productions");`
  This initial `executeQuery()` will retrieve the result set from the database. All of the subsequent methods will work on the result set that was retrieved at this time.

- [05] `whereAmI(rs);`
  The first call to `whereAmI()` causes `isBeforeFirst()` to return true. At this time, the cursor is not pointing to a valid row in the result set. To move to the first row, call the `next()` method.

- [06-07] title = rs.getString("PRODUCTION_TITLE");
  The getString() method is part of the try block. This method will fail because the cursor is not on a valid row. The catch will trap the error and return a message that there is an invalid cursor state.
- [08] rs.next();
  The cursor moves to the next row, which in this instance is the first row of the result set.
- [09] whereAmI(rs);
  The whereAmI() method shows that isFirst() is now true. At this time, the application can issue a get statement to retrieve information from the row in the result set.
- [10] title = rs.getString("PRODUCTION_TITLE");
  The getString() method retrieves the value of the Production_Title column in the current row.
- [11] rs.last();
  The last() method moves the cursor to the last row in the result set.
- [12] whereAmI(rs);
  The whereAmI() method now shows that the cursor is on the last row, because isLast() is true. When isLast() is true, data can still be read from the result set.
- [13] rs.next();
  The next() method now takes the cursor beyond the end of the result set. No SQL-Exception is raised when this occurs.
- [14] whereAmI(rs);
  The whereAmI() method shows that isAfterLast() is true. If an attempt were now made to retrieve a value from the result set, an SQLException would be raised.
- [15] rs.first();
  A call to first() resets the cursor to the beginning of the result set. In this case, the cursor is already on the first row, not on beforeFirst(). This is important if you are using the next() method to scroll through the list. If you use next() immediately after first(), the application bypasses the initial row.
- [16] title = rs.getString("PRODUCTION_TITLE");
  The application prints the first row of the PRODUCTIONS table.
- [17] rs.relative(3);
  The relative() method moves the cursor in either a positive (forward) or negative (backward) direction through the result set. This particular call moves the cursor forward by three rows from the current row. Because the cursor was on the first row, this places the cursor on the fourth row in the result set.
- [18] rs.relative(-3);
  The relative() method is used again to move three rows back to the original row on which we started.

- [19-22] `rs.relative(10);`

  This method forces the cursor to go beyond the end of the result set. Moving the cursor to an invalid position does not trigger an `SQLException`. The exception occurs on line 22, where the application attempts to retrieve something from the result set.

Retrieving Column Values

Many of the examples up to this point use the `getString()` method to turn a column value into a Java data type. As one might expect, `getString()` returns the contents of the column in the result set as a character string. There are a number of these methods, but before discussing the purpose of `getX()` methods, some understanding of SQL and Java data types is required.

Most SQL data types have a corresponding Java data type, and the following table lists all of the types available in Apache Derby, as well as the corresponding `getX()` methods associated with their retrieval.

Table 9-4 SQL versus Java Data Types

SQL Data Type	Java.sql.Types	getX() Method
SMALLINT	SMALLINT	getShort()
INTEGER	INTEGER	getInt()
BIGINT	BIGINT	getLong()
DECIMAL	DECIMAL or NUMERIC	getBigDecimal()
REAL	REAL	getFloat()
DOUBLE PRECISION	DOUBLE, FLOAT	getDouble(), getFloat()
DATE	DATE	getDate()
TIME	TIME	getTime()
TIMESTAMP	TIMESTAMP	getTimestamp()
CHAR	CHAR	getString()
VARCHAR	VARCHAR	getString()
LONG VARCHAR	LONG VARCHAR	getString()
CLOB	CLOB (JDBC 2.0 and up)	getClob()
BLOB	BLOB (JDBC 2.0 and up)	getBlob()
CHAR FOR BIT DATA	BINARY	getBytes()
VARCHAR FOR BIT DATA	VARBINARY	getBytes()
LONG VARCHAR FOR BIT DATA	LONGVARBINARY	getBytes()

All of these getX() methods are relatively similar in usage and are discussed in the following. The getBlob(), getClob(), and getByte() methods are slightly different and have separate sections dedicated to them.

getX() Usage

getX() methods take as input the name or ordinal of a column in the result set and retrieve the data in the specified format. For example, the following SELECT statement specifies three columns for the result set.

```
SELECT
  Production_No, Production_Title, Production_Start
FROM
  Productions;
```

To retrieve the Production_Title column into a string field, you could use the getString() method:

```
string prodTitle = rs.getString("Production_Title");
```

If the column name is not found, an SQLException is raised:

```
Error = S0022
Column 'PRODUCTION_TITLES' not found.
```

Another way to specify a column in the result set is to use an ordinal number. This refers to the position of the column in the result set. Column numbers begin at 1 for the first column in the select list and continue until the end of the list. In some cases, this might be the only way to access a column value. Consider the following SQL statement:

```
SELECT
  Production_No, COUNT(*) AS TOTAL_PROD
FROM
  Performances
GROUP BY Production_No;
```

An AS clause has been added to identify the COUNT(*) calculation. If this AS clause were not present, the database would have no way of distinguishing the result column. In other words, there would be no name for this column. Instead, the application can retrieve the second column value with the getInt(2) method.

```
int perfCount = 0;

rs = s.executeQuery( "SELECT Production_No, COUNT(*) AS TOTAL_PROD " +
                     " FROM Performances " +
                     " GROUP BY Production_No");
```

```
rs.next();
perfCount = rs.getInt(2);
System.out.println("Count = " + perfCount);
rs.next();
perfCount = rs.getInt("TOTAL_PROD");
System.out.println("Count = " + perfCount);
```

Both of the `getInt()` calls are equivalent and can be used interchangeably. However, the developer must be aware of the column names because an `SQLException` will be thrown if the column name is incorrect.

Mismatched Data Types

Normally a column in a result set would be retrieved to a similar column type in the Java application. There could be circumstances in which it would make sense to translate the object into something else to make it easier to manipulate. For example, an application might need to retrieve a date field but use it as part of a string rather than as a real date value. Unless the value being retrieved needs to be updated, converting it into a character string might be the easiest way to manipulate it.

The following SQL returns the start date of the first production in the YMLD database:

```
SELECT Production_Start FROM Productions WHERE Production_NO = 1;
```

The application wants to retrieve this date as a character string, so the `getString()` method is used:

```
rs = s.executeQuery( "SELECT Production_Start FROM Productions " +
                " WHERE Production_No=1");

rs.next();
String startDate = rs.getString(1);
System.out.println("StartDate = " + startDate);
```

The variable receiving the column value must match the data type of the `getX()` method; otherwise, the method will not compile properly.

Null Values

Null values need to be treated differently in Java than in SQL because the Java language does not have the corresponding concept. A Java null is completely different from an SQL `NULL`. There are two methods for detecting a null value that is returned in a result set. The one that works across all data types is `wasnull()`.

```
seat_no = rs.getInt("SEAT_NO");
if (rs.wasNull()) { ... }
```

This method should be used immediately after a getX() call to determine whether or not a column had a null value in it. The following example illustrates why the wasnull() method needs to be used to determine whether or not a column is null.

```
CREATE TABLE testnull
  (
  c1 int,
  c2 int,
  c3 varchar(1),
  c4 varchar(1)
  );

INSERT INTO testnull VALUES (NULL, 1, NULL, 'A');

SELECT * FROM testnull;

C1             |C2            |C3   |C4
--------------------------------------
NULL           |1            |NULL|A

1 row selected
```

The following code fragment prints the values that are retrieved from the table and whether or not they are null:

```
conn = DriverManager.getConnection("jdbc:derby:YMLD");
s = conn.createStatement();
rs = s.executeQuery( "SELECT C1, C2, C3, C4 FROM TESTNULL");
rs.next();
int c1 = rs.getInt("C1");
System.out.println("C1 Value="+c1 + " null=" + rs.wasNull());
int c2 = rs.getInt("C2");
System.out.println("C2 Value="+c2 + " null=" + rs.wasNull());
String c3 = rs.getString("C3");
System.out.println("C3 Value="+c3 + " null=" + rs.wasNull());
String c4 = rs.getString("C4");
System.out.println("C4 Value="+c4 + " null=" + rs.wasNull());
```

When executed, the code produces the following results:

```
C1 Value=0 null=true
C2 Value=1 null=false
C3 Value=null null=true
C4 Value=A null=false
```

Primitive Java data types, such as `integer`, are initialized to zero even when a value is not being returned from a column. String data types can be null, so this could be a way of determining whether or not a column was null. The `wasnull()` method continues to be the best way to determine the null values in a column because it works regardless of the data type being retrieved.

getByte() Usage

All strings within Apache Derby (CHAR, VARCHAR, or LONG VARCHAR) are stored in Unicode. The Unicode character encoding standard is a fixed-length character encoding scheme. Each character is 16 bits (2 bytes) wide, regardless of the language, and the resulting 65,536 code elements are sufficient for encoding most of the characters in the world's major languages.

Normally this will not impact the way your application sees the data because in Apache Derby, the data is stored in Unicode and manipulated as Unicode by a Java application. However, there will be instances in which you want to store data in a format that is not tied to Unicode encoding. For example, an application might need to store and retrieve binary data that contains the image of an employee.

To store and manipulate binary fields, an additional modifier to the character data types (CHAR, VARCHAR, and LONG VARCHAR) called FOR BIT DATA is available. Character columns that have this modifier in their definition are retrieved using the `getBytes()` method. The corresponding Java data type needs to be a byte array with sufficient storage for the field being retrieved. The `getBytes()` method is still required to retrieve a single-byte value.

```
byte [] bValue = new byte [1];
bValue = rs.getBytes(1);
System.out.println("Value=" + bValue[0]);
```

getBlob() and getClob() Usage

There are two varieties of LOBs: binary large objects (BLOBs) and character large objects (CLOBs). These objects are used to store large amounts of binary or character data, respectively. When a large column value needs to be retrieved, the application needs to use the `getBlob()` or `getClob()` method. These two methods provide a logical pointer to the large object, rather than a complete copy of the object. Usually, only portions of a LOB need to be processed anyway!

The retrieval methods supported by a BLOB object include:

- `InputStream getBinaryStream()`
  This method materializes the BLOB value as a byte stream containing binary bytes.

- `String getBytes(long position, int length)`
  This method retrieves a portion of the BLOB back to the application as a set of bytes. The byte array starts at `position` and includes `length` bytes.

- `long length()`
  This method returns the length of the string in bytes.
- `long position(byte[] bytepattern, long start)`
  This method returns the location of `bytepattern` in the `BLOB` object. The position at which to start searching is specified by `start`.

The `CLOB` object has similar retrieval methods:

- `InputStream getAsciiStream(), getUnicodeStream()`
  The `getAsciiStream()` method materializes the `CLOB` value as a character stream containing ASCII bytes, whereas `getUnicodeStream()` returns the data as Unicode characters.
- `String getSubString(long position, int length)`
  This method retrieves a portion of the `CLOB` back to the application as a string. The string starts at `position` and includes `length` characters.
- `long length()`
  This method returns the length of the string in characters (not bytes).
- `long position(String searchstr, long start)`
  This method returns the location of `searchstr` in the `CLOB` object. The position at which to start searching is specified by `start`.

The `SEATMAP` table in the YMLD database is defined as follows:

```
CREATE TABLE SeatMap
  (
  Seat_No              INTEGER NOT NULL,
  Seat_View            BLOB(50K),
  PRIMARY KEY (Seat_No)
  );
```

This table contains the theater view from the seats. When patrons are selecting seats, they can browse the views from the seats to decide which positions are best for them. To retrieve the information from the Seat_View column, the best approach is to use the `getBinaryStream()` method to materialize the object directly to disk. In addition, the `length()` function can be used to determine whether or not the size of the object might exceed the space available. Although this isn't usually an issue for personal computers and servers, embedded systems might be more limited on disk space.

The following SQL retrieves the seat image from the database and places it into a file for further use.

```
conn = DriverManager.getConnection("jdbc:derby:YMLD");
s = conn.createStatement();
rs = s.executeQuery("SELECT SEAT_VIEW FROM SEATMAP WHERE SEAT_NO = 1");
```

```
if (rs.next()) {
   InputStream in = rs.getBinaryStream("SEAT_VIEW");
   FileOutputStream fileOut =
      new FileOutputStream(".\\copy.jpg");
   int bytesRead = 0;
   byte[] buffer = new byte[4096];
   while ((bytesRead = in.read(buffer)) != -1) {
     fileOut.write(buffer, 0, bytesRead);
   }
   fileOut.close();
}
rs.close();
s.close();
```

The getBinaryStream() method returns an InputStream that can be used to retrieve bytes from the BLOB object. The use of a buffer is recommended from an efficiency perspective, but data could be transferred from the object one byte at a time. The alternative way of retrieving the data is to use the getBytes() method. The section of code within the IF block is modified to create a buffer for the entire image. This is practical only for large objects that don't take up too much memory.

```
if (rs.next()) {
  Blob blobOut = rs.getBlob("SEAT_VIEW");
  int blobLength = (int) blobOut.length();
  byte[] completeImage = blobOut.getBytes(1, blobLength);
  FileOutputStream fileOut = new FileOutputStream (".\\copy.jpg");
  fileOut.write(completeImage, 0, blobLength);
}
fileOut.close();
```

If the application didn't have enough storage for the entire object, portions of the BLOB could be retrieved by specifying a smaller value on the getBytes() call and keeping track of the current position in the BLOB. Note that the first argument in getBytes() is the offset in the BLOB from which the retrieval will start. The offset always starts at one (not zero).

Dynamically Determining Result Sets

All of the examples up to this point have assumed that the developer knows what data is to be retrieved from a table. The SELECT statement columns are known beforehand, so the application can be written to handle the number of columns being retrieved, along with the data types required to accept the column values. However, some applications need to dynamically determine the columns being retrieved based on user input. Consider also the case in which a SELECT * is issued against a table. When a table is created, the columns that are retrieved by a SELECT * might be known. But over time, the design of the table might change, so the order and even the number of columns might be different. Errors will result if an application does not adapt to such changes.

To allow for dynamic answer sets, Apache Derby supports the ResultSetMetaData interface. A developer would use this interface after issuing an executeQuery() method to query the column types.

```
conn = DriverManager.getConnection("jdbc:derby:YMLD");
s = conn.createStatement();
rs = s.executeQuery("SELECT * FROM TESTNULL");
ResultSetMetaData md = rs.getMetaData();
```

ResultSetMetaData() returns a host of information about the answer set. The possible information that can be returned includes the following:

- getColumnCount()—Returns the number of columns in a result set. Typically this value would be used as part of a loop to examine each column individually. The column parameter for each getX() method is the index of the column in the result set. The column index always starts at 1.

- getColumnClassName(column)—Returns the fully qualified Java class name of the object. For an integer column, for example, this method would return java .language.integer.

- getColumnDisplaySize(column)—Returns the maximum width required to display the column.

- getColumnName(), getColumnLabel(column)—The getColumnName() method returns the actual name of the column, whereas getColumnLabel() returns a suggested name for the column. In Apache Derby these two names are the same.

- getPrecision(column), getScale(column)—The getPrecision() and getScale() methods normally apply to DECIMAL and NUMERIC columns. For example, a DEC(14,2) column would have a precision of 14 and a scale of 2. For non-numeric columns, the scale is zero, and precision is usually the size of the field (in bytes) or the number of digits in the field. This differs from getColumnDisplaySize(), which usually includes extra bytes for the sign, mantissa, exponent, and other numeric symbols.

  In certain cases, the precision can be zero. This usually indicates that the field size is unknown or dependent on other system settings that cannot be determined at this time.

- getTableName(column)—Returns the name of the table or view from which the column has come. It is possible that this value will be different for columns that are returned as the result of a join. In this case, the column will belong to only one of the tables in the FROM clause.

- isAutoIncrement(column)—Returns true if the column is an identity column that automatically increments during each insert operation.

- isCaseSensitive(column)—Returns true for all character columns (CHAR, VARCHAR, LONG VARCHAR, or CLOB), and false otherwise. Note that character columns with the FOR BIT DATA modifier are not considered case-sensitive.

- isCurrency(column)—Returns true for columns that can hold currency values. In Apache Derby, only DECIMAL and NUMERIC columns return true.

- isNullable(column)—Returns true if a column can have null values assigned to it.

- isSearchable(column)—Returns true if a column can be used in a WHERE clause. The practical use of this method is limited because any column in the select list, even a calculated column, can be used in a WHERE clause.

- isSigned(column)—Returns true for any numeric column that can have a sign. Essentially, this means that SMALLINT, INT, BIGINT, DECIMAL, NUMERIC, FLOAT, REAL, and DOUBLE return true.

- getCatalogName(), getSchemaName(), isDefinitelyWritable(), isRead-Only(), isWritable()—These methods either return nothing (null) or false.

The following example creates a table named ALLTYPES, and then the ResultSetMeta-Data methods are used to generate Table 9-5.

```
CREATE TABLE ALLTYPES
  (
  F_CHAR                CHAR(10),
  F_VARCHAR             VARCHAR(5),
  F_LONGVARCHAR         LONG VARCHAR,
  F_CHAR_BIT            CHAR(9) FOR BIT DATA,
  F_VARCHAR_BIT         VARCHAR(3) FOR BIT DATA,
  F_LONGVARCHAR_BIT     LONG VARCHAR FOR BIT DATA,
  F_BLOB                BLOB(10K),
  F_CLOB                CLOB(5K),
  F_SMALLINT            SMALLINT,
  F_INT                 INT,
  F_BIGINT              BIGINT,
  F_FLOAT               FLOAT,
  F_REAL                REAL,
  F_DOUBLE              DOUBLE,
  F_DECIMAL             DEC(11,4),
  F_NUMERIC             NUMERIC(12,2),
```

```
F_DATE                  DATE,
F_TIME                  TIME,
F_TIMESTAMP             TIMESTAMP,
F_NOTNULL               CHAR(1) NOT NULL,
F_AUTOINCREMENT         INT NOT NULL GENERATED ALWAYS AS IDENTITY
);
```

Table 9-5 *ResultSetMetaData* Results

Column	Display	Precision	Scale	Incr	Case	$	Null	Search	Signed
CHAR(10)	10	10	0	F	T	F	T	T	F
VARCHAR(5)	5	5	0	F	T	F	T	T	F
LONG VARCHAR	32700	32700	0	F	T	F	T	T	F
CHAR(9) BIT	18	9	0	F	F	F	T	T	F
VARCHAR(3) BIT	6	3	0	F	F	F	T	T	F
LONGVARCHAR BIT	65400	32700	0	F	F	F	T	T	F
BLOB(10K)	20480	10240	0	F	F	F	T	T	F
CLOB(5K)	5120	5120	0	F	T	F	T	T	F
SMALLINT	6	5	0	F	F	F	T	T	T
INTEGER	11	10	0	F	F	F	T	T	T
BIGINT	20	19	0	F	F	F	T	T	T
FLOAT	22	15	0	F	F	F	T	T	T
REAL	13	7	0	F	F	F	T	T	T
DOUBLE	22	15	0	F	F	F	T	T	T
DECIMAL(11,4)	14	11	4	F	F	T	T	T	T
NUMERIC(12,2)	15	12	2	F	F	T	T	T	T
DATE	10	10	0	F	F	F	T	T	F
TIME	8	8	0	F	F	F	T	T	F
TIMESTAMP	26	26	0	F	F	F	T	T	F
CHAR(1) NOT NULL	1	1	0	F	T	F	F	T	F
INT INCREMENT	11	10	0	T	F	F	F	T	T

Prepared Statements

Much of the SQL that needs to be executed in an application can be handled with the `execute()`, `executeQuery()`, and `executeUpdate()` methods. However, each one of these methods requires the entire SQL string to be used as the input parameter. Aside from having to build the SQL statement, the application will need to deal with string constants. Strings within SQL statements are enclosed by single quotation marks ('). If a string contains single quotation marks or other control characters, it can be almost impossible to build an SQL statement.

During execution, an application will need to build the SQL statement dynamically and then submit it for processing. This process would have to be repeated each time, even if just one parameter changes. Although re-creating SQL statements for small parameter changes might not require much effort in the application itself, Apache Derby must parse and optimize the statements each time the `execute()` method is used. This means that any prior work done on the statement is lost. Reprocessing the request, even with a small change, can be expensive in terms of database optimization overhead. To minimize this overhead, and to simplify application development, use the `PreparedStatement()` method instead.

In a prepared statement, any values that need to be changed from call to call are replaced with the question mark character (?). These placeholders are commonly referred to as parameter markers. Parameter markers are variables within an SQL statement that need to have values supplied to them before the statement is executed.

Consider the task of populating a table with new records. One approach would be to code separate `INSERT` statements and then execute them individually.

```
s = conn.createStatement();
insertTESTPREP = "INSERT INTO TESTPREP VALUES ";
insertSQL = insertTESTPREP + "(1,1)";
s.executeUpdate(insertSQL);
insertSQL = insertTESTPREP + "(2,2)";
s.executeUpdate(insertSQL);
s.close();
```

Although this approach will work with small amounts of data, it becomes extremely unwieldy when working with hundreds of records. A better approach would be to use a prepared statement. A prepared statement can be executed after its parameter markers have been filled in. In the following example, the `createStatement()` method from the previous example is replaced with the `preparedStatement()` method.

```
PreparedStatement ps;
ps = conn.prepareStatement("INSERT INTO TESTPREP VALUES (?, ?)");
ps.setInt(1,1);
ps.setInt(2,1);
rows = ps.executeUpdate();
ps.setInt(1,2);
```

```
ps.setInt(2,2);
rows = ps.executeUpdate();
ps.close();
```

You can use the setInt() method to set the value of parameter markers. The first argument is the parameter marker, and the second argument is the actual value being inserted. There are a number of corresponding setX() methods similar to the getX() methods discussed in the section on handling result sets. Parameter numbers are numbered from 1 to n, starting at the first '?' that is found in a string.

Table 9-6 *setX()* Methods

SQL Data Type	Java.sql.Types	setX() Method
SMALLINT	SMALLINT	setShort()
INTEGER	INTEGER	setInt()
BIGINT	BIGINT	setLong()
DECIMAL	DECIMAL or NUMERIC	setBigDecimal()
REAL	REAL	setFloat()
DOUBLE PRECISION	DOUBLE, FLOAT	setDouble(), setFloat()
DATE	DATE	setDate()
TIME	TIME	setTime()
TIMESTAMP	TIMESTAMP	setTimestamp()
CHAR	CHAR	setString()
VARCHAR	VARCHAR	setString()
LONG VARCHAR	LONG VARCHAR	setString()
CLOB	CLOB (JDBC 2.0 and up)	setClob()
BLOB	BLOB (JDBC 2.0 and up)	setBlob()
CHAR FOR BIT DATA	BINARY	setBytes()
VARCHAR FOR BIT DATA	VARBINARY	setBytes()
LONG VARCHAR FOR BIT DATA	LONGVARBINARY	setBytes()

The setClob() and setBlob() methods do not set a value but rather set a locator to the CLOB or BLOB object. The setCharacterStream() or setBinaryStream() method must be used to actually update or set the value of a CLOB or a BLOB. Additional details on large object support can be found in the section on updating and inserting large objects.

Date, time, and timestamp objects might need to use corresponding `valueOf()` operators to convert strings to the proper representation. For instance, `setDate(1,"2005-05-05")` can result in an error because the `setDate()` method might not support a string argument for the statement that is being used. The `Date.valueOf()` operator could be used to create a proper date field within the `setDate()` method:

```
setDate(1,Date.valueOf("2005-05-05"));
```

Prepared statements can be used for INSERT, UPDATE, DELETE, and SELECT statements. For example, an application could create a statement that contains parameter markers for commonly requested information. The following example illustrates the use of a prepared statement that is subsequently used in a result set. The code returns a list of titles that contain a user-supplied keyword. This code can be reused until the statement is closed.

```
01   ps = conn.prepareStatement(
       "SELECT * FROM PRODUCTIONS WHERE PRODUCTION_TITLE LIKE ?");
02   search = " ";
03   while ( search != null ) {
       System.out.print("Enter a title to search for: ");
       search = br.readLine();
       if (search.length() == 0) break;
04     SQLsearch = "%" + search + "%";
05     ps.setString(1,SQLsearch);
06     rs = ps.executeQuery();
07     rows = 0;
08     while ( rs.next()) {
         if (rows == 0) {
           System.out.println();
           System.out.println("Productions found");
           System.out.println("----------------");
         }
         ++rows;
09       title = rs.getString("PRODUCTION_TITLE");
10       startDate = rs.getString("PRODUCTION_START");
         System.out.println(startDate + " : " + title);
       }
       if (rows == 0) {
        System.out.println("No titles found containing :" + search);
       }
       System.out.println();
11     rs.close();
     }
12   ps.close();
```

A detailed description of the example follows.

- [01] ps = conn.prepareStatement()
  The prepareStatement() method is passed to the SQL statement with parameter markers for the string that will be searched.

- [02] search = " "
  The search variable contains the string that will be searched for titles.

- [03] while (searchString != null) {}
  When the search variable is set to null, the program stops executing.

- [04] SQLsearch = "%" + search + "%"
  The actual SQL search string is set to the original text that was entered by the user, surrounded by percent signs (%). The LIKE predicate uses the percent sign as a wildcard character to match zero or more characters in a string. For example, '%the%' could match 'the', 'there', 'they', or 'leather' in a string.

- [05] ps.setString(1,SQLsearch);
  The first and only parameter marker is set to the value of the SQLsearch string.

- [06] rs = ps.executeQuery();
  The prepared statement is executed as a query with a corresponding result set. This is identical to creating a statement and issuing an executeQuery(string).

- [07] rows = 0;
  The rows that are returned by the query are counted in a while loop. This information is needed at the end of the loop to generate a message if no records were found.

- [08] while (rs.next()) {}
  The result set might contain multiple titles, so a loop needs to process every row.

- [09-10] title = rs.getString("PRODUCTION_TITLE")
  The columns in the result set are retrieved and printed out for the user to see.

- [11-12] rs.close(), ps.close()
  The result set should be closed at the end of the loop before another query is executed. Similarly, the prepared statement should be closed when the application is finished using it.

Running this application against the YMLD database produces the following output.

```
Enter a title to search for: the

Productions found
-----------------
2005-01-01 : Lilly of the Valley
2005-01-10 : Icing the Puck
2005-09-10 : Couched in Leather
```

```
Enter a title to search for: ask
No titles found containing: ask
```

AUTOCOMMIT, COMMITs, and ROLLBACKs

The SQL language has COMMIT and ROLLBACK statements that control when changes made to a database are physically committed to disk.

To ensure consistency of the data in a database, it is often necessary for applications to apply a number of changes together as a unit. This is called a unit of work. A unit of work is a recoverable sequence of operations within an application process. It is the basic mechanism that an application uses to ensure database integrity. At any given time, an application process has a single unit of work, but the life of an application process can involve many units of work. A unit of work is also known as a transaction.

Any application that successfully connects to a database automatically starts a transaction. The application must end the transaction by issuing a COMMIT or a ROLLBACK statement. The COMMIT statement tells Apache Derby to apply all database changes (inserts, updates, deletes, creates, alters) to the database at once. The ROLLBACK statement tells Apache Derby not to apply the changes and instead to return the affected rows back to their state before the beginning of the transaction.

The COMMIT and ROLLBACK statements are not used in JDBC. Instead, corresponding methods are available at the statement level called commit() and rollback(). In addition, the database has an autocommit setting.

Autocommit refers to the action that Apache Derby takes after every execute() operation. If autocommit is true, every statement is automatically committed after it completes execution. That means that there is no way of undoing the changes that were made.

Although it might appear that autocommit can cause problems for applications, it was originally intended to release locks and resources that continued to be held by SELECT statements. Even though SELECT statements do not change values, they still hold locks on the rows being read. This means that a SELECT statement could block another application trying to update a row by inadvertently preventing it from getting an update lock on that row. When autocommit is true, the SELECT statement commits immediately after reading the last row and releases the locks and resources that it was holding.

If an application wants to control the way in which commits are handled, it must turn autocommit off. This must be done at the connection level with the setAutoCommit(value) method. The current setting can also be queried using the getAutoCommit() method.

```
conn = DriverManager.getConnection("jdbc:derby:YMLD");
conn.setAutoCommit(false);
```

When an application wants to use a result set to update data, the autocommit value must be set to false, or else updates will fail.

Batching Requests

Issuing multiple INSERT or UPDATE statements against a database can be very inefficient, especially if the client is on a remote network. Each time the executeUpdate() method is called, the SQL is sent to the database engine and is processed, and then results are returned to the application. This process is repeated until all of the rows are inserted, deleted, or updated.

JDBC includes the addBatch(), clearBatch(), and executeBatch() methods to improve the efficiency of sending multiple SQL requests to the database engine. These batch methods are summarized in the following list.

- void addBatch(String sql)—This method allows a programmer to batch a number of statements together in one call to the database. To reduce the overhead of sending individual SQL calls to the database and waiting for a reply for each one, a programmer can batch all of the SQL into one group and have that set of statements executed as a block.

- void clearBatch()—After executing a set of statements in batch mode, the statements must be cleared before new statements are added. If the previous statements are not cleared after executing, they remain in the batch list and will be executed again.

- int[] executeBatch()—This method sends the entire set of SQL statements to the database engine for processing and returns an array of update counts if the SQL completed successfully.

These batch methods can be used with either a statement or a prepared statement. The following example was used in the prepared statement section to insert multiple records into a table:

```
s = conn.createStatement();
insertTESTPREP = "INSERT INTO TESTPREP VALUES ";
insertSQL = insertTESTPREP + "(1,1)";
s.executeUpdate(insertSQL);
insertSQL = insertTESTPREP + "(2,2)";
s.executeUpdate(insertSQL);
s.close();
```

This code could be rewritten as follows:

```
s = conn.createStatement();
insertTESTPREP = "INSERT INTO TESTPREP VALUES ";
insertSQL = insertTESTPREP + "(1,1)";
s.addBatch(insertSQL);
insertSQL = insertTESTPREP + "(2,2)";
s.addBatch(insertSQL);
int [] insertResults = s.executeBatch();
s.close();
```

The executeUpdate() methods have been replaced with addBatch() methods. The final executeBatch() method sends the entire block of SQL to Apache Derby for processing. The insertResults variable contains an array of integers that reflect the success or failure of the individual statements in the block. The application is responsible for checking each return code and deciding what do to.

The autocommit setting should also be considered when using a batch block. If the default auto-commit setting is used, every SQL statement will be committed individually. This means that the application will not have any control over whether all or none of the updates should be completed.

At the completion of the executeBatch() operation, the insertResults array will contain a set of return codes, one for each statement executed. The values in this array can be:

- 0 or greater—A successful execution of the statement with zero or more rows affected.
- -2—The statement succeeded, but the number of affected rows is unknown.
- -3—An error occured while processing the statement.

If an error occurs during batch processing, Apache Derby throws a BatchUpdateException. An application should use a corresponding try block to trap the error.

Another example of batch processing involves the use of prepared statements. The previous example added SQL strings to a batch request. In this example, the SQL strings are replaced with a prepared statement containing parameter markers.

```
ps = conn.prepareStatement("INSERT INTO TESTPREP VALUES (?, ?)");
ps.setInt(1,100); ps.setInt(2,100);
ps.addBatch();
ps.setInt(1,200); ps.setInt(2,200);
ps.addBatch();
results = ps.executeBatch();
ps.close();
```

Batch updates can add efficiency to the way large numbers of updates and inserts are processed by Apache Derby. The only drawback is that the application must check the individual return codes and decide how to handle any errors that might have occurred.

Using Result Sets to Modify Data

In many types of applications, users will scroll through a set of data before deciding when to update a record. The update could involve changing a value in a column or deleting an entire row. Using traditional result sets returned from an executeQuery() operation, an application can list all of the rows that are returned from a table. Unfortunately, these rows can't be updated dynamically, so the application would have to issue an UPDATE or a DELETE statement against the current row. The program would need logic similar to the following example:

```
rs = s.executeQuery("SELECT * FROM TESTCURSOR");
while (rs.next()) {
```

```
    ... populate display with all records found ...
}
... user selects a record to delete ...
rs = s.executeUpdate("DELETE FROM TESTCURSOR WHERE REC_NO = ...")
```

The first portion of the code would populate a display from which a user can select a row. When a particular row is selected for deletion, the key value for that row can be used in a subsequent DELETE statement. Although this approach will work, there is the chance that someone has a lock on the row that the user wants to delete. The reason for this is that the locks on the original SELECT statement are no longer active, and someone else can now lock this row. The other issue with this approach is that more SQL must be executed to delete the row. It would be much more convenient to request the deletion just by referring to the row that the user is currently browsing. This can be accomplished through the use of the FOR UPDATE clause within a SELECT statement, and an SQL cursor. A cursor is similar to the pointer found within a result set, except that it is used by the database to determine the record to which the change applies.

The FOR UPDATE clause is an optional part of a SELECT statement. The FOR UPDATE clause specifies whether the result set of a simple SELECT statement that meets the requirements for a cursor is updatable or not. Only simple, single-table SELECT cursors can be made updatable. For a cursor to be updatable:

- The SELECT statement must not include an ORDER BY, DISTINCT, GROUP BY, or HAVING clause.

- The underlying query must be a SELECT expression (not a VALUES clause).

- The FROM clause in the underlying query must specify only one table.

Cursors are read-only by default. For a cursor to be updatable, you must specify FOR UPDATE in the FOR clause. The FOR clause is added to the end of a SELECT statement and can have one of three formats:

- FOR READ ONLY or FOR FETCH ONLY—Specifying either of these two clauses tells Apache Derby that no updates will take place against the rows in the result set and that it can optimize access to these rows. This is the default setting for any SQL statement issued without the FOR clause.

- FOR UPDATE [OF column-names]—Specifying FOR UPDATE tells Apache Derby that the rows in the result set could be updated. If FOR UPDATE is used without any additional column qualifiers, all columns in the result set are eligible for update. If specific columns are listed after the FOR UPDATE clause, Apache Derby will restrict updates to only those columns. Restricting the columns can optimize access to these rows, but it will make your application less flexible.

The first step to enable the previous example to update data in the result set would be the addition of the FOR UPDATE clause to the SQL:

```
rs = s.executeQuery("SELECT * FROM TESTCURSOR FOR UPDATE");
```

Note that the application still needs to use the executeQuery() method because the SQL is not updating the actual rows at this time. Also, the autocommit setting must be turned off for the UPDATE clause to be valid:

```
conn.setAutoCommit(false);
```

The next step is to create a cursor. A cursor is an object within the result set to which the application refers when it must update the current row. A cursor is named using the setCursor-Name() method in the statement or prepared statement:

```
s.setCursorName("DeleteCursor");
```

After a cursor has been named, an SQL statement that will act on the cursor must be generated. This statement can be either a DELETE or an UPDATE statement. The format of the statements is:

```
DELETE FROM table WHERE CURRENT OF cursor-name
UPDATE table SET column=value WHERE CURRENT OF cursor-name
```

The statement that is used to execute these statements must not be the same one that was used to generate the result set! Otherwise, the original result set will be lost, and an SQLException will be raised. The table name must be the same as the one in the original result set. The cursor name refers to the setCursor() name defined as part of the statement. Finally, the SET clause is used as part of the UPDATE statement to change the column value. In the case of the UPDATE statement, this can be a prepared statement, and a parameter marker can be used for the value.

The following code demonstrates how the first record in the result set can be deleted using the CURRENT OF clause in a DELETE statement:

```
     conn = DriverManager.getConnection("jdbc:derby:YMLD");
01   conn.setAutoCommit(false);
02   s = conn.createStatement(
          ResultSet.TYPE_SCROLL_INSENSITIVE,ResultSet.CONCUR_UPDATABLE);
03   s = conn.createStatement();
04   s.setCursorName("DELETECURSOR");
05   rs = s.executeQuery("SELECT * FROM TESTCURSOR FOR UPDATE");
06   sd = conn.createStatement();
     rs.next() ;
     int recNo = rs.getInt("RECNO");
     System.out.println("RECNO=" + recNo);
```

```
07   rows = sd.executeUpdate(
        "DELETE FROM TESTCURSOR WHERE CURRENT OF DELETECURSOR");
     System.out.println("Number of rows deleted=" + rows);
08   conn.commit();
09   rs.close();
     sd.close();
     s.close();
```

- [01] `conn.setAutoCommit(false)`
  The autocommit mode is turned off so that the application can issue the FOR UPDATE clause in the result set.

- [02] `s = conn.createStatement(...)`
  This method does not need any parameters to work with the FOR UPDATE clause. However, if the application needs to scroll up and down the result set, TYPE_SCROLL_INSENSITIVE must be specified as the cursor type.

- [03] `s = conn.createStatement()`
  The first `createStatement()` method will be used for the SELECT statement result set.

- [04] `s.setCursorName("DELETECURSOR")`
  The cursor associated with the result set is called DELETECURSOR. The name of a cursor can be up to 18 characters long.

- [05] `rs = s.executeQuery("SELECT * FROM TESTCURSOR FOR UPDATE")`
  The SELECT statement has the FOR UPDATE clause to tell Apache Derby that the rows can be updated.

- [06] `sd = conn.createStatement();`
  A second `createStatement()` method will be used to execute the DELETE statements against the cursor.

- [07] `rows = sd.executeUpdate("DELETE ... WHERE CURRENT OF DELETECURSOR")`
  This method issues the actual DELETE statement against the cursor. The cursor must be properly positioned in the result set; otherwise, an SQLException is raised.

- [08] `conn.commit()`
  The updates to the rows will not take effect until the commit() method is called. If the application closes the result set before a commit, the changes will be lost. From an application perspective, the commit should occur before all of the underlying statement and result set objects are closed.

- [09] `rs.close();`
  All of the objects that are part of a transaction should be closed when they are no longer needed. This will ensure that no resources are left open on the database side.

The following example uses result sets and a prepared statement to perform updates. A prepared statement can be used for multiple updates, which allows for the use of parameter markers for values, rather than literals. This example updates the second column in the result set.

```
s.setCursorName("UPDATECURSOR");
rs = s.executeQuery("SELECT * FROM TESTCURSOR FOR UPDATE");
ps = conn.prepareStatement(
     "UPDATE TESTCURSOR SET RECVAL=? WHERE CURRENT OF UPDATECURSOR");
rs.next() ;
int recNo = rs.getInt("RECNO");
System.out.println("RECNO=" + recNo);
ps.setInt(1,100);
rows = ps.executeUpdate();
System.out.println("Number of rows updated=" + rows);
conn.commit();
```

Setting a Column to Null

A column can easily be set to null when an SQL statement is used directly to update a table:

```
UPDATE TESTCURSOR SET RECVAL = NULL WHERE RECNO = 1;
```

It's different when a prepared statement is used to update records because the value will be a parameter marker:

```
UPDATE TESTCURSOR SET RECVAL = ? WHERE CURRENT OF cursorname;
```

A null pointer does not have the same meaning in SQL as it might in Java. To set a value to null, the setNull() or updateNull() methods must be used. The updateNull() method is used with result sets and is the simpler of the two methods because it only needs the index of the column. The setNull() method requires the parameter marker number and the data type of the value that the null value is supposed to represent. The data types are listed in the following table.

Table 9-7 *setNull()* data types

SQL Data Type	Java.sql.Types
SMALLINT	SMALLINT
INTEGER	INTEGER
BIGINT	BIGINT
DECIMAL	DECIMAL or NUMERIC

Table 9-7   *setNull()* data types (*continued*)

SQL Data Type	Java.sql.Types
REAL	REAL
DOUBLE PRECISION	DOUBLE, FLOAT
DATE	DATE
TIME	TIME
TIMESTAMP	TIMESTAMP
CHAR	CHAR
VARCHAR	VARCHAR
LONG VARCHAR	LONG VARCHAR
CLOB	CLOB (JDBC 2.0 and up)
BLOB	BLOB (JDBC 2.0 and up)
CHAR FOR BIT DATA	BINARY
VARCHAR FOR BIT DATA	VARBINARY
LONG VARCHAR FOR BIT DATA	LONGVARBINARY

To set a column value to null, use the `setNull()` method with the appropriate data type value as the second parameter. The actual data type is part of the `Types` class, so you must use the form `Types.DATATYPE`. The following code sets the second parameter marker to a null integer value:

```
ps = conn.prepareStatement("INSERT INTO TESTPREP VALUES (?, ?)");
ps.setInt(1,1);
ps.setNull(2,Types.INTEGER);
rows = ps.executeUpdate();
```

Inserting and Updating Large Objects

Large objects need to be handled differently because of their size. Rather than assigning a value directly to a large object, output streams are used to move data into `CLOB`s and `BLOB`s. Three methods are available for creating output streams. Two methods are meant for character objects, and the third is for binary objects.

- `OutputStream setAsciiStream(long position)`,
  `setUnicodeStream(long position)`
  The `setAsciiStream()` method returns an output stream that contains ASCII bytes, and the `setUnicodeStream()` method is used for Unicode characters. The `position` parameter specifies the starting point for writing values in the `BLOB`.

- OutputStream setBinaryStream(long position)
  The setBinaryStream() method returns an output stream that writes the BLOB value from the specified starting point.

The easiest way to update or insert a BLOB or CLOB is to create an input stream to the object being inserted from the file system, and then to set the binary stream for the LOB to point to the input stream. The following code illustrates this approach:

```
01   File fileIn = new File(".\\theaterChair.jpg");
02   InputStream fis = new FileInputStream(fileIn);
     Connection conn = DriverManager.getConnection("jdbc:derby:YMLD");
03   ps = conn.prepareStatement(
            "UPDATE SEATMAP SET SEAT_VIEW = ? WHERE SEAT_NO = ?");
     ps.setInt(2,1);
04   int fileLength = (int) fileIn.length();
05   ps.setBinaryStream(1, fis, fileLength);
06   ps.executeUpdate();
     ps.close();
```

- [01] File fileIn = new File(".\\theaterChair.jpg");
  The file that will be inserted into the BLOB object is assigned to a variable.

- [02] InputStream fis = new FileInputStream(fileIn);
  An input stream to the existing file is created. The application should have appropriate try and catch blocks in the event that the file does not exist.

- [03] ps = conn.prepareStatement
  ("UPDATE SEATMAP SET SEAT_VIEW = ? WHERE SEAT_NO = ?");
  The prepared statement contains an UPDATE clause with two parameter markers. The SEAT_VIEW column is a BLOB object that contains a picture of a theater seat.

- [04] int fileLength = (int) fileIn.length();
  The length of the image is placed into the fileLength variable for use as part of the setBinaryStream statement.

- [05] ps.setBinaryStream(1, fis, fileLength);
  This method has three parameters. The first is the parameter marker being updated, the second is the input stream, and the third specifies the amount of data to be transfered from the input stream. It is possible to restrict the number of bytes being written into a BLOB, but in most cases, an application would be transferring entire files.

- [06] ps.executeUpdate();
  The final executeUpdate() method will transfer the data to the BLOB and complete the update.

In addition to using binary and character streams, BLOB objects can also use the setBytes()
method instead of updating the entire object.

Following are some additional points to remember about BLOB and CLOB objects:

- LOB types cannot be compared for equality (=) and non-equality (!=, <>).
- LOB values cannot be ordered, so <, <=, >, >= tests are not supported.
- LOB types cannot be used in indices or as primary key columns.
- DISTINCT, GROUP BY, and ORDER BY clauses are prohibited on LOB types.
- LOB types cannot be involved in implicit casting to other base types.

Stored Procedures

Stored procedures are a method for encapsulating SQL and logic on the database server. There
are many advantages to placing routines on the server, including access to large server resources,
minimizing network communication, reuse of code, and security. Placing frequently used code
in a stored procedure can also make it easier to develop applications because much of the logic
might already be coded.

Three steps are required to get a stored procedure to work:

- Create the server-side stored procedure.
- Define the stored procedure to the database.
- Create the application program that will use the stored procedure.

Each step is outlined in the following sections.

Creating a Stored Procedure

Writing a stored procedure is no different from writing a normal SQL application, aside from
three restrictions:

- Data types—A stored procedure cannot have long data types, such as LONG VARCHAR,
  LONG VARCHAR FOR BIT DATA, CLOB, and BLOB.
- Connection context—A stored procedure should use the connection context of the calling
  program. This means that the connection statement should use the following format:

  ```
  conn = DriverManager.getConnection("jdbc:default:connection");
  ```

  It is possible for a stored procedure to create its own connection context, but the calling program would not have any control over the commits and rollbacks that the stored
  procedure might perform.

- Returned results—A stored procedure must return its results through the parameters that
  were passed to it, including result sets. Result sets are a special case of passing information back to an application, and they are discussed in the section on handling result sets.

The stored procedure must be placed into a CLASSPATH that the database can find at execution time, or it must be placed into a .JAR file. In addition, the stored procedure must be defined to the database before it can be invoked. The following code illustrates a simple stored procedure that returns the number of productions that are stored in the YMLD database.

```
public static void getProdCount(int[] prodCount) throws SQLException {

  Statement s = null;
  Connection conn = null;
  ResultSet rs = null;

  try {
    conn = DriverManager.getConnection("jdbc:default: connection");
    s = conn.createStatement();
    rs = s.executeQuery("SELECT COUNT(*) FROM PRODUCTIONS");
    rs.next();
    prodCount[0] = rs.getInt(1);
  }
  catch (SQLException se) {
    prodCount[0] = 0;
  }
  finally {
    rs.close();
    s.close();
    conn.close();
  }
}
```

The prodCount parameter is an output parameter, so it must be defined as an array type (int [] prodCount). All assignments to this parameter should be done to the first element in the array (prodCount [0]). Arguments that are input parameters are defined with standard data types.

Defining a Stored Procedure

A stored procedure must be defined to the database with the CREATE PROCEDURE statement before being used by an application. The syntax of the CREATE PROCEDURE command is:

```
CREATE PROCEDURE procedure_name (parameters)
SPECIFIC [ schema-Name. ]SQL92 Identifier
[ DYNAMIC ] RESULT SETS integer
LANGUAGE JAVA
EXTERNAL NAME string
```

```
PARAMETER STYLE JAVA
{ NO SQL | MODIFIES SQL DATA | CONTAINS SQL | READS SQL DATA }
```

The CREATE PROCEDURE statement is followed by the procedure name and the optional parameter list. The procedure name must be a valid SQL identifier. Each parameter in the list has an input or output specification, a name, and a data type associated with it.

By default, all parameters are considered to be IN (input) parameters. If a parameter will be returned by the stored procedure, it should be coded as OUT. If the parameter will be sent to the stored procedure and possibly modified, it should be coded as INOUT. The parameter names are optional, but naming the parameters makes it easier to associate a parameter with its purpose. The parameters can be of any data type, except for LONG VARCHAR, CLOB, and BLOB.

DYNAMIC RESULT SETS integer indicates the estimated upper bound of returned result sets for the procedure. Default is no (0) dynamic result sets.

LANGUAGE JAVA tells Apache Derby to call the procedure as a public static method in a Java class.

The EXTERNAL NAME clause specifies the Java method to be called when the procedure is executed, and it takes the form class_name.method_name. The external name cannot have any extraneous spaces.

PARAMETER STYLE JAVA specifies that the procedure will use a parameter-passing convention that conforms to the Java language and SQL Routines specification. INOUT and OUT parameters will be passed as single-entry arrays to facilitate returning values. Result sets are returned through additional parameters to the Java method of type java.sql.ResultSet [], which is passed single entry arrays.

The SQL clause tells Apache Derby what SQL the procedure can perform. There are four options:

- CONTAINS SQL indicates that SQL statements that neither read nor modify SQL data can be executed by the stored procedure. Statements that are not supported in any stored procedure will return an error.

- NO SQL indicates that the stored procedure does not execute any SQL statements.

- READS SQL DATA indicates that some SQL statements that do not modify SQL data can be included in the stored procedure. Statements that are not supported in any stored procedure return an error.

- MODIFIES SQL DATA indicates that the stored procedure can execute any SQL statement except statements that are not supported in stored procedures. This is the default value.

A stored procedure definition must contain LANGUAGE, EXTERNAL NAME, and PARAMETER STYLE clauses. The CREATE PROCEDURE definition for the earlier example would be similar to the following code:

```
CREATE PROCEDURE getProdCount(OUT PRODCOUNT INT)
  PARAMETER STYLE JAVA
```

```
READS SQL DATA
LANGUAGE JAVA EXTERNAL NAME 'SP.getProdCount';
```

Calling a Stored Procedure

After a stored procedure has been written and cataloged in the database, the calling program can be written using the prepareCall() method.

Stored procedures are called using the callable statement:

```
CallableStatement csql = null;
csql = conn.prepareCall("{call procedurename(?, ?, ?) }");
```

The string that is passed to the prepareCall() method is a special escape sequence. The call statement is surrounded by braces ({ }), and the parameters are replaced with parameter markers (?). The SQL CALL statement can also be used for stored procedures that do not require any output parameters. These types of stored procedures can be tested from within the ij environment by using the CALL statement:

```
CALL getperformances('2005-01-01','2005-02-01');
```

The actual parameters passed to a stored procedure are input, output, or both input and output parameters. The output parameters must be registered using the registerOutParameter() method. This method takes two parameters: the first one is the parameter marker location in the statement, and the second one is the data type being passed to the stored procedure. The data types are listed in Table 9-7.

The following example shows how to execute the previously defined stored procedure:

```
conn = DriverManager.getConnection("jdbc:derby:YMLD");
CallableStatement cstmt = conn.prepareCall("call getProdCount(?)");
cstmt.registerOutParameter(1, Types.INTEGER);
cstmt.execute();
rows = cstmt.getInt(1);
System.out.println("Rows="+rows);
cstmt.close();
conn.close();
```

The registerOutParameter() method sets the only parameter marker to an integer type. Note that after the stored procedure returns, the getInt() method can be used to retrieve the value in this parameter.

Handling Result Sets

Another feature of stored procedures is their capability to return result sets. A result set can be opened by the stored procedure and passed back to the calling program. This allows the stored procedure to select data from the database without the calling program having to know the details of the SELECT statement. In some database implementations, the stored procedure has access to the tables, whereas the calling program does not have access.

If you want to return a result set from a stored procedure, the procedure definition must include the DYNAMIC RESULT SETS clause. By default, a stored procedure returns zero result sets. If a stored procedure must return a result set, the CREATE PROCEDURE statement must specify one or more result sets in the DYNAMIC RESULT SETS clause.

The last parameter of a stored procedure definition in Java must contain a result set array:

```
public static void getProdCount(int[] prodCount, ResultSet[] outRs) ...
```

The result set array holds the results. For example, the following code places the results of a SELECT statement into the result set for subsequent usc by the calling program:

```
s = conn.createStatement();
outRs[0] = s.executeQuery("SELECT * FROM PRODUCTIONS");
```

It is important that the stored procedure not close the result set or the statement when exiting the program; otherwise, the result set and all of the values within it are lost. The following example shows a stored procedure that returns a list of productions playing between two dates from the YMLD database. The calling program provides the start and end dates as input parameters, and the stored procedure returns the names and dates of the matching performances.

```
      public static void getPerformances(
         Date startDate,
         Date endDate,
01       ResultSet[] rsOut) throws SQLException {

         PreparedStatement ps = null;
         Connection conn = null;
         ResultSet rs = null;

         try {
02          conn = DriverManager.getConnection("jdbc:default:
              connection");
03          ps = conn.prepareStatement(
              "SELECT Production_Title, Production_Start,
                 Production_End " +
              " FROM Productions" +
              " WHERE (? Between Production_Start AND Production_End) OR " +
              "       (? Between Production_Start AND Production_End)") ;
04          ps.setDate(1, startDate);
            ps.setDate(2, endDate);
```

```
05      rsOut[0] = ps.executeQuery();
     }
   catch (SQLException se) {
      String SQLState = se.getSQLState();
      String SQLMessage = se.getMessage();
      System.out.println("Error = "+SQLState);
      System.out.println(SQLMessage);
   }
06   conn.close();
   }
```

The following notes provide additional information about key lines in the code.

- [01] ResultSet[] rsOut

  The result set must be the last parameter listed in the stored procedure definition. This is defined as an array of result sets so that the result set can be passed back to the calling program.

- [02] conn = DriverManager.getConnection("jdbc:default:
  connection");

  This stored procedure uses the connection from the calling program. This is what most stored procedures would use, but it is possible to create a different, independent connection here.

- [03] ps = conn.prepareStatement(
  "SELECT Production_Title, Production_Start, Production_End " +
  " FROM Productions" +
  " WHERE (? Between Production_Start AND Production_End) OR " +
  "   (? Between Production_Start AND Production_End)") ;

  This long SQL statement selects all of the productions that have start or end dates falling between the dates that are specified by the user.

- [04] ps.setDate(1, startDate);

  The two dates that are passed as parameters to the stored procedure are inserted into the parameter markers. The correct set routine (setDate()) must be used to correspond with the SQL data type in the SELECT statement.

- [05] rsOut[0] = ps.executeQuery();

  The results from executing the query are placed into the result set array. The first entry in the array always starts at position zero.

- [06] conn.close();

  The connection within the stored procedure can be closed without affecting the result set. However, closing the result set will destroy any data in the current result set.

The application that calls the stored procedure sets up the call in the normal way. The `prepare-Call()` method is used with the specified stored procedure, but excluding any reference to the result set array.

```
conn = DriverManager.getConnection("jdbc:derby:YMLD");
CallableStatement cstmt = conn.prepareCall("call getPerformances(?,?)");
cstmt.setDate(1,Date.valueOf("2005-03-31"));
cstmt.setDate(2,Date.valueOf("2005-05-15"));
cstmt.execute();
```

At this point, the application needs to access the result set that was generated by the stored procedure. A new method called `getResultSet()` is required to do this. A result set within the application is defined to use the result set being returned by the stored procedure:

```
ResultSet rs = cstmt.getResultset();
```

Now the contents of the result set can be manipulated like an ordinary result set. If the calling application does not know the contents of the cursor, the meta-data for the result set can be returned using `cstmt.getMetaData()`.

The remainder of the program can loop through and display the contents of the result set:

```
rows = 0;
while (rs.next()) {
  if (rows == 0) {
    System.out.println("Start Date End Date   Title" );
    System.out.println("--------------------------------");
  }
  ++rows;
  title = rs.getString("Production_Title");
  startDate = rs.getString("Production_Start");
  endDate = rs.getString("Production_End");
  System.out.println(startDate + " " + endDate + " " + title);
}
cstmt.close();
rs.close();
conn.close();
```

Trapping Errors in Stored Procedures and Functions

The previous example had a `try/catch` block within the stored procedure logic. Although this may be useful for debugging a stored procedure, you really don't want a stored procedure or SQL function to print an error message. The proper way to handle errors from within the stored procedure is to throw the exception to the caller and have the client code handle the problem.

If the stored procedure really needed to handle an exception, then it would catch errors that it could fix and rethrow any exceptions that cannot be handled back to the client.

Multiple Result Sets

Apache Derby supports multiple result sets, but their use is sequential. This means that the first result set must be used before moving to the second one. The `getMoreResults()` method is invoked on the statement to move to the second result set, and then a corresponding call to `getResultSet()` is required.

```
CallableStatement cstmt = conn.prepareCall("call getPerformances(?,?)");
cstmt.setDate(1,Date.valueOf("2005-03-31"));
cstmt.setDate(2,Date.valueOf("2005-05-15"));
cstmt.execute();
ResultSet rs = cstmt.getResultSet();
... process 1st result set
if (cstmt.getMoreResults()) {
  rs = cstmt.getResultSet();
  ... process 2nd result set
}
```

An `SQLException` will be raised if another result set is not available on the `getResult-Set()` call. For this reason, the `getMoreResults()` method should be checked to see if it is true before continuing to process the result set.

User-Defined Functions

Chapter 8 introduced user-defined functions (UDFs). UDFs allow you to extend the functionality of SQL by introducing new functions that can be used as part of the SQL syntax. Apache Derby comes with many built-in functions; however, it is possible to create your own scalar functions. Scalar functions accept one or more values and return another value. A UDF must be written in Java and then defined to the database. For example, the following SQL will register a `DSQRT` (double square root) function using existing Java libraries.

```
CREATE FUNCTION DSQRT (DATA DOUBLE)
  RETURNS DOUBLE
  EXTERNAL NAME 'java.lang.Math.sqrt'
  LANGUAGE JAVA
  PARAMETER STYLE JAVA;

values dsqrt(4);
```

```
1
---------------------
2.0

1 row selected
```

If a specific function is not available in Apache Derby, there might be a function available within the standard Java class libraries that could be used instead.

The previous function definition expects a double as an input argument and returns a double. Perhaps the application that is being developed requires the square root function to take integers as input and return a truncated integer value in return. This can be accomplished by writing a Java user-defined function, as follows:

```
import java.sql.*;

public class YMLDFunctions {

   public static int ISQRT(int sqrtvalue) {
      if (sqrtvalue < 0) throw new IllegalArgumentException();
      return (int)Math.sqrt(sqrtvalue);
   }
}
```

If an illegal value is used in the `ISQRT` function, an `IllegalArgumentException` will be thrown by the function. This will result in two errors being returned by Apache Derby to the calling program:

```
ERROR 38000: The exception 'java.lang.IllegalArgumentException'
  was thrown while evaluating an expression.
ERROR XJ001: Java exception: ':
  java.lang.IllegalArgumentException'.
```

Instead of returning a generic message, the function or stored procedure could throw a new `SQLException` with a specific error state and message.

```
import java.sql.*;

public class YMLDFunctions {

   public static int IRSQRT(int sqrtvalue) {
      if (sqrtvalue < 0) throw new SQLException(
          "You need a positive integer!",
          "38500");
```

```
    return (int)Math.sqrt(sqrtvalue);
  }
}
```

Now if an invalid value is passed to the function, a more meaningful message is returned to the application.

```
values irsqrt(-4);
1
-----------
ERROR 38500: You need a positive integer!
```

The first two characters of the SQLSTATE code ('38') represent the class assigned to external routine exceptions. When a method invoked by a user-defined function or procedure throws an exception, Apache Derby wraps it in an SQLException for the caller. If the method throws a specific SQLSTATE (i.e., 38500), Apache Derby returns it as is; otherwise, Derby returns a generic 38000 SQLSTATE.

Care should be taken to ensure that both the class name and the function name are declared as public. In addition, the function must be defined as static, or else the database won't be able to find the routine.

The class library is compiled using the appropriate development environment. This library could contain any number of functions that need to be defined to the database. If this example were placed in the file YMLDFunctions.java, it would be compiled with the following command:

```
javac YMLDFunctions.java
```

The name of the integer square root function is ISQRT. Although it would be desirable to overload the SQRT operator, Apache Derby only allows one definition of a function name. This means that there is no way to differentiate SQRT(double) and SQRT(int) in SQL statements or when using the DROP statement. Care should be taken to create unique function names that also give some hint of their usage. This will make it easier to code your SQL without having to resort to looking up the definitions.

The function can be registered in Apache Derby, and a test VALUES clause can be used to make sure that the function works.

```
CREATE FUNCTION ISQRT(GETSQRT INT)
   RETURNS INT
   PARAMETER STYLE JAVA
   NO SQL LANGUAGE JAVA
   EXTERNAL NAME 'YMLDFunctions.ISQRT';

values isqrt(4);

ERROR 42X50: No method was found to be able to match method call
YMLDFunctions.ISQRT(int), even tried all combinations of object and
```

primitive types and any possible type conversion for any parameters
the method call may have. It may be that the method exists, but it is
not public and/or static, or that the parameter types are not method
invocation convertible.

The function definition fails because the class library (`YMLDFunctions.class`) cannot be found in the `CLASSPATH` that is defined for the operating environment. One way to fix this is to make sure that `CLASSPATH` is set to the directory in which this code was developed. Alternatively, the class file could be copied to a directory to which `CLASSPATH` points. After the class file is copied to the proper location, Apache Derby will find the function, and it will be available to any SQL statement.

```
values isqrt(4);
```

```
1
-----------
2
```

```
1 row selected
```

Internal .JAR Files

The previous example highlights a problem with class files. Moving a user-defined function along with the database will prove troublesome if care isn't taken to place the class file in the proper location. One alternative is to create a .JAR file and place that directly into an Apache Derby database. Apache Derby has a command that lets you embed a .JAR file into the database; when the contents of the database are moved, the .JAR file is moved automatically.

The next three steps will generate the appropriate .JAR files and set the parameters in Apache Derby so that the function logic can be contained within the database itself.

The first step is to use the Java compiler to compile the class library:

```
javac YMLDFunctions.java
```

This step creates a class library called `YMLDFunctions.class`. The next step requires that the .JAR file be created from the class library. In this example, the only class library is `YMLDFunctions.class`:

```
jar cf YMLDFunctions.jar YMLDFunctions.class
```

There are numerous options in the `jar` command, but for our purposes, the `c` (create) and `f` (file) options are sufficient. The .JAR file is created from the `YMLDFunctions.class` and given the name `YMLDFunctions.jar`.

Finally, the .JAR file must be installed into the Apache Derby database, and the database parameters must be updated to search for the .JAR file from within the database. Using the `ij` command environment, the following function calls are required to register the .JAR file in

Apache Derby. This function will set up the database property to have Apache Derby look at the internal .JAR files first, rather than the CLASSPATH.

```
CALL sqlj.install_jar('YMLDFunctions.jar','YMLDFunctions',0);
CALL SYSCS_UTIL.SYSCS_SET_DATABASE_PROPERTY('derby.database.classpath',
   'APP.YMLDFunctions');
```

The first command registers the .JAR file in Apache Derby, and the second command enables the database to look at the internal .JAR files. For the qualified .JAR name and the database property setting, the schema is usually included as part of the name (APP.YMLDFunctions). The default schema for an embedded database is APP.

There are two other methods that let you update and delete .JAR files from within Apache Derby:

- Removing .JAR files—CALL sqlj.remove_jar('APP.YMLDFunctions',0);
- Updating .JAR files—CALL sqlj.replace_jar('YMLDFunctions.jar', 'YMLDFunctions',0);

After a .JAR file has been registered within Apache Derby, the new function can be used within SQL statements.

Create Function Details

The syntax of the CREATE FUNCTION statement can be broken down into a number of sections. The first section contains the name of the function (in this case, ISQRT) followed by the parameters being sent to the function itself. Each parameter has a name and data type associated with it. The parameter names are optional, but naming the parameters makes it easier to associate each parameter with its purpose. The parameters can be of any data type except LONG VARCHAR, CLOB, and BLOB.

The RETURNS clause defines the data type of the value that will be returned by the function. In this example, the ISQRT function will return an INT value. The return value has the same restrictions as the input parameters.

The EXTERNAL NAME clause specifies the Java method to be called when the function is executed, and it takes the form class_name.method_name. The external name cannot have any extraneous spaces.

LANGUAGE JAVA tells Apache Derby to call the function as a public static method in a Java class.

PARAMETER STYLE tells Apache Derby that the function will use a parameter passing convention that conforms to the Java language and SQL routines specification.

The SQL clause tells Apache Derby what SQL the function can perform. There are three options for this clause:

- CONTAINS SQL indicates that SQL statements that neither read nor modify SQL data can be executed by the function. Statements that are not supported in any function return an error.

- NO SQL indicates that the function cannot execute any SQL statements.
- READS SQL DATA indicates that some SQL statements that do not modify SQL data can be included in the function. Statements that are not supported in any function return a different error. This is the default value.

The RETURN clause specifies whether the function is called if any of the input arguments is null. There are two options for this clause:

- RETURNS NULL ON NULL INPUT specifies that the function should not be invoked if any of the input arguments is null. The result is the null value.
- CALLED ON NULL INPUT specifies that the function should be invoked if any or all input arguments are null. This specification means that the function must be coded to test for null argument values. The function can return a null or non-null value. This is the default setting.

A function definition must contain the EXTERNAL NAME, LANGUAGE, and PARAMETER STYLE clauses.

Using SQL Within a User-Defined Function

All of the prior UDFs have used simple logic and no SQL access. The following example demonstrates how SQL can be used within a UDF to expand the power of these functions. The YMLD Theater has a limited number of seats available per production. One of the most common queries requested by a patron is "What is the first date that I can get fives seats for this performance?" Although this is a relatively simple request, the underlying SQL requires a couple of joins, grouping, and sorting requests to get the answer.

A quick review of the YMLD schema shows the two tables that are required to determine the answer to this query.

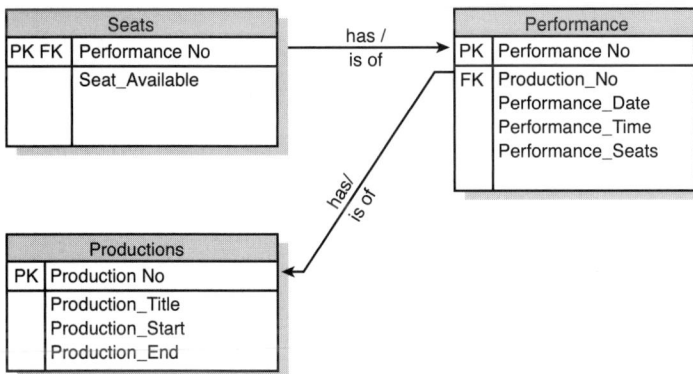

Figure 9-3 Production, Performance, Seat Relationship

The PRODUCTIONS table contains the title of a production. The production number can be determined from the production title, and then this number can be used to query the PERFORMANCES table. The PERFORMANCES table includes the date of each performance and the number of seats available. The number of seats could have been computed by running a query against the SEATS table. From a performance perspective, this is not the best database design! Requesting the availability of seats is probably the dominant request against a system like this. By placing the current number of available seats into the PERFORMANCES table, we can avoid doing costly queries against the SEATS table.

The earliest date of a performance can be retrieved using the following SQL. In this example, we are assuming that the title of the performance includes the word "Puck" and that the patron is looking for a large number of seats (14).

```
SELECT PROD.Production_Title, PERF.Performance_Date,
       MAX(PERF.Performance_Seats) AS Max_Seats
   FROM PRODUCTIONS PROD, PERFORMANCES PERF
  WHERE
    PROD.Production_Title LIKE '%Puck%' AND
    PERF.Production_No = PROD.Production_No
  GROUP BY
    PROD.Production_Title, PERF.Performance_Date
  HAVING
    MAX(PERF.Performance_Seats) >= 14
  ORDER BY
    PERF.Performance_Date ASC;


PRODUCTION_TITLE                      | PERFORMAN& | MAX_SEATS
-----------------------------------------------------------
Icing the Puck                        |2005-04-07|15
Icing the Puck                        |2005-04-16|15
Icing the Puck                        |2005-05-18|14

3 rows selected
```

A large portion of this SQL can be encapsulated in a function. The SQL that determines the earliest production date is shown next.

```
SELECT Performance_Date, max(Performance_Seats) AS Max_Seats
   FROM Performances
  WHERE
    Production_No = ?
  GROUP BY
    Performance_Date
```

```
HAVING
  MAX(Performance_Seats) >= ?
ORDER BY
  Performance_Date ASC;
```

The two parameters required to run this query are PRODUCTION_NO and the maximum number of seats required. Note that the MAX function is used to determine the maximum number of seats available for any performance. To be considered, the number of seats that someone is requesting must be less than or equal to this value.

If the number 4 is substituted for PRODUCTION_NO ("Icing the Puck"), and 14 is substituted for the number of seats, the query returns:

```
PERFORMAN&|MAX_SEATS
----------------------
2005-04-07|15
2005-04-16|15
2005-05-18|14


3 rows selected
```

This query is now placed into a function that returns the first available date based on the original production and seat criteria:

```
01 import java.sql.*;

02 public class GetPerformanceUDF {

03   public static Date GetPerfDate(int Prod_no, int Min_Seats)
       throws SQLException {

04     Connection conn = null;
05     Statement s = null;
06     ResultSet rs = null;
07     String SQL = null;
08     Date ResultDate = null;

09     conn = DriverManager.getConnection("jdbc:default:connection");
10     s = conn.createStatement();
11     SQL =
         "SELECT Performance_Date, " +
         "max(Performance_Seats) AS Max_Seats "+
         "FROM Performances " +
         "WHERE " +
```

```
           "   Production_No =  " + Prod_no + " " +
           "GROUP BY " +
           "  Performance_Date " +
           "HAVING " +
           "  MAX(Performance_Seats) >= " + Min_Seats + " " +
           "ORDER BY " +
           "  Performance_Date ASC";
12     rs = s.executeQuery(SQL);
13     if (rs.next()) {
14       ResultDate = rs.getDate("PERFORMANCE_DATE");
15       if (rs.wasNull()) {
16         ResultDate = null;
           }
17     rs.close(); // once we've iterated through the last row,
18     s.close();
19     return ResultDate;
         }
     }
```

The following notes provide additional information about key lines in the code.

- [01] import java.sql.*
  Any stored procedure, function, or application program that will be using JDBC function calls needs to include the java.sql.* import. Without this declaration, the compile step will fail because the proper JDBC definitions will not be available to the compiler.

- [02] public class GetPerformanceUDF {}
  The class must be public for the database to be able to use it. The name of the class does not have to be the same as the function. You can create a variety of functions within the same class file.

- [03] public static Date GetPerfDate(int Prod_no, int Min_Seats) throws SQLException{}
  The function declaration defines the input values to the function, as well as what the function will return. In this case, the two parameters, Prod_no and Min_Seats, will be used in the query to return the first performance that has the minimum number of required seats available. This function is defined with a throws SQLException clause so that errors will be returned to the calling application.

- [04-08] Declarations
  The variable block is defined outside the try statement to make the variables global to the function. The only variable that really needs to be defined in this section is the ResultDate field because it will be returned whether the function completes successfully or not.

- [09] conn = DriverManager.getConnection("jdbc:default:connection")

  If a stored procedure or function is accessing any SQL, it must establish a connection to the database first. Normally a stored procedure or function runs under the context of the calling application or SQL. In this case, the connection string does not refer directly to the database but rather to the default connection. This connect statement assumes that the calling program has already made a connection. If this is not true, an SQLException will be thrown and handled in the catch block. A stored procedure or function could create a connection outside of the context of the calling application, but this requires care in developing the application.

- [10] s = conn.createStatement();

  This method creates a statement handle that subsequently will be used to execute the SQL.

- [11] SQL Statement with parameters

  The SQL statement spans a number of lines in the function. Each line has a concatenation character at the end (+) to continue the string. In two portions of the SQL, the variables Prod_No and Min_seats are inserted into the string. Parameter markers could have been used as well, but because this statement is only being executed once, it is more efficient to use this approach.

- [12] rs = s.executeQuery(SQL);

  The SQL is executed immediately with this statement. The execute statement can be used for a variety of SQL statements, but it is particularly well suited for SELECT statements.

- [13] if (rs.next()) {}

  The rs.next call returns a value of true if a row is available in the result set. This means that at least one row was found matching the SELECT criteria in the SQL statement.

- [14] ResultDate = rs.getDate("PERFORMANCE_DATE");

  The getDate() function returns the contents of the Performance_Date column in the result set. The column name must be explicitly found in the result set for this to work. The date can also be returned by using the ordinal number of the column (position in the select list).

- [15] if (rs.wasNull()) { ResultDate = null;}

  If the returned date field is null, ResultDate will also be set to null. From a query perspective, this indicates that no rows were found. It could also mean that the production number was incorrect, but from a user perspective, no performances could be found that matched the criteria.

- [17-18] rs.close(); s.close();

  The statement and the connection are closed before the retrieved date value is returned.

- [19] return ResultDate;

  ResultDate is returned to the calling application.

Now that the function has been created, it needs to be defined within the database. The corresponding CREATE FUNCTION statement is shown next.

```
CREATE FUNCTION GetPerfDate(Prod_No INT, Min_Seats INT)
  RETURNS DATE
  PARAMETER STYLE JAVA
  READS SQL DATA LANGUAGE JAVA
  EXTERNAL NAME 'GetPerformanceUDF.GetPerfDate';
```

Any SQL INSERT, UPDATE, DELETE, or SELECT statement can now use this function as part of the SQL. For example, the following VALUES statement returns the first date on which production 3 has 5 available seats:

```
VALUES GetPerfDate(3,5);


1
----------
2005-03-08


1 row selected
```

The GetPerfDate() function can also be added to a SELECT statement. The following query returns the earliest date on which any production title with the word "the" in it will have 10 available seats:

```
SELECT Production_Title, GetPerfDate(Production_No, 10)
  FROM Productions
WHERE
  Production_Title like '%the%';


PRODUCTION_TITLE                       |2
-------------------------------------------------
Lilly of the Valley                    |2005-01-02
Icing the Puck                         |2005-01-18
Couched in Leather                     |2005-09-21


3 rows selected
```

Finally, the user-defined function can also be called from within an application to retrieve a value instead of issuing a SELECT statement. The following code uses the value returned from the function directly:

```
CallableStatement cstmt =
   conn.prepareCall("{? = CALL GetPerfDate(?,?)}");
cstmt.registerOutParameter(1, Types.DATE);
```

```
cstmt.setInt(2,2);
cstmt.setInt(3,10);
cstmt.execute();
Date dateGood = cstmt.getDate(1);
System.out.println("Date=" + dateGood);
```

Apache Derby Applets

You can create a Java applet that includes access to an Apache Derby database. To make this work, the applet must use a network driver to connect to the database. In addition, Apache Derby needs to be started as a network database.

The following example is an applet that retrieves the title and the start and end dates of all the productions running at the YMLD Theater:

```
01 public class DERBYAPPLT extends Applet {
02   Connection conn = null;

03   public void init() {
       try {
04       String url =
           "jdbc:derby:net://localhost/YMLD:user=APP;password=APP;";
05       Class.forName("com.ibm.db2.jcc.DB2Driver");
         conn = DriverManager.getConnection(url);
       }
       catch(Exception e) {
         e.printStackTrace();
       }
     }

     public void paint(Graphics g) {
       try {
         Font font = new Font("Arial",Font.PLAIN, 20);
         g.setFont(font);
         g.drawString("Your Momma Loves Drama Database",10,30);
         font = new Font("Lucida Console",Font.PLAIN, 16);
         g.setFont(font);
         g.drawString("Start Date  End Date    Title",10,60);
         g.drawString("_____",10,64);
06       Statement stmt = conn.createStatement();
07       ResultSet rs = stmt.executeQuery("SELECT * FROM Productions");
```

```
      int y = 85;
      while (rs.next()) {
        String dateStart = rs.getString("Production_Start");
        String dateEnd = rs.getString("Production_End");
        String title = rs.getString("Production_Title");
        String output = dateStart + "   " + dateEnd + "   " + title;
        g.drawString(output, 10, y);
         y = y + 20;
      }
      stmt.close();
    }
  catch(Exception e) {
      e.printStackTrace();
    }
  }
}
```

Most of this applet is identical to a normal Java program. A few differences are highlighted in the
following list.

- [01] public class DERBYAPPLET extends Applet {
  This example extends the Applet class, so a number of methods need to be handled
  within this class. The init() method is called when the applet is first initialized.
  This is where the connection to the database should be done. The second method is
  paint(), which is called as soon as the applet is displayed.

- [02] Connection conn = null;
  An applet has many methods associated with it; the connection should therefore be
  defined globally so that it can be accessed.

- [03] public void init() {
  The init() method initializes the connection to the database.

- [04] String url =
  "jdbc:derby:net://localhost/YMLD:user=APP;password=APP;";
  The applet needs to access the database through the network driver. In this example, the
  user ID and password are passed directly to the driver, but they could have been added
  to the connection string by using the Properties() method.

- [05] Class.forName("com.ibm.db2.jcc.DB2Driver");
  The network DB2 driver is used to connect to the Apache Derby database.

- [06] Statement stmt = conn.createStatement();
  A statement is allocated against the current connection. At this point, there is no difference between coding an application and an applet.

- [07] ResultSet rs = stmt.executeQuery("SELECT * FROM Productions");

  The result set is created from the SELECT statement; the rows are then retrieved and displayed on the screen.

The corresponding HTML (DerbyApplet.htm) that will launch this applet is shown next:

```html
<html>
<body>
<applet
   code="DERBYAPPLT.class" width=550 height=275
   archive="db2jcc_license_c.jar,db2jcc.jar">
</applet>
</body>
</html>
```

There are a number of parameters within the Applet tag that are required, including code, width, and height. The archive parameter is required to point to the proper JDBC drivers. When the HTML is opened in a suitable browser, it will display all of the productions playing at the YMLD Theater.

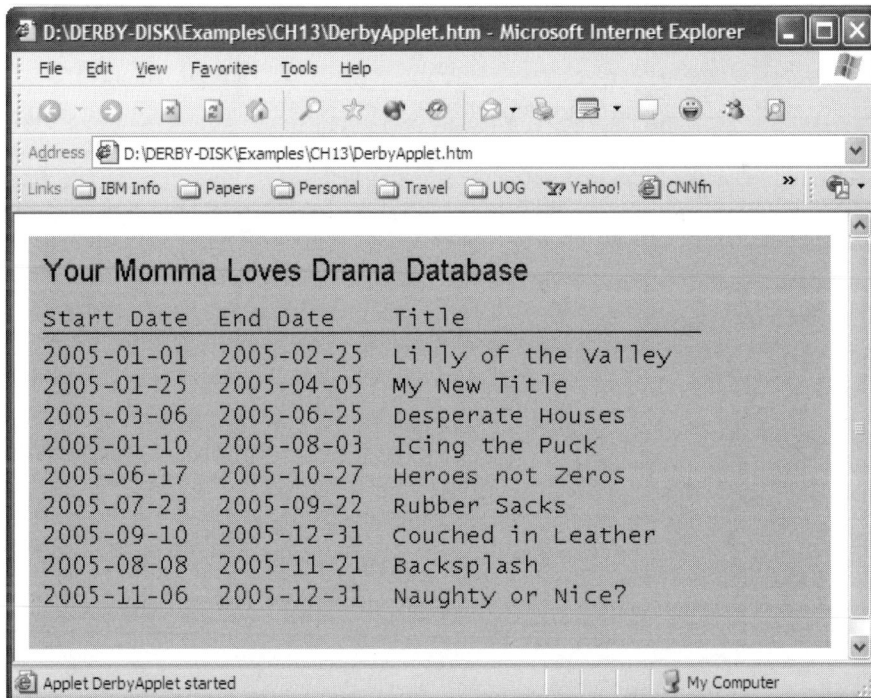

Figure 9-4   YMLD Applet

Locking Considerations

In a multi-user environment, record locking can become an issue that an application needs to handle. When one application is updating a record, that record is "locked" so that no other application can change it. This is critical in maintaining the integrity of the data.

Apache Derby supports four isolation levels: uncommitted read (UR), cursor stability (CS), read stability (RS), and repeatable read (RR). Insert, update, and delete operations always behave the same, no matter what the isolation level is. Only the behavior of SELECT statements varies depending on the isolation level.

Uncommitted Read

The uncommitted read isolation level, also known as dirty read, is the lowest level of isolation supported by Apache Derby. It can be used to access the uncommitted data changes made by other applications. For example, an application using the UR isolation level will retrieve all of the matching rows for a query, even if that data is in the process of being modified and has not yet been committed to the database.

If you decide to use this isolation level, your application might access incorrect data. There will be very few locks held by uncommitted read transactions.

Cursor Stability

The cursor stability isolation level locks any row on which the cursor is positioned during a transaction. The row lock is held until the next row is fetched or the transaction is terminated. If a row has been updated, the lock is held until the transaction is terminated. A transaction is terminated when either a COMMIT or a ROLLBACK statement has executed.

An application using the CS isolation level cannot read uncommitted data. In addition, the application locks the row that has just been fetched, and no other application can modify the contents of that row.

If you decide to use this isolation level, your application will always read consistent data, but you will lock the rows that you are updating or the rows that you are currently reading.

Read Stability

The read stability isolation level locks those rows that are part of a result set. If you have a table containing 10,000 rows and the query returns 10 rows, only 10 rows are locked.

An application using the RS isolation level cannot read uncommitted data. Instead of locking a single row, it locks all of the rows that are part of a result set, and no other application can modify the contents of those rows.

If you decide to use this isolation level, your application will get the same result every time the query executes during the same transaction.

Repeatable Read

The repeatable read isolation level is the highest isolation level available in Apache Derby. It locks all rows and application references within a transaction. Locks are held on all rows processed to build the result set, no matter how large the result set might be.

An application using the RR isolation level cannot read the uncommitted data of a concurrent application.

Choosing an Isolation Level

Choosing the proper isolation level is very important because the isolation level influences not only the concurrency but also the performance of the application. The more protection you have, the less concurrency is available.

Decide which concurrency problems are unacceptable for your application and then choose the isolation level that prevents these problems.

- Use the `uncommitted read isolation` level only if you run queries against read-only tables, or if you are only using `SELECT` statements and do not care whether you get uncommitted data from concurrent applications.

- Use the `cursor stability` isolation level if you want the maximum concurrency while seeing only committed data from concurrent applications.

- Use the `read stability` isolation level if your application operates in a concurrent environment. This means that qualified rows have to remain stable for the duration of the transaction.

- Use the `repeatable read` isolation level if changes to your result set are unacceptable.

Changing an Application's Isolation Level

When a connection does not specify an isolation level, it inherits the default isolation level for the Apache Derby system. The default is CS. To override the default, use the `setTransaction-Isolation()` method on a connection to change the value:

```
conn.setTransactionIsolation(TRANSACTION_READ_COMMITTED);
```

The four possible values are:

- `TRANSACTION_READ_COMMITTED`—cursor stability
- `TRANSACTION_SERIALIZABLE`—repeatable read
- `TRANSACTION_REPEATABLE_READ`—read stability
- `TRANSACTION_READ_UNCOMMITTED`—uncommitted read

Note that repeatable read from an SQL perspective is called `TRANSACTION_SERIALIZABLE` in JDBC.

In addition to using the `setTransactionIsolation()` method, you can also use the `SET CURRENT ISOLATION` statement in an application.

The SET CURRENT ISOLATION LEVEL statement allows you to change the isolation level for a user's connection. Valid levels are SERIALIZABLE, REPEATABLE READ, READ COMMITTED, and READ UNCOMMITTED. Issuing this statement commits the current transaction.

```
SET CURRENT ISOLATION =
  UR | DIRTY READ | READ UNCOMMITTED
  CS | READ COMMITTED | CURSOR STABILITY
  RS |
  RR | REPEATABLE READ | SERIALIZABLE
  RESET
```

The RESET option returns the isolation level back to the system default.

Lock Table

If an application has to change a large portion of a table, it might be faster to issue a LOCK TABLE statement instead of waiting for all locks to be acquired. Although locking a table will cause all other applications to wait, the processing of the table will be faster because the overhead of lock management will be eliminated.

The LOCK TABLE statement is issued from within an application.

```
LOCK TABLE table-Name IN { SHARE | EXCLUSIVE } MODE
```

SHARE mode is the default row-level locking for the table. EXCLUSIVE will lock the entire table for the duration of the commit scope, or until another LOCK TABLE statement with the SHARE option is issued.

Statement-Level Locking

Setting an isolation level for the entire duration of a connection through the setTransactionIsolation() method might not always be appropriate. There can be instances in which only a single SQL statement needs to exhibit a certain locking behavior. To support statement-level isolation, the WITH {lock-mode} clause can be used at the end of an SQL statement.

The syntax of the WITH clause is:

```
SELECT ...
WITH {RR | RS | CS | UR}
```

The WITH clause is optional on the SELECT statement, and by default, it is set to the system isolation level, or to the transaction level for the connection. For example, the following SELECT statement requests the uncommitted read isolation level. This means that it will read everything in the table, whether or not data has been committed by another application.

```
SELECT * FROM PERFORMANCES
WHERE PERFORMANCE_NO BETWEEN 122 AND 296
WITH UR;
```

The isolation level lasts only for the duration of this statement. Any subsequent SELECT statements will continue to use the default isolation level.

Summary

This chapter has covered a large amount of information on the use of the JDBC API within Apache Derby.

The first section of this chapter covered the basics of a JDBC application, including what imports to use, what driver is required, and how to connect to a database. Then the basic mechanics of allocating statements and executing simple DDL commands were reviewed, along with how to trap SQL errors and warnings in the application.

The second section examined the mechanics of creating, retrieving, and determining the contents of result sets. In particular, the ability to dynamically determine the data type, name, width, and other control information for columns in an answer set was explored in detail.

The third section examined prepared statements and how they can be used to simplify application design. In addition, the scope of commits within an application was examined, and special emphasis was given to how they relate to prepared statements and result set processing.

The fourth section dealt with the modification of data, including how to use result sets for updates, large object manipulation, and batching updates. Batching updates were shown to reduce network overhead and potentially improve performance.

The fifth section examined stored procedures, user-defined functions, and applets. These server-side objects can help to encapsulate logic for use by multiple applications. Each type of object was described in detail, including examples of usage.

The chapter concluded with a brief discussion on locking considerations and how connections, applications, and statements can have their isolation levels changed to suit an application's concurrency requirements.

Although this chapter has introduced many of the JDBC features available within Apache Derby, there are many more features. Additional information about JDBC features can be found in the Apache Derby manuals at http://incubator.apache.org/derby/manuals/index.html.

All of the examples in this chapter can be found on the book's Web site. The best way to learn how to use Apache Derby is to try running the examples yourself and experimenting with JDBC applications.

Developing Apache Derby Applications with Perl, PHP, Python, and ODBC

Communicating with an Apache Derby Network Server

The Apache Derby Network Server acts as a communication gateway for Apache Derby databases. It communicates through the Distributed Relational Database Architecture (DRDA) protocol to database clients and converts their requests to the native Apache Derby format. Because there are no functional open source application programming interfaces (APIs) that implement the DRDA protocol, Apache Derby relies on the IBM DB2 Universal Database (DB2 UDB) client to provide access through the Call Level Interface (CLI) and Open Database Connectivity (ODBC) APIs. The DB2 client converts CLI and ODBC requests into DRDA, enabling applications that are built against the DB2 client to connect to the Apache Derby Network Server. Given the similarity between the CLI and ODBC APIs, and due to the slight performance advantage offered by the single-layer CLI architecture, we will primarily discuss the means by which applications built on CLI can access the Apache Derby Network Server.

Distributed Relational Database Architecture (DRDA)

The DRDA protocol was adopted by the Open Group and has been a standard for database communications since 1998. The protocol enables application programs to connect to heterogeneous database managers to access distributed data. DRDA features high-performance network communications through an efficient data structure with thread-safe interoperability for relational databases. The Apache Derby Network Server communicates to remote clients through the DRDA protocol.

Call Level Interface (CLI)

The Call Level Interface is an X/Open standard API for accessing relational databases through SQL statements. In the DB2 UDB implementation of CLI, an application built on the CLI API directly accesses the relational database server by converting CLI calls into the DRDA protocol. The logical organization of CLI interfaces is divided roughly between *environment handles*, which provide access to the database environment, *connection handles*, which provide access to the database itself, and *statement handles*, which enable you to submit SQL statements, prepare and repeatedly execute statements with different parameters, and retrieve results sets from the database.

Open Database Connectivity (ODBC)

Based heavily on the CLI specification, ODBC is a database interface specification that was launched and successfully promoted by Microsoft Corporation for the early generations of its relational database products. Today the ODBC specification is one of the most common interfaces for accessing relational databases, and it is usually one of the first interfaces to be implemented for a database client and server. The relationship between CLI and ODBC extends not just to the conceptual elements of environment, connection, and statement handles, but also to the function names and arguments used to access the APIs. The APIs are so similar, in fact, that many CLI applications can be converted into ODBC applications by simply compiling against a different header file and linking against a different library. One significant difference between ODBC and CLI, however, is the architecture for ODBC communications: to connect to a database through ODBC, an application requires an ODBC driver and an ODBC driver manager.

The ODBC driver manager has the responsibility of loading the appropriate ODBC driver for the database to which the application has requested a connection. The application can either specify a full ODBC connection string (including the name of the ODBC driver) or simply reference a database that has been cataloged as an ODBC data source. In the first case, only the location of the ODBC driver must have been registered with the ODBC driver manager. In the second case, both the ODBC driver and the connection attributes for the database must have been registered with the ODBC driver manager.

Perl, PHP, and Python

Building on the practical and familiar framework of CLI and ODBC, the Perl, PHP, and Python extensions for database access have been implemented in C using CLI. Each language exposes the underlying CLI API in the scripting language's own simplified set of objects, methods, and functions, with the intention of presenting the database interface in a manner that is harmonious with the scripting language's own aesthetic and of easing the task of retrieving, inserting, and updating data from within a Perl, PHP, or Python program.

Installing the DB2 Runtime Client

ODBC, CLI, Perl, PHP, and Python applications all communicate with the Apache Derby Network Server through DRDA. Fortunately, the DB2 Runtime Client provides the runtime translation of CLI or ODBC calls to the DRDA protocol, which means that you must install the DB2 Runtime Client on the system from which you want to run your ODBC, CLI, Perl, PHP, or Python application. The DB2 Runtime Client is available for not only Linux and Windows operating systems running on 32-bit AMD and Intel architectures, but also for AIX, Solaris, and HP-UX operating systems, as well as for

Linux running on x86-64, OpenPOWER, pSeries, iSeries, and the zSeries hardware architectures. As a result, you can access your Apache Derby database from a CLI, ODBC, Perl, PHP, or Python application running on almost any major operating system available on the market today!

In general, only a single DB2 product (client or server) can be installed on a workstation at a time. If you have installed a DB2 server product, it contains the necessary client runtime functionality for CLI and ODBC connectivity, but you might have to start the installer to add the application development headers and libraries required for building the Perl, PHP, and Python database access extensions because these are not installed by default.

Linux Operating Systems

1. Download the DB2 Runtime Client for your Linux hardware architecture from http://ibm.com/db2/udb/support/downloadv8.html. In general, the most recent version of the DB2 Runtime Client provides the best interoperability and performance with your Apache Derby Network Server.

2. Decompress the DB2 Runtime Client for Linux using the following command:

```
bash$ tar xf FP8_MI00099_RTCL.tar
```

The `untar` operation creates a directory called `rtcl` in your current working directory.

3. Change the current directory to the `rtcl` directory.

4. Invoke the `db2setup` graphical installation program using the following the command:

```
bash$ su -c './setup'
```

Enter the root password at the prompt. At this point, either the graphical installer will be displayed, or you will run into one or more of several common problems:

- The operating system returns an error stating that the application cannot access the current display.

   This is a reasonably good sign; it means that the installer met all of the required dependencies and attempted to display itself but ran into a permission problem because the root user does not have access to the display process running under your login user ID. To solve this problem, try issuing the following set of commands instead of `su -c './setup'`:

   ```
   bash$ ssh -X root@localhost
   bash# cd /home/user/rtcl/
   bash# ./setup
   ```

- The operating system returns an error stating that it suffered from a segmentation fault.

   This is a sign that the threading model used by your Linux distribution differs from the threading model supported by the Java Virtual Machine (JVM) that is used in the

DB2 installation program. To overcome this problem, try issuing the following command to force Linux to use the older threading model that is used by the packaged JVM:

```
bash$ su -c 'LD_ASSUME_KERNEL=2.4.19 ./setup'
```

5. When the graphical installer displays, you must at a minimum select the **Application Development Headers and Libraries** option in addition to the mandatory components. The application development headers and libraries are required to compile the Perl, PHP, and Python extensions that enable those languages to access Apache Derby Network Servers. You should also consider installing the application development samples, which include sample code for creating CLI, Perl, and PHP applications that you can reuse for accessing Apache Derby databases. However, most of the graphical utilities are not useful for Apache Derby, so for the sake of minimizing your hard disk footprint, you should not install these components of the DB2 client.

6. Create a DB2 client instance. The examples in this book assume that you have created the default instance name db2inst1 in the default directory /home/db2inst1/. If you choose differently, ensure that you adjust the examples to match your choices.

After you have installed the DB2 Runtime Client and created a DB2 client instance, you can use that instance as a single repository, or *catalog*, of connection information for remote servers and databases on your system. Any user on your system can access the catalog and make use of the DB2 client connection infrastructure by inheriting the DB2 client profile with the following command:

```
bash$ . /home/db2inst1/sqllib/db2profile
```

Windows Operating Systems

Most users of Windows operating systems can install precompiled binary versions of the Perl, PHP, and Python database access extensions for Apache Derby, and in most cases they will also install precompiled binary versions of CLI and ODBC applications. For these users, DB2 Run-time Client Lite provides the perfect small footprint CLI or ODBC client for accessing the Apache Derby Network Server. The following instructions describe how to download and install DB2 Run-time Client Lite. However, a developer of CLI or ODBC applications needs the application development headers, which are only included with the full DB2 Run-time Client. Fortunately, the same Web site offers both clients for free download, so if you need to compile your own CLI or ODBC applications, you can adjust the following instructions accordingly.

1. Download DB2 Run-time Client Lite for Windows from http://ibm.com/db2/udb/support/downloadv8.html. In general, the most recent version of DB2 Run-time Client Lite provides the best interoperability and performance with your Apache Derby Network Server. During registration, you might have to choose which set of functionality you require; ensure that you specify the ODBC/CLI drivers.

2. Start the DB2 Run-time Client Lite package. The name of the package differs, depend-
    ing on the language of the package that you chose to download; for example, if you
    download the English package, the file name might be en_US_setup.exe. Double-
    click the file in Windows Explorer to start the graphical installer.

After you have installed DB2 Run-time Client Lite on your Windows operating system, you can
confirm that the installation was successful by running the db2cmd command from the command line. If a new command window with the title **DB2 CLP** opens, you are ready to begin
cataloging Apache Derby database connections.

Cataloging Apache Derby Network Servers

An Apache Derby Network Server is considered a *node* in a multi-tier database architecture.
Because the DRDA protocol is carried between the application requester (DB2 client that translates CLI calls into DRDA protocol flows) and the application server (Apache Derby Network
Server that translates DRDA protocol flows into relational database requests), the Apache Derby
Network Server is further categorized as a *TCP/IP node*. As you learned in Chapters 4 and 5,
when setting up your environment to run Apache Derby in network server mode, you have to
specify a port number on which the network server listens for connections and requests. When
you put all of that together, the syntax for cataloging an Apache Derby Network Server on the
DB2 client is relatively easy to understand:

```
bash$ db2 CATALOG TCPIP NODE node-name REMOTE hostname \
    SERVER port-number
```

For example, to catalog an Apache Derby Network Server running on a machine with the host
name pook.apache.org and serving requests on port 1527 with the nickname "derby", issue the
following command:

```
C:\> db2 CATALOG TCPIP NODE derby REMOTE pook.apache.org SERVER 1527
```

Notice that the command is exactly the same on both Linux and Windows operating systems. If
the command fails with an error message like "DB21061E Command line environment not initialized.", remember (on Linux) to inherit the DB2 client instance profile, or (on Windows) to start the
DB2 Command Window to ensure that your environment is ready to run DB2 client commands.

Cataloging Apache Derby Databases

In the DRDA topology, each Apache Derby database is known only in relation to the Apache
Derby Network Server that serves application requests to the database; therefore, to catalog a
single database, you must tell the DB2 client which node it must connect to in order to access the
database. Relative to all of the authentication methods available to the DB2 family of databases,
the only authentication method that the Apache Derby Network Server supports is server-based

authentication. Therefore, the syntax for cataloging an Apache Derby database on the DB2 client is as follows:

```
bash$ db2 CATALOG DATABASE database-name AT NODE node-name \
    AUTHENTICATION SERVER
```

For example, to catalog a database called YMLD on the Apache Derby Network Server that has been cataloged using the node name "derby", issue the following command:

```
bash$ db2 CATALOG DATABASE YMLD AT NODE derby AUTHENTICATION
    SERVER
```

ALWAYS CREATE DATABASES WITH UPPERCASE NAMES!

Apache Derby stores databases in directories created with the name specified in your `jdbc:derby:name;create=true` connection statement. Apache Derby faithfully creates directories with lowercase characters if that is what was requested in the connection statement. However, the DRDA standard states that all database names are to be folded to uppercase, so the DB2 client interprets a request to connect to the YmLd database as a request to connect to the YMLD database, and it requests a connection to the YMLD database from the Apache Derby Network Server.

On operating systems with case-sensitive file systems, such as Linux, Apache Derby tries to open the `YMLD` directory and returns an error to the client because only the `YmLd` directory exists on the file system. To avoid this problem, you should always create your Apache Derby databases with uppercase database names.

Testing Your Connection

To test your newly cataloged connection to the Apache Derby database, you can connect to the database from the DB2 command line as follows:

```
bash$ db2 CONNECT TO database USER user-name
```

The DB2 command line prompts you for a password and then tries to connect to the requested database. If the connection is successful, DB2 returns output like the following:

```
Enter current password for lynn:

   Database Connection Information

 Database server        = Apache Derby CSS10000
 SQL authorization ID   = lynn
 Local database alias   = YMLD
```

> **WHY DO I NEED TO SPECIFY A USER ID AND PASSWORD?**
>
> By default, Apache Derby does not enable any user authentication, so it might seem surprising that you have to specify a user ID and password for any connection to an Apache Derby database through the DB2 client. The reason you have to specify a user ID and password (which, for a database on which authentication has not been enabled, can be any string at all) is that the Apache Derby Network Server is only capable of performing authentication at the server.
>
> Of course, if you run Apache Derby in network server mode, you are strongly encouraged to enable some form of authentication (built-in, LDAP, or custom) because otherwise, any user with a TCP/IP connection to the Apache Derby Network Server can read or alter any row in any of the databases available to the network server.
>
> For more information on securing the Apache Derby environment, see Chapter 7, "Security."

Uncataloged Connections

Occasionally, you might want to write an application that enables users to create connections to databases without going through the hassle of cataloging the node and database from the command line. It is possible to create a data source name (DSN) for use within CLI, ODBC, Perl, PHP, and Python applications to connect to an Apache Derby database through the DB2 client without requiring a cataloged connection. The syntax for the uncataloged connection DSN is a single string; substitute the real host name, database name, and port number on which the Apache Derby Network Server is listening in the following example:

```
DRIVER={IBM DB2 ODBC DRIVER};HOSTNAME=pook.apache.org;
DATABASE=YMLD;PROTOCOL=TCPIP;PORT=1527;
```

Summary

The ODBC and CLI specifications are two very similar APIs for writing programs that connect to relational databases. Many popular programming languages have either adopted these APIs or built thin wrappers on top of them. In this chapter, you have learned:

- How the Apache Derby Network Server communicates with remote clients through DRDA
- How the DB2 Universal Database client enables applications written to the ODBC or the DB2 CLI specification to communicate with an Apache Derby Network Server
- How to install a DB2 client on Linux or Windows
- How to add an Apache Derby database to the DB2 client catalog of database connections
- How to test your connection to an Apache Derby database

"Your Momma Loves Drama" in JDBC

Introduction

This chapter introduces the "Your Momma Loves Drama" system and how you can develop its applications using Java and JDBC. Numerous APIs can be used to access the Apache Derby database, including PHP, Perl, Python, .NET, and ODBC. However, JDBC and Java have some key advantages over these APIs, including:

- JDBC is the native interface to Apache Derby
- JDBC and Java can be deployed on many different platforms without changes to the code
- All of the libraries, files, databases, and other resources can be embedded in one .JAR file for easy transport between systems

This chapter demonstrates how certain components of the YMLD system can be implemented. The code that is used throughout the chapter is meant to show certain techniques in JDBC coding and might not necessarily be the most elegant approach to Java development. However, the code has been tested, and the results are consistently correct. A developer should always get nervous when an SQL application returns different results from test to test!

From a development perspective, a number of tools were used to produce the final YMLD system. An open framework such as Eclipse (www.eclipse.org) is suitable for Apache Derby development. It includes a number of editing, testing, debugging, and deployment tools for Java. In addition, Apache Derby plug-ins are available (http://incubator.apache.org/derby/integrate/derby_plugin.html) for use within the Eclipse environment. Plug-ins give you the ability to manipulate and view Apache Derby objects within Eclipse.

Although Eclipse is generally suitable for major projects, those wanting to try out Java and JDBC development might want to use a less formal environment. The YMLD application was built using a few simple tools, including:

- jEdit—Java-based editor
- Thinlet—GUI toolkit that allows you to build applications with simple GUI screens
- ThinG—Thinlet graphical editor
- Nuvola—Icon set

More details about the development of the YMLD program and the use of these tools are provided in the application section.

Your Momma Loves Drama Database

The YMLD database was introduced earlier in the SQL chapter of the book. For reference, the database schema is reproduced in Figure 11-1.

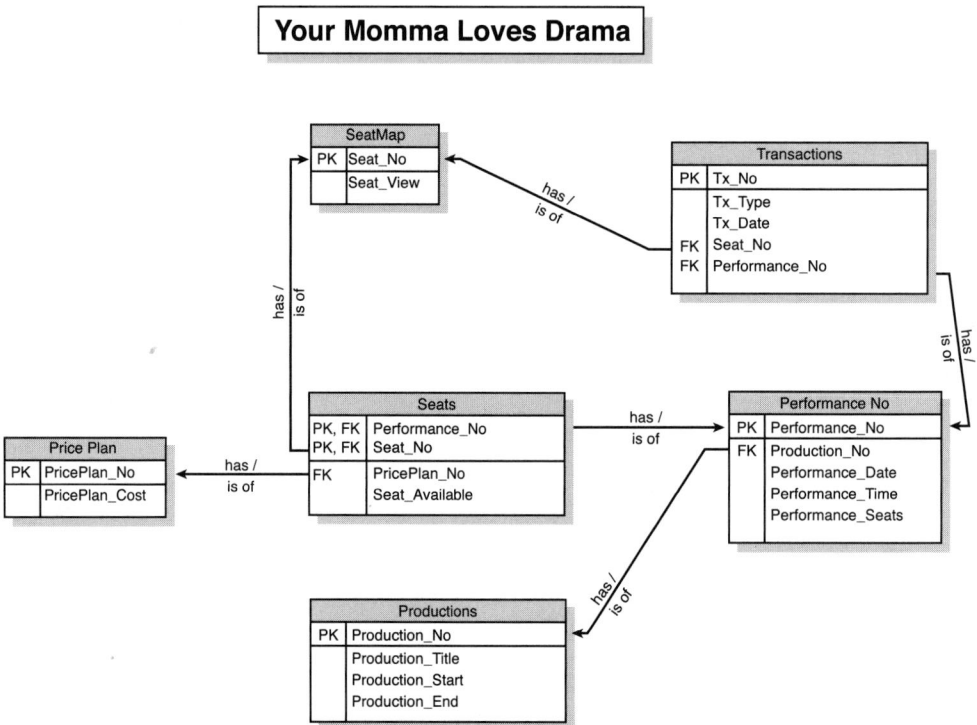

Figure 11-1   Your Momma Loves Drama schema

More details about the design of each of these tables are provided in the sections that follow.

PRODUCTIONS Table

YMLD is a very small and personal theater with a total of 20 seats. The theater runs a number of productions during the year. These productions are found in the PRODUCTIONS table.

```
CREATE TABLE Productions
  (
  Production_No      INTEGER NOT NULL GENERATED ALWAYS AS IDENTITY,
  Production_Title   VARCHAR(256),
  Production_Start   DATE,
  Production_End     DATE,
  PRIMARY KEY (Production_No)
  );
```

Each production has a production number, title, and start and end dates. The primary key is on the production number so that information on a particular production can be quickly accessed. In this implementation of the PRODUCTIONS table, the PRODUCTION_NO is a generated column. If you recall from Chapter 8, "SQL," generated columns automatically increment in value when a new row is added to the table. This simplifies programming because the programmer does not have to keep a separate "next value" table or use SELECT MAX(PRODUCTION_NO)+1 syntax to find the next suitable production number.

Data was loaded into the PRODUCTIONS table using the SYSCS_IMPORT_DATA utility.

```
CALL SYSCS_UTIL.SYSCS_IMPORT_DATA (null,
 'PRODUCTIONS',
 'PRODUCTION_TITLE,PRODUCTION_START,PRODUCTION_END',
 null,
 'PRODUCTIONS.DAT',
 null,null,null,0);
```

A data import was done rather than a table import because of the use of sequence numbers in the PRODUCTION_NO column. The import function cannot override a sequence number, so this import statement does not insert the PRODUCTION_NO column, but instead it relies on the database to generate it automatically. The corresponding PRODUCTIONS.DAT file contains a comma-delimited list of values to be inserted.

```
"Lilly of the Valley","2005-01-01","2005-02-25"
"My New Title",       "2005-01-25","2005-04-05"
"Desperate Houses",   "2005-03-06","2005-06-25"
"Icing the Puck",     "2005-01-10","2005-08-03"
"Heroes not Zeros",   "2005-06-17","2005-10-27"
"Rubber Sacks",       "2005-07-23","2005-09-22"
"Couched in Leather", "2005-09-10","2005-12-31"
```

```
"Backsplash",           "2005-08-08","2005-11-21"
"Naughty or Nice?",     "2005-11-06","2005-12-31"
```

PERFORMANCES Table

Every production has associated performances. Although a production has a start date and an end date, there is no guarantee that a production will run on all days that fall between these dates. For the data that is preloaded in this application, multiple productions can run during the same time. In some cases, as many as four productions can be active at any one time. Of course, the theater must have a minimum number of props to allow for a quick change of scenery between productions!

The performances are naturally found in the PERFORMANCES table.

```
CREATE TABLE Performances
  (
  Performance_No    INTEGER NOT NULL GENERATED ALWAYS AS IDENTITY,
  Production_No     INTEGER NOT NULL,
  Performance_Time  TIME NOT NULL,
  Performance_Date  DATE NOT NULL,
  Performance_Seats INTEGER NOT NULL,
  PRIMARY KEY (Performance_No),
  FOREIGN KEY (Production_No) REFERENCES Productions (Production_No) ON
    DELETE CASCADE
  );
```

Each performance during the year has a unique PERFORMANCE_NO. Some database designers might want to have performances within productions—for example, performances 1 through 10 for production 1, performances 1 through 20 for production 2, and so on. Although this can also be an acceptable approach, a single identifier has the advantage of allowing the use of sequences. This means that only the performance number is required when searching for available seats or for doing maintenance.

The final column in this table is PERFORMANCE_SEATS. One of the most common requests in a theater concerns the availability of seats for a performance. This request can be satisfied with one of two methods. The first method is to count the current number of allocated seats and subtract that from the total number of seats available. This method requires a significant amount of work on the part of the database. Rather than go through all that work, this column is used to keep track of the number of seats that are available for a performance. This means that some additional maintenance is required in an application to update this number.

Fortunately for Apache Derby developers, triggers can be used to achieve the same result. An update trigger can be created that will change the seat count when a seat changes status from empty to occupied (or vice versa). The definition of the trigger is shown here.

```
CREATE TRIGGER UPT_PERFORMANCES
  AFTER UPDATE OF SEAT_AVAILABLE
  ON SEATS
  REFERENCING
    NEW AS NEWROW
  FOR EACH ROW
  MODE DB2SQL
  UPDATE PERFORMANCES
    SET Performance_Seats =
         Performance_Seats +
           CASE
             WHEN NEWROW.SEAT_AVAILABLE = 1 THEN 1
             ELSE -1
           END
    WHERE Performance_no = NEWROW.Performance_no;
```

When an update to an existing seat record occurs, the associated performance record is also updated. The CASE expression is used to determine whether the count should be increased for refunds or decreased for purchases. Apache Derby triggers do not allow any form of logic within the trigger body itself, but fortunately using the CASE expression allows the trigger to achieve the desired result.

The design would change significantly if the application only stored seats that were available. In this case, an INSERT trigger would add to the seat count, while a DELETE trigger would decrease the seat count. For the sample data supplied with the YMLD application, 20 seats are automatically assigned to each performance, and the INSERT trigger decreases the total seat count when it inserts seats that are already occupied. Note that this is only done for the purpose of populating the YMLD database. A real application would only update the seat count when seats were inserted.

```
CREATE TRIGGER INS_PERFORMANCES
  AFTER INSERT
  ON SEATS
  REFERENCING
    NEW AS NEWROW
  FOR EACH ROW
  MODE DB2SQL
  UPDATE PERFORMANCES
    SET Performance_Seats =
         Performance_Seats +
           CASE
             WHEN NEWROW.SEAT_AVAILABLE = 0 THEN -1
             ELSE 0
           END
    WHERE Performance_no = NEWROW.Performance_no;
```

There is one referential constraint on the PERFORMANCES table.

```
FOREIGN KEY (Production_No) REFERENCES Productions(Production_No)
  ON DELETE CASCADE
```

If a production is deleted from the YMLD database (perhaps due to a lack of interest), all performances associated with this production are also automatically deleted. This clause could be changed to ON DELETE RESTRICT to force the programmer to refund all of the seats and delete individual performances before deleting the production. Having the delete cascade from the PRODUCTIONS to the PERFORMANCES table might cause the system to delete data that is critical to refunding money to existing ticket holders.

The PERFORMANCES table was loaded using the SYSCS_IMPORT_DATA utility.

```
CALL SYSCS_UTIL.SYSCS_IMPORT_DATA (
  null,
  'PERFORMANCES',
  'PRODUCTION_NO,PERFORMANCE_TIME,PERFORMANCE_DATE,PERFORMANCE_SEATS',
  null,
  'PERFORMANCES.DAT',null,null,null,0);
```

The same technique was used to load data into this table as was done for the PRODUCTIONS table. The PRODUCTION_NO column is generated automatically by the database, so it is not loaded as part of the command.

There are a total of 365 performances in the database (including a performance on Christmas Day!).

SEATS Table

The SEATS table tracks all of the currently allocated and occupied seats for a performance. Note that a record exists for every seat, whether it has been sold or not.

At this point there might be some questions about why seats are pre-allocated for a performance. An assumption was made that the number of seats available for a performance could change. For instance, seats may be unavailable because of an increased stage size, or some seats may need repair. A simple "total seats" column would not be specific enough in the PERFOR-MANCES table because it would not indicate which specific seats were unavailable. Instead, each seat for a performance is pre-allocated. A record for each available seat is created for every performance. Although there might be more efficient ways of tracking available seats, this approach does allow for the use of clever triggers to count the number of seats that are available!

The SEATS table is defined with the following SQL:

```
CREATE TABLE Seats
  (
  Performance_No    INTEGER NOT NULL,
```

```
Seat_No            INTEGER NOT NULL,
PricePlan_No       INTEGER NOT NULL,
Seat_Available     INTEGER NOT NULL,
CONSTRAINT Performances FOREIGN KEY (Performance_No)
  REFERENCES Performances(Performance_No) ON DELETE CASCADE,
CONSTRAINT PricePlan     FOREIGN KEY (PricePlan_No)
  REFERENCES PricePlan(PricePlan_No) ON DELETE RESTRICT,
CONSTRAINT SeatMap        FOREIGN KEY (Seat_No)
    REFERENCES SeatMap(Seat_No) ON DELETE RESTRICT,
CONSTRAINT SeatUnique   PRIMARY KEY (Performance_No, Seat_No)
);
```

Each performance has a total of 20 seats allocated for it. The PRICEPLAN_NO column refers to a table that contains the various prices that a seat could have. The SEAT_AVAILABLE column is set to 1 if a seat is available and 0 if it is not.

The final four statements are constraints that are defined against this table. The first constraint ensures that seats are tied to a particular performance and that they are deleted from the table if the corresponding performance is deleted.

```
CONSTRAINT Performances FOREIGN KEY (Performance_No)
  REFERENCES Performances(Performance_No) ON DELETE CASCADE
```

A developer might choose to use ON DELETE RESTRICT to ensure that the seats are deleted individually before the corresponding performance record is removed. Note that in the current YMLD design, there are two levels of CASCADE deletes that could occur. The PERFORMANCES table has an ON DELETE CASCADE constraint against the PRODUCTIONS table. This means that if a production is deleted, all performances associated with that production are deleted, and subsequently, all of the seats for these performances are also deleted. The CASCADE delete operation can cause a lot of activity in the database as a result of deleting only one production!

The next two constraints are used to check that the values being placed into the SEATS table are correct.

```
CONSTRAINT PricePlan     FOREIGN KEY (PricePlan_No)
  REFERENCES PricePlan(PricePlan_No) ON DELETE RESTRICT,
CONSTRAINT SeatMap        FOREIGN KEY (Seat_No)
  REFERENCES SeatMap(Seat_No) ON DELETE CASCADE
```

The ON DELETE RESTRICT clause makes much more sense for the PRICEPLAN column than an ON CASCADE DELETE. Deleting a particular price plan shouldn't delete all of the seats that are priced at this amount. Instead, seats that are tied to a PRICEPLAN that is being removed should be converted to something else.

The SEAT_NO column is checked against seats that are defined in the SEATMAP table. This column has ON DELETE CASCADE defined against it so that if a seat is deleted from the theater, it will be deleted from all performances. A developer might choose to use ON DELETE RESTRICT if refunds have to be given to people holding tickets for seats that are being removed.

The final constraint is a unique constraint on the combination of performance number and seat number. This constraint gives the database a quick way of accessing any seat and performance combination, as well as preventing any duplicate seats from being assigned to a performance.

The SEATS table is loaded using the SYSCS_IMPORT_TABLE utility. This utility loads the contents of the SEATS.DAT file into the SEATS table, and it assumes that each column in the data file will be placed into the table in the same sequence. Because the SEATS table does not have a sequence number, there is no need to specify which columns should be loaded.

```
CALL SYSCS_UTIL.SYSCS_IMPORT_TABLE
  (null,'SEATS','seats.dat',null,null,null,0);
```

PRICEPLAN Table

The PRICEPLAN table contains all of the prices that can be assigned to a seat.

```
CREATE TABLE PricePlan
  (
  PricePlan_No       INTEGER NOT NULL,
  PricePlan_Cost     DECIMAL(5,2) NOT NULL,
  PRIMARY KEY (PricePlan_No)
  );
```

Creating a separate pricing table makes it easier to control price increases and decreases. Only the PRICEPLAN entry has to be changed to affect the prices on all of the seats in the database. In addition, new prices can be added to this table without disrupting the existing system.

In more sophisticated systems, it might be better to separate price plans by production, or perhaps even by performance type. There might be cases in which the theater would want to charge more money for a production that requires additional staff or that is extremely popular. The theater might also want to differentiate pricing based on the actual time or day of the week that a performance takes place. Many theaters offer reduced rates for afternoon matinees or special student rates on "off" days. To create price differentiation by production, the PRICEPLAN table would require an extra column that points back to a valid production number. If differentiation is to be done by day of the week or time of production, then the performance number needs to be included as part of the PRICEPLAN table. In either case, the administration of the system will require more work. For the YMLD Theater, we have chosen to keep a simple pricing structure that remains consistent over all performances.

The PRICEPLAN table is loaded with four possible prices using a standard INSERT statement. The sample database distributes the seat prices randomly, but it attempts to limit price changes between seats to one level at a time (that is, it tries to put a price plan 1 seat beside a price plan 2 seat).

```
INSERT INTO PricePlan
  (PricePlan_No, PricePlan_Cost)
```

```
VALUES
   (1, 15.00), (2, 20.00), (3, 25.00), (4, 40.00);
```

SEATMAP Table

The SEATMAP table contains the valid seat numbers in the theater, along with an image of the front of the theater from each seat position. The key is the seat number.

```
CREATE TABLE SeatMap
   (
   Seat_No              INTEGER NOT NULL,
   Seat_View            BLOB(50K),
   PRIMARY KEY (Seat_No)
   );
```

All seat numbers in the theater need to be assigned to this table before they can be allocated to a performance. The actual image from the seat was intended to be used as an aid for someone purchasing a ticket to a performance. A theater patron could check the "view" from a seat before purchasing the ticket. A sample image was loaded into this table for demonstrating JDBC functionality in Chapter 9, "Developing Apache Derby Applications with JDBC," but the image has not been used in the YMLD demonstration program.

The current SEATMAP table contains 20 seats.

```
INSERT INTO SeatMap(Seat_No)
   VALUES
   1,2,3,4,5,6,7,8,9,10,11,12,13,14,15,16,17,18,19,20;
```

TRANSACTIONS Table

The TRANSACTIONS table is used to capture the ticket purchases that are made at the YMLD Theater. This table is also used for tracking other events, such as refunds, but for the most part, this table only contains seat purchase information.

```
CREATE TABLE Transactions
   (
   Tx_No              INTEGER NOT NULL GENERATED ALWAYS AS IDENTITY,
   Tx_Type            VARCHAR(32) NOT NULL,
   Tx_Date            DATE NOT NULL,
   Performance_No     INTEGER NOT NULL,
   Seat_No            INTEGER NOT NULL,
   FOREIGN KEY (Performance_No)
     REFERENCES Performances(Performance_No),
   FOREIGN KEY (Seat_No) REFERENCES SeatMap(Seat_No),
   PRIMARY KEY (Tx_No)
   );
```

The TX_NO column is automatically generated by the database, and it is used to uniquely identify a transaction that has taken place. The TX_TYPE column is usually set to 'PURCHASE', but it is reset to 'VOID' if a refund has been given. In addition, refund records are tagged with 'REFUND' in this field. The TX_DATE is the date on which the transaction occurred. If a developer wanted more granularity, a TIMESTAMP column could be used instead. The PERFORMANCE_NO and SEAT_NO uniquely identify the production for which a ticket was purchased.

There are two foreign keys in the TRANSACTIONS table. The PERFORMANCE_NO and SEAT_NO must both point to valid entries. Note that no DELETE rule is included on the foreign key references. The TRANSACTIONS table keeps historical track of what has happened in the database, so we don't want to lose any rows if the corresponding referential tables are changed.

The preloaded YMLD database does not contain any transactions. The transactions are generated as seats are reserved in the system.

The Your Momma Loves Drama Application

The YMLD application takes advantage of a number of technologies to deliver a theater reservation system. Although this application doesn't implement all aspects of a reservation system, it does demonstrate the use of Java and JDBC to communicate with an Apache Derby database.

The application is written entirely in Java, using the following components:

- jEdit—Java editor

  jEdit is described as a mature and well-designed programmer's text editor with seven years of development behind it. jEdit includes a number of plug-ins that facilitate the development of GUI applications, including a Thinlet viewer. More information on jEdit can be found at www.jedit.org.

- Thinlet—GUI toolkit

  Thinlet is a GUI toolkit in a single Java class, which parses the hierarchy and properties of the GUI, handles user interaction, and calls business logic. The graphical presentation of the panels and dialogs are described in an XML file, and the application methods are written as Java code. More information on Thinlet can be found at www.thinlet.com.

- ThinG—GUI design editor

  ThinG is a XUL GUI editor for Thinlet. ThinG can be found at http://thing.sourceforge.net.

- Nuvola—Icons

  The Nuvola icon set was originally intended for the KDE environment (www.kde-look.org). KDE is a powerful graphical desktop environment for Linux and UNIX workstations. The set of icons used by the YMLD application comes from the Nuvola icon set for KDE, and the original author of these icons can be found at http://www.icon-king.com.

- Apache Derby

  Of course, where would the YMLD application be without the database? The Apache Derby database can be found at the Apache Web site (www.apache.org) in the database section (http://db.apache.org/derby/).

For those projects that need to manage large numbers of class libraries, it might be better to develop applications under a framework similar to the Eclipse project (www.eclipse.org). To quote the Eclipse Web site, "Eclipse is a kind of universal tool platform - an open extensible IDE for anything and nothing in particular." Eclipse has a number of plug-ins that can extend the environment to support Apache Derby development. This can help to significantly reduce the time to develop applications against Apache Derby. The drawback is that Eclipse is a more structured environment and imposes a level of programming discipline that a developer might not be used to!

YMLD Overview

The YMLD application consists of six major functions that are displayed on the main introduction screen (see Figure 11-2). These functions include:

- Introduction—A brief overview of the system and the tools used to create it
- Current Performances—What's playing at the theater throughout the year
- Seat Pricing—The current price plans for seats at the theater
- Theater Seat Map—A visual display of how the seats are arranged
- Purchase Tickets—Select a production, date, and seats
- View Transaction Log—Examine the purchases history

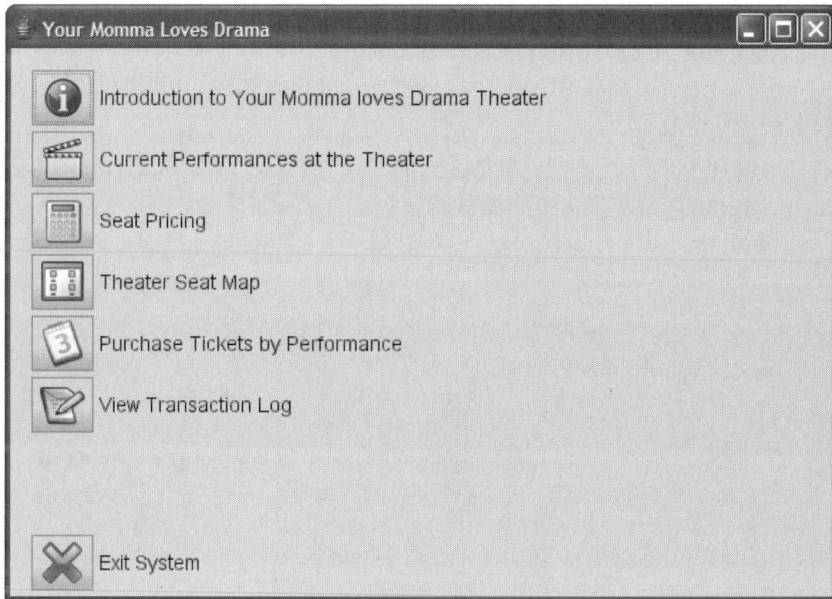

Figure 11-2   Your Momma Loves Drama main menu

Each of these functions is described later in this chapter.

Installing the YMLD Application

The source code (`YMLD.java`), panels, icons, and support files are found in the Chapter 11 link on the book's Web site (www.ibmpressbooks.com/title/0131855255). You don't have to compile this application on your machine because the executable image has been packaged as a .JAR file. The .JAR file contains the various class libraries and control information required to run the application.

Both program libraries and the YMLD database must be in the same directory as the application. The Web site includes a copy of the database in a zipped format (`YMLD.zip`). This file needs to be unzipped in the directory in which you've placed the `YMLD.jar` file. The YMLD database contains all of the data preloaded into the appropriate tables. If you don't want to use the zipped version of the database, you can re-create it by using the following command:

```
ij <create-YMLD.sql
```

Note that you must have set up the appropriate environment for the `ij` utility to work. The `setEmbeddedCP.bat` command (or shell) must be run before issuing the `ij` command.

When the `ij` command completes, it will have created the entire YMLD database. To start the YMLD application, issue the following command from a command line:

```
java -jar YMLD.jar
```

Once the application starts, you will see the main panel of the YMLD system, including the connection panel.

YMLD Initialization

The `main()` method of the YMLD program calls `FrameLauncher()`. This method is part of the Thinlet GUI library, and it sets up the environment in which the panels are to be displayed. The arguments to this method include the title of the application, the method that will be invoked to display the first panel, and the height and width dimensions of the screen.

```
public static void main(String[] args) throws Exception {
   new FrameLauncher("Your Momma Loves Drama", new YMLD(), 580, 375);
}
```

The `YMLD()` method displays two panels when it is invoked.

```
public YMLD() throws Exception {
   Object panel = parse(ymldMain);
   add(panel);
   panel = parse(ymldConnect);
   add(panel);
   requestFocus(find(panel, "bConnect"));
}
```

The parse() and add() methods are part of the Thinlet library. The parse(ymldMain) method returns an object that represents the main YMLD panel. The add(panel) method physically displays the panel on the screen. All of the routines that display information in the YMLD application use this technique.

The first panel (ymldMain) contains the main menu from which users can select an action. The second panel is the connection screen (ymldConnect) that a user must fill in with a user ID and password before being allowed to connect to the database. After the connection is made, the connection panel disappears, but the main menu remains.

Connecting to the YMLD System

An Apache Derby database can run with or without security. In the YMLD application, the default behavior is to request a user ID and password to connect to the system. The screen that initially appears when starting YMLD is shown in Figure 11-3.

Figure 11-3   Initial Connection Screen

You can change the user ID and password if you wish, but they must be registered in the derby.properties file to be accepted. By default, there is no defined properties file, so any user ID and password will do. However, if you want to try setting up users, add the following lines to the derby.properties file and include it in the directory in which the YMLD database is found.

```
derby.connection.requireAuthentication=true
derby.authentication.provider=BUILTIN
# Add your users here
derby.user.APP=app
```

When you click the **Connect** button, the `connectYMLD()` method is called to register the JDBC driver and to connect to the database with the specified user ID and password.

```
public void connectYMLD(Object panel, String uid, String pwd)
  throws Exception{
  String DerbyDriver = "org.apache.derby.jdbc.EmbeddedDriver";

  try {
    Class.forName(DerbyDriver).newInstance();
  }
  catch (Exception NoDriver) {
    showMessage("Error: No suitable Apache Derby driver found.");
    return;
  }

  try {
    String url = "jdbc:derby:YMLD";
    Properties properties = new Properties();
    properties.put("user", uid);
    properties.put("password", pwd);
    conn = DriverManager.getConnection(url,properties);
    Statement s = conn.createStatement();
    s.execute("SET SCHEMA APP");
    remove(panel);
  }
  catch(SQLException se) {
    getSQLError(se);
  }
  catch(Exception e) {
    showMessage("Error: Cannot connect to JDBC Driver.");
  }
}
```

The first `try` statement in the application attempts to register an embedded Apache Derby driver. You can change this to a network driver if the YMLD database will be accessed by multiple users. If an embedded driver cannot be found, the application raises an error (see Figure 11-4).

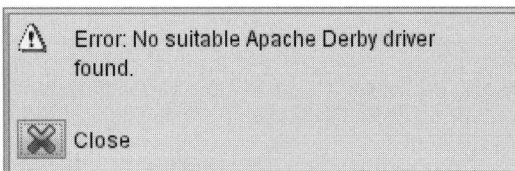

Figure 11-4   JDBC driver error

There are other ways of setting up the driver for Apache Derby. One method is to place the `derby.jar` file in the same directory as the YMLD application. Alternatively, the `setEmbeddedCP` command can be issued to set the `CLASSPATH` so that the YMLD application can find the appropriate Apache Derby libraries.

When the driver has successfully been loaded, the second `try` statement attempts to connect the user to the database. Two methods could be used to create the connection string. The method that is used in the YMLD application only generates the database URL string and then uses the properties field to add the user ID and password. Alternatively, the entire connection string, including the URL, userid, and password, can be generated and used to connect to the database. In either case, if the user ID and password are not valid, another error is raised (see Figure 11-5).

```
⚠  SQLState(08004): Connection refused :
    Invalid authentication.

✖  Close
```

Figure 11-5   User ID or password error

Note that an incorrect user ID or password generates the same error message. For the YMLD database, the default user ID is APP, with a password of app. After the connection completes, the current schema switches to APP. This ensures that all of the subsequent SQL statements will use APP as the high-level identifier. If the current schema was not changed, the application will append the user ID to the beginning of the table name. This will result in no tables or records being found.

One class variable is set in this code. The `conn` variable contains the connection context or handle to the database. This connection context will be used by all calls to the YMLD database, so it is best to have it available to all methods in the system.

Current Performances at the Theater

Clicking the **Current Performances** button gives you a list of productions at the YMLD Theater in a scrollable table (see Figure 11-6).

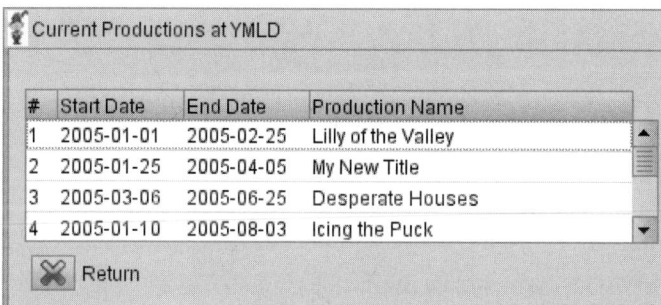

Current Productions at YMLD

#	Start Date	End Date	Production Name	
1	2005-01-01	2005-02-25	Lilly of the Valley	▲
2	2005-01-25	2005-04-05	My New Title	
3	2005-03-06	2005-06-25	Desperate Houses	
4	2005-01-10	2005-08-03	Icing the Puck	▼

✖ Return

Figure 11-6   Current productions at the YMLD Theater

This section of the YMLD application selects data from the PRODUCTIONS table by using a result set with JDBC. The pShowProductions() method uses a number of features of the Thinlet package to display a panel with multiple rows in a table. Although the purpose of this application is to demonstrate programming techniques for Apache Derby, the GUI interface affects the way the application needs to be written. These Thinlet interfaces will be discussed in this section only.

```
public void pShowProductions() throws Exception {
  Object panel = parse(ymldProductions);
  add(panel);

  try {
    Statement s = conn.createStatement();
    ResultSet rs = s.executeQuery( "SELECT * FROM Productions");
    while (rs.next()) {
      Object row = create("row");
      for (int i = 1; i < 5; ++i) {
        Object cell = create("cell");
        setString(cell,"text",rs.getString(i));
        add(row,cell);
      }
      Object tablep = find(panel,"Prodtable");
      add(tablep,row);
    }
    rs.close();
    s.close();
  }
  catch (SQLException se) {
    getSQLError(se);
  }
}
```

The initial portion of the pShowProductions() method retrieves, parses, and displays the production screen.

```
public void pShowProductions() throws Exception {
  Object panel = parse(ymldProductions);
  add(panel);
```

Each method in the YMLD application has the throws Exception specification. The Thinlet library requires access to external files that contain the specification for the dialogs, panels, tables, and other GUI objects. If a file is not available, the Thinlet library throws an exception.

None of the YMLD routines have `try` blocks around the Thinlet calls because the assumption is that the required files have already been included as part of the `YMLD.jar` file.

From an SQL perspective, all of the routines have `try` blocks around the SQL calls. If `try` blocks were not available to catch errors, `SQLExceptions` would be raised.

The SQL portion of the `pShowProductions()` routine creates a cursor into the PRO-DUCTIONS table and retrieves all of the current productions running at the YMLD Theater.

```
   try {
01   Statement s = conn.createStatement();
02   ResultSet rs = s.executeQuery( "SELECT * FROM
       Productions");
03   while (rs.next()) {
04     Object row = create("row");
05     for (int i = 1; i < 5; ++i) {
06       Object cell = create("cell");
07       setString(cell,"text",rs.getString(i));
08       add(row,cell);
       }
09     Object tablep = find(panel,"Prodtable");
10     add(tablep,row);
     }
11   rs.close();
     s.close();
   }
12 catch (SQLException se) {
13   getSQLError(se);
   }
```

- [01] `Statement s = conn.createStatement();`
  A statement must be allocated before any SQL can be executed against the database. Every routine that displays or manipulates SQL in the YMLD program will allocate a statement using the connection that was established when the application started.

- [02] `ResultSet rs = s.executeQuery( "SELECT * FROM Productions");`
  The result set contains a cursor that points to the results of the SELECT statement. In this method, the contents of the PRODUCTIONS table will be retrieved and displayed on the screen.

- [03] `while (rs.next()) { }`
  The application loops through all of the records that are found as a result of the SELECT statement. The `rs.next()` method returns true if a record is available to be read.

- [04] Object row = create("row");
  The create() method is part of the Thinlet library. The Productions panel contains a table that the application will load with values from the database. Tables contain a number of rows, and rows themselves are composed of many columns. Before a row can be added to a table, it must be populated with columns.
- [05] for (int i = 1; i < 5; ++i) {}
  Each row contains four columns of data from the PRODUCTIONS table. This loop is used to retrieve data from the result set and to place it into the different columns in the table.
- [06] Object cell = create("cell");
  A cell object needs to be created to hold the column value that will be inserted into the row.
- [07] setString(cell,"text",rs.getString(i));
  This method is another Thinlet routine. The various objects found within panels or dialogs have properties associated with them. Buttons, labels, and objects such as cells have "text" attributes that need to be set. The setString() method updates the value of the cell "text" with the contents of one of the columns retrieved from the PRODUCTIONS table.

  Each field that is retrieved by the SELECT statement must be extracted from the row. There are a number of approaches that can be used to do this. In this routine, the position of the column is used in the getString() method. The name of the column could be used instead of the ordinal number (location). For example, the first column, called PRODUCTION_NO, could be retrieved using getString("Production_ No"). The problem with using the name is that this makes it impossible to write generic retrieval routines. However, using ordinal positions can cause problems if the table definition changes. Although that is a remote possibility if you designed the table yourself, it can be an issue in larger systems where you do not control the table schema.

  As well as being cautious when using ordinal numbers, a developer should also consider using explicit column names rather than the all columns (*) specification. In this routine, the SELECT * FROM PRODUCTIONS statement will retrieve all columns from the table. It might be better to specify the exact columns and their desired order in the select list. For example, the following SELECT statement returns identical information:

```
SELECT
Production_No, Production_Title, Production_Start,
Production_End
FROM PRODUCTIONS
```

- [08] add(row,cell);
  The add() method adds the cell to the row object. Each column must be added to the row before the row itself can be added to the table. There are some special considerations

when reusing cells within a row. The loop that adds cells to the row initializes the cell object every time. However, if the cell object is reused before the row is added to the table, the only value that will get added is the last one that was defined. For example, a table with two columns might encounter the following code for inserting values:

```
Object cell = create("cell");
setString(cell,"text","1");
setString(cell,"text","2");
```

Only the last cell value will be placed into the row because the cell variable was reused. The expected result would be 1 and 2 in the two columns, respectively, but the actual result is 2 in the first column and nothing in the second column. An additional statement must be added to make this code work:

```
cell = create("cell");
```

The safest approach is to have a cell object for every column going into the table. Another acceptable approach is to use a loop where the cell object gets recreated every time. However, this might not work in all applications.

- [09] `Object tablep = find(panel,"Prodtable");`
  The find() method searches the panel or dialog for a specific object name. In this case, the program is searching for the Prodtable object. The Prodtable is the table list that is displayed as part of the panel. This is the object to which the row will be added.

- [10] `add(tablep,row);`
  The add() method adds the row to the table.

- [11] `rs.close();`
  All SQL statements and cursors, except for the database connection, should be closed when the program is finished using them. If an object is not closed, you might tie up resources in the database.

- [12] `catch (SQLException se) {}`
  All routines that issue any SQL statements should have a try or catch block. As a developer, you will probably not have any errors related to the SQL syntax. However, there is always a possibility that some database objects are missing because of administrative errors. In the event of an error, the catch block should be able to handle the problem.

- [13] `getSQLError(se);`
  A generic error handling routine was developed for the YMLD program. The getSQL-Error() routine displays an error message that contains all of the SQL diagnostic information.

getSQLError() Method

The pShowProductions() method relies on the getSQLError() routine to print any errors that occur during SQL processing. The catch block is similar in all of the YMLD methods.

```
catch (SQLException se) {
  getSQLError(se);
}
```

The SQLException is passed to getSQLError() to create and display the error string:

```
public void getSQLError(SQLException se) throws Exception {
  String SQLState = se.getSQLState();
  String SQLMessage - se.getMessage();
  showMessage("SQLState("+SQLState+ "): " + SQLMessage);
}
```

Whenever an error occurs within an SQL statement, an SQLException is raised, and information about the error needs to be returned to the user. Both the SQLState (error number) and the SQL message are available through separate methods. These two pieces of information are concatenated, and then the showdisplay() method is used to display the message for the user (see Figure 11-7).

Figure 11-7   Sample error message

Seat Pricing

Clicking the **Seat Pricing** button returns a tabular display of current seat prices at the YMLD Theater (see Figure 11-8).

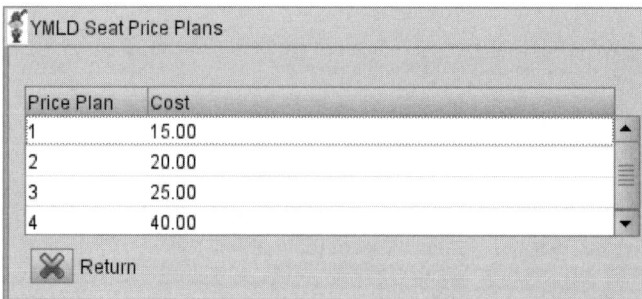

Figure 11-8   Current seat prices

The logic for retrieving the seat prices is identical to the logic for retrieving the current productions at the theater.

```
Statement s = conn.createStatement();
ResultSet rs = s.executeQuery( "SELECT * FROM PRICEPLAN");
while (rs.next()) {
  Object row = create("row");
  for (int  i = 1; i < 3; ++i) {
    Object cell = create("cell");
    setString(cell,"text",rs.getString(i));
    add(row,cell);
  }
  Object tablep = find(panel,"PriceTable");
  add(tablep,row);
}
```

In this routine, we are retrieving only two columns from the PRICEPLAN table and displaying the results.

Theater Seat Map

Clicking the **Theater Seat Map** button displays the current seating arrangements at the YMLD Theater (see Figure 11-9).

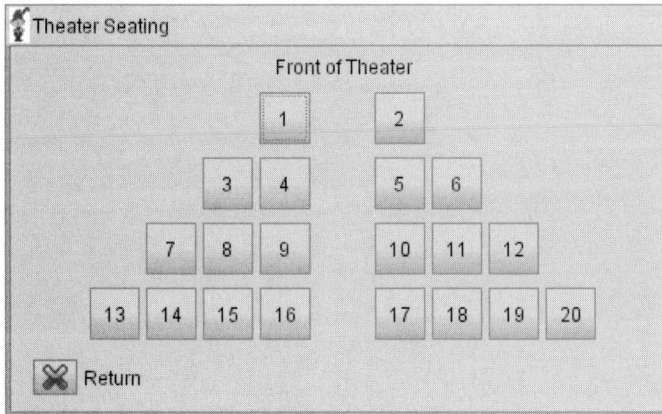

Figure 11-9   Seating plan

There is no additional logic behind the buttons shown on the screen. One of the possible uses for the seat buttons is to add a display of the theater "view" from this seat. The `SEATMAP` table has a column called `SEAT_VIEW`, which contains `LOB` objects. Pictures of the stage, as viewed from seats, could be stored in the database so that users can select a seat based on the view.

Purchase Tickets by Performance

Clicking the **Purchase Ticket** button takes you through a series of panels before a ticket purchase is finalized. There are five steps in purchasing a ticket:

- Select a production—The first panel asks you to select a production from the list of available productions.
- Select a date—The second panel displays a calendar and a seat map. No seat selection is available until you pick a performance date.
- Select a seat—After you have selected a performance date, the available seats for that performance are displayed, and you can select one or more seats to purchase.
- Confirm the order—The list of selected seats is shown for final confirmation.
- Finalize the transaction—The transaction is completed by updating the rows in the database.

Selecting a Production

The first step in purchasing a ticket is to select the production that you want to see (see Figure 11-10).

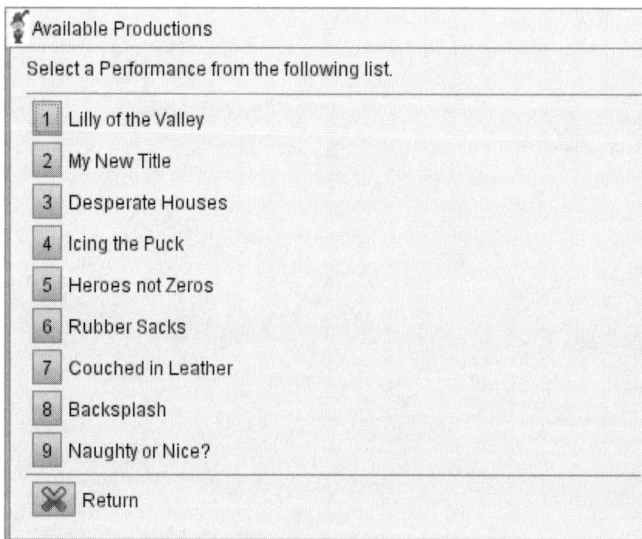

Available Productions

Select a Performance from the following list.

1. Lilly of the Valley
2. My New Title
3. Desperate Houses
4. Icing the Puck
5. Heroes not Zeros
6. Rubber Sacks
7. Couched in Leather
8. Backsplash
9. Naughty or Nice?

Return

Figure 11-10   Available productions

The list of productions is shown as a number of buttons with associated descriptions. This approach is different from the production and seat price lists. Rather than create a list of productions in a table, the application creates a menu from which the user can select. This approach provides a single view of all productions, rather than having the user scroll through a list in a table. The drawback of this approach is that it can handle only a small number of productions before the available space on the panel is used up.

The `pProdSelection()` method retrieves the current production list from the database and assigns titles to the labels beside the buttons on the screen. The SQL statement that retrieves this information is as follows:

```
SELECT PRODUCTION_NO, PRODUCTION_TITLE,
  MONTH(PRODUCTION_START) AS MONTH_START,
  MONTH(PRODUCTION_END) AS MONTH_END
FROM PRODUCTIONS
  ORDER BY PRODUCTION_NO;
```

Considerably more information is retrieved with this statement than you might expect. The `MONTH_START` and `MONTH_END` columns will be used for the next step in ticket selection. After a patron has selected a production, we want to be able to display a calendar from which to choose a performance date. Having the starting and ending months gives us information that we can use when initializing the next panel in this transaction.

The query also uses some built-in Apache Derby functions. The `MONTH` function strips only the month value from a date or a timestamp. This type of conversion could also be done in the application, but having it in the SQL is more convenient.

The assignment of titles to buttons is done within the `WHILE` loop:

```
01 Object buttons = find(panelProdSelection,"buttons");
02   int butpos = 0;
03   while (rs.next()) {
04     int production_no = rs.getInt("PRODUCTION_NO");
       String production_title = rs.getString("PRODUCTION_TITLE");
       String production_start = rs.getString("MONTH_START");
       String production_end = rs.getString("MONTH_END");
05     productionNames[production_no] = production_title;
06     Object button = getItem(buttons,index);
07     putProperty(button,"no",String.valueOf(production_no));
       putProperty(button,"start",production_start);
       putProperty(button,"end",production_end);
```

```
08    Object label = getItem(buttons,(butpos*2)+1);
09    setString(label,"text",production_title);
10    butpos += 1;
11    if (butpos == 9) break;
    }
```

- [01] Object buttons = find(panelProdSelection,"buttons");
  The find() function retrieves the panel object that contains button/label pairs on the screen.

- [02] int butpos = 0;
  The butpos variable is used to track which button number we are currently updating. This variable is also used to set some class variables with information that we are retrieving from the database. An application that uses input from a GUI needs to track information between changes in panels or dialogs. Unfortunately, context information between panels is not easily transferred because there is no direct call linkage between the panels. For this reason, a number of class variables are used to keep information as a user progresses through a series of panels.

- [03] while (rs.next()) {}
  The rs.next() method remains true as long as there are records to process.

- [04] int production_no = rs.getInt("PRODUCTION_NO");...
  The getInt() and getString() methods retrieve information from the result set. This information is used to set the production name beside each button, as well as to store some context information in the button property field. The PRODUCTION_NO is retrieved as an integer because it will be used as an index value for subsequent assignment statements.

- [05] productionNames[production_no] = production_title;
  The class variable productionNames contains the name of the productions currently in the database. The production name and production number are used in some of the ticket purchasing logic.

- [06] Object button = getItem(buttons,(butpos*2));
  The Thinlet package allows you to retrieve objects from a panel based on their position. The buttons panel contains nine buttons and nine labels. These objects are paired so that a label follows a button. The first object in the list has an index value of zero, so the first production button would be index position 0, and the label would be index position 1. To get the proper index position for the current button, we need to multiply the button number by 2.

- [07] putProperty(button,"no",String.valueOf(production_
  no)); ...
  There are three putProperty() statements in this block of code. Every object in
  a Thinlet GUI has a property field associated with it. The property field is available to
  an application to store additional information that is not associated with control of the
  object itself. This allows a developer to store information in the button definition that
  can be subsequently used by another program without having to store information in
  class variables. This technique is useful for storing limited character information in the
  control, but it is not recommended for large objects or numerous values.

  The production number (no), start month (start), and end month (end) are stored as
  button properties.

- [09] Object label = getItem(buttons,(butpos*2)+1);
  The button label is offset by one position from the button itself. For this reason, the
  index is set to butpos*2+1.

- [10] setString(label,"text",production_title);
  The label beside the button is set to the title of the production.

- [11] butpos += 1;
  The button position value increments by one for every production value read.

- [12] if (butpos == 9) break;
  Because of the design of this panel, a maximum of nine productions can be displayed
  at any one time. It is no coincidence that there are only nine productions in the YMLD
  database! A more generic approach would have been to create a table from which a user
  selects a production. Because of the limited number of slots, any productions past the
  ninth item would be ignored.

The final section of the code closes the open cursors and adds the panel to the screen display:

```
add(panelProdSelection);
rs.close();
s.close();
```

Selecting a Date

Both date and seat selections are done from one panel. This panel contains the name of the
selected production and the first month in which the production is playing (see Figure 11-11).

The date selection area is on the left side of the screen, and the seat selection area is on the
right side. The calendar has buttons that let you go forward or backward one month at a time. The
months are restricted to those in which the selected production is playing. The buttons on the calendar view change when you change the month. Note that buttons are only visible for the dates on
which there is a performance and seats are still available.

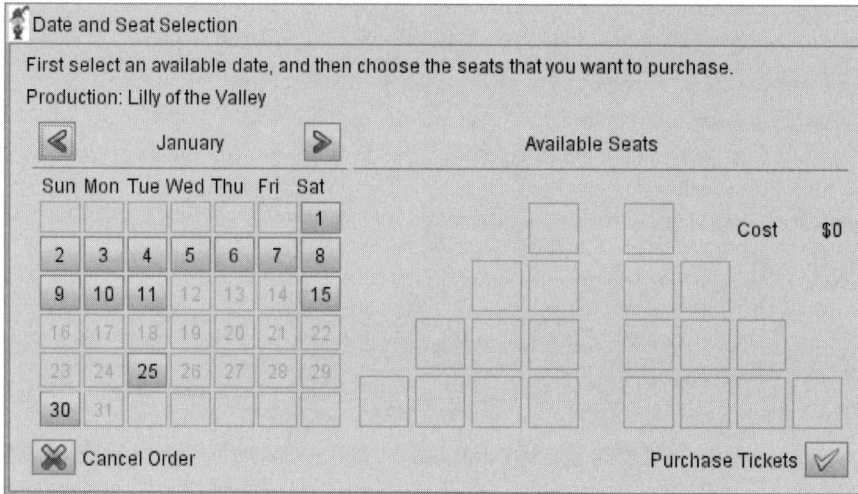

Figure 11-11   Date and seat selection

setCalendar()

The calendar is generated by the setCalendar() method. The logic is shown here.

```
   public void setCalendar() throws Exception {
01   getProdDates(selectedProdNo, selectedProdMonth);
02   Object objMonth = find(panelSeatSelection,"month");
     setString(objMonth,"text",monthNames[selectedProdMonth]);

03   Object daysPanel = find(panelSeatSelection,"days");
04   for (int i = 0; i <= 41; ++i) {
        Object dayButton = getItem(daysPanel,i);
        setString(dayButton,"text","");
        setBoolean(dayButton,"enabled",false);
     }
05   int dayofmonth = 1;
06   for (int i = monthDoW[selectedProdMonth];
           i < monthDoW[selectedProdMonth]+monthDays[selectedProdMonth];
           ++i) {
07      Object dayButton = getItem(daysPanel,i);
        setString(dayButton,"text",String.valueOf(dayofmonth));
08      if (prodDays[dayofmonth] == true) {
           setBoolean(dayButton,"enabled",true);
        }
```

```
      dayofmonth++;
   }

09  for (int i = 1; i <= 20; ++i) {
      Object seat = find(panelSeatSelection,String.valueOf(i));
      setIcon(seat,"icon",null);
      putProperty(seat,"selected","0");
      setBoolean(seat,"enabled",false);
   }
   totalCost = 0;
 }
```

- [01] `getProdDates(selectedProdNo, selectedProdMonth);`
  The `getProdDates()` method is described in detail in a later section. The purpose of the method is to return all of the dates on which a production is running during a particular month.

- [02] `Object objMonth = find(panelSeatSelection,"month");`
  The month object is retrieved from the panel so that the proper month can be displayed on top of the dates. The statement following this one places the name of the current month into the display. Three class variables are used to track the months, days, and beginning day of the week for each month.

```
static final int [] monthDays = {0,31,28,31,30,31,30,31,31,30,
   31,30,31};
static final int [] monthDoW  = {0,6,2,2,5,0,3,5,1,4,6,2,4};
static final String [] monthNames =
   {"","January","February","March","April",
    "May","June","July","August","September",
    "October","November","December"};
```

These three variables are initialized at the second position (index 1), rather than the first (index 0). This makes it easier to deal with months and days directly, instead of having to subtract one from every date calculation.

The `monthDoW` array refers to the day of the week on which a month begins. A zero represents Sunday, with Monday through Saturday being assigned successive values. These values are only valid for the year 2005. If the YMLD Theater had productions into 2006 and beyond, the algorithms would have to be modified to calculate the proper start dates, as well as the number of days in February during leap years.

- [03] `Object daysPanel = find(panelSeatSelection,"days");`
  The days object is retrieved from the panel so that the next loop can set the date on each of the buttons in the calendar.

- `[04] for (int i = 0; i <= 41; ++i) {}`
  Six weeks are displayed in the calendar. Remember that some months start on a Saturday and end on a Sunday or Monday six "weeks" later. For example, the month of January 2005 takes up six weeks on the calendar display (see Figure 11-12).

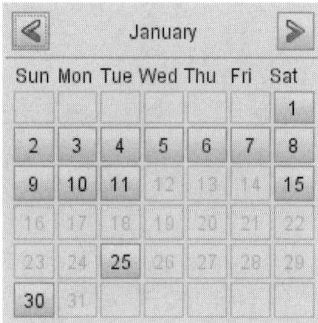

Figure 11-12　Date selection

The loop sets each button in the calendar to blank and disables it.

- `[05] int dayofmonth = 1;`
  The `dayofmonth` variable tracks which day on the screen is currently being modified. This variable is used for printing the current date, not for indexing the buttons on the screen.

- `[06] for (int i = monthDoW[selectedProdMonth]; ... )`
  This loop sets the actual dates of the month. The variable `i` is used to loop through the buttons on the screen. The starting value is the day of the week on which the month starts. In the case of January, this value is 6, which translates to the seventh button on the screen (Saturday). The loop continues for the total number of days in the month (`monthDays[]`).

- `[07] Object dayButton = getItem(daysPanel,i);`
  The current button is assigned to the `dayButton` variable. The statement that follows sets the button to the current day of the month.

- `[08] if (prodDays[dayofmonth] == true) {}`
  The `prodDays[]` array contains either a true or false value for each day of the month. If the value for a particular day is true, then a performance is scheduled for that day and seats are available, so the button is enabled and can be selected by the user. If the value is false, nothing has to be done because the buttons were initialized to be disabled at the beginning of the method.

- `[09] for (int i = 1; i <= 20; ++i) {}`
  The final loop disables all of the buttons that are associated with seats in the theater. The user must select a valid date before the available seats can be shown.

getProdDates()

The `setCalendar()` method relies on the `getProdDates()` routine to retrieve the dates (within a month) on which a performance is available. The important part of the routine is summarized in the following:

```
   Statement s = conn.createStatement();
   ResultSet rs = s.executeQuery(
01    "SELECT DAY(PERFORMANCE_DATE) AS DAYMONTH, PERFORMANCE_NO " +
      "FROM PERFORMANCES P " +
      "WHERE P.PRODUCTION_NO = " + prodNo + " AND " +
      "       MONTH(P.PERFORMANCE_DATE) = " + prodMonth + " AND " +
      "       P.PERFORMANCE_SEATS > 0 " +
      "ORDER BY PRODUCTION_NO");
02 for (int i = 1; i <= 31; ++i) prodDays[i] = false;
03 while (rs.next()) {
      int dayOfMonth = rs.getInt(1);
      int perfNo = rs.getInt(2);
      prodDays[dayOfMonth] = true;
      prodPerf[dayOfMonth] = perfNo;
   }
```

- `[01] SELECT statement`
  The `SELECT` statement that is used by the `getProdDates()` routine depends on `PRODUCTION_NO` and the month in which the performance is taking place.

  ```
  SELECT DAY(PERFORMANCE_DATE) AS DAYMONTH, PERFORMANCE_NO
    FROM PERFORMANCES P
  WHERE P.PRODUCTION_NO = prodNo AND
      MONTH(P.PERFORMANCE_DATE) = prodMonth AND
      P.PERFORMANCE_SEATS > 0
  ORDER BY PRODUCTION_NO;
  ```

  This query returns the day on which a performance is taking place and the performance number. The `WHERE` clause specifies that the rows for a particular month (`prodMonth`) and production (`prodNo`) are to be retrieved. In addition, there must be at least one seat available for a performance to be listed as available.

- `[02] for (int i = 1; i <= 31; ++i) prodDays[i] = false;`
  Each value of the `prodDays[]` array is set to false. A value in this array will be set to true if a performance for a particular day is found and if there are seats available.

- `[03] while (rs.next()) { }`
  The `prodDays[]` array will be set to true for each row that is returned from the `PERFORMANCES` table. In addition, the `prodPerf[]` array will contain the perfor-mance number for the production that is held on that day. This value is required later, when the user clicks on a particular date and needs to see what seats are available.

Selecting a Seat

After a user has selected a production and a performance date, the seats available for that performance are displayed on the screen (see Figure 11-13).

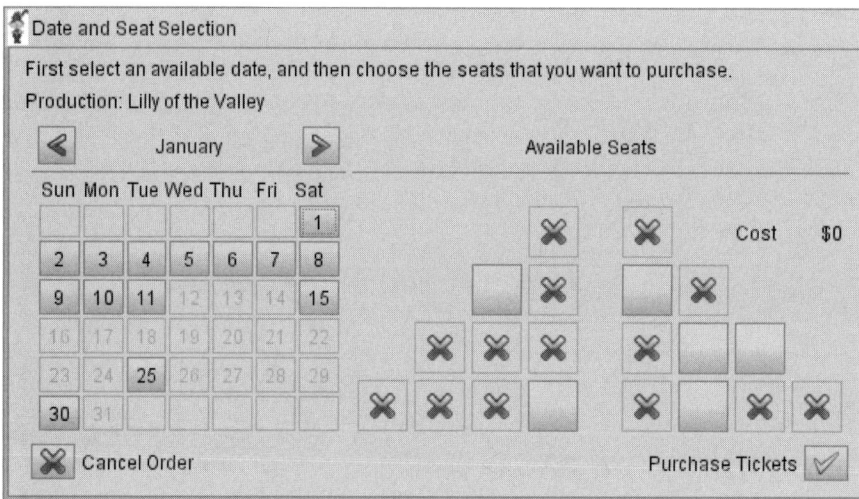

Figure 11-13   Seat selection

The `bCalendar()` method is called when a date button is clicked. This method finds all of the seats that are allocated for a particular performance and updates the display to show those seats. The routine first extracts the selected day, month, and performance number:

```
String whichDay = getString(objButton,"text");
selectedProdDay = Integer.parseInt(whichDay);
selectedProdDate = "2005-" +
                selectedProdMonth + "-" +
                selectedProdDay;
selectedPerfNo = prodPerf[selectedProdDay];
```

Using this information, the following SELECT statement is built to retrieve the seats that have been allocated for the specified performance:

```
SELECT SEAT_NO, SEAT_AVAILABLE, PRICEPLAN_COST
FROM SEATS S, PRICEPLAN P
WHERE PERFORMANCE_NO = selectedPerfNo AND
  S.PRICEPLAN_NO = P.PRICEPLAN_NO
ORDER BY SEAT_NO
```

The query returns the seat number, an indicator for whether the seat is available, and the current cost of the ticket for this seat. A join between the PRICEPLAN table and the SEATS table retrieves the pricing information for the seat.

The routine causes unavailable seats to display with a large X and available seats to remain unmarked and enabled for selection.

```
for (int i = 1; i <= 20; ++i) {
  Object seat = find(panelSeatSelection,String.valueOf(i));
  setIcon(seat,"icon",null);
  setBoolean(seat,"enabled",false);
}

while (rs.next()) {
  int seatNo = rs.getInt(1);
  int seatAvail = rs.getInt(2);
  int seatPrice = rs.getInt(3);
  Object seat = find(panelSeatSelection,String.valueOf (seatNo));
  if (seatAvail == 0) {
    setIcon(seat,"icon",getIcon("panels/I-Small-Cancel.png"));
    setBoolean(seat,"enabled",false);
  }
  else {
    setBoolean(seat,"enabled",true);
    putProperty(seat,"selected","0");
    putProperty(seat,"price",String.valueOf(seatPrice));
  }
}
```

The seat buttons have two additional properties assigned to them. The selected property is used to indicate whether a user has selected that seat for purchase. This will be important when the user confirms the order. The price property is used to display the price of the user's selection. Note that these properties could have been created as class arrays, but it is easier to attach these values to the button itself.

When a user clicks one of the seat buttons, the status of the selected property for that seat changes to true, and the button acquires a checkmark. If so desired, the user can click the seat button again to reset its status to unoccupied (see Figure 11-14).

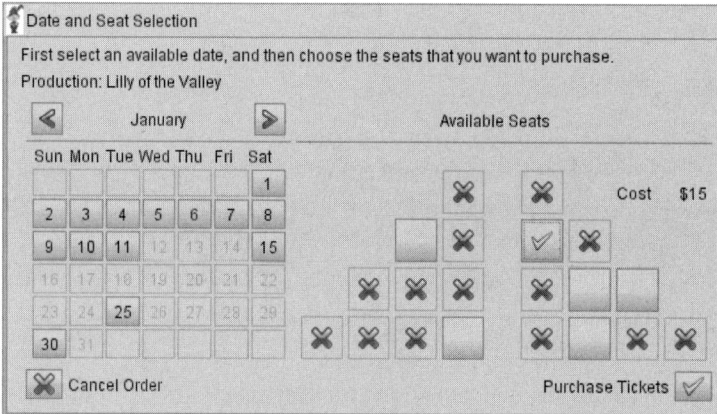

Figure 11-14   Seat selected

When a seat is selected, the cost field on the right side of the screen is updated. This value is updated whenever seats are added or subtracted. When all desired seats have been selected, the user can advance to the order confirmation step. If no seats have been selected, the system displays an error message (see Figure 11-15).

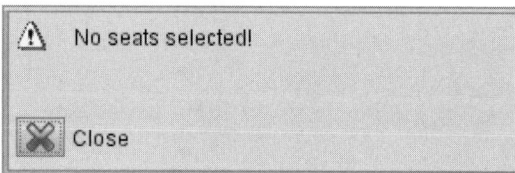

Figure 11-15   No seats selected

Confirming the Order

The confirmation screen is the last step in purchasing a ticket. This screen lists all of the tickets that a user has selected, and it requests confirmation of the order (see Figure 11-16).

The seat confirmation screen is created by the pShowTickets() method, which checks whether there are any selected seats before showing the confirmation screen.

```
if (totalCost == 0) {
  showMessage("No seats selected!");
  return;
}
```

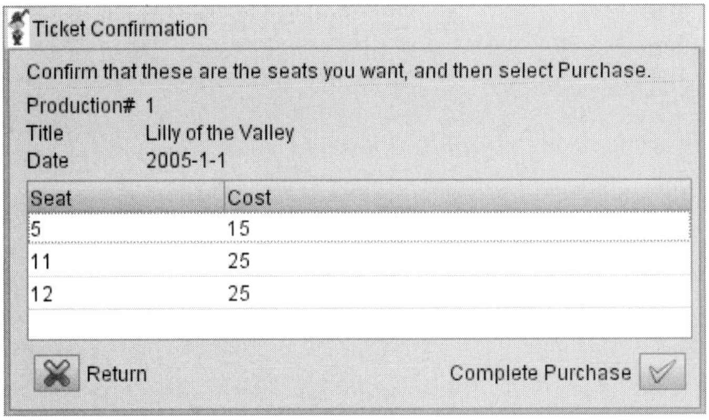

Figure 11-16   Order confirmation

There are two ways to determine whether any seats have been selected. The first method is to check whether the total value of seats selected so far is greater than zero. As seats are selected, their cost is added to the `totalCost` variable. If the total cost is zero, no seats have been selected. This method fails to take into account that some seats might have been given away; however, because the YMLD theater is a for-profit organization, we don't have to worry about that happening! To be absolutely sure that seats have been selected, the application could check the selected property on each seat button until one with a value of true was found.

The next section of the application populates the confirmation screen with the production number, title, and date of performance.

```
panelConfirmSelection = parse(ymldShowTickets);
add(panelConfirmSelection);
Object prodno = find(panelConfirmSelection,"prodno");
setString(prodno,"text",String.valueOf(selectedProdNo));
Object prodtitle = find(panelConfirmSelection,"prodtitle");
setString(prodtitle,"text",selectedProdName);
Object proddate = find(panelConfirmSelection,"date");
setString(proddate,"text",selectedProdDate);
```

At this point, each seat is checked to see whether it has been selected. If a seat has been selected, it is placed into a table that contains the seat number and the cost of the seat.

```
01 for (int i = 1; i <= 20; ++i) {
02   Object button = find(panelSeatSelection,String.valueOf(i));
03   if (getBoolean(button,"enabled") == false) continue;
04   Object selected = getProperty(button,"selected");
```

```
05      Object price = getProperty(button,"price");
06      if (String.valueOf(selected) == "1") {
07        Object row = create("row");
          Object cell = create("cell");
          setString(cell,"text",String.valueOf(i));
          add(row,cell);
          cell = create("cell");
          setString(cell,"text",String.valueOf(price));
          add(row,cell);
08        Object tablep = find(panelConfirmSelection,"tickets");
09        add(tablep,row);
        }
    }
```

- [01] for (int i = 1; i <= 20; ++i) {}
  There are twenty seats in the theater. Each seat is checked to see whether or not it has been selected for purchase. The application does not need to worry about seats being unavailable during a performance. By default, all seats are disabled, unless a record in the database shows that it is available.

- [02] Object button = find(panelSeatSelection, String.valueOf(i));
  Every button on the screen has a name associated with it. One technique for reading the buttons is to use an index into the panel, as we showed in the production list example. In the case of the theater seating example, there are empty labels between the buttons to help position them correctly. This means that there isn't an even number of spaces between button positions. Of course, this problem would not have occurred if the designer of the YMLD Theater had not been as creative with the seating arrangements! Instead of using the indexing technique, every button was given a unique name, which happened to be the numeric value of the seat. The find() method could then return an object that pointed to the nth button, and this object could then be used to check the status of the button.

- [03] if (getBoolean(button,"enabled") == false) continue;
  Only buttons that have been enabled are checked.

- [04] Object selected = getProperty(button,"selected");
  If a button was enabled, we also have to check whether it was selected by the user.

- [05] Object price = getProperty(button,"price");
  Each enabled button has a price associated with it. The application extracts the price at the same time that it retrieves the selected property.

- [06] if (String.valueOf(selected) == "1") {}
  Only records that are selected are added to the table.
- [07] Object row = create("row");
  The following statements create a row with two cells. The first cell contains the seat number, and the second cell contains the price of the seat.
- [08] Object tablep = find(panelConfirmSelection,"tickets");
  The table object on the confirmation panel is called tickets. This is the table to which the rows are added.

When the **Complete Purchase** button is clicked, the YMLD application finalizes the transaction, closes all of the intermediate windows, and displays the confirmation message (see Figure 11-17).

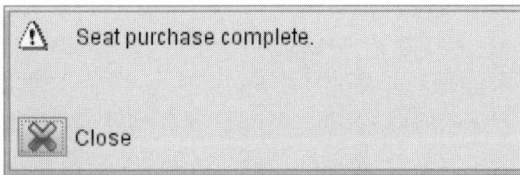

Figure 11-17 Purchase complete

Finalizing the Transaction

The routine that is called to finalize the transaction is named pFinishPurchase(). This method uses a prepared statement to update each selected seat to "occupied" and to write a transaction record to the TRANSACTIONS table. The first prepared statement updates the SEATS table.

```
PreparedStatement psUpdate = conn.prepareStatement(
  "UPDATE SEATS " +
  "  SET SEAT_AVAILABLE = 0 " +
  "WHERE  SEAT_NO = ? AND PERFORMANCE_NO = ?") ;
```

There are two parameter markers in this UPDATE statement. The first marker is for the seat being updated, and the second marker is for the performance number. This statement could be built dynamically by just creating an SQL statement with the concatenated seat number and performance number. Although this approach is perfectly acceptable, it isn't the most efficient way of executing repetitive SQL. With parameter markers, the database does not have to parse the SQL statement every time. This can reduce the amount of overhead.

The second prepared statement is an INSERT statement. This statement inserts a row into the TRANSACTIONS table. The TRANSACTIONS table keeps track of all tickets purchased at the YMLD Theater. This table is also used to refund patrons who change their minds.

```
PreparedStatement psLog = conn.prepareStatement(
    "INSERT INTO TRANSACTIONS(Tx_Type,Tx_Date,Performance_No,Seat_No) " +
    " VALUES ('UPDATE',CURRENT_DATE, ?, ?)");
```

Two parameter markers are associated with this INSERT statement. The TRANSACTIONS table actually has five columns in it. The first column is the transaction number, which is automatically generated by the database. For this reason, the INSERT statement cannot specify the actual transaction number. The TX_DATE column value is automatically created using the CURRENT_DATE special register. The TX_TYPE field is set to the value 'PURCHASE' to describe the purpose of the transaction record. The TRANSACTIONS table could become more important in the future if the owners of the YMLD Theater want to construct queries based on how quickly seats sell for a performance, or how often blocks of seats are sold. The last two columns, PERFORMANCE_NO and SEAT_NO, together uniquely identify the seats that were sold.

    The logic at this point in the routine scans through all 20 seats looking for the seats that were selected. These seats could also be determined by reading the table of selected seats that were already displayed, or by creating an array of available seats in a prior step. Any of these techniques would work.

```
     for (int i = 1; i <= 20; ++i) {
01     Object button = find(panelSeatSelection,
           String.valueOf(i));
       if (getBoolean(button,"enabled") == false) continue;
       Object selected = getProperty(button,"selected");
       if (String.valueOf(selected) == "1") {
         psUpdate.setInt(1,i);
         psUpdate.setInt(2,selectedPerfNo);
02       int rows = psUpdate.executeUpdate();
         psLog.setString(1,"PURCHASE");
         psLog.setInt(2,selectedPerfNo);
         psLog.setInt(3,i);
         rows = psLog.executeUpdate();
       }
     }
     psUpdate.close();
     psLog.close();
03   remove(panelConfirmSelection);
     remove(panelSeatSelection);
     remove(panelProdSelection);
04   showMessage("Seat purchase complete.");
```

- [01] `Object button = find(panelSeatSelection,`
  `String.valueOf(i));`
  Three panels are created during a ticket purchase transaction: `panelProdSelec-`
  `tion`, `panelSeatSelection`, and `panelConfirmSelection`. Whenever one
  of these panels is created, a class variable is assigned to the panel object. The reason for
  keeping track of the panels is to allow the ticket confirmation routine to close all of the
  intermediate panels automatically.

- [02] `int rows = psUpdate.executeUpdate();`
  After the parameter markers have been set, an `executeUpdate()` method is used to
  update the selected rows.

- [03] `remove(panelConfirmSelection);`
  After all of the updates have been completed, the panels associated with the ticket
  purchase transaction are closed.

- [04] `showMessage("Seat purchase complete.");`
  The final confirmation message, indicating that the tickets were successfully purchased,
  is displayed on the screen.

View Transaction Log

The transaction log contains records for each ticket that has been purchased. The transaction log
can be displayed if you want to see what purchases were made at the theater or if you need to
refund a ticket (see Figure 11-18).

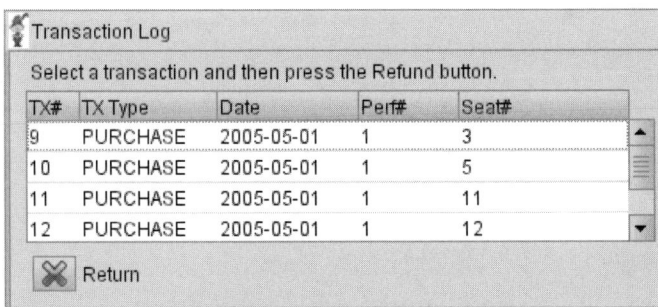

TX#	TX Type	Date	Perf#	Seat#
9	PURCHASE	2005-05-01	1	3
10	PURCHASE	2005-05-01	1	5
11	PURCHASE	2005-05-01	1	11
12	PURCHASE	2005-05-01	1	12

Figure 11-18   Transaction log

The routine that populates this screen with data is called `pShowTransactions()`. This
method retrieves all of the purchase transactions and displays them in a table on the screen.

```
ResultSet rs = s.executeQuery(
   "SELECT * FROM TRANSACTIONS WHERE TX_TYPE = 'PURCHASE'");
```

```
while (rs.next()) {
  String txNo   = rs.getString("TX_NO");
  String txType = rs.getString("TX_TYPE");
  String txDate = rs.getString("TX_DATE");
  String perfNo = rs.getString("PERFORMANCE_NO");
  String seatNo = rs.getString("SEAT_NO");
  Object row = create("row");
  Object cTxNo   = create("cell"); setString(cTxNo,"text",txNo);
  add(row,cTxNo);
  Object cTxType = create("cell"); setString(cTxType,"text",txType);
  add(row,cTxType);
  Object cTxDate = create("cell"); setString(cTxDate,"text",txDate);
  add(row,cTxDate);
  Object cPerfNo = create("cell"); setString(cPerfNo,"text",perfNo);
  add(row,cPerfNo);
  Object cSeatNo = create("cell"); setString(cSeatNo,"text",seatNo);
  add(row,cSeatNo);
  Object tablep = find(panel,"txTable");
  add(tablep,row);
}
```

The getString() method uses column names instead of column positions. Either technique will work, but this one allows us to explicitly state which columns we want to retrieve from the result set and which cell objects will contain them. The one advantage to this approach is that the cell locations in the row can be changed without modifying the SQL statement.

After the transaction log displays, you can click on any individual transaction to have it reversed. A message appears, prompting you to confirm the refund (see Figure 11-19).

Figure 11-19   Refund confirmation

The undo transaction operation takes information from the row that was selected in the transaction log.

```
public void selectRow(Object txTable) throws Exception {
  currentRow = getSelectedItem(txTable);
  Object pdeleteTxNo = getItem(currentRow,0);
  Object pdeleteDate = getItem(currentRow,2);
  Object pdeletePerfNo = getItem(currentRow,3);
  Object pdeleteSeatNo = getItem(currentRow,4);
  deleteDate    = getString(pdeleteDate,"text");
  deletePerfNo = getString(pdeletePerfNo,"text");
  deleteSeatNo = getString(pdeleteSeatNo,"text");
  deleteTxNo    = getString(pdeleteTxNo,"text");
  Object panel = parse(ymldUndo);
  add(panel);
  Object txtarea = find(panel,"msg");
  setString(txtarea,"text",
    "Do you want to undo the reservation for performance " +
    deletePerfNo + ", seat " + deleteSeatNo + " on " +
    deleteDate + "?");
  requestFocus(find(panel,"bCancel"));
}
```

Most of the logic in this method creates the confirmation screen and displays specific information about the performance and seat number that are associated with the refund request. Whenever a row object in a table is selected, it receives focus. This event enables an application to get the selected row and to retrieve the individual column values through the getItem() Thinlet method. The deleteVar set of class variables is initialized in this routine so that the application knows to which transaction the user was referring.

When you click the **Undo Transaction** button, the undoTx() method is called to finalize the refund.

```
   public void undoTx(Object panel) throws Exception {
     try {
01     conn.setAutoCommit(false);
02     PreparedStatement psUpdate = conn.prepareStatement(
         "UPDATE SEATS SET SEAT_AVAILABLE = 1" +
         "WHERE SEAT_NO = ? AND PERFORMANCE_NO = ?") ;
       psUpdate.setInt(1,Integer.parseInt(deleteSeatNo));
       psUpdate.setInt(2,Integer.parseInt(deletePerfNo));
       int rows = psUpdate.executeUpdate();
```

```
03     PreparedStatement psInsert = conn.prepareStatement(
         "INSERT INTO TRANSACTIONS " +
         " (Tx_Type,Tx_Date,Performance_No,Seat_No)" +
         " VALUES ('REFUND',CURRENT_DATE, ?, ?)");
       psInsert.setInt(1,Integer.parseInt(deletePerfNo));
       psInsert.setInt(2,Integer.parseInt(deleteSeatNo));
       rows = psInsert.executeUpdate();
04     PreparedStatement psUpdate2 = conn.prepareStatement(
         "UPDATE TRANSACTIONS SET TX_TYPE = 'VOID' " +
         "WHERE TX_NO = ?");
       psUpdate2.setInt(1,Integer.parseInt(deleteTxNo));
       rows = psUpdate2.executeUpdate();
05     conn.commit();
06     remove(currentRow);
       psInsert.close();
       psUpdate.close();
       psUpdate2.close();
07     conn.setAutoCommit(true);
     }
```

There are three distinct SQL statements within the undoTx() method. To ensure the integrity of the data in the TRANSACTIONS table, the three transactions must be either all committed or all rolled back at the same time. Statement [01] turns autocommit off for the database connection. Normally, autocommit is set to on, which means that every executed SQL statement is automatically committed in the database. If this were true in the undoTx() method, each insert or update operation would be committed before the others complete. This is not the behavior that we want, so autocommit is turned off.

The three SQL statements [02, 03, and 04] update various tables in the YMLD database. The first SQL statement updates the seat that is being refunded to indicate that the seat is again available. The second statement inserts a new row into the TRANSACTIONS table indicating that a refund has been processed for the seat. The third statement updates the original transaction record to indicate that it has been voided.

When the entire insert and update operations are complete, the SQL is committed [05], and the autocommit property is turned back on [07]. The remove() method [06] deletes the row from the TRANSACTIONS table so that the row associated with a refunded transaction can no longer be selected.

There are some additional considerations when using a transaction table to track all activity in a database. Although this approach is a great way of tracking activities in the system, it can become very expensive to query and maintain. In the YMLD application, transaction records are created for tickets purchased. In addition, refund records are created when patrons change their minds about the tickets that they have purchased. The TRANSACTIONS table can end up containing thousands of rows as the season progresses. A method is needed to prune the TRANSACTIONS table of old records that are no longer required. For example, transactions associated with performances that have already completed would be good candidates for deletion. In most cases, such information should be archived for auditing purposes or analysis.

Exit Routine

The final routine that is called when exiting the YMLD system is the exitYMLD() method, which closes the application.

```
public void exitYMLD() throws Exception {
  try {
    conn.close();
  }
  catch (Exception se) {
  }
  System.exit(0);
}
```

The database connection is closed before we exit the system. This ensures that any statements are properly terminated, especially if a transaction was started and no COMMIT statement was issued. Developers should make sure that all of their SQL statements are autocommitted, or that transactions, once complete, are committed explicitly.

Summary

This chapter has covered the development of the YMLD application using Java and JDBC. A variety of JDBC methods were used to access the YMLD database, including code to display current productions, seat prices, and transactions.

A series of GUI panels was developed to facilitate ticket purchasing activities, including the selection of a production, specifying a particular performance, picking available seats, and finally, confirming the seat selection. All of this development was done using various SQL statements and JDBC techniques.

A series of panels was also developed to allow transaction reversal. This topic also examined techniques for updating data, as well as implications of using a transaction log.

The source code and database can be found on the book's Web site. You are encouraged to experiment with the YMLD system and then to try some of these techniques with your own data.

CHAPTER **1 2**

"Your Momma Loves Drama" in Windows

Introduction

Chapter 11 introduced the "Your Momma Loves Drama" (YMLD) system and discussed how the applications can be developed using Java and JDBC. This chapter demonstrates how this application can be written using one of the data access APIs found in the Windows environment. Numerous APIs can be used to access the Apache Derby database, including ODBC, CLI, RDO, ADO, and .NET. Each of these APIs can access the Apache Derby database as long as the database is started as a network server and the DB2 client is used on the workstation.

This chapter demonstrates how certain components of the YMLD system can be implemented using Visual Basic .NET and ODBC (Open Database Connectivity). One of the reasons for using ODBC is to demonstrate some techniques that work against Apache Derby using a low-level API. ODBC gives the developer a lot of flexibility when dealing with a database system. However, coding in ODBC takes considerably more effort than using a built-in Visual Basic control that does all of the work for you. However, some of these controls cannot implement all of the features of the database, and they don't have as much flexibility as native ODBC commands.

This chapter also focuses on the implementation of features in the Microsoft Visual Basic .NET environment and covers many of the same features that were presented in Chapter 11. There will also be some repetition of logic in this section, but only where it needs to be modified to adapt to the Visual Basic .NET environment.

The Your Momma Loves Drama Application

The YMLD Windows application was written entirely in Visual Basic .NET. However, to access Apache Derby, some additional software is required:

- ODBC .NET Data Provider—The ODBC .NET Data Provider is an add-on component of the .NET Framework. This component provides access to native ODBC drivers. If

357

you do not have a copy of the ODBC .NET Data Provider, you can download it from the Microsoft Web site (http://www.microsoft.com).

- DB2 Client—Applications that are going to access the Apache Derby database across the network require the DB2 client. DB2 Run-time Client Lite is available from http://www-306.ibm.com/software/data/db2/runtime.html.

- Apache Derby—The Apache Derby database can be found at the Apache Web site (www.apache.org) in the database section (http://db.apache.org/derby/).

YMLD Overview

The YMLD application consists of six major functions that are displayed on the main introduction screen (Figure 12-1). These functions include:

- Introduction—A brief overview of the system and the tools used to create it
- Current Performances—What's playing at the theater throughout the year
- Seat Pricing—The current price plans for seats at the theater

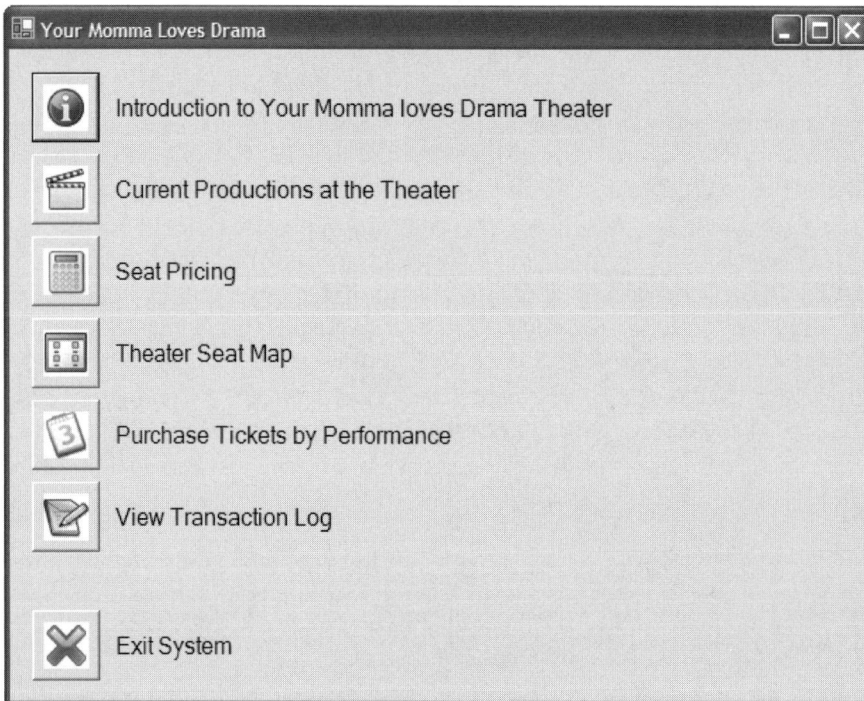

Figure 12-1   Your Momma Loves Drama main menu

- Theater Seat Map—A visual display of how the seats are arranged
- Purchase Tickets—Select a production, date, and seats
- View Transaction Log—Examine the purchases history

Each of these functions is described later in this chapter.

Installing the YMLD Application

Two versions of the YMLD Windows program are available on the book's Web site (www. ibmpressbooks.com/title/0131855255). The Visual Basic version is found in the Chapter 12 (VB6) link and uses RDO to access the YMLD database. The Visual Basic .NET version is found in the Chapter 12 (.NET) link and uses ODBC .NET support. Visual Basic and Visual Basic .NET share the same name and heritage, but there are significant differences between the development and programming models. This chapter does not discuss the design of the Visual Basic application, but it uses similar logic to the Visual Basic .NET version, so it should be easy to understand.

To run either version of this program, the YMLD database must first be created using the ij utility. The Web site includes a copy of the database in a zipped format (YMLD.zip) in the Chapter 12 directory. This file has to be unzipped in a directory on your hard drive, and then the network version of Apache Derby needs to be started. The YMLD database contains all of the data preloaded into the appropriate tables. If you don't want to use the zipped version of the database, you can re-create it by issuing the following command:

```
ij <create-YMLD.sql
```

Note that you must have set up the appropriate environment for the ij utility to work. The setEmbeddedCP.bat command (or shell) must be run before issuing the ij command.

When the ij command completes, it will have created the entire YMLD database. Before you start the YMLD application, you must start the Apache Derby network server and catalog the YMLD database. To start the network server, you must first set up the proper environment and then issue the start command from a command line.

```
setNetworkServerCP
startNetworkServer
```

These commands can be issued from either a Windows or Linux environment, but special care should be taken in Linux to ensure the proper spelling of the commands. The database can be run on either of these two operating systems as well, but the YMLD applications can only run from a Windows client.

After the network server has started, the YMLD database must be registered to ODBC. You must install DB2 Run-time Client Lite to issue these commands and to connect to the database. In a DB2 command line environment (initialized by issuing the db2cmd command), the catalog command can be used to register the database.

```
db2 => catalog tcpip node derby remote localhost server 1527
DB20000I  The CATALOG TCPIP NODE command completed successfully.
DB21056W  Directory changes may not be effective until the
  directory cache is refreshed.
db2 => catalog database ymld at node derby authentication
  server
DB20000I  The CATALOG DATABASE command completed successfully.
DB21056W  Directory changes may not be effective until the
  directory cache is refreshed.
db2 => catalog system odbc data source ymld
DB20000I  The CATALOG SYSTEM ODBC DATA SOURCE command completed
  successfully.
```

The initial catalog command tells the client that the Apache Derby server is on the local host and uses port 1527 to communicate with clients. The second catalog command tells the client that authentication of users is done at the server. This is always required when using Apache Derby as a network server. Finally, the YMLD database must be registered as an ODBC data source. All of these commands should be run from a DB2 command line.

After these catalog commands have executed, you can run the YMLD application. Both of these programs (RDO or .NET version) are named YMLD.exe. They have similar screens and actions, but the internal logic is slightly different. After the application starts, you will see the main panel of the YMLD system, including the connection panel.

YMLD Initialization

The main YMLD screen is displayed as the primary screen with the connection screen placed on top. A valid connection must be made to the YMLD database before you are allowed to issue any transactions against the system.

The first panel (ymldMain) contains the main menu from which users can select an action. The second panel is the connection screen (ymldConnect) that a user must first fill in with a user ID and password before being allowed to connect to the database. After the connection is made, the connection panel disappears, but the main menu remains.

Connecting to the YMLD System

An Apache Derby database can run with or without security, but when using the DB2 client, a user ID and password must be sent to the database. In the YMLD application, the default behavior is to request a user ID and password to connect to the system. The screen that initially appears when starting YMLD is shown in Figure 12-2.

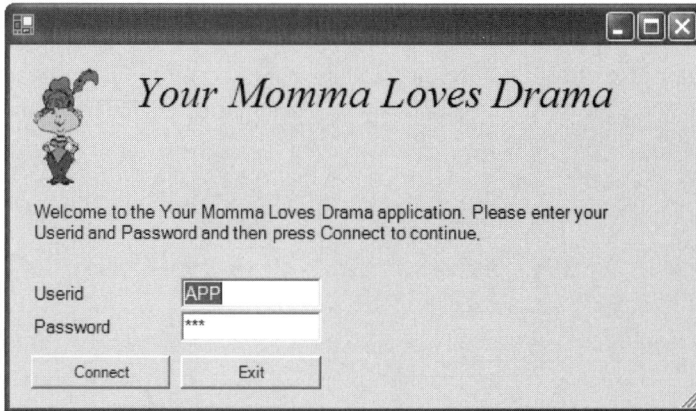

Figure 12-2   Initial connection screen

You can change the user ID and password if you wish, but they must be registered in the `derby` `.properties` file to be accepted. By default, there is no defined properties file, so any user ID and password will do. However, if you want to try setting up users, add the following lines to the `derby.properties` file and include it in the directory in which the YMLD database is found.

```
derby.connection.requireAuthentication=true
derby.authentication.provider=BUILTIN
# Add your users here
derby.user.APP=APP
```

When you click the **Connect** button, the program establishes a connection to the YMLD database.

The application checks the validity of the user ID and password to ensure that you've at least entered some information.

```
If (PWD.Text = "") Then
  MsgBox("You need to supply a password")
  Exit Sub
End If
```

```
If (UID.Text = "") Then
  MsgBox("You need to supply a userid")
  Exit Sub
End If
```

The program then enters a `try` block to connect to the database. In order for the program to recognize the ODBC-specific code, an `Imports` statement is placed at the beginning of the module:

```
Imports Microsoft.Data.Odbc
```

Without this statement, you must explicitly specify the fully qualified name of the function. This can lead to incredibly long statements that are very difficult to read!

```
Try
  Dim ymldConnectString As String = _
    "PROVIDER={IBM DB2 ODBC DRIVER};DSN=YMLD;UID=" & UID.Text & _
      ";PWD=" & PWD.Text & ";"
  YMLD.conn = New OdbcConnection(ymldConnectString)
  YMLD.conn.Open()
  Dim schema As OdbcCommand = _
    New OdbcCommand("SET SCHEMA APP", YMLD.conn)
  schema.ExecuteNonQuery()
  Me.Close()
Catch ex As System.Exception
  MsgBox(ex.Message)
End Try
```

Within the `try` block, `ymldConnectString` is set to contain the name of the ODBC driver, the database name, the current user ID, and the password. In this program, the following values are used in the connection statement:

- Driver—{IBM DB2 ODBC DRIVER}
- DSN (Database name)—YMLD
- UID (User ID)—Value from the dialog
- PWD (Password)—Value from the dialog

An ODBC connection is allocated with the `OdbcConnection()` method. `YMLD.conn` is a class variable that contains the connection information for the database. This connection information is used throughout the program, so a class (global) variable is the easiest way to keep track of it. The `YMLD.open` statement connects to the database.

If an error occurs while attempting to connect to the database, the `catch` block gains control and displays an error message (see Figure 12-3).

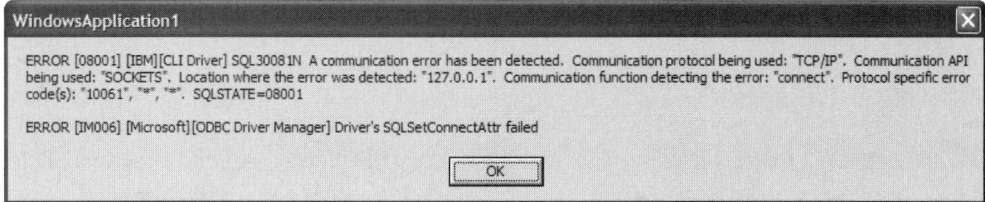

Figure 12-3   Connection error

ODBC calls should be placed in `try` blocks so that any potential errors can be trapped.

Bad User ID or Password

After the driver (either version) has been successfully loaded, the driver attempts to connect the user to the database. If the user ID and password are not valid, another error message is raised (see Figure 12-4).

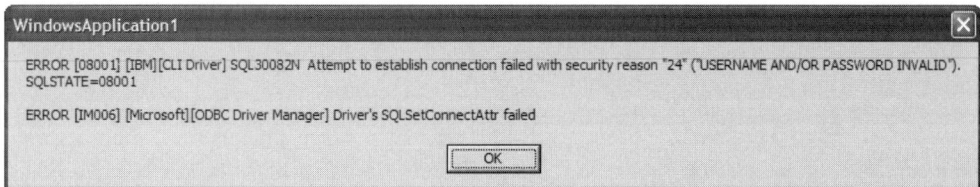

Figure 12-4   User ID or Password error

Note that an incorrect user ID or password generates the same error message.

Changing the Schema

When the YMLD database was created, all of its tables were created under the APP schema. When a user connects to a database, the default schema is the user ID; this would prevent the application from working. To ensure that the correct schema is used, the program issues a `SET SCHEMA` command immediately after the initial connection:

```
Dim schema As OdbcCommand = _
   New OdbcCommand("SET SCHEMA APP", YMLD.conn)
schema.ExecuteNonQuery()
```

`OdbcCommand` is used to immediately execute an SQL statement that does not return any rows. The statement might insert, update, or delete rows, or issue a command that alters objects in the database. `OdbcCommand` can have two parameters: the first one is the SQL string being executed, and the second is the connection to the database.

Error Handling

As mentioned previously, good programming practice includes `try` blocks around any ODBC statements being executed. The following block will catch all errors:

```
Catch ex As System.Exception
  MsgBox(ex.Message)
```

The initial connect dialog needs to catch all possible errors that occur while loading the ODBC drivers, so a system exception is the most appropriate one to use. The rest of the application uses `OdbcExceptions` to trap any errors while executing SQL statements:

```
Catch se As OdbcException
  MsgBox(se.Message)
```

Fortunately for developers, very little needs to be done in formatting an error message. `Odbc-Exception` already produces a descriptive error message that can be displayed to the user. Of course, the error message might not be that meaningful to a user who has no knowledge of the database system being used! In this case, the programmer could get individual error codes from the `OdbcException`. The `OdbcException.Errors.Count()` method returns the total number of errors encountered with a particular SQL statement. Each individual error can then be retrieved using the `OdbcException.Errors(i).SQLState` or `.NativeError` code. Error handling can be as simple or as complex as a developer wants it to be. The key consideration is what should be done when an error is encountered. The logic needs to determine whether the application can retry the SQL statement, attempt to reconnect to the database, or end the program. This information cannot be determined without accessing the underlying error codes of the database.

Current Performances at the Theater

Clicking the **Current Performances** button gives you a list of productions at the YMLD Theater in a scrollable table (see Figure 12-5).

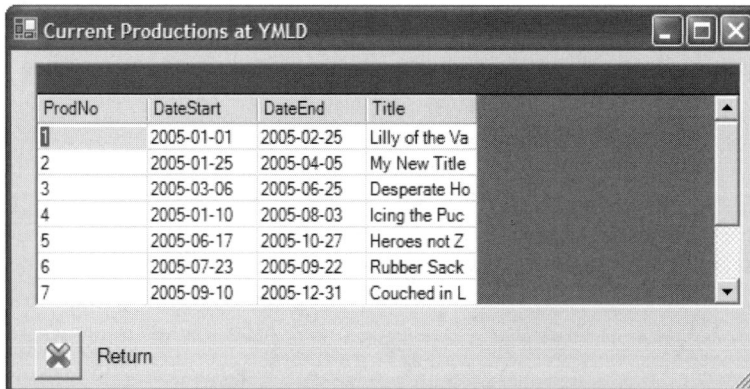

Figure 12-5   Current productions at the YMLD Theater

This section of the YMLD application selects data from the Productions table by using a result set with ODBC.

All of the panels in the YMLD application use two separate objects to display the data. The actual object on the form that displays the data is called a `DataGrid`, whereas the object that stores the temporary display data is called a `DataSet`. A data set contains a number of rows and columns that are defined within the control itself. The columns and result set name are created during the development of the application.

The YMLD application reads the results of an SQL statement and places the information directly into the data set. The `DataGrid` control is then refreshed with the information in the data set.

`OdbcDataReader` is used to retrieve a result set from a database. An `OdbcCommand` is created with the query (SELECT * FROM PRODUCTIONS) and the current connection (YMLD .conn). A `while` loop checks to see whether any data is present (`myReader.Read()`), subsequently retrieves all of the columns in the answer set, and populates the data set.

```
Dim myReader As OdbcDataReader
Dim mySelectQuery As String = _
     "SELECT PRODUCTION_NO, " & _
     "       PRODUCTION_START, " & _
     "       PRODUCTION_END, " & _
     "       PRODUCTION_TITLE " & _
     "FROM PRODUCTIONS"
Dim myCommand As New OdbcCommand(mySelectQuery, YMLD.conn)

myReader = myCommand.ExecuteReader()
While myReader.Read()
  ... process rows ...
End While
myReader.Close()
```

Each column is retrieved using a symbolic name, or an ordinal (position) within the answer set. The Get method (`GetInt`, `GetString`) specifies the type of data being returned from the column. In this example, only the PRODUCTION_NO is returned as an integer, and the other columns are all strings.

```
While myReader.Read()
  Dim newRow(3) As Object
  newRow(0) = myReader.GetInt32(0)
  newRow(1) = myReader.GetString(1)
  newRow(2) = myReader.GetString(2)
  newRow(3) = myReader.GetString(3)
  myRow = Prodtable.LoadDataRow(newRow, True)
End While
```

To retrieve a column based on the column name, use the `GetOrdinal()` method. `GetOrdinal(column_name)` returns the column position of the named column in the answer set. `GetOrdinal` can be combined with the `Get` method to retrieve data from the table by column name.

```
newRow(0) = myReader.GetInt32(myReader.GetOrdinal
   ("PRODUCTION_NO"))
```

There are a large number of `Get` methods available, depending on the data type. Table 12-1 summarizes the `Get` methods that are available to an application.

Table 12-1   SQL and Java Data Types

SQL Data Type	ODBC *Get()* Method
SMALLINT	GetInt16()
INTEGER	GetInt32()
BIGINT	GetInt64()
DECIMAL	GetDecimal()
REAL	GetFloat()
DOUBLE PRECISION	GetDouble(), GetFloat()
DATE	GetDate()
TIME	GetTime()
TIMESTAMP	GetDateTime()
CHAR	GetChar()
VARCHAR	GetString()
LONG VARCHAR	GetString()
CLOB	GetChars()
BLOB	GetBytes()
CHAR FOR BIT DATA	GetBytes()
VARCHAR FOR BIT DATA	GetBytes()
LONG VARCHAR FOR BIT DATA	GetBytes()

Because the data is read from the result set, the YMLD application must populate the data set so that the `DataGrid` can display the data. A data set is made up of a number of rows. To insert a new row into this table, a row object needs to be defined (new `myRow` as `DataRow`) and columns must be added to it. The `newrow(3)` variable is used to hold the columns that will be assigned to the row. The upper bound of the array size is used by the `LoadDataRow` method to determine how many columns are assigned to a row. In this example, four columns are added to the row, and the `LoadDataRow()` method adds the data to the DataGrid. Note that there must be a `BeginLoadData()` method at the beginning of the load operation and an `EndLoadData()` method when it completes.

```
Dim myRow As DataRow
Prodtable = Data.Tables(0)
myReader = myCommand.ExecuteReader()
Prodtable.BeginLoadData()
While myReader.Read()
  Dim newRow(3) As Object
  ...
  myRow = Prodtable.LoadDataRow(newRow, True)
End While
Prodtable.EndLoadData()
```

The `DataGrid` is mapped directly to the data set through the Data Source property. When the contents of the data set are changed, the `DataGrid` control immediately updates what is seen on the screen.

Try/Catch Block

All of the methods within the YMLD application rely on `try/catch` blocks to trap any errors that might occur when an SQL statement is issued. The `catch` block is identical in all of the YMLD methods.

```
try
  Odbc methods...
Catch se As OdbcException
  MsgBox(se.Message)
end try
```

There is no need to format the error message because the ODBC driver will create the complete message string. The `catch` block only displays the error message. A programmer might want to capture the error state to determine what should be done with the error. The YMLD application only displays the error message and then continues. A sample error message is shown in Figure 12-6.

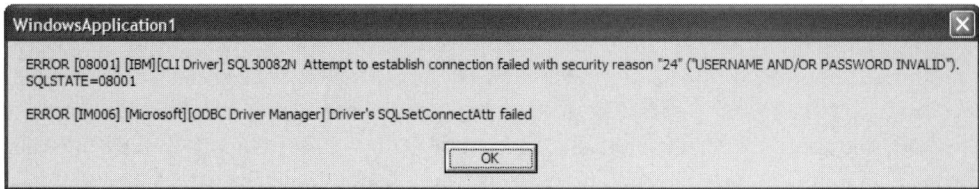

Figure 12-6   Sample error message

Seat Pricing

Clicking the **Seat Pricing** button returns a tabular display of current seat prices at the YMLD Theater (see Figure 12-7).

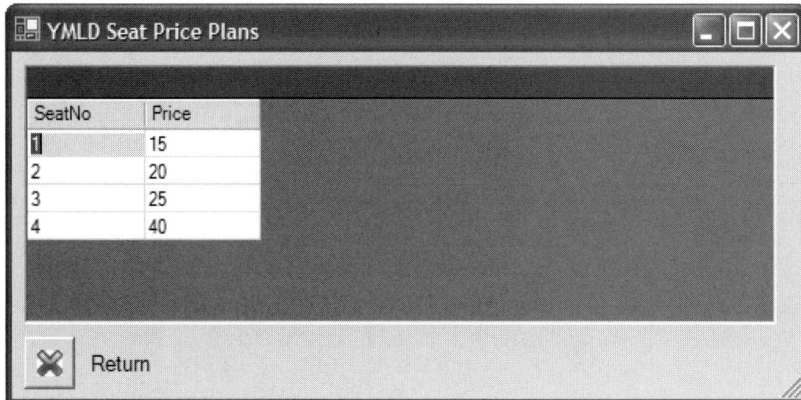

Figure 12-7   Current seat prices

The logic for returning the seat prices is identical to the logic for retrieving the current productions at the theater.

The Visual Basic .NET version loads the data into a data set and then maps the values to a data grid for display. The core portion of the logic is shown next.

```
Dim myReader As OdbcDataReader
Dim PriceTable As New DataTable()
Dim mySelectQuery As String = "SELECT * FROM PRICEPLAN"

Dim myCommand As New OdbcCommand(mySelectQuery, YMLD.conn)
Dim myRow As DataRow
PriceTable = Data.Tables(0)
```

```
myReader = myCommand.ExecuteReader()
PriceTable.BeginLoadData()
While myReader.Read()
  Dim newRow(1) As Object
  newRow(0) = myReader.GetInt32(0)
  newRow(1) = myReader.GetDecimal(1)
  myRow = PriceTable.LoadDataRow(newRow, True)
End While
PriceTable.EndLoadData()
myReader.Close()
```

In this routine, we are retrieving only two columns from the PRICEPLAN table and displaying the results. The first column (PRICEPLAN_NO) is an integer type, and the second column (PRICEPLAN_COST) is a decimal type.

Theater Seat Map

Clicking the **Theater Seat Map** button displays the current seating arrangements at the YMLD Theater (see Figure 12-8).

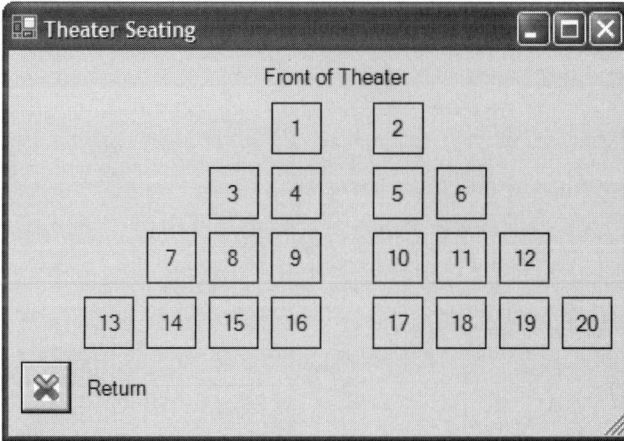

Figure 12-8 Seating plan

There is no additional logic behind the buttons shown on the screen. One of the possible uses for the seat buttons is to add a display of the theater "view" from this seat. The SEATMAP table has a column called SEAT_VIEW, which contains LOB objects. Pictures of the stage, as viewed from seats, could be stored in the database so that users can select a seat based on the view.

To retrieve large objects with ODBC, an application should use the GetBytes() method, which only retrieves a portion of the object, rather than the entire object. This minimizes the amount of memory required to manipulate these objects. Although it is possible to read an entire large object into memory at one time, this can be extremely inefficient, especially if only a portion of the object needs to be read.

Purchase Tickets by Performance

Clicking the **Purchase Ticket** button takes you through a series of panels before a ticket purchase is finalized. There are five steps in purchasing a ticket:

- Select a performance—The first panel asks you to select a performance from the list of available performances.

- Select a date—The second panel displays a calendar and a seat map. No seat selection is available until you pick a performance date.

- Select a seat—After you have selected a performance date, the available seats for that performance are displayed, and you can select one or more seats to purchase.

- Confirm the order—The list of selected seats is shown for final confirmation.

- Finalize the transaction—The seats are reserved in the system, and a record is placed in the transaction log for future refund or reporting activity.

Selecting a Production

The first step in purchasing a ticket is to select the production that you want to see (see Figure 12-9).

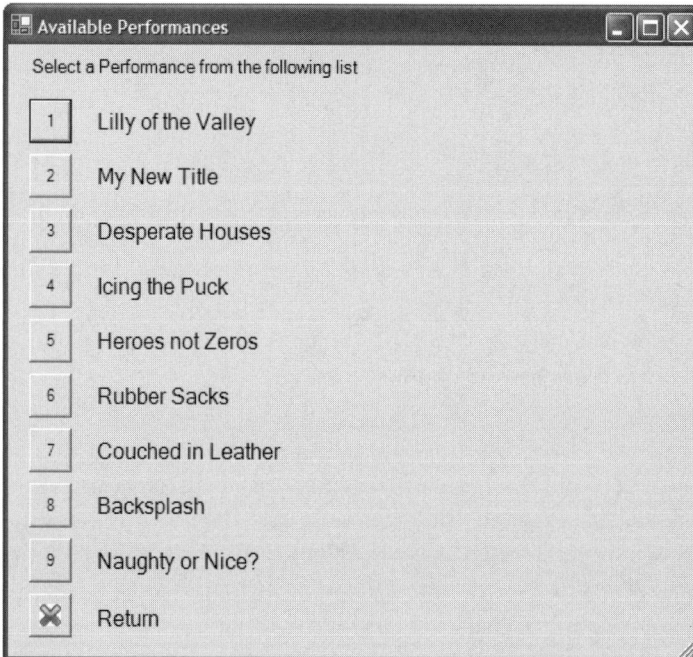

Figure 12-9 Available performances

The list of productions is shown as a number of buttons with associated descriptions. This approach is different from the production and seat price lists. Rather than create a list of productions in a table, the application creates a menu from which the user can select. This approach provides a single view of all productions instead of having the user scroll through a list in a table. The drawback of this approach is that it can only handle a small number of productions before the available space on the panel is used up.

The `ymldProdSection` dialog retrieves the current production list from the database and assigns titles to the labels beside the buttons on the screen. The SQL statement that retrieves this information is as follows:

```
Dim mySelectQuery As String = _
    "SELECT PRODUCTION_NO, " & _
    "        MONTH(PRODUCTION_START) AS MONTH_START, " & _
    "        MONTH(PRODUCTION_END) AS MONTH_END, " & _
    "        PRODUCTION_TITLE " & _
    "FROM PRODUCTIONS " & _
    "ORDER BY PRODUCTION_NO"
Dim myCommand As New OdbcCommand(mySelectQuery, YMLD.conn)

myReader = myCommand.ExecuteReader()
Dim but_count As Integer = 0
While myReader.Read()
    Dim newRow(3) As Object
    Dim Prodno As Integer = myReader.GetInt32(0)
    Dim ProdStart As String = myReader.GetInt32(1)
    Dim ProdEnd As String = myReader.GetInt32(2)
    Dim ProdTitle As String = myReader.GetString(3)
    Selection.setProduction(Prodno, ProdStart, ProdEnd,
      ProdTitle)
    Titles(but_count).Text = ProdTitle
    but_count = but_count + 1
End While
myReader.Close()
```

The SQL statement retrieves the production number, start date, end date, and title of all productions and places the information into a global class called `Selection`. The `MONTH_START` and `MONTH_END` columns will be used for the next step in ticket selection. After a patron has selected a production, we want to be able to display a calendar from which to choose a performance date. Having the starting and ending months gives us information that we can use when initializing the next panel in this transaction.

```
Public Class Selection
  Private Shared start_month(9) As Integer
  Private Shared end_month(9) As Integer
  Private Shared titles(9) As String
  Private Shared current_production As Integer
  Private Shared current_month As Integer
  Private Shared current_day As Integer
  Private Shared current_performance As Integer
  Private Shared seats_price(20) As Integer
  Private Shared seats_selected(20) As Integer

  Shared Sub setProduction(ByVal prodno As Integer, _
                           ByVal startmonth As Integer, _
                           ByVal endmonth As Integer, _
                           ByVal title As String)
      start_month(prodno) = startmonth
      end_month(prodno) = endmonth
      titles(prodno) = title
  End Sub

  Shared Sub setCurrentProduction(ByVal prodNo As Integer)
      current_production = prodNo
  End Sub

  Shared Function getProduction() As Integer
      Return current_production
  End Function
  ...
End Class
```

The setProduction method places production information into private variables that can be retrieved using other get methods. The private variables within the Selection class are used to store state information between the various panels in the YMLD application. As the user selects the production, performance, date, and seat information, it is all stored in these variables. Subsequent panels can retrieve information on the state of these variables by using the appropriate get method. This technique is similar to using global variables across all of the programs in an application.

The query also uses some built-in Apache Derby functions. The MONTH function strips only the month value from a date or a timestamp. This type of conversion could also be done in the application, but having it in the SQL is more convenient.

The assignment of titles to buttons is done using an array of labels:

```
Dim Titles() As System.Windows.Forms.Label = _
   {T1, T2, T3, T4, T5, T6, T7, T8, T9}
```

T1 through T9 are the dialog labels that contain the production titles. Rather than directly assigning a title to a label (T1.text = "Name of production"), the application can use the array of labels instead. Earlier versions of Visual Basic allowed labels and buttons to have the same name. Visual Basic would create a control array through which an application could loop to assign values. In Visual Basic .NET, this technique is no longer supported, so a workaround is to create an array that points to the underlying buttons or labels.

When a user clicks on a production to buy tickets, the ClickButton event is invoked. This is a general button handler that is responsible for each of the production buttons on the screen, and it is another example of a single method that supports multiple items. When the button is clicked, the tag information from the button is used to identify which production was selected. The tag field is available for all Visual Basic controls, and it allows you to uniquely identify a control. The actual text displayed on the button face could also have been used to determine which button had been clicked.

```
Private Sub ClickButton(ByVal sender As System.Object, _
                    ByVal e As System.EventArgs) _
    Handles B1.Click, B2.Click, B3.Click, B4.Click, B5.Click,
         B6.Click, B7.Click, B8.Click, B9.Click
    Dim btn As Button
    Dim whichProd As Integer
    Dim frmSeatSelect As Form
    btn = CType(sender, Button)
    Selection.setCurrentProduction(CInt(btn.Tag))
    frmSeatSelect = New ymldSeatSelection()
    frmSeatSelect.ShowDialog()
End Sub
```

Selecting a Date

Both date and seat selections are done from one panel. This panel contains the name of the selected production and the first month in which the production is playing (see Figure 12-10).

The date selection area is on the left side of the screen, and the seat selection area is on the right side. The calendar has buttons that let you go forward or backward one month at a time. The months are restricted to those in which the selected production is playing. The buttons on the calendar view change when you change the month. Note that buttons are only visible for the dates on which there is a performance and seats are still available.

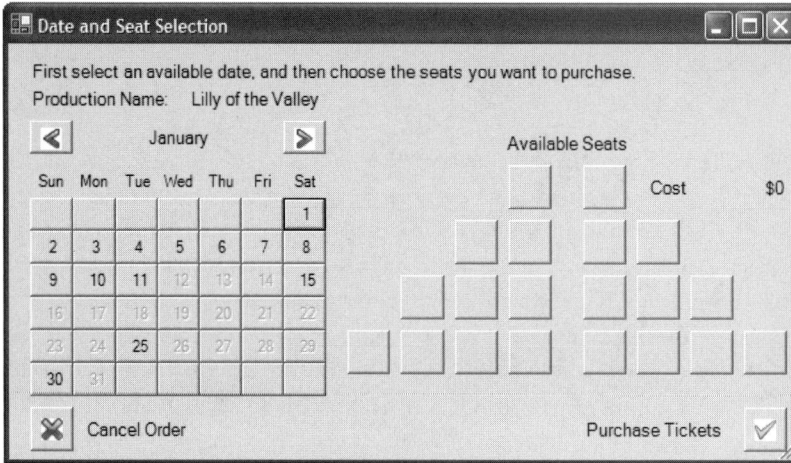

Figure 12-10   Date and seat selection

The seat selection dialog requires help from two methods: `setCalendar()` and `getProdDates()`.

setCalendar()

The calendar is generated by the `setCalendar()` method. The logic is shown here.

```
Public Sub setCalendar(ByVal whichMonth As Integer)
  Dim i As Integer

  For i = 0 To 41
      Days(i).Text = ""
      Days(i).Enabled = False
  Next

  Dim dayofmonth As Integer = 1
  For i = monthDoW(whichMonth) To monthDoW(whichMonth) + _
                  monthDays(whichMonth) - 1
      Days(i).Text = Str(dayofmonth)
      If (Productions.getProdDate(dayofmonth) <> 0) Then
          Days(i).Enabled = True
          Days(i).Tag = dayofmonth
      End If
```

```
      dayofmonth = dayofmonth + 1
   Next

   For i = 0 To 19
      Seats(i).Enabled = False
      Seats(i).Image = Nothing
   Next

   monthName.Text = monthNames(whichMonth)
   Total_cost = 0
   Cost.Text = "$0"
End Sub
```

A number of global variables are used to determine how a month should be formatted. These variables contain the days per month (`monthDays`), the starting day of the week (`monthDoW`), and the names of the months (`monthNames`):

```
Public monthDays() As Integer = {0, 31, 28, 31, 30, 31, _
                                 30, 31, 31, 30, 31, 30, 31}
Public monthDoW() As Integer = {0, 6, 2, 2, 5, 0, 3, 5, _
                                 1, 4, 6, 2, 4}
Public monthNames() As String = {"", "January", "February", "March", _
  "April", "May", "June", "July", "August", "September", "October", _
  "November", "December"}
```

The `monthDoW` array refers to the day of the week on which a month begins. A zero represents Sunday, with Monday through Saturday being assigned successive values. These values are only valid for the year 2005. If the YMLD Theater had productions into 2006 and beyond, the algorithms would have to be modified to calculate the proper start dates, as well as the number of days in February during leap years.

Six weeks are displayed in the calendar. Remember that some months start on a Saturday and end on a Sunday or Monday six "weeks" later. For example, the month of January 2005 takes up six weeks on the calendar display (see Figure 12-11).

The middle `for` loop sets the actual dates of the month. Each button is assigned a day of the month, based on the starting day of the week, and the number of days in the month. The starting value is the day of the week on which the month starts. In the case of January, this value is 6, which translates to the seventh button on the screen (Saturday). The loop continues for the total number of days in the month (`monthDays[]`).

Figure 12-11   Date selection

As the days of the month are placed on the screen, the `prodDays` array is checked to see whether a performance is available. If a value other than zero is found, then a performance is scheduled for that particular day and seats are available, so the button is enabled and can be selected by the user. If a value of zero is found, nothing has to be done because the buttons were initialized to be disabled at the beginning of the method.

The final loop disables all of the buttons that are associated with seats in the theater. The user must select a valid date before the available seats can be shown.

getProdDates()

The `setCalendar()` method relies on the `getProdDates()` routine to retrieve the dates (within a month) on which a performance is available. The `getProdDates()` method is shown here:

```
Shared Sub getProdDates(ByVal prodNo As Integer, ByVal prodMonth _
                        As Integer)
  Dim myReader As OdbcDataReader
  Dim i As Integer

  For i = 1 To 31
      PerfNoDay(i) = 0
  Next

  Try
```

```
    Dim mySelectQuery As String = _
      "SELECT DAY(PERFORMANCE_DATE) AS DAYMONTH,
        PERFORMANCE_NO "& _
      "FROM PERFORMANCES P " & _
      "WHERE P.PRODUCTION_NO = " & Str(prodNo) & " AND " & _
      "  MONTH(P.PERFORMANCE_DATE) = " & Str(prodMonth) & " AND " &_
      "  P.PERFORMANCE_SEATS > 0 " & _
      "ORDER BY PRODUCTION_NO"
    Dim myCommand As New OdbcCommand(mySelectQuery, YMLD.conn)
    Dim myRow As DataRow
    myReader = myCommand.ExecuteReader()
    While myReader.Read()
      Dim dayofmonth = myReader.GetInt32(0)
      Dim perfNo = myReader.GetInt32(1)
      PerfNoDay(dayofmonth) = perfNo
    End While
    myReader.Close()
  Catch se As OdbcException
    MsgBox(se.Message)
  End Try
End Sub
```

The SELECT statement that is used by the getProdDates() routine depends on PRODUCTION_NO and the month in which the performance is taking place.

```
SELECT DAY(PERFORMANCE_DATE) AS DAYMONTH, PERFORMANCE_NO
  FROM PERFORMANCES P
WHERE P.PRODUCTION_NO = prodNo AND
    MONTH(P.PERFORMANCE_DATE) = prodMonth AND
    P.PERFORMANCE_SEATS > 0
ORDER BY PRODUCTION_NO;
```

This query returns the day on which a performance is taking place and the performance number. The WHERE clause specifies that rows for a particular month (prodMonth) and production (prodNo) are to be retrieved. In addition, there must be at least one seat available for a performance to be listed as available.

The PerfNoDay array contains the performance number by day of the month. This is used to build a map of available seats. When a valid date for a performance is found, the corresponding button is enabled; otherwise, the button is disabled and appears grayed out.

Selecting a Seat

After a user has selected a production and a performance date, the seats available for that performance are displayed on the screen (see Figure 12-12).

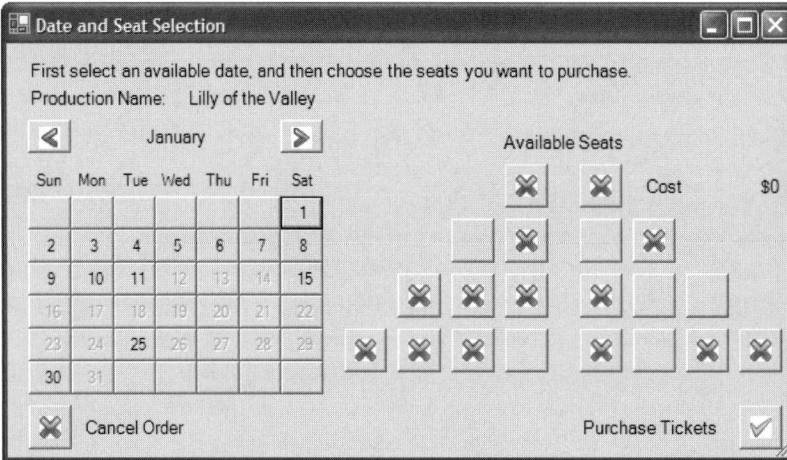

Figure 12-12   Seat selection

The `ClickButton` method is called when a date button is clicked. This method finds all of the seats that are allocated for a particular performance and updates the display to show those seats. The routine first extracts the selected day, month, and performance number:

```
Private Sub ClickButton(ByVal sender As System.Object, ByVal e As _
    System.EventArgs) Handles D1.Click, D2.Click, ..., D42.Click
  Dim btn As Button
  Dim dayofmonth As Integer
  Dim perfNo As Integer
  Dim i As Integer

  btn = CType(sender, Button)
  dayofmonth = CInt(btn.Tag)
  Total_cost = 0
  Cost.Text = "$0"
  perfNo = Productions.getProdDate(dayofmonth)
  Selection.setPerformance(perfNo)
  Selection.setDay(dayofmonth)
```

```
Selection.clearSeats()
For i = 0 To 19
  Seats(i).Image = Nothing
  Seats(i).Enabled = True
Next

Dim myReader As OdbcDataReader
Try
  Dim mySelectQuery As String = _
  "SELECT SEAT_NO, SEAT_AVAILABLE, PRICEPLAN_COST " & _
    "FROM SEATS S, PRICEPLAN P " & _
    "WHERE PERFORMANCE_NO = " & Str(perfNo) & " AND " & _
    "      S.PRICEPLAN_NO = P.PRICEPLAN_NO " & _
    "ORDER BY SEAT_NO"

  Dim myCommand As New OdbcCommand(mySelectQuery, YMLD.conn)

  myReader = myCommand.ExecuteReader()
  While myReader.Read()
    Dim seatNo As Integer = myReader.GetInt32(0)
    Dim seatAvail As Integer = myReader.GetInt32(1)
    Dim seatPrice As Integer = myReader.GetInt32(2)
    Selection.setSeat(seatNo - 1, seatAvail, seatPrice)
    If (seatAvail = 0) Then
      Seats(seatNo - 1).Image = ReturnBack.Image
    Else
      Selection.setSeat(seatNo - 1, 0, seatPrice)
      Seats(seatNo - 1).Image = Nothing
    End If
  End While
  ...
End Sub
```

Using this information, the following SELECT statement is built to retrieve the seats that have been allocated for the specified performance:

```
SELECT SEAT_NO, SEAT_AVAILABLE, PRICEPLAN_COST
FROM SEATS S, PRICEPLAN P
WHERE PERFORMANCE_NO = selectedPerfNo AND
  S.PRICEPLAN_NO = P.PRICEPLAN_NO
ORDER BY SEAT_NO
```

The query returns the seat number, an indicator for whether the seat is available, and the current cost of the ticket for this seat. A join between the PRICEPLAN table and the SEATS table retrieves the pricing information for the seat.

The routine causes unavailable seats to display with a large X and available seats to remain unmarked and enabled for selection. The Selection class is used to track the status of the seats.

The seat buttons have two additional properties assigned to them. The selected property is used to indicate whether a user has selected that seat for purchase. This will be important when the user confirms the order. The price property is used to display the price of the user's selection.

When a user clicks one of the seat buttons, the status of the selected property for that seat changes to 1, and the button acquires a checkmark. If so desired, the user can click the seat button again to reset its status to unoccupied.

```
Private Sub S1_Click(ByVal sender As System.Object, ByVal e As _
        System.EventArgs) Handles S1.Click, ..., S20.Click
    Dim btn As Button
    Dim seatNo As Integer
    Dim index As Integer

    btn = CType(sender, Button)
    seatNo = CInt(btn.Tag)
    index = seatNo - 1

    If (Selection.getSeatSelected(index) = -1) Then Exit Sub
    If (Selection.getSeatSelected(index) = 0) Then
        Seats(index).Image = Confirm.Image
        Total_cost = Total_cost + Selection
          .getSeatPrice(index)
        Selection.setSeatSelected(index, 1)
    Else
        Seats(index).Image = Nothing
        Selection.setSeatSelected(index, 0)
        Total_cost = Total_cost - Selection
          .getSeatPrice(index)
    End If
    Cost.Text = "$" + Str(Total_cost)
End Sub
```

Figure 12-13 shows the results of a user clicking one of the seat buttons.

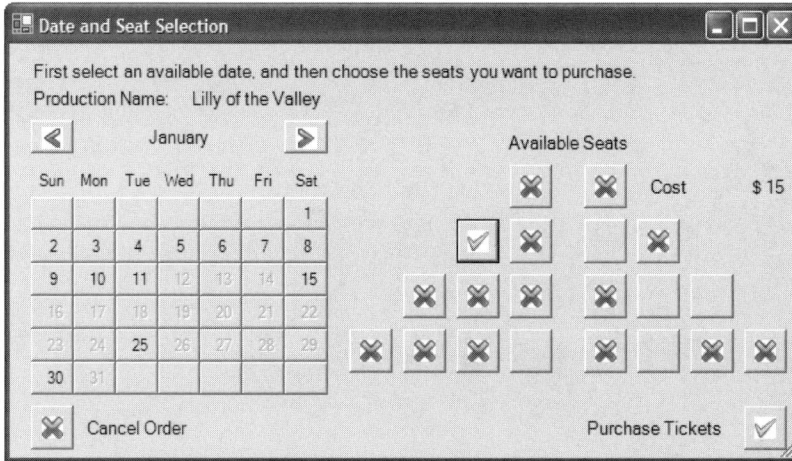

Figure 12-13 Seat selected

When a seat is selected, the cost field on the right side of the screen is updated. This value is updated whenever seats are added or subtracted. When all desired seats have been selected, the user can advance to the order confirmation step. If no seats have been selected, the system displays an error message (see Figure 12-14).

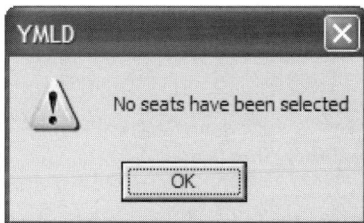

Figure 12-14 No seats selected

The ticket confirmation screen is not displayed unless there is a valid ticket order. There are two ways to determine whether any seats have been selected. The first method is to check whether the total value of seats selected so far is greater than zero. As seats are selected, their cost is added to the Total_Cost variable. If the total cost is zero, no seats have been selected. This method fails to take into account that some seats might have been given away. To be absolutely sure that seats have been selected, the application could check the selected property on each seat button until one with a value of true was found.

```
If (Total_cost = 0) Then
  MsgBox("No seats have been selected", MsgBoxStyle.Exclamation, "YMLD")
  Exit Sub
End If
```

Confirming the Order

The confirmation screen is the last step in purchasing a ticket. This screen lists all of the tickets that a user has selected and requests confirmation of the order (see Figure 12-15).

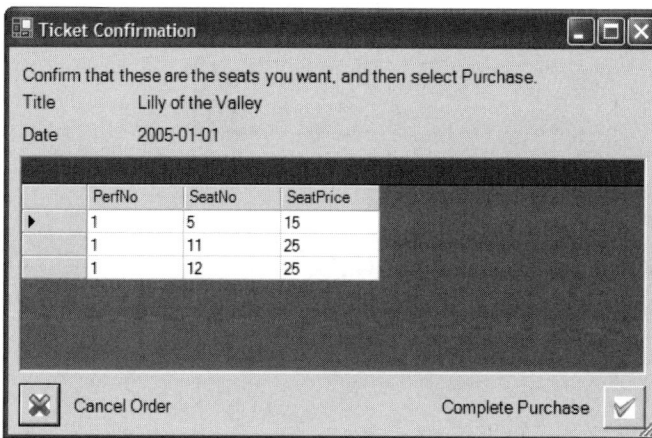

Figure 12-15   Order confirmation

At this point in the application, each seat is checked to see whether it has been selected. This is very similar logic to that used for listing current productions at the theater.

```
Private Sub ymldConfirmPurchase_Load(ByVal sender As System.Object, _
        ByVal e As System.EventArgs) Handles MyBase.Load
    Dim TicketTable As New DataTable()
    Dim seatNo As Integer
    Dim myRow As DataRow

    Display.addForm(Me)

    TicketTable = Data.Tables(0)
```

```
TicketTable.BeginLoadData()
For seatNo = 0 To 19
  If (Selection.getSeatSelected(seatNo) = 1) Then
    Dim newRow(2) As Object
    newRow(0) = Selection.getPerformance()
    newRow(1) = seatNo + 1
    newRow(2) = Selection.getSeatPrice(seatNo)
    myRow = TicketTable.LoadDataRow(newRow, True)
  End If
Next
TicketTable.EndLoadData()

ProdName.Text = Selection.getTitle()
ProdDate.Text = "2005-" & Format(Selection
  .getCurrentMonth, "00") &_
      "-" & Format(Selection.getDay, "00")
End Sub
```

There are twenty seats in the theater. Each seat is checked to see whether or not it has been selected for purchase. The application does not need to worry about seats being unavailable during a performance. By default, every seat is disabled, unless a record in the database shows that it is available.

As selected seats are found, the seat number, price, and performance number are placed into a data set control. These values are displayed by the DataGrid control for user confirmation.

When the **Complete Purchase** button is clicked, the YMLD application finalizes the transaction, closes all of the intermediate windows, and displays the confirmation message (see Figure 12-16).

Figure 12-16 Purchase complete

Finalizing the Transaction

The routine that is called to finalize the transaction within the `ymldlConfirmPurchase` panel is named `Confirm_Click()`. This method uses a prepared statement to update each selected seat to "occupied" and to write a transaction record to the TRANSACTIONS table. The first prepared statement updates the SEATS table.

```
Dim updateSeatSQL As String = _
    "UPDATE SEATS " & _
    "  SET SEAT_AVAILABLE = 0 " & _
    "WHERE  SEAT_NO = ? AND PERFORMANCE_NO = ?"

Dim updateSeat As OdbcCommand = New OdbcCommand(updateSeatSQL, YMLD.conn)
updateSeat.Parameters.Add("", OdbcType.Int)
updateSeat.Parameters.Add("", OdbcType.Int)
...
updateSeat.Parameters(0).Value = i + 1
updateSeat.Parameters(1).Value = Selection.getPerformance
updateSeat.ExecuteNonQuery()
```

There are two parameter markers in this UPDATE statement. The first marker is for the seat being updated, and the second marker is for the performance number. This statement could be built dynamically by just creating an SQL statement with the concatenated seat number and performance number. Although this approach is perfectly acceptable, it isn't the most efficient way of executing repetitive SQL. With parameter markers, the database does not have to parse the SQL statement every time. This can reduce the amount of overhead.

The parameter markers must be defined with the `Parameters()` method of the `OdbcCommand`. The `Parameters()` method requires two values. The first value refers to either the parameter name or, if blank, the parameter position in the statement. If the first string is blank, each successive add statement refers to the next parameter marker in the statement. In our example, there are two parameters in the statement, each of which is defined to be an integer type. If you name a parameter, it can be used in subsequent value assignments instead of referring to the position of the parameter marker. For instance, to set the value of the first parameter marker in the previous example, use the following code:

```
updateSeat.Parameters(0).Value = i + 1
```

However, this can be error-prone, especially if there are a lot of parameters to remember. Instead, the following code names the parameter marker and sets it using the same name:

```
updateSeat.Parameters.Add("@seatno", OdbcType.Int)
updateSeat.Parameters("@seatno").Value = i + 1
```

The second value in the `Parameters()` method is the data type of the parameter marker. The possible ODBC data types are summarized in Table 12-2.

Table 12-2 SQL and ODBC Data Types

SQL Data Type	ODBC Type
SMALLINT	Int16
INTEGER	Int32
BIGINT	Int64
DECIMAL	Decimal
REAL	Single
DOUBLE PRECISION	Double
DATE	DateTime
TIME	DateTime
TIMESTAMP	Array of Byte
CHAR	String
VARCHAR	String
LONG VARCHAR	String
CLOB	String or Array of Byte
BLOB	Array of Byte
CHAR FOR BIT DATA	Array of Byte
VARCHAR FOR BIT DATA	Array of Byte
LONG VARCHAR FOR BIT DATA	Array of Byte

The parameters are assigned values using the value clause of the parameter method:

```
insertTX.Parameters("@PERFNO").Value = Selection.getPerformance
```

After all of the parameters have been set, the `ExecuteNonQuery()` method is issued to run the SQL statement. The `ExecuteNonQuery()` method tells Apache Derby that this particular statement will not return any rows to the application. Although you can run INSERT, UPDATE, and DELETE statements using ExecuteQuery(), additional resources are required to create result sets, and this is unnecessary for statements that do not return any information. The ExecuteNonQuery() method returns the number of rows that were affected by the statement; this value can be useful when ensuring that the statement ran properly.

The second prepared statement is an INSERT statement. This statement inserts a row into the TRANSACTIONS table. The TRANSACTIONS table keeps track of all tickets purchased at the YMLD Theater. This table is also used to refund patrons who change their minds.

```
Dim insertTX As OdbcCommand = _
  New OdbcCommand(insertTransactionSQL, YMLD.conn)
insertTX.Parameters.Add("@SEATNO", OdbcType.Int)
insertTX.Parameters.Add("@PERFNO", OdbcType.Int)
...
insertTX.Parameters("@SEATNO").Value = i + 1
insertTX.Parameters("@PERFNO").Value = Selection
  .getPerformance
insertTX.ExecuteNonQuery()
```

Two parameter markers are associated with this INSERT statement. The TRANSACTIONS table actually has five columns in it. The first column is the transaction number, which is automatically generated by the database. For this reason, the INSERT statement cannot specify the actual transaction number. The TX_DATE column value is automatically created using the CURRENT_DATE special register. The TX_TYPE field is set to the value 'PURCHASE' to describe the purpose of the transaction record. The TRANSACTIONS table could become more important in the future if the owners of the YMLD Theater want to construct queries based on how quickly seats sell for a performance or how often blocks of seats are sold. The last two fields, PERFORMANCE_NO and SEAT_NO, together uniquely identify the seats that were sold.

The logic at this point in the application scans through all 20 seats looking for the seats that were selected. These seats could also be determined by reading the table of selected seats that were already displayed, or by creating an array of available seats in a prior step. Any of these techniques would work.

View Transaction Log

The transaction log contains records for each ticket that has been purchased. The transaction log can be displayed if you want to see what purchases were made at the theater, or if you need to refund a ticket (see Figure 12-17).

The ymldTransactions panel populates this screen with data using a DataGrid control and a data set. The logic is identical to that used in the ymldProductions panel. The application issues a SELECT statement against the TRANSACTIONS table and displays the result.

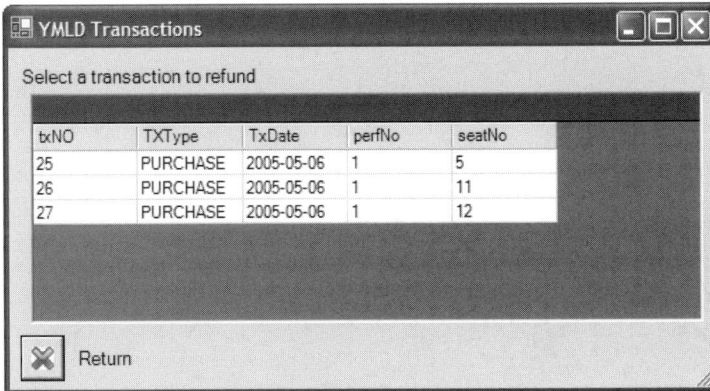

Figure 12-17 Transaction log

```
Dim TXS As New DataTable()
Dim mySelectQuery As String = _
      "SELECT * FROM TRANSACTIONS WHERE TX_TYPE='PURCHASE'"
Dim myCommand As New OdbcCommand(mySelectQuery, YMLD.conn)
Dim myRow As DataRow

TXS = Data.Tables(0)

myReader = myCommand.ExecuteReader()
TXS.BeginLoadData()
While myReader.Read()
  Dim newRow(4) As Object
  newRow(0) = myReader.GetInt32(0)
  newRow(1) = myReader.GetString(1)
  newRow(2) = myReader.GetString(2)
  newRow(3) = myReader.GetInt32(3)
  newRow(4) = myReader.GetInt32(4)
  myRow = TXS.LoadDataRow(newRow, True)
End While
TXS.EndLoadData()
myReader.Close()
```

After the transaction log displays, you can click on any individual transaction to have it reversed.

```
Dim answer As Integer =
  MsgBox("Do you want to undo the reservation for performance " + _
```

```
        Str(perfNo) + ", seat " + Str(seatNo) + " on " +
            txDate + "?",
        MsgBoxStyle.OKCancel, "Confirm Refund")
If (answer = vbCancel) Then Exit Sub
```

A message appears, prompting you to confirm the refund (see Figure 12-18).

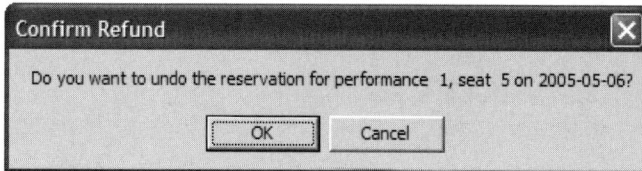

Figure 12-18   Refund confirmation

The undo transaction operation takes information from the row that was selected in the transaction log.

```
Dim doTX As OdbcTransaction = YMLD.conn().BeginTransaction
Dim updateSeatsSQL As String = _
    "UPDATE SEATS " & _
    "  SET SEAT_AVAILABLE = 1 " & _
    "WHERE  SEAT_NO = ? AND PERFORMANCE_NO = ?"

Dim updateTransactionSQL As String = _
    "UPDATE TRANSACTIONS SET TX_TYPE = 'VOID' " & _
    "WHERE TX_NO = ?"

Dim insertTransactionSQL As String = _
    "INSERT INTO TRANSACTIONS(Tx_Type,Tx_Date,Performance_No,Seat_No)"&_
    " VALUES ('REFUND',CURRENT_DATE, ?, ?)"


Dim updateSeat As OdbcCommand = New _
    OdbcCommand(updateSeatsSQL, YMLD.conn)
updateSeat.Parameters.Add("", OdbcType.Int).Value = seatNo
updateSeat.Parameters.Add("", OdbcType.Int).Value = perfNo
updateSeat.Transaction = doTX
updateSeat.ExecuteNonQuery()
```

```
Dim insertTX As OdbcCommand = New _
    OdbcCommand(insertTransactionSQL, YMLD.conn)
insertTX.Parameters.Add("", OdbcType.Int).Value = perfNo
insertTX.Parameters.Add("", OdbcType.Int).Value = seatNo
insertTX.Transaction = doTX
insertTX.ExecuteNonQuery()

Dim updateTX As OdbcCommand = New _
    OdbcCommand(updateTransactionSQL, YMLD.conn)
updateTX.Parameters.Add("", OdbcType.Int).Value = txNo
updateTX.Transaction = doTX
updateTX.ExecuteNonQuery()
doTX.Commit()
Data.Tables(0).Rows(row).Delete()
Data.AcceptChanges()
TxList.Refresh()
```

There are three distinct SQL statements within this method. To ensure the integrity of the data in the TRANSACTIONS table, the three transactions must be either all committed or all rolled back at the same time. The `OdbcTransaction` method must be used to create a transaction:

```
Dim doTX As OdbcTransaction = YMLD.conn().BeginTransaction
```

This statement creates a transaction context under which the statements execute. Each SQL statement includes the transaction context as part of the statement:

```
updateTX.Transaction = doTX
```

When all of the SQL statements have successfully completed, the transaction can be committed:

```
doTX.Commit()
```

The three SQL statements update various tables in the YMLD database. The first SQL statement updates the seat that is being refunded to indicate that the seat is again available. The second statement inserts a new record into the TRANSACTIONS table indicating that a refund has been processed for the seat. The third statement updates the original transaction record to indicate that it has been voided.

The `delete()` statement near the end of this logic removes the row from the data set in this panel. The data set contains a snapshot of the data and does not get refreshed when the database changes. Instead, the row is manually deleted by the system, and a `refresh()` is done against the `DataGrid` display so that the row is eliminated from view. If this were not done, a user might think that the ticket was still available for refund.

There are some additional considerations when using a transaction table to track all activity in a database. Although this approach is a great way of tracking activities in the system, it can become very expensive to query and maintain. In the YMLD application, transaction records are created for tickets purchased. In addition, refund records are created when patrons change their minds about the tickets that they have purchased. The TRANSACTIONS table can end up containing thousands of rows as the season progresses. A method is required to prune the TRANSACTIONS table of old records that are no longer required. For example, transactions associated with performances that have already completed would be good candidates for deletion. In most cases, such information should be archived for auditing purposes or analysis.

Exit Routine

The final routine that is called when exiting the YMLD system ensures that the connection is closed.

```
YMLD.conn().Close()
End
```

Closing the database connection ensures that any statements are properly terminated, especially if a transaction was started and no COMMIT statement was issued.

Summary

This chapter has covered the development of the YMLD application using Visual Basic .NET and ODBC. A variety of ODBC methods were used to access the YMLD database, including code to display current productions, seat prices, and transactions.

This version of the YMLD application is based on the Java version that was developed in Chapter 11. There are many similarities between building an application in Java with JDBC and building it using Visual Basic .NET and ODBC. The same steps are required to connect to a database and manipulate database objects; thus, someone familiar with JDBC syntax should be able to develop an ODBC application in Visual Basic .NET.

The source code and database can be found on the book's Web site. You are encouraged to experiment with the YMLD system and then to try some of these techniques with your own data.

"Your Momma Loves Drama" in PHP

PHP Overview

What Makes PHP Unique?

PHP is a popular free scripting language that was developed as a practical HTML template language with easy access to Web form variables and data stores such as relational databases. In 1995 Rasmus Lerdorf released the source code to the first version of the PHP template language, called Personal Home Page / Forms Interpreter (PHP/FI), and a small following of Web developers began to adopt the language. Over time, more programmers contributed to the PHP effort, porting the language and its extensions to Windows, improving database connectivity, and creating the infrastructure for the online PHP manual, and they released the improved version and renamed it PHP: Hypertext Preprocessor (PHP—a recursive acronym) in 1998. The current version of the language is PHP 5.0.4, but despite the subsequent addition of support for object-oriented programming and a stunning increase in the breadth of functionality, the core syntax of the language has remained relatively constant since 1998. At its core, PHP is still an extremely practical language for solving Web programming problems thanks to its built-in support for accessing Common Gateway Interface (CGI) variables, cookies, sessions, connectivity to a wide variety of databases, and its community of contributors of additional function and documentation.

In addition to the core extensions distributed with the PHP language itself, the PHP programming community has launched the PHP Extension and Archive Repository (PEAR) at http://pear.php.net and the PHP Extension Community Library (PECL) at http://pecl.php.net. Both projects are collections of extensions that have been developed by PHP enthusiasts and professionals who have offered the extensions to the PHP community for reuse in their own applications. The difference between the two projects is that PECL consists exclusively of extensions written in the C programming language, whereas many of the PEAR extensions are libraries of PHP code. Before you tackle any problem domain with PHP, you should check to see if someone else has already written an extension that will solve the problem for you. The existing extensions cover a wide range of functions, from database abstraction layers that rewrite SQL to suit the targeted database, to extensions that provide Web service interfaces to online search engines and retailers. To build the core of our PHP application, we will use one of the newest database abstraction layers, PHP Data Objects (PDO), that provides a common object-oriented data access interface for numerous databases through database drivers written in C for fast, memory-efficient operation. The PDO driver that we will use to access Apache Derby is the PDO::ODBC driver. Despite the name, you can compile PDO::ODBC directly against the IBM DB2 Runtime Client headers and libraries to access Apache Derby through the network-efficient DB2 Call Level Interface (CLI) layer.

Although this chapter teaches you the most common uses of PDO and PDO::ODBC—80% of the functions used by 80% of applications—you can find an excellent set of freely available documentation hosted by the PHP project at http://www.php.net/manual/. The PHP documentation is available in a variety of languages, and users are free to annotate any page of the manual with their own observations or examples to help improve the documentation.

Most Appropriate Uses for This Language

PHP overlaps with Perl and Python in some respects; however, Perl and Python are primarily known for system administration and text processing tasks that require only a simple command line interface, whereas PHP is probably the most popular choice for rapidly implementing forms-based dynamic Web sites. PHP does offer a command line scripting interface, but it tends to be used mostly by developers of the PHP language for automating their build and documentation system. Due to the popularity of the language for implementing dynamic Web sites, many extensions have been contributed to PEAR and PECL to provide function beyond the basic form handling requirements built into the language core. You can find extensions for such problem domains as Web page templates (even though PHP was originally implemented as an HTML template language, its functionality has grown to such an extent that some developers feel a need to add a template layer with less functionality above PHP itself), caching, and encryption, but the core CGI forms handling provided by PHP itself continues to be the basis of most of the Web extensions you will use.

PEAR and PECL also offer a number of extensions for creating GUI applications. However, unlike Python and Perl, no GUI extension available to PHP has yet achieved a level of stability or usage to become even a de facto standard, let alone an official standard extension for GUI applications. The profusion of choice and lack of maturity is compounded by the division of GUI extensions across operating system lines, with Windows GUI extensions focusing on the native Windows widgets and containers through extensions like WinBinder, while Unix GUI extensions focus on the GTK+ widgets and containers through the PHP-GTK and PHP-GTK2 extensions.

Purchaser Interface

The ticket purchaser interface for Your Mama Loves Drama is a forms-based Web application implemented with the PDO and PDO::ODBC extensions. Ticket purchasers will use their Web browsers to register themselves, search for events matching their date ranges and event type specifications, and order tickets.

Performance Characteristics

PHP is an interpreted language, which makes it an excellent choice for iterative prototyping or rapid application development. You can tweak the source code and immediately run your application to see the results of your change without having to compile or link the code. Just like Perl and Python, the PHP interpreter first converts the source code into object byte-code that is then executed by the PHP virtual machine. The interpreted nature of PHP applications means that most of your performance cost is derived from the first time you invoke the PHP interpreter.

Early Web applications built with CGI suffered from performance lags under heavy usage due to the resource demands of invoking the PHP interpreter for each requested Web page, but the developers of Apache and other Web servers quickly discovered how to keep a copy of the PHP interpreter running in memory at all times to bypass the start-up cost for every subsequently requested PHP-based Web page. With the Apache Web server, you can compile PHP as a dynamic shared object (DSO). This chapter describes how to compile and install PHP as an Apache DSO to improve the performance of your Web-based PHP applications. There are other approaches for maximizing the performance of PHP applications, such as using an opcode cache like Alternative PHP Cache (APC) or the Zend Optimizer to store a compiled version of each script for subsequent invocations, but those approaches are not covered here.

Popular Editing Environments

Because PHP is a scripting language, PHP applications are written using everything from the equivalent of text editors such as vi or Notepad for authoring throwaway scripts to integrated development environments (IDEs) that understand PHP development patterns and offer sophisticated support for collaborative programming efforts of large, complex PHP projects.

- Text editors such as VI Improved (http://vim.sourceforge.net) and Emacs offer features like syntax highlighting and easy customization.
- Open-source IDEs such as Kdevelop and Eclipse-based IDEs such as PHPEclipse (http://phpeclipse.sourceforge.net) offer syntax highlighting, code completion, the ability to browse your source code structure by function or object and method, and the ability to organize your files in projects.
- Full commercial IDEs like Komodo (http://activestate.com/komodo) or Zend Studio (http://www.zend.com/store/products/zend-studio/) offer all of the features of open-source IDEs with more complete help content, advanced debugging capabilities, regular expression scratchpads for testing and developing regular expressions, and integrated source code version control.

Learning the PHP Language

Delimiting PHP Code

PHP was developed as an HTML template language, with the intention of making it easy to intersperse snippets of executable PHP code amongst sections of static HTML output. For this reason, any section of PHP code starts with the processing instruction (PI) `<?php` and ends with the closing delimiter `?>`. So, for example, a PHP page that prints the current date could consist of the following code:

```
<html>
<head><title>Today's date</title></head>
<body>
<p>Today's date is:
<?php echo date('Y-m-d'); ?>
</p>
</body></html>
```

The PHP interpreter loads the page, automatically returns all of the HTML leading up to the PHP code `<?php echo date('Y-m-d'); ?>`, interprets and returns the results of the PHP code, and then returns the remaining HTML. This approach can be an extremely effective way of adding dynamic elements to Web pages in a large Web site, particularly as you create your own libraries of PHP functions that encapsulate more advanced functionality suited for your Web site's needs.

However, having dynamic PHP interspersed throughout HTML pages can make it difficult to track and debug your PHP code, or to provide more sophisticated control of the HTML output. For this reason, many more recent PHP programs consist of a single block of PHP code that is responsible for creating all of the HTML output along with the dynamic code. Ultimately, the approach you choose to use for each project depends on the requirements of your particular application.

Variables

Variable Names

You can easily identify a variable in PHP programs, as every variable name is prefixed with the signifier character $. Variable names consist of alphanumeric strings, where the name must begin with an alphabetical or underscore character, and the PHP interpreter determines through the syntax of the expression when a variable name has been assigned or is being used.

```
<?php
// Valid variable names:
$student = '00093456';
$database2 = 'SAMPLE';
$_name = 'Jennifer';
```

```
// Invalid variable name: PHP interpreter will die with an error
$3student = '00093456';
?>
```

Declaring Variables

PHP variables do not need to be declared before they are used; they will auto-vivify (spring into existence) when you assign a value to them. If you try to access the value of a variable that has not had a value assigned to it, the PHP interpreter will consider the value of the variable to be NULL. In the following example, $newvar is treated as an empty string and is invisible in the output of the script:

```
<?php
echo "The date is $newvar" . date('Y-m-d');
?>
```

The output of the preceding example is:

```
The date is 2005-08-22
```

Data Types

Boolean

The simplest data type is the Boolean data type, which is capable of holding only one of two different values: TRUE or FALSE. To explicitly assign a true or false value to a variable, you can use the case-insensitive True and False values. However, most PHP control structures evaluate the return value of an expression to determine whether a given condition is true or false.

```
<?php
# False is equal to numeric 0
  if (False == 0){
    print "FALSE is equal to 0\n";
  }
  # NULL is neither True nor False
  if (NULL == False) {
    print "NULL is equal to FALSE\n";
  }
  if (NULL == True) {
    print "NULL is equal to TRUE\n";
  }
?>
```

The output of the preceding example is:

```
FALSE is equal to 0
NULL is equal to FALSE
```

The following values evaluate to FALSE in the context of a Boolean operation or control flow statement: NULL, False, numeric types that evaluate to zero, empty arrays, empty strings, and strings that contain only the character 0.

Numeric Types

PHP offers two different types of numeric variables: integers and floats. Plain integers can represent at least 32 bits of precision (up to a signed value of 2,147,483,647) or more, depending on the machine and operating system on which the PHP interpreter is running. Any integer value greater than the maximum value for a 32-bit signed integer is automatically converted to a float. Floats represent floating point numbers, such as decimals or exponentials.

```php
<?php
  // Integers
  $age = 32;
  $circumference = 500000000;

  // Floats
  $decimal = 2.6;
  $exponent = 2E32;

  print $exponent;
?>
```

The output of the preceding example is:

```
2E+032
```

Arrays

Arrays are structures that map keys to values. You can explicitly define the keys to effectively create a hash structure, or you can allow PHP to implicitly define the keys to provide 0-based indices to the values in your array. All arrays are composed of zero or more elements, and individual elements can be accessed by appending the number of the 0-indexed element to the name of the array between square brackets. For example, to return the eighth element of a array object named '$kittens', use $kittens[7].

To create a simple array, assign a comma-delimited set of elements to your variable: $array = array(1, 2, 3);. The elements of an array can be any other PHP object, including other arrays. To create nested arrays, enclose the elements of a nested array in parentheses:

$nested = array(1, array(1, 2, 3), 2, 3);. To create an empty array, assign a empty set of parentheses to your array: $empty = array(). In the following example, we create three different arrays and use the built-in var_dump() function to display all of the elements of the $nested array:

```php
<?php
    // Arrays
    $array = array(1, 2, 3);
    $nested = array(1, 2, 3, array(1, 2, 3), 5);
    var_dump($array);
    $empty = array();
?>
```

The output of the preceding example is:

```
array(5) {
  [0]=>
  int(1)
  [1]=>
  int(2)
  [2]=>
  int(3)
  [3]=>
  array(3) {
    [0]=>
    int(1)
    [1]=>
    int(2)
    [2]=>
    int(3)
  }
  [4]=>
  int(5)
}
```

Strings

Strings in PHP are a series of characters. As PHP does not provide native support for Unicode or other multi-byte character encodings, each character in a string is mapped to a single byte. You can create strings by using three different delimiting methods: single quotes, double quotes, and HEREDOC notation. To concatenate sting variables, use the . operator.

Single quote-delimited strings prevent any interpolation of their contents, with the sole exception of a backslash character preceding a single-quote character to enable you to embed single quote characters within single quoted strings. If your single quoted string includes multiple lines, those linefeed characters will be reproduced in any output of that string.

Double quote-delimited strings enable interpolation to allow you to include PHP variables or escaped characters inside the string content. Just as in single quoted strings, if your double quoted string includes multiple lines, those linefeed characters will be reproduced in any output of that string. An alternate means of including linefeeds in a string is to use the escaped \n character, which represents an embedded line feed. To take advantage of PHP variable interpolation, you can assign the value of the date() function to a PHP variable and then use it as an interpolated part of double quoted strings throughout your PHP script to avoid the overhead of calling the date() function multiple times:

```php
<?php
  // Double quoted strings
  $today = date('Y-m-d');
  print "<html>
  <head><title>$today: News of the day</title></head>
  <body><p>Today's date is $today.\n</p></body>
  </html>";
?>
```

The output of the preceding example is:

```
<html>
  <head><title>2005-04-03: News of the day</title></head>
  <body><p>Today's date is 2005-04-03.
</p></body>
</html>
```

To assign a long string containing single quotes, double quotes, escaped characters, and PHP variables, consider using HEREDOC notation. HEREDOC notation interpolates escaped characters and PHP variables in the same way as double quoted strings, but the opening delimiter is `<<<identifier;`, where `identifier` represents the character sequence that will be used in the closing delimiter for the HEREDOC string. The closing delimiter consists of the delimiter identifier on an empty line with no other characters on the same line.

```php
<?php
  // HEREDOC string
  $today = date('Y-m-d');
  print <<<HTML
<html>
  <head><title>$today: News of the day</title></head>
  <body><p>Today's date is $today.\n</p></body>
```

```
</html>
HTML;
?>
```

The output of the preceding example is:

```
<html>
  <head><title>2005-04-03: News of the day</title></head>
  <body><p>Today's date is 2005-04-03.
</p></body>
</html>
```

Control Structures

Control structures help you structure the flow of your code by restricting the execution of a block of code unless a condition you have specified evaluates to true. Your condition can explicitly invoke the typical comparison operators: < (less than), > (greater than), == (is equal to), != (is not equal to), <= (less than or equal to), and >= (greater than or equal to). Your condition can also be a simple expression. A simple expression that evaluates to any non-zero value, or a non-empty sequence, is considered true.

The general syntax for a control structure is as follows:

```
control-keyword (condition) {
      <block of code>
}
<block of code>
```

The control keyword specifies the kind of control structure that is defined. The condition expression, terminated by a statement, specifies the condition that must be evaluated to true before the following indented code block will be executed.

while and *do/while* Loops

A while loop executes a block of code as long as the condition specified for the while statement evaluates to TRUE. The following example decrements the value of an integer variable using the -- postfix operator within a while loop, terminating the loop once the value of $x reaches 0.

```
<?php
  // While loops
  $x = 5;
  while ($x) {
    print $x-- . "\n";
  }
?>
```

The output of the preceding example is:

```
5
4
3
2
1
```

You can invert the order of execution and condition testing by enclosing a code block in a do control structure, with the while() condition occurring after the code block. The do/while structure ensures that the code block will always be executed at least once before the condition is tested.

if ... elseif ... else

An if statement executes a block of code if the specified condition evaluates to true. The elseif keyword identifies an alternate condition block of code that will be executed if the if condition and any preceding elseif conditions evaluate to false. The else keyword identifies an alternate block of code that will be executed if the if condition and all elseif conditions in the same control structure evaluate to false.

```php
<?php
  // if ... elseif ... else blocks
  $x = 5;
  if ($x > 6) {
    print "x is large";
  }
  elseif ($x > 5) {
    print "x is pretty big";
  }
  elseif ($x > 0) {
    print "x is enough";
  }
  else {
    print "x is little";
  }
?>
```

The output of the preceding example is:

```
x is enough
```

switch

The `switch` control structure in PHP acts as a specialized form of `if` statement, in that it executes a number of comparisons against the same value. The syntax for a `switch` control structure is as follows:

```
switch (test-value) {
  case expression-1:
    statement;
    break;
  case expression-2:
    statement;
    break;
  default:
    statement;
}
```

The *test-value* for the `switch` control structure is a simple type (boolean, integer, float, string) that is tested against the *expression* for each `case` statement until a case matches. If a case matches, the interpreter executes every PHP statement following the matching `case` statement until it encounters either a `break` statement, in which case control is returned to the next PHP statement following the `switch` structure. If the `switch` control structure contains a `default` statement, the PHP interpreter always executes statements contained in the `default` statement unless it encounters a `break` statement.

FALLING THROUGH *SWITCH* CONTROL STRUCTURES

Just to re-emphasize the importance of including `break` statements in your `switch` control structures, once a case matches the test value for the `switch` control structure, the PHP interpreter executes every subsequent statement in the structure, including those for `case` statements that do not match the test value.

---

for Iterators

The `for` control structure in PHP is used as a C-style iterator control structure, so its condition breaks PHP conventions by requiring three related expressions: `for (expression1; expression2; expression3)`. The first expression typically declares the starting value for some variable and is only executed the first time the `for` control structure is encountered. The second expression is used as a truth value test for determining whether the code block should be executed. The third expression is executed at the end of the code block and is typically used to increment or decrement the variable declared in the first expression in the condition.

```php
<?php
  // for loops
```

```
  for ($x = 1; $x < 5; $x++) {
    print $x . "\n";
  }
?>
```

The output of the preceding example is:

```
1
2
3
4
```

foreach Iterators

The `foreach` control structure in PHP is an iterator that iterates through every element in an array, or in an object that has publicly visible variables, or in an object that implements the `Iterator` interface. Each iteration returns the element value and optionally the key for each element as named variables that you can access within the containing code block.

```
<?php
  // foreach loops: returning element values

  $array = array(
    'name' => 'Dan Scott',
    'age'  => 32,
    'languages' => array('Perl', 'PHP', 'Python')
  );

  print "Returning array values:\n";
  foreach ($array as $value) {
    print "$value\n";
  }

  print "\n";
  // foreach loops: returning keys and values
  print "Returning array keys and values:\n";
  foreach ($array as $key => $value) {
    print "Key: $key; value: $value\n";
  }
?>
```

The output of the preceding example is:

```
Returning array values:
Dan Scott
```

```
32
Array
```

```
Returning array keys and values:
Key: name; value: Dan Scott
Key: age; value: 32
Key: languages; value: Array
```

Note that the nested array cannot be represented as a string directly, so PHP substitutes the string "Array" to indicate that the returned value was an array type. To handle array types (or any type) specially, you can use the built-in is_type() functions to determine which type a variable contains. For example, to handle one level of nested arrays, we can modify our foreach() loop to include a test for a nested array using the is_array() function:

```php
<?php
  // foreach loops: returning element values

  $array = array(
    'name' => 'Dan Scott',
    'age'  => 32,
    'languages' => array('Perl', 'PHP', 'Python')
  );

  print "Returning array values:\n";
  foreach ($array as $value) {
    if (is_array($value)) {
      foreach ($value as $nextval) {
        print "[$nextval] ";
      }
      print "\n";
    }
    print "$value\n";
  }
?>
```

The output of the preceding example is:

```
Returning array values:
Dan Scott
32
[Perl] [PHP] [Python]
```

break and *continue*

The break and continue keywords enable you to exercise a finer degree of control over your control structures. The break keyword interrupts the normal flow of a for iterator or while loop and returns control to the enclosing scope. The break keyword also accepts an integer value that tells the PHP interpreter how many levels of nested scope it should break out of. The continue keyword, in comparison, maintains the flow within the same scope but immediately forces the next iteration of the enclosing loop.

Defining Functions

Defining your own functions in PHP consists of five easy steps:

1. Use the function keyword to indicate that you are defining a function.

2. Specify the name of the function you are defining.

3. Specify the input arguments that the function accepts within parentheses, along with any default values for unspecified arguments.

4. Define the function body. This generally involves manipulating the input arguments in some way.

5. *Optionally*: Return a literal value or an object. If you do not explicitly return a value or object, the function will always return NULL.

For example, we can define a new function named additup that accepts three integer values and returns their sum to the caller in just a few lines of code:

```
// Defining functions
function additup($a, $b, $c=0) {
  return $a + $b + $c;
}

print additup(3, 2, 1) . "\n";
print additup(3, 2) . "\n";
```

Note that the third input argument has a default value of 0; this makes the third argument to our very simple function optional. Like any function, you can assign the results that were returned to a variable, or you can use the results directly in the caller. Calling the additup() function as shown in the preceding example results in the following output:

```
6
5
```

Creating Classes

With the release of PHP version 4, classes and object-oriented syntax were added to the language, but the implementation relied heavily on references to variables and functions to graft object orientation on top of the existing procedural syntax. PHP version 5, however, implemented the syntax and semantics directly within the core interpreter, improving the performance and functionality of classes in PHP. This chapter briefly documents how to define your own classes and methods using the PHP version 5 syntax. The recipe for cooking up your own class is:

1. Use the `class` keyword to indicate that you are defining a class.

2. Specify the name of the class you are defining. By convention, PHP class names are capitalized to distinguish them from variable or method names.

3. *Optional:* Use the `extends` keyword to indicate the class from which your new class inherits functions and variables.

4. Enclose the code block that defines the members and methods of the class within braces.

5. Declare any class member variables using the `public`, `private`, or `protected` keywords to define the visibility of the method. If you do not specify the visibility of the method, the default level is `public`. Note that although PHP allows public class member variables to be accessed directly by callers, it is a good idea to provide wrapper methods to set and get the class member variables. This gives you the opportunity to normalize the values rather than passing raw values to or from the class member variables.

6. Declare a `__construct` method to automatically initialize the class member variables. The variables defined for the `__construct` method map to the arguments passed in when a new instance of the class is instantiated.

7. Declare any class methods to implement the behavior of the class using the `public`, `private`, or `protected` keywords to define the visibility of the method. If you do not specify the visibility of the method, the default level is `public`.

Within the scope of a class definition, you can use the `$this` operator to refer to class member variables and methods. In the following example, we define a generic class called `Horse` that represents the attributes and methods for all horses, and then we define the `Thoroughbred` class that inherits from the `Horse` base class to add its own specialization. Although the base class defines all of the methods, child classes can override those methods, define new methods, or add new member variables to their definition.

```php
<?php
  // Defining classes

  class Horse {
    function __construct($hands, $color) {
      $this->hands = $hands;
      $this->color = $color;
    }
```

```php
  function getHands() {
    return $this->hands;
  }

  function getColor() {
    return $this->color;
  }

  function getBreed() {
    return $this->breed;
  }
}

class Thoroughbred extends Horse {
  function __construct($hands, $color) {
    parent::__construct($hands, $color);
    $this->breed = 'standardbred';
  }
}

$derby = new Thoroughbred(15, 'blood bay');
print $derby->getHands() . "\n";
print $derby->getColor() . "\n";
print $derby->getBreed() . "\n";
?>
```

Now that we have defined our new classes, instantiating a new object and accessing some of its methods is easy. When we instantiate a new `Thoroughbred` object, the constructor first calls the `Horse` constructor using the special `parent::` keyword to access its parent class' member methods and variables, and then it adds its specialized attribute for the breed. When we invoke the `getHands()` method on the instance, you can confirm that the base class constructor did indeed initialize the `$hands` member variable as expected:

```
15
blood bay
standardbred
```

Including Libraries of PHP Code

Although you can define all of your functions, classes, and actual program code in a single file, this approach makes it impossible to reuse your custom functions and classes in other applications. Instead, you can collect functions and classes into one or more *include files*: files that contain related groups of functions and variables.

As an example, consider the `Horse` class that we defined during our discussion of classes. Let's assume we want to reuse the `Horse` class in many of our applications, so we have placed it in its own file called `horse.php`. To access the classes and functions defined in the `Horse` class, issue the `include()`, `include_once()`, `require()`, or `require_once()` statement and specify the name of the file you want to import. The classes and functions in the included file are available to the code following the `include` or `require` statement. In the following example, we access the `Thoroughbred` class defined in the `horse.php` file extension to the constructor for the `HTTPServer` object.

```php
<?php
  require('horse.php');

  $derby = new Thoroughbred(15, 'blood bay');
  print $derby->getHands() . "\n";
  print $derby->getColor() . "\n";
  print $derby->getBreed() . "\n";
?>
```

INCLUDE, INCLUDE_ONCE, REQUIRE, AND REQUIRE_ONCE

The difference between the include and require statements is that if the file cannot be found, the `include()` and `include_once()` statements return a `Warning` but allow the script to continue executing, whereas the `require()` and `require_once()` statements return an `Error` and stop execution of the script.

The difference between the `include()`/`require()` and `include_once()`/`require_once()` statements is that the `include_once()`/`require_once()` statements silently prevent the same file from being included multiple times within the same PHP script.

Include files are useful for helping to organize even small projects, but for large projects, they are absolutely essential.

Installing and Configuring PHP

Before you can install and configure PHP to create Apache Derby applications, you must:

1. Install and configure Apache Derby as described in Chapter 4, "Installing Apache Derby and IBM Cloudscape on Windows," or Chapter 5, "Installing Apache Derby and IBM Cloudscape on Linux."

2. Start the Apache Derby Network Server as described in the install chapter.

3. Install and configure the IBM DB2 Application Development Client to enable Open Database Connectivity (ODBC) access to Apache Derby databases as described in Chapter 10, "Developing Apache Derby Applications with Perl, PHP, Python, and ODBC."

Once you have successfully made an ODBC connection to your Apache Derby database, you can proceed with installing and configuring PHP on your system.

Installing PHP on Linux

Normally, your best option is to locate and install the version of PHP offered by your chosen Linux distribution. However, to use PDO and PDO::ODBC to access our Apache Derby database, we need to install a minimum level of PHP 5.0.4. For a relatively recent example, Red Hat Enterprise Linux 4.0 offers php-4.3.9-3.2.i386 as an RPM Package Manager (RPM) package, which is too old for our purposes. To satisfy the prerequisites of PDO and PDO::ODBC, we need to compile and install a newer version of PHP from the freely available PHP source—and to avoid conflicting with the Linux distribution's binary version of PHP, we must first remove those binary packages.

To remove the binary PHP package, or any other RPM package on an RPM-based Linux distribution such as Red Hat Enterprise Linux, issue the following command as a user with root authority:

```
# rpm -ev php
```

On Debian or other apt-based Linux distributions, issue the following command as a user with root authority to remove an APT package:

```
# apt-get remove php
```

On Gentoo, a source-based Linux distribution, issue the following command as a user with root authority:

```
# emerge unmerge php
```

To compile PHP from source, you must have installed the Apache, autoconf, automake, bison, flex, gcc, and libxml2 packages, along with any corresponding development packages. Then perform the following steps:

1. Download the PHP source from http://www.php.net/downloads.php. For PDO support, you must download at least PHP 5.0.4.

2. Uncompress the PHP source. If you downloaded the bzip2 compressed version of the PHP, issue the following command:

   ```
   bash$ tar xjf php-5.0.4.tar.bz2
   ```

   If you downloaded the gzip compressed version of the PHP source, issue the following command:

   ```
   bash$ tar xzf php-5.0.4.tar.bz2
   ```

3. Configure the PHP source, pointing to the Apache apxs configuration script that enables you to build PHP as an Apache DSO module.

```
bash$ cd php-5.0.4
bash$ ./configure --with-apxs=/usr/sbin/apxs --enable-cli
```

Note that if your distribution bundles Apache 2, your configure option must specify `--with-apxs2` instead of `--with-apxs`.

4. Build the PHP source.

```
bash$ make
```

5. Install the PHP binaries that you have compiled, using root authority. The executable files will be installed in the `/usr/local/bin` directory, while any extensions will be installed in the `/usr/local/lib/php` directory.

```
bash$ su -c 'make install'
```

6. Copy `php.ini-recommended` from the source directory to a new file called `/usr/local/lib/php.ini` to set the right default values for your PHP configuration.

7. Ensure that you can invoke PHP from the command line by issuing the following command to display the PHP version:

```
bash$ php -v
```

Configuring PHP on Linux

The PDO and PDO::ODBC extensions are currently not shipped with any Linux distributions, which means you have to download and install them yourself. This is not as much hard work as it sounds: we'll guide you through the steps and help you avoid the most common pitfalls. First, ensure that you have the following packages installed on your system:

1. DB2 Runtime Client, with application development headers, must be installed to provide the ODBC driver and the ODBC libraries.

2. gcc (the Gnu C compiler) must be installed, as the PDO and PDO::ODBC extensions consist largely of C code that must be linked against the DB2 Application Development Client libraries to produce the C extension.

To successfully build and install the PDO and PDO::ODBC extensions for Apache Derby, perform the following steps:

1. As a user with root authority, issue the following commands to download, compile, and install the latest versions of the PDO extension:

```
bash# pear upgrade pear
bash# pear install PDO
bash# pear install PDO::ODBC
```

2. Edit your PHP configuration file to tell PHP to automatically load the PDO extension when the PHP interpreter is invoked. As a user with root authority, edit or create /usr/local/lib/php.ini and ensure that it contains the following entry:

```
; Load extensions
extension=pdo.so
```

3. As a user with root authority, issue the following commands to download, compile, and install the latest versions of the PDO::ODBC extension:

```
bash# pear install PDO::ODBC
```

4. Edit your PHP configuration file to tell PHP to automatically load the new extension when the PHP interpreter is invoked. As a user with root authority, edit or create /usr/local/lib/php.ini and ensure that it contains the following entry:

```
extension=pdo::odbc.so
```

5. Check that PHP has successfully loaded the new extensions by issuing the following command to list the loaded modules:

```
bash$ php -m
```

PDO and PDO::ODBC should be among the module list.

Installing PHP on Windows

Setting up PHP access to Apache Derby on Windows is easy because the PHP project makes all of the required binary packages freely available for your use.

Downloading PHP

The PHP Web site offers a freely available PHP interpreter that includes a complete set of documentation and base packages. Download the zipped PHP package from the PHP Web site (http://www.php.net/downloads.php).

Installing PHP

Once you have downloaded the zipped PHP package, extract the package to a directory. For the purposes of this chapter, we will assume that you have extracted the PHP package into the C:\php5 directory. Add C:\php5 to your system or user %PATH% environment variable so that you can invoke it directly from the command line. You should also copy php.ini-recommended to a new file called php.ini to set the right default values for your PHP configuration.

Configuring PHP

Now that you have installed PHP, you need to download and install the PDO and PDO::ODBC extensions to be able to connect to your Apache Derby database through the IBM DB2 Universal

Database client. Perform the following steps to install the PDO and PDO::ODBC extensions:

1. Download the zipped collection of PECL Windows binary extensions from http://www.php.net/downloads.php.

2. Extract the PECL Windows binary extensions into your `C:\php5\ext\` directory.

3. Edit your PHP configuration file to specify the location of your new extensions, and to tell it to load the new extensions. As a user with root authority, edit `C:\php5\php.ini` and ensure that it contains the following entries:

   ```
   ; Extension directory
   extension_dir='C:\php5\ext\'
   ; Load extensions
   extension=php_pdo.dll
   extension=php_pdo::odbc.dll
   ```

4. Check that PHP has successfully loaded the new extensions by issuing the following command to list the loaded modules:

   ```
   C:\php5\> php -m
   ```

   PDO and PDO::ODBC should be among the module list.

Now that you have installed both PHP and the PDO and PDO::ODBC extensions, you are ready to start writing PHP applications that connect to Apache Derby.

Creating Apache Derby Applications with PHP

For the purposes of testing your PHP installation, create a file called `'hello-derby.php'` containing the following lines:

```php
<?php
  echo "Hello, Apache Derby world!";
?>
```

Running PHP Scripts from the Command Line

To run a PHP script on Windows operating systems, you can explicitly invoke the PHP interpreter to run `hello-derby.php` from the command line by invoking the name of the PHP interpreter, followed by the name of the script. The name of the PHP interpreter for CGI applications is normally `php.exe`, while the name of the PHP interpreter for command line (CLI) applications is normally `php-cli.exe`. To run our example script as a PHP CLI application, issue the following command:

```
C:/> php-cli hello-derby.php
```

To run a PHP script on Linux operating systems, invoke the name of the PHP interpreter, followed by the name of the script. The name of the PHP interpreter for CGI applications is normally php, while the name of the PHP interpreter for command line (CLI) applications is normally php-cli. If the PHP interpreter is not in a directory specified by your PATH environment variable, you will have to specify the path to the PHP interpreter. To run the script in your current working directory, issue the following command:

```
$ php hello-derby.php
```

To run the script contained in the /home/lynn/ directory as a CLI application:

```
$ php-cli /home/lynn/hello-derby.php
```

Connecting to an Apache Derby Database

Single Connections

In the PDO extension, PDO objects represent connections to databases. To connect to an Apache Derby database, create a PDO object by invoking the PDO constructor with a PDO data source name (DSN) consisting of the PDO driver identifier and database name, your user name, and password as arguments. The following code example illustrates a function in which those arguments are assigned explicit values. We use this function in our PHP library to create all of the PDO objects for our applications so that changing the connection information from a development database to a production database requires us to modify only one file. Other PHP applications could retrieve the appropriate argument values from the command line interface or from the values submitted from a Web form.

```php
<?php

function YMLD_databaseConnect() {
  $database = 'YMLD';
  $user = 'db2inst1';
  $password = 'ibmdb2';

  try {
    $conn = new PDO("odbc:$database", $user, $password);
    $conn->exec("SET CURRENT SCHEMA APP");
  }
  catch (PDOException $e) {
    print $e;
  }
  return $conn;
}
?>
```

Note that immediately after connecting to the database, we issue the SET CURRENT SCHEMA statement to ensure that we automatically qualify the names of any database objects, such as tables, views, or stored procedures, within the APP schema, rather than the default schema matching the user name. This enables us to connect to the database using different user names, yet still work with the same sets of data without having to change the database object names throughout the rest of our code. You can also use this approach to qualify your test and production schemas in case you want to experiment with new PHP functions that might alter your data in unexpected ways.

All of the actual PDO calls are wrapped in a try { } block so that we can catch any PDO-Exception object that might be thrown and handle them appropriately; in our case, we simply print the exception statement and return the connection $conn (which will be FALSE if the connection failed). In a real application, you can execute code in a try block and catch any exceptions at a much higher level so that the exception can contain more context about what went wrong and so that the application can choose the right method of handling the exception. For example, a Web application might simply log the error message, whereas a GUI application might display a dialog box to the user to alert him or her to the problem.

Disconnecting from a Database

To disconnect from a database, set the value of the PDO object to NULL to close the connection and free up system resources. Compared to most PHP operations, connecting to a database is a time- and network-intensive operation, so you should reuse the PDO object as much as possible. In a typical PHP script, you create a PDO object at the start of the script and reuse that connection throughout the rest of the script, then disconnect from the database at the end of the script to ensure that the system resources are returned to the database server promptly. If you do not explicitly close the connection, PDO will close the connection for you when the script completes.

Pooling Connections

Creating a database connection is probably the single largest drain on your system's resources and performance. For applications that must support a high volume of database access, you might want to consider connection pooling—reusing existing database connections instead of destroying and re-creating them. The PDO::ODBC driver offers built-in connection pooling support at the ODBC driver manager level if you run PHP on Windows. Your Web application can reuse an existing Apache Derby connection to perform its work.

Issuing SQL Statements

Whereas PDO objects represent the connection to a database in the PDO, PDOStatement objects provide the mechanism for issuing SQL statements and retrieving results from the database.

Executing a Single Statement

To issue a single SQL statement, call the `exec()` method of the PDO object. For example, to add a new production to the list of productions, you can insert a row into the `PRODUCTIONS` table as follows:

```
function YMLD_insertOne($conn) {
  $sql = "INSERT INTO PRODUCTIONS (Production_Title,
    Production_StartDate, Production_EndDate)
    VALUES ('Lily of the Valley', '2005-01-18', '2005-02-13')";
  $conn->exec($sql);
}
```

Issuing SQL Statements with Placeholders

Most SQL statements that you issue in your applications will be built with user input, rather than simple predetermined SQL statements like the previous example. And for each user, those statements may differ only slightly: for example, in a message forum, you might retrieve a list of messages written by a particular user by issuing a `SELECT` statement with a `WHERE` clause that limits the scope of rows to those that match the user's ID. You could build the SQL statement by interpolating PHP variables, concatenating the strings using the `.` operator, or using `printf`-style `%` parameters, but those approaches introduce the risk that your user input might (intentionally or otherwise) invalidate or corrupt your SQL statement. To avoid this situation, PDO supports parameterized SQL statements through the use of placeholders. A placeholder in an SQL statement can be either a question mark (`?`) character or a named parameter (`:name`). You can use multiple placeholders of the same type in a single SQL statement as long as you pass one argument per placeholder when you execute the statement.

To create a `PDOStatement` object, call the `prepare()` method of the PDO object and pass the SQL statement as the method argument. You can pass parameters to the statement either by binding each parameter using the `PDOStatement::bindParam()` method or by passing the parameters as an array option to the `PDOStatement::execute()` statement when you execute the statement.

Reissuing the Same SQL Statement with Different Parameters

Executing a single statement at a time is fine for low-volume applications, but sometimes you must repeatedly reissue an SQL statement with only slight variations. For example, assume you want to add ten more productions to your database. You could manually build ten different `INSERT` statements and issue the `PDO::exec()` method once for each statement, but there is an alternate approach that requires less work from both the PHP database driver and the Derby network server. To use this optimized method of executing the same statement with different parameter values, prepare the SQL statement once using the `PDO::prepare()` method, then call the `execute()` method on the resulting `PDOStatement` object. The `PDOStatement::execute()`

method accepts the SQL statement and an array containing one or more parameters. The following function iterates through an array of parameters to insert seven new rows into the PRODUCTIONS table.

```
function YMLD_insertMany($conn) {
  $sql = "INSERT INTO PRODUCTIONS (Production_Title,
    Production_StartDate, Production_EndDate)
    VALUES (?, ?, ?)";
  $stmt = $conn->prepare($sql);

  $productions = array(
    array('Cats and Dogs', '2005-04-01', '2005-05-01'),
    array('Desperate Houses', '2005-05-02', '2005-06-01'),
    array('Icing the Puck', '2005-06-02', '2005-07-01'),
    array('Heroes', '2005-07-02', '2005-08-01'),
    array('Rubber Sacks', '2005-08-02', '2005-09-01'),
    array('Couched in Leather', '2005-09-02', '2005-10-01'),
    array('Backsplash', '2005-10-02', '2005-11-01'),
  );

  foreach ($productions as $row) {
    $stmt->execute($row);
  }

  $stmt = NULL;
}
```

The previous code example begins by creating a PDOStatement object from the PDO object by preparing the INSERT statement that we want to issue multiple times. Notice the three parameter markers within the VALUES clause; these will be replaced by the values of each array nested within the $productions array. Each time we iterate over the array in the foreach control structure, we invoke the execute() method on the PDOStatement object and pass the $row array to the method to pass into the INSERT statement. Finally, we set the $stmt object to NULL to return its resources back to the system.

Counting the Number of Changed Rows

The PDOStatement object offers a rowCount() method that returns the integer value of the number of rows affected by the last execute() call. If the execute() method has not been called, or if the last call did not affect any rows, the value returned is -1. Note that the rowcount() method only returns the number of rows affected by non-SELECT statements. If you must determine how many rows would be returned by a SELECT statement, you can issue the same

SELECT statement with the returned columns wrapped in a COUNT() scalar function—but then you must retrieve the results of the SELECT statement, which we will discuss in the following section.

Retrieving Data

The previous section discussed how to issue SQL statements, including how to most efficiently execute the same statement multiple times. But beyond finding out how many rows were affected by a given non-SELECT SQL statement, we have not yet talked about how to issue a SELECT statement and retrieve the results of the SELECT operation. The same principles apply to retrieving data returned as the result of calling a stored procedure with a CALL statement. After all, as much fun as it can be to modify database schemas and insert, update, or delete data in the database, you need to be able to get data out of the database to write a useful application.

Retrieving a Single Result Set

Every SELECT statement that you issue will return a single result set—a set of rows that matched the conditions of your SELECT statement. Calling a fetch method on the PDOStatement object after an execute() call automatically retrieves the first row from that result set. Here is an example of how to fetch a row into a set of variables:

```
function YMLD_selectNextShow($conn) {
  $sql = 'SELECT Production_No, Production_Title,
    Production_StartDate, Production_EndDate
    FROM Productions
    WHERE Production_StartDate > CURRENT_DATE
    ORDER BY Production_StartDate';

  $stmt = $conn->query($sql);
  $row = $stmt->fetch();
  $stmt = NULL;
  return $row;
}
```

You have already seen the PDO::prepare() and PDOStatement::execute() pattern in our examples of issuing INSERT statements. For SELECT statements without parameters, however, we also have the option of calling the PDO::query() method to immediately issue the SELECT statement and return a PDOStatement object. To retrieve the row, we must call the PDOStatement::fetch() method, optionally specifying the format in which the row should be returned. If there are no rows in the result set, the fetch method returns NULL.

In the preceding example, we issue a simple SELECT statement to retrieve all of the productions from our Apache Derby database in the order of their start date, ensuring that only those productions that begin their run after today's date (using the CURRENT_DATE special register in the WHERE clause) will be returned. We then fetch only the first row of the result set by invoking the `fetch()` method on the `PDOStatement` object, close the cursor by setting the `PDOStatement` object to `NULL`, and return the `$row` variable to the caller. The onus is on the caller, therefore, to correctly handle the result.

Formats for Returning Rows

PDO defines a number of constants that enable you to specify the format in which the row should be returned by passing the constant as an argument to the `PDOStatement::fetch()` method:

- `PDO::FETCH_BOTH` (default): Returns an array indexed by both column name and column number as returned in your result set

- `PDO::FETCH_NUM`: Returns an array indexed by column number as returned in your result set, starting at column 0

- `PDO::FETCH_ASSOC`: Returns an array indexed by column name as returned in your result set

- `PDO::FETCH_BOUND`: Returns `TRUE` and assigns the values of the columns in your result set to the PHP variables to which they were bound with the `PDOStatement::bindParam()` method

- `PDO::FETCH_LAZY`: Combines `PDO::FETCH_BOTH` and `PDO::FETCH_OBJ`, creating the object variable names as they are accessed

- `PDO::FETCH_OBJ`: Returns an anonymous object with property names that correspond to the column names returned in your result set

Calling Stored Procedures

Stored procedures encapsulate complex logic or commonly required actions as database server objects. Apache Derby uses stored procedures to great effect as the primary administration interface for the database, so it is important to learn how to call stored procedures in your applications. You can call stored procedures from any number of different client applications without having to re-implement the logic in each client application. A stored procedure can accept zero or more parameters, and each parameter can be declared as an input-only (`IN`) parameter, an output-only (`OUT`) parameter, or a parameter that accepts an input value and returns an output value (`INOUT`). Along with returning values for `OUT` and `INOUT` parameters, a single stored procedure can also return multiple result sets. In addition to the built-in stored procedures that are available with Apache Derby, you can write your own stored procedures in Java using the Java Database Connectivity (JDBC) API. The PDO::ODBC extension offers support for calling any stored procedure and handling the results appropriately.

Calling Stored Procedures with *IN* Parameters

To call a stored procedure with `IN` parameters using PDO, you can prepare and execute the `CALL` statement using parameter markers just as you would for a `SELECT` statement or any other SQL statement. For example, given a stored procedure named `DOUBLE_IN` that accepts two `IN` parameters of type VARCHAR(32) representing the old title and the new title, respectively, of a production that you want to update in the Productions table, you could call the stored procedure with the following function:

```
function YMLD_callProcedureDoubleIn($conn) {
  $sql = 'CALL double_in(?, ?)';

  $stmt = $conn->prepare($sql);
  $stmt->execute(array('Cats and Dogs', 'My New Title'));
  $stmt = NULL;
}
```

We create a PDOStatement object by preparing the CALL statement for the stored procedure, using parameter markers to represent the stored procedure parameters. You might have noticed that the stored procedure name is lowercase, even though we had said that the stored procedure name was DOUBLE_IN. In Apache Derby, stored procedure names are not case-sensitive; the database automatically converts your stored procedure name to uppercase. Then, in the same way that we can execute any other SQL statement with parameter markers, we pass an array of input values to the PDOStatement::execute() method for PDO to bind to the CALL statement.

Retrieving a Single Result Set

Calling a stored procedure that returns a single result set is just like calling any other stored procedure through PDO: execute the SQL statement with the appropriate parameters to call the stored procedure. Then, to handle the result set returned by the stored procedure, invoke the PDOStatement::fetch() method to retrieve one or more rows from the result set. The following example demonstrates how to call a stored procedure named SINGLE_RESULT that returns a single result set and that accepts no parameters.

```
function YMLD_callProcedureSingleResult($conn) {
  $sql = 'CALL SINGLE_RESULT()';
  $rows = array();

  $stmt = $conn->query($sql);
  while ($row = $stmt->fetch(PDO::FETCH_NUM)) {
    $rows[] = $row;
  }

  $stmt = NULL;
            return $rows;
}
```

The preceding function calls the stored procedure using the PDO::query() method to return a PDOStatement object and then retrieves all of the rows into a variable (cleverly named

$rows) using a while loop around the PDO::fetch() method before cleaning up the cursor resources and returning the rows to the function caller.

Passing *OUT* and *INOUT* Parameters

To call a stored procedure that accepts OUT or INOUT parameters, you must learn how to use a new, slightly more complex way of issuing an SQL statement containing parameter markers. PDO supports the use of IN and INOUT parameters in stored procedures by allowing you to explicitly bind parameters in an SQL statement to a PHP variable. When you execute the SQL statement, PDO passes in the value of the PHP variable as the input value for an INOUT parameter and ignores the value of the PHP variable for an OUT parameter. When the stored procedure returns, the output values of OUT and INOUT parameters are stored in the values of the bound PHP variables.

The syntax for the PDOStatement::bindParam() method is bindParam (*parameter-ID, variable, parameter-type, parameter-length*) where:

- *parameter-ID* identifies the SQL parameter either as a 1-indexed integer (for question mark placeholders) or a string (for named parameters)
- *variable* is the PHP variable that you want to bind to the specified SQL parameter
- *parameter-type* identifies the PDO type mapping for the SQL parameter
- *parameter-length* identifies the maximum length of the SQL parameter

PDO defines four different constants that represent data types of SQL parameters. Although this seems quite limited compared to the vast number of SQL data types that Apache Derby supports, PDO determines the SQL data type before issuing the SQL statement and converts the specified PDO type to the correct SQL data type to prevent losing data or precision. The four PDO type constants are:

- PDO::PARAM_NULL: Use this type to represent the special SQL NULL value.
- PDO::PARAM_STR: Use this type to represent CHAR, DATE, DECIMAL, DOUBLE, FLOAT, NUMERIC, REAL, TIME, TIMESTAMP, and VARCHAR SQL types.
- PDO::PARAM_INT: Use this type to represent SMALLINT, INTEGER, and BIGINT SQL types.
- PDO::PARAM_LOB: Use this type to represent LOB and CLOB SQL types.

To pass an OUT parameter to a CALL statement, invoke the PDOStatement::bindParam() method with all four arguments. To pass an INOUT parameter to a CALL statement, invoke the PDOStatement::bindParam() method with all four arguments, but append | PDO:: PARAM_INPUT_OUTPUT to the *parameter-type* argument to indicate that the parameter is an INOUT parameter. For example, the following function calls a stored procedure named PRODUCTION_LISTS2 that accepts a single INOUT parameter of type DATE.

```
function YMLD_callProcedureInout($conn) {
  $sql = 'CALL production_lists2(:date)';
```

```
$value = '2029-02-04';
$stmt = $conn->prepare($sql);

// Bind the INOUT parameter
$stmt->bindParam(':date', $value,
   PDO::PARAM_STR|PDO::PARAM_INPUT_OUTPUT, 14);
$stmt->execute();

$stmt = NULL;
         return $value;
}
```

We bind the `$value` variable to the named `INOUT` parameter in our `CALL` statement as a PHP string data type (`PDO::PARAM_STR`) INOUT parameter. If you are wondering about the strange syntax in the `PDOStatement::bindParam()` method call, `PDO::PARAM_STR` and `PDO::PARAM_INPUT_OUTPUT` are PDO module constants that map to a bitmask, and the `|` operator is a bitwise `OR` operator that sets the corresponding bit that maps to each constant. When PDO handles the `PDOStatement::bindParam()` call, it checks the value of the *parameter-type* parameter to determine the data type of the parameter and to see whether the `PDO::PARAM_INPUT_OUTPUT` bit has been set. When we call the stored procedure with the `PDOStatement::execute()` method, the input value of the `$value` PHP variable is passed in to the `PRODUCTION_LISTS2` stored procedure and then is set to a new value by the stored procedure. After cleaning up the cursor resources, we return the value of the `$value` variable to the caller of the function.

Retrieving Multiple Result Sets

Whereas `SELECT` statements can only return a single result set, stored procedures can return multiple result sets. When you call a stored procedure that returns a single result set, just iterate through the rows of the result set by calling the `PDOStatement::fetch()` methods as though you were retrieving rows from a `SELECT` statement. When you call a stored procedure that returns multiple result sets, you can iterate through the rows of the first result set using the `PDOStatement::fetch()` method, then invoke the `PDOStatement::nextRowset()` method of the `Cursor` object to retrieve the next result set from the stored procedure. If there are no more result sets to retrieve from the stored procedure, `PDOStatement::nextRowset()` returns `NULL`. If you do not know how many results sets a given stored procedure will return, you can simply iterate over the `PDOStatement::nextRowset()` method using a `while` loop control structure. The following example demonstrates a call to a stored procedure that returns three result sets, with different sets of columns in each result set.

```
function YMLD_callProcedureResults($conn) {
  $sql = 'CALL PRODUCTION_LISTS()';
  $stmt = $conn->query($sql);
```

```
$rows = $stmt->fetchAll(PDO::FETCH_NUM);
do {
  YMLD_printResults($rows);
  $rows = $stmt->fetchAll(PDO::FETCH_NUM);
} while ($rows && $stmt->nextRowset());

$stmt = NULL;
}

function YMLD_printResults($rows) {
  print "\nNew result set:\n";
  foreach ($rows as $row) {
    foreach ($row as $col) {
      print "$col ";
    }
    print "\n";
  }
}
```

In the `callProcedureResults()` function, we prepare, execute, and return the statement directly through the `PDO::query()` method, then enter a do loop to iterate through the result sets. Rather than fetching and printing a row at a time, we have chosen to use the `PDOStatement::fetchAll()` method to return the complete result set as an array of arrays. If `$rows` contains a non-NULL value, we pass the variable to our helper function, `YMLD_printResults()`, which simply iterates through the rows and columns and prints each row on its own line. The `while()` condition for the do loop attempts to advance to the next result set associated with the `PDOStatement` object; if there is no subsequent result set, then the method returns `false` and the do loop is completed.

Managing Transactions

A transaction is a set of one or more database operations that must all succeed for any changes to be reflected in the database. When all of the database operations in a transaction succeed, the corresponding changes are committed to the database. If one of the operations fails, all of the operations in the transaction can be rolled back so that the database appears to be unmodified. When you create a database connection with the PDO extension, your connection is set to commit automatically after every statement. If your application ends unexpectedly, none of the SQL statements that your application has issued to that point will be lost.

However, there are times when you want either all of a set of SQL statements or none of them to succeed; for example, if you are responsible for developing an application that sells tickets online, you do not want the SQL statement that sends tickets to a purchaser to succeed if the SQL statement that changes the seat status to unavailable subsequently fails—you might end up selling tickets for the same seats twice, which would cause an unpleasant situation for your customers and your theater manager. To force all or none of a set of SQL statements to succeed, you can begin a *transaction* by turning off autocommit mode with the `PDO::beginTransaction()` method. Every subsequent SQL statement that your application issues through that PDO object will not modify the database irrevocably until you issue a `PDO::commit()` method. Alternately, if your application dies unexpectedly or some event occurs (such as a user clicking a 'CANCEL' button), you can issue the `PDO::rollBack()` method to reverse the changes to the database back to the point in time where the transaction began. PDO automatically rolls back a transaction if your script dies before you issue `PDO::commit()`.

Note that you can have multiple connections to your Apache Derby database at a time, even from within the same application, simply by creating new PDO objects, and each connection can have a different transaction. Rolling back the work performed on one PDO object does not affect the SQL statements issued through the other PDO objects in your application. Be aware that using transactions can impose significant locking overhead on your database, though, so if you are modifying data or your database schema, you should either explicitly commit your work regularly or leave your PDO object in autocommit mode.

HAVING TROUBLE MAKING IT STICK?

After you begin a transaction, if you do not issue an explicit commit after modifying your database schema or data, none of the changes you have made will be visible after the application ends. So, if you want to make your changes permanent, invoke the `PDO::commit()` method before the end of your application.

Explicitly Committing and Rolling Back Transactions

The PDO specification provides a standard set of methods that you can call to start and end transactions. To begin a transaction, call the `PDO::beginTransaction()` method. To roll back a transaction, call the `PDO::rollBack()` method. To commit a transaction, call the `PDO::commit()` method. Once you begin a transaction, a rollback will only roll back work to that commit point. The following example demonstrates how to perform some database operations in a transaction and then either commit the work or roll back all of the statements that have been performed since the transaction began:

```
function YMLD_dropTables($conn) {
  $sql = 'DROP TABLE ';
  $tables = array('TRANSACTIONLOG', 'SEATS', 'SEATMAP',
             'PRICEPLAN', 'PERFORMANCES', 'PRODUCTIONS');

  // Begin a new transaction, turning off autocommit
  $conn->beginTransaction();
```

```
foreach ($tables as $table) {
    try {
      $conn->exec("$sql $table");
    }
    catch (PDOException $e) {
      print "Failed to drop table $table\n";
    }
  }

  // We always want to commit this transaction
  if (TRUE) {
    $conn->commit();
  }
  else {
    $conn->rollBack();
  }
}
```

Setting Autocommit

You can explicitly turn autocommit off for a specific PDO object by passing `PDO::ATTR_AUTO-COMMIT, FALSE` as the parameters to the `PDO::setAttribute()` method. To check the current value of the autocommit behavior for the PDO object, invoke the `PDO::getAttribute()` method with `PDO::ATTR_COMMIT` as the argument. If autocommit is off, the method returns the value `FALSE`:

```
function YMLD_setAutocommit($conn) {
  // Turn autocommit off
  $conn->setAttribute(PDO::ATTR_AUTOCOMMIT, TRUE);
  print checkAutocommit($conn);

  // Turn autocommit on
  $conn->setAttribute(PDO::ATTR_AUTOCOMMIT, TRUE);
  print checkAutocommit($conn);
}

function YMLD_checkAutocommit($conn) {
  if ($conn->getAttribute(PDO::ATTR_AUTOCOMMIT)) {
    return "Autocommit is ON";
  }
```

```
  else {
    return "Autocommit is OFF";
  }
}

YMLD_setAutocommit($conn);
```

Special Data Types

Although many organizations use databases to store nothing more complicated than strings and numbers—customer relationship management applications, university transcripts, results from scientific experiments, and so on—some organizations have found databases invaluable for storing less traditional kinds of data. In the following section, we consider the support that PDO offers Apache Derby for storing non-traditional data types.

Large Objects: *BLOBs* and *CLOBs*

Large object data types are used to represent data that can consist of hundreds of megabytes of binary or character data per column. To build a database-driven jukebox, you might decide to store all of your audio files as binary large object (BLOB) data types in your database along with a few other columns representing the genre, title, artist, length, and year in which the song was released. An alternative design for this application simply stores the files on the file system and stores the location of each file in the database instead. The advantage of storing large object data in the database is that you avoid having to develop two different backup procedures for your data and deploying your application is simply a matter of copying your database.

One disadvantage of storing large object data in the database is that your database backups may be much larger. In addition, the PDO extension currently only supports retrieving BLOB data starting from the first byte of the BLOB. The lack of random access to BLOB data through PHP means that operations requiring the equivalent of file-seek and file-read behavior are best implemented through separate files on the file system. Our application stores images as BLOB objects in the database for the convenience of backing up and deploying the application.

The scientific field of life sciences provides a more likely scenario for storing character large object (CLOB) data in a database. Genetic analysis depends in large part upon analyzing DNA sequences—long strings consisting of combinations of the characters 'A', 'C', 'T', and 'G'—to understand the roles that individual genes play in various illnesses and to find potential cures. Much of the analysis can be carried out through SQL statements with user-defined functions that understand how to compare DNA sequences.

To extract a BLOB value from a database using the PDO extension, use the `PDOStatement::bindColumn()` method to explicitly specify the `PDO::PARAM_LOB` type, and optionally bind the BLOB directly into a file handle you create using the PHP `fopen()` function. `PDOStatement::bindColumn()` is used to bind output values from a column in a result set to a PHP variable, and the syntax for the PDOStatement::bindColumn() method is bindColumn(*column, variable, parameter-type, parameter-length*) where:

- *column* identifies the column in the row as a 1-indexed integer
- *variable* is the PHP variable that you want to bind to the specified SQL parameter
- *parameter-type* identifies the PDO type mapping for the SQL parameter
- *parameter-length* identifies the maximum length of the SQL parameter—note that this has no meaning for LOB columns

When you pass a file handle to PDOStatement::bindColumn() for the *variable* argument, you avoid the overhead of storing the entire LOB in memory (remember, a large object can be gigabytes in size) and instead stream the data directly into a file. In the following example, the BLOB data for each row is stored as a file on the local file system.

The most efficient way to insert a BLOB value into a database with PDO is to use the PDOStatement::bindParam() method to bind the BLOB directly from a file handle you create using the PHP fopen() function. PDOStatement::bindParam() is used to bind output values from a column in a result set to a PHP variable, and the syntax for the PDOStatement:: bindParam() method is bindParam(*parameter, variable, parameter-type, parameter-length*) where:

- *parameter* identifies the SQL statement parameter to which the input value will be bound, identified as a 1-indexed integer for question mark placeholders or as the name of a named parameter
- *variable* is the PHP variable that you want to bind to the specified SQL parameter
- *parameter-type* identifies the PDO type mapping for the SQL parameter
- *parameter-length* identifies the maximum length of the SQL parameter

When you pass a file handle to PDOStatement::bindParam(), you avoid the overhead of first reading the entire LOB in memory (remember, a large object can be gigabytes in size) and instead stream the data into the database directly from a file or other stream object. In the following example, we define a function that accepts a seat number and filename as arguments:

```
function YMLD_insertSeatImage($conn, $seat_number, $image) {
  $sql = 'INSERT INTO SeatMap (Seat_No, Seat_View) VALUES
    (?, ?)';

  $fh = fopen($image, 'r');
  $stmt = $conn->prepare($sql);
  $stmt->bindParam(1, $seat_number, PDO::PARAM_INT);
  $stmt->bindParam(2, $fh, PDO::PARAM_LOB);
  $rc = $stmt->execute();
  return $rc;
}
```

Creating Web Interfaces

The Web was designed to be simple. All that a basic Web application needs to do is receive plain-text requests from the Web server and return the appropriate header and HTML to the requestor. In the late 1990s, it was common for authors of Web applications to create their own routines for handling these basics. However, as requirements grew more complex with the advent of HTTP 1.1, Common Gateway Interface (CGI) forms handling, authentication, cookies, secure socket layer (SSL) protocols, JavaScript, and other enhancements to the user experience, most Web application authors realized that their time was better spent focusing on creating a usable interface and leaving the underlying implementation details to a common set of libraries.

Setting the XHTML Header

To comply with the Hypertext Transfer Protocol (HTTP), any object that a Web server transfers must be prefaced by one or more HTTP headers. The HTTP headers contain metadata to identify the kind of content that is being returned, along with optional metadata such as the date when the content expires, the character encoding for the content, or other metadata that helps the Web browser or other HTTP client understand how to handle the object that is being returned. The only mandatory HTTP header is the content type header, which enables your Web browser to decide whether to display the object inside the browser as HTML, invoke a third party program or extension to display the object in a special viewer such as a multimedia player, or download the object to save on your file system.

When compiled as a CGI executable or as an extension to a Web server API (such as an Apache module), PHP automatically returns all of the required HTTP headers first, followed by any optional headers you set with the PHP `header()` function or through PHP's built-in session, cookie, or form variable support, followed by the actual object. The HTTP headers are simple text strings that follow a standard format. The most important HTTP header for our purpose, the content type header, follows the format `Content-type:` *text/html* where *text/html* represents the Multipurpose Internet Mail Extension (MIME) type of the content returned by the script. The most common MIME type for Web pages is `text/html`, representing HTML and XHTML content, but other MIME types include `text/plain` and `text/xml` for plain text and XML content, respectively.

Handling *POST* and *GET* Variables

Every application accepts some form of input and produces some form of output. In the case of Web applications, the output normally takes the form of an HTML page, and the input is provided by CGI form variables submitted from an HTML form. There are two kinds of CGI variables: GET variables, which are visible in the URL as key=value pairs, and POST variables, which are passed in the HTTP header and thus are not normally visible to the user. Whereas GET variables are limited by the maximum total URL length that Web servers or browsers will accept without truncation, POST variables have the advantage of being able to pass much longer fields.

Every Web application requires a caller (normally the HTML form that specifies the CGI variables) and a handler (the PHP script that accepts the CGI variables and generates some response based on the input values). The caller and the handler can be the same PHP script, of course; you have probably seen this approach in action if you have ever filled out a Web form incorrectly and received the same form back in response with the missing fields highlighted and your "good" data already filling out the rest of the fields. In this case, your Web browser was the initial caller to the PHP script that accepts input from the Web form. The PHP script handles the request, validates your input, and if it is not satisfied with the input, calls itself with an extra parameter so that it can highlight the missing fields.

Let's look at a sample HTML form to understand how data is passed from the form to the handler script.

```
<form action='ymld.php' method='POST'>
  <input type="radio" name="performance" value="1"
    checked="checked">
    Cats and Dogs</input><br />
  <input type="radio" name="performance" value="2">
    Desperate Houses</input><br />
  <input type="radio" name="performance" value="3">
    Icing the Puck</input><br />
  <input type="submit" /> <input type="reset" />
</form>
```

The `action` attribute of the form element specifies the URL to which the form submits its variables. The `method` attribute specifies that the variables will be passed using the `POST` method. The first three input elements are of type `"radio"`, meaning that they will be rendered as radio buttons. As all of the radio buttons have the same `name` attribute, they will be mutually exclusive. The browser passes the value of the `name` attribute to the handler script as the parameter name and passes the `value` attribute as the parameter value. In this form, the `value` attribute holds the ID number of the corresponding production in the Productions table and the associated production title. Finally, the submit and reset buttons offer mechanisms for submitting the form values and resetting the form values, respectively.

You can find the complete yet concise specification for HTML forms hosted by the World Wide Web Consortium at http://www.w3.org/TR/REC-html40/interact/forms.html.

PHP: AUTOMATIC GLOBAL ARRAYS FOR FORM AND SERVER VARIABLES
To make it as easy as possible for you to retrieve the values of GET and POST variables in a PHP script, the PHP interpreter automatically creates global arrays called $_GET[] and $_POST[] that contain the values for any form variables that have been submitted to the script, indexed by the form variable name. For example, if a script receives the POST variable 'username' with the value 'Daniel', you can access that value through $_POST['username'].

Another convenient automatic global array is $_SERVER, which contains server environment variables. The most important element of this array for our purposes is PHP_SELF, which returns the relative URL for the PHP script. Passing the escaped value of $_SERVER['PHP_SELF'] as a form action URL enables a script to call itself, no matter what the hostname of the Web server is or where in the file system hierarchy the script is placed.

Later in the chapter we discuss the $_COOKIE[] and $_SESSION[] automatic global arrays, which provide extremely convenient cookie and session functionality. The creators of PHP really do want to make your Web application development as easy as possible! However, it is your responsibility to use these variables securely, and for that reason it is a best practice to consider the contents of any of these automatic global arrays user input and to filter the contents using strip_tags() and htmlentities() before using them in your own script.

Due to the potential for mistakenly assigning the wrong ID to a production title, and the likelihood that productions will be added and removed on a regular basis, this is a form that you would not want to maintain by hand. You should either dynamically generate the page containing this form for every page request or, if the overhead of that approach is too high, set up a maintenance job to generate the page through cron on Linux or through the system scheduler on Windows.

Let's look at a PHP script that uses the performance POST variable in a query of the YMLD database to retrieve the list of performances for the requested production that still have seats available for purchase:

```php
<?php
require('ymldlib.php');

if (!array_key_exists('page', $_GET) or
    !array_key_exists('page', $_GET)) {
  YMLD_index_page();
  exit();
}

$page = $_GET['page'];
$id = $_GET['id'];

if (!is_numeric($id)) {
  YMLD_index_page();
  exit();
}

if ($page == 'show') {
  YMLD_show_page($id);
```

```
}
else if ($page == 'view') {
  YMLD_display_seat_info($id);
}
else {
  YMLD_index_page($conn);
}

function YMLD_index_page() {
  print YMLD_header('YourMamaLovesDrama:: Home');
  $conn = YMLD_databaseConnect();
  if ($conn) {
    $productions = YMLD_select_all_shows($conn);
    print YMLD_display_productions($productions);
  }
  else {
    print "Sorry, we are unable to serve your request at this time.";
  }
  print YMLD_footer();
}

function YMLD_show_page($id) {
  print YMLD_header('YourMamaLovesDrama:: Display Performance');
  $conn = YMLD_databaseConnect();
  $performances = YMLD_select_performance_data($conn, $id);
  $seats = YMLD_select_available_seats($conn, $performances);
  print YMLD_display_performances($performances, $seats);
  print YMLD_footer();
}

function YMLD_header($title) {
  $header = <<<HERE
<?xml version="1.0" encoding="iso-8859-1"?>
<!DOCTYPE html
  PUBLIC "-//W3C//DTD XHTML 1.0 Transitional//EN"
   "http://www.w3.org/TR/xhtml1/DTD/xhtml1-transitional.dtd">
<html xmlns="http://www.w3.org/1999/xhtml" lang="en-US"
 xml:lang="en-US">
  <head><title>$title</title></head>
  <body><h1>$title</h1>
```

```
HERE;
  return $header;
}


function YMLD_footer() {
  return "</body>\n</html>";
}


?>
```

In this simple dispatch script we use the standard PHP include mechanism `require` (`'ymldlib.php'`); this makes the functions that we have defined in our custom `ymldlib.php` file available to our script. Our first operation checks the special global `$_GET[]` array to determine whether any of the `GET` form variables that have been passed to the page have a name of `'page'`. We check the value of the `page` form variable to determine whether the user has requested the page for the first time or whether they are in the middle of a session with our database. We check the value of the `id` form using the `is_int()` function to ensure that the value is numeric. The `page` parameter is used as the basis of our dispatch script: depending on the value of the `page` parameter, the same script performs different operations. In this script, if the page parameter is not defined, the script hands control to the `YMLD_index_page()` function to display the welcome page for the YMLD Web application, whereas if the `page` parameter value is `'show'`, the script hands control to the `YMLD_show_page()` function to display the list of performances that have tickets remaining for purchase.

Checking User Input for Tainted Values

Before taking any significant action, we verify that the value of the `POST` variable `id` resolves to an integer. Malicious users could directly submit requests to our script using a non-integer value, so we use the PHP built-in `is_int()` function to ensure that the parameter only contains an integer value—nothing more and nothing less. If `is_int()` returns false, the script avoids the overhead of creating a new database connection and simply returns an error message. If the test returns true, however, then the function calls the `YMLD_show_page()` function, creates a new database connection using the YMLD extension's `YMLD_databaseConnect()` method, and passes the performance value to the `YMLD_select_performance_data()` and `YMLD_select_available_seats()` functions. The function then passes the data into the `YMLD_display_performances()` function to format the resulting XHTML.

The process of checking form input to ensure that it does not include any unexpected or harmful data is called *taint-checking*. Along with simple type-checking functions like `is_int()` or `is_numeric()`, PHP offers the ability to validate extremely complex patterns in expected input using the regular expression capabilities of the Perl Compatible Regular Expressions (PCRE) extension. SQL injection attacks are a specific type of malicious form input that typically prey on scripts that, instead of using statements with parameterized queries, simply interpolate user input into a directly executed statement. The problem with concatenating user input is that it potentially opens a major security hole by enabling your users to enter input including single quote characters followed by other SQL clauses. For example, imagine a script that retrieves a list of a given user's purchase orders by concatenating user input to an SQL statement stub:

```
// Security hole if input value = "16' OR 1 > 0"
$stmt = "SELECT order_no, cost FROM purchases
  WHERE user_id = '{$_POST['id']}'";
$conn->exec($stmt);
```

If the user passes in a user ID value of `16' OR 1 > 0` this snippet of code would end up returning every purchase order in the database because 1 is always greater than 0. However, our taint-checking regular expression in the `YMLD_show_page()` function ensures that every character in the input value is a digit. And by using a parameter marker in the `PDO::prepare()` and `PDOStatement::execute()` methods, we further ensure that the input value will be matched against a single field and cannot be used to inject unwanted SQL into the method. Always protect your application by making the effort to issue SQL statements with parameter markers and by checking your form variables for malicious user input as described in the next section.

Input-Filtering Functions

PHP includes a number of fast built-in functions to test whether the value contained by a PHP variable matches the type you expect:

- `is_bool()`—The variable contains either a `TRUE` or `FALSE` value
- `is_float()`—The variable contains a float value
- `is_int()`—The variable contains an integer value
- `is_numeric()`—The variable contains a numeric (float or integer) value
- `is_string()`—The variable contains a string

To validate more complex patterns, such as a Canadian postal code, you can use PHP's Perl Compatible Regular Expression (PCRE) functions to determine whether the value matches the pattern. In the case of a Canadian postal code, you could use the `preg_match()` function to test for three pairs of alternating uppercase letters and digits, surrounded by an arbitrary amount of white space, and including one space after the third character, using the following regular expression:

```
$pcode = 'M4P 1T6';
$pattern = '/^\s*[A-Z]\d[A-Z] \d[A-Z]\d\s*$/';
if (preg_match($pattern, $pcode)) {
  // contains a Canadian postal code
}
```

The pattern is conventionally delimited by forward slashes (/), although other delimiters such as
(), <>, and [] are also supported. ^ tells the regular expression engine to start matching at the
beginning of the string; without ^, the pattern will attempt to match anywhere in the string. The
character class \s matches any white space character in case our users accidentally insert a space or
tab in the Web form. * indicates that the preceding character class should be matched any number
of times in case the user leaned on the space bar for a minute or two. [A-Z] creates a character
class that matches any alphabetic characters between and including A through Z. \d is a character
class that matches any digit. Finally, we repeat the 0 or more white space character match at the end of
the pattern, followed by $ to indicate the end of the string. This pattern prevents anything other than a
string matching our definition of a Canadian postal code from being accepted by our application.

Web Application Summary

Almost any CGI Web application is just a variation on this basic theme: retrieve CGI variables
using the automatic global arrays, perform some actions based on the value of the CGI variables,
and print your XHTML content. For completeness, this section illustrates the YMLD_select_
performance_data(), YMLD_select_available_seats(), and YMLD_display_
performances() methods.

```
function YMLD_select_performance_data($conn, $production) {
  /* Return an array of all performances for a given production
  that still have seats available. */

  $sql = '
    SELECT Performance_No, Production_Title,
    Performance_Date, Performance_Time
    FROM Productions INNER JOIN Performances
    ON Productions.Production_No = Performances.Production_No
    WHERE Productions.Production_No = ?
    AND Performance_Seats > 1
  ';

  $stmt = $conn->prepare($sql);
  $stmt->execute(array($production));
  $performances = $stmt->fetchAll(PDO::FETCH_NUM);
  $stmt = NULL;
  return $performances;
}
```

When we call the YMLD_select_performance_data() function from our dispatch script,
the function accepts the value of the $id POST variable as the $production parameter and
passes that parameter to the placeholder in the SELECT statement. The method assigns all of the

rows in the result set to the `performances` list using the `$stmt->fetchAll()` method and returns that array to the caller. Passing `PDO::FETCH_NUM` to `$stmt->fetchAll()` tells PDO to return an array of arrays indexed by number, rather than the default of arrays indexed by both number and column name; for large result sets, this can save your application a significant amount of memory.

```
function YMLD_select_available_seats($conn, $performances) {
  /* Return an array of all available seats and prices for a
  given performance of a show. */

  $sql = '
    SELECT Seat_No, PricePlan_Cost
    FROM Seats INNER JOIN PricePlan
    ON Seats.PricePlan_No = PricePlan.PricePlan_No
    WHERE Performance_No = 20
    AND Seat_Available = 1
  ';

  $stmt = $conn->prepare($sql);

  $seats = array();
  foreach ($performances as $show) {
    $show_num = intval($show[0]);
    $stmt->execute(array($show_num));
    $row = $stmt->fetch(PDO::FETCH_NUM);
    while ($row) {
      $seats[$show_num] = array($row[0], $row[1]);
      $row = $stmt->fetch(PDO::FETCH_NUM);
    }
  }

  $stmt = NULL;
  return $seats;
}
```

The YMLD_select_available_seats() method also passes a variable to the placeholder in a SELECT statement. The second argument of the function, &$perfomances, is the array we returned from YMLD_select_performance_data(). We iterate through that array using a foreach statement to pass the performance ID ($show[0] means the first element of the array referenced by the $show variable, and to ensure that PHP passed the right value to our SQL statement, we assign the integer value to the $show_num variable using the PHP built-in intval() function) to the execute statement. The method assigns the resulting values to the $seats hash using the performance ID ($show_num) as the hash key, with the seat number and seat cost as the members of an array that are added to the hash.

> **MANIPULATING DATA THROUGH SQL STATEMENTS OR PHP FUNCTIONS**
>
> In this example we use SELECT statements in two separate PHP functions to retrieve data from the YMLD database and store that data in separate PHP data structures. We then pass those structures to a formatting function that generates the core XHTML output. Although this approach enables us to break the script into easily understandable and reusable functions, a more efficient application structure would retrieve the required data through a single SELECT statement. Databases like Apache Derby are optimized to retrieve and manipulate data faster than multi-purpose programming languages. Retrieving all data from a single SELECT statement also avoids race conditions that could arise in this scenario if a given performance that had seats available when the YMLD_select_performance_data() SELECT statement was issued sold all of its tickets before the YMLD_select_available_seats() SELECT statement was issued. When you write your own applications, keep this balance of simplicity and efficiency in mind and make any design trade-offs consciously.

```php
function YMLD_display_performances($performances, $seats) {
  /*
  Display performances for a given production with radio buttons
  so a user can display the seats that are available for a given
  performance.
  */

  $self = strip_tags(htmlentities($_SERVER['PHP_SELF']));
  $form = <<<HERE
<table>
  <tr><th>Title</th><th>Date</th><th>Time</th><th>Seats</th></tr>
HERE;
  foreach ($performances as $show) {
    $form .= "<tr><td>{$show[0]}</td><td>{$show[1]}</td>";
    $form .= "<td>{$show[2]}</td><td><$form ";
    $form .= "action='{$self}?page=view' method='POST'>";
    $form .= "<select name='seat'>";
    foreach ($seats[$show[3]] as $seat) {
      $form .= "<option value='{$seat[0]}'>";
      $form .= "{$seat[1]}</option>\n";
    }
```

```
    $form .= "</select><input type='submit' value='Display' />";
    $form .= "</$form></td></tr>\n";
  }
  $form .= "</table>";
  return $form;
}
```

The `YMLD_display_performances()` function demonstrates the caution that is required to generate valid XHTML output. In this XHTML, the performances are formatted in a table, with each row representing a performance for a different time on the requested day. To complicate matters, the final column in each row contains an XHTML form that displays the available seats by price in a drop-down form element. You must be careful to ensure that your XHTML is valid—for example, ensuring that every `<table>` start tag has a matching `</table>` end tag—or else your Web page may not display in the format that you or your Web designers expected.

Note that although we could have directly issued `print` statements within the `YMLD_display_performances()` function, we instead created a single string variable that contains all of the XHTML and returned that XHTML to the caller. We prefer this method of creating Web applications because it affords you much more flexibility if you decide to change the layout of your Web site. In the case of the `YMLD_display_performances()` function, we return a single self-contained `<table>` XHTML element. For the purposes of our sample application, we are simply printing that table as the body of our XHTML page, but a more sophisticated Web site might decide to display that table as just one element of a complete portal page. Returning the XHTML content from a method as a string variable gives you the ability to collect all of the XHTML elements you want to display in a single Web page in any order before displaying them. If you chose to simply print the XHTML content from within each method, you would have to call each method in the exact order required by your Web design—and that might cause problems if the results of some element you want to display on the bottom of your Web page are required as input to an element you want to display at the top of your Web page.

To give us the flexibility to rename this script or to import this extension into other scripts, we avoid hard coding a specific URL into the form returned from the `YMLD_display_performances()` function. Instead, we rely on the escaped value of the `$_SERVER['PHP_SELF']` automatic global value to return the dynamic URL for the Web page that invoked `YMLD_display_performances()`.

Customizing Web Sites with Sessions

Sessions bring statefulness to the Web by making it possible for a user to add, for example, three items to a shopping cart in an online store, browse through several other Web pages, and return to the Web site a few minutes later to continue adding items to her cart or to complete her purchase without forcing you to explicitly pass the complete list of items she has chosen to purchase between Web pages in the online store. Although adding statefulness to the Web offers a dramatic improvement to the user experience and eases your coding effort immensely, the design principles of sessions are quite simple:

1. The Web application assigns a random identifier to the user when she first accesses the site during a given browser session.

2. This identifier is stored as a cookie in the user's Web browser or encoded in the URL.

3. The identifier is then used as a key to remember user-specific information in a server-side external storage system (file systems, shared memory, or databases are common repositories).

Because the session variables are stored on the server, they provide a relatively secure means of storing user information. Once again, PHP demonstrates its focus on rapid Web application development by building support for session management right into the core of the language through the `$_SESSION[]` automatic global array and the `session_start()` function. To begin a session, call the `session_start()` function to ask PHP to try to set the session in a cookie or, if the user has disabled cookies, to encode the session ID in the URL. Once you have initiated a session in your application, you can add a new variable to the user's session, or if this is not the first time the user has visited your application during this browser session, you can retrieve or modify the existing information in the user's session:

```php
<?php
session_start();
if (!isset($_SESSION['visits'])) {
  $_SESSION['visits'] = 1;
}
else {
  $_SESSION['visits']++;
}
print "You have been here {$_SESSION['visits']} times this session.";
?>
```

You can combine sessions with information stored in an Apache Derby database to enable your users to customize the appearance of your Web site to their liking. Assume that you design your Web site to provide user-customizable values for such aspects as font size, background color, geographic location, and language. When a user accesses your Web site for the first time, she views the Web site with all of the default values. After the user registers and successfully logs in to your Web site, your application can retrieve a set of preferences from the database, issue `session_start()`, and load `$_SESSION[]` with the key / value pairs for her preferences. For the rest of her browser session, every subsequent page of your Web site can simply poll `$_SESSION[]` for any of her customizations.

Summary

This chapter has led you through the process of installing and configuring the PHP interpreter with Apache Derby support on your server. You learned the basic building blocks of database-driven PHP applications, including how to connect to the database, issue SQL statements, and fetch results from the database. The chapter presented the core elements of Web applications, including how to retrieve form variables, check form variables for tainted input, and design a Web application based on a page dispatch controller pattern with the PHP functions divided between business logic and presentation logic. Finally, you learned how to create a PHP application that uses sessions to customize the user experience.

"Your Momma Loves Drama" in Perl

Perl Overview

What Makes Perl Unique?

Perl was originally designed as an extremely practical language for developing solutions to system administration and text manipulation problems. Originally written for UNIX operating systems, Perl has been ported to every commonly used operating system because of its usefulness in a wide range of applications. As a practical language, it adopted the syntax of many of the more specialized utilities it had been designed to replace—for example, the implicit variable handling of awk and the regular expressions of sed—and this led to the impression that Perl scripts were naturally messy and difficult to read. When written with care and consideration for future maintenance, however, the source for a Perl application can be just as easy to understand as an application written in any other language.

One great advantage of Perl as a programming language is the Comprehensive Perl Archive Network (CPAN) at www.cpan.org. CPAN is a collection of modules and applications developed by Perl enthusiasts and offered to the Perl community for reuse in their own applications. Before you tackle any problem domain with Perl, you should check to see if someone else has already written a module that will solve the problem for you. Existing modules solve problems such as calculating the number of days between two arbitrary dates or sequencing genetic data. We will take advantage of four commonly used modules to build the core of our Perl application:

- CGI, a module that provides a set of functions for creating Web applications through the Common Gateway Interface for exchanging data between a browser and an application
- DBI, the database interface module that defines the standard interface for access to relational and non-relational sources of data

439

- DBD::DB2, the DB2 database driver that implements the DBI specification and that enables you to connect to Apache Derby through Derby's ODBC driver

- Tk, a module that embeds the Tcl scripting language's graphical user interface (GUI) toolkit and exposes an object-oriented Perl interface to enable you to easily create GUI applications

Although this chapter teaches you the most common uses for each of these modules—80% of the functions used by 80% of applications—you can find additional reference documentation for any of the modules available from CPAN by issuing the `perldoc module-name` command to view text help files or by viewing the nicely formatted XHTML version of the module documentation online at http://search.cpan.org. The Perl applications developed in this chapter separate common functions into a custom Perl module to demonstrate how you can reuse application logic between both a Web application and a GUI application.

Most Appropriate Uses for This Language

Perl remains true to its roots and continues to be an extremely popular language for system administration and text processing tasks that require only a simple command line interface. With the immense popularity of the Web in the 1990s, Perl was also adopted as the de facto language for implementing forms-based dynamic Web sites. The popular Web site Slashdot (www.slashdot.org) is an example of a database-driven site that handles all user interactions through Perl. Due to the popularity of the language for implementing dynamic Web sites, many modules have been contributed to CPAN to provide function beyond the basic form handling requirements met by the CGI module. You can find modules for such problem domains as Web page templates, caching, and session handling, but the CGI module continues to be the basis of most of the Web modules you will use.

CPAN also offers a number of modules that ease the burden of creating GUIs for applications. Although the wealth of options means that none of the modules can arguably be called a standard, the Perl::Tk interface to the Tk graphical toolkit is one popular solution for creating cross-platform GUIs.

Administrator Interface

The administrator interface will consist of a single GUI panel implemented with the Perl::Tk module, which enables you to view and add events stored in the Your Momma Loves Drama (YMLD) application database. This will be enough application code for you to learn the basics of building a GUI application with Perl::Tk that links GUI actions to data stored in an Apache Derby database.

Purchaser Interface

The ticket purchasing interface for YMLD is a forms-based Web application that is implemented with the CGI module. Ticket purchasers will use their Web browser to register, search for events matching their date ranges and event type specifications, and order tickets.

Performance Characteristics

Perl is an interpreted language, which makes it an excellent choice for iterative prototyping or rapid application development. You can tweak the source code and immediately run your application to see the results of your change without having to compile or link the code. The interpreted nature of Perl applications means that most of your performance cost is derived from invoking the Perl interpreter.

Early Web applications built with CGI suffered from performance lags under heavy usage due to the resource demands of invoking the Perl interpreter for each requested Web page, but the developers of Apache and other Web servers quickly discovered how to keep a copy of the Perl interpreter running in memory at all times to bypass the start-up cost for every subsequently requested Perl-based Web page. In the Apache Web server, this option is called `mod_perl`. It requires you to write your Perl code using slightly stricter syntax to run properly under this environment. This chapter discusses the key aspects of the choices made in developing the YMLD application to comply with the `mod_perl` requirements.

Popular Editing Environments

Perl applications are written using everything from the equivalent of text editors, such as vi or Notepad for authoring throwaway scripts, to integrated development environments (IDEs) that understand Perl development patterns and offer sophisticated support for collaborative programming efforts on large, complex Perl projects.

- Text editors, such as VI Improved (http://vim.sourceforge.net) and Emacs, offer syntax highlighting and easy customization, among other features.

- Open-source IDEs, such as Kdevelop, and plug-ins for the Eclipse platform, such as EPIC (http://e-p-i-c.sourceforge.net), offer syntax highlighting, code completion, integrated debugging, the ability to browse your source code structure by function or object and method, and the ability to organize your files in projects.

- Full commercial IDEs, such as Komodo (http://activestate.com/komodo), offer all of the features of open-source IDEs with more complete help content, advanced debugging capabilities, regular expression scratchpads for testing and developing regular expressions, and integrated source code version control.

Installing and Configuring Perl

Before you can install and configure Perl to create Apache Derby applications, you must:

1. Install and configure Apache Derby as described in Chapter 4, "Installing Apache Derby and IBM Cloudscape on Windows," or Chapter 5, "Installing Apache Derby and IBM Cloudscape on Linux."

2. Start the Apache Derby Network Server as described in the installation chapter.

3. Install and configure the IBM DB2 Application Development Client to enable Open Database Connectivity (ODBC) access to Apache Derby databases, as described in Chapter 10, "Developing Apache Derby Applications with Perl, PHP, Python, and ODBC."

After you have successfully made an ODBC connection to your Apache Derby database, you can proceed with installing and configuring Perl on your system.

Installing Perl on Linux

Your best option is to locate and install the version of Perl that is offered by your chosen Linux distribution. For example, Red Hat Enterprise Linux 4.0 offers perl-5.8.5-12.1 as an RPM Package Manager (RPM) package. To install this package, or any other RPM package on an RPM-based Linux distribution, issue the following command as a user with root authority:

```
# rpm -ivh perl-5.8.5-12.1.i385.rpm
```

On Debian or other apt-based Linux distributions, issue the following command as a user with root authority to install an APT package:

```
# apt-get install perl
```

On Gentoo, a source-based Linux distribution, issue the following command as a user with root authority:

```
# emerge perl
```

Follow the same approach to install your distribution's packages for the Perl CPAN, CGI, DBI, and Tk modules. Linux distributions normally name modules or extensions for languages following a *language-module* naming convention, so to find the Perl CGI module for your Linux distribution, search for perl-cgi* or perl-CGI* in your package repository.

Configuring Perl on Linux

The DBD::DB2 module is not shipped with any Linux distributions, which means you have to download and install it yourself. This is not as much hard work as it sounds: we'll guide you through the steps and help you avoid the most common pitfalls. First, ensure that you have the following packages installed on your system.

1. DB2 Runtime Client, with application development headers, must be installed to provide the CLI driver.

2. gcc (the Gnu C compiler) must be installed because the DBD::DB2 module consists largely of C code that must be linked against the DB2 Runtime Client libraries to produce the C module.

To successfully build and install the DBD::DB2 module for Apache Derby, perform the following steps as a user with root authority while connected to the Internet:

1. Inherit the DB2 client environment by running the DB2 environment setup script, where *db2inst1* represents the DB2 instance user name:

    ```
    # . /home/db2inst1/sqllib/db2profile
    ```

2. Set the *DB2_HOME* environment variable to point to the location of the DB2 instance:

    ```
    # export DB2_HOME=/home/db2inst1/sqllib
    ```

3. Invoke the CPAN module install command for DBD::DB2 from the command line. The CPAN module will automatically search for, download, and install the module you have requested after asking you a number of one-time configuration questions. Note that you can just accept the default answers for all of the CPAN questions.

    ```
    # perl -MCPAN -e 'install DBD::DB2'
    ```

Installing Perl on Windows

Setting up Perl access to Apache Derby on Windows is easy because companies and individuals have made all of the required packages freely available for your use.

Downloading Perl

ActiveState offers the ActivePerl distribution for free download from http://activestate.com/ActivePerl/. ActivePerl is a freely available Perl interpreter that includes a complete set of documentation and, most importantly, the Perl Package Manager (PPM). PPM helps you download and install Perl modules from ActiveState's servers by resolving dependencies on other modules and by giving you access to most of the Perl modules available from CPAN without requiring a C compiler. Download the Microsoft Installer (MSI) ActivePerl package from ActiveState for the best installation experience.

Installing ActivePerl

After you have downloaded the ActivePerl MSI package, double-click the package to invoke the installer and perform a complete installation of all of the ActivePerl components.

Configuring Perl

Now that you have installed ActivePerl with PPM support, use PPM to install the DBI and DBD::DB2 modules. ActiveState does not host binary versions of the database drivers, but Jeff Urlwin has graciously offered binary versions of the database drivers, which are available through PPM at http://ftp.esoftmatic.com/outgoing/DBI/.

To install the DBI and DBD::DB2 modules, issue the following commands (substituting 5.8.4 with the version of ActivePerl that you have installed):

1. Install the DBI package from esoftmatic.com's repository:

```
C:\> ppm install
http://ftp.esoftmatic.com/outgoing/DBI/5.8.4/DBI.ppd
```

2. Install the DBD::DB2 package from esoftmatic.com's repository:

```
C:\> ppm install
http://ftp.esoftmatic.com/outgoing/DBI/5.8.4/DBD-DB2.ppd
```

By issuing an install command, you tell PPM to download the corresponding package and install it in your system's Perl modules directory so that the module will be available the next time you run a Perl script.

Creating Apache Derby Applications with Perl

Using Perl Modules

To use a Perl module in a Perl script, you must tell the Perl interpreter to load the module through the use statement. Most Perl scripts collect their use statements at the top of the script to ensure that all of the dependencies are met before the rest of the script is run. It is also an easy way to inform other users of your script about the required modules.

All of the Perl scripts that are developed in this chapter start with the following lines:

```
#!/usr/bin/perl -w
use strict;
use DBI qw{ :sql_types };
```

When you invoke a script on Windows operating systems, the first line is ignored. However, on UNIX-based operating systems, the special #! (or "hash-bang") line tells the operating system to use the command /usr/bin/perl -w to interpret the rest of the script. The -w flag tells the Perl interpreter to issue extra warnings if it discovers non-fatal inconsistencies in your code, such as variable declarations that override an existing variable in the same scope.

use strict tells the Perl interpreter to adhere to strict Perl semantics, such as requiring every variable to be declared before it is used. Invoking Perl's strictness pragma helps ensure that your script operates in the manner that you expect, rather than taking liberties to try to do what you mean. As a pleasant side effect, Perl programs coded with use strict tend to be easier to read than programs that expect variables to spring into existence on demand.

use DBI imports all of the objects and methods that the DBI module normally exports to programs. The qw(:sql_types) modifier tells the program to include a set of constants representing SQL data types, such as SQL_INTEGER and SQL_VARCHAR. We use some of these constants in our sample application.

Running Perl Scripts from the Command Line

Copy all three lines from the first example into a new text file called `hello-derby.pl` and try running the Perl script to ensure that your Perl environment is set up correctly.

To run a Perl script on Windows operating systems, you should be able to simply invoke the file name from the command line. The ActivePerl installer associates the `.pl` file name extension with the ActivePerl interpreter by default, so an alternative is to double-click the `hello-derby.pl` file in Windows Explorer—but this causes a command window to open briefly and then disappear as soon as the script finishes, so you will have no way of knowing whether an error occurred. If the script fails to run because the operating system did not associate Active-Perl with the `.pl` extension, you can either create that association yourself by using the "Open with..." context menu item in Windows Explorer or explicitly invoke the Perl interpreter from the command line:

```
C:/> perl hello-derby.pl
```

To run a Perl script on Linux operating systems:

1. Grant execute permission to the script using the `chmod` command. You only need to do this once for a given script:

   ```
   $ chmod u+x hello-derby.pl
   ```

2. Run the script by issuing the script's name at the command line. If the script is not in a directory specified by your *PATH* environment variable, you will have to specify the path to the script.

   - To run the script in your current working directory, issue the following command:

     ```
     $ ./hello-derby.pl
     ```

   - To run the script contained in the `/home/lynn/` directory, for example, issue the following command:

     ```
     $ /home/lynn/hello-derby.pl
     ```

Connecting to an Apache Derby Database

Single Connections

In the Perl DBI, database handle objects represent connections to databases. To connect to an Apache Derby database, create a database handle by calling the `connect()` method of the DBI object with the database name, user name, and password as arguments. The following code example illustrates a subroutine in which those arguments are assigned explicit values. We use this subroutine in our custom Perl module to create all of the connections for our applications.

Other Perl applications could retrieve the appropriate argument values from the command line interface or from the values specified in a Web form.

```perl
sub db_connect {
    my $database = 'TESTDB';
    my $user = 'db2inst1';
    my $password = 'ibmdb2';

    # Connect to the database
    my $dbh = DBI->connect("dbi:DB2:$database", $user,
      $password, { AutoCommit => 1, RaiseError => 1 });

    return $dbh;
}
```

If you are wondering what that `{ AutoCommit => 1, RaiseError => 1 }` argument is for, the anonymous hash is the standard way to specify connection properties when you create a database handle. The set of connection properties that you can specify in the anonymous hash includes `AutoCommit` and `RaiseError`, and by setting their value to 1, you tell the database driver to ensure that those properties are turned on. When your Perl program is ready to go into production, you might want to set `RaiseError` to 0 instead to prevent the program from dying completely when an error occurs in the database interactions.

Disconnecting from a Database

To disconnect from a database, call the `disconnect()` method on the database handle object.

```perl
$dbh->disconnect();
```

Compared to most Perl operations, connecting to a database is a time- and network-intensive operation, so you should reuse the database handle as much as possible. In a typical Perl script, you create a database handle at the start of the script and reuse that connection throughout the rest of the script, then disconnect from the database at the end of the script to ensure that the system resources are promptly returned to the database server.

Pooling Connections

Creating a database connection is probably the single largest drain on your system's resources and performance. For applications that must support a high volume of database access, you might want to consider connection pooling—reusing existing database connections instead of destroying and re-creating connections. The Perl DBI supports a limited form of connection pooling called *cached connections*: if you create connections using the `DBI->connect_` `cached()` method, and you specify exactly the same connection parameters with each call to DBI->connect_cached(), the database driver will reuse an existing connection to perform its work.

Of course, if you plan to issue any INSERT, UPDATE, or DELETE statements, or if you plan to issue any SQL statements that modify the database schema, you should reconsider using a cached connection—particularly for a connection in which the AutoCommit property is turned off. Imagine the confusion that would result if two applications were in the middle of modifying the database schema, and one of the applications decided to issue a ROLLBACK. Because both applications are using the same database connection, the ROLLBACK in one application would affect the work of both applications.

If you encounter a situation in which a cached connection makes sense for your application, substitute the DBI->cached_connect() method for the DBI->connect() method. In all other cases, simply use the DBI->connect() method to create a database handle object and reuse that object in the rest of your script.

Issuing SQL Statements

Executing a Single Statement Immediately

After you create a database handle to the YMLD database, you can start issuing SQL statements to modify data or the database schema. To issue a single SQL statement, call the do() method on the database handle. For example, to add a new production to the list of productions, you can insert a row into the PRODUCTIONS table as follows:

```
my $insert_stmt = q{
    INSERT INTO PRODUCTIONS (Production_Title,
    Production_StartDate, Production_EndDate)
    VALUES ('Lily of the Valley', '2005-01-18', '2005-02-13')
};
my $result = $dbh->do($insert_stmt);
```

The q{} syntax delimits a string that is assigned to the $insert_stmt variable. SQL statements use single quotation marks to delimit values, so delimiting the entire string with single quotation marks would force you to add backslash characters to escape the single quotation marks inside the string. Even wrapping the statement in double quotation marks can be hard to read due to the preponderance of vertical characters. The q{} syntax gives you a way to avoid having to escape quotation marks inside of quotation marks.

Preparing Statements for Reuse

Executing a single statement at a time is fine for low-volume applications, but sometimes you have to repeatedly reissue an SQL statement with only slight variations. For example, assume that you want to add ten more productions to your database. You could manually build ten different

INSERT statements and issue the do() database handle method once for each statement, but there is an alternate approach that requires less work from both the Perl database driver and the Apache Derby network server.

You can create a prepared statement object by calling the prepare() method on the database handle and then repeatedly calling the prepared method's execute() method. The prepare() method accepts an SQL statement in which each variable value has been replaced by a parameter marker—a question mark (?) symbol. Each time that you call the execute() method, you pass a different set of parameters that substitute for the parameter markers you included in your prepared statement. In the following example, a while loop iterates through a list of parameters to insert ten new rows into the PRODUCTIONS table.

```
# Add our productions to the database
my $insert_production = q{
    INSERT INTO Productions
    (Production_Title, Production_StartDate, Production_EndDate)
    VALUES (?, ?, ?)
};

my @productions = (
  ['Cats and Dogs', '2005-04-01', '2005-05-01'],
  ['Desperate Houses', '2005-05-02', '2005-06-01'],
  ['Icing the Puck', '2005-06-02', '2005-07-01'],
  ['Heroes', '2005-07-02', '2005-08-01'],
  ['Rubber Sacks', '2005-08-02', '2005-09-01'],
  ['Couched in Leather', '2005-09-02', '2005-10-01'],
  ['Backsplash', '2005-10-02', '2005-11-01'],
);

my $sth = $dbh->prepare($insert_production);
foreach my $show (@productions) {
  my $rows_affected =  $sth->execute(@$show);
}
$sth->finish();
```

The previous code example begins by declaring the INSERT statement that we want to issue multiple times. Note the three parameter markers within the VALUES clause; these will be replaced by the values of each array within the @productions array of arrays. We create the prepared statement by calling the prepare() method on the database handle. We iterate through each row of the @productions array, converting the array reference $show back into an explicit array by prepending the @ symbol. Finally, we call the finish() method to destroy the statement handle and return its resources to the system.

Binding Parameters to Prepared Statements

When you execute a prepared SQL statement, the Perl DBI tries to automatically bind the data type of each variable to the corresponding parameter marker in the SQL statement. You can help the Perl DBI do its job correctly by explicitly binding parameters to specific data types. To bind a parameter to a data type, call the `bind_param()` method of the statement handle and specify:

1. The parameter number (starting at 1)
2. The value of the parameter
3. *Optional*: The type of the parameter

When all of the parameters have been bound, call the `execute()` method on the statement handle without any arguments. In the following example, we bind the parameter values with an explicit data type and then issue the statement by calling the `execute()` method without any parameters:

```
my $sth = $dbh->prepare($insert_production);
foreach my $show (@productions) {
  $sth->bind_param(1, @$show[0], SQL_VARCHAR);
  $sth->bind_param(2, @$show[1], SQL_DATE);
  $sth->bind_param(3, @$show[2], SQL_DATE);
  my $rows_affected = $sth->execute();
}
```

If you are wondering where to find data type values like `SQL_VARCHAR` and `SQL_DATE`, all of the data types are defined in the DBD::DB2::Constants Perl module. In general, however, you can define an explicit data type by prepending `SQL_` to the data type name.

Executing Prepared Statements

To execute a prepared statement, you must call the `execute()` method on the statement handle. If the prepared statement contains parameter markers, you must either pass an array of values that will be implicitly bound to the corresponding parameter markers, or explicitly bind the value and data type of each parameter using the `bind_param()` method, and then call `execute()` without any arguments.

The `execute()` method returns the number of rows affected by non-`SELECT` statements. If no rows were affected, the `execute()` method returns `'0E0'` to trick Perl into treating the boolean value as true, but the numeric value as zero.

If you must determine how many rows would be returned by a `SELECT` statement, you can issue the same `SELECT` statement with the returned columns wrapped in a `COUNT()` scalar function—but then you have to retrieve the results of the `SELECT` statement, which we will discuss in the following section.

Retrieving Data

The previous section discussed how to issue SQL statements, including how to prepare a statement and bind parameter markers in the statement to values in your Perl script. But, beyond finding out how many rows were affected by a given non-SELECT SQL statement, we have not yet talked about how to issue a SELECT statement and retrieve the results of the query. The same principles apply to retrieving data returned as the result of calling a stored procedure with a CALL statement. After all, as much fun as it can be to modify database schemas and insert, update, or delete data in the database, you need to be able to get data out of the database to write a useful application.

Retrieving a Single Result Set

Every SELECT statement that you issue will return a single result set—a set of rows that matched the conditions of your SELECT statement. Any fetch methods that you call on the statement handle after an execute() call automatically retrieve rows from that first result set. Here is an example of how to fetch a row into a set of variables:

```
# Select all rows from the Productions table
sub select_productions {
  my ($dbh, $results) = @_;

  my $select = q{
    SELECT Production_No, Production_Title,
    Production_StartDate, Production_EndDate
    FROM Productions
  };
  my $sth = $dbh->prepare($select);

  my $rc = $sth->execute();
  my ($id, $title, $start, $end);
  $rc = $sth->bind_columns(\($id, $title, $start, $end));
  while ($sth->fetch()) {
      push(@$results, [$id, $title, $start, $end]);
  }

  $sth->finish();
}
```

You have already seen the prepare() and execute() pattern in our examples of issuing INSERT statements. For SELECT statements, however, we add the bind_columns() and fetch() calls so that we can retrieve the results of the statement. After binding the columns of the result set to the $title, $start, and $end variables, each successful fetch() call replaces the values of the variables with the corresponding values from the row that has been returned. Binding result set columns to variables results in the best performance for your script because this approach avoids the overhead of creating new variables with each `fetch()` call.

If there are no more rows left to fetch in the result set, the `fetch()` call returns a false value and ends the `while` loop.

Calling Stored Procedures

Stored procedures encapsulate complex logic or commonly required actions as database server objects. Apache Derby uses stored procedures to great effect as the primary administration interface for the database, so it is important to learn how to call stored procedures in your applications. You can call stored procedures from any number of different client applications without having to reimplement the logic in each client application. A stored procedure can accept zero or more parameters, and each parameter can be declared as an input only (`IN`) parameter, an output only (`OUT`) parameter, or a parameter that accepts an input value and returns an output value (`INOUT`). Along with returning values for `OUT` and `INOUT` parameters, a single stored procedure can also return multiple result sets.

Although Apache Derby only allows you to create JDBC stored procedures, you can easily call stored procedures from Perl scripts. Treat stored procedures that only accept `IN` parameters and that do not return any result sets the same way you would treat an `INSERT` statement; either call the `do()` method on the database handle or prepare and execute the `CALL` statement.

Passing *OUT* and *INOUT* Parameters

When you call a stored procedure that accepts `OUT` or `INOUT` parameters, you have to perform the additional steps of declaring variables that will accept the output values and binding the parameters to those variables using the `bind_param_inout()` method of the statement handle. Yes, despite the name of the method, you do have to call the `bind_param_inout()` method to bind `OUT` parameters! In the following example, the script calls a stored procedure that accepts one `INOUT` parameter of type `DATE`.

```perl
sub call_procedure_inout {
  my ($dbh, $results) = @_;

  my $call = q{
    CALL production_lists2(?)
  };
  # Declare scalar that will pass in IN value and hold OUT value
  my $value = '2029-02-04';
  $results->{"IN"} = $value;

  my $sth = $dbh->prepare($call);
  my $rc = $sth->bind_param_inout(1, \$value, 16);
```

```
    $rc = $sth->execute();
    $sth->finish();

    $results->{"OUT"} = $value;
}
```

In the preceding example, the variable $value is declared with a value of '2029-02-04'. After preparing the CALL statement, we bind the variable using the bind_param_inout() method. The bind_param_inout() method accepts three arguments: parameter number, a reference to the variable (created by prepending a backslash to the variable name), and the maximum length in bytes that will be returned in the output value. In the example, we specify 16 bytes for the maximum length, even though we know that the DATE type requires only 10 bytes. To prevent data truncation, it is safest to round the estimate up to a higher value. Note that the same variable $value also receives the output value of the INOUT parameter when the stored procedure returns.

Retrieving a Single Result Set

Calling a stored procedure that returns a single result set is just like issuing a SELECT statement that returns a result set, with only a slight difference if the stored procedure has OUT or INOUT parameters. The following example demonstrates how to call a stored procedure that returns a single result set and that accepts two parameters: an IN parameter of type DATE and an OUT parameter of type VARCHAR(32). The result set consists of a single column.

INITIALIZING VARIABLES FOR MOD_PERL

To enhance the execution speed of Perl scripts, the mod_perl Apache module maintains a single copy of the Perl interpreter in memory and retains the byte-optimized code for each Perl script it loads, including the values of any variables after the script finishes executing. What does this mean to you? To avoid inheriting variable values from previous scripts, you must explicitly initialize every variable in the script. In the call_procedure_in_out_result subroutine, $value is initialized to undef.

```
sub call_procedure_in_out_result {
  my ($dbh, $results) = @_;
  my $call = q{
    CALL production_lists3(?, ?)
  };
  # Declare scalar that will hold OUT value
  my $value = undef;
  my $sth = $dbh->prepare($call);
  my $rc = $sth->bind_param(1, '2004-01-01');
  $rc = $sth->bind_param_inout(2, \$value, 64);
```

```
$rc = $sth->execute();
$results->{"OUT"} = $value;

# Get result set by binding to $value
$rc = $sth->bind_columns(\($value));
while ($sth->fetch()) {
  push(@{$results->{"SET"}}, $value);
}
$sth->finish();
}
```

Retrieving Multiple Result Sets

Although SELECT statements can only return a single result set, stored procedures can return multiple result sets. When you call a stored procedure that returns a single result set, just iterate through the rows of the result set by calling the fetch() method on the statement handle as though you were retrieving rows from a SELECT statement. When you call a stored procedure that returns multiple result sets, you can iterate through the rows of the first result set using fetch() and then access the db2_more_results attribute of the statement handle to retrieve the next result set from the stored procedure. The following example demonstrates a call to a stored procedure that returns three result sets, with different sets of columns in each result set.

```
sub call_procedure_results {
  my ($dbh, $results) = @_;

  # Call a stored procedure that returns three result sets
  my $call = q{
    CALL production_lists()
  };
  my $sth = $dbh->prepare($call);
  my $rc = $sth->execute();
  my ($title, $number, $end);

  $rc = $sth->bind_columns(\($title));
  while ($sth->fetch()) {
    push @{$results->[0]}, $title;
  }

  if ($sth->{db2_more_results}) {
    $rc = $sth->bind_columns(\($title, $number));
    while ($sth->fetch()) {
```

```
      push @{$results->[1]}, [$title, $number];
    }
  }

  if ($sth->{db2_more_results}) {
    $rc = $sth->bind_columns(\($number, $end));
    while ($sth->fetch()) {
      push @{$results->[2]}, [$number, $end];
    }
  }
  $sth->finish();

}
```

Managing Transactions

A transaction is a set of one or more database operations that must all succeed for any changes to be reflected in the database. When all of the database operations in a transaction succeed, the corresponding changes are committed to the database. If one of the operations fails, all of the operations in the transaction can be rolled back so that the database appears to be unmodified. Transactions can impose significant locking overhead on your database, however, so when you connect to a database in a Perl application, the DBD::DB2 driver immediately commits each discrete database operation.

Explicitly Committing and Rolling Back Transactions

The Perl DBI provides a standard set of methods that you can call on the database handle to start and end transactions. To begin a transaction, call the begin_work() method on the database handle. To roll back a transaction, call the rollback() method on the database handle. To commit a transaction, call the commit() method on the database handle. The following example demonstrates how to begin a transaction, perform some database operations, and then either commit the work or roll back all of the statements that have been performed since the transaction began:

```
sub transactions {
    my ($dbh) = @_;

    my @cleanup = (
      'DROP TABLE Productions',
      'DROP PROCEDURE production_lists',
      'DROP PROCEDURE production_lists2',
      'DROP PROCEDURE production_lists3',
    );
```

```
$dbh->begin_work();
foreach my $stmt (@cleanup) {
    my $result = $dbh->do($stmt);
}
# We always want to roll back this transaction
if (1) {
    $dbh->rollback();
}
else {
    $dbh->commit();
}
}
```

Setting *Autocommit*

You should explicitly turn AutoCommit on or off when you create the connection handle by passing the AutoCommit attribute as part of the connection attribute hash argument for the connect() method. We briefly discussed the AutoCommit attribute in the "Connecting to an Apache Derby Database" section, so as a reminder: Setting any connection attribute to the value 1 turns on the associated behavior, whereas setting any connection attribute to the value 0 turns off the associated behavior. Following is an example that creates a database handle with AutoCommit turned on:

```
my $dbh = DBI->connect($database, $user, $password,
    {AutoCommit => 1 });
```

After you have created the database handle, you can change the AutoCommit behavior at any time by directly setting the corresponding database handle attribute. For example, to turn off AutoCommit, you could include either of the following statements:

```
$dbh->{"AutoCommit"} = 0;
$dbh->begin_work();
```

Remember that when you turn AutoCommit off, none of the changes to the database are made permanent until you either explicitly call the commit() method on the database handle or turn AutoCommit back on.

Special Data Types

Although many organizations use databases to store nothing more complicated than strings and numbers—customer relationship management applications, university transcripts, results from scientific experiments, and so on—some organizations have found databases invaluable for storing less traditional kinds of data. In the following section, we consider the support that DBD:: DB2 offers Apache Derby for storing non-traditional data types.

Large Objects: *BLOBs* and *CLOBs*

Large object data types are used to represent data that can consist of hundreds of megabytes of binary or character data per value. To build a database-driven jukebox, you might decide to store all of your audio files as binary large object (BLOB) data types in your database, along with a few other columns representing the genre, title, artist, length, and year in which the song was released. An alternative design for this application simply stores the files on the file system and stores the location of each file in the database. The advantage of storing large object data in the database is that you avoid having to develop two different backup procedures for your data, and deploying your application is simply a matter of copying your database.

One disadvantage of storing large object data in the database is that your database backups might be much larger. In addition, the DBD::DB2 driver only supports retrieving BLOB data starting from the first byte of the BLOB. The lack of random access to BLOB data through Perl means that operations requiring the equivalent of file-seek and file-read behavior are best implemented through separate files on the file system. Our application stores images as BLOB objects in the database for the convenience of backing up and deploying the application.

The life sciences provide a more likely scenario for storing character large object (CLOB) data in a database. Genetic analysis depends in large part upon analyzing DNA sequences—long strings consisting of combinations of the characters 'A', 'C', 'T', and 'G'—to understand the roles that individual genes play in various illnesses and to find potential cures. Much of the analysis can be carried out through SQL statements with user-defined functions that understand how to compare DNA sequences.

The most efficient way to extract a BLOB value from a database using the Perl DBD:: DB2 driver is to call the blob_read() method on the statement handle. The blob_read() method takes three arguments: a column number identifying the position of the BLOB in the row, starting at position 1; an offset value that is currently ignored; and a length value that specifies how many bytes at a time to retrieve from the database. By reading one piece of the BLOB at a time, blob_read() prevents your application from having to store potentially hundreds of megabytes of data in memory.

In the following example, the BLOB data for each row is stored as a file on the local file system.

```perl
sub save_blob_to_file {
    my ($dbh) = @_;

    print "creating blob file\n" if $debug;
    #Remember what the LongReadLen setting was
    my $store_lrl = $dbh->{"LongReadLen"};
```

```perl
    #Prevent any LOB data being returned by fetch
    $dbh->{"LongReadLen"} = 0;

    # Retrieve 1024 bytes at a time
    my $len = 1024;
    my $stmt = "SELECT Seat_View FROM SeatMap
        WHERE Seat_No = 1";
    my $sth = $dbh->prepare($stmt);
    $sth->execute();

    while (my @row = $sth->fetchrow()) {
      open(FH, '>', 'seat.gif') or warn "Could not open file:
        $!\n";
      #Read $len bytes into $buf from column 1 until finished
      while (my $buf = $sth->blob_read(1, 0, $len)) {
        print FH $buf;
      }
      close(FH);
    }

    #Reset LongReadLen to previous value
    $dbh->{"LongReadLen"} = $store_lrl;

    $sth->finish();
}
```

The simplest way to insert a large object is to treat it as you would any other INSERT statement. The following example reads the contents of a Portable Network Graphic (PNG) file into a variable and then passes that variable to the execute() method of the statement handle to insert the string as a BLOB.

```perl
sub insert_blob {
    my ($dbh) = @_;

    my $stmt = "INSERT INTO SeatMap(seat_view)
                VALUES (?)";
    my $sth = $dbh->prepare($stmt);

    open(FH, '<', 're16.png');

    # read the file in binary mode
    binmode(FH);
```

```
    # read the entire file into memory at once
    local undef $/;
    my $resume = <FH>;

    close(FH);

    # Insert the row using implicit data type binding
    my $rows_affected = $sth->execute($resume);
    $sth->finish();
    return $rows_affected;
}
```

However, for very large objects, you might not want to temporarily store hundreds of megabytes of data in memory simply to insert the object. In that case, you can bind a file directly to the INSERT statement placeholder by calling the bind_param_inout() method on the statement handle and passing the db2_file => 1 attribute. The following example inserts an HTML file into the database as a BLOB by reference.

```
sub insert_blob_by_file_reference {
    my ($dbh) = @_;

    my $length = 32000;

    my $stmt = "INSERT INTO SeatMap(Seat_View)
                VALUES (?)";
    my $sth = $dbh->prepare($stmt);

    my $filename = 're16.png';

    $sth->bind_param_inout(1, \$filename, $length,
        {db2_file => 1});
    my $rows_affected = $sth->execute();
    $sth->finish();
    return $rows_affected;
}
```

Creating Web Interfaces

The Web was designed to be simple. All that a basic Web application needs to do is receive plain text requests from the Web server and return the appropriate header and HTML to the requestor. In the late 1990s, it was common for developers of Web applications to create their own routines for handling these basics. However, as requirements grew more complex with the advent of HTTP 1.1, Common Gateway Interface (CGI) forms handling, authentication, cookies, secure socket layer (SSL) protocols, JavaScript, and other enhancements to the user experience, most Web application developers realized that their time was better spent focusing on creating a usable interface and leaving the underlying implementation details to a common set of libraries.

Using Common Web Modules

In the world of Web applications written in Perl, CGI is the most common module used by Web authors. Many other modules extend CGI or provide a simplified interface to CGI, but at the core of Perl's Web capabilities is CGI.pm. In this section we demonstrate the most important features of the CGI module, but we encourage you to delve into the many other features that this module offers.

Handling *POST* and *GET* Variables

Every application accepts some form of input and produces some form of output. In the case of CGI Web applications, the output normally takes the form of an HTML page, and the input is provided by CGI variables submitted from an HTML form. There are two kinds of CGI variables: GET variables, which are visible in the URL as key=value pairs, and POST variables, which are passed in the HTTP header and thus not normally visible to the user. Although GET variables are limited by the maximum URL length that Web servers or browsers will accept without trunca-tion, POST variables have the advantage of being able to pass much longer fields.

Every CGI Web application requires a caller (normally the HTML form that specifies the CGI variables) and a handler (the Perl script that accepts the CGI variables and generates some response based on the input values). The caller and the handler can be the same Perl script, of course; you have probably seen this approach in action if you have ever filled out a Web form incorrectly and received the same form back in response with the missing fields highlighted and your "good" data already filling out the rest of the fields. In fact, CPAN includes a very handy module called CGI:: QuickForm that helps you generate and validate forms in a user-friendly fashion.

Let's look at a sample HTML form to understand how data is passed from the form to the handler script.

```
<form action='/available.pl' method='POST'>
  <input type="radio" name="performance" value="1"
    checked="checked">
    Cats and Dogs</input><br />
  <input type="radio" name="performance" value="2">
    Desperate Houses</input><br />
  <input type="radio" name="performance" value="3">
    Icing the Puck</input><br />
  <input type="submit" /> <input type="reset" />
</form>
```

The action attribute of the form element specifies the name of the handler script to which the form submits its variables. The method attribute specifies that the variables will be passed using the POST method. The first three input elements are of type "radio", meaning that they will be rendered as radio buttons. Because all of the radio buttons have the same name attribute, they will be mutually exclusive. The browser passes the value of the name attribute to the handler script as the parameter name and passes the value attribute as the parameter value. In this form, the value attribute holds the ID number of the corresponding production in the PRODUCTIONS table and the associated production title. Finally, the submit and reset buttons offer mechanisms for submitting the form values and resetting the form values, respectively.

You can find the complete yet concise specification for HTML forms hosted by the World Wide Web Consortium at http://www.w3.org/TR/REC-html40/interact/forms.html.

Due to the potential for mistakenly assigning the wrong ID to a production title and the likelihood that productions will be added and removed on a regular basis, this is a form that you would not want to maintain by hand. You should either dynamically generate the page containing this form for every page request or, if the overhead of that approach is too high, set up a maintenance job to generate the page through cron on Linux or through the system scheduler on Windows operating systems.

Let's look at a CGI script that uses the performance POST variable in a query of the YMLD database to retrieve the list of performances for the requested production that still have seats available for purchase:

```perl
#!/usr/bin/perl -w
use strict;
use warnings;
use DBI qw{ :sql_types };
use CGI qw{ *table };
use YMLD qw{
    db_connect
    display_performances
    display_productions
    display_seat_info
    select_available_seats
    select_performance_data
    select_productions
    select_seat_info
};

my $cgi = new CGI;
print $cgi->header();

my $page = $cgi->param('page');
```

```
if (!$page) {
    index_page();
}
elsif ($page eq 'show') {
    display_page();
}

sub display_page {
    print $cgi->start_html(-title=>'YourMamaLovesDrama:
        Display performance');
    print $cgi->h1('YourMamaLovesDrama: Display performance');
    my $id = $cgi->param('id');
    if ($id =~ m/^(\d+)$/) {
        my $dbh = db_connect();
        my @performances = qw{};
        my %seats;
        select_performance_data($dbh, $id, \@performances);
        select_available_seats($dbh, \@performances, \%seats);
        display_performances($cgi, \@performances, \%seats);
        $dbh->disconnect();
    }
    else {
        print $cgi->p('Requested performance does not exist');
    }
    print $cgi->end_html();
}
```

In this simple dispatch script, we use both the DBI and CGI modules. One difference from our basic CGI script header is that we have specified use CGI qw{ *table } to provide start and end methods for table elements. You might also notice the call to use YMLD with a long list of imported references; this call imports the functions that we have defined in our custom YMLD.pm module. Our first operation instantiates a new CGI object so we can start accessing the methods provided by the CGI module, and because every invocation of this script must return some HTML response, our first call to the CGI object prints the HTTP header required for a valid HTTP response. Our second call to the CGI object retrieves the value of the page parameter that the XHTML form passed to the script. The page parameter is used as the basis of our dispatch script: depending on the value of the page parameter, the same script performs different operations. In this script, if the page parameter is not defined, the script hands control to the index_page() subroutine to display the welcome page for the YMLD Web application; if the page parameter value is 'show', the script hands control to the show_page() subroutine to display the list of performances that have tickets available for purchase.

Checking User Input for Tainted Values

Within the `show_page()` subroutine, our second and third calls to the CGI object create the title and heading of the XHTML content. Before taking any further action, we verify that the value of the `POST` variable resolves to an integer. Malicious users could submit requests directly to our script using a non-integer value, so we use a regular expression to ensure that the parameter only contains digit (`\d`) characters. If the regular expression does not return any matches, the subroutine avoids the overhead of creating a new database connection and simply returns an error message. If the regular expression returns a match, however, the subroutine creates a new database connection and passes the performance value to the `select_performance_data()` and `select_available_seats()` subroutines. The subroutine then passes the data to the `display_performances()` subroutine to format the resulting XHTML.

The process of checking form input to ensure that it does not include any unexpected or harmful data is called *taint-checking*. SQL injection attacks are a specific type of malicious form input that typically prey on scripts that, instead of using prepared statements with parameterized queries, simply concatenate user input into a directly executed statement. The problem with concatenating user input is that it potentially opens a major security hole by enabling your users to enter input, including single quotation mark characters followed by other SQL clauses. For example, imagine a script that retrieves a list of a given user's purchase orders by concatenating user input to an SQL statement stub:

```
# Security hole if input value = ' OR 1 > 0
my $stmt = "SELECT order_no, cost FROM purchases WHERE user_id = ';
my $id = $cgi->param('user_id');
$dbh->do($stmt . "$id'");
```

If the user passes in a user ID value of `' OR 1 > 0` this snippet of code would end up returning every purchase order in the database because 1 is always greater than 0. Protect your application by making the effort to issue the `prepare()` and `execute()` statements with parameter markers and by checking your form variables for malicious user input.

Web Application Summary

Almost any CGI Web application is just a variation on this basic theme: create the CGI object, print the HTTP header using the `header()` method of the CGI object, retrieve the CGI variables using the `param()` method of the CGI object, and print your XHTML content. For completeness, here are the `select_performance_data()`, `select_available_seats()`, and `display_performances()` subroutines:

```
sub select_performance_data {
  my ($dbh, $performance, $results) = @_;

  my $select = q{
    SELECT Performance_No, Production_Title,
```

```
    Performance_Date, Performance_Time
    FROM Productions INNER JOIN Performances
    ON Productions.Production_No = Performances.Production_No
    WHERE Productions.Production_No = ?
    AND Performances.Performance_SeatsAve = 1
  };
  my $sth = $dbh->prepare($select);

  my $rc = $sth->execute($performance);
  my ($id, $title, $date, $time);
  $rc = $sth->bind_columns(\($id, $title, $date, $time));
  while ($sth->fetch()) {
      push(@$results, [$id, $title, $date, $time]);
  }

  $sth->finish();
}
```

The `select_performance_data()` subroutine passes the value of the `id` POST variable
to the placeholder in the prepared SELECT statement. The subroutine binds the columns to local
variables and adds each row of results as an anonymous array to the `$results` array reference
that we passed to the subroutine.

```
sub select_available_seats {
  my ($dbh, $performances, $seats) = @_;

  my $select = q{
    SELECT Seat_No, CAST(PricePlan_Cost AS DECIMAL(5, 2))
    FROM Seats INNER JOIN PricePlan
    ON Seats.PricePlan_No = PricePlan.PricePlan_No
    WHERE Performance_No = ?
    AND Seats.Seat_Available = 1
  };
  my $sth = $dbh->prepare($select);

  foreach my $show (@$performances) {
      my $rc = $sth->execute($show->[0]);
      my ($id, $price);
      $rc = $sth->bind_columns(\($id, $price));
      while ($sth->fetch()) {
          $seats->{$show->[0]}{$id} = $price;
```

```
    }
  }
  $sth->finish();
}
```

The `select_available_seats()` subroutine also passes a variable to the placeholder in a prepared SELECT statement. We cast the value of the `PricePlan_Cost` column to a DECIMAL(5, 2) data type to return values like 79.25, instead of +7.92500000000000E+001. The second parameter of the subroutine is a reference to the array that we returned from `select_performance_data()`, and we iterate through that array using a `foreach` statement to pass the performance ID to the execute statement (`$show->[0]` means the first element of the array referenced by the `$show` variable). The subroutine binds the result set columns to local variables and assigns the values to the `$seats` hash reference using the performance ID (`$show->[0]`) as the first hash key, the seat number as the second hash key, and the seat cost as the value of the hash key.

MANIPULATING DATA THROUGH SQL STATEMENTS OR PERL SUBROUTINES

In this example, we use SELECT statements in two separate Perl subroutines to retrieve data from the YMLD database and store that data in separate Perl data structures. We then pass those structures to a formatting subroutine that generates the core XHTML output. Although this approach enables us to break the script into easily understandable and reusable subroutines, a more efficient application structure would retrieve the required data through a single SELECT statement. Databases like Apache Derby are optimized to retrieve and manipulate data faster than multi-purpose programming languages. Retrieving all data from a single SELECT statement also avoids race conditions that could arise in this scenario if a given performance that had seats available when the `select_performance_data()` SELECT statement was issued sold all of its tickets before the `select_available_seats()` SELECT statement was issued. When you write your own applications, keep this balance of simplicity and efficiency in mind and make any design trade-offs consciously.

```
sub display_performances {
    my ($cgi, $performances, $seats) = @_;

    print $cgi->start_table();
    print $cgi->Tr(
        $cgi->th('Title'),
        $cgi->th('Date'),
        $cgi->th('Time'),
        $cgi->th('Seats'),
    );
```

```
foreach my $show (@$performances) {
    my @seat_list = $seats->{$show->[0]};
    $cgi->param(-name=>'page', -value=>'view');
    print $cgi->Tr(
        $cgi->td($show->[1]),
        $cgi->td($show->[2]),
        $cgi->td($show->[3]),
        $cgi->td($cgi->start_form({-method=>'POST',
                    -action=>$cgi->self_url}),
            $cgi->popup_menu(-name=>'seat',
                -values=>$seats->{$show->[0]},
                -default=>$seat_list[0]
            ),
            $cgi->submit({-value=>'Display'}),
            $cgi->end_form()
        )
    );
    print "\n";
}
print $cgi->end_table();
}
```

The `display_performances()` subroutine introduces another capability of the CGI object: the ability to generate XHTML output by calling the method using the same element name as the one you want to create. You could also generate the XHTML content by issuing `print()` statements, but you should be familiar with the CGI technique so that you can understand other Perl applications that do use this feature of the CGI module. The general approach to creating an XHTML element through the CGI object is to call the method by element name, passing in a list of the contents of that XHTML element as the arguments to that method. Of course, most XHTML elements can, in turn, contain other XHTML elements, so you can see that the first call to `$cgi->Tr()` contains a number of `$cgi->th()` elements. You can also see some calls such as `$cgi->start_table()` and `$cgi->end_form()`; by default, the CGI module only defines start and end methods for the `html` and `form` XHTML elements, but by passing `qw{ *table }` to the `use CGI` request, we ensured that start and end methods would be defined for the `table` XHTML element as well.

XHTML ELEMENTS THAT CONFLICT WITH RESERVED PERL NAMES

Some XHTML elements conflict with reserved Perl keywords or Perl built-in functions. For example, the `tr` XHTML element for table rows conflicts with the `tr()` function for translating characters. In these cases, you must call the corresponding CGI method name with an uppercase initial character.

Customizing Web Sites with Sessions

Sessions bring statefulness to the Web by making it possible for a user to add, for example, three items to a shopping cart in an online store, browse through several other Web pages, and then return to the Web site a few minutes later to continue adding items to the cart or to complete the purchase without forcing you to explicitly pass the complete list of chosen items between Web pages in the online store. Although adding statefulness to the Web can dramatically improve the user experience and ease your coding effort immensely, the design principles of sessions are quite simple:

1. The Web application assigns a random identifier to the user when she first accesses the site during a given browser session.

2. This identifier is stored as a cookie in her Web browser.

3. The identifier is then used as a key to remember user-specific information in a server-side external storage system (file systems, shared memory, or databases are common repositories).

You could create your own Perl subroutines to generate unique session identifiers and track the user data associated with each session, but as usual in Perl, someone has already contributed a module called CGI::Session to perform exactly those functions. Let's take a look at how you can use CGI::Session to add statefulness to your own Apache Derby application.

To begin, install the CGI::Session module following the techniques outlined at the start of this chapter. Issue the `use CGI::Session;` statement at the start of your Web application to make the module features available to your script. When you have created the CGI object in your application, you can create a new session ID or, if this is not the first time the user has visited your application in this browser session, you can retrieve the existing session ID for your user.

```
my $session = new CGI::Session(undef, $cgi, {Directory=>File::
   Spec->tmpdir()});
```

To prevent users from being able to masquerade as other users (by predicting session identifier strings), CGI::Session generates session identifiers using the MD5 module to create a random string of numbers and letters. In the preceding example, CGI::Session stores the session identifier in the `$session` object. Your Web application can then store or retrieve session parameters from the `$session` object by calling the `param()` method.

```
# store the user's preferred background color
$session->param('bgcolor', 'cyan');
# retrieve the user's preferred background color
my $background = $session->param('bgcolor');
```

Creating GUI Interfaces

Perl does not offer a native graphical toolkit of its own. Instead, it borrows graphical toolkits from several other languages and projects and offers modules that provide Perl interfaces to those toolkits. The most popular cross-platform graphical toolkit is Tk, the counterpart to the Tcl programming language. The Tk module in CPAN provides an interface to Tk that is powerful, easy for users to understand, and with some study, relatively easy to program.

To write a Perl/Tk application, you must initialize the application window in the main method and then call the `MainLoop` function to act as an event handler until the user dismisses the application window. During the life of the application window, the event handler can create new top-level windows, modify the data that is displayed in the main application window, or perform other functions, as determined by the callback methods that you define for the active GUI widgets. After the user dismisses the application window, the application can perform any required resource cleanup before exiting. Following is the sample main method from our YLMD administration application:

```perl
#!/usr/bin/perl -w
use warnings;
use strict;
use Tk;
use Tk::Table;
use DBI qw{ :sql_types };


my $dbh = db_connect();
if ($dbh->errstr) {
    print $dbh->errstr;
    exit;
}
my $main = display_productions($dbh);

MainLoop;

$dbh->disconnect();
exit;
```

The Tk module provides the basic objects required to create a Perl/Tk application, whereas the Tk::Table module adds an advanced layout manager for displaying tabular data. We use the Tk::Table layout to display the list of productions that are stored in the YMLD database because it provides conveniences (such as automatic scrollbars) that would be laborious to program ourselves. Notice that in this new script, we connect and disconnect from the database in the same way that we do in our Web applications. You could easily improve the administration application by adding a connection dialog that enables administrators to specify their preferred user names, passwords, and databases. The `display_productions()` subroutine contains the bulk of our GUI layout, so let's take a look:

```perl
sub display_productions {
  my ($dbh) = @_;

  my $main = MainWindow->new(-title=>'YourMamaLovesDrama ' .
      'Administration Panel');
  my @columns = ('Title', 'Start Date', 'End Date');
  my @select_data;
  select_productions($dbh, \@select_data);
  my $row_count = scalar(@select_data);

  my $menuitems = [
      [Cascade=>"~File", -menuitems=>[
        [Button=>"~Refresh", -command=>[\&refresh, $main, $dbh]],
        [Button=>"~Exit", -command=>[\&exit]],
      ]],
      [Cascade=>"~Productions", -menuitems=>[
        [Button=>"~Add", -command=>[\&add_production, $main]],
      ]]
  ];

  my $menubar = $main->Menu(-menuitems=>$menuitems);
  $main->configure(-menu=>$menubar);

  my $table = $main->Table(-rows=>$row_count,
      -columns=>scalar(@columns) + 1, -scrollbars=>'se',
      -fixedrows=>1, -fixedcolumns=>1, -takefocus=>1)->pack;

  foreach my $column (1 .. scalar(@columns)) {
    my $column_header = $main->Button(
        -text=>$columns[$column - 1]
    );
    $table->put(0, $column, $column_header);
  }
```

```
  foreach my $row (1 .. $row_count) {
    my $row_header = $main->Button(-text=>"Row $row");
    $table->put($row, 0, $row_header);
    foreach my $column (1 .. scalar(@columns)) {
#Label objects are read-only, while Entry objects are editable
      my $cell = $main->Entry(-width=>20,
          -text=>$select_data[$row - 1][$column - 1]
      );
      $table->put($row, $column, $cell);
    }
  }
  return $main;
}
```

Every Perl/Tk application starts by instantiating a MainWindow object. After creating our MainWindow, cleverly called $main, we retrieve all of the rows from the PRODUCTIONS table.

IMPROVING THE DESIGN

A more advanced design would limit the number of returned rows to prevent your system from using too much memory while working with a large database.

We then create a list of menu items that will appear on the main window. The Cascade entry declares the top-level menu item that will appear under the window title bar. Each Button object that is nested within the Cascade list declares a text attribute and a reference to the associated subroutine that will be called if the user selects that menu item. We declare the subroutine within an anonymous list so that we can also pass arguments to the subroutine: for example, we pass the MainWindow instance and the database handle to the refresh() subroutine so that we can get a new set of results from the database and replace the current MainWindow object with a new MainWindow object. To complete the menu, we pass the menuitems list to the Menu constructor method of the MainWindow instance and set the resulting object as the application window menu by invoking the configure() method on the MainWindow instance.

To create the Tk::Table object, we call the Table constructor on the MainWindow instance and pass in the following attribute values:

1. Number of rows (derived from the results of our SELECT statement)

2. Number of columns (one for each field in our SELECT statement, plus one more for the row identifiers)

3. Scrollbar location ('se' means south-east, so the scrollbars are placed in the bottom-right corner of the table; the default location is the top-left, which looks rather strange)

4. Number of fixed rows (one, for our column headers)

5. Number of fixed columns (one, for our row identifiers)

6. Whether the table should take focus from the keyboard and mouse (yes)

When the Tk::Table object (cleverly called $table) has been instantiated, we can add cells to the table by calling the put() method of the Tk::Table object and passing in the row number, column number, and Tk object to place in that cell. For the column headers and row identifiers, we create immutable Button objects, and for the actual data cells, we create Entry objects. Entry objects are editable text fields, so to enable your users to edit the data directly in the table, you could define a callback method that updates any changed fields.

Now let's look at the add_production() subroutine to understand how the event callback from the Perl/Tk menu item works.

```perl
sub add_production {
  my ($main) = @_;
  my $dialog = $main->Toplevel(
      -title=>'Add Production',
      );
  my $top = $dialog->Frame()->pack(-side=>'top');
  my $bottom = $dialog->Frame()->pack(-side=>'bottom');

  my $labels = $top->Frame()->pack(-side=>'left');
  my $entries = $top->Frame()->pack(-side=>'right');

  $labels->Label(-text=>'Title:')->pack(
      -side=>'top', -anchor=>'e'
  );
  my $title = $entries->Entry(-width=>20,
      -text=>'Title')->pack(-anchor=>'w'
  );
  $labels->Label(-text=>'Start date:')->pack(
      -side=>'top', -anchor=>'e'
  );
  my $start = $entries->Entry(-width=>10,
      -text=>'Start date')->pack(-anchor=>'w'
  );
  $labels->Label(-text=>'End date:')->pack(
      -side=>'top', -anchor=>'e'
  );
```

```perl
my $end = $entries->Entry(-width=>10,
    -text=>'End date')->pack(-anchor=>'w'
);

$bottom->Button(-text=>"OK", -command=>[\&insert_production,
    $main, $dialog, $title, $start, $end])->pack(
    -side=>'left'
);
$bottom->Button(-text=>"Cancel", -command=>[\&dismiss,
    $dialog])->pack(-side=>'right'
);
}
```

The add_production() subroutine receives one argument, the MainWindow instance itself, matching our specification in the corresponding Button object in the main window menu. In the add_production() subroutine, we create a new dialog that accepts user input for a new production in the YMLD database. In Perl/Tk, you create a new window by instantiating a TopLevel object from the MainWindow or another TopLevel instance. So far, we have avoided GUI layout discussions by using the Tk::Table layout manager for the main window, but in this dialog, we want to add three text fields and their corresponding labels, as well as an **OK** button and a **Cancel** button to the bottom of the dialog. This application, like most Perl/Tk applications, uses the pack layout manager to create each window.

The pack layout manager's default layout method is to add each object in the center of the window, with each successive object added underneath the previous object. A stack of labels, text fields, and buttons would hardly be usable, so we need to override the default layout attributes in the pack() method to improve the layout design. To group collections of GUI widgets together, we use the standard Perl/Tk method of instantiating Frame objects as containers. Each Frame instance can have its own location in the window, so we start by instantiating the Frame object $top to hold our Label objects and Entry objects at the top of the window, and a Frame object $bottom to hold our buttons at the bottom of the window. The -side attribute for the pack() method declares the location where the layout manager will attempt to position the object.

Now we need to ensure that the labels and text fields line up beside each other, rather than appearing in a vertical stack. Not surprisingly, this means that we create two more Frame objects positioned to the left side and right side, respectively—but notice that we instantiate the new Frame objects on the $top Frame instance. By containing the Label and Entry object Frame objects in the top frame, we ensure that our buttons will appear at the bottom of the window. If you try to create the left-positioned and right-positioned Frame objects outside of a top-positioned Frame, your buttons appear between the labels and Entry objects rather than underneath them.

When we instantiate each Label and Entry object, we specify the -anchor attribute of the pack() method as 'e' and 'w' to assign their alignment to the east (right) and west (left), respectively. This results in labels that are positioned tightly against their associated text entry field. Finally, we add the `Button` objects to control the behavior of the dialog. Each button object is added to the `$bottom Frame` instance so that they sit below the labels and text fields, and we position the **OK** button to the left side and the **Cancel** button to the right side, in accordance with normal user interface design principles.

The **OK** button defines a `-command` attribute that passes all of the pertinent objects to the referenced subroutine `insert_production()` so that the values entered in the `Entry` objects can be retrieved through their `get()` methods and passed into the `INSERT` statement that creates the new production in the YMLD database. The `insert_production()` subroutine can contain validation logic to ensure that the values are acceptable before trying to insert the new production—for example, the end date should not fall before the start date—and can, in turn, instantiate its own `TopLevel` objects to display error messages or otherwise interact with the GUI and the database.

Summary

This chapter has led you through the process of installing and configuring the Perl interpreter with Apache Derby support on your server. You learned the basic building blocks of database-driven Perl applications, including how to connect to the database, issue SQL statements, and fetch results from the database. The chapter presented the core elements of Web applications, including how to retrieve form variables, check form variables for tainted input, and design a Web application based on a page dispatch controller pattern, with the Perl subroutines divided between business logic and presentation logic. Finally, you learned how to create a Perl application with a graphical user interface using the Tk module.

"Your Momma Loves Drama" in Python

Python Overview

What Makes Python Unique?

Python is a free object-oriented scripting language that offers high-level data types such as dictionaries and arrays, tightly integrated code documentation and unit testing, and dynamic variables. In the early 1990s, Guido van Rossum introduced the world to the Python programming language, and the world began to adopt and extend this efficient new language. The programming community first spent a great deal of energy arguing for and against Python's use of indentation instead of braces to group statements, but many in the community embraced this minor source formatting requirement as an aid to the legibility of the Python source. The language distribution includes an astonishing number of base modules to help Python programmers solve their problems quickly, including the `cgi` module for manipulating Common Gateway Interface (CGI) variables in Web applications, the `Tkinter` module that wraps the Tk graphical user interface (GUI) toolkit for creating GUI applications in Python, and parsers for SGML, HTML, XML, and URLs.

In addition to the base modules, the Python programming community has launched the Python Package Index (PyPi) at http://www.python.org/pypi. PyPi is an index of modules and applications that have been developed by Python enthusiasts and offered to the Python community for reuse in their own applications. Before you tackle any problem domain with Python, you should check whether someone else has already written a module that will solve the problem for you. Existing modules cover a wide range of functions, from interfaces that generate project plan Gantt charts to complete end-user applications such as multimedia jukeboxes. We will take advantage of a commonly used module to build the core of our Python application: `pyDB2`, a module that provides a Python DB-API 2.0 compliant interface to Apache Derby through the IBM DB2 Universal Database run-time client.

473

Although this chapter teaches you the most common uses for each of these modules—80% of the functions used by 80% of applications—you can find an excellent set of freely available documentation hosted by the Python project at http://python.org/doc/. Your Python distribution typically includes a complete set of XHTML-formatted documentation that has been extracted from each base module. On Windows operating systems, you can invoke the `pydocgui.pyw` script to start a Web server running entirely in Python (using the BaseHTTPServer base module) and invoke your default Web browser to view the locally installed Python documentation.

Most Appropriate Uses for This Language

Python overlaps with Perl in many respects; Python has become a popular language for system administration and text processing tasks that require only a simple command line interface. Python is also a popular language for implementing forms-based dynamic Web sites. Red Hat adopted Python as the scripting language of choice for their Linux distribution system utilities. Due to the popularity of the language for implementing dynamic Web sites, many modules have been contributed to PyPi to provide function beyond the basic form handling requirements met by the `cgi` module. You can find modules for such problem domains as Web page templates, caching, and session handling, but the `cgi` module continues to be the basis of most of the Web modules that you will use.

PyPi also offers a number of modules that ease the burden of creating GUI applications. Although the wealth of options means that none of the modules can arguably be called a standard, the Tkinter interface to the Tk graphical toolkit is the most popular solution for creating cross-platform GUI applications in Python.

Administrator Interface

The administrator interface will consist of a single GUI panel implemented with the `Tkinter` module, which enables you to view and add events stored in the Your Momma Loves Drama (YMLD) application database. This will be enough application code for you to learn the basics of building a GUI application with Tkinter that links GUI actions to data stored in an Apache Derby database.

Purchaser Interface

The ticket purchasing interface for YMLD is a forms-based Web application that is implemented with the `cgi` module. Ticket purchasers will use their Web browser to register, search for events matching their date ranges and event type specifications, and order tickets.

Performance Characteristics

Python is an interpreted language, which makes it an excellent choice for iterative prototyping or rapid application development. You can tweak the source code and immediately run your application to see the results of your change without having to compile or link the code. Just like Perl and PHP, the Python interpreter first converts the source code into object byte-code that is then executed by the Python virtual machine. However, a characteristic unique to Python is that the

Python interpreter automatically saves the byte-code of a script or module as a `.pyc` file so that the next time you invoke that script or module, Python will send the cached byte-code directly to the Python virtual machine. The interpreted nature of Python applications means that most of your performance cost is derived from invoking the Python interpreter.

Early Web applications built with CGI suffered from performance lags under heavy usage due to the resource demands of invoking the Python interpreter for each requested Web page, but the developers of Apache and other Web servers quickly discovered how to keep a copy of the Python interpreter running in memory at all times to bypass the start-up cost for every subsequently requested Python-based Web page. In the Apache Web server, this option is called mod_python. It requires you to write your Python code using slightly stricter syntax to run properly under this environment. This chapter uses the `cgi` module as a means of illustrating the principles of developing Web applications with Python, and it provides a good basis of understanding for creating a Web application that complies with the mod_python requirements.

Popular Editing Environments

Python applications are written using everything from the equivalent of text editors, such as vi or Notepad for authoring throwaway scripts, to integrated development environments (IDEs) that understand Python development patterns and offer sophisticated support for collaborative programming efforts on large, complex Python projects.

- Text editors, such as VI Improved (http://vim.sourceforge.net) and Emacs, offer syntax highlighting and easy customization, among other features.

- Open-source IDEs, such as Kdevelop, and plug-ins for the Eclipse platform, such as PyDev (http://pydev.sourceforge.net/), offer syntax highlighting, code completion, the ability to browse your source code structure by function or object and method, and the ability to organize your files in projects.

- Full commercial IDEs, such as Komodo (http://activestate.com/komodo), offer all of the features of open-source IDEs with more complete help content, advanced debugging capabilities, regular expression scratchpads for testing and developing regular expressions, and integrated source code version control.

Learning the Python Language

Variables

Variable Names

Unlike many other programming languages, Python does not require you to prefix variable names with a special signifier character. Variable names consist of alphanumeric strings, where the name must begin with an alphabetical or underscore character, and the Python interpreter determines through the syntax of the expression when a variable name has been assigned or is being used.

By convention, variable names in Python programs consist of all lowercase characters. Underscore characters or camelCaps are not used to differentiate words within most Python programs. The underscore character is prefixed to variable names by convention to indicate that a given class variable should not be accessed directly from outside of the class; however, the Python interpreter does not enforce this convention.

```
>>> # Valid variable names:
... student = '00093456'
>>> database2 = 'SAMPLE'
_name = 'Jennifer' # '_' usually indicates a class member variable
>>>
>>> # Invalid variable names:
... 3student = '00093456'
  File "<stdin>", line 1
    3student = '00093456'
            ^
SyntaxError: invalid syntax
```

Declaring Variables

Python variables do not need to be declared before they are used; they will auto-vivify (spring into existence) when you assign a value to them. However, if you try to access the value of a variable that has not had a value assigned to it, the Python interpreter will return an error message complaining that the variable has not been defined.

```
>>> print noname # noname has not been initialized with a value
Traceback (most recent call last):
  File "<stdin>", line 1, in ?
NameError: name 'noname' is not defined
```

Data Types

Boolean

The simplest data type is the Boolean data type, which is capable of holding only one of two values: true or false. To explicitly assign a true or false value to a variable, you can use the `True` and `False` values. However, most Python control structures evaluate the return value of an expression to determine whether a given condition is true or false. Interestingly, if you explicitly compare the value of a variable or expression against `True` or `False` with the `==` operator, most results will be neither true nor false.

```
>>> # False is equal to numeric 0
>>> if (False == 0):
```

```
...       print "True... no, false... argh!"
...
True... no, false... argh!
>>> # None is neither True nor False
>>> if (None == False) or (None == True):
...       print "True... no, false... argh!"
...
>>> # However, None evaluates to False
>>> if (None):
...       print "True... no, false... argh!"
...
True... no, false... argh!
```

Outside of an explicit comparison, the following values evaluate to `False` in the context of a Boolean operation or control flow statement: `None`, `False`, numeric zero, empty sequences, and empty strings.

Numeric Types

Python offers four different types of numeric variables: plain integers, long integers, floats, and complex numbers. Plain integers can represent at least 32 bits of precision (up to a signed value of 2,147,483,647) or more, depending on the machine and operating system on which the Python interpreter is running. Any integer value greater than the maximum value for a plain integer is automatically converted to a long integer. Long integers are represented by an integer value with the suffix 'L'; you can assign a long integer to a variable by applying the 'L' suffix yourself. Floats represent floating point numbers, such as decimals or exponentials. Complex numbers contain a real and an imaginary part, accessible by the `real` and `imag` properties of the variable holding the complex number.

```
>>> # Plain integers
...
>>> age = 32
>>> circumference = 500000000
>>> circumference
500000000
>>>
>>> # Long integer
...
>>> total = age * circumference
>>> total
16000000000L
>>>
>>> # Floats
...
```

```
>>> decimal = 2.6
>>> decimal
2.6000000000000001
>>> exponent = 2E32
>>> exponent
2.0000000000000001e+032
>>> int(exponent)
200000000000000010732324408786944L
>>>
>>> # Complex numbers
...
>>> complex = 10.6+9.2J
>>> complex
(10.6+9.1999999999999993j)
>>> complex.real
10.6
>>> complex.imag
9.1999999999999993
```

Sequences

Sequence objects have the following properties in common:

- They are composed of zero or more elements.
- Individual elements can be accessed by appending the number of the 0-indexed element to the name of the sequence between square brackets. For example, to return the eighth element of a sequence object named 'kittens', use `kittens[7]`.
- Segments, or *slices*, of a sequence can be returned by specifying the starting and ending elements of the slice around a colon. If you do not specify the starting element, the first element is assumed; if you do not specify the ending element, the final element is assumed. If you only supply a colon, a copy of the complete sequence is returned. For example, to return the third through fifth elements of a sequence object named 'kittens', use `kittens[2:4]`.

Tuples are the simplest form of sequence object. To create a tuple, assign a comma-delimited set of elements to your variable: `tuple = 1, 2, 3`. The elements of a tuple can be any other object, including other tuples. To create nested tuples, enclose the elements of a nested tuple in parentheses: `nested = 1, (1, 2, 3), 2, 3`. To create an empty tuple, assign an empty set of parentheses to your tuple: `empty = ()`. Tuples are *immutable* objects: you cannot modify an element of a tuple.

```
>>> # Tuples
...
>>> tuple = 1,2,3
```

```
>>> tuple
(1, 2, 3)
>>> # Attempt to modify a tuple element
... tuple[0] = 4
Traceback (most recent call last):
  File "<stdin>", line 1, in ?
TypeError: object does not support item assignment
```

Lists are *mutable* sequence objects. To create a list, assign a comma-delimited set of elements to your variable. To differentiate a list from a tuple, enclose the list elements within square brackets: `list = [1, 2, 3]`. You can modify the elements of a list by assigning a new value directly to the list element: `list[0] = 6` changes the first element of `list` to an integer value of 6.

```
>>> # Lists
...
>>> list = [1,2,3]
>>> list
[1, 2, 3]
>>> # Attempt to modify a list element
>>> list[0] = 6
>>> list
[6, 2, 3]
```

Strings

Strings are a special form of immutable sequence objects. The elements of strings are individual characters. For simple strings, the set of characters is delimited by single quotation marks or double quotation marks: the only difference is that to enclose a quotation mark of the same type as the delimiter, you have to escape the quotation mark with a backslash character. For example, to assign the string `He said "stop"` to a variable, you could use `phrase = 'He said "stop"'` or `phrase = "He said \"stop\""`. The former method is probably easier to read.

To assign a long string literal to a variable, you can use the `\` line continuation operator to avoid very wide columns in your program. The `\n` character represents an embedded linefeed character. If you want to assign a multi-line string to a variable that retains all white space and linefeed characters, delimit the string with triple quotation marks (three single or double quotation mark characters) instead.

```
>>> # Strings
...
>>> phrase = 'He said "Stop!"'
>>> print phrase
He said "Stop!"
>>> phrase = 'He said "Stop!", \
```

```
... but the light was green.'
>>> print phrase
He said "Stop!", but the light was green.
>>> phrase = 'He said "Stop!",\n\
... but the light was green.'
>>> print phrase
He said "Stop!",
but the light was green.
>>> phrase = """He said "Stop!",
... but the light was green, so
... he drove on without hesitation.
... """
>>> print phrase
He said "Stop!",
but the light was green, so
he drove on without hesitation.

>>>
```

To concatenate stings, use the + operator. To embed variables within a string, you can use the `printf`-style formatting placeholders within the string and append the tuple of variables (corresponding to the placeholders) to the end of the string using the % operator.

```
>>> # Concatenating and formatting strings
...
>>> age = 32
>>> weight = 200.5
>>> name = 'Dan' + " " + 'Scott'
>>> print 'Name: %s. Age: %d. Weight: %3.1f' % (name, age, weight)
Name: Dan Scott. Age: 32. Weight: 200.5
>>>
```

Dictionaries

A *dictionary* is an object that holds zero or more key:value pairs. Think of a dictionary as a sequence object that enables you to retrieve values by a named key, rather than by the index position of the element. Keys can be any immutable type, although strings are probably the most commonly used type. Keys within a given dictionary object are unique; if you attempt to create a new key:value pair using a key that already exists, the new value will overwrite the assignment for the existing key. Keys and values within a dictionary object can be of different types, so the value for one key might be a string, and the value for another key can be a tuple, or even another dictionary.

To create a dictionary object, assign a set of key:value pairs, delimited by commas, to your variable. Enclose the set of key:value pairs with curly braces. To retrieve the value of a given key, specify the key as the index of the variable. To add a new key:value pair to an existing dictionary object, specify the new key as the index of the variable and assign the new value. To list all of the keys within a dictionary object, invoke the `keys()` method. To determine whether a dictionary object already includes a given key, invoke the `has_key()` method.

```
>>> # Dictionaries
...
>>> employee = {'name': 'Dan Scott', 'age': 32, 'employer': 'IBM'}
>>> print employee['age']
32
>>> employee['languages'] = ('Perl', 'PHP', 'Python')
>>> print employee.keys()
['languages', 'age', 'name', 'employer']
>>> print employee.has_key('age')
True
>>>
```

Control Structures

Control structures help you structure the flow of your code by restricting the execution of a block of code unless a condition you have specified evaluates to true. Your condition can explicitly invoke the typical comparison operators: < (less than), > (greater than), == (equal to), != (not equal to), <= (less than or equal to), or >= (greater than or equal to). Your condition can also be a simple expression. A simple expression that evaluates to any non-zero value, or a non-empty sequence, is considered true.

The general syntax for a control structure is as follows:

```
control-keyword condition:
    <block of code>
<block of code>
```

The control keyword specifies the kind of control structure that is defined. The condition expression, terminated by a statement, specifies the condition that must be evaluated to true before the following indented code block will be executed.

while Loops

A `while` loop executes a block of code as long as the condition specified for the `while` statement evaluates to true.

```
>>> # While loops
...
>>> x = 5
```

```
>>> while x:
...       x = x - 1
...       print x
...
4
3
2
1
0
```

if ... elif ... else

An `if` statement executes a block of code if the specified condition evaluates to true. The `elif` keyword identifies an alternate condition block of code that will be executed if the `if` condition and all preceding `elif` conditions evaluate to false. The `else` keyword identifies an alternate block of code that will be executed if the `if` condition and all `elif` conditions in the same control structure evaluate to false.

```
>>> # if ... elif ... else blocks
...
>>> x = 5
>>> if x > 6:
...       print "x is large"
... elif x > 5:
...       print "x is pretty big"
... elif x > 0:
...       print "x is enough"
... else:
...       print "x is little"
...
x is enough
>>>
```

for Iterators

The `for` control structure in Python is used to iterate over all of the elements of an object. The `for` statement returns an element of the object for each loop through a block of code.

```
>>> # for iterators
...
>>> employee = {'languages': ('Perl', 'PHP', 'Python'), 'age': 32,\
 'name': 'Dan Scott', 'employer': 'IBM'}
>>> for k in employee:
```

```
...        print '%s: %s' % (k, employee[k])
...
languages: ('Perl', 'PHP', 'Python')
age: 32
name: Dan Scott
employer: IBM
>>>
```

pass, break, and continue

The pass, break, and continue keywords enable you to exercise a finer degree of control over your control structures. The pass keyword tells the Python interpreter to do absolutely nothing; pass is commonly used to satisfy Python's requirement for a code block within a control structure because a comment alone does not satisfy the Python interpreter in this context.

```
>>> from time import localtime
>>> while localtime()[3] < 15:
...        pass # Waiting for 3:00 pm
...
>>>
```

The break keyword interrupts the normal flow of a for iterator or while loop and returns control to the enclosing scope. The continue keyword, in comparison, maintains the flow within the same scope but immediately forces the next iteration of the for iterator or while loop.

Defining Functions

Defining your own functions in Python consists of five easy steps:

1. Use the def keyword to indicate that you are defining a function.
2. Specify the name of the function that you are defining.
3. Specify the input arguments that the function accepts, along with any default values for unspecified arguments, followed by a colon.
4. Define the function body. This generally involves manipulating the input arguments in some way.
5. *Optionally*: Return a literal value or an object. If you do not explicitly return a value or an object, the function will always return 'None'.

For example, we can define a new function named additup(), which accepts three integer values and returns their sum to the caller in just a few lines of code:

```
def additup(a, b, c=0):
  'Return the sum of the input arguments.'
  return a + b + c
```

The first statement in the function body can be a string literal, called a *docstring*, that serves as the internal documentation for the function. There are a number of utilities that can generate sets of reference documentation from docstrings in your custom modules. Note that the third input argument has a default value of 0; this makes the third argument to our very simple function optional. Like any function, you can assign the returned results to a variable or use the results directly in the caller. Calling the `additup()` function results in the following output:

```
>>> x = additup(3, 2, 1)
>>> print x
6
>>> print additup(3, 2)
5
```

Creating Classes

As a language designed to be object-oriented and easily extensible from the ground up, Python makes it easy to define your own classes. The recipe for cooking up your own class is:

1. Use the `class` keyword to indicate that you are defining a class.

2. Specify the name of the class that you are defining. By convention, Python class names are capitalized to distinguish them from variable or method names.

3. *Optional:* Enclose the comma-delimited list of classes from which your new class inherits, if any, in parentheses.

4. Append a colon to the class name and inheritance list, and begin the code block that defines the members and methods of the class.

5. Declare any class member variables. Note that, although Python allows class member variables to be accessed directly by callers, it is a good idea to provide wrapper methods to set and get the class member variables. This gives you the opportunity to normalize the values rather than passing raw values to or from the class member variables.

6. Declare an __init__ method to automatically initialize the class member variables. The variables defined for the __init__ method map to the arguments passed in when a new instance of the class is instantiated.

7. Declare any class methods to implement the behavior of the class. The first argument to any class method is always `self`, representing the instance; any other arguments are optional.

In the following example, we define a generic class called `Horse` that represents the attributes and methods for all horses, and then we define the `Thoroughbred` and `Standardbred` classes that inherit from the `Horse` base class to add their own specialization. Although the base class defines all of the methods, child classes can override those methods, define new methods, or add new member variables to their definition.

```
class Horse:
    'Defines a horse object'
```

```
  def __init__(self, hands, color):
    self.hands = hands
    self.color = color

  def gethands(self):
    'Return the horse height in hands'
    return self.hands

  def getcolor(self):
    'Return the color of the horse'
    return self.color

  def getbreed(self):
    'Returns the breed of the horse'
    return self.breed

class Thoroughbred(Horse):
  'Defines a thoroughbred horse'

  def __init__(self, hands, color):
    Horse.__init__(self, hands, color)
    self.breed = 'thoroughbred'

class Standardbred(Horse):
  'Defines a standardbred horse'

  def __init__(self, hands, color):
    Horse.__init__(self, hands, color)
    self.breed = 'standardbred'
```

Now that we have defined our new classes, instantiating a new object and accessing some of its methods is easy. When we instantiate a new Thoroughbred object, the constructor first calls the Horse constructor and then adds its specialized attribute for the breed. When we invoke the gethands() method on the instance, you can confirm that the base class constructor did indeed initialize the hands member variable as expected:

```
>>> derby = Thoroughbred(15, 'blood bay')
>>> print derby.gethands()
15
>>> print derby.getbreed()
thoroughbred
```

Importing Modules

Although you can define all of your functions, classes, and actual program code in a single file, this approach makes it impossible to reuse your custom functions and classes. Instead, you can collect functions and classes into one or more *modules*: files that contain related groups of functions and classes collected into a namespace defined by the file name (ignoring the `.py` extension). Most of the functionality that is bundled with the standard Python distribution is collected into modules, rather than being available within the default language namespace, so you need to become familiar with using modules to get the most out of Python. To access an element contained within a given namespace, use the dot (`.`) operator in a standard *namespace.element* addressing syntax, similar to how you access methods and member variables of classes.

As an example, consider the `CGIHTTPServer` module, which offers a complete HTTP server with the capability to run CGI scripts implemented in Python. To access the classes and functions that are defined in the `CGIHTTPServer` class, issue the `import` statement and specify the name of the module that you want to import. The classes and functions will be available within the namespace of the module; in this example, we pass the `CGIHTTPRequestHandler` class contained within the `CGIHTTPServer` module to the constructor for the `HTTPServer` object.

```python
#!/usr/bin/python
import BaseHTTPServer
import CGIHTTPServer

server_address = ('', 8000)
httpd = BaseHTTPServer.HTTPServer(server_address, \
  CGIHTTPServer.CGIHTTPRequestHandler)
httpd.serve_forever()
```

Modules are useful for organizing even small projects, but for large projects, they are absolutely essential. It can be cumbersome to always fully qualify the namespace for the objects you access—`CGIHTTPServer.CGIHTTPRequestHandler` is a lot to type—so there are a few alternate import syntaxes that can ease your work with modules. The first is to assign an easier to type or more meaningful alias for the namespace as part of your import statement, using the `as` clause. For example, rather than having to refer to the CGIHTTPServer namespace, you could have issued the statement `import CGIHTTPServer as cgih` and referred to the elements of the CGIHTTPServer namespace using the `cgih` prefix instead.

The second option is to import the module's elements directly into your main program namespace using the `from` *module* `import` *tuple* syntax. The tuple can be a single element, a set of multiple comma-delimited elements, or an asterisk (`*`) to import all of the elements into your main program namespace. In the following example, we import the `HTTPServer` object from the `BaseHTTPServer` module and import all of the elements of the `CGIHTTPServer` module:

```python
#!/usr/bin/python
import BaseHTTPServer import HTTPServer
from CGIHTTPServer import *
```

```
server_address = ('', 8000)
httpd = HTTPServer(server_address, CGIHTTPRequestHandler)
httpd.serve_forever()
```

Note that we did not have to prefix the module name to the module elements when we used them in the main program. Although importing elements into your main program namespace can ease your typing effort, it can lead to confusing namespace collisions if, for example, two modules define elements by the same name. For this reason, we generally recommend that you alias the namespace to provide a shorthand reference to the module rather than importing the module elements directly into your main program namespace.

Installing and Configuring Python

Before you can install and configure Python to create Apache Derby applications, you must:

1. Install and configure Apache Derby as described in Chapter 4, "Installing Apache Derby and IBM Cloudscape on Windows," or Chapter 5, "Installing Apache Derby and IBM Cloudscape on Linux."
2. Start the Apache Derby Network Server as described in the installation chapter.
3. Install and configure the IBM DB2 Application Development Client to enable Open Database Connectivity (ODBC) access to Apache Derby databases, as described in Chapter 10, "Developing Apache Derby Applications with Perl, PHP, Python, and ODBC."

After you have successfully made an ODBC connection to your Apache Derby database, you can proceed with installing and configuring Python on your system.

Installing Python on Linux

Your best option is to locate and install the version of Python that is offered by your chosen Linux distribution. For example, Red Hat Enterprise Linux 4.0 offers python-2.3.4-14 as an RPM Package Manager (RPM) package. To install this package, or any other RPM package on an RPM-based Linux distribution, issue the following command as a user with root authority:

```
# rpm -ivh python-2.3.4-14.i386.rpm
```

On Debian or other apt-based Linux distributions, issue the following command as a user with root authority to install an APT package:

```
# apt-get install python
```

On Gentoo, a source-based Linux distribution, issue the following command as a user with root authority:

```
# emerge python
```

Configuring Python on Linux

The pyDB2 module is not shipped with any Linux distributions, which means you have to download and install it yourself. This is not as much hard work as it sounds: we'll guide you through the steps and help you avoid the most common pitfalls. First, ensure that you have the following packages installed on your system.

1. DB2 Runtime Client, with application development headers, must be installed to provide the ODBC driver and the ODBC libraries.

2. gcc (the Gnu C compiler) must be installed because the pyDB2 module consists largely of C code that must be linked against the DB2 Application Development Client libraries to produce the C module.

To successfully build and install the pyDB2 module for Apache Derby, perform the following steps:

1. Download the pyDB2 module from http://sourceforge.net/projects/pyDB2/. The latest version available at the time of this writing is 0.996a; however, the version of the code stored in the Concurrent Versioning System (CVS) repository includes a number of critical fixes. If the released version has not been updated when you read these instructions, use the CVS repository instead; otherwise, replace 0.996a in the following steps with the latest version of pyDB2.

2. Extract the source files from the pyDB2 tar.gz file, creating a subdirectory called DB2-0.996a:

   ```
   $ tar xzf pyDB2-0.996a.tar.gz
   ```

3. Alternatively, you can retrieve the latest files directly from the CVS repository. Perform the following steps to create a directory called PyDB2 containing the source files. Press Enter when you are prompted for a password.

   ```
   $ export PSERVER=pserver:anonymous@cvs.sourceforge.net
   $ cvs -d:$PSERVER:/cvsroot/pyDB2 login
   $ cvs -d:$PSERVER:/cvsroot/pyDB2 co PyDB2
   ```

4. Build the pyDB2 module:

   ```
   $ cd 0.996a; python setup.v81.py build
   ```

5. Install the pyDB2 module:

   ```
   $ su -c "python setup.v81.py install"
   ```

Installing Python on Windows

Setting up Python access to Apache Derby on Windows is easy because companies and individuals have made all of the required binary packages freely available for your use.

Downloading Python

The Python Web site offers a free Python interpreter that includes a complete set of documentation and base packages. Download the Microsoft Installer (MSI) Python package from the Python Web site (http://www.python.org/download/).

RETRIEVING THE CORRECT VERSION OF PYTHON FOR PYDB2

The binary version of the `pyDB2` module for access to Apache Derby databases must match the version of Python that you install on Windows. Check the files available at ftp://people.linuxkorea.co.kr/pub/DB2/win32; a file ending in `-py2.3.exe` will work correctly only with Python 2.3.x. At the time of this writing, Python 2.4.1 was available, but only the `pyDB2` binary for Python 2.3.x was available.

Installing Python

After you have downloaded the Python MSI package, double-click the package to invoke the installer and perform a complete installation of all of the Python components.

Configuring Python

Now that you have installed Python, you need to download and install the `pyDB2` module to be able to connect to your Apache Derby database through the IBM DB2 Universal Database client. Perform the following steps to install the `pyDB2` module:

1. Download the `pyDB2` Windows binary module from ftp://people.linuxkorea.co.kr/pub/DB2/win32.

2. Install the `pyDB2` package by double-clicking the `.EXE` file that you downloaded. The installer automatically determines the location of your Python language modules.

Now that you have installed both Python and the `pyDB2` module, you are ready to start writing Python applications that connect to Apache Derby.

Creating Apache Derby Applications with Python

Using Python Modules

To use a Python module in a Python script, you must tell the Python interpreter to load the module through the `import` statement. Most Python scripts collect their `import` statements at the top of the script to ensure that all of the dependencies are met before the rest of the script is run. It is also an easy way to inform other users of your script about the required modules.

All of the Python scripts developed in this chapter start with the following lines:

```
#!/usr/bin/python
import DB2
```

When you invoke a script on Windows operating systems from the command line, the first line is ignored. However, on UNIX-based operating systems and in a Web server's CGI handler, the special #! (or "hash-bang") line tells the operating system to use the command /usr/bin/python to interpret the rest of the script.

Running Python Scripts from the Command Line

Copy both lines from the previous example into a new text file called hello-derby.py and try running the Python script to ensure that your Python environment is set up correctly.

To run a Python script on Windows operating systems, you should be able to simply invoke the file name from the command line. The Python installer associates the .py file name extension with the Python interpreter by default, so an alternative is to double-click the hello-derby.py file in Windows Explorer—but this causes a command window to open briefly and then disappear as soon as the script finishes, so you will have no way of knowing whether an error occurred. If the script fails to run because the operating system did not associate Python with the .py extension, you can either create that association yourself by using the "Open with..." context menu item in Windows Explorer or explicitly invoke the Python interpreter from the command line:

```
C:/> python hello-derby.py
```

To run a Python script on Linux operating systems:

1. Grant execute permission to the script using the chmod command. You only need to do this once for a given script:

   ```
   $ chmod u+x hello-derby.py
   ```

2. Run the script by issuing the script's name at the command line. If the script is not in a directory specified by your *PATH* environment variable, you will have to specify the path to the script.

   - To run the script in your current working directory, issue the following command:

     ```
     $ ./hello-derby.py
     ```

   - To run the script contained in the /home/lynn/ directory, for example, issue the following command:

     ```
     $ /home/lynn/hello-derby.py
     ```

Connecting to an Apache Derby Database

Single Connections

In the Python DBI-API 2.0, Connection objects represent connections to databases. To connect to an Apache Derby database, create a Connection by calling the connect() method of the DB2 object with the database name, user name, and password as arguments. The following code example illustrates a function in which those arguments are assigned explicit values. We use this function in our custom Python module to create all of the `Connection` objects for our applications so that changing the connection information from a development database to a production database requires us to modify only one file. Other Python applications could retrieve the appropriate argument values from the command line interface or from the values specified in a Web form.

```
def database_connect():
    """
    Create a connection to the Apache Derby database.
    """

    database = 'TESTDB'
    user = 'db2inst1'
    password = 'ibmdb2'
    conn = DB2.connect(database, user, password)
    return conn
```

Disconnecting from a Database

To disconnect from a database, call the `close()` method on the `Connection` object: `conn.close()`.

Compared to most Python operations, connecting to a database is a time- and network-intensive operation, so you should reuse the `Connection` object as much as possible. In a typical Python script, you create a `Connection` at the start of the script and reuse that connection throughout the rest of the script, then disconnect from the database at the end of the script to ensure that the system resources are promptly returned to the database server.

Pooling Connections

Creating a database connection is probably the single largest drain on your system's resources and performance. For applications that must support a high volume of database access, you might want to consider connection pooling—reusing existing database connections instead of destroying and re-creating connections. Although the Python DB-API 2.0 does not define support for connection pooling in the API itself, an open source project called SQL Relay does offer connection pooling support. By combining the Python DB-API 2.0 with SQL Relay, your Web application can reuse an existing Apache Derby connection to perform its work.

Of course, if you plan to issue any INSERT, UPDATE, or DELETE statements, or if you plan to issue any SQL statements that modify the database schema, you should reconsider using a cached connection. Imagine the confusion that would result if two applications were in the middle of modifying the database schema, and one of the applications decided to issue a ROLLBACK.

Because both applications are using the same database connection, the ROLLBACK in one application would affect the work of both applications.

Issuing SQL Statements

Although Connection objects represent the connection to a database in the Python DB-API 2.0,
Cursor objects provide the mechanism for issuing SQL statements and retrieving results from
the database.

Executing a Single Statement

To issue a single SQL statement, call the cursor() method on the Connection object to
create a Cursor object, then call the execute() method on the Cursor object and pass the
SQL statement as the parameter. For example, to add a new production to the list of productions,
you can insert a row into the PRODUCTIONS table as follows:

```
def insert_one(conn):
    """
    Insert one row into the database.
    """

    curs = conn.cursor()
    stmt = """
    INSERT INTO PRODUCTIONS (Production_Title,
        Production_StartDate, Production_EndDate)
        VALUES ('Lily of the Valley', '2005-01-18', '2005-02-13')
    """
    curs.execute(stmt)
    curs.close()
```

The three double quotation marks (""") delimit the start and end of a string that is assigned to
the stmt variable. SQL statements use single quotation marks to delimit values, so delimiting
the entire string with single quotation marks would force you to add backslash characters to
escape the single quotation marks inside the string. Wrapping the statement in double quotation
marks would force you to add backslash characters to the end of each line of the SQL statement
to prevent Python from parsing the first line as a complete line instead of a continuation. Using
three double quotation mark delimiters enables you to include long SQL statements in your code
without having to include numerous backslash characters.

Issuing SQL Statements with Placeholders

Most SQL statements that you issue in your applications will be built with user input, rather than
simple predetermined SQL statements like the previous example. And for each user, those statements might differ only slightly: for example, in a message forum, you might retrieve a list of
messages written by a particular user by issuing a SELECT statement with a WHERE clause that

limits the scope of rows to those that match the user's ID. You could build the SQL statement by simply concatenating the strings using the + operator or `printf`-style `%` parameters, but that approach introduces the risk that your user input might (intentionally or otherwise) invalidate or corrupt your SQL statement. To avoid this situation, the Python DB-API 2.0 supports parameterized SQL statements through the use of placeholders. A placeholder in an SQL statement is a question mark (?) character that must be replaced by exactly one argument. You can use multiple placeholders in a single SQL statement, as long as you pass one argument per placeholder each time you invoke the `execute()` or `executemany()` method.

Reissuing the Same SQL Statement with Different Parameters

Executing a single statement at a time is fine for low-volume applications, but sometimes you must repeatedly reissue an SQL statement with only slight variations. For example, assume that you want to add ten more productions to your database. You could manually build ten different `INSERT` statements and issue the `execute()` `Cursor` method once for each statement, but there is an alternate approach that requires less work from both the Python database driver and the Apache Derby network server. To use this optimized method of executing the same statement with different parameter values, call the `executemany()` method on the `Cursor` object. The `executemany()` method accepts the SQL statement and a list object containing one or more lists of parameters. The `pyDB2` module issues the SQL statement as many times as it takes to exhaust the list of parameters that you passed to the `executemany()` method. The following example iterates through a list of parameters to insert seven new rows into the `PRODUCTIONS` table.

```python
def insert_many(conn):
    """
    Insert multiple rows into the database using values from a
      list of lists.
    """

    curs = conn.cursor()
    stmt = """
    INSERT INTO Productions
    (Production_Title, Production_StartDate, Production_EndDate)
    VALUES (?, ?, ?)"""

    productions = [
      ['Cats and Dogs', '2005-04-01', '2005-05-01'],
      ['Desperate Houses', '2005-05-02', '2005-06-01'],
      ['Icing the Puck', '2005-06-02', '2005-07-01'],
      ['Heroes', '2005-07-02', '2005-08-01'],
      ['Rubber Sacks', '2005-08-02', '2005-09-01'],
      ['Couched in Leather', '2005-09-02', '2005-10-01'],
      ['Backsplash', '2005-10-02', '2005-11-01'],
```

```
]

curs.executemany(stmt, productions)
curs.close()
```

The previous code example begins by creating a Cursor object and declaring the INSERT statement that we want to issue multiple times. Note the three parameter markers within the VALUES clause; these will be replaced by the values of each list within the productions list. When we invoke the executemany() method on the Cursor object and pass the productions list to the method, pyDB2 issues the INSERT statement for each list within the productions list. Finally, we call the close() method to destroy the Cursor object and return its resources to the system.

Counting the Number of Changed Rows

The Cursor object contains a .rowcount property that holds the integer value of the number of rows affected by the last execute() or executemany() call. If the execute() or executemany() methods have not been called, or if the last call did not affect any rows, the value of .rowcount is -1. Note that the .rowcount property only holds the number of rows affected by non-SELECT statements. If you must determine how many rows would be returned by a SELECT statement, you can issue the same SELECT statement with the returned columns wrapped in a COUNT() scalar function—but then you have to retrieve the results of the SELECT statement, which we will discuss in the following section.

Retrieving Data

The previous section discussed how to issue SQL statements, including how to most efficiently execute the same statement multiple times. But, beyond finding out how many rows were affected by a given non-SELECT SQL statement, we have not yet talked about how to issue a SELECT statement and retrieve the results of the query. The same principles apply to retrieving data returned as the result of calling a stored procedure with a CALL statement. After all, as much fun as it can be to modify database schemas and insert, update, or delete data in the database, you need to be able to get data out of the database to write a useful application.

Retrieving a Single Result Set

Every SELECT statement that you issue will return a single result set—a set of rows that matched the conditions of your SELECT statement. Any fetch methods that you call on the statement handle after an execute() or executemany() call automatically retrieve rows from that first result set. Here is an example of how to fetch a row into a set of variables:

```
def select_next_show(conn):
    """
    Select the next show from the Productions table, based on
    today's date. If there are no future shows starting after
    today, return None.
    """
```

```
curs = conn.cursor()
stmt = """
SELECT Production_No, Production_Title,
    Production_StartDate, Production_EndDate
    FROM Productions
    WHERE Production_StartDate > CURRENT_DATE
    ORDER BY Production_StartDate
"""

curs.execute(stmt)
row = curs.fetchone()
curs.close()
return row
```

You have already seen the `execute()` pattern in our examples of issuing `INSERT` statements. For `SELECT` statements, however, we have to call one of the `fetchone()`, `fetchmany()`, or `fetchall()` `Cursor` methods to retrieve the results of the statement. As their names suggest, `fetchone()` retrieves a single row from the result set as a sequence object, `fetchmany()` retrieves one or more rows from the database as a nested sequence object, and `fetchall()` retrieves all of the remaining rows from the result set as a nested sequence object. If there are no rows in the result set, the fetch methods return the special Python value `None`.

In the preceding example, we issue a simple `SELECT` statement to retrieve all of the productions from our Apache Derby database in the order of their start date, ensuring that only those productions that begin their run after today's date (using the `CURRENT_DATE` special register in the `WHERE` clause) will be returned. We then fetch only the first row of the result set by invoking the `fetchone()` method on the `Cursor` object, close the cursor, and return the `row` variable to the caller. In the docstring, we warn the caller that the method will return `None` if no productions satisfy the search criteria. The onus is on the caller, therefore, to correctly handle the result.

Calling Stored Procedures

Stored procedures encapsulate complex logic or commonly required actions as database server objects. Apache Derby uses stored procedures to great effect as the primary administration interface for the database, so it is important to learn how to call stored procedures in your applications. You can call stored procedures from any number of different client applications without having to reimplement the logic in each client application. A stored procedure can accept zero or more parameters, and each parameter can be declared as either an input only (`IN`) parameter, an output only (`OUT`) parameter, or a parameter that accepts an input value and returns an output value (`INOUT`). Along with returning values for `OUT` and `INOUT` parameters, a single stored procedure can also return multiple result sets.

However, although Apache Derby allows you to write powerful stored procedures in JDBC, the pyDB2 module currently offers only a subset of the capabilities required to call stored procedures. With pyDB2, you can:

- Call stored procedures that only accept IN parameters, including stored procedures that accept no parameters at all. The implementation of the callproc() method in pyDB2 does not return a modified sequence containing the returned values of your input parameters.

- Call stored procedures that return zero or one result sets. pyDB2 currently does not support the nextset() method for requesting the next result set after a stored procedure call.

By the time you read this, the pyDB2 module might already have been extended to remove these limitations with stored procedures—that's the wonderful fluidity of open source software. For now, however, you must keep these limitations in mind as you develop your application. The majority of database applications never issue a single call to a stored procedure, so you might very well be able to code your application in Python without having to make significant design concessions. After all, if the pyDB2 module authors never found it necessary to address these limitations, you probably won't need to use stored procedures in your application either.

Calling Stored Procedures with *IN* Parameters

To call a stored procedure through the pyDB2 module, call the callproc() method of the Cursor object and pass the name of the stored procedure as the first argument, followed by the parameters (if any) that the stored procedure requires for input. For example, consider a stored procedure named DOUBLE_IN that accepts two IN parameters of type VARCHAR(32). The parameters represent the old title and the new title, respectively, of a production that you want to update in the PRODUCTIONS table. You could call the stored procedure with the following function:

```
def call_procedure_double_in(conn):
    """
    Call a procedure that only accepts IN parameters.
    """

    curs = conn.cursor()
    stmt = 'double_in'
    old = 'Cats and Dogs'
    new = 'My New Title'
    curs.callproc(stmt, old, new)
    curs.close()
```

We create a Cursor object and then assign the name of the stored procedure to the stmt variable. You might have noticed that the stored procedure name is specified in lowercase characters, even though we had said that the stored procedure name was DOUBLE_IN. In pyDB2, stored procedure names are not case-sensitive; the module automatically converts your stored procedure name to uppercase. Unlike a standard UPDATE, DELETE, INSERT, or SELECT statement, you do not use placeholders to indicate the number of parameters that you are passing to the stored procedure. The callproc() method automatically assigns any arguments after the name of the stored procedure to the stored procedure as input parameters. Also, unlike a standard SQL statement, do not pass the parameters as a sequence object to the callproc() method; simply pass the parameters in order as discrete arguments.

Retrieving a Single Result Set

Calling a stored procedure that returns a single result set is just like calling any other stored procedure through pyDB2: you invoke the callproc() method on the Cursor object with the appropriate parameters to call the stored procedure. Then, to handle the result set returned by the stored procedure, invoke the fetchone(), fetchmany(), or fetchall() method, as appropriate, to retrieve one or more rows from the result set. The following example demonstrates how to call a stored procedure named SINGLE_RESULT that returns a single result set and accepts no parameters:

```
def call_procedure_single_result_set(conn):
    """
    Call a procedure that returns a single result set.
    """

    curs = conn.cursor()
    stmt = 'SINGLE_RESULT'
    curs.callproc(stmt)
    rows = curs.fetchall()
    curs.close()
    return rows
```

The preceding function calls the stored procedure using the callproc() Cursor method. The function then retrieves all of the rows into a variable (cleverly named rows), using the fetchall() method. Finally, it cleans up the cursor resources and returns the rows to the function caller.

Passing *OUT* and *INOUT* Parameters

UNIMPLEMENTED AT THE TIME THIS WAS WRITTEN
Although the Python DB-API 2.0 specification defines the interface for passing OUT and INOUT parameters to a stored procedure, the pyDB2 module had not implemented that functionality at the time this book was written. This functionality is documented according to the Python DB-API 2.0 specification in the event that the pyDB2 developers complete the stored procedure support offered by the module.

To call a stored procedure that accepts OUT or INOUT parameters, follow the same steps that you follow to call a stored procedure that accepts zero or more IN parameters. The return value of the callproc() method is a sequence containing the modified OUT and INOUT parameter values. For example, the following function calls a stored procedure named TEST_OUT_VARCHAR that accepts a single OUT parameter of type VARCHAR(32).

```
def call_procedure_out_varchar(conn):
    """
    Call a procedure that returns one OUT VARCHAR parameter.
    """

    curs=conn.cursor()
    stmt = 'TEST_OUT_VARCHAR'
    parm = None
    res = curs.callproc(stmt, parm)
    curs.close()
    return res
```

We set the value of the parm variable, which will hold the OUT parameter value, to None, although we could set it to any value that fits within the VARCHAR(32) parameter definition. When we call the stored procedure through the callproc() method, we assign the sequence returned by callproc() to the variable named res. The res sequence will have exactly one entry containing the string that was set by the TEST_OUT_VARCHAR stored procedure. After cleaning up the cursor resources, we return the res sequence to the caller of the function.

Retrieving Multiple Result Sets

UNIMPLEMENTED AT THE TIME THIS WAS WRITTEN

Although the Python DB-API 2.0 specification defines the interface for retrieving multiple result sets returned by a call to a single stored procedure, the pyDB2 module had not implemented that functionality at the time this book was written. This functionality is documented according to the Python DB-API 2.0 specification in the event that the pyDB2 developers complete the stored procedure support offered by the module.

Although SELECT statements can only return a single result set, stored procedures can return multiple result sets. When you call a stored procedure that returns a single result set, just iterate through the rows of the result set by calling the fetchone(), fetchmany(), or fetchall() methods on the Cursor object as though you were retrieving rows from a SELECT statement. When you call a stored procedure that returns multiple result sets, you can iterate through the rows of the first result set using the fetchone(), fetchmany(), or fetchall() method, then invoke the nextset() method of the Cursor object to retrieve the next result set from the stored procedure. If there are no more result sets to retrieve from the stored procedure, nextset() returns None. If you do not know how many results sets a given stored procedure will return, you can simply iterate over the nextset() method using a while loop control structure. The following example demonstrates a call to a stored procedure that returns three result sets with different sets of columns in each result set.

```
def call_procedure_results(conn):
    """
    Call a procedure that returns three result sets.
    Just print the contents of each result set.
    """

    curs = conn.cursor()
    stmt = 'PRODUCTION_LISTS'
    curs.callproc(stmt)
    print curs.fetchall()
    while curs.nextset():
      print curs.fetchall()
    curs.close()
```

Managing Transactions

A transaction is a set of one or more database operations that must all succeed for any changes to be reflected in the database. When all of the database operations in a transaction succeed, the corresponding changes are committed to the database. If one of the operations fails, all of the operations in the transaction can be rolled back so that the database appears to be unmodified. When you create a database connection with the pyDB2 module, you immediately begin a transaction, so if your application ends unexpectedly or without explicitly committing changes to the database, none of the changes will take effect. Transactions can impose significant locking overhead on your database, however, so if you are modifying data or your database schema, you should either explicitly commit your work regularly or turn autocommit on through the autocommit() Connection method.

HAVING TROUBLE MAKING IT STICK?

By default, the Python DB-API 2.0 specifies that any database connection will automatically start a transaction. If you do not issue an explicit commit after modifying your database schema or data, none of the changes you have made will be visible after the application ends. So, if you want to make your changes permanent, invoke the commit() method on the Connection object before the end of your application.

Explicitly Committing and Rolling Back Transactions

The Python DB-API 2.0 specification provides a standard set of methods that you can call on the Connection object to start and end transactions. To roll back a transaction, call the `rollback()` method on the Connection object. To commit a transaction, call the `commit()` method on the Connection object. Once you commit a transaction, a rollback will only roll back work to that commit point. The following example demonstrates how to perform some database operations in a transaction and then either commit the work or roll back all of the statements that have been performed since the transaction began:

```
def drop_tables(conn):
  """
  Remove the tables from the database.
  """

  curs = conn.cursor()
  stmt = 'DROP TABLE '
  tables = ('TRANSACTIONLOG', 'SEATS', 'SEATMAP', 'PRICEPLAN', \
   'PERFORMANCES', 'PRODUCTIONS')

  for table in tables:
    try:
      curs.execute(stmt + table)
    except:
      print 'Failed to drop table ' + table
  curs.close()

# We always want to commit this transaction
  if 1:
    conn.commit()
  else:
    conn.rollback()
```

Setting Autocommit

You can explicitly turn autocommit on after you create the Connection object handle by invoking the `autocommit()` method of the Connection object. To check the current value of the autocommit behavior for the Connection object, invoke the `autocommit()` method without any arguments. If autocommit is off, the method returns the value 0:

```
>>> import DB2
>>> conn = DB2.connect(database, user, password)
>>> print conn.autocommit()
0
```

To turn autocommit on, pass the value 1 to the `autocommit()` method:

```
>>> import DB2
>>> conn = DB2.connect(database, user, password)
>>> conn.autocommit(1)
```

Special Data Types

Although many organizations use databases to store nothing more complicated than strings and numbers—customer relationship management applications, university transcripts, results from scientific experiments, and so on—some organizations have found databases invaluable for storing less traditional kinds of data. In the following section, we consider the support that pyDB2 offers Apache Derby for storing non-traditional data types.

Large Objects: *BLOBs* and *CLOBs*

Large object data types are used to represent data that can consist of hundreds of megabytes of binary or character data per value. To build a database-driven jukebox, you might decide to store all of your audio files as binary large object (BLOB) data types in your database, along with a few other columns representing the genre, title, artist, length, and year in which the song was released. An alternative design for this application simply stores the files on the file system and stores the location of each file in the database. The advantage of storing large object data in the database is that you avoid having to develop two different backup procedures for your data, and deploying your application is simply a matter of copying your database.

One disadvantage of storing large object data in the database is that your database backups might be much larger. In addition, the pyDB2 module only supports retrieving BLOB data starting from the first byte of the BLOB. The lack of random access to BLOB data through Python means that operations requiring the equivalent of file-seek and file-read behavior are best implemented through separate files on the file system. Our application stores images as BLOB objects in the database for the convenience of backing up and deploying the application.

The life sciences provide a more likely scenario for storing character large object (CLOB) data in a database. Genetic analysis depends in large part upon analyzing DNA sequences—long strings consisting of combinations of the characters 'A', 'C', 'T', and 'G'—to understand the roles that individual genes play in various illnesses and to find potential cures. Much of the analysis can be carried out through SQL statements with user-defined functions that understand how to compare DNA sequences.

The pyDB2 module currently treats BLOB data types as any other data type, allowing you to extract a BLOB value from a database as one of the columns in a row returned from a query. By reading the entire BLOB with each `fetch` statement, be aware that your application may have to store hundreds of megabytes of data in memory.

In the following example, the BLOB data for each row is stored as a file on the local file system.

```
def retrieve_blob(conn, filename):
    """
    Save a BLOB from the database into a file.
    """

    curs = conn.cursor()
    stmt = """
    SELECT Seat_View FROM SeatMap
    """
    row = curs.fetchone()
    pic_data = str(row[0])
    curs.close()

    output = file(filename, 'wb')
    output.write(pic_data)
    output.close()}
```

The simplest way to insert a large object is to insert it directly from a file on disk into the table. The pyDB2 module provides three different methods, listed in Table 15-1, that you can use to wrap a file name when you pass it to the execute() method of the Cursor object to tell pyDB2 what kind of large object you are inserting.

Table 15-1 Large Object File Insertion Methods

DB2 Large Object Type	pyDB2 Method
Binary large object (BLOB)	DB2.BLOB()
Character large object (CLOB)	DB2.CLOB()
Double-byte character large object (DBCLOB)	DB2.DBCLOB()

In the following example, we define a function that you can use to insert PNG files into the YMLD database as BLOB files by simply passing the database connection and the file name for the PNG file:

```
def insert_seat_view(conn, seatnumber, filename):
    """
    Insert a picture (BLOB) into the database from a file.
    """
```

```
curs = conn.cursor()
stmt = """
INSERT INTO SeatMap(Seat_No, Seat_View)
VALUES (?, ?)
"""
curs.execute(stmt, seatnumber, DB2.BLOB(filename))
curs.close()
```

Creating Web Interfaces

The Web was designed to be simple. All that a basic Web application needs to do is receive plain text requests from the Web server and return the appropriate header and HTML to the requestor. In the late 1990s, it was common for developers of Web applications to create their own routines for handling these basics. However, as requirements grew more complex with the advent of HTTP 1.1, Common Gateway Interface (CGI) forms handling, authentication, cookies, secure socket layer (SSL) protocols, JavaScript, and other enhancements to the user experience, most Web application developers realized that their time was better spent focusing on creating a usable interface and leaving the underlying implementation details to a common set of libraries.

Setting the XHTML Header

To comply with the Hypertext Transfer Protocol (HTTP), any object that a Web server transfers must be prefaced by one or more HTTP headers. The HTTP headers contain meta-data to identify the kind of content that is being returned, along with optional meta-data, such as the date when the content expires, the character encoding for the content, or other meta-data that helps the Web browser or other HTTP client understand how to handle the object that is being returned. The only mandatory HTTP header is the content type header, which enables your Web browser to decide whether to display the object inside the browser as HTML, invoke a third party program or extension to display the object in a special viewer such as a multimedia player, or download and save the object on your file system.

Your Python script must return all of the required and optional HTTP headers first, followed by two linefeed characters (\n), followed by the actual object. The HTTP headers are simple text strings that follow a standard format. The most important HTTP header for our purpose, the content type header, follows the format *Content-type: text/html*, where *text/html* represents the Multipurpose Internet Mail Extension (MIME) type of the content returned by the script. The most common MIME type for Web pages is text/html, representing HTML and XHTML content, but other MIME types include text/plain and text/xml for plain text and XML content, respectively.

Because all of our Web pages will return XHTML content, and we want to create a standard look and feel for our XHTML content, we will define a convenience method that returns not only the HTTP content type header but also the XHTML title and header based on the single parameter title. Note the two linefeed characters (\n) that separate the HTTP header from the actual XHTML content.

```
def header(title):
  header = "Content-type: text/html\n\n"
  header = header + """<?xml version="1.0" encoding="iso-8859-1"?>
<!DOCTYPE html
  PUBLIC "-//W3C//DTD XHTML 1.0 Transitional//EN"
    "http://www.w3.org/TR/xhtml1/DTD/xhtml1-transitional.dtd">
<html xmlns="http://www.w3.org/1999/xhtml" lang="en-US"
 xml:lang="en-US">
  <head><title>""" + title + """</title></head>
  <body><h1>""" + title + '</h1>'
  return header
```

Using Common Web Modules

In the world of Web applications written in Python, `cgi` is the most common module used by Web authors. Many other modules extend `cgi` to provide more complex capabilities, but at the core of Python's Web capabilities is the `cgi` module. In this section we demonstrate how to use the `FieldStorage` class to retrieve CGI script variable input from your users' Web browser submissions.

Handling *POST* and *GET* Variables

Any application accepts some form of input and produces some form of output. In the case of CGI Web applications, the output normally takes the form of an HTML page, and the input is provided by CGI variables submitted from an HTML form. There are two kinds of CGI variables: GET variables, which are visible in the URL as key=value pairs, and POST variables, which are passed in the HTTP header and thus not normally visible to the user. Although GET variables are limited by the maximum URL length that Web servers or browsers will accept without truncation, POST variables have the advantage of being able to pass much longer fields.

Every CGI Web application requires a caller (normally the HTML form that specifies the CGI variables) and a handler (the Python script that accepts the CGI variables and generates some response based on the input values). The caller and the handler can be the same Python script, of course; you have probably seen this approach in action if you have ever filled out a Web form incorrectly and received the same form back in response with the missing fields highlighted and your "good" data already filling out the rest of the fields. In this case, your Web browser was the initial caller to the Python script that accepts input from the Web form. The Python script handles the request, validates your input, and if it is not satisfied with the input, calls itself with an extra parameter so that it can highlight the missing fields.

Let's look at a sample HTML form to understand how data is passed from the form to the handler script.

```
<form action='/cgi-bin/ymld.py' method='POST'>
  <input type="radio" name="performance" value="1"
    checked="checked">
    Cats and Dogs</input><br />
  <input type="radio" name="performance" value="2">
    Desperate Houses</input><br />
  <input type="radio" name="performance" value="3">
    Icing the Puck</input><br />
  <input type="submit" /> <input type="reset" />
</form>
```

The `action` attribute of the form element specifies the name of the handler script to which the form submits its variables. The `method` attribute specifies that the variables will be passed using the `POST` method. The first three input elements are of type `"radio"`, meaning that they will be rendered as radio buttons. Because all of the radio buttons have the same `name` attribute, they will be mutually exclusive. The browser passes the value of the `name` attribute to the handler script as the parameter name and passes the `value` attribute as the parameter value. In this form, the `value` attribute holds the ID number of the corresponding production in the `PRODUCTIONS` table and the associated production title. Finally, the submit and reset buttons offer mechanisms for submitting the form values and resetting the form values, respectively.

You can find the complete yet concise specification for HTML forms hosted by the World Wide Web Consortium at http://www.w3.org/TR/REC-html40/interact/forms.html.

Due to the potential for mistakenly assigning the wrong ID to a production title and the likelihood that productions will be added and removed on a regular basis, this is a form that you would not want to maintain by hand. You should either dynamically generate the page containing this form for every page request or, if the overhead of that approach is too high, set up a maintenance job to generate the page through `cron` on Linux or through the system scheduler on Windows operating systems.

Let's look at a CGI script that uses the performance `POST` variable in a query of the YMLD database to retrieve a list of performances for the requested production that still have seats available for purchase:

```
#!c:/local/python2.3/pythonw.exe
import YMLD
import cgi
import cgitb; cgitb.enable()
import re

def show_page(id):
  print header('YourMamaLovesDrama:: Display Performance')
  num = re.compile('^(\d+)$')
  m = num.search(id)
```

```
   if (m):
     conn = YMLD.database_connect()
     performances = YMLD.select_performance_data(conn, int(id))
     seats = YMLD.select_available_seats(conn, performances)
     print display_performances(performances, seats)
   else:
     print "<p>Invalid parameter.</p>"
   print footer()

def header(title):
   header = "Content-type: text/html\n\n"
   header = header + """<?xml version="1.0" encoding="iso-8859-1"?>
<!DOCTYPE html
   PUBLIC "-//W3C//DTD XHTML 1.0 Transitional//EN"
    "http://www.w3.org/TR/xhtml1/DTD/xhtml1-transitional.dtd">
<html xmlns="http://www.w3.org/1999/xhtml" lang="en-US"
 xml:lang="en-US">
   <head><title>""" + title + """</title></head>
   <body><h1>""" + title + '</h1>'
   return header

def footer():
   return """</body>\n</html>"""

if __name__ == '__main__':
   form = cgi.FieldStorage()

   if (not form.has_key('page')):
     index_page()
   elif (form.getvalue('page') == 'show'):
     show_page(form.getvalue('id'))
   elif (form.getvalue('page') == 'view'):
     display_seat_info(form.getvalue('id'))
   else:
     index_page(conn)
```

In this simple dispatch script, we use the standard Python cgi, cgitb, and re modules. The cgitb module offers enhanced debugging information in case an exception occurs in your Python script. Calling cgitb.enable() returns that complete set of exception information as XHTML output to the Web browser, which is extremely useful during development, but which should be disabled when your program is put into production (and hopefully free from any bugs).

You might also notice the call to `import YMLD`; this imports the methods that we have defined in our custom `YMLD.py` module. Our first operation instantiates the `FieldStorage` object to automatically parse and hold the values of the `POST` and `GET` variables. We check the value of the `page` form variable to determine whether the user has requested the page for the first time or whether they are in the middle of a transaction against our database. The `page` parameter is used as the basis of our dispatch script: depending on the value of the `page` parameter, the same script performs different operations. In this script, if the `page` parameter is not defined, the script hands control to the `index_page()` function to display the welcome page for the YMLD Web application; if the `page` parameter value is `'show'`, the script hands control to the `show_page()` function to display the list of performances that have tickets available for purchase.

Checking User Input for Tainted Values

Within the `show_page()` function, we begin by creating the title and heading of the XHTML content. Before taking any further action, we verify that the value of the `POST` variable resolves to an integer. Malicious users could submit requests directly to our script using a non-integer value, so we use the regular expression capabilities offered by the `re` module to ensure that the parameter only contains digit (`\d`) characters. If the regular expression does not return any matches, the function avoids the overhead of creating a new database connection and simply returns an error message. If the regular expression returns a match, however, the function creates a new database connection using the `YMLD` module's `database_connect()` method and passes the performance value to the `select_performance_data()` and `select_available_seats()` functions. The function then passes the data into the `display_performances()` function to format the resulting XHTML.

The process of checking form input to ensure that it does not include any unexpected or harmful data is called *taint-checking*. SQL injection attacks are a specific type of malicious form input that typically prey on scripts that, instead of using statements with parameterized queries, simply concatenate user input into a directly executed statement. The problem with concatenating user input is that it potentially opens a major security hole by enabling your users to enter input, including single quotation mark characters followed by other SQL clauses. For example, imagine a script that retrieves a list of a given user's purchase orders by concatenating user input to an SQL statement stub:

```
# Security hole if input value = "16' OR 1 > 0"
curs = conn.cursor
form = cgi.FieldStorage()
stmt = "SELECT order_no, cost FROM purchases WHERE user_id = '%s'" \
 % (form.getvalue('id'))
curs.execute(stmt)
```

If the user passes in a user ID value of `16' OR 1 > 0` this snippet of code would end up returning every purchase order in the database because 1 is always greater than 0. However, our taint-checking regular expression in the `show_page()` method ensures that every character in the input value is a digit. And by using a parameter marker in the `curs.execute()` method, we further ensure that the input value will be matched against a single field and cannot be used to inject unwanted SQL into the method. Always protect your application by making the effort to issue SQL statements with parameter markers and by checking your form variables for malicious user input.

Web Application Summary

Almost any CGI Web application is just a variation on this basic theme: retrieve CGI variables using the `FieldStorage` object of the `cgi` module, perform some actions based on the value of the CGI variables, and print your HTTP headers and XHTML content. For completeness, here are the `select_performance_data()`, `select_available_seats()`, and `display_performances()` methods:

```python
def select_performance_data(conn, production):
    """
    Get a list of all performances for a given production
    that still have seats available.
    """

    curs = conn.cursor()
    stmt = """
      SELECT Performance_No, Production_Title,
      Performance_Date, Performance_Time
      FROM Productions INNER JOIN Performances
      ON Productions.Production_No = Performances.Production_No
      WHERE Productions.Production_No = ?
      AND Performances.Performance_SeatsAve = 1
    """

    curs.execute(stmt, production)
    performances = curs.fetchall()
    curs.close()
    return performances
```

The `select_performance_data()` method passes the value of the `id` POST variable to the placeholder in the `SELECT` statement. The method assigns all of the rows in the result set to the `performances` list using the `curs.fetchall()` method and returns that list to the caller.

```python
def select_available_seats(conn, performances):
    """
    Get a list of all available seats and prices for a
    given performance of a show.
    """
```

```
curs = conn.cursor()
stmt = """
  SELECT Seat_No, CAST(PricePlan_Cost AS DECIMAL(5, 2))
  FROM Seats INNER JOIN PricePlan
  ON Seats.PricePlan_No = PricePlan.PricePlan_No
  WHERE Performance_No = ?
  AND Seats.Seat_Available = 1
"""

seats = {}
for show in performances:
  seats[str(show[0])] = []
  curs.execute(stmt, show[0])
  row = curs.fetchone()
  while row:
    seats[str(show[0])].append((row[0], row[1]))
    row = curs.fetchone()
curs.close()
return seats
```

The `select_available_seats()` method also passes a variable to the placeholder in a
SELECT statement. We cast the value of the `PricePlan_Cost` column to a DECIMAL(5,
2) data type to return values like 79.25 instead of +7.92500000000000E+001. The second
parameter of the function is the list we returned from `select_performance_data()`, and
we iterate through that array using a `for` statement to pass the performance ID to the `execute`
statement (`show[0]` means the first element of the list referenced by the `show` variable).
The method assigns the resulting values to the `seats` dictionary using the performance ID
(`str(show[0])`) as the dictionary key, with the seat number and seat cost as the members of a
tuple that are added to the list referred to by the `seats` dictionary key.

MANIPULATING DATA THROUGH SQL STATEMENTS OR PYTHON FUNCTIONS

In this example, we use SELECT statements in two separate Python functions to retrieve
data from the YMLD database and store that data in separate Python data structures. We
then pass those structures to a formatting function that generates the core XHTML output.
Although this approach enables us to break the script into easily understandable and
reusable functions, a more efficient application structure would retrieve the required data
through a single SELECT statement. Databases like Apache Derby are optimized to retrieve
and manipulate data faster than multi-purpose programming languages. Retrieving all data
from a single SELECT statement also avoids race conditions that could arise in this scenario
if a given performance that had seats available when the `select_performance_data()`
SELECT statement was issued sold all of its tickets before the `select_available_`
`seats()` SELECT statement was issued. When you write your own applications, keep this
balance of simplicity and efficiency in mind and make any design trade-offs consciously.

```
def display_performances(performances, seats):
    """

    Display performances for a given production with radio buttons
    so a user can display the seats that are available for a given
    performance.
    """

    form = """<table>
    <tr><th>Title</th><th>Date</th><th>Time</th><th>Seats</th>
    </tr>\n"""
    for shownum, title, date, time in performances:
        form = form + "<tr>"
        form = form + "<td>" + title + "</td>"
        form = form + "<td>" + date + "</td>"
        form = form + "<td>" + time + "</td>"
        form = form + "<td><form action='" + url() + \
           "?page=view' method='POST'>"
        form = form + "<select name='seat'>"
        for seat, price in seats[str(shownum)]:
            form = form + "<option value='" + str(seat) + "'>"
            form = form + str(price) + "</option>\n"
        form = form + "</select><input type='submit' value='Display' />"
        form = form + "</form></td></tr>\n"
    form = form + "</table>"
    return form

def url():
    import os

    return os.environ['SCRIPT_NAME']
```

The display_performances() function demonstrates the caution that is required to generate valid XHTML output. In this XHTML, the performances are formatted in a table, with each row representing a performance for a different time on the requested day. To complicate matters, the final column in each row contains an XHTML form that displays the available seats by price in a drop-down form element. You must be careful to ensure that your XHTML is valid—for example, ensuring that every <table> start tag has a matching </table> end tag—or else your Web page might not display in the format that you or your Web designers expect.

Note that although we could have directly issued print statements within the display_performances() method, we instead created a single string variable that contains all of the

XHTML and returned that XHTML to the caller. We prefer this method of creating Web applications because it affords you much more flexibility if you decide to change the layout of your Web site. In the case of the `display_performances()` method, we return a single self-contained `<table>` XHTML element. For the purposes of our sample application, we are simply printing that table as the body of our XHTML page, but a more sophisticated Web site might display that table as just one element of a complete portal page. Returning the XHTML content from a method as a string variable gives you the ability to collect all of the XHTML elements you want to display in a single Web page in any order before displaying them. If you chose to simply print the XHTML content from within each method, you would have to call each method in the exact order required by your Web design—and that might cause problems if the results of some element you want to display on the bottom of your Web page are required as input to an element you want to display at the top of your Web page.

To give us the flexibility to rename this script or to import this module into other scripts, we avoid hard coding a specific URL into the form returned from the `display_performances()` function. Instead, we create a new function `url()` to return the full path and name of the script from the HTTP headers. The HTTP headers are stored as environment variables, and fortunately the standard `os` module offers the `environ` dictionary element to provide access to the environment variables by name.

Customizing Web Sites with Sessions

Sessions bring statefulness to the Web by making it possible for a user to add, for example, three items to a shopping cart in an online store, browse through several other Web pages, and then return to the online store a few minutes later to continue adding items to the cart or to complete the purchase without forcing you to explicitly pass the complete list of chosen items between Web pages in the online store. Although adding statefulness to the Web can dramatically improve the user experience and ease your coding effort immensely, the design principles of sessions are quite simple:

1. The Web application assigns a random identifier to the user when she first accesses the site during a given browser session.
2. This identifier is stored as a cookie in the Web browser.
3. The identifier is then used as a key to remember user-specific information in a server-side external storage system (file systems, shared memory, or databases are common repositories).

Unfortunately, Python currently does not include any standard module that provides session support for Web-based Python applications; instead, a wide variety of frameworks for building Web applications have created different implementations of session support. mod_python, for example, defines a set of `Session` classes to implement sessions backed by memory or a simple database format. However, these classes are not compatible with the `web.session` classes offered by the Web Modules project (http://www.pythonweb.org/projects/webmodules/). In an effort to impose some regularity and modularity in this space, the Web Server Gateway Interface (WSGI) proposal at http://www.python.org/peps/pep-0333.html seeks to define a standard interface between Web servers and Python Web frameworks.

Creating GUI Interfaces

Python does not offer a native graphical toolkit of its own. Instead, it borrows graphical toolkits from several other languages and projects and offers modules that provide Python interfaces to those toolkits. The most popular cross-platform graphical toolkit is Tk, the counterpart to the Tcl programming language. The Tkinter module included with most Python distributions provides an interface to Tk that is powerful, easy for users to understand and, with some study, relatively easy to program.

To write a Tkinter application, you must instantiate and initialize the main application window (the Tk() class) in the main method and then call the mainloop() function to act as an event handler until the user dismisses the application window. During the life of the application window, the event handler can create new top-level windows, modify the data that is displayed in the main application window, or perform other functions, as determined by the callback methods that you define for the active GUI widgets. After the user dismisses the application window, the application can perform any required resource cleanup before exiting. Following is the sample main method from our YMLD administration application:

```
import Tkinter as Tk
import YMLD
import DB2


if __name__ == '__main__':
  root = Tk.Tk()
  app = Administration(root)
  root.mainloop()
```

The Tkinter module provides the basic objects required to create a Tkinter application. The YMLD module is our custom module that, because we have taken the time to design and implement the data access methods separately from our presentation methods, we can use in both our Web and GUI applications. The Administration class contains the bulk of our GUI layout, so let's take a look at the class constructor method:

```
class Administration:
  """
  Create an administrative GUI for the YMLD application.
  """
  def __init__(self, root):
    self.root = root
```

```python
        self.conn = YMLD.database_connect()
        root.title("YourMamaLovesDrama Administration Panel")
        menubar = Tk.Menu(self.root)

        # Menu items
        filemenu = Tk.Menu(menubar, tearoff=0)
        menubar.add_cascade(label="File", menu=filemenu)
        filemenu.add_command(label="Refresh", command=self.refresh)
        filemenu.add_command(label="Exit", command=self.exit)

        productions = Tk.Menu(menubar, tearoff=0)
        menubar.add_cascade(label="Productions", menu=productions)
        productions.add_command(label="Add",
          command=self.addproduction)

        self.root.config(menu=menubar)

        self.display_productions()

    def refresh(self):
        """
        Refresh the main window with the latest production
        data from the YMLD database.
        """
        self.frame.destroy()
        self.display_productions()

    def exit(self):
        """
        Quit the YMLD administration application, cleaning up
        all resources.
        """
        self.conn.close()
        self.root.quit()
        self.root.destroy()

    def addproduction(self):
        """
        Create the pop-up AddProduction dialog.
        """
        add = AddProduction(self, self.root)
```

Notice that in this object-oriented GUI application, we connect to the database the same way that we do from our Web applications, by calling a method that contains hard coded values for the database name, user name, and password. When you understand the basics of Tkinter, you can easily improve the administration application by adding a connection dialog that enables administrators to specify their preferred user names, passwords, and databases.

We begin by setting the title of the root Tk window to something meaningful. This title will be displayed in the YMLD administration window title bar, and your window manager might also use the title to identify minimized versions of the running application. To provide the standard look and feel of a modern GUI application, we instantiate a `Menu` object called `menubar` that will hold further `Menu` objects representing the usual "File" and "About" menu items. We then create a set of menu items that will appear on the main window contained by the Tkinter `Menu` object. The `add_cascade()` method declares the label for the top-level menu item that will appear under the window title bar, and each `add_command()` method for a given `Menu` object declares a text label and the associated method that will be called if the user selects that menu item. To complete the menu, we assign `menubar` as the value of the `menu` configuration variable by calling the `config()` method of the root Tk window. Finally, we call the `display_productions()` method to actually display the productions on our root Tk window.

The `refresh()`, `exit()`, and `addproduction()` methods represent relatively simple implementations of commands that correspond to the `Menu` items that we have just added. The `refresh()` method destroys the `Frame` object created by the `display_productions()` method to remove the old data displayed in the YMLD administration GUI and then calls the `display_productions()` method to refresh the data in the GUI. The `exit()` method closes the `Administration` instance database connection, stops the root Tk window event-handling loop, and destroys the root Tk window and all of its resources. The `addproduction()` method instantiates a new instance of our custom `AddProduction` class, which results in a pop-up secondary dialog that grabs the user input focus until the user either submits the new production information or cancels the dialog.

Now let's look at the `display_productions()` method so that we can discover how to present tabular data in Tkinter applications:

```python
def display_productions(self):
    """
    Display the productions in a table in the main window.
    """
    self.frame = Tk.Frame(root)
    self.frame.pack()

    # Display all productions on main window
    columns = ('ID', 'Title', 'Start Date', 'End Date')
    y = 0
```

```
for header in columns:
  c = Tk.Button(self.frame, text=header, font='Helvetica 10 bold')
  c.grid(row=0, column=y, sticky=Tk.E+Tk.W)
  y = y + 1
shows = YMLD.select_all_shows(self.conn)
x = 1
for row in shows:
  y = 0
  for col in row:
    c = Tk.Button(self.frame, text=col, font='Helvetica 10')
    c.grid(row=x, column=y, sticky=Tk.E+Tk.W)
    y = y + 1
  x = x + 1
```

First we instantiate a `Frame` object within our root Tk window to hold our table and call the `pack()` method to place the `Frame` in the window. Although the `pack()` layout method allows for more sophisticated layout options, we can just accept the defaults for the root frame of the GUI. The tabular data itself will be laid out as a grid of `Button` objects, where each `Button` object represents a cell in the table. A `Button` object can be associated with a command—for example, clicking on a production title could invoke a secondary dialog that displays the complete list of performances for that production—but for our purposes, we simply want to display text in each cell and rely on the border of each `Button` to present a well-defined table. The `grid()` layout allows for more refined control over the layout of your GUI than the `pack()` method, and because `grid()` deals with rows and columns, it is ideal for tabular data. To create a table, we simply iterate through the columns in each row returned from the `select_all_shows()` method and create a `Button` with the corresponding text in the appropriate place in the table using the `grid()` layout method.

IMPROVING THE DESIGN
A more advanced design would limit the number of returned rows to prevent your system from using too much memory while working with a large database.

There are only two complex parts to this method. The first is that we use explicit font styles to differentiate the table headers from the table contents by setting the font attribute of the table header `Button` objects to a bold style. The second is that we achieve a uniform cell size for each `Button` object in a given column by setting the sticky attribute to `Tk.E+Tk.W`—meaning that the `Button` objects should "stick" to both the east (E) side and the west (W) side of the column, rather than collapse to fit the text that would otherwise be displayed.

Now let's look at the `AddProduction` class definition to understand how to create modal dialogs in Tkinter applications.

```python
class AddProduction(Tk.Toplevel):
    """
    Pop-up dialog that disables the main parent window and enables
    users to type in the information for a new YMLD production.
    """
    def __init__(self, parent, root):
        Tk.Toplevel.__init__(self, root)
        self.transient(root)
        self.root = root
        self.parent = parent
        self.title('Add Production')

        bottom = Tk.Frame(self)
        bottom.pack(side=Tk.BOTTOM)

        top = Tk.Frame(self)
        top.pack(side=Tk.TOP)

        labels = Tk.Frame(top)
        labels.pack(side=Tk.LEFT)

        entries = Tk.Frame(top)
        entries.pack(side=Tk.RIGHT)

        titlelabel = Tk.Label(labels, text='Title:')
        titlelabel.pack(anchor=Tk.E)
        self.titleentry = Tk.Entry(entries)
        self.titleentry.insert(0, 'Title')
        self.titleentry.pack(anchor=Tk.W)

        startlabel = Tk.Label(labels, text='Start date:')
        startlabel.pack(anchor=Tk.E)
        self.startentry = Tk.Entry(entries)
        self.startentry.insert(0, 'YYYY-MM-DD')
        self.startentry.pack(anchor=Tk.W)

        endlabel = Tk.Label(labels, text='End date:')
        endlabel.pack(anchor=Tk.E)
        self.endentry = Tk.Entry(entries)
```

```
    self.endentry.insert(0, 'YYYY-MM-DD')
    self.endentry.pack(anchor=Tk.W)

    # Add standard OK/Cancel buttons
    ok = Tk.Button(bottom, text='OK', command=self.addproduction)
    ok.pack(side=Tk.LEFT)
    cancel = Tk.Button(bottom, text='Cancel', command=self.cancel)
    cancel.pack(side=Tk.RIGHT)

    # Prevent root window from operating
    self.grab_set()
    self.initial_focus = self.titleentry
    self.initial_focus.focus_set()
    self.wait_window(root)

def addproduction(self):
    """
    Add one new production to the YMLD database.
    """
    YMLD.insert_one(self.parent.conn, (self.titleentry.get(), \
        self.startentry.get(), self.endentry.get()))
    self.parent.refresh()
    self.cancel()

def cancel(self):
    """
    Standard method for cancelling an operation and
    removing the dialog that contained the Cancel button.
    """
    self.root.focus_set()
    self.destroy()
```

In Tkinter, you create a new window by instantiating a TopLevel object from the root Tk window or another TopLevel instance. The purpose of the AddProduction class is to create a new dialog that accepts user input for a new production in the YMLD database, so the AddProduction class inherits methods and properties from the Tkinter TopLevel object. So far, we have avoided advanced GUI layout discussions with the pack() method by using the grid() layout method for the main window instead. However, in this dialog, we want to add three text fields and their corresponding labels, as well as an **OK** button and a **Cancel** button to the bottom of the dialog, and although the grid() layout method could be made to work, the pack() layout method is more suited to this kind of GUI element flow. By understanding both of these layout methods, you will be better equipped to choose the right layout method for your needs in each dialog that you create.

The pack layout manager's default layout method is to add each object in the center of the window, with each successive object added underneath the previous object. A stack of labels, text fields, and buttons would hardly be usable, so we need to override the default layout attributes in the pack() method to improve the layout design. To group collections of GUI widgets together, we use the standard Tkinter method of instantiating Frame objects as containers. Each Frame instance can have its own location in the window, so we start by instantiating the Frame object top to hold our Label objects and Entry objects at the top of the window, and the Frame object bottom to hold our buttons at the bottom of the window. The side attribute for the pack() method declares the location where the layout manager will attempt to position an object.

Now we need to ensure that the labels and text fields line up beside each other, rather than appearing in a vertical stack. Not surprisingly, this means that we create two more Frame objects positioned to the left side and right side, respectively—but notice that we instantiate the new Frame objects on the top Frame instance. By containing the Label and Entry object Frame objects in the top frame, we ensure that our buttons will appear at the bottom of the window. If you try to create the left-positioned and right-positioned Frame objects outside of a top-positioned Frame, your buttons will appear between the labels and Entry objects, rather than underneath them.

When we instantiate each Label and Entry object, we specify the anchor attribute of the pack() method as 'Tk.E' and 'tk.W' to assign their alignment to the east (right) and west (left), respectively. This results in labels that are positioned tightly against their associated text entry field. Finally, we add the Button objects to control the behavior of the dialog. Each button object is added to the bottom Frame instance so that it sits below the labels and text fields, and we position the **OK** button to the left side and the **Cancel** button to the right side, in accordance with normal user interface design principles.

The **OK** button defines a command attribute that calls the addproduction() instance method so that the values entered in the Entry objects can be retrieved through their get() methods and passed to the INSERT statement that creates a new production in the YMLD database. The addproduction() method can contain validation logic to ensure that the values are acceptable before trying to insert the new production—for example, the end date should not fall before the start date—and can, in turn, instantiate its own TopLevel objects to display error messages or otherwise interact with the GUI and the database.

Summary

This chapter has led you through the process of installing and configuring the Python interpreter with Apache Derby support on your server. You learned the basic building blocks of database-driven Python applications, including how to connect to the database, issue SQL statements, and fetch results from the database. The chapter presented the core elements of Web applications, including how to retrieve form variables, check form variables for tainted input, and design a Web application based on a page dispatch controller pattern, with the Python functions divided between business logic and presentation logic. Finally, you learned how to create a Python application with a graphical user interface using the Tkinter module.

Web Site Contents

Introduction

This book contains a number of examples and sample SQL for you try out on your own Cloudscape/Derby system. These examples can be found on the book's Web site: www.ibmpressbooks.com/title/0131855255.

Web Site Contents

The Web site contains links to a number of resources that can help you get started with Apache Derby.

- Articles—A number of developerWorks articles about Apache Derby are available at www.ibm.com/developerworks/.

- Cloudscape—Three different copies of the IBM Version of Apache Derby (Cloudscape) are found at www.ibm.com/developerworks/db2/library/techarticle/dm-0408cline/index.html.

- Network Client—If Apache Derby is to be used as a network server, a suitable client must be used to connect to it. Information on the DB2 Client can be found at www.ibm.com/developerworks/db2/library/techarticle/dm-0409cline2/.

- Documentation—The IBM Cloudscape Information Center is available at http://publib.boulder.ibm.com/infocenter/cscv/v10r1/index.jsp.

- EclipseDemo—The Eclipse framework has various plug-ins available to simplify development against an Apache Derby database. This demo demonstrates the use of Eclipse to create an Apache Derby application and can be found at www-128.ibm.com/developerworks/db2/library/techarticle/dm-0509cline/

- Examples—A number of the chapters have examples that demonstrate Apache Derby functionality. Each chapter has a link in this Web site that allows you download all of the sample code for that chapter.
- YMLD Database—The YMLD database is reproduced in a number of the chapters. This link includes a full copy of the YMLD database, including scripts that can reproduce the database by using the ij command.

Summary

The reader is encouraged to try out the various examples found within the sample code on the Web site. These examples are an excellent way of learning how to use Apache Derby!

Apache Derby and IBM Cloudscape Resources

A community can be thought of as a group of people that share a common interest, or a common place to live. Whatever definition you want to use for this term, one characteristic common to communities is that their commonality more often than not synergizes into a strong support structure. The following is a list of resources that you can use to reach out to the rest of *your* Apache Derby community members, learn how to build applications, and generally become more of an Apache Derby expert.

General Information

- IBM Cloudscape product at: http://www.ibm.com/software/data/cloudscape
- DeveloperWorks Scholars' Program at:
  http://www.ibm.com/software/info/university/products
- Apache Derby Incubator Project site at: http://incubator.apache.org/derby/
- IBM Cloudscape online documentation at:
  http://publib.boulder.ibm.com/infocenter/cldscp10/index.jsp
- Migrating databases to IBM Cloudscape at:
  http://publib.boulder.ibm.com/epubs/html/c1894710.html

Application Development

- IBM Cloudscape Developer's Domain corner at:
  http://www-106.ibm.com/developerworks/db2/zones/cloudscape/
- IBM Developer Works IBM Cloudscape Web site at:
  http://www-128.ibm.com/developerworks/db2/zones/cloudscape/

- "Using DB2 Plug-ins for Eclipse with Apache Derby" by Susan Cline at:
  http://www-128.ibm.com/developerworks/db2/library/techarticle/dm-0410cline/
- "Using DB2 Plug-ins for Eclipse with Apache Derby, Part II" by Susan Cline and Gilles Roux at:
  http://www-128.ibm.com/developerworks/db2/library/techarticle/dm-0411cline/
- "Connect to Apache Derby Databases Using Jython" by Bob Gibson at:
  http://www-106.ibm.com/developerworks/db2/library/techarticle/dm-0502gibson/
- "Cloudscape and ODBC" by Susan Cline at:
  http://www-106.ibm.com/developerworks/db2/library/techarticle/dm-0409cline2/index.html
- "ODBC Programming Using Apache Derby" by Rajesh Kartha at: http://www-128.ibm
  .com/developerworks/db2/library/techarticle/dm-0409kartha/index.html
- "Develop IBM Cloudscape and DB2 Universal Database Applications with PHP" by Dan Scott at:
  http://www-128.ibm.com/developerworks/db2/library/techarticle/dm-0502scott/index.html
- "Apache Derby Database Development with Apache Ant" by James Snell at:
  http://www-128.ibm.com/developerworks/db2/library/techarticle/dm-0412snell/
- "Developing Perl Applications with Apache Derby" by Moria Casey at:
  http://www-128.ibm.com/developerworks/db2/library/techarticle/dm-0410casey/
- "Connecting PHP Applications to Apache Derby" by Moira Casey at:
  http://www-128.ibm.com/developerworks/db2/library/techarticle/dm-0409casey/
- "ADO.NET and IBM Cloudscape" by Yip-Hing Ng and Rob Reuben at:
  http://www-128.ibm.com/developerworks/db2/library/techarticle/dm-0410ng/

Getting to Know the IBM Cloudscape and Apache Derby Databases

- The Cloudscape Detective Game at: http://www-128.ibm.com/developerworks/edu/
  dm-dw-dm-0412kubasta-i.html?S_TACT=104AHW11&S_CMP=LIB
- "An Introduction to BACKUP, RESTORE, and ROLLFORWARD Recovery in IBM Cloudscape/Apache Derby" by Suresh Thalamati at: http://www-128.ibm.com/
  developerworks/db2/library/techarticle/dm-0502thalamati/
- "IBM Cloudscape Version 10: A Technical Overview" by Jean Anderson and Kathy Saunders at:http://www-106.ibm.com/developerworks/db2/library/techarticle/dm-0408anderson/
  index.html
- "IBM Cloudscape: Understanding Java CLASSPATH" by Jean Anderson and Susan Cline at: http://www-106.ibm.com/developerworks/db2/library/techarticle/dm-0408anderson2/

Support

- Online IBM-hosted technical support resources at:
  http://www.ibm.com/software/data/cloudscape/support
- "A Compendium of Frequently Asked Questions" by Stanley Bradbury at:
  http://www-106.ibm.com/developerworks/db2/library/techarticle/dm-0408bradbury/
  index.html

Newsgroups and Mailing Lists

- Apache mailing lists at: http://www.apache.org/foundation/mailinglists.html
- IBM Cloudscape community forum at:
  http://www-106.ibm.com/developerworks/forums/dw_forum.jsp?forum=370&cat=19

Troubleshooting Hints and Tips

Introduction

This appendix contains some hints and tips gathered from various chapters in this book; it is divided into sections based on topics such as installation, performance tuning, SQL, and application development. If you've run across a problem with Apache Derby, you might find the solution in this section!

Installation

Performing a Graphical Installation and Saving Disk Space

If you know that you have a JRE running on your system, you can use the generic graphical installation program to set up an Apache Derby environment. This is a useful option if your workstation or target device has a shortage of available disk space because this installation program has a significantly smaller footprint than its Windows-native counterpart.

Setting Environment Variables on Linux

Don't forget to include the colon (:) separation character between directory paths and ensure that you enter the path to the JRE that you want to use at the start of the PATH system variable declaration. Also note that the path to your JRE must include the /bin directory. In addition, ensure that you append the $PATH parameter after the colon that separates entries in this variable on Linux. Otherwise, all paths will resolve to this location. And remember, Linux is case-sensitive. Finally, ensure that you've sourced your profile so that the kernel will pick up the changes that you have made. For example, use the source .bashrc command.

Setting Environment Variables on Windows

Don't forget to include the semi-colon (;) separation character between directory paths, and ensure that you enter the path to the JRE that you want to use at the start of the PATH system variable declaration. Also note that the path to your JRE must include the /bin directory.

If You're Installing the Apache Derby Code on a Linux System Using the 2.6 Kernel

As of the writing of this book, the Apache Derby installation program does not work with the 2.6 kernel with certain JVMs. The 2.6 kernel changes the threading model and creates the incompatibility. Certain distributions (for example, RHEL3 and SuSE Linux Pro 9.2) backport the 2.6 kernel, and the Apache Derby installation program will not work with these distributions. If the Apache Derby installation program for Linux doesn't start, use the export LD_ASSUME_KERNEL=2.4.19 command to set the kernel level for the session that will perform the installation.

Choosing a Target Directory for the Apache Derby Installation

You cannot select a path name that includes spaces.

If You Can't Start Your Apache Derby Database

If you can't seem to get your Apache Derby database to start correctly, try running the appropriate scripts to solve the problem. These scripts are covered in the installation chapters. You should always start troubleshooting by ensuring that you have a JRE on your system (enter the java -version command) and ensuring that the CLASSPATH environment variable is set up correctly.

If You Can't Connect to Your Apache Derby Database

Ninety-five percent of the time, you've failed to start the Apache Derby Network Server. Remember, if you are using any one of the external APIs (Java Common Client, PHP, and so on), you need to start the Apache Derby Network Server. If you want to support two separate connections to your database, you also need to start an Apache Derby Network Server. For example, if you are testing your application and start the Apache Derby database with it, and you want to work with the database schema using one of the Eclipse tools, you will need the Apache Derby Network Server because the application requires two connections, one from the application and one from the Integrated Development Environment.

Performance Tuning

You need to properly size Apache Derby memory. If you find that performance is sluggish, or if you encounter OutOfMemory exceptions (OOMEs), the first thing you should do is to adjust the Apache Derby pageCache. The amount of memory that you can safely allocate to the page cache depends on a combination of many factors: the amount of physical memory on your machine, the average `pageSize`, and the `maxHeap` of the JVM. The basic calculation is to compute the number of pages to allocate to the `pageCache` as a ratio of the JVM to the `maxHeap` size.

You set the `maxHeap` size using the Java parameter `-Xmx#m`. In this example, # is the size in MB that you want to allocate to this heap. For example, the command `java -Xmx128m` allocates 128 MB to `maxHeap`. If you need to change this parameter for performance reasons or to avoid OOMEs, be sure that the JVM maximum heap size specified is less than the total physical memory of the machine.

We've seen internal tests with Apache Derby and Java 1.4.0 that showed good results with a 20:1 ratio for the JVM `heapSize` to the Apache Derby `pageCache`. This ratio was used for a very "active" application; smaller ratios might be better suited to your application.

If your application processes a lot of transactions per second, you might experience more OOMEs with a larger JVM `heapSize` to Apache Derby `pageCache` ratio. We recommend starting with a ratio of 20:1 and stress testing your application with lower and lower ratios. For example, if you didn't experience any OOMEs with a 20:1 ratio, you can try a 10:1 ratio to see if it still yields acceptable performance without any memory errors. We've seen very lightweight applications run with a JVM `heapSize` to Apache Derby `pageCache` ratio of 2.5:1. The Apache Derby default settings are `pageCache=1000` (4-MB cache) and `maxHeap=64KB`, which yield a 16:1 ratio.

Security

Database File Security

Physical security for an Apache Derby database is controlled through the operating system and the database startup parameters. An Apache Derby database places all of the data and control information within a directory structure in the underlying file system. Control to the file system is then established through operating system commands so that only specific applications or users can access the data.

Database File Encryption

Apache Derby includes a number of options for encrypting a database. Encrypting the database might be a requirement for many sensitive applications, especially if unauthorized users could access the actual database files. To encrypt a database, encryption must be turned on at database creation time. There is no option to encrypt a database after it has been created.

Booting Encrypted Databases

Encrypted databases cannot be booted automatically, along with all other databases on system startup. Instead, encrypted databases are booted when you first connect to them. Once the database is booted, all connections can access the database without the boot password. The boot password is not meant to prevent unauthorized connections to the database once it has been booted. Database encryption is meant to prevent fraudulent access to data outside of the database engine.

Remote Authentication

By default, user authentication is not active in Apache Derby. In some cases, this can cause a problem, especially when accessing Apache Derby from a remote client. The client that is used to communicate with the database requires a user ID and password to be specified as part of the connection. In this case, any user ID and password are acceptable to the database.

Built-in Authentication

The simplest authentication scheme is provided within Apache Derby itself. Apache Derby provides a simple, built-in repository of user names and passwords. To use the built-in repository, set `derby.authentication.provider` to `BUILTIN`. Using the built-in repository is an alternative to using an external directory service such as LDAP.

Security Hierarchy

Because Apache Derby supports two levels of authentication, you need to know which level takes precedence and how they interact.

- Authentication set at the system level only—When the `derby.properties` file contains `requireAuthentication=true`, all users defined at the system level will have access to all databases. Attempting to connect to any database will fail unless a user ID and password are specified.

- Authentication set at the database level only—When `requireAuthentication` is set to true for an individual database (and not set in the `derby.properties` file), access to the database is restricted to users who are defined in the database. Therefore, it is a good idea to create a user in the database before restricting access to the database! If you've made a mistake and this hasn't been done, you can turn on system-level authentication, add the user ID, and then connect to the database.

- Authentication set at both system and database level—System-level users are able to connect to the database, along with users identified at the database level. If there is a conflict involving passwords, the database-level password takes precedence. For example, you might have created user T1 with password t1 at the system level, and user T1 with password t2 at the database level. Connecting as T1 with the t1 password fails because the database-level password takes precedence over the system-level password.

Database Features

Database Structure

An Apache Derby database contains objects such as tables, columns, indexes, and .JAR files. An Apache Derby database can also store its own configuration information.

An Apache Derby database is stored in files that live in a directory with the same name as the database (that is, the SAMPLE database is found in the SAMPLE directory). Database directories typically live in system directories.

Creating an Apache Derby Database

There is no CREATE DATABASE command within the Apache Derby environment. Instead, databases are created and accessed via the Apache Derby connection URL. The create=true option can be added to the connect statement to create the database.

Database Names

Database names within Apache Derby can cause you grief depending on your environment. Database names in a Windows environment are not case-sensitive, so SAMPLE and sample are exactly the same database from an Apache Derby perspective. However, if you are running on Linux, names are case-sensitive, so make sure that you spell the name exactly the way you created it. To minimize confusion on local and remote applications, you should use uppercase names for databases. The SQL standard converts the database name to uppercase characters when a DB2 client tries to connect to the Apache Derby database running in network server mode, so a best practice is to always specify an uppercase database name in your connection string and when you are actually creating the database.

Deleting an Apache Derby Database

Apache Derby does not have a DROP DATABASE command. Instead, you must use operating system commands to delete the directory in which the database resides. The Apache Derby catalog tables for the deleted database are independent of any other database that you might have created. Other databases have their own unique directory structure and do not share catalog tables.

Special Characters in the Apache Derby Properties File

When editing the Apache Derby services.properties file, remember that forward and backward slashes in file definitions are interchangeable. However, two backward slashes are required to represent one backward slash because the backward slash is considered an escape character.

SQL

Ensure That Your Environment Variables Are Properly Set

Make sure that you have issued the setEmbbeddedCP command in Windows or setEmbeddedCP.sh in Linux. These commands are case-sensitive in Linux, so make sure you type the shell command correctly. This command sets up the appropriate environment variables for running Apache Derby on your operating system.

Use Declared Tables for Temporary Storage

The DECLARE statement is very similar to the CREATE statement, except that it is used to create temporary tables that are used only during a session. The only object that can be declared is a table, and it exists only for the current user who created it.

The creation of a temporary table does not update the catalog, so locking, logging, and other forms of contention are avoided with this object. The temporary table is dropped when you disconnect from the database.

Select the Right Data Types

Knowledge of the possible data values and their usage is required to be able to select the correct data type. Specifying an inappropriate data type when defining tables can result in wasted disk space, improper expression evaluation, and performance problems.

When using character data types, the choice between CHAR and VARCHAR is determined by the range of column lengths. For example, if the range of column lengths is relatively small, use a fixed CHAR defined with the maximum length. This will reduce storage requirements and could improve performance.

Large Object Support

If you would like to manipulate textual data that is greater than 32 KB in length, you can use CLOB, the character large object data type. For example, if you need to store an employee's resume, the resume could be stored in a CLOB column, along with the rest of the employee's information. There are many SQL functions that can be used to manipulate large character data columns, but there are a few restrictions that you should be aware of:

- LOB types cannot be compared for equality (=) and non-equality (! =, < >)
- LOB types cannot be ordered, so <, <=, >, and >= tests are not supported
- LOB types cannot be used in indices or as primary key columns
- LOB types cannot be used with the DISTINCT, GROUP BY, or ORDER BY clause
- LOB types cannot be involved in implicit casting to other base types
- CLOBs and LONG VARCHARs are not allowed as parameter values for many of the conversion functions
- CLOBs, BLOBs, or LONG VARCHARs cannot be used in the CREATE FUNCTION or the CREATE PROCEDURE statement

Null Considerations

A null value represents an unknown state. Therefore, when columns containing null values are used in calculations, the result is unknown. Special considerations are required to properly handle nulls when coding an Apache Derby application. Apache Derby treats nulls differently than it treats other values. To define a column to not accept null values, add the NOT NULL clause to the end of the column definition. For example:

```
CREATE TABLE T1 (C1 INT NOT NULL, ...)
```

In general, avoid using nullable columns, unless they are required to implement the database design. There is overhead storage to consider: An extra byte per nullable column is needed if nulls are allowed.

Identity Column

Consider using an identity column for values that need to be incremented whenever a new record is added to the table. It is possible to have Apache Derby automatically generate sequential values. Once a table has been created with an identity column, the starting value cannot be changed.

Indexes

An index is a list of the locations of rows sorted by the contents of one or more specified columns. Indexes are typically used to improve query performance. More than one index can be defined on a particular table, which can have a beneficial effect on the performance of queries. However, the more indexes there are, the more the database manager must work to keep the indexes current during update, delete, and insert operations. Creating a large number of indexes for a table that receives many updates can slow down processing.

Null Values and Indexes

Nulls, when it comes to indexing, are treated the same way as any other null value. You cannot insert a null value twice if the column is a key for a unique index because this violates the uniqueness rule for the index.

General Indexing Guidelines

Indexes consume disk space. The amount of disk space will vary depending on the length of the key columns and the number of rows being indexed. The size of the index will increase as more data is inserted into the table. Therefore, consider the disk space required for indexes when planning the size of your database.

Searching for Null Values

A null value represents an unknown value for a particular occurrence of an entity. You can use a null value in cases where you don't know a particular column value.

To select rows that have null values in a column, the IS NULL predicate must be used instead of the equals operator. Similarly, the IS NOT NULL predicate selects rows that have a non-null value in the column.

Use Parentheses in Expressions

It is always good practice to use parentheses to specify the order of operations for any mathematical or logical expression in your SQL. In addition, query performance can significantly improve if join columns are appropriately indexed.

Case Expressions

You can add some logic to your SQL using CASE expressions. The order of the conditions for a CASE expression is very important. Apache Derby will process the first condition first, then the second, and so on. If you do not pay attention to the order in which the conditions are processed, you might retrieve the same result for every row in your table. For example, if you coded the "<20000" condition before the "<15000" condition, all the data that is less than 15000 will execute the code in "<20000" block and will never reach the "<15000" block.

Every condition in a CASE expression starts with the WHEN clause, and the set of conditions finishes with the END clause. The ELSE clause is optional but recommended in the event that none of the conditions is met.

Schema

A schema is a database object that represents a collection of named objects within an Apache Derby database. If no schema is supplied, the default schema name is APP.

Trigger Data View

Multiple triggers defined on the same table will see the same image of the row, even though one trigger after another might fire. It might make sense to place some data type checking, rather than a trigger, into a column constraint.

JDBC Application Development

Using Embedded JDBC Drivers

Every Apache Derby embedded application must load the JDBC driver before issuing any connects or SQL statements. Stored procedures and user-defined functions do not need to load the JDBC driver because it is assumed that they are running under the context of another program.

The class that loads the Apache Derby local JDBC driver is the org.apache.derby.jdbc.EmbeddedDriver class. There are a variety of ways to create an instance of the Apache Derby driver class, but do not use the class directly through the java.sql.Driver interface. The preferred method is to use the DriverManager class to create connections using the Class.forName() method: Class.forName("org.apache.derby.jdbc.EmbeddedDriver").

IBM DB2 JDBC Universal Driver for Apache Derby

The IBM DB2 JDBC Universal Driver for Apache Derby is the same JDBC driver that is included with the Cloudscape 10.0 product for accessing the network server. If Apache Derby is being used as a network server, this driver allows you to connect through JDBC, using Distributed Relational Database Architecture (DRDA). DRDA is the Open Group's (www.opengroup.org) client/server architecture for accessing remote relational data across multiple platforms.

Apache Derby Network Servers

By default, the Apache Derby network servers will only listen on the `localhost`. Clients must use the `localhost` host name to connect. By default, clients cannot access the network server from another host. To enable connections from other hosts, you can set the `derby.drda.host` property, or you can start the Network Server with the `-h` option in the `java org.apache .derby.drda.NetworkServerControl start` command.

To start the Network Server so that it will listen on all interfaces, start with an IP address of 0.0.0.0. A server started with the 0.0.0.0 option will listen to client requests that originate from both `localhost` and other machines.

Universal Driver Attributes

The DB2 Universal JDBC Driver supports a number of optional database connection URL attributes. The DB2 JDBC Universal Driver requires that you set the Universal Driver user and password attributes to non-null values. There are two options that might be of interest to an application developer. The `readOnly` option will prevent an application from updating any tables in the database, and the `retrieveMessages` option will retrieve the full SQL error messages, rather than just the error code, from the server. This is extremely useful when the reason for the error is unknown and the message text might be more meaningful.

Accessing Result Sets in a Random Order

Applications that need to retrieve rows from a result set in a random order should use a scrollable cursor (`TYPE_SCROLL_INSENSITIVE`). This method offers much more flexibility than the default forward cursor, but it requires more application logic.

Closing Statements

When an application is finished using a statement, it is good practice to close the statement to free resources in the application and in the database. A statement is closed using the `close` method.

try Blocks

A `try` block should always be placed around any SQL statement that might cause an error. Although it is unlikely that your SQL syntax is incorrect, there is always the possibility that underlying objects are missing. Moreover, SQL that is submitted directly by a user can be error-prone.

Multiple *SQLExceptions*

Apache Derby sometimes returns multiple `SQLExceptions`. Use the `getNextException()` chain to process all of the exceptions. The first exception is always the most severe exception, with SQL92 Standard exceptions preceding those that are specific to Apache Derby.

The most severe error is usually the one that needs to be addressed, but for diagnostic purposes, it might be good practice to list all of the errors that occurred in an SQL statement.

SQLWarnings Versus *SQLExceptions*

Apache Derby can generate warnings in certain circumstances. A warning is generated if, for example, you try to connect to a database with the create attribute set to true, and the database already exists. Aggregates such as SUM also raise a warning if null values are encountered during the evaluation. Another example is an UPDATE or DELETE statement that affects no rows.

An SQLWarning will remain in affect until another SQL statement is issued. If you want to clear all existing warnings, use the clearWarnings() method.

Mismatched Data Types

A column in a result set is normally retrieved to a similar column type by an application. However, sometimes it's easier to translate the object into something else to make it easier to manipulate. For example, an application might need to retrieve a date field but use it as part of a string, rather than as a real date value. Unless the value being retrieved needs to be manipulated or updated, converting it into a character string might be the easiest way to manipulate it.

Null Values in Java

Null values need to be treated differently in Java than in SQL because the Java language does not have a corresponding concept. A Java null is completely different from an SQL null. There are two methods for detecting a null value that has been returned in a result set. The one that will work across all data types is wasnull().

Autocommit Settings

Autocommit refers to the action that Apache Derby takes after every execute() statement. If autocommit is true, every statement is automatically committed after it completes execution. That means that there is no way of undoing the changes that were made.

If an application wants to control the way that commits are handled, it must turn autocommit off. This must be done at the connection level with the setAutoCommit(value) method. The current setting can also be queried using the getAutoCommit() method.

When an application wants to use a result set to update data, the autocommit value must be set to false or else updates will fail.

Inserting and Updating Large Objects

Large objects need to be handled differently because of their size. Rather than assigning a value directly to a large object, output streams are used to move data into CLOBs and BLOBs. Three methods are available for creating output streams. Two methods are meant for character objects, and the third is for binary objects.

The easiest method for updating or inserting a `BLOB` or a `CLOB` value is to create an `InputStream` to the object being inserted from the file system and then to set the `Binary-Stream` for the `BLOB` to point to the `InputStream`.

User-Defined Functions

If a specific function is not available in Apache Derby, a function might be available within the standard Java class libraries that could be used instead.

Care should be taken to ensure that both the class name and the function name are declared as `public` in the function definition. In addition, the function must be defined as `static`, or else the database will not find the routine. In addition, make sure that `CLASSPATH` is set to the directory in which this code was stored.

Connecting to a Database from a Stored Procedure

If a stored procedure or function accesses any SQL, it must first establish a connection to the database. Normally a stored procedure or function runs under the context of the calling application or SQL. In this case, the connection string does not refer directly to the database but to the default connection. It is assumed that the calling program has already made a connection. If this is not true, an `SQLException` will be thrown and handled in the `catch` block. To connect to the default connection, use the following syntax:

```
conn = DriverManager.getConnection("jdbc:default:connection")
```

Summary

This chapter has provided you with a number of hints and tips for dealing with Apache Derby. Hopefully you won't have any problems when using this technology!

Index

informIT